Rome's Cultural Revolution

The period of Rome's imperial expansion, the late republic and earlier empire, saw transformations of its society, culture and identity. Drawing equally on archaeological and literary evidence, this book offers an original and provocative interpretation of these changes. Moving from recent debates about colonialism and cultural identity, both in the Roman world and more broadly, and challenging the traditional picture of 'romanisation' and 'hellenisation', it offers instead a model of overlapping cultural identities in dialogue with one another. It attributes a central role to cultural change in the process of redefinition of Roman identity, represented politically by the crisis of the republican system and the establishment of the new Augustan order. Romans are shown using Greek culture creatively to create new systems of knowledge which render the old ruling class powerless, and give authority to the new imperial system. The discussion follows a number of principal themes, including the cultural transformations of Italy, the role of Vitruvius' treatise on architecture in building a new Roman identity, the role of antiquarian writers in transforming the idea of Roman tradition, the transformation by Augustus of ways of knowing and controlling the city of Rome and, above all, the growth of luxury, the Roman debate on the issue, and the archaeological evidence for transformations of Roman material culture. Whether or not it is right to see these changes as 'revolutionary', they involve a profound transformation of Roman life and identity, one that lies at the heart of understanding the nature of the Roman empire.

ANDREW WALLACE-HADRILL is Professor of Classics at the University of Reading and has been Director of the British School at Rome since 1995. His previous books are *Suetonius. The Scholar and his Caesars* (1983), *Houses and Society in Pompeii and Herculaneum* (1994) and *Domestic Space in the Roman World. Pompeii and Beyond* (co-edited with Ray Laurence, 1997). He is currently directing a major project on a Pompeian neighbourhood with Michael Fulford and, since 2001, has directed the Herculaneum Conservation Project. He frequently contributes to radio and television programmes on various aspects of Roman life and in 2004 was awarded an OBE for services to Anglo-Italian cultural relations.

Rome's Cultural Revolution

ANDREW WALLACE-HADRILL

CAMBRIDGE
UNIVERSITY PRESS

CAMBRIDGE
UNIVERSITY PRESS

University Printing House, Cambridge CB2 8BS, United Kingdom

Cambridge University Press is part of the University of Cambridge.

It furthers the University's mission by disseminating knowledge in the pursuit of education, learning and research at the highest international levels of excellence.

www.cambridge.org
Information on this title: www.cambridge.org/9780521721608

© Andrew Wallace-Hadrill 2008

First published 2008
Reprinted with corrections 2010

A catalogue record for this publication is available from the British Library

Library of Congress Cataloguing in Publication data
Wallace-Hadrill, Andrew.
Rome's cultural revolution / Andrew Wallace-Hadrill.
    p. cm.
Includes bibliographical references and index.
ISBN 978-0-521-89684-9 (hardback)
1. Rome–Civilization.   2. Group identity–Rome.   3. Rome–Social life and customs.
4. National characteristics, Roman.   I. Title.
DG77.W35   2008
937 – dc22   2008021910

ISBN 978-0-521-89684-9 Hardback
ISBN 978-0-521-72160-8 Paperback

To the British School at Rome

Contents

Figures and table

Figures

Table

Colour plates

Preface

This book is about a transformation of Roman society, culture and identity, in the time span we can characterise (without precision) as the later Republic and earlier Empire. To call it a 'cultural revolution' is to invite debate. The reference to Ronald Syme's ironically-titled *Roman Revolution* is also a reference to the debates that title provoked. The question of whether one can legitimately speak of a political 'revolution' at Rome is semantic: why we choose to hail particular moments as 'revolutions' is a question of our own ideologies and rhetorical agendas.[1] The challenge of the title, however, lies not in deciding what qualifies as a revolution, but what role 'culture' might play. That we are far from the world of Mao's China is evident. 'Culture' is an exceptionally complex concept, and, as I hope to show, has at its heart a tension between competing conceptions of how societies are, or should be, constructed. But beyond all these semantic doubts, the core of my argument is simple enough: that the political transformation of the Roman world is integrally connected to its cultural transformation. The claim is not that cultural change caused political change, nor that it mirrored it; but that the two are so intimately connected that without its cultural components, the political story is two-dimensional.

Nothing in my treatment is intended as definitive. There are many large areas touched on in passing which could have been developed at length: I have tried to focus on a number of themes where I felt I might have a contribution to make. I am fully aware of how much more there is to say about Roman literature, Roman art, and Roman religion. My interest in hellenisation goes back to studying Plautus with Eduard Fraenkel, Horace with Robin Nisbet, and the Second Sophistic with Ewen Bowie. I have watched with admiration while a number of friends, including Mary Beard and Denis Feeney, have changed our approaches to Roman religion. I have witnessed with awe the sea-change to the study of the Mediterranean brought about by Peregrine Horden and Nicholas Purcell. If I do not pursue certain themes, it is not for lack appreciation of their interest and importance.

---

[1] Goldhill and Osborne (2006).

This project has spent painfully long in gestation. The stages of its development often show through the final text, and are in any case marked by a series of publications over the last two decades. The idea of writing a book on this theme grew in the early 1980s in Cambridge while writing about emperors and culture in Suetonius, and wishing my canvas were broader. The title comes from a jesting comment by Brent Shaw on an early outline: I have been unable to get it out of my head. I have been deflected along the way by numerous distractions: the houses of Pompeii and Herculaneum took on a life of their own, the challenges of teaching and of running a department (in Reading) and an institution (in Rome) proved more demanding than my worst fears. For significant steps forward in the project I have always depended on periods of research leave. A semester in the Classics department at Princeton in 1991 gave me the chance to share my ideas with a bright and critical group of graduate students, and to sketch a first draft, long since submerged (to Elaine Fantham I owe not only my invitation, but the chance to read and think in her own peaceful and well-stocked study). A later period in 1994–5 supported by a British Academy Research Readership allowed me to visit Munich and deepen my knowledge of Roman luxury (my understanding of Roman art has been transformed by discussions then and later with Paul Zanker). The text incorporates material from these earlier drafts, and from earlier publications, but as is stands was completely rewritten in subsequent periods of leave from the British School at Rome, first in the Getty Research Centre in Los Angeles (Marion True's kindness to me as to many others is not forgotten), then in the Sackler Library in Oxford (I thank Ewen Bowie for the hospitality of the SCR of Corpus Christi College).

The advantage, and disadvantage, about taking too long over a project is that major publications have continued to appear which change the complexion of the question. In the early stages, Paul Zanker's *Power of Images in the Age of Augustus*, Elizabeth Rawson *Intellectual Life in the Late Roman Republic*, and Erich Gruen's *Culture and National Identity in Republican Rome* reset my agendas. As I tried to finish off the text, major new works continued to appear, including Emma Dench's *Romulus' Asylum* and Denis Feeney's *Caesar's Calendar*. As I have struggled to keep the bibliography in any sense up to date, I have had to concede that the longer I spend updating, the more out of date the text will become.

I have had the benefit and stimulus of the advice of more friends than I can list. Those who have helped me with comments on individual chapters include Michael Fulford, Martin Millett, John Papadopoulos, Simon Keay and Paul Zanker. Many Italian friends have let me pick their brains about their sites, and have proved generous in helping me with illustrations, especially Francesco Cifarelli and Federica Colaiacomo for Segni, Sandra

Gatti for Palestrina and Alatri, Piero Guzzo and Maria Paola Guidobaldi for Pompeii and Herculaneum, Adriano La Regina for Pietrabbondante, and Eugenio La Rocca and Claudi Parisi Presicce for Rome. A vital help over recent years has been provided by a sequence of research assistants in Rome, without whom my bibliography would be very much thinner: Sarah Court, Rosie Harman, Sophy Downes, and above all Amy Richardson, whose support over the illustrations has proved indispensable. At the final stage, Chris Siwicki helped me out with the index. I am particularly indebted to those who undertook the labour of reading the entire text, and in doing so have saved me on countless occasions from my careless errors, ignorance and forgetfulness: these are Mary Beard, Filippo Coarelli, Jas Elsner, Denis Feeney, Fergus Millar, and Peter Wiseman. It would be no repayment for their great kindness to lay the numerous imperfections that remain at their door. Michael Sharp and his sharp-eyed team at Cambridge University Press have helped to remove many other flaws, and have made the process of production remarkably swift and painless.

One final debt is summed up in the dedication. It would not have been possible to write this book as it is without the extraordinary opportunity of living for twelve years in Rome provided to me by the British School. For over a century, this institution has given British (and other) scholars a chance to see the Roman world from a different perspective, to engage with the materiality of Roman Italy, and to get to know different worlds of scholarship, above all that of Italy, but also that of the international cluster of academies in Rome. If this book has a good deal to say about people who find themselves between cultures, it is because I have found myself so. Possibly I place too much weight on language as a model of cultural identity: that is an outcome of living between languages, and being daily confronted with my own limitations and rootedness. I am deeply obliged to the generous help of many colleagues, in particular to Valerie Scott and her staff in the School's superb library, to Sue Russell, for her calm skill in deputising in my absences, to Maria Pia Malvezzi, for arranging permissions for me as for so many others, to Elly Murkett, for keeping administrative distractions at bay, and to four successive Chairmen, Fergus Millar, Geoffrey Rickman, Peter Wiseman and Ivor Roberts, for support in tough times. My final and greatest thanks are to my wife, Jo, who has cheerfully put up with being 'institutionalised' in Rome, and given me unfailing support and encouragement throughout the protracted conception, gestation, and birthpangs of this volume.

AWH

1 May 2008

Acknowledgements for illustrations

Every attempt has been made to trace copyright holders for all illustrations used in this book; any omissions are unintentional, and result from the difficulties of identifying copyright in older publications. I am deeply appreciative of the readiness of numerous individuals and institutions to provide illustrations and permissions.

Research institutions

British School at Rome (figs. 3.13, 8.1, 8.15, 8.21, 8.22, 8.33, 8.35, 8.36, 8.37, Plate XXIV); Deutsches Archäologisches Institut, Rome (figs. 2.2, 2.3, 2.4, 2.5, 2.6, 2.7, 2.10, 6.9, 6.11, 6.12, 6.13, 6.15); Ecole Française de Rome (figs. 6.1, 6.2, 6.21, 6.22, 6.23, 6.24, 6.25).

Publishing houses

Cambridge University Press (figs. 4.14, 6.19); Edizioni Quasar (fig. 3.25); Gangemi Editore (fig. 4.4); Istituto Poligrafico e Zecca dello Stato (figs. 6.7, 6.8, 8.16, 8.17, 8.18, Plates XV, XVI); MIT Press (fig. 4.11); Omega Edizioni (figs. 3.2 and 3.3); Oxford University Press (figs. 4.1, 4.2); Princeton University Press (figs. 4.8, 4.13, 4.15); Rudolf Habelt GMBH, Bonn (fig. 8.39); Sagep Editori, Genova (figs. 6.3, 6.4); Verlag Walter de Gruyter, Berlin (fig. 4.12).

Museums and heritage authorities

Ashmolean Museum, Oxford (fig. 8.38); British Museum (figs. 2.1, 2.9, 5.6, 5.7); Fitzwilliam Museum, Cambridge (fig. 8.45); Getty Museum (fig. 8.4, Plate XXI); Munich, Phototek des Museums für Abgüsse Klassischer Bildwerke (fig. 5.4); Ny Carlsberg Glyptotek, Copenhagen (figs. 2.1, 5.3, 5.5); Rheinisches Landesmuseum Bonn and Museée Nationale du Bardo, Tunis (figs. 8.3, 8.6, 8.8, 8.10, 8.12, 8.17, 8.23, 8.25, 8.27, 8.41, Plate XX); Comune di Roma, Sovraintendenza ai Beni Culturali (figs. 6.21, 6.22, 6.23, 6.25); Musei Capitolini, Roma (figs. 6.17, 6.18, 8.42, 8.43, 8.44,

Plates XXIX, XXX, XXXI); Comuna di Segni, Museo Archeologico (figs. 3.19, 3.20); Soprintendenza per i Beni Archeologici dell'Etruria Meridionale (fig. 3.8); Soprintendenza Archeologica del Lazio, Museo di Palestrina (figs. 3.9, 3.10, 3.11); Soprintendenza Archeologica del Lazio, Museo di Alatri (fig. 3.14); Soprintendenza Speciale per i Beni Archeologici di Napoli e Pompei (figs. 3.24, 3.26, 3.28, 3.34, 4.7a, 4.7b, 4.9, 4.16, 4.17, 4.19, 4.20, 6.6, 6.10, 7.1, 7.2, 7.3, 7.5, 8.5, 8.7, 8.13, 8.14, 8.15, 8.21, 8.22, 8.24, 8.32, 8.33, 8.34, 8.36, 8.37, Plates VI, X, XIV, XV, XVI, XVIII, XXII, XXIII, XXIV, XXV, XXVI, XXVII, XXVIII, XXXVII); Soprintendenza Archeologica di Salerno, Museo di Paestum (fig. 7.4, Plate XVII).

Authors, photographers and illustrators

Filippo Coarelli (fig. 5.2); Zeno Colantoni (fig. 8.44, Plate XXXI); Katherine Dunbabin (fig. 8.29); Araldo De Luca, Roma (figs. 8.42, 8.43, Plates XXIX, XXX); Alfredo Foglia, Naples (figs. 7.5, 8.5, 8.13, 8.32, Plates XVIII, XXII); Michael Harvey (figs. 7.1, 7.2, 7.3, Plates XIV, XV, XVI); Sophie Hay and Anthony Sibthorpe (figs. 8.21, 8.22, 8.33, 8.36, 8.37, Plates XXIV, XXVII, XXVIII); Adolf Hoffmann (fig. 3.27); Adriano La Regina (figs. 3.5, 3.30); Lorenzo Quilici (figs. 6.26, 6.27); Amy Richardson (figs. 3.1, 3.4, 3.6, 3.7, 3.23, 4.5, 4.6, 8.2, 8.31, 8.35, 8.40, 8.46, 8.47, 8.48); Frank Sear (figs. 4.1, 4.2, 4.3); Nicholas Wood (fig. 8.1, Plate XIX).

PART I

Cultures and identities

1 | Culture, identity and power

> Quintus Ennius used to say he had three hearts, because he knew how to speak in Greek and Oscan and Latin.
>
> (Aulus Gellius, *Attic Nights* 17.17.1)

> In this respect he [Favorinus] seems to have been equipped by the gods themselves for this very purpose: to give a model to the locals of Hellas that there is no difference between education and birth; to teach the Romans that not even those with high social standing can overlook the standing brought by education; and to teach the Celts that none of the barbarians should feel alienated from Hellenic culture, with him as their model.
>
> (Dio of Prusa, Oration 37, 26–7)

Two literary figures, spanning the period with which this book is concerned, embody the complex layering of Roman cultural identities. Ennius, whose epic vision of Roman history in the *Annales* was among the pioneering works of the new Latin literature, came from Rudiae in the heel of Italy, the Salento, close to the modern Lecce.[1] Though in an area heavily colonised by the Greeks since the seventh century, in the ambit of Tarentum, it was in origin a settlement of the local tribe, the Messapi, one which spoke its own distinctive variant of the Italic language. By Ennius' birth in 239 BCE, the town had been under Roman control for half a century; but the Romans acknowledged South Italy, or 'Magna Graecia' as a Greek-speaking territory.[2] In a famous anecdote transmitted by the second-century CE antiquarian, Aulus Gellius, Ennius is reported to have described himself as having three hearts, *tria corda*, because he knew how to speak in Greek and Oscan and Latin.[3] What is so striking is not his trilingual skill, but the fact that he felt that these languages represented *hearts*: what should be unique was triple. It went to the core of his identity. There are puzzles about this saying. Oscan is treated by linguists as a separate language group from Messapic. Perhaps because Oscan was the most dominant of the central Italian languages, it

---

[1] See Skutsch (1985), Rawson (1989) 444–8.   [2] Lomas (1993), Crawford (1996a) 981–3.

[3] Aulus Gellius 17.17.1; see Skutsch (1985) 749–50.

stood proxy for any local dialect; or perhaps Ennius actually was brought up in a family of Oscan speakers, though in Messapian territory. In any case, 'Oscan' stands for the local Italic language, neither Greek nor Roman. His Greek came from his education, probably at Tarentum, his Latin from the realities of Roman domination: he is said to have been taken to Rome under the wing of no less a figure than Cato, the future Censor, and his writings show ample proof not only of his mastery of Latin, but his ability to represent the Romans to themselves with pride. He became a Roman citizen in 184 BCE, and celebrated his change of citizenship in the line

Nos sumus Romani qui fuimus ante Rudini
We are Romans who were once Rudians.[4]

His pride in being Roman, correctly defined by citizenship, was no impediment to retaining his Oscan heart.

The second figure is Favorinus of Arelate (modern Arles): the Romans called this area Provincia Nostra, *our* province, though indeed Greek influence goes back to the foundation of the Greek colony of Massilia. Prominent as a member of the Greek literary movement which adopted the label of 'sophists', called in modern scholarship the Second Sophistic, he moved among the notable literary figures of Hadrianic Rome, including Plutarch and Herodes Atticus on the Greek side, Cornelius Fronto and Aulus Gellius on the Latin.[5] The biographical sketch of him in Philostratus' *Lives of the Sophists* (8) reports the three 'paradoxes' he claimed to have marked his life: that though a Gaul he spoke Greek (ἑλληνίζειν/*hellēnizein*), though a eunuch he had been tried for adultery, and though he had quarrelled with the emperor Hadrian, he was still alive.

On the first of these paradoxes, he has more to say in the speech that survives among the works of his teacher, Dio of Prusa (*Oration* 37, the 'Corinthian Oration'). Indeed, the phrasing of the paradox is opaque, for it is not immediately clear how far *hellēnizein* shades beyond its root sense of 'speaking Greek' to one more charged with cultural identity, of 'behaving/ living like a Greek'. Trying to persuade the Corinthians not to take down the statue erected in his honour, now that he is out of favour with the emperor, he points to the model of a Lucanian who was honoured with a statue by the people of Tarentum because his Doric dialect was so pure. The Messapian Ennius, of course, would equally have needed to prove his linguistic purity to the Tarentines, whose purist intolerance was also shown by their abuse of

[4] Fr. 525, see Feeney (2007) 143.
[5] Illuminatingly discussed by Gleason (1995) 3–20, 131–68; also Whitmarsh (2001a) 119–21.

a third-century Roman ambassador for his poor Greek.[6] As for Favorinus himself, surely he deserves a bronze statue:

If someone who is not a Lucanian, but a Roman, not one of the plebs, but of the equestrian order, and who has imitated not only the language, but the thinking and way of life and dress of the Greeks, and has done so with such conspicuous mastery as to have no rival either among the Romans before him or the Greeks of his own day . . . should he not have a bronze statue set up by you? Yes, and city by city: by you [Corinthians], because though a Roman he has become perfectly Hellenic (*aphēllēnisthē*), just as has your city; by the Athenians, because he speaks Attic dialect; by the Spartans because he is devoted to gymnastics; by all because he philosophises and has already inspired many of the Hellenes to philosophise with him, and has in addition pulled in no small number of barbarians. (25–6)

He makes quite clear that it is an issue of cultural identity. He is more Greek than any Roman, even more Greek than any Greek of his day (he would naturally concede superiority to the classics of the past) because his *hellēnizein* goes beyond language to an entire way of life. His Roman identity is guaranteed by his membership of the *ordo equester*. Here he is not a Gaul who has made himself a perfect Greek (*aphēllēnisthē*), but a Roman. Similarly the Corinthians represent a colony of Roman citizens who nevertheless have learned to live like perfect Greeks. His philosophical activity as a sophist makes him not merely a good convert, but a notable recruiter for the cause of hellenism.

His enthusiasm for his own cultural ambidexterity carries him to higher extremes: he goes on to assert (in the passage cited at the start), that the gods themselves have given him a role as model to all three cultures. He can teach the Greeks the importance of their own παιδεία/*paideia*, because he is an example of being Greek through education not birth. He can teach the Romans the same lesson – because, despite his social standing as an *eques Romanus*, he acquires more standing through his fame as a man of learning. He can teach his own Gauls that the barbarian has no need to feel inferior: the standing and achievements brought by *paideia* are open to all. Thus he drives home the idea that *paideia*, the education at the heart of hellenic culture, gives the barbarian a claim to hellenic identity no weaker than that of the native. It is not enough to be born hellenic: you must make yourself so by education. Equally, it is not enough to be born to Roman social rank: you must acquire standing through education.

What Ennius and Favorinus have in common is a form of cultural triangulation that is one of the most remarkable features of the Roman world,

---

[6] See ch. 2, p. 59.

whether of the second century BCE or of the second century CE. This goes beyond bilingualism. Because both Roman and Greek represent universal cultural poles, they need to triangulate their local identity, as Messapians, Lucanians, Gauls, or whatever, with both the world of Greek culture and that of Roman power. They reveal no sense (let alone fear) that in 'hellenising' they are sacrificing their local identity. You can have three hearts. You can be more Greek than the Greeks, and more Roman than the Romans, without ceasing to be a Gaul from Arelate. Above all, identity is seen as a process. The Greek termination (ζειν-/-izein) suggests not *being* something but *becoming* it by repetitive action, what Bourdieu calls *habitus*.[7] If you *hellēnizein*, you make yourself continuously into a hellene by behaving like a hellene, in language and culture. The passive form with the prefix ἀπο-/apo- indicates completion of a process: you have made yourself fully hellenic (without ceasing to be Roman or Gallic). The instrument of this process is education, *paideia*: it is by practising, not just language, but ways of thinking, ways of living, ways of dressing, that you make yourself into a perfect hellene. There is always hope for the barbarian: the gods want him to know as much. It is a providential order with racist roots, but some refreshingly un-racist aspirations.

Those who study the Second Sophistic, the movement of Greek literary revival under the Roman empire to which Favorinus belonged, draw attention to the complexities of Greek identity under Roman rule, to dialogue and multiple identities rather than fusion.[8] Ewen Bowie, in a ground-breaking paper, suggested that in reaction to Roman dominance, Greeks relocated identity in their prestigious past, in a way that also appealed to a Roman construction of the Greek.[9] Simon Swain pointed to the linguistic model of code-switching for the bilingual fluency between which the Greek elite of the second century CE shuttle between Greek and Roman identities.[10] Tim Whitmarsh has explored the use of *paideia* by Favorinus and his contemporaries to redefine Greek identity.[11] Greg Woolf has examined strategies of staying Greek while becoming Roman.[12] Nobody looking at the Greece of the high Roman Empire could imagine that Roman conquest swamped hellenic culture, though it impacted on it deeply, as Susan Alcock's study of the Greek landscape under Roman rule has shown.[13]

---

[7] Bourdieu (1977).   [8] In general, see Goldhill (2001).

[9] Bowie (1970), reprinted as Bowie (1974).

[10] Swain (1996), see also Adams, Janse and Swain (2002).

[11] Whitmarsh (2001b), and see now Borg (2004).

[12] Woolf (1996), cf. Woolf (1997).   [13] Alcock (1993), Alcock (1997).

The Roman world is a rewarding space (surprisingly so to those who think Roman culture dull and monotonous) in which to reflect on the complexities of cultural identity, especially the subtle layering of identities in the wake of passages of conquest and colonisation. The ancient world has its contribution to make to the burgeoning literature on 'cultural identity'.[14] Favorinus' Provence, like Ennius' Salento, was colonised by Greeks long before its conquest by Rome. Ancient Mediterranean cultures are as stratified as any archaeological sequence, and the traces of each episode could remain for many centuries: the Phoenician/Punic colonisation of North Africa and the west, the Greek colonisation of South Italy, Sicily and southern France form visible substrates under Roman rule, and at some points like western Sicily and Malta many layers intersect. These progressive waves do not wash out what has gone before, nor churn up new and old to form a homogeneous new entity, but remain in superimposition, in a coexistent complexity.

Too often in cultural history, recourse is made to one of two metaphors: the metallurgical 'fusion', or the biological 'hybridity'. In fusion, two metals form an alloy, a new and distinct metal which takes characteristics from its components but blends them completely. In hybridisation, different species from the animal or plant kingdom are cross-fertilised: their offspring is genetically different from both parents, while retaining characteristics of both – though the hybrid is provisional, normally sterile in the animal kingdom, and taking as many as fifty–sixty generations to form a new species in the plant kingdom.[15] The strata of archaeology may intersect, but they never fuse; and human history suggests that successive cultural influences rarely cancel the traces and memories of the past. The survival of minority languages or religions centuries after conquest suggests that the production of a rapid and homogeneous fusion after conquest is certainly not to be taken for granted, if indeed it ever happens.

The archaeology of cultural identity

There has been enormous debate in recent years, in rather different fields, about both hellenic culture and identity and about the Roman cultural impact in Italy and the provinces. Both debates take their impulse from broader debates, in anthropology, in archaeology and in the emergent field of cultural studies. Cross-over between disciplines, like other forms of cultural contact takes place at specific points and times, and it is the debate in

---

[14] Cf. Goldhill (2001) 15, and now particularly Dench (2005).   [15] Cf. Young (1995).

British (non-classical) archaeology, that stimulated a reassessment of Roman provincial archaeology.

For archaeologists, the issue of culture and national identity is particularly fraught.[16] As a corollary of the anthropological view that each people has its own culture, twentieth-century archaeologists widely assumed that each people had its own distinctive material culture, and that a distinctive material-culture therefore indicated ethnic boundaries. The very early use of the idea by Gustav Kossinna, based on the premise that 'sharply defined archaeological culture areas correspond unquestionably with the areas of particular peoples or tribes', enabled a prehistory of the Germani that directly served the First World War *Kulturpropaganda* of German cultural superiority, and led after his death to fuel Nazi racist theory.[17] Even though Kossinna was discredited along with Aryanism, the underlying premise was widely shared. V. Gordon Childe was widely influential in his definition of an archaeological culture:

We find certain types of remains – pots, implements, ornaments, burial rites, house forms – constantly recurring together. Such a complex of regularly associated traits we shall term a 'cultural group' or just a 'culture' ... We assume that such a complex is the material expression of what would today be called a 'people'.[18]

Apart from the obvious dangers of using such material to fuel nationalist claims, there are a number of basic objections to the theory of the coincidence of 'archaeological cultures' with ethnic boundaries. First, the groupings involved are not necessarily ethnic, and it is a product of modern nationalism to construct such closed boundaries for the past. Second, the material record normally shows a flux of change, and it may be impossible to distinguish whether an important change (e.g. in burial customs) reflects the arrival of a new people, or the dissemination of new ideas, and what power relations may lay behind the latter (conquest, commercial contact, internal changes in social structure, etc.). Third, the assemblage of an archaeological culture is not so much a set of unique types as variations on widely shared types, and distinctive associations of those types, which may occur elsewhere but not in that precise association: that can make the identification of a separate 'archaeological culture' more or less arbitrary.[19]

These difficulties may be particularly acute for prehistory in the absence of evidence outside the material record for the nature of groupings. It is absolutely clear that archaeological cultures may fail to overlap with linguistic

[16] See Shennan (1989a), Graves-Brown, Jones and Gamble (1996), Jones (1997).
[17] Veit (1989).   [18] Childe (1929) v–vi.   [19] Wiessner (1983), cf. Shennan (1989b).

boundaries, as Colin Renfrew has demonstrated for the Celts,[20] and may also fail to coincide with tribal boundaries recorded by ethnographers.[21] Ethnic identity is by no means easy to define, and relies on various combinations of common factors – shared land, descent, language, customs, religion, name and history – but above all the prerequisite is a self-awareness and wish to identify the participants as an entity, a condition not satisfied either by the imposition of identity from outside, whether in the past or by ourselves now.[22] We can express this by saying, with Jonathan Hall, that ethnic identity, and surely identities in general, are 'discursively constructed', created by the discourse of the participants themselves.[23]

How can such self-identification be inferred from the material record alone? The question is helped, but not resolved, by the distinction of cultural artefacts which aim explicitly to mark identity from those which may be taken to reflect it. So Polly Wiessner proposed the category of 'emblematic style' to distinguish 'formal variation in material-culture that has a distinct referent and transmits a clear message to a defined target population about conscious affiliation or identity'.[24] But, again, how is one to distinguish artefacts that mark ethnic, as opposed to other sorts of identity?

While these points create a difficulty for the archaeologist who has only material culture as a guide to human groupings, they also have relevance in the historical period when we are much better informed about what self-definitions of identity the participants offered. Tonio Hölscher rightly and articulately remonstrates against simple equations of culture and identity on the grounds that, even within a defined political unit, identity is not simple and bounded. He prefers to speak of a multiplicity of competing identities, ethnic, social, religious and so on, which may intersect without coinciding.[25]

The 'romanisation' debate

At this point, we need to confront the difficulties inherent in the framework by which cultural change in the Roman world has been approached. Our

---

[20] Renfrew (1996).　[21] E.g. Bursche (1996) on the Vistula mouth.

[22] For the definition, see Renfrew (1996) 130. For an example of the difficulties of accepting an external imposed identity in the case of the identification by Romans of the 'Samnites', see Dench (1995).

[23] Hall (1997) 2.　[24] Cited by Shennan (1989b) 18.

[25] Hölscher (2000), Hölscher (2008). For the history of the concept of identity, see Gleason (1983); for an attack on modern usage, see Niethammer (2000).

standard terminology implies a dual process, whereby the values of Greek culture are first absorbed by the Romans ('hellenisation') and then diffused through Roman conquest across the western Mediterranean ('romanisation'). The vocabulary is implicated in a whole view of the place of Greek and Roman culture in the building of modern Europe, for which Greek culture is the foundation of western civilisation, the transmission of this culture to Rome appears a necessary step, the value of which to the Romans must be self-evident, just as the value of Roman civilisation to the western barbarians is self-evident.

As Martin Millett and a growing number of voices working on Roman provinces have pointed out, the language of 'romanisation' that seemed self-evident to Francis Haverfield at the beginning of the twentieth century incorporated models of European colonialism which are no longer easy to accept.[26] It is not enough to redress the balance by pointing out the survival of 'native' elements and locating in them either a sense of local identity or of 'resistance' to external domination.[27] Acculturation cannot be taken as an either/or process whereby individual aspects of 'native' culture either are or are not replaced by elements of Roman culture. The interest lies rather in understanding the dialectic of appropriation by which cultural goods and traits of the conquering power are taken on by the conquered to serve specific ends, and one may add reciprocally the process whereby the conquering power takes over traits from the conquered to accommodate conquest.

Millett's rethinking of romanisation in Britain takes distance from any assumption of inherent Roman cultural superiority, and of any model which sees acculturation as a top-down imposition by the conqueror on the conquered.[28] Instead, he emphasises how local elites embraced certain elements of Roman culture for their own purposes. The choices flow from the structures of pre-existing late Iron Age societies. Roman culture is re-contextualised in the structures of power-relations, not just between Roman and native, but between native elites and the societies they sought to dominate. But though Millett thus distances 'romanisation' from the colonialist mould in which the concept was formed, he has opened a Pandora's box. Given the outdated ideology from which 'romanisation' springs, would we not do better to abandon the concept, as David Mattingly has repeatedly urged?[29] But, if so, what language can we use? 'Acculturation', too, is

---

[26] On problems of the concept of 'romanisation' in provincial contexts, see e.g. Millett (1990), Metzler *et al.* (1995), Terrenato (1998), Woolf (1998) 4–7, Keay and Terrenato (2001).

[27] Bénabou (1976).   [28] Millett (1990).

[29] Barrett (1997), Mattingly (2002), Mattingly (2004), Mattingly (2006) 14–17.

suspect: its Eurocentric parentage presupposes too easily a model whereby the superior (Roman/European) culture spreads by osmosis over the native (barbarian/third world).

A recent case has been made for 'creolisation'.[30] As an instrument for reassessing the culture of the colonised, 'hybridity' has proved powerful in the field of post-colonial studies. Critics like Homi Bhabha or Gyatri Spivak have shown a way to recover the subaltern voice, and recreate a 'third space' between coloniser and colonised, in which the coloniser does not simply destroy existing cultures and impose his own, and the colonised is not simply passive victim, or stubbornly resistant, but which rather, in the partial appropriation and partial subversion of the colonist culture, creates a hybrid that articulates his ambivalence.[31] 'Creolisation' is a specific example of hybridity that has been developed in studies of the Caribbean and the southern slave-owning states of America. Its point of departure is linguistic studies: the creation among those of African origin of new language formed from elements both of French and African.[32] As often, language offers a model for study of material-culture, and it has been shown that European forms are reappropriated into African ritual practices, and that a new form of religious practice is created by the deliberate juxtaposition of certain Catholic elements with others of African origin. What this model offers is a 'bottom-up' view of culture, which allows popular elements of the native to reassert themselves against the 'top-down' model implicit in romanisation.[33]

But this view in turn runs into numerous objections. Replacing the word 'romanisation' with 'creolisation' scarcely enables by itself the sub-elite populations of Britain or Gaul to recover their voices. The Caribbean analogy leaves room for a significant misfit, with a starting point of a historical situation of two colonising populations, distinguished by origin (Europe/Africa), status (master/slave), and the construction of race that justifies the inequality (white/black). The Roman provincial situation is only partly analogous. Conquest does not reduce the native population to slavery: Rome recruits the existing Iron Age societies to its own support. Those societies come complete with their own social structures and inequalities, which the Romans deliberately promote. This sort of 'top-down' is the product of Roman power structures, not of a failure in modern analysis.

But we might go further and question whether the implicit structure of 'romanising' behaviour as elite, and 'creole' as sub-elite, in fact holds.

---

[30] Webster (2001), Webster (2003).   [31] Bhabha (1990), Bhabha (1994); Spivak (1987).
[32] Abrahams (1983).
[33] For the use of the Creole analogy in the early nineteenth century by Niebuhr, see p. 20.

Why assume that Roman culture is an elite culture? Part of the argument of the present book is that this very assumption is the product of a modern construction of the 'Classics' as a discipline. If used as an educational tool for defining an elite,[34] it does not mean that the Roman culture under study was in fact produced exclusively by and for an elite. Take baths and amphitheatres, characteristic Roman structures that appear in Britain as a result of 'romanisation'. Both types of public structure evidently served to recruit to the system, and hence define, a portion of the population extending considerably beyond the elite. It may indeed be the case that the spectacles in the amphitheatre were a prime instrument by which local elites defined their standing *vis-à-vis* the local population; but that mechanism of elite construction could not have worked if it had not enjoyed a mass appeal. The flip side of the assumed top-down/bottom-up contrast is equally suspect. Why should Gallic gods like Epona be assumed to be the outcome of popular, sub-elite religiosity, and not of the elite? Given the importance of priesthood in defining elites in the ancient world, why suppose that these native or 'creole' cults are other than elite-driven?[35]

Variants have been proposed more recently on the creolisation model. Patrick Le Roux prefers the term *métissage*, one which since the sixteenth century has been used to describe the sort of 'cross-breeding' or 'mixed blood' encountered in colonial circumstances.[36] It has the advantage, like Homi Bhabha's 'third space', of allowing for an ongoing dialogue between the component parts. Such a model has considerable attractions, not least in 're-empowering' the role of the colonised in shaping their own cultures. But what it has in common with the acculturation model it seeks to replace is the assumption that the end product is a single, 'blended' culture, derived from two 'pure' parents. In the case of the meeting of two cultures, it attributed a sort of initial 'purity' to each culture, which is only subsequently 'contaminated'. It underestimates the capacity of cultures to redefine themselves as a direct result of contact with the other. The colonial experience can define the coloniser as well as the colonised. As Chris Gosden puts it:

The English were Anglicised through their empire at least as much as through events that happened at 'home'. The same may also be true for the Romans, Aztecs or Chinese.[37]

In this vision, the process of cross-cultural fertilisation is creative, not merely generating a cross-bred offspring with an awkward mixture of features of

---

[34] Freeman (1997); Stray (1998).   [35] Beard and North (1990), Derks (1998).

[36] Le Roux (2004) 301, taken up by Cecconi (2006), Traina (2006).

[37] Gosden (2004) 4; see 60–72 for a critique of 'hybridisation'.

both parents, but allowing both sides to engage in a continuous process of redefinition of self. The Roman empire becomes a great 'middle ground', not simply of the 'Roman' versus the 'other' (in various degrees assimilated to Rome), but an enormous multi-sided exchange across a vast territory, in which 'influences came from everywhere and flowed to everywhere'.[38]

We might, with Gosden, consider another possibility: that in colonialist circumstances, different cultures do not simply blend to form a single new entity (fusion, hybridisation, creolisation, *métissage*), but that the elements can survive in plurality alongside each other, perhaps as 'discrepant identities',[39] or even simply as parallel and coexistent ones. The specific model for 'creole' culture is a linguistic one: a Creole language is an independent language formed from elements of two languages to become something new. But it is not by any means the only possibility. A commoner historical phenomenon is bilingualism, whereby two (or more) languages remain in use alongside each other, often in a pattern of oscillation characterised as 'code-switching' whereby the user moves from one language to another not only from sentence to sentence, but from phrase to phrase.[40] A sentence spoken by a bilingual code-switcher may like a Creole sentence contain elements drawn from two languages. But the switching is always an improvisation, by players who understand the component languages as distinct; whereas a Creole follows the predictable patterns of a true language, with the same combinations of the component elements used by many speakers. What if the outcome of Roman imperial rule was not to create a new consistent blend at local level, but to enable the coexistence of elements of Roman and native culture, with code-switching as an improvisation?

One thesis pursued by this book is that bilingualism is at least as interesting a model as fusion or creolisation.[41] We are fortunate that the linguistic phenomenon in the Roman world has recently been subjected to exhaustive analysis.[42] One firm conclusion is that the Roman world produces no evidence of Creole languages, but abundant evidence of bilingualism and code-switching, and at all social levels: Latin and Greek, Latin and Italic dialects, Latin and Punic, Latin and Gaelic. While there is clear evidence that Roman rule extended the use of Latin across the Mediterranean, there is little of the suppression of local languages. It is rather quaint that, while we regard the Romans has having been rather tolerant in allowing Greek to remain the dominant language of the eastern Mediterranean, the fact that

---

[38] Gosden (2004) 105.   [39] The expression of Mattingly (2006) 491ff.
[40] Myers-Scotton (1990), Heller (1995), Adams, Janse and Swain (2002).   [41] See chs. 2 and 3.
[42] Adams (2003).

African clergy still needed Punic to address their fourth-century congregations is seen as a limit or shortcoming of 'incomplete' romanisation. But that is to assume that the project of romanisation was to substitute one cultural package with another, rather than to introduce the Roman *in addition to* the local.

What Fergus Millar's study of the Roman Near East has shown in great detail is a world in which many cultures remain active alongside each other: Latin, Greek, Syriac coexist linguistically and culturally.[43] Antioch, Jerusalem, Edessa, Emesa, Palmyra and Petra retain highly distinctive local identities alongside new and old common elements. The same can be said of North Africa, where Latin, Greek and Punic coexist. If a doctor, Boncar Clodius son of Mecrasius, and his mother Byrycth daughter of Balsilech, put up tombstones in late first-century CE Lepcis inscribed in Latin, Greek and Punic, it does not make him a Creole, but someone conscious of several identities.[44] The same effect can be reproduced all round the Empire. We must surely deduce that Roman culture was not totalising. The spread of Latin may eventually have resulted in language death for many Italic dialects; but there is a long period of bilinguality before that happens.

Hellenic culture and ethnicity

The focus of the present study is not the romanisation of the provinces, but rather the transformations of Roman culture within Italy itself. But the same set of debates which have made archaeological study of the provinces more lively and dynamic, and more engaged in the critical issues of our own world, are equally relevant for all aspects of cultural change in the ancient world. There has been a curious fragmentation of a set of issues that are closely interrelated, between specialists in different fields of antiquity. Roman provincial archaeologists have only exceptionally engaged with the archaeologists of Roman Italy, and have encountered considerable suspicion in doing so.[45] Hellenisation in Italy has separately been the province of archaeologists, especially art historians, on the one hand, and of philologists

---

[43] Millar (1993).

[44] Reynolds and Ward Perkins (1952) 654–5. See also Traina (2006) 153 for the case of the Tingitanian M.Valerius Severus, son of the (Punic) Bostar, maternal grandson of the (Berber) Izelta.

[45] Terrenato (2001); Sisani (2007) for rejection. I am grateful to Filippo Coarelli for showing me an advanced copy of this book. For other recent reactions, see the dossiers in *Annales, histoire, sciences sociales* 59–2 (2004), 285–383 and *Mélanges de l'École Française de Rome Antiquités* 118–1 (2006), 81–166; Alföldy (2005), Inglebert (2005).

on the other. And the lively debate on culture and identity in the Greek world has had curiously little impact on those looking at the impact of the Greek on the Roman world.

Similar debates are being conducted over the pre-Roman Greek world as over the western provinces of the Roman empire. Both take as their starting point a broader debate in the archaeological discipline about material-culture and ethnicity, which in its turn moves from a wider discussion in sociology, social anthropology and cultural theory about identity. The key issue is how the material-culture record does and does not illuminate issues of identity. The fundamental insight comes from Berger and Luckmann's *Social Construction of Reality*.[46] If social realities are the outcome of our own constructions and not immanent, then the nineteenth-century idea of race, as carrying certain inherent characteristics, potentials and limitations, must be replaced. If the identity of an ethnic group is expressed in its culture, including its material culture, that is only because the group has chosen to construct itself in opposition to other groups.

The 'objective' ascription of identity to groups underpins racist theory; the new ethnicity empowers groups and subgroups to define themselves 'subjectively'. That principle underlies Jonathan Hall's application of such theory to ancient Greece, and in particular to the ethnic groupings of Dorian, Ionian, Aeolian and Achaean.[47] But the insistence on the 'emic' over the 'etic', the 'subjective' over the 'objective' definition of ethnicity, leads in the end to great obstacles in the use of the material-culture record. Only in the discursive self-definition of myth does Hall feel confident of true ethnic identity. Others have urged that even in the literary texts, especially Herodotus, there is awareness of the deliberate use of material culture to distinguish groups:[48] so he depicts the Ionian Athenians as consciously adopting a different form of dress pin to distinguish themselves from their Dorian enemies, the Aeginetans and Argives, who in turn ban offerings of the Attic type in their sanctuaries (Herodotus 5.88), or the Argives and Spartans distinguishing themselves by short and long hair in the aftermath of the battle of the champions (Herodotus 1.82.7).

A related problem is what we mean by an 'ethnic group'. Josh Ober distinguishes different levels: umbrella groups, societal and subsocietal.[49] At the level of umbrella group, we may be looking at those the Greeks themselves characterised as 'ethnic', Dorian, Ionian, etc.; or indeed at the broader grouping of hellenic, to which they ascribed a racial–cultural identity (Herodotus

---

[46] Berger and Luckmann (1966).   [47] Hall (1997), Hall (2002).   [48] Antonaccio (2003).
[49] Ober (2003).

8.144.2, defining the hellene by common descent, language, religions and customs). But as the passages cited above suggest, the most bitter enmities could be between neighbouring *poleis*, and it is these societal groups we might expect to see distinguish themselves in their material culture. Yet in the modern world, it is perhaps above all distinctions of subsocietal groups where ethnicity is most telling: not at the level of the nation-state, but of different ethnic, religious and ideological groupings within the state. These have proved harder to trace in the world of the Greek *polis*, and Morris' attempt to detect distinctiveness in the slave-dominated Attic *deme* of Thorikos drew a blank.[50]

The outcome of such debate in Greek studies has been a more dynamic conceptualisation of culture. No longer taken as a given, a stable matrix inherited from the past and necessarily reproduced, culture becomes a field of energy and dispute:

And so, even if culture is conceptualised as a coherent system, it manifests itself as contradictory practices, members of different subcultures confront each other, clash, reconcile, contest value and meaning, and that contestation forms the material record that is available to us.[51]

Not only the cultural distinctions and conflicts within the Greek world have undergone reassessment, but – and this is of particular significance for the study of Rome – the oppositions of Greek/other. Edith Hall showed convincingly that the opposition of Greek to barbarian was not fully formulated till after (and in response to) the Persian wars.[52] The 'orientalising' world of the seventh and sixth centuries CE was one in which the Greeks were open to innumerable cultural influences from the east. But Burkert's *The Orientalising Revolution* (1992) or West's *East Face of Helicon* (1997) slip, so Dougherty urges, into a model to which commentators on hellenisation in Roman Italy are prone: that culture flows downhill, from high to low, to fill a vacuum, introducing culture where no culture had been.[53] That is exactly the nineteenth-century image of civilisation of the savage: the inferior, primitive races lack civilisation, and Christianity and European culture fill the void, to their benefit. That fails to allow for the active participation of the Greeks in their appropriation and transformation of the 'oriental', just as much as the Romans must be seen as active players in their hellenisation. The opening chapters of Herodotus' histories might point the way:

---

[50] Morris (1998).   [51] Dougherty and Kurke (2003) 1.   [52] Hall (1989).
[53] Burkert (1992), West (1997).

Instead of a one-way voyage of influence from the Near East to Greece, we prefer to describe cross-cultural contact as a series of expeditions moving from west to east as well as east to west, carrying cargo, craftsmen, and colonists; exchanging goods, ideas, and customs; transforming, bartering, and teaching.[54]

In a striking illustration of the risks of buying into the reductive us/them ideologies of the texts, Hagemajer Allen points to the derivation of the iconography of classical Attic grave *stelai* from Achaemenid rock-cut tombs.[55] The totalising anti-barbarian ideology paraded by the Athenians is a mask for continued contact and exchange of ideas. As Margaret Miller, too, has shown, at the very moment of classic conflict with Persia, Athens appropriates Persian idioms.[56]

One point which such studies underline is the danger of monolithic constructions of cultures and identities. Identities are multiple and over-lapping. They exist simultaneously at numerous levels: Greek/barbarian, Dorian/Ionian, Athenian/Aeginetan, Athenian citizen/metic/slave. But it is also false to assume that the various indicators of identity coincide: descent, religion, language and custom, the four elements to which Herodotus points, cross-cut rather than proving coterminous. Religion may divide groups within a community, and it may cut across the boundaries of community. Language, always one of the most potent identifiers, may define submerged ethnic groups within a nation (as Basque, Breton or Welsh), may coexist in multilingual groups (Belgium, Switzerland), and may cut across national boundaries (German speakers). Material-culture must be assumed to be as protean as language or religion. To say that it is not single, fixed, ascribed or bounded is not to say that it is not eloquent, and capable of potent claims to identity. It may, in Bourdieu's terms, leave a trace of the praxis by which the habitus embodied in ideology produces and reproduces itself. But it may conflict with ideology, or coexist in tension with it.

Hellenisation and romanisation

Where do these debates impact on the question of cultural change and identity in Italy itself? An underlying problem is that of fragmentation of disciplines. From the viewpoint of the Italian local archaeologist, the roman-isation of the diverse populations of the Italian peninsula is a vast subject, with innumerable case-studies, and a number of syntheses, which for all their differences regard the diverse and conflicting case-study evidence as

[54] Dougherty and Kurke (2003) 5.   [55] Hagemajer Allen (2003).   [56] Miller (1997).

pointing to a single, overarching process.[57] It is this branch of study that stands closest to discussions of provincial romanisation, and where doubts about a 'top-down' model of universal acculturation have been articulated.[58]

But a closely overlapping domain is that of the art historian, concerned with monumental architecture, sculpture and the 'fine arts', whether at Rome itself or in the cities of Italy. Here the emphasis has been rather on hellenisation: that is, not on the impact of Roman culture on communities beyond Rome, but on the importation of skills, styles and ideas from the hellenistic East. Since the classic Göttingen conference on *Hellenismus in Mittelitalien* (1974), it has been common ground that Italy witnesses a widespread transformation, especially in the aftermath of the Punic wars, with many common features, that cannot be taken as an imposition of Roman culture but which is indeed the direct consequence of the Roman unification of Italy, of the common experience of eastern campaigns by Rome and her allies, in which Rome played a dominant role. From this point of view, '*Hellenisierung*' is an aspect of '*Romanisierung*'.[59] For those in this field there has been little hesitation in associating cultural change with political power, and the ideological element of public building and art has always been to the fore: the great exhibition held in Berlin on *Kaiser Augustus und die verlorene Republik* (1988) and its associated publication firmly locates artistic change in the political context of the collapse of the political system of the republic and the establishment of a new order by Augustus.[60] The argument of Paul Zanker brings this set of approaches to its clearest expression: a transformation of the visual language of the world of imagery, that abandons a hellenistic idiom in exchange for a classicising one, is the outcome of a change in Roman ideology on which the new imperial order is based.[61] Any worries that hellenisation as a process inverts the normal power-relationship or that acculturation reflects the hegemony of the conquerors are put to rest by an argument which shows the conquerors manipulating cultural idiom for their own ideological ends.[62]

We may ask why discussion of this process of hellenisation has remained distinct from that of romanisation in Italy. Studies in each area are undertaken in full awareness of the other. But the two are conceptualised as distinct processes. So even a study which underlines the diversity of the phenomena

---

[57] David (1994), Vallat (1995), Torelli (1999).   [58] Keay and Terrenato (2001).

[59] Zanker (1976) 11–20. Note the formulation (at p. xx): 'Einheimische Traditionen *verschmelzen* in dieser Zeit endgültig mit Lebensformen der hellenistischen Koine.'

[60] Hofter (1988).   [61] Zanker (1988).

[62] For the inversion of power relations, see Gallini (1973), and below.

described as 'romanisation' sees hellenisation as a separate but similar phenomenon:

> The closest parallel for Romanization is Italy is perhaps Hellenization, in the sense that it was a process that reduced differences across a range of disparate phenomena such as elite taste, the organization of land or political systems, across a peninsula where local and ethnic peculiarities always played the strongest role.[63]

But if it is true that it was hellenisation that made the diverse populations of Italy more similar in taste, economic relations and politics, how can one distinguish it at all from romanisation? Of course, the answer is that it depends whom you are imitating, Greeks or Romans. In this, the idea of hellenisation as a distinctive cultural phenomenon gains much strength from the parallel phenomenon in literature and intellectual life: again, this is a separate debate, but one conducted in full awareness of its correlate in material-culture. The 'debt' of Roman literature to Greek has always been one of the central concerns of Latin literary critics, and from the early twentieth-century attempts to isolate 'das Römische', there has been an unwillingness to view the Romans as passive victims of an acculturation process. Critics are also happy to see literature in the context of a broader transformation of intellectual life, magisterially charted by Elizabeth Rawson.[64] Changing fashions in the study of material culture have had a direct impact on the interpretation of hellenisation in literature, particularly in its political and ideological implications.[65]

In the case of literature or intellectual life, the category of hellenisation seems self-evident. One could hardly apply the term romanisation to the use by Latin writers of Greek models and concepts. But that is achieved by defining it in terms of its cultural 'sources'. Focus instead on the geographical origins of the writers of Latin literature, and we have what is a particularly striking aspect of the romanisation of Italy: from the *semigraeci*, like Livius Andronicus or Ennius of Rudiae in the heel of Italy, with his three hearts, Greek, Oscan and Latin, to Plautus of Umbrian Sarsina, or the Cisalpines of the late first century BCE, Catullus and Virgil, we have a consistent picture whereby the production of Latin literature at Rome is pioneered by Italian 'outsiders' – apart, that is, from the 'public' genres of Roman history and oratory. The continuation of the phenomenon into the empire, together with the pattern whereby authors are the vanguard of new waves of political participation (Spaniards in the first century CE, Africans in the second),

---

[63] Keay and Terrenato (2001) 3.   [64] Rawson (1985).
[65] Galinsky (1996), Habinek and Schiesaro (1997), Feeney (1998).

makes it hard not to recognise literature and intellectual life as a fundamental feature of the romanisation process, if by that we mean the spread to the cities of Italy and the provinces of a common language and culture in which all were active participants.

Why, then, are we so keen to analyse them as separate processes? The spread throughout Italy of architectural monuments, luxury goods, domestic forms, ways of writing and ways of thinking that are all deeply impregnated with the 'Greek' tells us more about the power of Rome than the power of the hellenic. It is as if the frequency of Greek slave names in Italy were to qualify slavery as an aspect of hellenisation: as if where they came from mattered more than why they got there and what functions they served.

The answers to these questions lie in the periodisation of the ancient world established in the early nineteenth century, and to the potent influence of Johannes Gottlieb Droysen in articulating a model of the cultural transformations of the ancient Mediterranean. In his *Geschichte des Hellenismus* (1836), Droysen used 'hellenism' and 'hellenistic' to denote a period which he saw as characterised by the extension of hellenic culture, in the aftermath of Alexander's conquests, to the East, and the creation of a new '*Verschmelzung*' or 'fusion' of East and West. The historical mission of the Hellene, having taken inspiration from the Orient (orientalisation), is to civilise the eastern Mediterranean (hellenisation), reaching a climax in the late hellenisation of Rome. Rome's mission, then, once hellenised, is to Romanise the west, and so lay the ground for European civilisation – which of course in its turn will westernise/Christianise/secularise/industrialise/modernise its colonies on other continents and the third world at large, culminating in globalisation. On that scheme, hellenisation is the necessary *logical* precondition for romanisation, even if the two seem to run *chronologically* parallel in the Italy of the late republic.

Interestingly enough, Droysen's thinking already showed the direct impact of the European colonialist experience. As Luciano Canfora has shown, Droysen owed a particular debt to the Roman historian Niebuhr, who in publishing a number of inscriptions from Egypt and the East, had pointed to the emergence of a 'bastardised' form of the Greek language, with rules different from that of classical Greek, one which from Droysen onwards would be called 'hellenistic Greek', formed in his view from the experience of Greek spoken in oriental lands, the result of a fusion or *Verschmelzung*.[66] Droysen had an explicit colonial model in mind: thanks in part to the influence of his teacher, the Danish ethnographer Father Carsten, Niebuhr could point

---

[66] Canfora (1987). I owe this important reference to Filippo Coarelli.

to the parallel of the Creole spoken in French Haiti and San Domingo, to explain the transformation of Greek in Egypt and the Orient.[67] Creolisation, far from being a new model to transform the models of cultural change in antiquity, appears to lie at the roots of their formation.

Droysen, in giving currency to the term 'hellenism' to characterise not only the distinctive form of Greek language, but also the entire culture of the Greek-speaking, or 'hellenistic', world created by Alexander's conquests, gave rise to much controversy. One controversy was over his use of the word 'hellenism'. Richard Laqueur maintained that in Greek texts *hellēnizein* and *hellēnismos*, referred overwhelmingly to linguistic usage, especially correct linguistic usage, in contrast to *barbarismos*, the incorrect language of a foreigner, or *soloecismos*, the speech of those like the citizens of Soloi whose Greek was not proper.[68] He argued that Droysen had misread a passage in the *Acts of the Apostles* (6.1) distinguishing Jews from *hellēnistai*, or simply Greek-speakers. The charge has been frequently repeated; but, as Canfora showed, not only did Droysen never refer to the *Acts*, but he believed he had authority for his usage in the title of a (lost) treatise by Irenaeus Pacatus, 'On the dialect of the Alexandrians, or *hellēnismos*'.[69] But despite Canfora's defence (and the title may be interpreted not as 'the Alexandrian dialect as a new form of Greek', but 'Alexandrian dialect in contrast to proper grammatical Greek'), neither hellenistic Greek nor hellenistic culture is a convincing product of a fusion or creolisation (there are no Egyptian or Syrian elements), and the fusion model was inappropriate from the start.

There is more to be learned from the usage of the term *hellēnismos*. Since Laqueur, the digitisation of Greek Literature by the Thesaurus Linguae Graecae (TLG) has rendered Greek usage far easier to control. Searching the word-group *hellēnizein*, *hellēnistēs*, *hellēnismos* only bears out Laqueur's analysis. 'Hellenising' is what Greeks do when they speak Greek. With considerable frequency, the words are used of foreigners: so the Attic orator Aeschines can attack Demosthenes as 'the son of a barbarian Scythian mother, hellenising in his speech', the geographer Agatharchides refers to the Persian Boxos who left his country for Athens 'and hellenised in his speech and thinking', while Plutarch mentions that the philosopher Clitomachus was born a Carthaginian, named Hasdrubal, and 'was taught to hellenise'.[70] At one point, Greek usage differs sharply from modern: the verb is active and

---

[67] Canfora (1987) 24, 71–6.　　[68] Laqueur (1928); see further Bichler (1983) 5–32.

[69] Canfora (1987) 12–14.

[70] Aeschines, *in Ctesiphonten* 172.11; Agatharchides, *de mari Erythraeo* 5; Plutarch, *de Alexandri fortuna* 328d2.

intransitive: 'hellenising' is what the foreign Greek-speaker does for himself, not something that he does to others, or that is done to him. The modern transitive usage, whereby a colonial power 'hellenises' (or 'romanises') another people is simply never met. When we rarely encounter a situation of forced hellenisation, such as the pressure brought to bear by Antiochus IV Epiphanes of Syria on the Jews to adopt Greek ways, it is expressed as 'he forced the Jews to hellenise', *not* 'he hellenised the Jews'.[71] This pattern holds good in over 440 uses of the verb *hellēnizein*.[72]

The exception to this rule is in the rare use of the compound, ἀφελλη-νιζειν/*aphellēnizein*. We met at the outset Favorinus, who regarded himself as having become, despite being Roman, completely Greek, *aphellēnisthē*, through his *paideia*. Here his adoption of another culture is evidently voluntary, not imposed from outside. But the Jewish author Philo, in a highly panegyrical account of the reign of Augustus in his *Embassy to Gaius*, goes rather further. His Augustus had the ultimate civilising mission: he brought an end to wars and brigandage, cleared the seas of pirates and promoted trade, restored the liberty of every city, brought order in the place of disorder, domesticated the brutality of uncivilised tribes, boosted Hellas with many a new Hellas, and rendered hellenic (*aphellēnisas*) the vital parts of barbarian lands.[73] It is ironical that the one passage suggesting the imposition of Greek culture on barbarian peoples is by a Roman emperor, whose business we might otherwise suppose to be romanisation.[74]

Droysen's vision of hellenism, which has done so much to shape our periodisation of ancient history, is the outcome of a historically determined set of ideologies; on the one hand colonialist in its vision of cultural fusion, on the other hand, as Momigliano argued, stamped with Hegelian Protestant teleology, in its vision of the process of history as a cultural preparation for the arrival of Christianity.[75] That Alexander's conquests, in dramatically extending Greek power in the East, generated a series of important cultural transformations, we may accept. It is the characterisation of such transformation as a 'fusion' that is most in doubt. The doubts rise most acutely to the fore when we consider the effects of this transformation in the western Mediterranean, and specifically in the cultural interaction with Roman power.

---

[71] So Eusebius, *Demonstratio Evangelica* 10.1, and numerous similar passages in Church writers.

[72] The exceptional passive form, *hēllēnisthēsan*, used by Thucydides 2.68 of the Acarnanians, indicates that they became Greek in their speech, not that they were made so by others.

[73] Philo, *Legatio ad Gaium* 147, 'tēn de barbaron en tois anagkaiotatois tmēmasin aphellēnisas'.

[74] See Veyne (1980) 123, Marotta (2006) 105.

[75] Gilbert (1931); Momigliano (1955), Momigliano (1977); Bichler (1983) esp. 96–105.

The difficulties that surround the application of the hellenisation model to Rome can be addressed once we acknowledge the underlying flaws in Droysen's fusion model, and his perverse reading of '*hellēnismos*' not as the attempt to reinforce a model of correct Greek language and culture, in the face of colonial expansion, in lands where it stood in danger of 'corruption', but as the fusion of Greek with other languages, the very debasement the hellenists sought to avoid. Scholars have pointed to three principal problem areas in the idea of hellenisation at Rome.[76] First, there is the formidable problem of the inverse flow of culture and power, summed up in the Horatian line, 'Graecia capta ferum victorem cepit'. Captive Greece turns on its 'uncouth' conqueror, and inverts the process of military conquest through cultural conquest.[77] This model of hellenisation implies an essentially passive role for the Romans. Willing victims, as if in some perverse game of sexual domination, they accept that Greek culture is 'superior' and surrender their 'primitive' culture to its control. Such a model is evidently unsatisfactory. As Clara Gallini puts the dilemma in classic Marxist terms, a change at the level of superstructure ought to reflect changes at the level of structure: a conquest state will hardly transform its culture except to serve the purposes of its conquest. Because the colonial experience of acculturation has been marked by spread of culture from the dominant powers downwards, we must look to modes of appropriation where external cultural models are deliberately taken over to serve the purposes of the society concerned. Both Gallini and Veyne point to the post-war appropriation by Japan of western cultural values as part of a strategy of aggressive competition with western economic dominance; but not even here do we escape from the model of the transformation of the 'loser'.

Here, Gosden's idea of a 'middle ground', in which cultures stand in dialectic with one another, provides a way out. If we focus on the reciprocity of the process whereby the colonial power not only provides powerful new cultural models to the colonised, but in turn takes to itself cultural models from the colonised (enough to refer to the spread of tea and curry in colonial Britain, and the fashions for oriental art and religion), we can allow that Roman conquest of Greece led not to fusion but reciprocal exchange. The cultures do not fuse (any more than they did in the 'hellenistic east'), but enter into a vigorous and continuous process of dialogue with one another. Romans can 'hellenise' (speak Greek, imitate Greek culture) without becoming less

---

[76] Gallini (1973); Veyne (1979); Hölscher (1990); Curti, Dench and Patterson (1996) 181ff.

[77] Horace, *Epistles* 2.1.156f.: 'Graecia capta ferum victorem cepit et artes/intulit agresti Latio.' The whole epistle is concerned with the relationship of Greek and Latin literature.

Roman: indeed, the mutual awareness may have the effect of defining their
Romanness more sharply by contrast. Reciprocally, the Greeks under Roman
rule define their own identity more sharply by *paideia* even as they become
Roman in other ways.

This may account for the apparent ambivalence of Romans about the process. As Erich Gruen has demonstrated in detail, numerous Roman voices
of protest about the imitation of Greek and the intrusion of eastern ways
did not diminish the vigour and confidence with which the Roman elite
appropriated what suited its own purposes.[78] The voices of the Romans
commenting on the process are shot through with an irony that reflects the
fact of dialogue (not fusion). Horace, the son of a freedman who learned
from his father that you could become a good Roman the Roman way by
following *exemplum,* and whose poetic output depends on a ransacking of
Greek literature as thorough as that of a Mummius, exposed the contradiction by representing the conquering power as captive. His wording echoes
some earlier formulations of the problem.[79] In contact with Greek sophistication, the Roman represents himself as 'wild' and 'uncivilised': so Porcius
Licinus in the late second century represents the Muse arriving in the second
Punic war with winged step among the bellicose and wild race of Romulus.[80] The language of an external force bringing culture into a primitive, but
successfully bellicose, race ('intulit se bellicosam in Romuli gentem feram')
is picked up by Horace ('ferum victorem cepit et artis/intulit'). Equally,
he reflects Cicero's extensive discussion of the competition between Greek
and Latin literature in the *Tusculan Disputations* (1.1): He is willing to concede defeat (doctrina Graecia nos . . . superabat), but only in so far as the
Romans were not interested in winning this particular battle ('facile vin-
cere non repugnantes', it is easy to defeat those who do not fight back).
But while the arrival of Greek culture in Rome may be represented as a
defeat, it can equally be seen as a conquest. Against the Horatian 'Graecia
capta' should always be set the alternative image expressed by Ovid (but
rarely cited): the Roman boasts to have robbed the Greek of his culture by
conquest:

Nondum tradiderat victas victoribus artes/Graecia
Greece had not yet surrendered its conquered arts to the conquerors.[81]

---

[78] Gruen (1990), Gruen (1992). Also, Hölscher (1990).   [79] Cf. Whitmarsh (2001b) 9–14.
[80] Cited by Aulus Gellius 17,21,45, fr. 1 in *Fragmenta Poetarum Latinorum*: 'Poenico bello secundo
Musa pinnato gradu/intulit se bellicosam in Romuli gentem feram.'
[81] Ovid, *Fasti* 3.101f.

Acknowledge that the process is in fact a continuous dialogue, with no winners and no losers, and it is more evident why the same phenomenon can be represented at will as victory or defeat.

This links to a second set of problems inherent in the term 'hellenisation'. It is used to describe the changes of a specific period, starting approximately in the late third century BCE, that corresponds to the period characterised by Droysen as 'hellenistic'. In Roman terms, it is marked by the beginnings of Latin literature, and in some senses of 'Roman art'. The perception that before this date, say some time in the second Punic war, the Romans were uncouth barbarians is an idea, as we have seen, promoted by the Romans themselves. That this period is marked by a quantum leap in terms of cultural change is beyond doubt; but it must be said at once that the idea of Rome before 200 BCE as 'rustic', untouched by Greek influence, and more authentically 'Roman' than what follows it, is purest myth, a false image of the past generated in the second century BCE for rhetorical purposes.[82] The archaeology of early Rome and the middle republic definitively refutes that image. Early Rome was very far from wild and uncouth: Greek culture leaves its mark on Rome at every moment we can document, and the more we learn about archaic Rome, the more we are inclined to accept, even if in a rather different sense, the argument of the Augustan historian, Dionysius of Halicarnassus, that Rome was from the first a Greek city.[83] It is no longer possible to think of the 'grande Roma dei Tarquini' except in terms of close contact with a world of Greek culture, whether or not mediated by the Etruscans.[84] Nor is it convincing to posit a sort of 'Dark Age' between archaic Rome and the late republic when hellenising culture dries up. The problem is rather one of shortage of evidence; but the material assembled, for instance, in the *Roma medio-repubblicana* exhibition of 1973 shows a Rome open at all points to contemporary Greek currents.[85]

The apparent contradiction, of a Rome not barbarian and uncivilised, but already exposed to centuries of Greek influence, embarking like a neophyte on a new experience of hellenisation, can be resolved once we free ourselves from the fusion model. Rather than seeing hellenisation as an irreversible

---

[82] See, e.g., Horsfall (1993), Wiseman (1994) 26–9, Feeney (1998) 25–8, 50–2, Wiseman (2004) 13ff. For a masterly analysis of successive waves of hellenism, see Coarelli (1996c) 15–84.

[83] Cf. Fox (1993), revised in Fox (1996). Cf. Musti (1988).

[84] See Cristofani (1990) for the exhibition catalogue on *La Grande Roma dei Tarquini*. Cornell (1995) 86ff. argues for direct Greek influence in the rise of the city-state of Rome. Eduard Fraenkel's Oxford inaugural of 1935, 'Greek and Roman culture', Fraenkel (1964), had already emphasised the early start of Greek influence.

[85] Various authors (1973). The point is made by Gallini (1973) 184. See also Dondero and Pensabene (1982).

conversion, a passage from barbarian to hellenic, we may see it instead as a perpetually renewable dialogue, a set of exchanges whereby the hellenic (or, rather, the dominant variant thereof at any one time, Euboean, Corinthian, Attic, South Italian, Alexandrian, Pergamene, etc.) is constantly imitated, without in any way diminishing Roman or Italic identity. The intensity of the dialogue is surely greater in the last two centuries BCE, enabled by the wholesale transfer of resources, human, intellectual and material, that results from Roman conquest in the eastern Mediterranean. But even at the end of the period, the process is no more complete than at its outset: the exchange will continue with equal vigour for at least another four centuries, so long as a cross-Mediterranean traffic remains intense. Rome can continue to absorb from the East without becoming eastern, just as the Greek East can continuously absorb from Rome without becoming less Greek.

The third difficulty, that of extricating the process of 'hellenisation' from that of 'romanisation', is one we have already seen. The two processes of cultural exchange are not separable but interdependent. The spread of 'hellenistic' urban models in central Italy follows the spread of Roman roads and control: here hellenisation is synonymous with romanisation.[86] The *political* fact of Roman domination is expressed through the *stylistic* adoption of hellenistic forms. In this sense, if Rome has a cultural 'mission civilisatrice', it depends on the borrowing of hellenic culture, so that Augustus may, not unreasonably, be seen by Philo as hellenising, not romanising, the entire Roman world, Greek and barbarian. As cultural missionaries, the Romans are middle-men, buying civilisation at a discount in the East, to sell it on at a premium in the West. 'Hellenisation' and 'romanisation' are not sequential, but two closely interrelated aspects of the same phenomenon.

But the same problem applies even if we consider the central aspects of Roman 'high culture' itself. Is it that Roman art is 'hellenised' by using the language of Greek art, or that Romans, in appropriating Greek art forms, 'romanise' them? Here the doubts raised long ago by Otto Brendel remain to the point: is there really any such thing as 'Roman' art? While the pursuit of an essential 'Roman' style that characterises and unifies Roman art is highly tendentious, we can indeed speak meaningfully of Rome as a major centre of artistic production, or the Roman empire as a specific period when art is produced under Roman control. 'Greek' art, on the other hand, can be identified stylistically (even when produced in Rome), and belongs to no single centre of production.[87] It would appear that not only for art,

---

[86] Zanker (1976); Curti, Dench and Patterson (1996).   [87] Brendel (1953 (n.p. 1973)).

but more broadly, 'Greek' and 'Roman' are not strictly parallel as types of cultural identity: while the 'Greek' is defined precisely by its hellenic culture, the 'Roman' is defined by political structures. Everything under Roman control may be taken as 'Roman', whereas within that control, the 'Greek' may remain culturally distinctive.

Hence 'hellenisation' may refer to a stylistic change at the very same time that 'romanisation' describes its political effect. It is a contradiction with which we can live, provided we do not trap ourselves in a model of *Verschmelzung*. Rome transforms both itself and the rest of Italy by opening itself to a new intensity of influence through conquest of the east, undertaken hand in hand with the Italian allies. But what is perhaps most striking about the double process is the perpetual transformational power of the heart of power at Rome itself. To pursue an anatomic metaphor, it is as if hellenisation and romanisation represented the two phases of the circulation of the blood. If hellenisation is the diastolic phase, by which blood is drawn in to the centre, romanisation is the systolic phase, that pumps the oxygenated blood back to the extremities. It is not enough to have one single, prolonged phase of the one, followed by a similar, single, long phase of the other, because the two need to alternate constantly, to keep the system alive.[88]

The principal stumbling block thus appears to be the tacit assumption that culture is unitary, that you must be one thing or another, or even a blend of the two, but not both at the same time. Whether we follow the late-nineteenth-century reading of culture as the assemblage of ascriptive identifiers of an ethnic group (its language, beliefs, customs and assemblage of material culture), or the more recent reading as the set of choices and practices by which a group constructs, interprets and reproduces its own identity, it is hard to talk about any form of acculturation (in the sense of cultural appropriations from one group to another) without raising fundamental questions about identity itself. Whether colonial acculturation is seen as positive (the civilising of the savage) or negative (the suppression of native traditions by the homogenising force of an external power), it is assumed that culture is a zero-sum game: one culture (savage/native) is displaced by another (civilising/colonialist). Hybridisation only reintroduces the initial problem: it allows an active role to the native in creating a new assemblage, but still assumes that the old (native) is displaced by the new (hybrid).

The alternative model of bilingualism, or rather multilingualism, points the way to other possibilities: of populations that can sustain simultaneously

---

[88] See ch. 8 for further exploration of this image.

diverse culture-systems, in full awareness of their difference, and code-switch between them. Feeney has argued that one of the most striking characteristics of Roman culture from the earliest stage – that is, the first waves of Greek colonisation in Italy – is the ability to maintain its difference from the Greek while constantly modifying itself in directions assimilable to the Greek.[89] The close contact between two cultures allows endless possibilities for contamination (call it 'creolisation' if preferred), but so long as the Roman constructs itself as different from the Greek, the Greek elements it has borrowed/appropriated/imitated/stolen/hijacked are romanised by an act of self-redefinition.

Culture does not merely say who you are. It says who you are *in relation to others*. It states proximities as well as differences. Italic hellenisers do not state that they are Greeks. They reveal that they are in contact with Greeks, that they know, and can speak, something of their cultural language. Speaking the language does not of itself betray a power-relationship; but an understanding of what that power-relationship is changes the way you read multi-linguality. There are (as we shall see) Roman hesitations over the speaking of Greek as a possible admission of weakness; but the Greek spoken by a Roman conscious of superiority is a signal of strength. The Oscan-speaker who also speaks Latin knows it is the language of the conqueror, and may, according to circumstance, regret the loss of independence or rejoice in being on the winning side: the Oscan who speaks Latin as an Italiote on Delos has the advantage, and in speaking Greek in addition only strengthens the advantage, since Greek enjoys currency without dominance. Should the Oscan-speaking Italiote find himself speaking Greek to a Latin-speaking Italiote, he enjoys an additional advantage, of distance from the language of domination. To this argument we shall return in later chapters.[90]

Ideas of culture

Terms like 'hellenisation' and 'romanisation' are fraught with difficulties, though this is no reason for avoiding them completely, but rather for unpacking them carefully and not using them unreflectingly.[91] These difficulties, however, reflect the much graver problems that surround the word 'culture' itself.

---

[89] Feeney (1998) 25–8.   [90] See esp. ch. 3.

[91] *Pace* Syme (1988) 64: 'In modern textbooks the term "Romanisation" is put to frequent employment. It is ugly and vulgar, worse than that, anachronistic and misleading.' Cited by Keay in Keay and Terrenato (2001), 122.

Far from being a stable and agreed concept, 'culture' is fluid and disputed; and the history of the word holds within itself a reflection of the class-conflict of the post-industrial society which created and used it. As Raymond Williams has shown, modern English usage dates back only to the late eighteenth century, when the vital extension from its previous application to husbandry ('the culture of crops') took place in close conjunction with the emergence of a group of other keywords: industry, democracy, class and art.[92] The division of society by class came to substitute the older division by rank: as we will see in examining 'luxury' (ch. 7), the long historical objections to luxury lay in its confusion of social hierarchy. As the hierarchy of rank collapsed in industrialised society, 'class' emerged as a new form of distinction, and 'culture' played a key role in underpinning the differences of class. From its origins down to current usage, 'culture' has been not a neutrally descriptive term, but a highly charged concept, embodying emotions, values, and conflicts that must be understood in the context of the social framework within which it has been produced.

The English idea of culture belongs to a Continental context, to ideas of 'culture' and 'civilisation' that emerged in France and Germany in the second half of the eighteenth century. As Norbert Elias showed in his study of 'The Civilising Process',[93] *civilisation* emerges as a positive term, opposed to barbarism, in French writing of around 1760, with a consciously wider reference than the *civilité* or *politesse* which were the characteristic virtues of court society. In French, *civilisation* was a process affecting the whole people including, crucially, the bourgeoisie. In German society, in which by contrast there was no integration of the German-speaking middle class with the French-speaking court circles, the term *Zivilisation* remained closely associated with the values of the court circles, and *Bildung* and *Kultur* (originally *Cultur*) became the watchwords of the middle-class intellectuals engaged in pioneering of a new German literature and culture. The legitimating ideals of the intelligentsia, '*das rein Geistige* (the purely spiritual), in books, scholarship, religion, art, philosophy, in the inner enrichment, the intellectual formation (*Bildung*) of the individual' were evolved in conscious conflict with what appeared the empty and superficial manners of the court aristocracies.[94]

But though this image of *Kultur* is idealising, the more neutral concept of culture as what characterises a people emerged very early. Already in the

---

[92] Williams (1961); supplemented and modified by Williams (1983) esp. 87–93; see also Eagleton (2000) 1–31.

[93] Elias (1978) ch. 1. On Elias' contribution, see also Kuper (1998).

[94] Elias (1978) 27; cf. Kroeber and Kluckholm (1952).

late eighteenth century Johann Gottlieb Herder in his universal history of mankind had resisted the idea that human history represented a unilinear process of development of civilisation or culture towards a culmination in contemporary European culture.[95] 'The very thought of a superior European culture is a blatant insult to the majesty of Nature.'[96] On the contrary, he saw every people (*Volk*) as having its own 'culture'. Yet (unlike many who later used the term less cautiously), he recognised that 'Nothing is more indeterminate than this word, nothing more deceptive than its application to entire peoples and epochs'.[97]

'Culture' as a high ideal was rather slower to emerge in England than in Germany, but does so in full polemic vigour in Matthew Arnold's *Culture and Anarchy* (1869). Arnold stands in a tradition of English thinkers deeply concerned with the perceived growth in the gulf between classes consequent upon industrialisation.[98] Culture is his antidote to the anarchy that threatens a society split by class division; and it is locked in conflict with the 'Philistinism' promoted by the external values of a 'mechanical' society concerned with Wealth, Industry, Production and Progress. Arnold's culture belongs to no one social class: neither to the barbarous aristocracy, with their vested interest in the *status quo*, nor the philistine middle classes, nor to the degraded and brutal populace. It is offered as a common solution to all classes, 'as the great help out of our present difficulties; culture being a pursuit of our total perfection by means of getting to know, on all the matters which most concern us, the best which has been thought or said in the world'. Arnold's culture is an ideal, and one which requires commitment: 'Culture is the passion for sweetness and light, and (what is more) the passion for making them prevail.' But Arnold's recipe for culture, with its heavy stress on classical education, and its dismissal of scientific culture implicit in the polemic against the Philistine and mechanical, provoked sharp reaction in England against the whole notion of culture, dismissed by its opponents as unEnglish ('this same . . . *sauerkraut* or *culture*').[99]

When Edward Tylor in his pioneering work of anthropology, *Primitive Culture* (1871) offered an alternative definition of the word, he did so in this context of controversy. '*Culture* or *civilisation*, taken in its wide ethnographic sense, is that complex whole which includes knowledge, belief, art, morals, law, custom and any other capabilities and habits acquired by man as a member of society.' Precisely in denying that culture is an ideal, and

---

[95] See Kroeber and Kluckholm (1952) 22–3.

[96] *Ideas on the Philosophy of the History of Mankind* (1784–91), cited by Williams (1983) 89.

[97] Cited by Williams (1983) 89, and by Díaz-Andreu (1996) 52.   [98] Williams (1961) ch. 6.

[99] See Young (1995) for Arnold from a post-colonial perspective.

one delimited by the traditions of western civilisation, and seeing it as an inescapable feature of living in any human society, Tylor reverts to Herder's image of a world of many cultures, and thereby subverts the key feature of Arnold's missionary zeal.

This 'ethnographic' approach to culture, inherited by Tylor from Herder and subsequent German writers, blossomed among the anthropologists of the twentieth century,[100] not only becoming a dominant concept within the discipline, but so diverse in its usage that, by the 1950s, Kroeber and Kluckhohn could chart and categorise 154 different definitions of the term.[101] The last half-century of cultural anthropology would make that count seem modest now. The more recent explosion of interest in popular culture, sub-cultures, class cultures and subaltern cultures have continuously extended the application of the concept, though the underlying idea remains constant that 'culture' cannot be restricted to the higher values of an elite group, but is the complex of behavioural characteristics and values which identify a group of any sort. Such a 'value-free' definition of culture wears a false appearance of objectivity: for the identification of such patterns of behaviour as systems, as coherent packages which make sense in themselves, and deserve respect and study in their own right, constitutes a challenge to the implicit assumptions of 'high culture', that the classical intellectual and artistic tradition of western civilisation is superior and morally improving.[102]

What emerges from the history of the word 'culture' is not two separate usages, which sit almost by coincidence within the same lexeme, but a contestation inherent from the first in both usages. The 'unmarked', 'value-free' usage resists the claims of the 'marked' usage to superior value, while the marked usage rebuffs the claims of the unmarked usage to any true coherence or value. This background is of particular significance to the student of the ancient Mediterranean world, since 'classical culture' is historically implicated in the debate. It is the model and the legitimation of the claims to validity of the 'higher culture' of nineteenth-century western societies; and simultaneously it is the victim of a twentieth-century rebellion against those values and the social systems that drew their legitimation from it. Paradoxically, it is the overthrow of the claims to dominance of the classical within modern culture that liberates the student of ancient societies to

---

[100] Díaz-Andreu (1996) 54–5. Note the debt to Pasteur's concept of culture in the biological sphere: Herbert (1991).

[101] Kroeber and Kluckholm (1952) 41–79.

[102] Compare the inbuilt contestation in the idea of 'popular' versus 'high' culture: Frow (1995) 60–88.

recover their cultural diversity and their multiplicity across place and time, and to look afresh at how culture in its unmarked sense served to mark changing identities, to legitimate and reproduce systems of power.

Paideia and mores

To acknowledge both the cultural specificity of the concept of culture (it is *our* way of interpreting experience) and the still unresolved tension that lies at its heart does not disqualify it as a tool for approaching antiquity, at least so long as we do not confuse our conceptual categories with theirs. It is consequently revealing to ask what concepts were available in Greek and Latin to describe what we call 'cultural change' at Rome. The matter is not, however, so simple as establishing two alternative conceptual frameworks, one modern, one ancient. For one crucial complication (underestimated in the discussion of the modern concept) is that the ideas of 'civilisation' and 'culture' were developed by men across Europe steeped in knowledge of classical literature, and for whom, as we have seen, classical literature itself could represent a central value in the ideal of a modern culture.[103]

The word 'culture' itself is a conscious Latin derivative. The base sense of 'cultivation of the fields' that Williams detects in earlier English usage of the word is the base sense of Latin *cultura*; and the extension to the idea of the cultivation of the mind that Williams sees as the first step in its extension derives directly from Latin. If Bacon could speak of 'the culture and manurance of minds' (1605),[104] it was because he knew his Cicero: philosophy was the cultivation of the mind ('cultura animi philosophia est').[105] The metaphor of cultivation implies a parallelism of human life with nature. As nature may be wild and uncultivated, and is perceived as tamed and improved by human cultivation, so human life itself ranges from the wild and uncultivated to the civilised. This idea is expressed by the words which are the roots of our 'civilisation' and 'culture': 'to bring men from a wild and rustic way of life to humane and civil culture',[106] already contains the roots of western notions of culture (*cultum*), civilisation (*civilem*) and humanity (*humanum*). *Cultus*, in this sense, is explicitly a value, something which may be present or absent from human life, and which enriches and improves from its presence. Cicero invokes such ideas precisely where he is

---

[103] See Dench (2005) 65–9.   [104] Cited by Williams (1983) 77.

[105] *Tusculan Disputations* 2.13; cf. *de Finibus* 5.54, etc.

[106] Cicero, *Orator* 1.33: 'homines a fera agrestique vita ad humanum cultum civilemque deducere.'

justifying the appropriation into Latin of features of Greek culture perceived to be alien.

The Romans were quite capable of conceding that they had once been uncivilised. So Virgil's Evander explains to Aeneas that, before the reign of Saturn, Fauns and Nymphs had lived in Latium without custom or culture: 'quis neque mos neque cultus erat' (*Aeneid* 8.316). It was Saturn who brought together a scattered race, and gave them laws. The twin ideas of *mos*, the implicitly superior customary behaviour, including the reliance on laws, that marks the Roman, and *cultus*, the cultivation that distances from savagery, lie at the origins of our twin senses of 'culture', as both that which defines and that which improves. *Cultus* already incorporates the strange mixture of references that makes the idea of 'culture' so protean, from knowledge of a tradition of classical literature to the manners, including sexual manners, of a polite society: thus Ovid's celebration of the golden Roman of his day, welcomes its 'culture' in contrast to the primitive Rome of Romulus, 'quia cultus adest' (*Ars Amatoria* 3.127). Augustan Rome already had 'culture'.

Cultura/cultus offer the immediate etymological roots of the modern 'culture' but by no means exhaust its classical conceptualisation. A whole complex of ideas needs to be taken into account; the local boundaries between these ideas are of importance for the construction of any ancient conceptual framework. What in the present context is perhaps most striking and significant is the profound difference in construction of these ideas between Greek and Latin.

For the Greek, as Favorinus has already illustrated, it is the twin concepts of *hellēnismos* and *paideia* that lie at the heart of any concept of culture. The assumption of the natural superiority of the hellene to the barbarian, which has its origins in the Persian wars of the fifth century BCE,[107] and set out as a matter of scientific doctrine by the fifth-century treatise on *Airs, Waters and Places* preserved in the Hippocratic *corpus*, meant that Greek ways of doing things, the nexus of language, religion and custom (*nomoi*), were not merely different, but superior. Hence the barbarian (maybe a Gallo-Roman like Favorinus) who spoke Greek and followed Greek ways, in a word, a *hellēnistēs*, was denying his lower nature as barbarian, and rising to a high ideal. *Paideia* was the mechanism for this transformation, at once *Bildung*, the educational system of the gymnasium, and *Kultur*, the superior state of one thus educated.[108] Only through *Bildung* is *Kultur* possible: only through

---

[107] See Hall (1989).

[108] Classically defined by Werner Jaeger in his three volumes of *Paideia*: Jaeger (1946–7). On education, see Marrou (1956), Morgan (1998).

paideia can you attain the *paideia* that marks the hellene in contrast to the *barbaros*.

The transmission of this bundle of ideas and values to the Romans necessarily required major transpositions. Neither *hellēnismos* nor *paideia* could translate into Latin without major change. *Latinitas* echoes *hellēnismos*, but only in the limited sense of pure linguistic usage, the avoidance of linguistic barbarisms. Speaking Latin, unlike speaking Greek, did not make a man superior, or indeed Roman.[109] Superiority lay in morality. As Cicero explains in the introduction to the *Tusculan Disputations*, even if Greece had superior literature, Roman *mores* were self-evidently superior to Greek *mores*. At the same time, *paideia* is dismantled into its components: *studia* or *doctrina* (sometimes *studia doctrinae*), the literary and intellectual pursuits which the Romans willingly adapt (though neither of these terms is used in the sense of an absolute value as *paideia*); and the *artes*, particularly the plastic arts, which 'rustic Latium' is conceded to have lacked, though since they are perceived as without moral value, the lack hardly matters. There is no Latin word to express *paideia* in its sense of superior cultural formation.

The two conflicting elements which make up the modern idea of culture thus stand in different relationships in Greek and Latin. The Greek readily acknowledged that different peoples had different ways of living, and could be non-judgemental about it: Greek ethnography anticipates cultural anthropology in its relatively value-free descriptions of different cultures. Greek superiority lay not in a general way of life but *paideia*, a formation in literature, music and the arts, an Arnoldian high culture. Romans by reaction located their identity in their way of life, the complex pattern of traditions they called *mores*;[110] and the appropriation of Greek *paideia* is always qualified by the insistence that this sort of 'high culture' is not the definition of Roman identity. There is a perpetual lopsidedness between the 'Greek' and the 'Roman' that flows from the fact that Rome is a citizen state, with a legally defined membership, and Greece a geographic area defined by its common language (ch. 2).

Unlike Greek *paideia*, Roman culture fails to develop itself as a proselytising system of values, with the ambition to convert barbarian lands. In its place, we see the emergence in the age of Cicero of a new concept, *humanitas*.[111] It corresponded to no one concept in Greek, since it involved simultaneously the gentleness of behaviour that contrasted with the

---

[109] See ch. 2. On *paideia* in Cicero, see now Gildenhard (2007).

[110] Discussed at length in ch. 5.

[111] Schadewaldt (1973) for the extensive discussion in German scholarship of this 'Wertbegriff'.

barbarian's savage ferocity (*philanthrōpia, epieikeia* or *praotēs* in Greek), and the cultivation of the intellect that contrasts with the barbarian's uncouth ignorance (*paideia*). But without being a Greek concept, *humanitas* is created in response to Greek culture. It allows a re-integration of *studia* and *mores*. The humane man is superior to the inhumane barbarian simultaneously because of his education and 'high' culture and because his way of life, his habits and morals, are civilised not barbarous. Humanity is not the prerogative of one people: one is not superior as Greek, nor indeed as Roman. Any human may be humane, though many (the barbarous) tend to bestiality, in their ferocity and lack of education. The concept thus actually creates the possibility of 'culture' that is not confined by the local boundaries of a particular community – though in effect you must join the Greco-Roman club to achieve it.

This is the term Tacitus employs, with a remarkable degree of irony, in the one rare passage on the export of Roman culture to the provinces. Agricola as governor of Britain introduces the local elite to what we would term 'Roman culture'. It consists both in education, the liberal arts, the Latin language and rhetoric, and in the Roman way of life, dress (the *toga*), entertainments, baths and dinner parties. It is this combination of education and a way of life, of a high ideal (the liberal arts), and the all-too-suspect aspects of life that can ironically be described as temptations, *delenimenta vitiorum*, that together compose *humanitas*. That at least is the innocent reading, what these without the cynical realism of the historian would like to believe; but Tacitus recognises culture as an instrument of control, *pars servitutis*, the more effective because perceived not as a form of enslavement but as value shared by mankind.[112]

Political and cultural revolutions

The following chapters will explore these suggestions in greater detail. But the force of the central argument is to align cultural with political change. It is suggested that the wide-ranging transformations of Roman material and intellectual culture that (without being limited to this period) reach a peak in the last two centuries BCE and the first century CE, spanning the late Republic and early Empire, can be read as an integral expression and instrument of a realignment of 'identities' and construction of power within

---

[112] *Agricola* 21: 'idque apud imperitos humanitas vocabatur, cum pars servitutis esset.' See ch. 4, n. 91. Cf. Woolf (1998) 54–60, 67–71; Lo Cascio (2007).

Roman society. This hypothesis contests a widely assumed model of cultural change in Rome, that is 'top-down' in the narrowest sense. On this model Roman culture is defined and redefined by an elite, the same one familiar from political analysis. This 'nobility' not only leads conquest, but is the principal beneficiary of it, using new wealth to reinforce its own dominance. The cultural innovations are a result and expression of that success: from the villas of the rich to the patronage of arts and literature, the elite articulates the expression of its hegemony through cultural hegemony, and consolidates its power in society. Any broader percolation of this culture beyond elite circles is the result of a trickle-down effect, which only reinforces further the power structure.

The alternative model I offer is not strictly bottom-up. Just as the concept of 'the Roman revolution' is questionable in political terms because there is no move towards democracy or proletarian power, so it would be incredible to suggest that the changes in culture are driven by the ordinary citizen body, let alone the masses. But what *can* be sustained is a cultural revolution exactly parallel to Syme's political one: the elite is challenged by groups immediately below and outside the elite, which successfully establish their claim to belong to a redefined elite. The imperial elite is only superficially a reproduction of the republican elite. It is the outcome of a series of violent contests (including four civil wars), which challenged the exclusion from power, first of the local elites of the Italian allied cities, then more broadly of the provinces. Even if Trajanic Rome is run by an elite just as much as Scipionic Rome, it makes all the difference that the successful colonial has risen to the top. This remains one of the historically most remarkable features of the Roman empire, that the power system was constantly permeable to the energy of new elites from the peripheries. The correlate of that social revolution is a cultural one. 'Being Roman' is only superficially the same thing in 100 CE as in 100 BCE, despite the determination of Roman ideology to mask that transformation and present continuity.

Political power on its own is not enough to define an elite. Polybius acknowledged that much in his brilliant description of a Roman noble funeral: the ritual and parade of the family masks was an essential mechanism of reproduction of social superiority. It is by the criss-crossing practices, gestures and rituals that we call 'culture' that not only is group membership expressed, but social power within the group is claimed and contested. Had any group actually enjoyed a stability of dominance within Roman society across the generations, cultural innovation would have been pointless. Change flows from the fact that new, successful groups are laying claim to power. Their success may be attributed to the capacity of empire to generate new wealth, and in that sense it is military and economic. But it is in the conversion of wealth into social prestige that new forms of culture emerge.

The social and cultural revolution, on this hypothesis, falls into two phases. In the first, 'late republican' phase, the hegemony of the metropolitan elite was challenged by 'new men' both within the citizen body (characteristically members of the group of *equites*), and in particular by the local elites of the Italian cities. Syme's *The Roman Revolution* saw the ascendancy of Augustus as sealing the success of this wider elite. The second, early imperial phase, sees the successful challenge of the elites of specific western Mediterranean provinces, especially the Spains, Narbonese Gaul and Africa. But a parallel and more controversial phenomenon is the challenge of rich freemen to elite status, that sees its political climax in the success of Claudius' secretariat, and its classic cultural commentary in Petronius' *Satyricon*. The extraordinary social transformation of at least some of the cities of Roman Italy, conspicuously attested on the Bay of Naples, which enables the rich freedman to gain social prestige, for instance as an Augustalis, cannot be disentangled from the transformation of material culture observable in those cities. Not even these ex-slaves can be represented as a proletariat: they are precisely a sub-elite group, excluded from overt power by the rules of the game, which vigorously (some might say 'stridently') asserts its elite status. The same set of political and economic changes unleashed by empire renders the elite potentially permeable to both groups; though in this case the refusal of the provincial elites to make common cause leaves the contestation of the freedmen only partially successful. But equally the social revolution threatened by the rise of freedmen is only partially contained: and the record of material-culture points to a spread of a cultural language that is all about assertion of status, to circles far beyond what can reasonably be described as an elite. It is perhaps here that the revolutionary impact of the new culture is most clearly seen.

2 | Dress, language and identity

The imperial biographer Suetonius depicts the aged Augustus approaching his final hours. In an unusually festive mood, he takes himself to the Bay of Naples. He is delighted by an incident when outside Puteoli, a newly arrived boat from Alexandria spots the emperor, and the crew and passengers offer sacrifice in gratitude for the gifts of freedom and fortune. He rewards his suite with a gift of forty gold pieces a head, to be spent on Alexandrian goods. To this donative, he adds further gifts:

Every day he distributed to his companions a variety of small presents, including togas and *pallia*, setting the condition that the Romans should both dress and speak in Greek, and the Greeks in Roman clothes and language.[1]

The vignette is richly evocative of a Roman sense of cultural identity and its relationship to hellenic contact. The process normally described as 'hellenisation' has been under way for two full centuries,[2] and there is palpably a sense of easy familiarity which a Roman emperor and his companions display with the Greek world. Goods are flowing freely from Alexandria to the coast of Italy, thanks to Augustus' own conquest of thirty-three years previously. But this is a part of the Italian coast which he himself chooses to treat like a 'little Greece'. The narrative continues to describe the emperor watching the exercises of '*ephebes*' on Capri, following ancient practice (*ex vetere instituto*). It is 'traditional' in this part of the world for the young to be educated in the characteristic style of the Greek *polis*. He distributes to the *ephebes* presents 'scattered at dinner' – this, too, a Greek practice. He calls Capri '*Apragopolis*' ('Donothing city'), his own coinage for the city of the idle that endows it with the dignity of a *polis*. He improvises Greek verses over dinner, and tests the skills of Thrasyllus, astrologer and grammarian from Rhodes. And his dying words are the coda of a Greek comedy that invites applause for the player.

---

[1] Suetonius, *Augustus* 98: 'sed et ceteros continuos dies inter varia munuscula togas insuper et pallia distribuit, lege proposita ut Romani Graeco, Graeci Romano habitu et sermone uterentur.' For the context, see D'Arms (1970) 74f.

[2] See ch. 1.

The Augustus whom Suetonius evokes is at the same time deeply immersed in Greek language and culture, and yet acutely conscious of his own standing as a Roman, and the differences that implies. In drawing us this picture, Suetonius was not quite a neutral witness.[3] We need only think of the cultural profile of the author himself, probably from Hippo Regius in North Africa, on the one hand a member of the equestrian order and an imperial official, on the other a scholar immersed in Greek learning, with titles in Greek to his credit, as well as an essay *De veste gentium*, 'On national costume'. Stylistically, he allows himself occasional citations of Greek words in his Latin text, a freedom encountered in letter-writing and satirical works, but not in the Roman 'high' genres of oratory or history. Suetonius can sympathise with Augustus' ambidexterity. But he is also summoning up an Augustus who is a good model for Hadrian, the emperor whom he served as secretary *ab epistulis*. Hadrian's cultural crossovers as a Graeculus do much to define his style. Hadrian's choice to wear a beard has been widely interpreted as the adoption of a Greek style though, as the lively discussion it has provoked has shown, it may be read in many ways, including a reversion to an older Roman style.[4] Hadrian is one of only two emperors, along with Julian the Apostate, who are represented by surviving statues as wearing the *pallium* (figures 2.1, 2.2): even if his statue comes from Greek Cyrene, it is the exception among the hundreds of surviving statues of emperors from Greek cities.[5]

For all this easy and playful intimacy with Greek culture, whether by Augustus, or the Hadrianic Suetonius, there is no mistaking Augustus, or for that matter Hadrian, for a Greek. Roman identity has not become elided with Greek identity: the very game played of swapping clothes, languages, and thus identities, underlines how distinct they remain. From a conventional 'essentialist' view of ethnic and cultural identity, this may seem self-evident. Greeks and Romans simply are different peoples, with different ways of doing things: they can 'borrow' or even 'exchange' items of their culture with one another, but the difference will remain because 'in their blood'. But such a view of ethnicity will no longer ring true. If we start instead from the axiom that ethnicity is made, not given, that peoples construct and reconstruct their own identities, and do so in a huge variety of ways by different means, with different emphases, our Suetonian passage will invite instead reflection on how Roman identity is here being made. If ethnicity is, as Jonathan Hall

---

[3] Wallace-Hadrill (1983) 181–5.   [4] See Zanker (1995) 206–21, Smith (1998), Vout (2006).
[5] See Bieber (1959) 399–400. On the sensitivity in the Greek east to the *toga* as proper uniform for a Roman citizen, see Smith (1998) 65–6.

Figure 2.1 Hadrian wearing the *pallium*, from Cyrene (© Copyright the Trustees of the British Museum)

Figure 2.2 Augustus as *pontifex maximus* (DAI Neg. 65.1111)

has argued for the archaic Greeks, 'discursively constructed', this is surely an example of the discourse by which 'Roman-ness' was made.[6]

The anecdote, by no coincidence, highlights two key markers of identity, dress and language. Neither, of course, is a necessary marker of ethnicity. National costume is a familiar concept, but though members of a population may happen to dress similarly (in this sense have a common archaeological culture), until a form of dress is consciously adopted as a sign of difference from others, it does not mark ethnicity. Thus, however the peoples of Scotland may have dressed in the past, it is not until the kilt, with its variant tartans for each clan, is 'invented' in the nineteenth century that it becomes a mark of Scottish identity, long after political union with England, and after the final defeat of aspirations to restore the house of Stuart.[7]

---

[6] Hall (1997).

[7] Trevor-Roper (1983). On the relevance of Hobsbawm and Ranger (1983), see now Dench (2005) 15.

Equally, language, while exceptionally potent in creating a sense of identity, frequently fails in its boundaries to coincide with the political boundaries of nationalism.[8]

In this case, dress and language prove to have quite different weightings as markers of the Greek and the Roman. Indeed, they stand in an inverse relationship to each other. In dress, the *toga* overtly distinguishes the Roman in a sense that neither *pallium* nor any other form of dress marks the Greek; while, conversely, the Greek language is a critical marker of Greek identity in a way that is not quite the same for Latin language and Roman identity.

Both contrasts deserve to be explored in greater detail; but it is worth bringing out first an underlying difference that is obvious but fundamental. Roman discussion repeatedly offers us 'Roman' and 'Greek' as a balanced and matching pair; and so accustomed are we to dividing the ancient world into Greek and Roman that we take the balance for granted. But in terms of ethnic identity, they are radically different: 'Roman' is a juridical category, defined by citizenship, by membership of the *populus Romanus*, or by relationship to Roman *imperium*, in a way never true for 'Greek', which never until the modern period describes a political entity; whereas 'hellenic' existed as a cultural category, to describe people with a shared language and culture, in a way never true for the peoples of the Roman empire. The point is not hair-splitting, because it is basic to our understanding of what is at stake in the Roman discourse of 'us' and 'them', of creating a set of oppositions between 'Roman' and 'Greek'. The pair are deeply unbalanced, because all is seen from a Roman perspective, and the aim is not a Roman understanding of the Greeks, but a Roman definition of self. Just as Hartog showed that Herodotus' history of the barbarian peoples beyond Greece functions as a mirror, a set of oppositions, by which the Greeks are defined, so the Roman representation of the 'Greeks' is their own mirror, in which they reflect their difference.[9]

Dressing and cross-dressing

We may start with Roman dress, or rather, dress sense. The *toga* has an intimate symbolic link with the sense of Roman identity because of its explicit use as a marker of Roman citizenship.[10] It is a classic example of

---

[8] See esp. Colin Renfrew on the 'Indo-European' debate: Renfrew (1987) and Renfrew (1996) 125–37.

[9] Hartog (1988). See Thomas (2000).

[10] See in general Dench (2005) 35, 274ff., on 'national costume', Goette (1990), Stone (1994), Davies (2005).

'emblemic style', an artefact marked with a distinctive form that 'transmits a clear message to a defined target population about conscious affiliation or identity'.[11] This is more than to say that it was the 'national costume' for the Roman male, for in practice Romans might wear different types of clothing for different occasions, and notoriously for many of the poor this formal dress was unaffordable, a garment worn by most of Italy, as Juvenal puts it, only to be carried out in at a funeral.[12] More significantly, it carried an explicit symbolic charge, and one that was to the fore in the Augustan period to which the anecdote belongs.[13] It is in one of the passages of the *Aeneid* mostly overtly concerned with providing a charter for Roman identity, Jupiter's prophecy at the start of the epic of the future greatness of the Roman race, that Virgil describes the Romans as 'Masters of the world and people of the *toga*' ('Romanos, rerum dominos, gentemque togatam').[14]

Added symbolic weight is lent by Suetonius' anecdote of Augustus indignantly reacting to a crowd of men in dark dress, *pullati*, at a *contio*, by citing the line of Virgil and instructing the aediles to ensure in future that nobody was to enter the Forum unless *togati* and without cloaks (*lacernae*).[15] How long, and how effectively, this insistence on the *toga* as formal wear to formal assemblies of Roman citizens was enforced, we cannot tell, though Hadrian is credited with reviving the injunction, insisting that senators and equestrians should always wear the *toga* in public except when returning from dinner (an exception that acknowledged that dinner dress, *synthesis*, was a different code).[16]

The mirror image of the idea that Roman citizens *ought* to wear the *toga* is the enforcement of the rule that those who were not citizens were banned from wearing it. So we find Claudius bizarrely ruling that in a trial for falsely pretending to citizenship, the defendant was permitted to wear the *toga* when speaking in his own defence (and asserting that he was a citizen), but forced to change out of it while the prosecution were speaking (asserting that he was not a citizen).[17] Later, we find the younger Pliny mentioning that the ex-praetor Valerius Licinianus, now teaching rhetoric in exile in Sicily, wore a Greek *pallium*, 'because one to whom water and fire has been

---

[11] Wiessner (1983) 257, Shennan (1989b) 18; see chapter 1.

[12] Juvenal, *Satires* 3,171–2 'pars magna Italiae est, si verum admittimus, in qua/nemo togam sumit nisi mortus'. See Stone (1994).

[13] Vout (1996), Dench (2005) 276–9.

[14] *Aeneid* 1.282. Bender (1994) 151 notes that this is the only occurrence of the word in the epic.

[15] Suetonius, *Augustus* 40,5. On the *lacerna*, see Kolb (1973).

[16] SHA, *Hadrian* 22.2–3. See Harlow (2005).   [17] Suetonius, *Claudius* 15.2.

forbidden lacks the right to a *toga*' (*Epist.* 4.11.3), and the legal force behind this is confirmed by a passage in the *Digest* noting that hostages resident in Rome should not wear the *toga* unless explicitly granted as this privilege by the emperor (*Digest* 49.14.32). The *toga* has become a closely guarded legal right of the full Roman citizen.[18]

It is therefore the 'discursive construction' of the *toga* which lends it its symbolic significance, though the innumerable grave reliefs and statues from the first centuries BCE and CE which ritually depict dead Romans in togas are themselves a vigorous contribution to that discursive practice, as their emphatic deployment by persons of freedman status suggests.[19] It is precisely in the period of supposed 'hellenisation' that the garment comes to the fore as a conscious marker, and specifically in the context of contrasting the Roman with the Greek. The first mocking reference to *Graeci palliati* is in a comedy of Plautus, doubtless with self-conscious irony since the actors were in Greek costume, in a form of comedy that became known as the *fabula palliata* in contrast to the 'native' *togata*.[20]

The *toga* was one of a number of formal indicators, along with the use of a name form referred to as *tria nomina*, with praenomen, gentilicium and cognomen, that by the end of the first century BCE came to be construed as the 'traditional' Roman way. In the case of the *tria nomina*, we can demonstrate that naming practices were fluid, evolving continuously throughout Roman history, and that the three-name convention enjoyed a relatively brief heyday.[21] In the case of the *toga*, we have, and we may suspect the Romans themselves had, too little iconographic evidence to say how dress conventions actually evolved over the period before the first century BCE, though they firmly attributed its use to the kings, and the elder Pliny believed that Servius Tullius' *toga praetexta* survived in Rome down to Sejanus' day.[22] Romans regarded the *toga* as derived from the Etruscan dress called *tebenna*, distinct from the rectangular *himation* in its rounded form. Yet that distinction in Etruscan dress only emerged gradually in the archaic period during a heavily hellenising phase, though it suited the Romans to point to the Etruscans for a 'native', and by implication non-hellenic, origin.[23] The first surviving statue of a *togatus*, the Arringatore of Florence, is an Etruscan magistrate explicitly designated with an Etruscan name form, Aule Meteli[24] (figure 2.3). It is clear that, as a dress form, the *toga* was not unique to Rome in the republican period, but widespread through central

---

[18] Stone (1994).   [19] Zanker (1975), Kleiner (1977), Zanker (1981), Zanker (1988) 163.
[20] Plautus, *Curculio* 288; see Gowers (1993) on Plautine irony.   [21] Salway (1994).
[22] Pliny, *Natural History* 8.197.   [23] Bonfante Warren (1973), Bontante Warren (1975) 48–53.
[24] Dohrn (1968), Crawford (1996) 418, Dench (2005) 278.

Figure 2.3 Statue of *togatus*,
'Arringatore', Museo Archeologico
Firenze (DAI Neg. 63.599)

Figure 2.4 Roman *togati* on Ara Pacis frieze (DAI Neg. 72.2401)

Italy, just as the *atrium* house, to which we shall return, seems to be a more general Italian phenomenon before it is marked as 'Roman'. Paradoxically, the best evidence for the diffusion of the *toga* in Italy is the legal expression, *ex formula togatorum*, which is used in the agrarian law of 111 BCE to indicate those who were not Romans or Latins, but Italian allies supplying troops to Rome.[25] On one of its first encounters, then, the *toga* is not the marker of the Roman citizen, but of the Italian who is *not* a Roman citizen.

When, in the first century BCE, the iconographic evidence for *togati* becomes abundant, what strikes art historians is the degree of change of style over time. The 'classic' style with which we are most familiar emerges, by no coincidence, precisely under Augustus.[26] Moreover, as represented, it is often not radically distinct from Greek dress-forms: the Athenian citizens wearing their *himatia* on the Parthenon frieze are closely comparable to the Roman *togati* on the Augustan Ara Pacis frieze (figure 2.4).[27] That is partly due to direct imitation by the artists, but also to direct Greek influence on how the *toga* was actually worn.[28] It is illuminating to note the debate between art historians over the clothes worn by the man on a well-known republican grave relief from the via Statilia (figure 2.5). Margareta Bieber took it for a *pallium*, imitated from Greek sculpture; Diana Kleiner affirmed that it must be a *toga*, since it would be so odd to find a Roman citizen dressed (for his funeral, Juvenal might add) in anything else.[29]

This uncertainty is not a simple product of our ignorance. On the contrary, it is because the precise style of wearing the *toga* affected in the first century BCE involved a conscious imitation of the Greek *pallium*. The *toga* of this period, or rather the style of wearing it, is marked by two features: the tight loop, the *sinus* or arm-sling, in which the right arm is held high and close to the chest, and the length of fall of the garment, almost reaching the shoes. Margaret Bieber showed that the tight arm-sling closely copies a type of which the earliest example is a statue of the fourth-century Athenian orator Aeschines, one which we know from a Roman copy in the Villa of the Papyri at Herculaneum, dated to the mid first century BCE (figure 2.6).[30] It is no

---

[25] *Corpus Inscriptionum Latinarum* 1² 585 = Crawford, *Roman Statutes* no. 2, line 21: '[ceivis] Romanus sociumve nominisve Latini, quibus ex formula togatorum [milites in terra Italiae imperare solent].

[26] Bieber (1973) 441–3, Goette (1990) 24–31.

[27] Hölscher (1987) 46.   [28] Stone (1994) 16.

[29] Stone (1994) 40, at n. 24 summarises the debate; see Goette (1990) 24–6 for the type.

[30] Bieber (1959).

Figure 2.5 Grave relief from the via Statilia showing *togatus/palliatus* (DAI Neg. 2001.2051)

Figure 2.6 Aeschines in *pallium*, Naples Museum (Villa of the Papyri) (DAI Neg. 85.486)

coincidence that the model is a classic Attic orator, for the first century BCE, as Cicero's rhetorical treatises testify, was a period of intensive imitation by Roman orators of Attic models. It makes good sense, too, that a dress-fashion of this sort should be driven by the practice of orators, especially in the period when a pursuit of Attic purity was sought to counteract supposed Asianic excess. The *toga* was above all the formal wear of the public speaker in the Forum, addressing a court, the senate, or the Roman people. Cicero's generation turned to Greek rhetorical theory to improve their technique; and one lesson they learned was that the orator must think not only of his words, but his dress and gesture. It was Demosthenes who said that the three most important things for an orator were delivery, delivery and delivery. Gesture was a key to good delivery.

The most explicit account of the principles of delivery and gesture that survives is over a century later, in Quintilian's advice to the young orator (*Institutio Oratoria* 11.3.65–149). Frequently citing Cicero, he makes clear that while gesture is critical to good delivery, the orator is treading a tightrope between gesturing too little (and so appearing unemotional) and gesturing too much (and so appearing exaggerated, like a comic actor, or effeminate, and sacrificing his stance as a true man of dignity). The rules on how to wear your *toga* (or *pallium*) are closely bound up with self-control and moderate gesticulation. Thigh-slapping is too much, a model set by the demagogue Cleon. The tight wrapping of the right arm, whether in *pallium* or *toga*, is about maintaining your dignity in speaking. The orator shouldn't look like a dancer, like Titius who gave his name to a dance.

It is in the context of this concern for the well-tempered gesture that Quintilian sets out (mostly helpfully for us), his rules on how to wear a *toga* properly. It is all about striking a balance. The *sinus* or arm-sling should not be too high or too low. The *balteus* or belt should not be too tight or too loose. The fold should be thrown over the shoulder, but not cover the throat, otherwise the dress will be tight and lose the dignity lent by a broad chest (11.3.140–1). The reader becomes increasingly conscious of the sheer awkwardness of the garment, the difficulty of speaking in public with a minimum of animation without throwing the clothing into disarray, when Quintilian admits that his rules apply above all to the introduction to the speech: gradually, as you move into narrative, you can let the fold slip off the shoulder, and pull the *toga* away from your throat and upper chest as the argument hots up (but you should avoid, needless to say, the foppish and effeminate gesture of throwing the bottom fold over your tight shoulder); by the end of the speech, almost anything goes, sweat, disordered clothing, the *toga* loose and falling off all round (11.3.144–6).

Had we but such detailed instructions of gesture and dress for the age of Demosthenes, and that of Cicero, we might understand with precision the unspoken codes of gestural propriety that underlay the first-century fashion of the tight arm-sling. But Quintilian helps us further by his sensitivity to change of dress styles over time:

There is an element of dress-style which has changed to some extent with the changing circumstances: for the ancients had no arm-sling, and those after them had very short ones. Therefore they must necessarily have used different gestures from ours in the Prooemium since their arms were contained in the cloth, as with the Greeks. (11.3.137–8)

He knows that the tight arm-sling would have impeded the rhetorical flourishes of a century later, and that this was the Greek style, too. Moreover, he can cite authorities of the first century who laid down the law on dress-style:

The ancients used to let the *toga* reach right down to the heels, as the Greeks do with the *pallium*: this is the recommendation of the writers of that day on gesture, namely Plotius and Nigidius. (*ibid.* 143)

Both the length of drop and the tight arm-wrap of the late republican *toga* were driven by the conscious desire to imitate good Greek rhetorical practice; and they imitated key features of the *pallium* so closely as to render the garments harder to distinguish. Yet at precisely the same period, we find them obsessed with the difference of the garments, and the impropriety of confusing them.

A significant series of passages and anecdotes from the late republican period explores the problematic nature of the wearing of 'Greek' clothes by Romans.[31] First, historical accounts report the denunciation of Publius Scipio (Africanus to be), while the Roman armies are mustering in Sicily for the invasion of Africa, for parading in the gymnasium at Syracuse wearing the *pallium* and the boots called *crēpides*. If these are taken as the 'correct dress' for a Greek gymnasium, the anxieties about dress belong in the context of wider anxieties about the gymnasium; to its importance as a cultural marker of Greek identity I shall return. The defence is that a Roman should wear the right dress for the occasion: as the *toga* belongs to the Forum, distinguished from the *vestis domestica* of home dress, the convivial dress of evening entertainment, and above all the armour of warfare, so in a marked Greek context, Greek clothes are appropriate. The same defence will apply to Scipio's brother, Lucius, who is depicted on a statue on the Capitoline wearing *chlamys* and *crēpides*, or to Sulla in the same garb at Greek festivals in Naples.[32] We meet the defence in its most elaborate form in Cicero's speech for Rabirius, who is accused of abandoning the *toga* for the *pallium* while serving in Egypt as steward of Ptolemy. Foolish he may have been, Cicero concedes, but he did it in a good cause, for his survival depended on it: he wore the *pallium* at Alexandria to permit him to wear the *toga* at Rome, for had he stuck to the *toga* he would have lost everything.[33] Cicero could cite the Scipios as precedent for Rabirius; and also the case of Rutilius Rufus, model of old-fashioned virtue, who avoided the massacre by Mithridates of Roman citizens, *togati*, by changing his clothes. Wearing the *pallium* is hateful (*odiosum*), but done under duress.

---

[31] Heskell (1994). On gesture and gait, see Corbeill (2004) 107–39.

[32] For the significance of the *chlamys* as the purple cloak of kings, see Hallett (2005a) 102ff., esp. 151–3 on Scipio.

[33] Cicero, *pro Rabirio Postumo* 26–7.

If Cicero knows how to defend a Roman for wearing the *pallium*, he knows equally how to attack him: Verres is excoriated in half a dozen passages for wearing the *pallium* in Sicily:

A praetor of the Roman people stood on the shore wearing Greek sandals (*soleae*), with a purple *pallium* and a sweeping tunic, drooped over his girlfriend. There were many occasions when both Sicilians and many Roman citizens saw him in this outfit.[34]

Prima facie, it was a charge to stir indignation in a Roman jury of the first century BCE. Indeed, it was the very sentence Quintilian would cite as exemplary in his chapters on gesture, urging the orator to refrain from actually imitating Verres' regrettable pose while reciting (11.3.90).

The question raised by these incidents, and implicit in the Augustan enforcement of 'traditional' dress-code, is whether Roman identity is threatened or undermined by the temporary abandonment of so charged a marker as the *toga*. From one point of view, it is a surrender to Greek practice; from another, implicit in the positive encouragement given to his Roman companions by Augustus, that model of homespun *toga*-wearing authenticity, to dress and talk Greek, it is a code which has its time and place. But in the very process of setting up the *pallium* as the opposite of the *toga*, the Romans are engaged in a mirrored construction of 'culture through the looking glass'.

In this context, it becomes interesting to look again to the most important shift in dress-style registered by studies of the Roman *toga*. We have already met Quintilian's observation that the imitation of the tight arm-sling of the Greeks had significant implications for their gesture. Chronologically, the watershed lies between Cicero and Quintilian, in the reign of Augustus. By a series of changes apparent even to the inexpert eye, the *toga* became considerably fuller, and the arm-sling was loosened gradually, until, by the late Augustan period, it fell in a great loop just above the right knee (figure 2.6). The change starts in the early Augustan period, as is seen in the tomb of the baker Eurysaces (figure 2.7); and, once made, it remains astonishing stable for the next three centuries, until late antiquity brings in changes of its own. If we can associate late republican *toga* style with Greek rhetoric, to what should we attribute the Augustan shift, and its tenacious hold through the imperial period?

One context for the change worth considering is precisely the debate on the proprieties of *toga* and *pallium*. If public figures could be criticised for wearing the *pallium*, was it not risky to allow an assimilation of the *toga* to

[34] Cicero, *in Verrem* 2.5.86; similarly 2.4.54–55; 2.5.31; 40; 137. See Heskell (1994).

Figure 2.7 Tombstone of the baker Eurysaces,
outside the Porta Maggiore (DAI Neg. 33.749)

the Aeschines-type, one which leaves us scratching our heads about which a
freedman buried on the via Statilia is actually wearing? If you want the *toga*
to symbolise Roman identity, in explicit contrast to Greek, it is as well to wear
it in as distinctive a way as possible. From the moment the Augustan style
with the long, loose *sinus* comes in, doubts over which is which evaporate:
the national costumes have become polarised. Augustus and his friends,
playing cross-dressing on the bay of Naples, no longer stood in danger of
being confused one with another. That is to say, at precisely the period at
which Augustus not merely encourages the use of the *toga*, but backs it with
the force of law in the Forum, the *toga* makes a sharp movement away from
its immediately preceding phase of 'hellenisation'.

The sensibility to dress difference on the Roman side seems to have no
echoing sensibility on the Greek side. The first surprise must be to register
the fact that *pallium* is a Latin word without Greek derivation. *Pallion* has
no entry in the classical Greek lexicon, though interestingly it is met in a
range of Greek writings of the imperial period, notably Christian writings,

where it is taken to be a derivative of the Latin word.[35] The dress so labelled by the Romans is usually referred to as the ἱμάτιον/*himation*; but so little loading does the word carry in Greek that authors like Plutarch are happy to use it refer to the Roman *toga*.[36] There is little sign in Greek authors of consciousness of the *himation* as a form of 'national costume'. If any word is marked, it is the τρίβων/*tribōn*, the 'worn' cloak that marks out the Spartans and, after Socrates, philosophers, especially Stoics and Cynics. Latin authors, in using *pallium* or *palliolum* for the philosopher's cloak, elide what in Greek is an important distinction, and it seems to be a matter of indifference whether *pallium* is used contemptuously of a mean, worn garment, or with outrage of the purple attire of a Verres.[37]

That the opposition of *toga* and *pallium* is lopsided is an outcome of the lopsided balance of 'Roman' and 'Greek'. If the *toga* is a marker quite specifically of citizenship, there is no corresponding Greek citizenship to be marked. The hellene cannot be defined juridically, only as in Herodotus' classic definition by shared descent, cults, language and customs (8.144). The critical definitions of the hellenic are cultural, and dress appears not to carry a heavy marking in this context. If anything, dress marked local differences, the 'dialect' of dress, rather than a national language.[38] On the contrary, the dress distinction which the Greeks knew to mark them apart from the barbarian was nudity.[39] In Herodotus' mirror, it is the shock experienced by barbarians at male nudity that creates the knowledge of difference.[40] Just as the *toga* is the uniform which in Roman sculpture is used to connote citizenship, sculptured nudity, of gods, heroes, athletes and rulers, is a ritual affirmation of Greek difference.[41] Depictions of naked Greeks fighting against Persians in their elaborate costumes, and even parodically subjecting them to sexual assault, underlined pride in a distinctive costume.[42]

---

[35] See Liddle Scott Jones, *Greek–English Lexicon*, Supplement s.v., citing Aesopica *Proverbs* 120 and inscriptions. A search of the *Thesaurus Linguae Graecae* now produces some seventy-six further references, none earlier than the second century CE, overwhelmingly from late antique and Byzantine sources.

[36] Plutarch, *Brutus* 17, *Coriolanus* 14.

[37] For *tribōn*, see Liddle Scott Jones, *Greek–English Lexicon*, e.g. Demosthenes 54.34 equates wearing the tribon to Laconisation. For *pallium* as a poor garment, cf. Cicero, *Tusculan Disputations* 3,59, 'saepe est etiam sub palliolo sordido sapientia'. See further Daremberg and Saglio (1877–1912) s.v. *pallium*.

[38] Herodotus 5, 87–8 distinguishes 'Doric' from 'Ionian' dress styles; Thucydides 1,6 sees Ionian and Doric styles in terms of evolution through time. Cf. Harrison (1989).

[39] Bonfante Warren (1989), Himmelmann (1990), Osborne (1997), Hallett (2005a) 6–8.

[40] Herodotus 1.10.3 for the shame of nudity among Lydians 'and just about all the other barbarians'; developed by Thucydides 1.6, who sees the differentiation from barbarians as the result of historical development.

[41] Hallett (2005a) 20–60 on nudity as a 'costume'.   [42] See Hallett (2005a) 5–14.

Nakedness is a dress code which is heavily visual, and 'emblemic' in the sense that those who adopted it were aware of, and indeed provocatively paraded it as a sign.

Nudity, then, raises a new level of problematic relation between Greek and Roman.[43] From the Greek point of view, the Romans shared the barbarian distaste: so it is the Greek Plutarch who provides commentary to the elder Cato's avoidance of bathing naked in front of his son:

> This indeed appears to have been a shared practice among the Romans: even fathers-in-law avoided bathing with sons-in-law since they looked askance at undressing and nakedness. Subsequently, however, they learned to strip from the Hellenes, and in return refashioned the Hellenes to do this in company with women. (*Cato the Elder* 20,5)

The passage is notable for the awareness that cultural influence could flow both ways, and assumes that the practice of stripping in public had to be 'learned' by the Romans from the Greeks. That fits in with a strongly expressed passage of Cicero which associates as a package of decadent traits taught by the Greeks the gymnasium, nakedness, and homosexual love, citing in support a line of a tragedy of Ennius:

> Flagitii principium est nudare cives corpora.
> The beginning of outrage is for citizens to strip.[44]

Not only here, but in several public speeches, Cicero can trade on the assumption that nakedness is shocking, and particularly so in a Roman magistrate like Antony, whose undress (or half-dress) at the crowning of Caesar at the Lupercalia is held up for derision, like the drunken and naked dancing of the consul Aulus Gabinius.[45]

Textual evidence of strong disapproval of nudity creates a seeming contradiction with iconographic evidence, since Romans too are portrayed nude in sculptures (figure 2.8). The contradiction has been 'resolved' in a number of ways. Paul Zanker took the juxtaposition of Roman portrait heads with heroising nude torsos as one of a number of signs of discordant elements generated by hellenisation in the late Republic, a conflict which he saw as resolved by Augustus' creation of a new stylistic language. Erich Gruen, by contrast, denies the conflict, arguing that prominent Romans would scarcely have had themselves portrayed in this fashion if it was regarded as shocking, and

---

[43] See now Hallett (2005a) 61–101 on Roman attitudes to nudity.

[44] Cicero, *Tusculan Disputations* 4,70. See below on the gymnasium. Also Crowther (1980–1).

[45] Cicero, *Philippics* 2,86, *in Pisonem* 22. Heskel (1994) 137–9.

Figure 2.9 Denarius of Octavian as naked hero, with foot on globe (photo courtesy British Museum, BMRR Rome 4341)

Figure 2.8 Statue of a Roman as naked hero, Chieti Museum (DAI Neg. 67.841)

Figure 2.10 Augustus in 'hip-mantle', Ravenna relief (DAI Neg. 38.1407)

that the adoption of this Greek style points to their self-confidence.[46] Chris Hallett argues that no conflict was felt because the Romans, by a suspension of disbelief, could accept nudity or semi-nudity as a costume which marked the subject as like a hero of Greek mythology, an Achilles.[47] Yet the fact that the elder Pliny explicitly contrasts the nudity of Greek statues with the military breastplates of the Roman, underlining that it was Greek to conceal nothing, implying specifically the genitals,[48] and that Augustus, after a brief flirtation with total nudity in the triumviral period (figure 2.9), then established the genital-veiling 'hip-mantle' as his definitive heroic uniform (figure 2.10),[49] suggests that at least some of the shock of nudity remained in the Roman mind in the face of any artistic conventions.

The debate illustrates the enormous difficulty both of extrapolating cultural attitudes and values from the material record in the absence of written records and of reconciling the partial records we have with the fragmentary material-culture record. It reflects much broader problems experienced by archaeologists in moving from the record of material culture to inferences about ethnicity and cultural identity, and of pinning down, if ethnicity is 'discursively constructed', just what the discourse was. There are clear methodological risks in drawing inferences from the material record of what attitudes 'must have' been. Granted that there was a well-established Roman republican convention of representing Roman generals naked, can we safely infer that this *must have* been acceptable, any more than inferring, granted that Cicero voices standard Roman prejudice against public nudity, that such statues *must have* been disturbing or discordant?

I bring out this problem because it runs closely parallel to the discourse of the propriety of the toga. If we simply accept those passages of Cicero which represent the wearing of Greek clothes by a Roman as shocking, then the statue of Lucius Scipio in Greek military uniform *must have* been shocking; on the other hand, if we started from the statue, put up confidently by one of a pair of flamboyant and successful brothers who constantly ran a gauntlet of controversy, we will infer that a few voices of criticism were not enough to put them off. Romans did controversial things, took risks, even revelled in stirring outrage: a long line of *exempla* from Scipio to Caesar to

---

[46] Zanker (1988) 5–11, Gruen (1996) 219; the debate is reviewed by Stevenson (1998).

[47] See Hallett (2005b) 101ff., esp. 218.

[48] *Natural History* 34.18: 'togatae effigies antiquitus ita dicabantur. Placuere et nudae tenentes hastam ab epheborum e gymnasiis exemplaribus: quas Achilleas vocant. Graeca res nil velare, at contra Romana ac militares thoraces addere.'

[49] Hallett (2005a) 160–3.

Nero to Hadrian should warn us from thinking that Roman morality was ever so normative as to constrain the bold. On the contrary, morality was instrumental: a means of humiliating your enemies and glorifying yourself.[50] Cicero has no qualms in attacking Verres and defending Rabirius for the same behaviour.

The conclusion should surely be that we should not attempt to construct for the Romans what they failed to construct for themselves, a homogeneous and uncontroversial cultural identity. Nor should we swallow their own tendentious oppositions of 'us' and 'them'.[51] The very process of defining Greek culture in opposition to Roman, in 'inventing', as we may say, the *pallium* as symbolically charged as negative to the positive of the *toga*, enables the Roman to transgress, or to switch from one charge to the other. The explicit voices that associate nudity with moral depravity and Greek ways make it extremely likely that the charge was felt by a Roman looking at a statue of a nude Roman: the buzz came from getting away with it.

Another aspect of the process is worth underlining: the charges cannot remain the same over the course of time. The more frequent and 'normal' the transgression, the less effective the gesture. If Augustus felt enough qualms about being portrayed naked to compromise on the hip-mantle, his equally 'old-fashioned' and 'morally upright' successor Vespasian reverted to full frontal nudity.[52] Plutarch's comment on Roman bathing practices implies a sort of leap-frogging: as if having learned to be shameless about public nudity, the next buzz came from going a step further and introducing mixed nudity, a practice which will first shock, then affect, the Greeks (of course, the story is a good deal more complicated than that). It is ironical confirmation of Plutarch's thesis that the Romans, having 'learned' to portray males nude, developed nude female portraiture, a category that comes up against the rather stronger Greek taboo on female nudity.[53] There may be only sixteen examples of nude female portraits, but the bizarre sensation of seeing a Flavian society lady, possibly Marcia Furnilla, wife of the emperor Titus, with her tightly-curled coiffure half-covering her breasts and pudenda with the gesture of Venus Pudica, and almost certainly from her tomb, cannot be washed away by telling ourselves it was not so bizarre to the Roman (figure 2.11).[54] The very openness which allows the Roman to incorporate bilingually two potential conflicting cultural traditions in the same image leaves tangible the story of that conflict.

[50] Edwards (1993).   [51] See further ch. 5.   [52] Hallett (2005a) 178–83.
[53] Hallett (2005a) 219.   [54] D'Ambra (1996) for this fashion.

Figure 2.11 Statue of Flavian lady as
Venus Pudica, from villa near Lago
Albano (Ny Carlsberg Glyptotek,
Copenhagen)

Similarly, we can witness the *pallium* take its revenge. Tertullian's *de Pallio*
confirms that in third-century CE Carthage, a Roman citizen could still be
criticised for wearing the *pallium*. The old oppositions are still to the fore, but
can be inverted: 'even if the *pallium* is a Greek thing, the word is under Latin
control, *penes Latium*: the garment came in with the word' (*de Pallio* 3,7).
The elder Cato is paradoxically cited as one who, for all his censorious
expulsions of Greeks, learned not only to speak Greek, but favoured Greek
clothing by baring his shoulder like a *palliatus* (*ibid.* 3,8). If *Romanitas* is
salvation, one can at least imitate the Greeks in the more honourable aspects
of their culture: how absurd for North Africa to imitate Greek athletics and
body-hair removal, and to spurn their clothing – to be depilated, not be
clothed, in Greek style (*ibid.* 4,1). The *toga* is then associated with Roman
luxury and decadence (5,5); the *pallium* is the garb of philosophers, teachers
and artists, and can proclaim, 'all the liberal arts are contained in my four

corners' (6,2). To this Tertullian adds a new boast, that it is now the garb of a Christian. The later history of the word is a long and vigorous one, and it flourishes in both Greek and Latin Christian writers as a symbol of a man of God, a disciple or a monk; and its use spreads to a variety of Church vestments that mark out priests, bishops and popes.[55]

Switching tongues

If dress was more critical as a marker of identity to the Roman than the Greek, the situation is the reverse with language.[56] If Latin was the language normally associated of a Roman citizen, speaking Latin was neither a necessary nor a sufficient condition of being a Roman. The emperor Claudius' act as censor in depriving a leading Greek of his Roman citizenship on the grounds of inability to speak Latin is recorded as an eccentricity (Suetonius, *Claudius* 16.2);[57] by that period there must have been many Greek speakers holding Roman citizenship who shared his deficiency. Conversely, there had always been Latin speakers, starting with the members of the archaic *nomen Latinum*, who spoke Latin without claiming Roman citizenship, including slaves. Indeed, for Artemidorus, for a Greek to dream of learning Latin could be a sign of impending slavery, 'for no slave is taught Greek'.[58]

By contrast, to 'speak hellenic', *hellēnizein*, is at all times a core definition of being a hellene. While for Herodotus, common descent has a place alongside language, cult and customs in distinguishing Hellenes from barbarians, by the fourth century BCE, the idea of common descent could be dropped. The classic declaration is that of Isocrates in the *Panegyricus* (50), in praise of Athenian cultural leadership:

So far has our city [Athens] left behind the rest of the world in matters of thought and speech that its pupils have become the teachers of others, and it has changed the name of Hellene to appear no longer a matter of descent but of mental formation, and the people who are called Hellenes are those who share our culture (*paideia*) rather than those who share common blood (*physis*).[59]

Athenian hegemonic claims over Greek language and culture could be contested, as in the attempt of Heraclides to argue that the Athenians did not speak hellenic at all:

---

[55] See DuCange, *Lexicon*, and Lampe (1961).
[56] See now the subtle discussion of Dench (2005) 302–29.
[57] Suetonius, *Claudius* 16.2, cf. Dio 60.17.3f., cf. Dench (2005) 138.
[58] Artemidorus, *Oneirocrita* 1.53.   [59] Hall (1997) xiii.

Hellas was originally a *polis* founded in Thessaly by Hellen son of Aeolus . . . the descendants of Hellen are Hellenes by race, and hellenize in their language; the Athenians living in Attica are Attic by descent and atticize in their dialectic, just as the Dorians descended from Dorus doricize.[60]

But by this date any attempt to restrict 'hellenic' to a tribal descent group ran in the face of usage, and the centrality of language in the construction of identity is evident in the passage, and its assumptions about the word 'hellenise'.

A criticism long levelled against Droysen, as we have seen (ch. 1), was that he was using the word '*Hellenismus*' in a way not justified by Greek writers. Droysen's usage, following Niebuhr, assumed that *Hellenismus* was the product of a hybridisation, a new form of Greek created by a colonial encounter in the orient. The objections are not merely linguistic, that *hellēnismos* refers to a proper, grammatical usage of the Greek language. It is that it understates both the insistence on linguistic purity as a guarantee of hellenic identity, and the willingness of this redefined identity to sit alongside other, local identities. What is relevant is the centrality of language in the Greeks' own idea of their identity. If identity can be constructed in many different ways, one of the most significant variants is the role played by language.[61] To adhere to Greek identity by 'hellenizing' demanded above all the use of the hellenic tongue, and beyond that more broadly *paideia*, Greek education and culture. Hellenism never requires the natives to abandon their own tongue.

The hellenisation of Judaea is a good test-case. The vocabulary is met in Jewish authors describing the long-standing disputes between Jews who did or did not hellenize. To do so was to use the Greek language and such aspects of Greek custom and culture as were compatible with Judaism. As modern scholarship sees it, neither hellenism nor Judaism were fixed categories, but the objects of continuous negotiation. A 'hellenising' Jew believed himself no less Jewish for that, though his enemies might dispute the point.[62] For Jews living in the Greek-run cities of the hellenistic kingdoms, accommodation was a necessity; but if hellenism was the medium of accommodation, it did not demand loss of Jewish identity, but provided the instrument for redefining it.

What then becomes significant to observe is the Roman reaction to the linguistic demands of 'hellenism'. There is a notable contrast between the

---

[60] Heracleides the Critic, *On the Cities in Greece* fr. 3.   [61] Edwards (1985).

[62] Hengel (1980), Millar (1987) 110f., Dench (2005) 312–13. Gruen (1998) 1–40, and more broadly Gruen (2002).

Jewish and Roman responses. Whereas the 'hellenising' Jew, despite the previous elaboration of Hebrew as a religious and literary language, uses Greek
without compromise to identity, Romans repeatedly voice considerable
concern about Greek as a threat to Latin, and paradoxically the 'hellenisation' in the literary field is the process of creating a literature on a Greek
model but in the Latin language.

Roman voices do not speak in unison on this question: they may contradict themselves as well as each other. The common feature is that the
Greek cultural achievement is conceived as a problem, whatever solution
may be offered. Something of the complexity of the issues at stake emerges
in an extraordinary passage of Valerius Maximus, in his survey of the good
institutions of the Romans' ancestors (2.2.2–3):

The extent to which magistrates in former times acted to protect their own and the
Roman people's majesty, can be seen in this: among other signs of maintenance of
gravity, they adhered with the greatest perseverance to the principle of never giving
responses to Greeks except in Latin. On the contrary, they eliminated the volubility
of speech that is their particular strong point by forcing them to speak through
interpreters, not only in our own city, but even in Greece and Asia. Their aim was
evidently to achieve the greater respect and diffusion for the Latin language among
all peoples. It was not that they [the magistrates of old] lacked application to learning
(*doctrina*), but they thought there was no single respect in which the *pallium* should
not be subject to the *toga*; and they thought it unworthy for the weight and authority
of empire to be granted to the enticements and sweetness of letters.

As a statement of the actual situation in the second century BCE, to which it
presumably is meant to apply, the passage is richly misleading. Valerius suppresses in this context the humiliating incident in 282 BCE when Postumius
Megellus is supposed to have provoked the ridicule of the Tarentines by his
use of Greek, though he records in a subsequent chapter that Postumius' *toga*
was bespattered with shit by the Tarentines.[63] The mastery and deployment
of Greek by generals like Flamininus is one of their most striking achievements, and the contrary view has been put from Strabo to Momigliano that
it was to this mastery (while the Greeks proudly refused to learn Latin) that
the Romans owed their success.[64] Given the rich crop of official Roman documents in Greek that survive from this period, the 'principle' claimed by
Valerius has little point: even if decisions were made in Latin and translated
into Greek, allowing translation would frustrate the purpose of spreading

---

[63] Kaimio (1979) 96; see Dionysius of Halicarnassus, *Roman Antiquities* 19.5 and Appian,
   Samnitica 7.2 for the story.
[64] Strabo 9.2.3; Momigliano (1975) 38, Rawson (1985) 321.

the knowledge of Latin.[65] But the principle of displacing Greek by Latin is confuted by the facts.

Vastly though the use of Latin did spread, it was not in the Greek east. The main desire of Roman government was to make itself understood, and it did so by regularly communicating in Greek. There was full awareness in the first century BCE that Greek functioned as a world language in a way denied to Latin. The acknowledgement of the universality of Greek is explicit in Cicero, who could defend the value of the Greek poet Archias to the Roman generals he praised on the grounds of the wider diffusion of Greek than Latin:

If anyone imagines that Greek verses bring in a smaller return in glory than Latin ones, he is gravely mistaken: for this reason, that Greek is read in virtually all nations, whereas Latin is confined within its own boundaries, which are frankly restricted. (Cicero, *pro Archia* 23)

The value of the Valerius passage lies not as a statement of actual Roman policy, but in its underlying cultural assumptions. Greek language, rhetorical proficiency (*volubilitas*) and culture (*doctrina*) are linked together as a threat to Rome. It may be a real threat of being outwitted and outmanoeuvred in negotiation; but it is also a symbolic threat of diminution of the *maiestas*, *gravitas*, and *auctoritas* of Roman power. The use of the Greek language would be as much of a symbolic defeat as the use of the *pallium*. Greeks must be subjected, not merely militarily, but in everything; and Romans must beware the seduction implicit in their culture.

These views surely do have their origins in the second century BCE. The elder Cato may have insisted on addressing the Athenian assembly in Latin, though even this is not certain, since Plutarch, who asserts it, finds himself contradicting other sources who claimed that Cato addressed them in Greek.[66] Valerius' views would doubtless have been welcome to Cato. But, instead of arguing (implausibly) that Valerius is right, or that such views were traditional, it is worth focusing on what he himself is doing in a contemporary context. Writing under Tiberius when the use of Greek in the Roman senate and Roman government had been long since established as normal, he nevertheless presents an attitude of hostile jealousy towards hellenism not as an outmoded curiosity, but as an ideal. It is the present age that has got it wrong.

---

[65] Kaimio (1979) 94ff. discusses the evidence for the use of Greek in detail. Gruen's (1996) 'appeal of Hellas' glosses over it.

[66] Plutarch, *Cato ma* 12.4–5; discussed by Kaimio (1979) 98, and by Gruen (1996) 'Cato and hellenism' (at n. 110), who suppresses the doubts.

He continues by pointing to the example of Marius, who refused in his old age to involve himself in Greek culture. This is something for which Plutarch sharply criticised Marius at the start of his life ('if he had sacrificed to the Muses' his old age would not have resulted in the disaster of the civil war), and it is likely that the criticism goes back to Posidonius' history.[67] Valerius is apologetic on the issue: he should not be condemned for rustic rigour, for he did not wish 'as victor to become more polished through the eloquence of a conquered people'. Here is the same epigrammatically expressed issue of military versus cultural conquest met in Horace and Ovid. And Valerius offers his solution to the problem with his next example:

> Who then opened the doors of the senate to the custom by which nowadays the ears of the houses are deafened by pleas in Greek? It was, I think, the rhetor Molo, who sharpened the studies of M. Cicero. It is established that he was the first of all foreign nationals to be given a hearing in the senate without an interpreter. The honour was not inappropriate, considering that he had assisted the supreme force of Roman eloquence. (Valerius Maximus 2.2.3)

Apollonius Molon was Cicero's tutor in rhetoric on Rhodes in the 90s BCE. He is deployed here as symbol of a double transition. On the one hand he introduces the use of Greek to the senate; on the other, he is responsible for handing over the palm for eloquence to the Romans through his teaching of Cicero. The point may be elaborated via Plutarch's account of Cicero and Molon. Not understanding Latin, Molon requests Cicero to declaim in Greek, which the young man does with resounding success. But, to Cicero's distress, the rhetor sits long in silence, until he at last delivers his verdict:

> Indeed I praise and admire you, Cicero; but I pity the fate of Greece, seeing that the only fine things that were left to us, our *paideia* and *logos*, thanks to you have fallen to the Romans. (Plutarch, *Cicero* 4.6–7)

Molon symbolises the cultural defeat of Greece: it is not only that Cicero's *corpus* of Latin speeches challenged comparison with those of Demosthenes, in his own eyes and in those of subsequent critics, but even that Cicero could beat the Greeks at oratory in their own tongue. His mastery of Latin rhetoric is founded on wresting this prize from the Greeks.

It seems almost pedantic to say that this whole viewpoint is a construct based on hindsight. In 87 and 81 BCE, when Molon is attested as having visited Rome, Cicero had no name even as a Latin orator, and his debt to Molon cannot have influenced the senate. Indeed, the whole idea that to

---

[67] Plutarch, *Marius* 2.2.

address the senate in Greek *without interpreter* was a privilege is nonsensical. It is well attested that others addressed the senate *with interpreters*, notably the three heads of philosophical schools, Carneades, Diogenes and Critolaos, who in 155 BCE addressed the senate with C. Acilius, who had written a history of Rome in Greek, as their interpreter.[68] It could be no privilege to the Greek speaker to dispense with an interpreter unless all the senators understood Greek; and the dropping of interpreters is testimony to the extraordinary spread of knowledge of Greek in the Roman upper classes. Even so, Cicero commented, that there was always someone who called for an interpreter.[69]

Valerius offers not a reliable historical account, but a model for Roman cultural imperialism. He approves of two contrary examples: one, encapsulated in Marius, is the rejection of Greek culture on the grounds that it is demeaning to the victor to be put at a disadvantage. The other, embodied in Cicero, is the conquest of Greek culture by its own weapons. Either way there is a battle, and either way Rome wins: 'O lucky town of Arpinum!' as Valerius winds up his piece, 'whether you wish to look at the most glorious despiser of letters or their richest font!' Whether or not he understands the attitudes of the second and early first centuries, he articulates a viewpoint characteristic of the late first century BCE and early first century CE. As in Cicero's *Tusculan Disputations*, and in the familiar passages of Virgil, Horace and Ovid, Rome is seen as locked in a cultural war with Greece, in which victory may be claimed for either side.

That the Romans saw themselves as engaged in a power struggle over linguistic usage seems evident; but it is a warfare more complex than Valerius admits. He does, however, seem to reflect a point of view that was current by the reign of Tiberius about linguistic etiquette.[70] A number of anecdotes are told, as it happens, about Tiberius and the use of language. The fullest source is Suetonius.[71]

In Greek language he was normally fluent, but he did not employ it in all contexts, and particularly avoided it in the senate: to the extent that before using the word '*monopolium*', he begged pardon for using a foreign word; and when a draft senatorial decree was read containing the word '*emblema*', he put in an amendment to change

[68] Kaimio (1979) 104.   [69] *de Finibus* 5.89; Kaimio (1979) 105.   [70] Kaimio (1979) 94f.

[71] Suetonius, *Tiberius* 71: 'sermone Graeco quamquam alioqui promptus et facilis, non tamen usque quaqua usus est, abstinuitque maxime in senatu: adeo quidem, ut "monopolium" nominaturus veniam prius postularet, quod sibi verbo peregrino utendum esset; atque etiam cum in quodam decreto patrum "emblema" recitaretur, commutandam censuit vocem, et pro peregrina nostratem requirendam aut si non reperiretur, vel pluribus et per ambitum verborum rem enuntiandam.'

the foreign word for one in our language, or if none could be found, substitute a periphrasis.

The scruples of linguistic etiquette which Valerius attributed to the past were a mirror of those of the emperor of his day. Whereas in 282 BCE a Roman might indeed risk humiliation, the learned Tiberius, the exile in Rhodes, friend of grammarians and astrologers, who quizzed the experts on the song the Sirens sang, could make a show of sustaining the linguistic purity of Rome's most official voice.

The link between this anecdote and the story of Augustus and his friends swapping clothes and languages is obvious enough. It sees language as a dress, that can be put on and off at will. But it also sees it as deeply implicated in cultural identity. You run a real risk of letting the side down by using the wrong language or wearing the wrong clothes.

Code-switching[72]

The complexities of linguistic practice and allegiance may stand as a sample of the complex processes of cultural change that we so simplify in the word 'hellenisation'. In recent linguistic studies of bilingualism, the concept of 'code-switching' has attracted much discussion, and it offers a particularly fruitful model of how two cultures may sit alongside each other, interacting rather than 'assimilating'.

Such studies look at the ways that the bilingual deploy languages tactically according to social context. There exists a power-relationship between languages that is determined by social and historical context: frequently one is the language of dominant power, one of subjection. As Carol Myers-Scotton puts it, each language presupposes a 'set of rights and obligations' between the speakers. In any situation, one choice of language will be 'unmarked', the other 'marked': the unmarked language is the normal, expected language, the marked choice signals something abnormal. Switching to the marked language flags a negotiation: 'switching away from the unmarked choice in a conventional exchange signals that the speaker is trying to negotiate a marked rights and obligations balance to replace the unmarked one current in the exchange'.[73]

---

[72] See ch. 1. I owe a particular debt to Simon Swain for introducing me to the concept of code-switching, to my former colleague Jim Adams for bibliographical guidance, and to colleagues in Canada for adding a Canadian dimension to my reading. The code-switching literature is reviewed by Adams (2003) 18–28.

[73] Myers-Scotton (1990) 98; see further Myers-Scotton (1993).

Establishing one language as dominant is a key to hegemonic practice, as Monica Heller observes, working on the use of English and French in Canada, an arena where the contested political dimensions of language are particularly explicit. It is precisely the fact that using one language is 'normal' or 'unmarked' that establishes the rules of the game, the underlying power-relationship. By using the dominant language you buy into the rules of the game. But the fact it is unmarked means you take the dominance for granted. 'Buying into the game means buying into the rules, it means accepting them as routine, as normal, indeed as universal, rather than as conventions set up by dominant groups in order to place themselves in the privileged position of regulating access to the resources they control. Bourdieu has insisted over and over again that it is precisely by appearing not to wield power that dominant groups wield it most effectively.'[74]

Given this underlying power-relationship (and it must surely be clear from everything we have seen about Roman thoughts on linguistic practice that they would have accepted this analysis), switching into the non-dominant language is bound to have significance in context. It signals that the speaker is negotiating, not simply taking the power-relationship for granted. The ambidextrous user can negotiate by the facility of flicking at will between languages to meet the demands of different social contexts. It is this sort of ambidexterity we can see again and again in a Flamininus or Cicero or Tiberius. The key to success is knowledge of the social contexts that demand or permit the change of language. In Syracuse in the gymnasium, or Naples, or your private *hortus* or peristyle, go Greek; but woe betide if you let your *crēpides* show in the senate. Similarly, we may think of the difference between the language of Cicero's speeches, steeped of course in hellenistic rhetorical and grammatical form, but pure in their Latinity, and the letters interlarded with Greek words.

Latin as an imperial language

Valerius Maximus' supposed principle of the universal Roman insistence on the use of Latin over Greek tells at best half of the story, of a pride in Latin as a marker of identity, oscillating with a willingness to embrace the communications opportunities offered by Greek, and an adept use of code-switching to get the best of both worlds. Valerius' nationalistic principle in fact proves more pertinent to the relationship of Latin to non-Greek

---

[74] Heller (1995) 160–1. See also Heller (1988).

languages. We take it almost for granted that Latin emerges as the dominant language of the western empire, displacing not only the other local dialects of Italy, but Celtic, Punic and other historically established local languages. It is here in the west indeed that Latin is *the* language of official discourse, and that a principle of consciously maximising its spread is uncontestable. One has only to consider the impact of the Social War in Italy on the epigraphy of Italian towns to see how dramatically languages like Oscan and Etruscan fall out of use after 80 BCE, whereas by significant contrast the official use of Greek in Neapolis and other South Italian towns is not only permitted but encouraged.[75]

While the spread of Latin in the west may seem in retrospect self-evident, the corollary is a transformation of the Latin language itself which makes it indebted to Greek linguistic theory and structures.[76] How closely inter-linked are the phenomena of linguistic imperialism and national language formation can be seen from the example of Spain and Latin America. The deliberate spread of Spanish throughout the Latin American colonies, and the suppression of local 'Indian' languages to subaltern tongues, spoken by the powerless classes excluded from government, goes hand in hand with the imposition of Castilian as the dominant version of Spanish, both in America and at home in Spain. Basque and Galician are reduced to subaltern tongues just as much as native South American languages.[77]

The process by which Latin emerges as a language of imperial domination is rather more complex than the victory of Latin over Oscan and other Italic dialects, and in this sense the Castilian example is inadequate. The essential process is a redefinition of the Latin language itself: for hand in hand with the insistence that others use one's language is the establishment of authoritative standards by which to lay down what that language is. Here both the precedent and the model of the transformation of Latin is the transformation of Greek. If pure linguistic usage, *hellēnismos*, is a mark of the extension of hellenic culture to non-hellenic peoples, it is necessary to establish a mechanism, a structure of authority, by which correct usage is defined. It was precisely the role of the grammarian, *grammatikos*, to enter upon the dismaying variety of alphabets, spelling, pronunciation, morphology and usage presented by the traditional dialects of Greek, and establish agreed standards. It seems so obvious to moderns learning ancient Greek that 'Greek grammar' exists that it is easy to overlook that this grammar is the formulation of the age we call 'hellenistic'.

---

[75] Crawford (1996a).   [76] Adams (2003) 762–74 questions whether Latin was 'hellenised'.
[77] Mar-Molinero (2000); also, in general, Edwards (1985).

The parallel transformation that takes place in Latin, above all in the first century BCE, involves a fundamental shift of location of linguistic authority. The well-regulated forms of Latin enshrined for us in compilations like Kennedy's *Latin Primer* are hewn only at the cost of much debate from what L. R. Palmer called 'the morphological uncertainties of archaic Latin, the confusions of gender, the fluctuating forms of declension, conjugation and word-formation'.[78] At issue is not merely whether the language is used consistently, but who is entitled to say what is or is not correct usage.

Cicero grasps the issue in his discussion of *Latinitas*, the 'pure usage' in Latin which he insists on for the Roman orator just as much as the Greek orator is bound by *hellēnismos*.

> Hitherto pure Latin was not a matter of reason and science, *rationis et scientiae*, but of good usage, *bonae consuetudinis*. I pass over Laelius and Scipio; in that period men were praised for their pure Latin as for their innocence (though there did exist those who spoke badly). But virtually everyone in those days who neither lived outside this city [i.e. Rome], nor was tainted by domestic barbarity, used to speak correctly. But this has been corrupted in Rome as in Greece. Both Athens and this city have received a flood of peoples from a diversity of origins whose language is polluted (*inquinate loquentes*). This is why our talk needs purging, and some sort of rationality needs to be applied like a touchstone, which cannot be changed, nor are we to go by the perverted rule of usage.[79]

Cicero's schematised account sees the foreigner as the source of corruption of what would otherwise be a pure tongue. The initial standard for good usage is topographical, 'this city', and it is the flood of speakers from outside who are seen to have changed linguistic practice even within Rome itself to the extent that there is no longer a local touchstone. The fallacy of this as a historical account is admitted by the concessions about the age of Scipio. Even then, though you might trust the Roman aristocracy to speak proper Latin, there were Latin speakers outside the city, and even within the city, the presence of slaves, especially those in contact with the young, risks importing 'domestic barbarity'. That particular source of corruption was to continue to worry rhetorical theorists and, over a century later, Tacitus could still point to the corrupting influence of slave nursemaids and pedagogues as a cause for the perceived decline of Latin oratory.[80]

The fallacy of course lies in the myth of an originally 'pure' language which is only subsequently 'corrupted' and so in need of purging. Diversity of usage is the norm, whether between different populations of language users, or

---

[78] Palmer (1954) 125.   [79] Cicero, *Brutus* 258.   [80] Tacitus, *Dialogus* 29.

over the course of time, and 'purism' can be imposed on language only by the imposition of external authority. That new authority is only won gradually, as the outcome of an extended debate in which both the politicians who used the language in the Forum and the theorists who trained them to do so, participated vigorously. The debate is visible in all of Cicero's theoretical discussions of oratory, but its fullest and most technical articulation is to be found in Varro's *De Lingua Latina.*[81]

Only six of Varro's twenty-five books on the Latin language survive, but these (esp. 8–10) centrally concern the theoretical debate over the nature of authority in language that goes back to Aristarchus and the grammarians of Alexandria on one side, and the Stoic school of Pergamum represented by Crates of Mallos on the other. The issue between Aristarchus' principle of *analogia* and Crates' principle of *anomalia* is clear enough. It goes to the heart of the function of the grammarian. Is he merely observing how people actually speak, in all the variety and inconsistency of actual practice (*anomalia*), and extrapolating standards from that usage, or is he sifting through the chaos of usage to refine patterns of consistency and sets of predictable rules (*analogia*)? Varro's position on the debate is carefully nuanced, and indeed he doubtless understates the extent to which the original Greek debate was nuanced, and allowed that neither observation of usage nor principles of consistency provided by themselves an adequate answer. On the one hand, he acknowledges the desirability of consistency; on the other, he is at pains to point out that considerable variety of usage is possible within patterns of consistency, that it is offensive to the majority of users to insist on changing standard usage in favour of consistency, and that language is subject to continuous and legitimate innovation.

One of the most interesting features of his presentation is the repeated set of analogies he draws between linguistic practice and material culture, especially dress, personal adornment, housing and furnishings. One passage (*De Lingua Latina* 8.27–32) argues that usage (*consuetudo*) rather than logical rules (*analogia*) must be invoked to explain certain arbitrary differences. Similarly in clothing, where there is no rule of similarity in the types of clothing worn by men (*toga* and tunic) and women (*stola* and *pallium*); or in houses, which show great contrasts within types of spaces (the *atrium* versus the peristyle, or even the summer versus the winter *triclinium*). Nor, he insists, can these contrasts simply be explained functionally (by *utilitas*). Dress, housing and tableware exist indeed for functional reasons, but their elaboration is a matter of *humanitas*. A thirsty man (*homo*) needs a cup, but

---

[81] See Dench (2005) 316–21.

considerations of *humanitas* require a beautiful cup (31). Even within the same house, *triclinia* are not all furnished with couches of the same style; they are decorated with different materials (ivory, etc.).

He returns to these points later (9,18–21). Following *consuetudo*, traditional practice, cannot be an adequate answer: one follows good examples (*exempla*), not bad (9,18). Old practice does not stop innovation in clothing, building, or furniture: does love of habit persuade us to wear worn-out old clothes rather than new ones? (9,20). Has not traditional usage in types of vessels, called *sini* and *capulae*, been rendered obsolete by new forms of vessels imported from Greece? If so, why not allow new words? (9,21)

Here Varro is evidently able to draw on his other antiquarian studies: it is precisely because he had written about changing Roman practice in the *Antiquities* that he can observe the changing vocabulary that goes with changing ways (he returned again to this material in his *De vita populi Romani*). But the link goes deeper than that: language and material culture are seen as subject to the same laws and the same historical process by which Roman *consuetudo*, normal practice, far from being fixed, is in a state of flux: *consuetudo loquendi est in motu* (9,17). The parallel from which we started between dress and language, between *toga/pallium* and Latin/Greek, broadens in Varro's hands from a polarity of 'us' and 'them' to an awareness of cultural change that creates the need for definitions.

The debate did not start with Varro in the 40s BCE. He refers back to the position on the debate of his master Aelius Stilo in the early first century BCE. Chance has preserved, along with the more famous Lives of the Caesars, the summary Lives of Grammarians (*de Grammaticis*) of Suetonius. His account gives particular significance to the pioneering role of Stilo as an amateur and gentleman, an *eques Romanus*, unlike the often slave-born professionals who followed him. In Suetonius' account, interest in grammar goes back at Rome to the visit of the grammarian Crates of Mallos, who comes to Rome in the mid second century BCE on an embassy, breaks a leg in an open sewer on the Palatine, and stays to lecture. It would be interesting to know how his views on the dominance of customary practice, and hence *anomalia*, went down with an audience so ideologically wedded to *mos maiorum*; but certainly it is his side of the debate that Aelius Stilo is said to have favoured.[82]

What deserves emphasis, then, is that over the course of less than a century, Latin moves sharply away from a model based on 'customary usage' and endorses the principle of analogical consistency. One author known to have championed the principle explicitly is Julius Caesar, who wrote a now lost

---

[82] See Kaster (1995) 68–70 on Aelius Stilo.

treatise *de Analogia*, referred to in complimentary terms by Cicero. The essay was penned, Fronto informs us, during the Gallic campaigns. Here too is a paradox which Fronto does not miss: he wrote 'amidst the volleys about how to decline nouns, between the trumpet blasts about aspiration'.[83] The wordplay brings out a real parallelism: between conquests that reduced the barbarous Gaul to Roman order, and a treatise designed to keep Latin pure of barbarism, and to reduce it to an order that would enable it to become the language of Gaul itself.[84]

There is no need here to rehearse the individual details of the transformation of the Latin language which came out of these debates. If the 'rationalisation' of Latin is deeply indebted to Greek linguistic theory and practice, that is not because of an automatic assimilation that comes with 'hellenisation', but because Latin is being consciously set up in competition with Greek to serve as a language of Mediterranean-wide communication, and is availing itself of an effective technology. Any implicit compromise to ethnic identity is warded off by a scrupulousness about loan-words. Tiberius' avoidance of loan words in a senatorial decree runs parallel to Cicero's creation of an entire vocabulary of philosophical Latin. But one only has to read Latin technical writing, from Vitruvius to Celsus or the elder Pliny and Frontinus, to see that the scruples over loan-words do not reach far into daily usage.

The point I wish to underline, however, is the implicit shift of authority in this linguistic reform. The touchstone, as Cicero puts it, is no longer 'this city'. Authority in local usage is necessarily linked to authority in local society; those within the society who can claim most authority, in Rome's case the nobility which claimed to be the living incorporation of ancestral practice, wield most influence over how the language is used, and their repeated public performances in the Forum were definitive. The subjection of language to fixed grammatical rules, whether based on consistency or on interpretations of what constituted 'customary practice', *consuetudo*, shifts authority to the grammarians themselves. The protagonists in the late republican debate are still closely linked into the republic ruling class: Aelius Stilo, an *eques Romanus*, and friend and political ally of some of the leading political figures of the day (he accompanied Metellus Numidicus into exile), M. Terentius Varro, senator of praetorian rank, and the unexceptionably patrician Caesar himself. But in practice, the experts are the emergent

---

[83] Fronto 221N: 'scripsise inter tela volantia de nominibus declinandis, de verborum aspirationibus et rationibus inter classica et tubas'.

[84] Note, however, that the standard grammars of the imperial period were not primarily (or effectively) designed for teaching Latin as a foreign language: McKitterick (1989) 13ff.

profession of grammarians, who constitute themselves as the 'guardians of the language', *custodes linguae latinae,* from the first century BCE into late antiquity.[85]

The issue of authority is spelled out in an anecdote in Suetonius' biographical notice on Pomponius Marcellus, a grammarian of the early empire famed for his fearless pugnacity, and with a reputation as a former boxing champion.[86] There is debate over whether a word used by the emperor Tiberius is proper Latin. One expert, the grammarian Ateius Capito, ingratiatingly remarks that even if the word was not good Latin before, now Tiberius has used it, it will be. Marcellus contradicts him flatly: 'Capito lies. You, Caesar, can give citizenship to a man, but not to a word.'[87] In the exchange, there is truth on both sides. Ateius' observation is correct in so far that the emperor possesses an overwhelming authority over the definition of the 'Roman', and that language is tied up in the sense of identity that is juridically defined by citizenship.

---

[85] Kaster (1988).   [86] Suetonius, *de Grammaticis* 22; see the discussion of Kaster (1995) 222–8.
[87] The same anecdote is told by Cassius Dio 57.17.2, Kaster (1995) 226–7.

PART II

Building identities

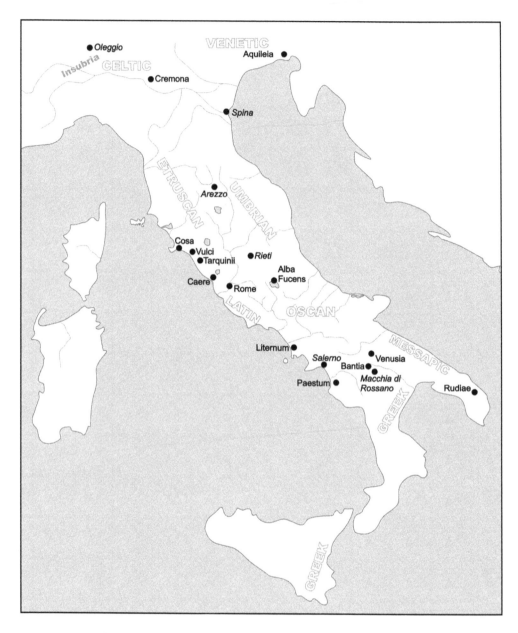

Figure 3.1 Map of Italy with principal language groups (drawn by Amy Richardson)

3 | Roman Italy: between Roman, Greek and local

Oleggio is a sleepy market town in the former territory of the Celtic tribe, the Insubres, on the west bank of the river Ticino (figure 3.1). ('Insubria' is still a potent local label in an area stretching from Milan into Switzerland.) A necropolis with 268 burials excavated there in the 1990s offers a vivid snapshot of the changes in material culture brought by romanisation.[1] It spans in time the passage from the late La Tène culture met in Celtic areas across continental Europe at the end of the second century BCE to the late empire. The area had been in alliance with Rome since 194 BCE, a treaty which, according to Cicero, stipulated that Rome would not offer its citizenship to their people (*pro Balbo* 32); it was granted *ius Latii* in 89 BCE under the lex Pompeia, and full Roman citizenship in 49 BCE by Caesar. The most striking transformation takes place between the late second and late first centuries BCE. The earliest graves have numerous features of the standard Celtic warrior tradition. The men (even in one case a woman) are buried with their panoply of armour ritually deformed: the swords bent in two or broken (figure 3.2). Their main ornaments are large iron *fibulae* of a standard Celtic type, suitable for pinning the heavy woollen cloak or *sagum Gallicum*. In Northern Gaul, the same late La Tène swords are found, markers of a martial society in which elite status is signalled by such weapons.[2] Yet, alongside these clear ethnic markers are signs of the incipient impact of the Roman world. Strigils, razors and hair-cutting shears point to bathing and the care of the body. The odd silver mirror and alabaster *ungentarium* points to the same luxurious vanities. And vessels in black-glaze ware, modelled on the standard types of Etruria, indicate the consumption of wine. Feasting and bathing in the Mediterranean tradition sit alongside the symbols of the kilted warrior. With the passing of time, the balance tilts (figure 3.3). In the early first century, the panoplies and bent swords disappear; the brooches turn into lighter types in bronze, and the ornaments grow richer, with rings, necklaces and bracelets of hellenistic types characterising female burials. By the Augustan period the transformation is complete. This picture can be replicated throughout the Insubrian territory.[3]

---

[1] Spagnolo Garzoli (1999).   [2] Roymans (1996) 13–20.   [3] Grassi (1995).

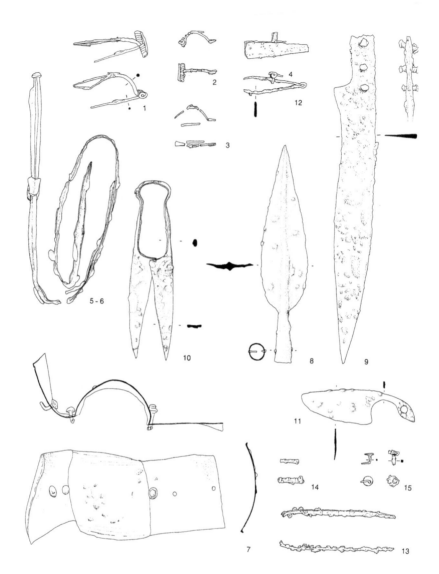

Figure 3.2 Burial assemblage from Oleggio with La Tène items, deformed sword, brooch, etc. (after Spagnolo Garzoli 1999, figure 157, with permission, Omega Edizioni)

It is hard not to read these grave-goods as statements of identity: 'through the elements of costume the local peoples wished to reassert their membership of the Celtic *ethnos* at the culminating moment of the encounter with the Roman world.'[4] But what exactly is the identity they wish to assert: of Celts *rather than* Romans? Or is it a hybrid identity, part-Celt, part-Roman?

[4] Spagnolo Garzoli (1999) 357.

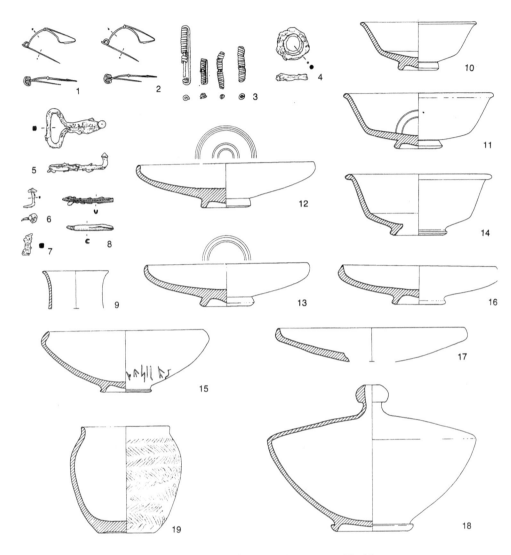

Figure 3.3 Burial assemblage from Oleggio with Campanian ware and bathing equipment (after Spagnolo Garzoli 1999, figure 102, with permission, Omega Edizioni)

Or is it a bilingual identity, people who manage to be Celts and Romans at the same time? Certainly, the strength of the Celtic assertion fades, in neat synchronisation with the abandonment of the treaty clause protecting them from being turned into Romans, to acceptance of Latin, then of Roman legal standing. We may be reminded of a pattern of intergenerational change met often across the empire: instance the African Apuleius Maxssimus alias Rideus, whose Latin/Punic bilingual epitaph shows his grandfather (Iuzale), father (Iurathe) and wife (Thanubra) with Punic names, while he himself has separate Punic and Roman names, and his sons, Pudens, Severus and Maximus, sound like standard Romans.[5]

The fundamental study by Adams of bilingualism in the Roman world underlines repeatedly the importance of this intergenerational pattern of bilingualism: the first generation (in our world typically the immigrant) speaks their own language (L_1) with fluency, but acquires the standard language (L_2); the second generation is equally fluent in L_1 and L_2; the third is fluent in L_2, less so in L_1. The bilingual has a vital role to play of contact between the two languages (or cultures, or identities); each may influence the other, and frequent code-switching between the two is a powerful assertion of dual identity. Exceptionally, a trilingual will underline the importance of multiple identity: we have met Ennius as a man with three hearts, trilingual in Greek, Oscan and Latin, and Favorinus the Roman Gaul, more Greek than the Greeks (ch. 1); or we may think of the remarkable Palmyrenes, operating from the Janiculum in Rome to South Shields in north England, who commemorate themselves in Latin, Greek and Aramaic; or the doctor Boncar who speaks Greek as a doctor, Roman as a citizen, and Punic as an African; or the Jews buried in Rome and Venusia in late Antiquity who speak Greek and Latin, but strain to add Hebrew tags to their graves however poor their grasp of that language.[6] These triple-switchers rub in the point: they wish *all* their identities to be visible or audible. They do not regard subsidiary identities as diminishing their primary identity (if one such there is), but as enriching it.

To return to the Insubrians. The models recently offered of hybridisation (Creoles or pidgins) have implications quite different from that of bilingualism (ch. 1). A hybrid language, though derived from two source languages, has its own rules, requires specific learning (so cannot be picked effortlessly up by speakers of the source languages), and is transmitted across generations. The bilingual, by contrast, is fully aware of the difference of the two languages between which he/she switches, comprehends their separate identities and rules, and uses them appropriately to specific situations (thus: Latin to a magistrate, Greek in a medical consultation, Punic to a fellow-African). There is nothing to say that our Insubrians were not equally alive to context, equally aware of when to pin on the *sagum* and when to strip down for the bath. Moreover, the progressively shifting make-up of the grave-goods is a strong argument against the formation of a separate, hybrid, identity, that is neither Celtic nor Roman.

Indeed, the linguistic model should be followed with due caution. Language is frequently a critical component of cultural identity; but that does

---

[5] Millar (1968) 132, Adams (2003) 217.   [6] Noy (1999), Adams (2003) 22–3.

not mean that other components automatically correspond with it, or obey the same rules. You could, as we have seen (ch. 2), learn Latin without turning into a Roman, and indeed could in some cases be a Roman without speaking Latin. Patterns of influence, or the possibilities of code-switching, may function differently for aspects of material culture and language. That bilingualism was a standard phenomenon linguistically does not imply automatically that the same principles applied to material culture: it is only a possible model, a hypothesis to evaluate.

There is a further caution which should give pause before accepting too easy an equation of the type, brooch = Celt: strigil = Roman. The Celts were not new to contact with the Mediterranean world in the second century BCE. The necropolis of the Gallic settlement of Monte Bibele near Monterenzio, which dates from the fourth to second century BCE, already demonstrates a pattern of lively exchange between Celts and Etruscans. Etruscan female names show a busy marriage trade between the peoples, *conubia gentium*. Here, in nine of the 113 tombs, dating to the late fourth/early third century BCE, bronze or iron strigils, together with other athletic instruments, are found in place of the traditional Celtic armour; in one case (tomb no. 103), linked to an Etruscan name, *Laθialu*.[7] The Celts may have been aware of bathing long before contact with Romans, as an Etruscan practice. Do strigils and razors and ointment jars point to a specifically Roman culture at Oleggio? We make that assumption because at that time the Romans were the prime contact to the south. Yet what would the Roman historian Sallust have made of these Celtic burials? Would he have welcomed the transition from martial virtues to luxury? It is precisely his complaint that the Roman ruling class had abandoned its self-definition in terms of martial virtues, and been corrupted by the new status language of Asiatic luxury (Sallust, *Catilina* 10–12). He might have been more comfortable with our alternative label of 'hellenisation': the Celtic nobility was corrupted by foreign ways just as much as the Roman. Caesar, too, saw the martial spirit of the Gallic Celts as softening by comparison with the Germans (*Bellum Gallicum* 6.24).

This chapter looks again at some of the processes illustrated by Oleggio in Italy at large. The subject is vast, and much debated. Discussion here will focus on the issue of identity: what does language change and material-culture change tell us about the changing identities of an area which only latterly came to think of itself as a unity? In what follows, I shall attempt to develop the model hinted at above in the case of the Insubrians. Rather than a model of change across three generations, we are looking at a long period of some three centuries. At the outset, say in the mid fourth century

---

[7] Vitali (1987) 365–76, Torelli (1999) 3–4.

BCE, the peoples of Italy are talking local languages, following local cultures (L_1). At the close, say in the late first century BCE, we can broadly speak of a unified culture, based on the single language of Latin, or more accurately on an agreed bilingualism or *diglossia* of Latin and Greek (L_2). The interest lies in understanding the long bilingual transition, when Latin (/Greek) sits alongside the local languages. Our chances of understanding what that transition meant in terms of identities are much reduced if we start from the unitary view of culture that supposes that every step towards the acquisition of a new language represents a loss to the old. Once we grasp that the culturally multilingual, who could orient themselves in diverse circumstances in different languages, enjoyed a powerful advantage rather than a loss of identity, we can begin to unpick much of the confusion implicit in theories of romanisation and hellenisation, and understand better how from this matrix Roman culture emerged no less transformed than that of any Italic people.

Direct and indirect romanisation

Discussion of romanisation in Italy, generally seen as a process stretching from the beginning of major territorial expansion of Rome in the fourth century to the symbolic unification of the Tota Italia of Augustus,[8] involves so complex a range of interrelated aspects that it is necessary to draw some distinctions. In doing so, my aim is not to define the process of romanisation (which is rather our own interpretative framework), but to clarify the issue here under discussion, namely the relationship of cultural change to identity. From this point of view, it is important to distinguish *direct* from *indirect* romanisation – that is, those actions by which the Roman state deliberately, consciously and directly transformed parts of Italy into parts of the Roman state, from the broader and vaguer set of changes which may or may not have been willed by Rome, but which brought progressive cultural assimilation of all parts of Italy to a single, Roman model, what Gramsci called 'hegemony'.[9]

Direct romanisation is fundamental for understanding indirect assimilation, but paradoxically is less revealing for the issue of cultural identity. At its core lies colonisation: the conquest of territory, followed by the definition of that territory as the property of the Roman people (*ager Romanus*), sometimes occupied by individual Roman settlers (viritane assignments), but also consolidated by the settling of new cities formed from Roman citizens,

---

[8] E.g. Salmon (1982), David (1994), Torelli (1999).   [9] Cf. Gabba (1994).

supplemented by Latins, operating under Roman law, but normally as self-governing cities independent of Rome, involving loss of Roman citizenship (*coloniae Latinae*), and more rarely until the second century retaining full Roman rights as parts of the Roman state (*coloniae Romanae*). Such colonisation literally changed the landscape of Italy.[10] The process of division of territory and assignation of plots, ritualised by Etruscan lore, has left the enduring traces of centuriation on the landscape of the country. So powerfully does the division of land mark the romanisation of Italy that it is possible to publish an entire book entitled *La romanizzazione della Campania antica* without discussing any issue other than land-distribution.[11] Division of the land is closely allied, by the same set of Etruscan rituals, to the layout and division of the newly founded city. Often, as in the case of Cosa or Alba Fucens, the city and countryside are laid out on the same axes. Colonies might be established in the place of existing cities (like Paestum) or create new centres (like Cosa); in any case, the hundred or so colonies established by Rome between the fourth and second centuries enormously increased the number of urban centres in Italy, so that urbanisation hangs closely together with colonisation and land-division. Part and parcel of such urbanisation are programmes of major building and engineering works: fortifications, temples and public, political spaces (*fora, comitia*) characterise the city, major engineering works mark the landscape, above all the great network of roads, with its vast implications for communications and exchange within Italy, and water management works (aqueducts). To grasp the awesome impact of such works on the landscape, it is enough to stand beneath the Cascate delle Marmore near Terni, where M'. Curius Dentatus after his conquest in 290 BCE released the waters of the flooded basin of the Sabina around Rieti, diverting the water into the valley of the Nera in Umbria, enabling major land-reclamation.

Vast though the impact of all these processes was on Italy, they are not in themselves, except in their indirect effects, the dialogue between Roman and non-Roman that constitutes acculturation. There is never a surprise to find the inhabitants of the *ager Romanus* or the citizens of the colonies speaking Latin, following Roman law, Roman political institutions or Roman customs. On the other hand, the colonies and the diaspora of Roman citizens in Italy were an essential part of the acculturative discourse. Internally, they found themselves in dialogue with the existing traditions and culture of the population of their area. Externally, they offered reference points for allied communities in their dialogue with Rome, and could stand in close dialogue,

[10] Gambaro (1999).   [11] Franciosi (2002).

like the colony of Cales with allied Teanum Sidicinum, or the colony of Puteoli with Cumae or that of Venusia with Lucanian Bantia. The excavations of the Latin colonies of Cosa, Alba Fucens, Paestum and Fregellae have made a fundamental contribution over the last thirty years to the understanding of how such colonies offered models of the Roman at local level: with their formulae of layout – the grid pattern within irregular wall-circuit, dominated by the peripheral siting-points of temples and *auguracula*, their core features of Forum, and circular *comitium*, and the regular patterns of *atrium* and terraced houses, they constituted a formula suitable for diffusion in a way that Rome itself never could.[12] We may question whether Cosa is the simple mirror of Rome, *parvae effigies simulacraque*, for which Frank Brown took it;[13] on the other hand, the copy-book similarity of the finest house of early second-century Cosa, the House of Diana, with the House of Sallust in Pompeii illustrates how the same formulae are found in allied cities as in colonies.[14]

It is an inherent function of a colony to be an extension of the mother-city. Rome here is inheritor of a Greek tradition, and it is important to remember that despite the culturally distinctive language with which Roman colonisation surrounded itself, from the legal distinctions of Roman and Latin, to the Etruscan rites of ploughing the *pomerium*, and the division with the *groma* of the land by *decumani* and *cardines*, the model of colonisation, including urban and rural divisions, is the extension of the pattern brought to South Italy by the Greeks in the archaic period, and concurrently applied in the new eastern kingdoms of Alexander and his successors. Colonisation has its own claim to be regarded as an aspect of hellenisation.

If the story were simply one of the imposition of a Roman identity on Italy through colonisation, it would be less complex, and less interesting. The complications arise through the indirect impact of colonisation on adjoining areas that had not been made part of the Roman state. The decision not to colonise is as interesting and important as the decision to colonise, and it is the creation of a network of independent allied states (*socii*), with their dismaying variety of statuses and treaty conditions, that is perhaps the most original and historically remarkable feature of the 'making of Roman Italy'. To put it provocatively (and with conscious exaggeration): the founding of colonies is part of the hellenisation of Italy (Roman power expressed in a hellenic idiom), the creation of a network of independent allies is the true romanisation (Roman power expressed in a Roman way). Too paradoxical, of course: but it is necessary, to counter the sheer deadweight of historical

[12] Torelli (1999).   [13] Fentress (2000).   [14] Fentress (2003).

inevitability that makes it appear to us that Rome always wanted to make Italy fully Roman, that we should underline the consistency with which for at least three centuries, the Romans ignored, and eventually actively resisted, the idea of making the allied states Roman. From a later perspective, one might imagine a scenario by which from the beginning of the fourth century, Rome created a network of fully Roman cities, subject to Roman law and institutions, speaking the Latin language, in each of the territories it progressively conquered. Instead it sustains a continuous antinomy of Romans and non-Romans within the area under its military control. That is not compatible with any sort of policy or strategy of 'making Roman' the Etruscans, Umbrians, Oscans, Greeks and others who formed part of their alliance.

The critical turning point is the Social War (91–89 BCE). It was only at the end of the second and beginning of the first centuries BCE that the debate was launched over whether the allies should become part of the Roman state. The endless modern debate over what was at stake in that conflict (the legal protections afforded by Roman citizenship, the right to be treated with respect by Roman magistrates, the political participation of the local elites, economic advantages, especially the fairer sharing of the costs and benefits of war, etc.) surely reflects how unclear the issues were even to the participants. What would it mean to call all the citizens of allied states 'Roman citizens'? Was it clear in advance to any of them? Mouritsen has argued that the allies cannot have been fighting for citizenship since it could not have satisfied their needs, and hence were fighting for independence.[15] But, as Brunt maintained forcefully, political rights are always worth fighting for: to become Roman citizens with votes was to become active participants in the debate over what that citizenship involved, to give them the right and means to satisfy their needs. What is evident on any interpretation of the conflict is that it was the allies who were challenging Rome for a more advantageous integration into the Roman state, not the Romans attempting to impose it on the allies. The lex Iulia of 90 BCE conceded citizenship to Latins and allies in order to retain their loyalty in this crucial conflict: it is perverse to argue that the demand for citizenship did not come from the beneficiaries themselves, whatever their motives.[16] The Social War destroyed the basis of the dialectic, between Roman and non-Roman, that had characterised Italy for at least two centuries, a dialectic which presupposed, and thereby promoted, a separation of identities.

[15] Mouritsen (1998).   [16] *Pace* Mouritsen (1998) 153ff.

Languages and identities

The correlate of lack of Roman interest in imposing Roman institutions on allied states is the absence of a policy of Latinisation. There is no evidence, as Adams has stressed, of any Roman policy to wipe out local languages or to impose the use of Latin, whether on the peoples of Italy under the republic, or the provinces under the empire.[17] For lack of other explicit evidence on Roman thinking on this issue, the case of Cumae must be the crucial test-case.[18] In 180 BCE, Livy reports, Cumae sent a successful delegation to the senate to request permission 'to speak Latin in public and for the right for auctioneers to conduct sales in Latin'.[19] Cumae, though one of the earliest Greek colonies, had been overwhelmed by the Samnites in the late fifth century BCE, and had been Oscan-speaking thereafter. In close proximity to the Roman colony of Puteoli (since 196 BCE), with Scipio's *colonia* of Liternum to the north, Cumae found itself in the growing epicentre of Roman power in Campania. The disgrace of Oscan Capua provided a model from which to take distance. Cumae might have recalled Greek origins and revived Greek, on the model of nearby Neapolis, had it wished to assert an independent identity not tainted by Oscan, but preferred Latin.

There is no surprise, but what makes the episode striking is that Cumae felt it necessary to ask formal permission of the senate to use Latin in formal public acts. That presupposes that there was no standing invitation or encouragement by Rome to its allies to take up the use of Latin. It may not have been legally necessary to ask the senate permission: the delegation is an ostentatious display of loyalty, or flattery. But it does imply that Rome was seen to enjoy proprietary rights over the Latin tongue: it was *their* language, and especially as used formally in public, the language of power, and the Cumaeans wished to underline that theirs was an act of respect, not of theft. Only five years before the senate, in its vigorous repression of the cult of Bacchus, had circulated its ban throughout Italy, to allies as well as citizens and Latins, in the Latin language: the surviving copy was found at Tiriolo in Calabria.[20] The allies could recognise Latin as the language of insistent power. At the same time, we cannot leap to the conclusion that Cumae now abandoned Oscan: the numerous Oscan inscriptions of Cumae cannot be made to terminate with 180 BCE.[21]

---

[17] Adams (2003) 113, 289.   [18] Cf. Kaimio (1975) 99f.

[19] Livy 40.43.1, 'ut publice Latine loquerentur et praeconibus Latine vendendi ius esset'.

[20] *Corpus Inscriptionum Latinarum* 1² 581, Livy 39.18; I owe this point to Filippo Coarelli.

[21] Vetter (1953) nos. 108–14, Poccetti (1979) nos. 129–34.

Against this isolated episode we might be tempted to set the passage of Valerius Maximus discussed above (ch. 2) which claims a consistent policy of promoting the international use of Latin by insisting on the public use of Latin by its magistrates. This oversimplified claim reveals only part of the picture.[22] The alternative language presupposed by Valerius is Greek; and there was, as we have seen, a degree of Roman anxiety about being overwhelmed by a language that paraded itself as superior. Even so, the most remarkable point is the lack of Roman insistence on Latin, and the constant use of Greek as the twin language of the empire: Greek was regularly used in the Roman army and in provincial administration under the empire, to judge from Egypt. If there is generally an opposition of High–Low between two languages in a context of diglossia, Greek cannot be shown to have been treated by the Romans as low: Adams sees the status of Latin rather as 'super-high', the ultimate language of power, but Greek accepted practically, in at least the east, as the effective language of business and administration.

On the other hand, the exceptional respect afforded by the Romans to what they could describe as 'our other language' cannot be generalised. There is no trace of respect for the Italic dialects, or of Roman attempts to learn the languages of their neighbours. A case can be made for limited respect for Etruscan, especially in the context of religious learning. A case can also be made for Punic, which was acknowledged to have its own literature (notably the twenty-eight volumes of Mago on agriculture, translated into Latin after the sack of Carthage, Pliny, *Natural History* 18.22). Plautus' *Poenulus*, with its parody of a Punic accent, also shows familiarity at Rome with Punic. Etruscan and Punic were the two languages (apart from Latin and Greek, *utraque lingua nostra*), which the emperor Claudius learned (Suetonius, *Claudius* 34). Punic is the subject of the most eloquent expression from antiquity of respect for non Greco-Latin tongues, in a letter of Augustine to Maximus of Madaura:

Nor could you so forget yourself, writing as an African to a fellow-African, since we are both settled in Africa, as to think that Punic names should be belittled . . . or you would surely regret your birth in the cradle of that language. (*Epist.* 17.2)

Few passages articulate so clearly the concept of identity (*te ipsum oblivisci* is the opposite of *gnōthi seauton*, not merely not to know who you are but to forget who you are). The argument is surely convincing that, even if non-African Romans did not learn Punic as a rule, they respected the right

---

[22] Adams (2003) 558–9.

of those born in traditionally Punic-speaking territory to use and identify themselves with that language.[23]

One reason for a lack of Roman effort in learning the other languages of Italy apart from Greek was their sheer number. While Greece may have characterised by the diversity of its dialects, they were recognisably members of the same family, and the hellenic tongue was one of the common features that for Herodotus identified the Hellenes. Italic 'dialects' were separate languages, even if closely related, and there is no sign that Latin and Oscan speakers sensed an underlying community. Apart from the gaps between Latin, Oscan, Umbrian, Venetic and Messapic, the Italian peninsula had substantial populations of three non-Italic groups: Etruscans, Greeks and Celts. Latin as the conquest language offered itself in the role of the common tongue, while conceding superiority to Greek as a common tongue on a Mediterranean-wide level.

If Romans had little incentive to learn other Italic languages, Italic-speakers had plenty of incentive to learn both Latin and Greek. The most visible example is the community of traders (*negotiatores*) from Italy operating in the great slave market of Delos between 166 and 87 BCE.[24] The rich crop of inscriptions, especially the dedications from what is consequently named the Agora of the Italians, illustrates their bilingual use of Latin and Greek. As a group, they identify themselves as *Italici*, as did the traders of North Africa and elsewhere.[25] They include Roman citizens and members of the Italian allied states: it was once maintained these came largely from the South, but it has been shown that many came from central Italy, from cities like Praeneste and Aletrium.[26] In Greek documents, individual Roman citizens and inhabitants of the city of Rome are referred to as *Romaioi*, but the corporate group is always referred to as *Italikoi/Italicei*. They include freeborn, freed and slaves. The slaves, especially when acting as a group as the *Competaliastai*, tend to use Greek, but not even Roman citizens making dedications to the likes of Scipio Africanus have any compunction about using Greek. The *Italici* acting as a formal group have a preference for Latin. There is no trace of Oscan or any other local Italic language.[27]

Delos is the conspicuous example of how empire generated profits; the entire eastern Mediterranean will have had its significant population of *negotiatores Italici*, and the alleged death toll of 80,000 in the massacre organised in Asia Minor in 88 by Mithridates points to the scale.[28] It is self-evident

---

[23] Adams (2003) 239–44.   [24] Rauh (1993).

[25] E.g. Sallust, *Jugurtha* 26, 47 on Cirta and Vaga in N. Africa; see Wilson (1966).

[26] Coarelli, Musti and Solin (1982).   [27] Adams (2003) 642ff.

[28] See Brunt (1971) 224–7 on the likely exaggeration of the number.

that, in this context, the assertion of local identities by use of Italic dialects had no place; in fact no example of these languages is found outside a local Italic context (contrast the Palmyrenes, who flaunted their Aramaic in Rome and South Shields). Because there is no example of a trilingual inscription including an Italic language, it is easy to forget how many trilingual speakers of (say) Oscan, Latin and Greek there must have been. We can see them as bilinguals, in Oscan and Latin at home, in Latin and Greek abroad. The context determined language choice, and the place for local languages and assertion of local identity was at home. It was abroad that a new identity was created as '*Italici*', expressing the Latin-speaking communality of Romans and *socii*. The power of multiple identities lies in their strategic deployment in diverse contexts.

There is considerable evidence for bilinguality between Italic languages and Latin, especially in the second and early first centuries BCE, not only from bilingual inscriptions (which are rare), but from the simultaneous use of both languages in the same communities, implying choice. Torelli has observed the dichotomy in modern approaches between pre-historians looking at pre-Roman cultures, for whom romanisation spells the deletion of native culture, and romanists, for whom it represents the effective construction of an integrated society.[29] The same dichotomy applies to linguistics: for students of Italic dialects, Latinisation, whether the appearance of Latin usages in Italic languages, or the use of Latin script, or ultimately the use of Latin language, is negative. Nostalgia for diversity and triumphalism over integration are equally partial as viewpoints. They understate the extent and interest of the transitional periods in which two languages (and, by extension, two cultures) may sit alongside each other and interact. The question is not why one language/culture deletes another, but how and why a bilingual situation is first created, then abandoned.

The best-documented situation is that for Etruria, thanks to the abundance of the *corpus* of Etruscan inscriptions (over 10,000), and has been thoroughly analysed from this point of view.[30] Evidence for the spread of Latin in Etruria in the second century is limited, despite the standard (and surely correct) observation that military service as Roman allies must have rendered knowledge of Latin essential at least for the ruling class from the early third century.[31] Two sets of fragments of Roman statutes found in the territory of Clusium, the second group with Etruscan script on the

[29] Torelli (1999) 13.
[30] Harris (1971), Kaimio (1975), Benelli (1994), Benelli (2001), Adams (2003) 169ff.
[31] Homeyer (1957).

reverse, are normally dated to the late second or early first century BCE; but though they document the diffusion of Roman law in the Latin language, they say rather less than the use of Latin in public inscriptions by local municipal authorities, something attested in Umbria but not Etruria.[32] The bulk of evidence for the use of Latin alongside Etruscan belongs to the first century BCE, particularly in the context of family burials, suggesting that the shift to Latin only starts with the grant of Roman citizenship by the lex Iulia of 90 BCE.[33] Especially in the bilingual inscriptions of Clusium and Perugia, which are relatively common,[34] there seems to be a gradual shift over three generations: Etruscan remains standard in the first part of the first century, bilingual Etruscan and Latin inscriptions are common in the middle of the century, Etruscan becomes progressively rarer towards the end of the century.[35] Etruscan forms are heavily affected by Latinisms in the bilingual period, but Latin only rarely by Etruscan.

The sense remains in the bilingual inscriptions that different values may be expressed by the two languages. In Latin, filiation and tribe are properly used as signals of Roman citizenship: Q. Folnius A.f. Pom. (Quintus Folnius, son of Aulus, of the Pomptine tribe).[36] In Etruscan, the matronymic has a force alien to the Roman tradition, and the same man is given as *velχe fulni velχes ciarθialisa* – Velche Fulni (son of) Velche (born of) Ciarthia. The two languages express different cultural usages and different identities. But there is continuous interchange between the two. Thus the Etruscan matronymic practice affects Latin usage, and a non-Roman form is generated: *C. Treboni Q.f. Gellia natus* – Gaius Trebonius, son of Quintus, born by Gellia – and even in the innovative *Gelliae natus* – born of Gellia – where the genitive is the standard case in the standard Latin expression, *Caii filius* – son of Gaius – though the verb form *natus* normally requires the ablative.[37] The subtlety with which this generation experiments with name forms, and reveals sensitivity to the requirements of two cultural traditions, suggests that the dual identity is consciously embraced. When it disappears, under Augustus, it does so, as we shall see, as part of a widespread pattern in Italy.

The pattern from Etruria cannot be generalised for other areas. Even within Etruria, the cities of the south, led by Caere, the first Etruscan city to be granted Roman citizenship, seem to take up Latin earlier than those of the north. The evidence for the spread of Latin in Umbria is significantly earlier, from the second century BCE.[38] There are no major groups of bilingual

---

[32] Harris (1971) 173–5.   [33] Kaimio (1975) 227.   [34] Benelli (1994).   [35] Benelli (2001) 11.
[36] Benelli (2001) no. 4.   [37] Adams (2003) 169ff.
[38] Bradley (2000) 203–17. For Umbrian texts, see Rix (2002) 47–66.

grave inscriptions as in Etruria, though a cluster of grave tiles from Tuder (Todi) perfectly illustrates intergenerational shift, with the father's name form (la.ma.tvplei, Lars Dupleius son of Marcus) given in Umbrian in standard Umbrian form, those of the daughter and her husband in Umbrian form but Latin script, that of the grandson (ca puplece ma fel, C. Publicius Marci filius) in Latin script and Latin name form.[39] What is particularly striking about the Umbrian situation is that public inscriptions were put up using Latin in place of Umbrian script well before the Social War, and that the Latin language was used by 'a considerable number of allied Umbrian communities' in the same period.[40] There is evidently a period in the late second and early first centuries when the public voice of Umbrian authorities was bilingual. Six *marones* of Asisium advertised the improvement of the town amenities with a cistern, wall and arch in Latin: their standard Umbrian title of office shows that this must predate the Social War, and it forms part of a programme of terracing that belongs to the second century.[41] The names of two of the same *marones* appear on a boundary stone from the territory of Asisium that was inscribed in Umbrian but in Latin script.[42] It is surely right to conclude that language choice was a matter of context: Umbrian was still fully alive as the local language, but the magistrates of Asisium, like those of Cumae, might prefer that the public image of their town should follow their Latin neighbours.[43] At the same time, around 100 BCE, the Iguvines in inscribing their ancient rituals in Umbrian, a clear declaration of religious identity, used the Latin script.[44]

Here the geography of the Umbrian valley is significant (figure 3.4). The southern half of the valley was controlled by the Latin colony of Spoletium from 241 BCE, whereas the northern half remained split between the small Umbrian hill towns of Asisium, Fulginiae, Hispellum, Mevania, Trebiae and Urvinum. Their close juxtaposition, in an area that invited intimate communication, provided incentive for both assimilation and differentiation. A dual identity, Umbrian and Latin, allowed both close links with Roman neighbours, and a distance from them. There is no need to read the early spread of Latin in Umbria as a sign of the weakness of Umbrian culture (compared to Etruscan);[45] there are quite enough Umbrian inscriptions of

---

[39] Vetter (1953) 232, Bradley (2000) 205.

[40] Bradley (2000) 209. Sisani (2007) 275–97 ('I processi acculturativi') and IX for a *corpus* of all pre-Social War inscriptions from Umbria in Latin lettering or language, and a careful analysis of Latinisation.

[41] *Corpus Inscriptionum Latinarum* I², 2112; for the dating, see Coarelli (1996a) 249.

[42] Vetter (1953) 236.   [43] Bradley (2000) 210.

[44] Sisani (2001b) 237ff.   [45] Harris (1971) 184–7.

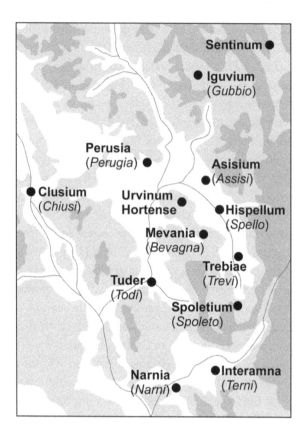

Figure 3.4 Map of Umbria (drawn by Amy Richardson)

the late second century to show that the language itself was still alive.[46] The Umbrian language survives the disappearance of the Umbrian script in the late second century; and though Latin inscriptions come to predominate, those in the Umbrian language continue.[47] On the other hand, the speed with which after the Social War Umbrian not only disappears as a public language, but is completely replaced by Latin as the language of private funerary epigraphy, even if it does not entail a deletion of Umbrian identity, shows that tenacity to the local language ceased to be an important marker of identity.[48]

The language *we* associate most closely with a separate and indeed separatist identity is Oscan, thanks to its use in the Social War as one language of the rebel Italia. Here the classic expression of bilingual identity is precisely the series of coinage issues of the rebel forces of 91–89 BCE. The symbol of

---

[46] Bradley (2000) 213.   [47] For full analysis, see now Sisani (2007) 301–407.
[48] Bradley (2000) 215.

the Italian bull trampling the Roman wolf could scarcely be more expressive of a sense of separate identity; especially when the Italian bull, *vitellus*, was etymologically linked with Italia, and the point emphasised by the Oscan version of the legend, *viteliu*. The Roman wolf as symbol gained added force for Oscan speakers who knew that the Hirpini, prominent among the rebels, owed their name to the Oscan for wolf, *irpu*:[49] the Roman wolf resisted by the folk who had always protected their flocks from the local wolves. But, for all the anti-Roman message, the coinage is deeply bilingual. Oscan *viteliu* twins with Latin Italia; *Paapi embratur* with Papius Imperator. At all points the rebel coinage is a mirror image of Roman coinage: in its weight and denomination, in its designs and in its circulation pattern.[50] At the very moment of expression of difference, the anti-Romans prove to be cast in a Roman mould, and fluent in their language and symbolic currency.

Oscan epigraphy is at its peak in the second century, especially in the heartland of Samnium. Abundant material has emerged from the excavation of the great mountain sanctuaries like Pietrabbondante, Vastogirardi and Schiavi d'Abruzzo,[51] as in the Lucanian equivalent at Macchia di Rossano di Vaglio where the lettering is Greek.[52] They show the local elites busy building shrines, dedicating pavements, podia, statues, thank-offerings and so on. They certainly point to a strong pride in local identity. Yet formulae like UPST. LEGU. TANGINUD. AAMANAFED. ESIDUM. PRUFATTED, which echo verbally the Roman practice and Latin formula, *senatus sententia faciundum curavit eidem probavit* ('following the decision of the senate, he supervised its construction and the same man conducted the final inspection'), show again the local expression of thoughts and ways that come from Rome. The Oscan suffers repeated interference from Latin usages in a way that only makes sense in a bilingual context.[53] The Samnites, unlike the Umbrians, do not seem to have opted for Latin in their public voices before the Social War; but they were evidently highly conversant with the Latin language, and with the ways in which the Roman elite marked its status by the dedication of public works.

It is natural to imagine that the Samnite elite learned Latin in the second century, whether to carry out their function of commanding local contingents in the Roman army, or for any sort of business with fellow *Italici*. The general assumption is that beneath elite level, knowledge of Latin was rare.

---

[49] Festus 93L (106M).   [50] Burnett (1998); Rix (2007) 76–7.

[51] Poccetti (1979) nos. 13–32 (Pietrabbondante), Poccetti (1979) no. 33 (Vastogirardi), Poccetti (1979) no. 34 (Schiavi d'Abruzzo); see also Rix (2002) 81–91.

[52] Lejeune (1990) nos. 154–83, Poccetti (1979) nos. 154–83. See also Rix (2002) 123–34.

[53] Campanile (1976), Adams (2003) 127 ff.

This belief in a two-class linguistic system is partly encouraged by the nature of the evidence (it was the elite who supervised public works, and who could afford lavish graves with inscriptions), though also by the evidence of the long survival among the peasantry of languages like Celtic and Punic. It is the more necessary to pay close attention to the rare cases of inscriptions clearly made by workers. In early imperial Gaul, La Graufesenque provides comprehensive and explicit evidence of potters operating bilingually in Latin and Gallic: they are aware that Latin is the language of the 'export market', but frequently switch into Gaulish for internal purposes:[54]

Even in this lower-class community the Gauls had been provided with the tools of Latin literacy, and although they often used those tools to write Gaulish, they were revealing in various ways a regard for the status of Latin, and an awareness of commercial advantages. Knowledge of Latin was bound to spread, assisted by the framework of literacy which had already been put in place.[55]

The same point can been made for pre-Social War Samnium, in the great sanctuary complex of Pietrabbondante. In the main temple and the theatre below it, the inscriptions and dedications were exclusively in Oscan.[56] Even if the formulae and grammatical constructions they used showed the impact of the elite's knowledge of Latin, they ostentatiously displayed Samnite identity. But up in the roof of the temple, where nobody could see, a roof tile betrayed a bilingual reality (figure 3.5). Two workers in the tile factory 'signed' their work by imprinting with their footprints, and by incising their names and slightly different messages from opposite edges of the tile, one in Oscan, the other in Latin:

HN. SATTIIEIS DETFRI
SEGANATTED. PLAVTAD
(Detfri slave of Herennius Sattius/signed with a footprint)
Herenneis Amica
signavit qando
ponebamus tegila.
(Amica slave of Herennius/signed when/we were placing the tile).[57]

(Poccetti no. 21)

The Oscan worker, Detfri, a name otherwise unknown, was a female slave of Herennius Sattius. Her Latin fellow-worker, Amica, was a female slave of the same Herennius. The master is shown to be Samnite by his names. Interestingly, his Latin-speaking slave gives his name in an Oscan form of

---

[54] Adams (2003) 687ff.   [55] Adams (2003) 719.   [56] La Regina (1966).
[57] Poccetti (1979) no. 21; see La Regina (1966).

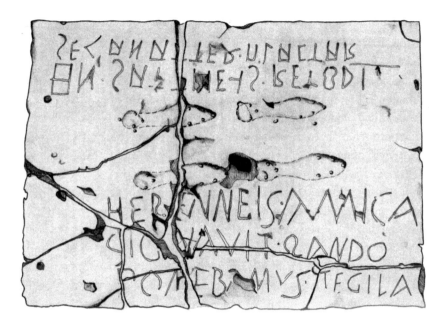

Figure 3.5 Roof tile from Pietrabbondante with bilingual inscription in Oscan and Latin (after La Regina, *Studi Etrusci* 44, 1976: 285)

the genitive, Herenn-*eis* rather than-*i*, a type of linguistic influence that can be described as 'accommodation', whereby the user of one language makes deferential acknowledgement of another. Conversely, the Oscan *seganatted* appears to be modelled innovatively on the standard Latin *signavit*.[58]

This remarkable bilingual document is eloquent of two languages operating in intimate contact. Usages in each language are influenced by the other. In playful exchange, the two workers engage in a sort of mirror writing: indeed, the fact that they write from opposite edges of the tile, so that one message is the other way up from the other, means that the writing of the two travels in the same direction, since Oscan script flows to the left, Latin to the right. Their separate tongues make complementary points: the word 'footprint' (*plavtad*) is used only in the Oscan, though Latin *planta* was familiar in the context of the signature of ceramics, *in planta pedis*. Only the Latin text refers to 'us', the pair of workers (*qando ponebamus*). The two footprints themselves happen to be of a type of shoe typical of Samnium.[59] There is an evident awareness here of contrasting identities, and a playful banter between them. That banter is conducted by two female slaves.

[58] Adams (2003) 124f.   [59] Morel (1991b) 195–99.

It has been suggested that the tile was manufactured in Venafrum, a town famed for its tiles, where the Sattii are attested;[60] given the extreme logistical problems of transporting the weight of tiles required for a temple roof over a considerable distance up into the mountains, the most we can reasonably imagine is that workers from a tile factory in Venafrum came up to Pietrabbondante to take part in the construction project. Either way, it underlines the point that there is likely to have been constant contact in Samnium between Latin- and Oscan-speaking neighbours, and that this contact was by no means limited to the elite but could affect even their workers. We are not dealing with two completely separate zones, each characterised by its own language and usages, but between a situation of exchange in full mutual awareness.

A similar point can be made on the basis of the pottery of Campanian Teanum Sidicinum and its neighbour, Cales, a Latin colony since 334 BCE.[61] Cales was a major centre of production of black-glazed pottery, which achieved considerable diffusion. Calene ware is common in dedications at the sanctuaries of Teanum; but Teanum also has its own pottery production which mimics Calene forms. Forms and decoration apart, the potters of Cales had a distinctive idiom for signing their ware in a long version that spelled out who and where:

Retus Gabinius C.s. Calebus fecit.
(Retus Gabinius slave of Caius of Cales made it.)

The pottery of Teanum also has a long form of signature in Oscan:

Beriiumen anei upsatuh sent tiianei.

The interpretation of the Oscan is debated, but is approximately, 'Of the Berii, made with the wheel at Teanum'. It is not completely clear who is influencing whom (Morel allows for the possibility of the Sidicine potters setting the model with the long form), but the point is that the workshops of potters in two neighbouring towns, one Sidicine and one Latin, operated in full awareness of one another and exchanged ideas and idioms.

These texts from Pietrabbondante/Venafrum and Teanum/Cales may be no more than hints, but like the potters of La Graufesenque, they are enough to put us on our guard against the assumption that bilingual contact and exchange was limited to the elites. The question is of critical importance, since we need to account for the apparent language death of Oscan. Evidence for the survival of Oscan into the early Empire is limited and debatable.

---

[60] Cato, *de Agricultura* 135.1; Coarelli and La Regina (1984) 172–6.   [61] Morel (1991a) 136–9.

Literary sources (Strabo and Suetonius) seem to indicate that Atellan farces were still performed in Oscan under Augustus: particularly interesting is the suggestion that they survived as a form of street theatre, which would indicate plebeian roots.[62] Painted messages in Oscan survive from Pompeii, but the argument that they must have been recent to survive is fallacious: one of the most famous examples, which shows a gladiator with the Oscan label 'SPARTAKS', survived because covered with a later layer of plaster. Similarly, the *eituns* painted inscriptions are legible still today, long after excavation, and long after their use either before or during the Social War.[63]

For lack of evidence, it is virtually impossible to say whether there was a grass-roots survival of Oscan in the period after the Social War when Latin had become the only (Italic) language of public life. But we should leave room for the possibility that Latin became widespread in Italy in the third and second centuries BCE at sub-elite levels, both through service together in the army, by neighbourly relations with Latin colonies, and by the diverse possibilities of the world of work and commerce. The network of consular roads is rightly seen as an instrument of romanisation: their function is precisely to facilitate exchange and interconnections of all types. Trunk roads, and their vital subsystem of side-roads or *diverticula*, spread inland patterns of connectivity which traditionally characterised coastal areas.[64] Even if we cannot define how many of what rank and description moved around the roads, we can confidently predict that such exchanges increased in scale and in social spread.

What was the effect on linguistic identity? There is a considerable danger of reading the epigraphic record as a snapshot of an actual linguistic situation: that Latin spread to the extent that we find Latin inscriptions, and local languages survived to the extent we find local or 'epichoric' inscriptions. But the inscriptions are not neutral evidence to the extent that they act as conscious expressions of identity. We can see this most clearly when we can see that the authors are bilingual. The six *marones* of Asisium were capable of putting up a significant inscription in public in Umbrian: they chose Latin not because they had forgotten Umbrian, but because they wished to underline their links with Rome. Conversely, the *medices* of the Frentani at Pietrabbondante, or those of Pompeii, consistently chose to underline a Samnite identity, though it is incredible that they were not capable of Latin if they wanted. The slave girls in the tile yard thought it was a bit

---

[62] Rawson (1991) 476, citing Strabo 5.3.6, Suetonius, *Iulius* 39.1, *Augustus* 43.1.
[63] Crawford (1996b) 985.
[64] Coarelli (1988), Laurence (1999) 11–26, Horden and Purcell (2000) 124–32.

of a game. What language contact and language choice enables is a greater reflexivity about linguistic identity: the proliferation of Oscan inscriptions in the second century can be read not simply as evidence of language survival, but of enhanced awareness of cultural diversity.[65]

How close this interchange between Latin and local was, and how subtle the expressions of identity involved, is illustrated by the bronze tablets from the Lucanian town of Bantia, and the endless modern debate to which they have given rise. The two faces of the bronze tablet are inscribed, one with a Roman law in Latin, the other with local Bantian legislation in Oscan. The uncertainties are multiple. The expected sequence of the laws, which might have led us to expect a local law effaced by a central Roman law after the Social war, was controverted by the discovery of a fragment with a nail hole: on the Latin side it occupied a blank at the bottom, on the Oscan side the text is written skirting around it, implying that it was the Oscan side to be inscribed second, after the Latin side had been already inscribed, nailed to the wall, then taken down. Then it is wholly unclear which the Roman law is: possibly of the tribune Saturninus whose agrarian law of 103 BCE required the magistrates and senators to swear allegiance in a similar way to that prescribed by the text, but it might be a law of any point in the final decades of the second century, on a range of issues.[66] Equally, it is unclear in what context the Oscan law was made: as an independent ally before the Social war, but heavily reliant on a Latin model, possibly that of the neighbouring Latin colony of Venusia, or after the war as a municipium, directly dependent on Rome. The balance of probability is in favour of the pre-war context, but it is a close call.[67]

Perhaps the most telling lesson is that we could be in such doubt. This is an Oscan Bantia in the most intimate contact with Rome. It inscribes its own laws on the flip side of a Roman text, however acquired (it is often assumed it came from Venusia, but it is not to be excluded that allied cities posted Roman laws that were felt to concern them). It uses Latin not Oscan script to do so, writing like Romans from left to right. The very concept of inscribing laws to prescribe the constitutional basis of a community is Roman, and the specific topics (trials before the assembly, procedures for census of citizens, civil law procedures and the sequence of magistracies) were ones of current concern at Rome. The titles of the magistracies (censor, praetor, quaestor and tribunus plebis) are all Roman. And the language itself

---

[65] Tagliamonte (1996) 221–34.
[66] Crawford (1996b) no. 7, 193ff. See Adamesteanu and Torelli (1969) for the new fragment.
[67] Crawford (1996b) no. 13, 271ff.

is deeply infected with Latinisms, more so than other Oscan documents, in a way that suggests the attempt to find an equivalent of specific Latin legal formulae.[68] It may well be that their model was a set of regulations from Venusia, where the bronze itself may have originated. But the more the evidence piles up to show the Bantians could not have conceived their law without an almost slavish adherence to a Roman thought-world, the more significant their choice of Oscan becomes. It seems that the choice 'was intended to symbolise independence from Rome', and that it is the work of a ruling elite fully conversant with Latin, yet 'desperate to assert an Oscan identity'.[69]

What this means is that the spread of Latin did not in itself lead to the death of Oscan and of awareness of local identity. It actually made it more acute, or perhaps one should say that it redefined its parameters. It evidently was possible to be both Latin and Oscan. To borrow a Latin alphabet and Latinate words, a set of Roman political institutions, and even a reused Roman inscription, was of course to admit the power of another culture. At the same moment, to translate this all into Oscan was to reassert the local. It is neither the language of submission nor of resistance, but of dialogue and dual identity. A casual find in Banzi revealed a close parallel in what has been identified as the *auguraculum*, the ritually defined area marked out, in close correspondence to Etruscan augural rites, with *cippi*, each marked, in Latin script, with the name of a god.[70] The inclusion of a familiar Oscan goddess, Flusa (the Latin Flora), raises the same debate: is this monument after the establishment of a Roman *municipium*, marked by Roman–Etruscan ritual, or before, marked by a local goddess? It is the dialogue between the two that prevents us turning the Social War into a watershed between absolutes: neither absolutely Oscan before, not absolutely Roman after.

We have seen several times, in Oleggio, in the tombs of Chiusi, in the grave tiles of Todi, the pattern of intergenerational shift, whereby the first generation operates in the local language (L_1), the second bilingually in the local and Latin (L_1 and L_2), the third primarily in Latin (L_2). More important, we have seen a much slower rhythm, that lasts over some three centuries, from the Roman expansion of the late fourth century to the new order of Augustan Italy. The intermediate stage of bilingualism (L_1 and L_2) stretches from the beginning of the third to the end of the first century BCE. It varies enormously from region to region. In some areas, notably Campania and Umbria, the substitution of Latin as a language of public discourse is

---

[68] Crawford (1996b) 274, Adams (2003) 137f.
[69] Crawford (1996b) 276.   [70] Torelli (1995) 97ff.

easier and swifter than others (Etruria and Samnium). Language usage, as registered by the kind of epigraphic material that survives, is not an adequate mirror of the spread of dual-language abilities. Studies of bilingual practice emphasise that code-switching is context-bound. There may have been many local Italian elites capable of putting up inscriptions in Greek who would not have dreamt of doing so; equally, many of the *negotiatores* on Delos will have known Oscan or Umbrian or Messapic without dreaming of inscribing those languages in the Agora of the *Italici*. In a long period of bilingualism, there was abundant interference between languages: the more that Rome influences local institutions (the system of magistracies, local constitutions, the expression of elite status through benefactions and public works), the more the language used to express those institutions is coloured by Latin. This is not necessarily a sign of language death, nor of death of identity.

Above all, language emerges as a powerful expression of identity in the Italy of this period. There are conflicting aspects of identity that need to be conveyed. Latin carried high prestige as the language of the conqueror: there were good reasons for Rome's Italian allies to ally themselves with that prestige as Latin-speaking *Italici*. There were surely advantages in non-military contexts such as trade in mastering Latin; our instinctive association of Latin with the local elites should be questioned in view of clear evidence of its knowledge among workers and slaves. It is not wholly easy to imagine Asisium of the late second century BCE with Latin inscriptions on its walls populated by stubborn Umbrian monolinguals. The potency of language in expressing identity is most dramatically illustrated by the coinage of the Social Wars: the Italic bull speaks Oscan to spite the Roman wolf. But the same coinage underlines their ambivalence: they use Latin, too, because it is in fact their common tongue. As we move to consider the interpretation of material culture, these ambivalences should be borne in mind.

Bilingualism and material culture

Among all the cultural markers of identity, language is accepted to have a special place. 'It is often argued in linguistic literature that language is the most important marker of identity that there is.'[71] Bilingual contexts heighten this awareness rather than diminish it: 'This book is overwhelmingly about identity, and that is because bilinguals of different types are often particularly aware of the conflicts of identity determined by their belonging

---

[71] Adams (2003) 751, referring to Crystal (2000) 40.

to more than one speech community.'[72] But language is by no means the only marker, nor even a necessary marker; its potency in this respect lies in the close association between language and the concepts it expresses. If we find the Etruscan language expressing the Etruscan usage of naming the mother, or Umbrian describing local ritual and religious practice, or Latin expressing Roman institutions like tribal affiliation, names of magistrates and legal structures, the sense of identity is the more marked. So when we find North African city coinages of the early Empire with the city names inscribed in neo-Punic, but the imperial titulature in Latin, language and content are matched: 'there is nothing more 'Roman' than Roman imperial names and titles, and Latin language and script were used to convey those elements.'[73] Language performs its marking function best where the culture (in the sense of customary practices and values) is imbedded in the language, and the language in the culture.

The difficulty is to make the leap from language to material culture. Different markers of culture cannot all be assumed to be orchestrated and harmonious expressions of a single absolute of 'cultural identity'. Many attempts have been made to use language as an analogy, from Levi-Strauss's employment of the linguistic theories of de Saussure to Geertz's reading of culture as a web of signification.[74] Nevertheless, material culture has its own grammar, and does not always shadow the rules of language. Cultural goods are appropriated with extraordinary ease and frequency into different contexts, and separated from their original context and significance to be endowed with local meaning.[75] We have only, with Sahlins, to observe the appropriation of western goods into the local social structures of the Sandwich Island chieftains, or the potlatch ceremonies of the Kwakiutl of north-west America, to see that using other people's goods does not necessarily make you more like them.[76] The same phenomenon may be observed with loan-words which, in their passage from one language to another, may acquire radically different context and signification. To borrow a word is one thing, to learn a language another, and if material culture behaves like a language, it is only when an entire series of interrelated artefacts is in association with a set of practices and values, not when isolated features are borrowed.

[72] Adams (2003) 751–2.   [73] Adams (2003) 244.

[74] Geertz (1973) 5: 'Believing, with Max Weber, that man is an animal suspended in webs of significance he himself has spun, I take culture to be those webs, and the analysis of it to be therefore not an experimental science in search of law but an interpretative one in search of meaning.'

[75] Appadurai (1986).   [76] Sahlins (1981).

These difficulties are not always appreciated in discussions of the romanisation of material cultures in Italy. A Celtic brooch may point to a Gallic
war-cloak, and thus to the values of a warrior society; a strigil, especially
when accompanied by ointment jars, may point to the practice of bathing,
and thus to the values of a Greco-Roman city. Found together, they are
reminiscent of a bilingual inscription, with tribe and affiliation given in
Latin, matronymic in Venetic. What is enormously much harder to assess is
whether they expressed two identities, whether in conflict or in harmony, or
the absorption of new practices, like loan-words, into a single identity. And
if the strigil gave the Insubrian a dual identity, did it make him feel specifically Roman, like the colonists of nearby Cremona, or rather associate with a
broader Mediterranean cultural *koinē*, already met centuries before through
the Etruscans?

The overwhelming tendency has been to assume that the acquired identity
was specifically Roman, even though its origins might be manifestly non-
Roman. The assumption flows from the big picture, that recognizes that the
end result is to provide a common cultural identity to the Italian peninsula
associated with Roman citizenship, and therefore reads each step towards
that common identity as a conscious step in pursuit of that eventual identity.
Not the least of the difficulties about this assumption is that the material
aspect of this common culture was both derived from, and often consciously
evocative of, the hellenistic east. The solution is to give Rome the role of the
channel of transmission:

> Hellenistic sculpture, painting and architectural details, Hellenistic writing and
> modes of thought came to be quickly noted and eclectically imitated at Rome,
> and Rome's hegemony ensured their rapid transmission into other parts of Italy.[77]

In point of fact, it is questionable whether Rome did indeed play this role as
the channel of transmission; but even if it could be demonstrated, it would
remain an open question whether Italians acquiring Greek ways through
Roman mediation would consequently perceive them to flag a Roman identity. The Stabian baths in Pompeii, which Eschebach believed went back to
the fourth century BCE, but substantially achieved their present form in the
second, serve in the modern literature as one of the earliest surviving specimens of *Roman* baths. Yet there is every reason to suppose that the models
were South Italian, and if they were Roman, that they came not from the
metropolis, but from elsewhere in Campania. Oscan Pompeii was associating itself with a model of luxury surely familiar on the Bay of Naples, but

---

[77] Salmon (1982) 100.

would this make the Pompeian feel more Roman, and would that conflict with his Samnite sensibilities?

The last decade or so has seen an enormous increase in our knowledge of the record of cultural change in Italy. Area after area has seen high-quality monographs and exhibitions of the archaeological record of romanisation: in the north, Liguria[78], Transpadana[79] and the Veneto;[80] in the centre, Etruria,[81] Umbria,[82] the Apennines, including Picenum,[83] the Ager Praetutianus,[84] Samnium[85] and the Sabina;[86] and in the south Daunia,[87] Apulia and Lucania.[88] There is little need here to add to the abundant material assembled by such case-studies, but rather to address the implicit issues of identity-change.

The question of whether the adoption of hellenistic cultural features was a direct result of romanisation was addressed perceptively by Jean-Paul Morel in a discussion of the romanisation of Samnium and Lucania in the fourth and third centuries BCE.[89] He raised serious doubts about the standard picture of Latin colonies as the instrument of diffusion of Roman ways across the peninsula. Not even the colonies emerge as reliable importers of goods and styles from Rome. While Alba Fucens in this period has a certain amount of specifically Roman pottery, like Genucilia plates and black ware with '*petites estampilles*', Cales and Paestum, Morel maintains, show no trace of Roman imports at all. As Johannowsky observed, if the Romans could not extend their cultural influence at this period to northern Campania, what hope had they of penetrating the highlands of Samnium? But equally striking is the contrast between the Latin colony of Aesernia, the advance post of Rome in Samnium, with the Samnite site of Pietrabbondante. The third-century BCE temple of Aesernia, with its backward-looking Romano-Italic style, met in other Roman sites like Sora, is a sharp contrast with the first phase of temple-building at Pietrabbondante, with a sophisticated use of the Ionic that points to direct hellenistic influences. This particular case-study contradicts the thesis of Rome as the advance guard of the new waves of hellenistic style; on the contrary, Rome gives the impression of being retrograde.

Morel rightly cautions against generalising the results of a case-study based on a limited period and a specific area. Elsewhere he subscribes to the view of Rome as model ('Rome was the intermediary through which

[78] Gambaro (1999).   [79] Grassi (1995), Spagnolo Garzoli (1999).

[80] Cresci Marrone and Tirelli (1999).   [81] Carandini (1985), Terrenato (1998).

[82] Coarelli (1996a), Bradley (2000), Sisani (2007).   [83] Delplace (1993).

[84] Guidobaldi, M. P. (1995).   [85] Various authors (1991), Capelli (2000).   [86] Sternini (2004).

[87] Volpe (1990).   [88] Russo Tagliente (1992).   [89] Morel (1991).

Greek art conquered the west and fundamentally shaped its civilisation'), while noting the Roman tendency to counteract and block new borrowings from the east.[90] It is hard indeed to know what weight to give to the Roman rhetoric of rejection of luxury (ch. 7). Luxury laws are two-edged evidence, pointing both to a perception of certain aspects of hellenistic culture as alien and threatening, and to the enthusiasm with which they were embraced. Luxurious housing was a particular focus of Roman moralising protest: but the fragmentary record of republican housing from Rome hardly allows us to judge whether Pesando was right to argue that the House of the Faun at Pompeii reached a level of luxury and hellenistic sophistication not to be encountered in mid-second century BCE Rome.[91]

Roman disapproval of the luxury of bathing, and the extended resistance to the building of permanent theatres, meant, as we have seen, that some of the most characteristic features of the Roman urban landscape, public baths, theatres and amphitheatres, made their appearance at Rome only in the mid first century BCE. But that need not exclude Rome's role as a model through magnificent private baths, as developed by Sergius Orata and his like in Campania, and through the spectacular investments in temporary wooden theatre buildings. As an architectural form, the amphitheatre was certainly not developed at Rome; but the dramatic development of importance of gladiatorial combat from its original connection with private funerals, and its combination with beast-hunts, was directly and recognizably attributable to Rome.[92] When the language (amphitheatre as architectural form) and social practice/value system (deadly spectacles) coincide, we feel on secure ground. But just as *amφι-θeatron* was a loan-word in Latin, flagged as Greek by its recognizable phi and theta, so the building appears to have been a loan-form in Rome.[93]

Two explanatory models would appear to be at work. If we look at the *longue durée* of tendencies over several centuries, we can say that cultural change in Italy, seen in urbanisation, monumental building, increasing luxury of material goods and the prevailing use of a consistent artistic language, was the direct result of Roman conquest, promoted through road-building and colonisation and the desire of local elites to imitate the fashions embraced by the successful conqueror. But look in closer focus at local situations, area by area, period by period, and the value of the equation of hellenisation with romanisation decreases. We need to allow for the possibility that local elites were imitating the same eastern models as the Roman

[90] Morel (1989) 515.   [91] Pesando (1997) 268–71, Torelli (1999) 8.
[92] Welch (1994), Welch (2007).   [93] Etienne (1966).

elite, with direct, unmediated access of their own; that the imitation was not an act of respect to Rome ('cultural cringe'), but a competitive claim to respect in their own right; and that even if the Romans did get there first in the game of imitative appropriation, the reference points remained eastern. To return to the trilingual model: if we think of the Italic elites as having three hearts like Ennius – local, Greek and Latin – they might play off their identities against each other, too fluent in Greek to need to feel their hellenising culture had turned them into Romans, too fluent in Latin to feel it had reduced them to the status of the defeated Greeks.

One major contribution has been Torelli's studies of the distribution of various artefacts and styles, which have shown that Italy is very far from homogeneous in its reception of hellenistic styles associated with Roman power. A striking example is the widespread diffusion of a particular type of funerary monument, characterised by a Doric frieze of triglyphs alternating with designs, most commonly ox-skulls (*bucrania*), sacrificial instruments (like *paterae*) and flowers, all of which evoke the act of sacrifice. This Doric frieze is often combined with an Ionic cornice, in an idiom familiar from late hellenistic monuments like the altar of the lower sanctuary at Praeneste. But while this idiom is widespread in central Italy, in a zone stretching from Latium and Campania across the Apennines and up into the Po valley, and even round to Aquileia and Istria, it is notably absent both from Etruria and much of the south, especially Apulia and Bruttium.[94] There is evidently cultural choice at work, but to what shall we attribute it? Torelli offers two or three factors: that these areas already had strong traditions of funerary practices of their own, and that they were characterised economically by large estates; whereas the areas of diffusion of Doric friezes are those where military colonisation was most intense.[95] Interestingly, the 'blank' areas are those most receptive to hellenic culture in the archaic period of Greek colonisation, so that one could argue that Roman settlement brought its own separate wave of hellenisation to less hellenised areas, though that is an argument that would break down in Campania. And other artefacts produce other patterns.

So Torelli has shown a striking correlation between the distribution of anatomical *ex voto* offerings and the spread of Roman settlers, either in colonies or *viritim*, though the original model is developed in the strip from Etruria through Latium to northern Campania.[96] He has also suggested a significant pattern in the distribution of architectural terracottas of the Etrusco-Italic type: originating in Etruria and Latium, these spread through

---

[94] Torelli (1995) 159–89.   [95] Torelli (1995) 177.   [96] Torelli (1999) 121.

central Italy, notably Umbria,[97] and are limited in the north and south to actual colonies.[98] But these patterns, though similar, are not the same: especially in Umbria, while architectural terracottas were spread enthusiastically by imitation to allied cities, anatomical *ex votos* appear to be limited to actual Romans or Latins.

The failure of these distribution patterns to map onto each other makes interpretation the more difficult. Some features seem to be limited to Roman settlers, others to spread via them to neighbouring areas. Sometimes (as with architectural terracottas) Etruria and Latium are close cultural allies; at other times (Doric friezes) they offer contrasts. When we factor in the no less interesting study of distribution of building techniques, namely *opus incertum* and *opus reticulatum*, we meet yet other patterns: the second- and early first-century BCE building boom in *opus incertum* has surprisingly limited concentration in Latium and Campania, and leaves the colonies looking backward and underdeveloped,[99] while *opus reticulatum*, the characteristic style of the later first century BCE and first century CE, concentrates around epicentres in Rome and the Bay of Naples, and is exceptional in Samnium, Bruttium and Lucania and Etruria north of Tarquinii.[100]

Certainly, these patterns show that there is no such thing as a homogeneous process of romanisation. Areas differ sharply, depending on the nature and strength of the Roman presence, geographical character (coast versus highlands) and cultural background. But no single feature of material culture can present itself as the litmus of romanisation. Artefacts and styles are not simply reflections of a generalised acculturation process, but individually tell specific stories which can be difficult to decipher. To return briefly to the burials of Oleggio, black-glaze pottery has been described strikingly as the *fossile guida*, or index fossil, of romanisation.[101] From the perspective of a Celtic site in the Po valley, that may be so; but when we consider that two of the primary centres of production of *vernice nera* were in Etruria (especially Arezzo) and Campania, and more specifically Naples, manufactured by potters whose first languages were respectively Etruscan and Greek, albeit alongside the Rome workshops producing *petites estampilles*, we may ask whether either black-glaze pottery, which gains very wide diffusion, was perceived by their users as tell-tale sign of being Roman. On the other hand, the anatomic *ex voto*, with its narrow spread, does indeed seem to be associated with Romans and Latins, but fails to influence the behaviour of

---

[97] Cf. Bradley (2000) 158ff., 270ff.   [98] Torelli (1999) 122ff.   [99] Torelli (1995) 191–210.
[100] Torelli (1995) 212–45.
[101] Grassi (1991) 50, Grassi (1995) 32; cf. A. Deodato in Spagnolo Garzoli (1999) 20.

their allies. We have noted Wiessner's identification of 'emblematic style' to distinguish 'formal variation in material culture that has a distinct referent and transmits a clear message to a defined target population about conscious affiliation or identity' (ch. 1). There is all the difference in the world between the style which flags to the archaeologist Roman influence, like black-glaze pottery, and that which was felt by the users themselves to be emblematic of a particular identity, which is arguably the case with anatomical offerings. The discussion of romanisation has paid far too little attention to this vital distinction.

Monumental building

The erection of conspicuous public buildings, and the urbanisation of which it is frequently, but not always, a part, have a central role to play in accounts of the romanisation of Italy. Promotion of the role of urban centres rates as one of the fundamental features of the romanisation of Italy; at the same time, use of the language of hellenistic art and architecture which is an inextricable part of such monumentalisation rates as a fundamental feature of hellenisation. It is therefore worth turning to the phenomenon with Wiessner's distinction in mind, and asking what such building has to say emblematically about the identity of the builders. Before looking at some examples, it is worth drawing attention to two general points, about 'self-romanisation' and the distinction between city and non-city.

It is above all in the context of monumental building that the idea of 'self-romanisation' or *autoromanizzazione* has been developed. We saw above the distinction between direct and indirect romanisation. There are only certain circumstances in which we can speak of Rome as deliberately and consciously making parts of Italy Roman, such a colonisation, land-division and road-building. There are other areas where we can be reasonably confident that Rome had no strategy of imposing its ways, notably in the use of Latin. In the case of artefactual styles, it is frequently impossible to tell whether an act of imitation is voluntary or imposed, conscious or unconscious, significant of identity or not. But monumental building requires such a concerted attempt on the part of a community, is such a commitment of resource, and leaves behind so conspicuous a public symbol, that it is hard not to read it as a significant statement of identity. On the other hand, except possibly when under the Empire buildings are erected through imperial patronage, it is hard to read them as an imposition from outside; even when supported by imperial patronage, major public buildings are likely to represent a communal expression of communal identity. So Coarelli used the case-study of Asisium, which through the second century BCE develops an impressive system of terraces and walls, culminating in an inscription in Latin (see p. 87), to illustrate an Umbrian community voluntarily trans-forming itself in imitation of its Roman neighbours.[102] With this analysis we may fully agree, and go further to question whether the implicit converse of **auto**-*romanizzazione*, namely cultural and identity change imposed from outside, can have much reality. The doubts are rather over how local and Roman identity collide, collude and interplay.

The second point is about the basic distinction often drawn between the urbanised and non-urbanised areas of Italy. It is a familiar feature of the geography of Italy that much of the Apennines, especially Samnium, is far tougher terrain that the coastal areas, and that this is linked to the widespread custom observed by the ancient sources of living scattered in villages (*kata komas*, *vicatim*) rather than concentrated in cities. This dis-tinction is mapped by Torelli as a threefold one: between the privileged and developed coastal strip, from Etruria to Latium to Campania and Magna Graecia, the underdeveloped Apennine interior, and an intermediary zone between the two to which the urban ways of the coast spread most easily.[103] Doubters of the contrast are urged to spend more time in the rigours of the interior,[104] though one may suspect it is precisely a fondness for non-urbanised areas like the moors or Lake District that has long attracted the British to Samnium.

These contrasts are not merely geographical but a matter of emphatic cultural choice. The terrain of Samnium is extensive and varied (figure 3.6). Some spots are more suitable for urbanisation: several, like Venafrum or Aesernia, were colonised or occupied by the Romans. But while Umbria developed numerous lesser urban centres in response to neighbouring colonies, the Samnites of the interior appear to have made a deliberate choice not to do so. There were abundant Samnite cities on the coast to set the model, including Capua, Cumae, Pompeii, Nuceria Alfaterna and Teanum Sidicinum. The lack of comparable settlements in the interior, cou-pled with the dramatic phenomenon of the monumentalisation of sanctuary sites in relatively remote spots, has led to the term, 'non-cities'. It is not merely that these communities are in a pre-urban stage of their formation, and have yet to embark on a developmental stage we call 'urbanisation'. It is rather that they have the model of urbanisation firmly in mind and reject it; the monumentalisation of sites that are not cities is in this sense as strong a

---

[102] Coarelli (1996a).   [103] Torelli (1995) 1–15, Torelli (1999) 5–8.   [104] Torelli (1999) 5, n. 26.

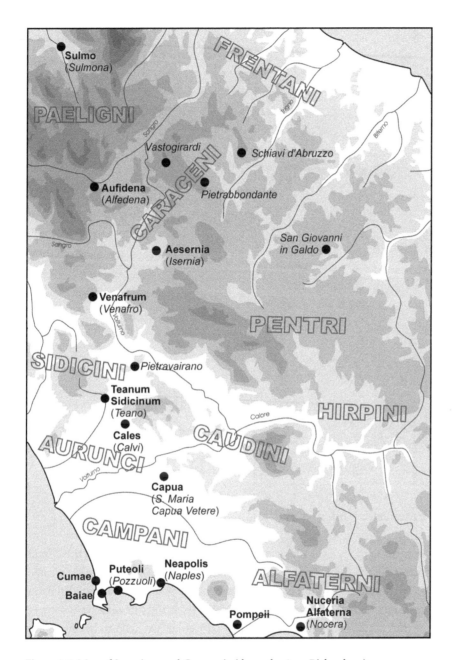

Figure 3.6 Map of Samnium and Campania (drawn by Amy Richardson)

statement of ethnic identity as is conceivable. We might take this as a sign of being less romanised; alternatively, we could say that the dual identities of Roman/Samnite interact differently from those of Roman/Umbrian, and enable a strong expression of difference.

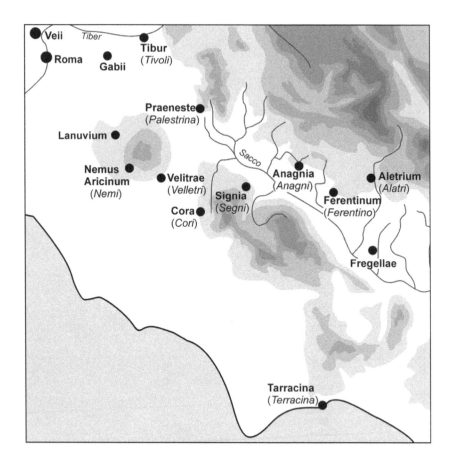

Figure 3.7 Map of Latium and the Sacco valley (drawn by Amy Richardson)

Praeneste: Hellenistic, Roman and Italic

In turning to review some well-known and much-debated sites, this discussion will focus on the relationship between form, style and identity. We need to be more alert to what is 'emblematic', in the sense of deliberately flagging messages about identity, and what only to us as outside observers seems to fit into certain cultural categories. In particular, we need to be alert to the possibility of 'bilingualism' in the sense of multiple and ambivalent identities. Praeneste has long, and deservedly, enjoyed a reputation as a type-site for Italic hellenisation, and is a good place to start in confronting the question of what sort of statements about identity can be extracted from monuments and artefacts (figure 3.7).

The extraordinary richness of Praeneste, in terms of material culture, goes back to the eighth century. Indeed, this continuity alone gives the lie to the Horatian myth of a rustic Latium importing the arts only after the conquest of Greece ('Graecia capta . . . artis intulit *agresti Latio*').[105] Beyond question, the second century BCE brought an impressive boom; but we can distinguish at least two previous waves of influence from the east. The first is in the archaic period, corresponding closely to the colonisation of Magna Graecia from the eighth to sixth centuries BCE. Here Praeneste is conspicuous for its '*tombe principesche*', magnificent aristocratic burials with rich, 'orientalising', grave-goods, largely imported from the east. The Tomba Bernardini of the late eighth century ranks as the finest of these 'princely' burials in Lazio: Rome itself has nothing to compare (the tombs of its kings are lost), though Castel di Decima has an impressive array of tombs.[106] The real comparanda are in Etruria, and specifically at Caere, where the Tomba Regolini-Galassi is so close in its grave-goods that it seems reasonable to deduce that the material from Praeneste was imported by the same channels with Caere as intermediary. What identity might the chiefs of Praeneste be signalling with such burials: Greek, Etruscan, or even oriental? The choice makes little sense, because the important point is that burials of this type are a widespread phenomenon in Italy, stretching down to Campania and Pontecagnano, and with close links with contemporary burials on the Greek mainland.[107] They point to an Odyssean pattern of travel and gift-exchange across the Mediterranean, of chieftains marking their power locally by the display of rich objects that advertise their connections to a wider world. Locals might or might not recognise rich Phoenician metalwork as oriental – that would depend on what stories came, as in the Odyssey, attached to the gifts. They would surely not recognise it as a statement of oriental, or Greek, or Etruscan, identity, but of links to those worlds.

At the same time, there were evidently links to Rome, which belongs to the same matrix of eastern influence with strong Etruscan ties. The late sixth-century architectural terracottas, showing a parade of chariots, that come from an unidentified shrine below the city at S. Rocco alla Colombella, are close in style and not inferior in quality to terracottas showing chariot races from Veii, Velletri and Rome. In Colonna's view, this is a representation of a triumph, and the most explicit that survives, intimately connected with the sacred topography of the city, and the processional route from the extra-mural shrine of Fortuna to the temple of Jupiter Imperator beneath the modern cathedral, and possibility with the layout of a New City with grid-pattern on Greek colonial model.[108] Greek urbanism and Latin victory are already intertwined.

---

[105] See ch. 2.   [106] Canciani and von Hase (1979), Colonna (1992).
[107] Cornell (1995) 82ff., Smith (1996) 93–7; for Pontecagnano, see d'Agostino (1977).
[108] Colonna (1992) 36–43.

Praeneste's relations to Rome under the early republic are unclear; never a member of the Latin League, it is possible that the city, like Tibur, fell under the control of the Aequi of the interior in the fifth century.[109] From the confusion of the Latin and Samnite wars of the fourth century, and episodes of alignment with Rome's enemies, Praeneste emerges in firm alliance with Rome, with its large territory diminished, but with complete independence, not Latin status. It is in the fourth and third centuries that the necropolis of la Colombella offers its richest harvest of burials, and the extraordinary series of bronze cists which, along with engraved mirrors, ivory combs, strigils and bathing equipment, attest the material culture of a large and flourishing elite.[110]

If these burials do not quite match the magnificence of the 'princely' tombs of the archaic period, the *corpus* of over 138 bronze cists that have emerged from them and elsewhere represent perhaps the most important example of the artistic production of central Italy of the period.[111] The quality of line-drawing matches that of any contemporary body of material known from Greek ceramics. The mythological and generic subject matter shows close engagement with Greek mythology, while offering what is not simply a reflection of a generalised Greco-Italic mythology, but a specific local appropriation. The *corpus* of *cistae*, and the closely related series of engraved mirrors, plays a central role in the argument for the existence of a distinctive 'Roman' mythology; depictions of themes like the wolf and twins, evoking the cluster of festivals of Lupercalia, Feralia and Quirinalia, have an evident local relevance to Rome, while many figures like Castor and Pollux, Marsyas, Liber and hairy-suited satyrs reflect Latin versions of such myths.[112]

The links with Rome are nowhere more explicit than on the cista Ficoroni with its striking inscription (figure 3.8):

NOVIOS. PLAVTIOS. MED. ROMAI. FECID
DINDIA. MACOLNIA. FILEAI. DEDIT.
Novius Plautius made me at Rome.
Dindia gave to her daughter Magulnia.

The cist, the first found at Praeneste in 1738, is part of the series that characterizes the site, yet clearly states Rome as the place for production, and points to the sort of marriage links between the local elite and that of Rome

---

[109] Cornell (1995) 306.   [110] Quilici (1992), Lorenzini (2002).
[111] Battaglia and Emiliozzi (1979), Battaglia and Emiliozzi (1990).
[112] Wiseman (2004) 87–118.

Figure 3.8 Cista Ficoroni, Villa Giulia Museum, Rome (courtesy Soprintendenza per i Beni Archeologici dell'Etruria Meridionale, foto n. 9152D)

that might occasion such commissions. It may be that Rome was a major production centre for such material, though the surviving record does little to encourage that deduction. But in any case, we see a Praeneste with an independent elite that is tied by links of marriage and exchange to Rome, familiar with its mythology, and associated in artistic patronage and production.

We can describe this elite as romanising, in virtue of such links; and as hellenising in virtue of the artistic style of its production. And while 'emblematically' the style and mythological content do indeed parade the links to the Roman and to the Greek world, it would be hard to argue that the ethnic consciousness expressed is anything other than a local one. The array of grave goods is a distinctive local one, even if its components find parallels elsewhere. The art world long treated the *cistae* as an aspect of Etruscan art, and it took the major exhibition on *Roma medio-repubblicana* of 1973 to reassert the independence of Lazio.[113] Mirrors are standard in Etruscan burials, and indeed the earliest phases at Praeneste use imported Etruscan mirrors. In the earliest phase, in the fifth century, the *cistae* are made of wood covered with leather; the metal attachments, both figurative handles and feet, are strongly influenced by Etruscan production: the models for the feet come from early fifth-century Vulci,[114] while the handles have strong links to early fourth-century Spina.[115] But as the tradition develops, the artistic links are numerous, to Magna Graecia as well as Etruria, and a distinctive local tradition emerges. It is as the use of bronze extends to the entire body of the *cista* that the practice of incision, already familiar from mirror backs, takes hold, and establishes a distinctive local product with its distinctive artistic forms.[116] The style and themes of the cists and the mirrors are so close that they come to form a new ensemble. Restored to the context of the graveyards, with their stone pinecone markers and simplified female heads, a context so compromised by the nineteenth-century excavators,[117] they exemplify a quite recognisable local style that could never be confused with Roman or Etruscan.

The graveyards express the self-awareness of a local elite, of a group of families whose names the burials attest as a continuous presence from the fourth to late second centuries. Among the over 1,000 *cippi* (grave-markers) of the cemetery, about a third have names inscribed (c. 350); and among these 138 different *gentes* are attested (they use the standard Latin system of *praenomen* plus *nomen* plus patronymic, so we are talking about 138 *nomina*). The great families that dominate the record from the fourth century onwards, like the Anicii, Dindii, Feidenatii, Magulnii, Orcevii, Saufeii and

---

[113] Battaglia and Emiliozzi (1979) xxi.   [114] Jurgheit (1986) 153.
[115] Coppola (2000) 105.   [116] Battaglia and Emiliozzi (1992).   [117] Baglione (1992).

Tampii, repeatedly hold local magistracies, and strengthen their hold locally and abroad by marriage links.[118]

The identity expressed can be defined as a specific one of citizenship, or membership of the *classis* of those equipped socially and economically for hoplite warfare.[119] While women are marked by the set of toiletries that comes with the *cista*, men are characterised by the combination of lance with bathing gear, the strigil set (sometimes inscribed) and bronze oil jar shaped like a cage (to contain a leather pouch). On one mirror, we see a young man approaching his bride with exactly this combination of accoutrements, lance and bathing set. We may recall the combination of military and bathing equipment met in the Celtic burials of Oleggio. As Torelli pertinently comments, these are the symbols of the *ephebeia*, the young citizen trained in the gymnasium, and in combination mark the citizen who has passed through his military and gymnastic training.[120] It is a standard hellenic idiom for expressing citizenship; the wars in which they are training to fight are ones fought in alliance with Rome; the citizenship is that of the independent city of Praeneste. The necropolis of la Colombella may indeed bear witness to the links of Praeneste with the wider world but, as for identities, it is local social structures and local religiosity which are at stake.

The last and most spectacular wave of hellenism at Praeneste is that of the second century BCE. There is a change both in scale and style, though the burials dry up, to give way, presumably, to roadside tombs as at Rome. The change in style is most immediately visible in the figure of the goddess Fortuna herself, who in this period abandons the old Etrusco-Italic image of the mother-goddess, and takes on instead the features of the hellenistic Tyche, the Fortune of victory with wings and crown, and is partially assimilated to Isis.[121] But it is in the monumental development of the sanctuary of Fortuna Primigenia that the self-confidence of the new style proclaims itself (figure 3.9). Ever since Delbrück's *Hellenistische Bauten*, Praeneste has enjoyed its reputation as the touchstone of the new hellenisation of second-century Italy, though indeed Fasolo and Gullini in their publication of the sanctuary as exposed by bombing in the war urged that it should be seen as a specifically Italic expression of hellenism.[122] From the awesome axial planning of the layout, with its orchestrated sequence of terraces and ramps,[123] to the architectural language of the colonnades and entablatures, the sanctuary displays deep indebtedness to eastern Mediterranean models (figure 3.10). Perhaps the most striking image of hellenisation is not from the sanctuary,

---

[118] Harvey (1975), Coarelli (1992) 260. [119] Pairault Massa (1992) 111–15.
[120] Torelli (1992) 275–6. [121] Agnoli (2002) 23–6, Various authors (1994).
[122] Delbrück (1907) 47–90, Fasolo and Gullini (1953) 441–8, cf. Hanson (1959) 36.
[123] Coarelli (1987a), Coarelli (1992).

Figure 3.9 Model of the sanctuary of Fortuna at Praeneste, Museo Archeologico di Palestrina (author's photo)

Figure 3.10 Detail of mosaic from Praeneste, Museo Archeologico di Palestrina: party of revellers (author's photo)

but from the late second-century buildings of the Forum: from the Doric frieze of the altar,[124] to the culmination in the decorative details of the mosaics in *opus vermiculatum*, with its explicitly Alexandrian presentation of the Nile and its temples, peoples, flora and fauna, neatly labelled in Greek.[125]

The observation that it was precisely members of the old elite families, like the Anicii, Magulnii, Orcevii, Samiarii, Satricanii and Saufeii, who emerge from the dedications of Delos and other eastern sites as *negotiatores*,[126] provides a context both for the economy of the building, and the evident knowledge of and attraction to eastern models. These families are deeply implicated in the processes of Roman imperialism; it is telling that at end of the second century and in the early first century, Saufeii are also found active in Roman politics: a *monetalis* in 150, a likely Gracchan tribune, a quaestor in 100 who was killed as a partisan of Saturninus, and another tribune in 91 giving his name to a *lex agraria*.[127] The *cohors Praenestina* distinguished itself in various campaigns (Livy 9.16.17–18; 23.19.17–18); and it is on the nexus of direct military involvement and access to booty, and indirect profiteering from the slave and art trades of Delos and elsewhere, that the gigantic financial investment represented by the monumental sanctuary must rest.

Hellenisation, then, is seen in the artistic expression, and romanisation in the collusion with conquest, though neither of these is a new tendency, for Praeneste had been hellenising and romanising for many centuries already. But what is at issue is the expression of identity. Is Praeneste submerging its local character in subscribing to the new hellenistic *koinē*? That is a conclusion one can reach only if wedded to a model of identity that allows no ambivalence and no bilingualism. The sanctuary is hellenistic from the point of view of its axial monumentality: the supposed models are complexes like the Asclepieion at Cos, or the combination of temples and theatre at Pergamum, or the sanctuary of Dea Syria on Delos, though the truth is that neither these nor any other eastern site are a real model for the way the theatre–temple formula was developed in Italy.[128] The scale and monumentality of the construction is inconceivable without the specific Roman development of concrete construction techniques: here it is more Roman than hellenistic, and Praeneste is one of a well-defined cluster of sites in Latium and Campania which pushed *opus incertum* construction to new limits. In Rome, it is met in porticoes and basilicas, notably the great concrete structure beneath

---

[124] Coarelli (1978).

[125] Coarelli (1983) = Coarelli (1996b) 312–26, Zevi (1994), Meyboom (1995), Versluys (2002) 52–3.

[126] Wilson (1966) 110, Solin (1982) 113, Müller and Hasenohr (2002).   [127] Harvey (1975).

[128] Hanson (1959), Coarelli (1996b) 328–31.

Figure 3.11 Polygonal walling of terrace from the sanctuary of
Fortuna at Praeneste (author's photo)

the Aventine, long known as the Porticus Aemilia, now identified as the
Navalia.[129] Outside Rome, *opus incertum* is the language of great sanctuaries, from Praeneste to Tibur to Tarracina.[130] Yet alongside the *opus incertum*,
the local use of massive polygonal blocks of limestone to support the great
terraces aligns Praeneste with other central Italian sites, and distinguishes it
from Rome (figure 3.11).[131]

But it is at this point that it becomes most apparent that this new architecture is not merely a reflection of what is happening in the Greek east, nor
a replication of the reinterpretation of that by Rome, but a vigorous and

---

[129] Tucci (2006).   [130] Torelli (1995) 191–210.   [131] Cifarelli (2003), 88–96.

innovative movement in which the Italic cities play their own role. In terms
of expression of identity, it is highly significant that so many of these sites are
sanctuaries: religion has always rated alongside language as one of the most
visceral expressions of ethnic identity. Praeneste forms part of a recognisable group, the sanctuaries of Lazio, represented by Gabii, Fregellae, Tibur,
Tarracina, Lanuvium and the Nemus Aricinum; since these are all Roman, it
might be seen as a response to Roman influence.[132] But it is also part of a phenomenon that is met throughout central and southern Italy: the great hilltop
sanctuary sites of which Pietrabbondante for Pentrian Samnium, Hercules
Curinus at Sulmona for the Paelignians, the shrine of Mefitis at Macchia di
Rossano for Lucania, and the sanctuary of Pupluna (Populonia) at Teanum
for the northern Campanian Sidicini, are each only the most conspicuous
example of a repetitive phenomenon. Such widespread monumentalisation
of local cults reflects an enormous investment in local religiosity and local
pride which is in no way diminished by the existence of stylistic evocations
of the east, or dependence on participation in Roman imperialism and constructional technique. It seems to cut across the distinctions between the
urbanised and 'non-cities' areas: sanctuaries were the most potent physical
embodiment of local beliefs and values.

We may note another feature that makes the erection of the sanctuary of
Fortuna Primigenia unlike what was happening in Rome. The inscriptional
evidence shows clearly that the responsibility for the erection of the sanctuary
complex was one shared between many members of the local elite families:
this was the observation which led Degrassi to argue that it could not have
been put up after the Sullan sack of the city, after which the evidence for these
families collapses (only 20 of 138 families are attested after Sulla).[133] It is true
that this coincides with the end of the great cemeteries, especially that of la
Colombella, which had flourished from the fourth century onwards.[134] But
that is only another way of stating the same thing: the Sullan sack spelled the
end of a period of a cluster of families, and their cultural expression in burials
and in monuments. The fact that the sanctuary had multiple patrons is what
makes it so unlike contemporary Rome, where individual temples are erected
competitively by individual members of the elite. There was no complex in
Rome of comparable scale and ambition, and no collaboration between the
rich to achieve it. Pompey's theatre in 55 BCE was not only Rome's first ven-
ture into the idiom of the theatre–temple complex, but the first attempt to
break from the scale of the individual *monumentum* (see ch. 4). The collaboration of the Praenestine elite has an exact parallel in the collaboration of

[132] Coarelli (1987).   [133] Degrassi (1969).   [134] Clauss (1977).

the Samnite elite at Pietrabbondante, and is surely eloquent of the awareness of local collaboration as the basis for the assertion of local pride.

Urban renewal in the Sacco valley

Praeneste's Sanctuary of Fortune was a phenomenal success. Its relevance spread far beyond the local population. We know that it was visited by king Prusias of Bithynia in 167 BCE, and by the philosopher Carneades in 154 while on a mission to Rome: these visits were before the likely date of the major phase of monumentalisation.[135] What is impressive is not simply that famous people from the eastern Mediterranean visited Praeneste, but that their visits should enter the historical record: we know not because they left casual inscriptions behind, but because Livy and Cicero thought it worthwhile mentioning the fact: that is indeed to leave ripples behind. The monumentalisation of the sanctuary expresses an ambition to make ripples at a Mediterranean level, to become one of the great holy places that would attract pilgrims in its own right, to be more than a mere satellite of the great centre of attraction in Rome.

Praeneste exemplifies at least three distinguishable patterns for which several parallels can be offered in the second century. One is of the specifically Italic combination of theatre and temple in a single major complex, that we meet not only in Latium, especially nearby at Gabii and Tibur, but further afield in Samnium (Pietrabbondante) and Campania, as dramatically revealed by the discovery of a site on a ridge top at Pietravairano.[136] A second is the embellishment of hilltop sanctuaries in general: here again Tibur or Pietrabbondante are parallels, but not Gabii, and numerous other sites come into consideration, like the memorable *opus incertum* vaulting of the terraces of the sanctuary at Tarracina, once identified with Jupiter Anxur, or further-flung sites like Hercules Curinus at Sulmona and Mefitis at Macchia di Rossano. A third is the monumental enhancement of a series of urban centres (whether or not these were also sanctuaries), which we may exemplify from the string of little hilltop centres that followed the valley of the Sacco river, the main corridor connecting Latium with Campania, to the east the territory of the Hernici in the foothills of the Apennines, to the west the Latin colonies of the Monti Lepini.

There is a close parallel here to the cluster of Umbrian towns around Assisi which passed through a significant phase of urbanisation in the second

---

[135] Livy 45.44.8 for Prusias, Cicero, *de Divinatione* 2.87 for Carneades.
[136] Guaitoli (2003) 295–6, see Caiazza (2004) 47–9 for plans.

century. Coarelli used Asisium as a test case for the process of self-romanisation, seeing in the major engineering works of terracing and walling that redefined the urban layout the impact of a Roman model of urbanism.[137] The Hernican cities, too, especially Aletrium and Ferentinum, show a notable outbreak of building and engineering frenzy in the second century BCE. Each of these sites (and many others in the general area) are characterised by their outer defensive circuits in polygonal or 'Cyclopean' walling. The dating of such structures is notoriously problematic, since the tradition extends at least from the fifth to first centuries, and the distinction of the four manners of walling has all-too-little basis in stratigraphic exploration for reliable dating. But the general consensus is that the fortification of these sites goes back to the fourth century, a phase in which after rebellion against Rome in 362, and continued tensions, Aletrium and Ferentinum (unlike Anagnia) were rewarded for their loyalty by independent Latin status.

The renewed building activity of these towns belongs to the late second century. Aletrium (figures 3.12, 3.13) renews the circuit of its walls, and embarks on a major monumentalisation of its acropolis, with an imposing wall in polygonal masonry supporting the upper terrace.[138] A firm historical context is supplied by the remarkable inscription of Betilienus Varus, one of the most eloquent testimonies to the urbanisation process of this period (figure 3.14)

Lucius Betilienus Varus, son of Lucius, on the decision of the senate supervised the construction of the following list: all roads in the town, the portico that leads to the citadel, the exercise ground, the sundial, the market, the plastering (?) of the basilica, the seating, the cistern for the baths, the cistern at the gate, the supply of water to the town to the height of 340 feet, and he made the aqueduct and he made solid pipes. Because of these things they made him censor twice, and the senate granted to his son exemption from military service, and the people donated a statue to Censorinus.[139]

It is the fact that the senate of Aletrium can still grant exemption from military service that demonstrates that it must predate the Social War; once the town became a *municipium* with Roman citizenship, only Rome could

---

[137] Coarelli (1996a).   [138] Zevi (1976), Coarelli (1982) 193–200.

[139] *Corpus Inscriptionum Latinarum* 1², 1529: 'l(ucius) Betilienus L(uci) f(ilius) Vaarus/haec quae infera scripta/sont de senatu sententia/facienda coiravit: semitas/in oppido omnis, porticum qua/in arcem eitur, campum ubei/ludunt, horologium, macelum,/basilicam calecandam, seedes,/[l]acum balinearium, lacum ad/[p]ortam, aquam in opidum adqu(e)/arduom pedes CCCXL fornicesq(ue)/fecit, fistulas soledas fecit./Ob hasce res censorem fecere bis/senatus, filio stipendia mereta/ese iousit, populusque/statuam donavit Censorino'.

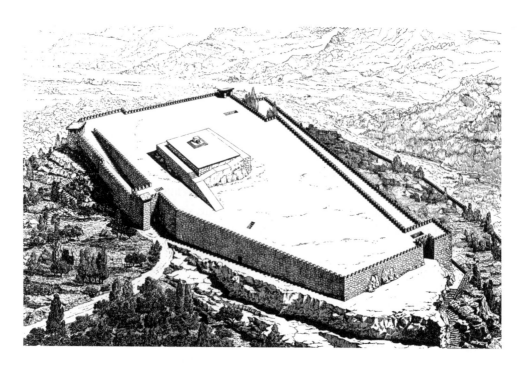

Figure 3.12 Aletrium, view of citadel (reconstruction drawing by G. B. Giovenale, 1889)

Figure 3.13 Aletrium, gate (photo Fr P. P. Mackey, BSR Archive Mackey.1 Alatri.1)

Figure 3.14 Inscription of Betilienus Varus from Aletrium
(drawing, Alatri Museum, Soprintendenza del Lazio)

grant such a privilege. Betilienus Varus' programme of works is a remarkably
extensive episode of urban renewal: it affects the road network, a series of
major central facilities – market and basilica were certainly central, and the
sundial and seating probably associated with them, and a transformation of
the water supply. The focus is civic and not religious: only the portico to the
arx is connected to a sanctuary area. As Zevi argued, his programme must
be after the monumental work on the *arx*, since his new portico which led
to it seems to have been revealed by excavation in neat alignment with the
new access rampart to the citadel.[140] As in the other cases considered, we can
speak both of hellenisation, in the sense of the underlying concept of urban
embellishment, and of the architectural detail, and romanisation in the sense
of the military/economic engine that drives it. The concern with water supply and bathing, just as the choice of a *campus* as exercise ground, rather
than gymnasium, point to a specifically Roman model. The element of local
pride is not only implicit in the ambitious scheme of local improvement,
but here as elsewhere in the apparent ideological choice implicit in the use of
polygonal masonry. *Opus incertum* was widely available as a technique by the

---

[140] Zevi (1976).

second century, and was far less labour-intensive than polygonal masonry.[141] Aletrium offers this local technique at its peak: the 'third manner' involves the accurate cutting and fitting of enormous blocks of limestone, with straight edges forming perfect joins with neighbouring blocks. The walling of the citadel is among the finest examples of the technique, undertaken with great pride and skill. Whereas one might have predicted that the development of new concrete construction techniques would spell the demise of the local craft tradition of masonry, we see it here and elsewhere at its apogee, expressing a visual continuity with the structures that had defined the city for at least two centuries.

The family of Betilienus emerge with particular prominence from the inscriptions of Aletrium. An inscription preserved in the wall of the cathedral on the *arx* itself records a dedication of money to Jupiter by Marcus and Gaius Betilienus, the sons of Marcus: presumably the temple beneath the cathedral was dedicated to Jupiter, if not to the Capitoline triad. Another block, set in the city wall, records the contribution of Publius Betilienus Hapalus, son of Marcus; since he is a quattuorvir, he belongs to the period after the Social War. At least four members of this family are active as benefactors and magistrates in the late second and early first century BCE. It has been suggested that they, like the nobles of Praeneste, owed their wealth to trade on Delos,[142] though the only attestation of their name on Delos is on oil amphorae from Brindisi exported across the Mediterranean.[143] But more confidently we can say that at Aletrium, as at Praeneste, collaboration with Rome allowed the emergence of dominant families which survive for several generations, and which both express and reinforce their dominance through public building schemes, as was the case in Rome. Romanisation expresses itself in social and economic relations, and the reproduction of Roman urban features, while Hernican identity finds its alibi in the reassuring continuity of polygonal masonry.

At Ferentinum, by contrast, there is a mixture of constructional languages.[144] Here, too, the polygonal defences are extensively renewed, and as at the Porta Sanguinaria we see the improved technique of the 'third manner' sitting on the cruder blocks of the 'second manner' (figure 3.15). Here, too, the *arx* was embellished, by a towering bastion supporting what we may assume to have been a temple, in the position subsequently occupied by the bishop's palace (figure 3.16). In this case, the core of the construction and its inner vaulting are in concrete *opus caementicium*, but the outer facing is

[141] Coarelli (1977b).   [142] Coarelli, Musti and Solin (1982) 198.
[143] Zevi (1976) 88; cf. Hatzfeld (1919) 386.   [144] Coarelli (1982) 183–93.

in polygonal work of the 'fourth manner', in which the cut of the blocks is mostly rectangular, while the upper body is in smaller peperino blocks in *opus quadratum*. This 'fourth manner' might be seen as the final refinement of the polygonal building tradition, bringing it closer to the 'look' of buildings in the hellenistic tradition; but if so, it is also a step away from assertion of local difference. The inscription that runs the full width of the façade records the work of the two censors (an office not possible after the Social War), Aulus Hirtius and Marcus Lollius (figure 3.17).[145] The fact that their descendants held consulships at Rome in the late first century may be taken to illustrate the familiar process whereby the *domi nobiles* move into power in Rome. Even so, they succeeded in making their Ferentinum impressive for a tiny hill-town, and in full consciousness of its Hernican heritage. The impression is not of a choice and contrast between Hernican and Roman identity, but of a cosy duality.

This small cross-section of the Sacco valley would not be complete without crossing the valley to the west bank, where from the heights of the Monti Lepini the early Latin colony of Signia (Segni) looked down to the Hernican hill-tops (figure 3.18).[146] In archaeological terms, if we did not know from historical sources that this town was Latin not Hernican, it would be difficult to tell them apart culturally: the formula of outer circuit of defences in polygonal masonry and upper terrace with citadel or *arx* is identical. The historical sources report Signia as twice settled as a colony, under Tarquinius Superbus (Livy 1.56.3) and again in the early republic (Livy 2.21.7). Such dates are impossible to confirm without the sort of extensive archaeological investigation which these sites lack. Nevertheless, Segni has been particularly well served, both by the project of the University of Salerno, and by the exemplary study of Francesco Cifarelli.[147]

It is now clear that the entire monumental complex of the acropolis, including the tripled-celled 'Capitolium', the vast circular basin on alignment with it, and the *auguraculum* above, underwent its present monumentalisation in the second half of the second century BCE (figure 3.19). The polygonal masonry has been taken, since Edward Dodwell in 1834, who drew

---

[145] *Corpus Inscriptionum Latinarum* 10, 5837–5838: 'A(ulus) Hirtius A(uli) f(ilius), M(arcus) Lollius C(ai) f(ilius) ce(n)s(ores) fundamenta murosque af solo faciunda coeravere idemque probavere. In terram fundamentum est pedes XXXIII, in terram ad/idem exemplum quod supra terram silici.' 'Aulus Hirtius son of Aulus (and) Marcus Lollius son of Gaius as censors supervised the construction of the substructures and walls from the ground up, and the same approved it. The substructure is 33 feet deep into the earth, and is built in hard stone on the same pattern as what is above ground.'

[146] Coarelli (1982) 173–8.　　[147] De Rossi (1992), Cifarelli (2003).

Figure 3.15 Ferentinum, Porta Sanguinaria (photo Fr P. P. Mackey, BSR Archive Mackey. 509 Ferentino. 2)

Figure 3.16 Ferentinum, substructure and citadel erected by Hirtius and Lollius (author's photo)

Figure 3.17 Ferentinum citadel, detail of dedicatory inscription (author's photo)

the Cyclopean parallels with Mycenae, to be a sign of antiquity.[148] But both the massive podium of the temple, and the elaboration of the surrounding terrace, can be shown to be second century by the stratigraphy, with foundation trenches that cut deposits of votive offerings stretching from the fourth to the second centuries.[149] The temple itself beneath the church of S. Pietro, now accepted on the basis of a dedicatory inscription to be that of Juno Moneta, had walls built in imported tufo ashlar; yet its podium built at the same time emphatically underlines the local polygonal limestone tradition (figure 3.18). The circular basin is an integral part of the same complex: it is lined in the same tufo ashlar as the temple, but the real structure is a thick lining of concrete, very precisely *opus signinum*, the waterproof lining technique to which Signia gave its name.[150] Again, constructional techniques and styles sit together, and if identities were flagged (what could be more emblematic than *signinum* at Signia, the call-sign of this Signal station?), they cohabited in an effortless performance of code-switching.

The late second-century monumentalisation of the acropolis, in its dominant position above the Sacco valley and the route from Rome into Samnite territory, reads as an assertion of local pride, in almost antiphonal response

---

[148] Dodwell (1834) plates 81–87. Dodwell provided no commentary, but the design of including Greek and Italian 'Cyclopean' walls in the same volume implies his view.
[149] Cifarelli (2003) 75–8.   [150] De Rossi (1992) 89–94.

REMAINS OF A TEMPLE at SIGNIA .

Figure 3.18 Segni, church of S. Pietro (Edward Dodwell, c.1834)

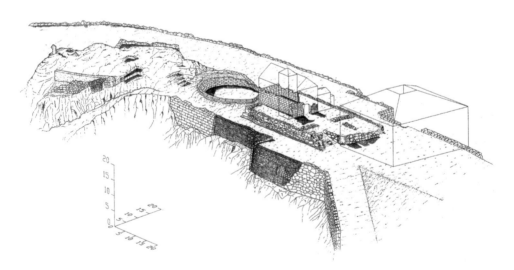

Figure 3.19 Signia (Segni), reconstruction of buildings on citadel (Comune di Segni, Museo Archeologico, after Cifarelli 2003, figure 20)

Figure 3.20 Signia (Segni), drawing of nymphaeum with inscription by architect (Comune di Segni, Museo Archeologico, after Cifarelli 1995, figures 8, 13–14)

to the statements of the Hernican towns visible across the valley, or of Praeneste itself at the head of the valley. The element of 'hellenisation' is neatly captured in a *nymphaeum* structure below the acropolis (figure 3.20). An inscription forming part of the mosaic pebble decoration gives us the name of the architect, Quintus Mutius, but uses Greek language, or an erratic form thereof, less surprising in a bilingual, to do so: ΚΟΙΝΤΟΣ ΜΟΥΤΙΟΣ ΗΡΧΙΤΗΚΤΟΝΕ [. . .].[151] Cifarelli assumes that this shows his Greek origin; but just as Greek could be felt to be the correct professional language for a

---

[151] Assuming the verb to be ἀρχιτεκτονέω/ *architektoneō*, the second eta is erroneous.

doctor, it might for an architect.[152] In either case, there is a cultural decision involving patron as much as architect in the choice of this language for a Roman name.

A brilliant study by Zevi links this Q. Mutius to Q. Mucius Scaevola, and to the architect of Marius' temple of Honos and Virtus, and suggests a series of ties between the Marians, the leading families of towns like Signia and Praeneste, and the hellenising architecture of the late second century BCE, and identifies C. Mucius as the architect of the sanctuary of Fortuna at Praeneste.[153] If this must remain speculation, it remains completely plausible to suggest that behind the rebuilding of centres like Signia, Aletrium and Praeneste lay a network of ties, between local dominant families and the leading political figures at Rome, and that the architectural expertise that underpinned these ambitious schemes was of an international level, supported by patronage at Rome, and drawing on the knowledge base of the hellenistic architectural profession. Again, romanisation and hellenisation seem to converge; but the point at which they meet is a local expression of continuity with a past which they at least imagined stretched back to the regal age.

The phenomenon we are looking at is one that ends abruptly with the Social and Civil wars of the 80s BCE. Sulla's sack of Praeneste was notorious for its brutality (Appian, *BC* 1.397–439); and though the sanctuary continued to attract interest in the early imperial period (we will turn later to the Augustan grammarian Verrius Flaccus and his Praenestine calendars), it is evident that the conjunction between a flourishing local elite stretching back several centuries, and the wealth generated by war-booty, the profits of eastern trade and the richness of the sanctuary itself, was never replicated, and that Fortuna Primigenia froze in its second-century form. Aletrium, Ferentinum and Signia equally seem to have passed their moment of glory. Signia's neighbour, the Latin colony of Cora (Cori) in the Monti Lepini, shows the same formula of the polygonal stronghold of the early colony, and a reflowering of the main sanctuary on the *arx* in the second century (figure 3.21).[154] The elegant tetrastyle Doric temple (traditionally, the temple of Hercules, but plausibly identified by Coarelli as that of Juno Moneta) was built on a new podium of concrete faced in *opus incertum*, while the surrounding terrace had third-manner polygonal walling: votive deposits within its fill dating from the fourth to second centuries show both the continuity of the temple site, and the late second-/early first-century dating of its reconstruction (figure 3.22).[155] The dedicatory inscription by the duumviri,

[152] Adams (2003) 356.   [153] Zevi (1996b).   [154] Coarelli (1982) 254–65.
[155] Brandizzi Vittucci (1968) 77–96, Coarelli (1982) 264.

Figure 3.21 Cora (Cori), polygonal masonry (drawing by Edward Dodwell, c.1834)

Figure 3.22 Cora (Cori), temple of Hercules (author's photo)

M. Matlius and L. Turpilius, shows that the colony had not yet been made a *municipium*, as it was after the Social War.

After the wars, Cora became a by-word for decline. Lucan lists Cora with Veii and Gabii as towns now dusty, ruined and deserted:

> Ruins covered with dust could scarce reveal Gabii, Veii and Cora . . .
> It is not corroding time that ate them away,
> and left them crumbling monuments of the past:
> It is Civil War's crime we see so many empty cities.[156]

In Lucan's gloomy vision, what changed the face of Italy was not the *longue durée* (for *aetas edax*, we might substitute 'the romanisation of Italy from the fourth to second centuries'), but the traumatic convulsions of the first century BCE. The archaeological evidence strongly supports that vision.

Two faces of the Samnite: Pompeii and Pietrabbondante

The argument to this point has urged that the various cultural influences and processes described as romanisation and hellenisation cannot be seen as a progressive erosion of local cultural identities. The language of Greek art and architecture, and the social structures and economic muscle generated by collaboration in Roman conquest, gave to at least some allied Italic cities the means to assert themselves more effectively in a rapidly expanding Mediterranean context. It is surely significant that all the sites discussed, along with others like Tibur discussed only in passing, where major building projects were launched in the second and early first centuries BCE, were all independent *socii* with their own responsibility for raising and supplying troops for Roman campaigns. In the extraordinary patchwork of statuses of central Italy, these cities stand out as oases of independence in a sea of direct subordination to Rome (figure 3.23). That is precisely what must have made Roman citizenship such an uncertain goal: the monuments suggest that at least in the second century there had been advantages also to independence.

In passing now to the Oscan-speaking territory of the Samnites, we may address another issue, the assumption that the impact of Roman power and Greek cultural influence was homogenising, and that by spreading a common cultural language or *koinē*, it tended to eradicate local differences. This

---

[156] Lucan, *Bellum Civile* 7. 392–9: 'Gabios Veiosque Coramque/pulvere vix tectae poterunt monstrare ruinae . . ./non aetas haec carpsit edax monimentaque rerum/ putria desistit: crimen civile videmus/ tot vacuas urbes.'

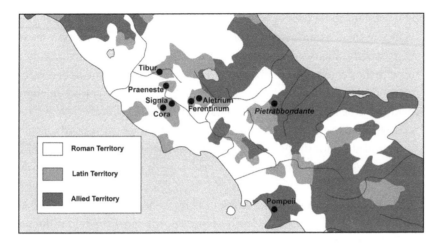

Figure 3.23 Map of allied, Latin and Roman territory in central Italy on the eve of the Social War (drawn by Amy Richardson)

flows from the assumption that a common language inherently spells the death of local languages. It does not allow for the possibility that a new common language is appropriated in different ways in different local contexts, and can thereby be recruited to heightening the sense of local specificity rather than eroding it. Pompeii and Pietrabbondante offer strikingly different appropriations of the hellenistic in the same time frame, but in areas with quite different socio-economic backgrounds. We have seen the importance of the distinction, underscored by Torelli, between urbanised coastal zones and the non-urbanised Apennine interior. We have noted that the two tendencies, of monumentalisation of urban centres, and of development of hill-top sanctuaries, sometimes overlap but sometimes form sharp distinctions. In Pompeii and Pietrabbondante we can see closely related stylistic tendencies, and similar Rome-promoted elite involvement, resulting in quite different outcomes.

Pompeii

Pompeii may stand conveniently for the long tradition of Greco-Italic urbanism. Its position on the Bay of Naples led to a history of close contacts with multiple influences sustained over many centuries. In the archaic period, from the seventh century BCE onwards, we can infer close contact with Greek colonists, reflected most clearly in the choice of Apollo and Minerva/Hercules for the main cults. But numerous Etruscan inscriptions and the frequency of *bucchero* point to equally strong Etruscan contacts, shown by Cristofani to be part of a pattern that spreads from Capua to Salerno, including the Sorrentine peninsula. The old thesis of concentration in the Altstadt of the 'Etruscan' city of Pompeii can no longer be sustained, conflicting with the demonstration that the wall circuit goes back to the sixth century BCE, and to firm evidence for linear structures of the same period on alignment with the layout of the eastern half of the city. Even if the assumption is current that the grid-pattern of this 'new city' belongs to the third century, we should allow for the possibility that it goes back to the sixth century BCE, and represents a local reception of the grid-pattern model offered by nearby Greek colonies.[157]

By the third century BCE, Pompeii's primary identity can be described as Samnite, in so far as it is clearly subject to the same wave of influence from the interior that swept over Cumae and Capua in the late fifth century BCE, that its language of public life in unhesitatingly Oscan, and that the names of the dominant families show ties with the interior.[158] Nevertheless, the sense of strong common identity between Oscan speakers as Samnite has been exaggerated by a combination of Roman and modern myth: the romanticised image of tough, independent Samnites overlooks the deep contrasts between Campanians, Hirpini, Pentri and other groupings.[159] The Campanians had an exceptional history of intimate contact with Greeks, and hellenisation may well have had different resonances for them than for the Pentri. We do not even know whether they would have labelled themselves ethnically as Samnites, Campani, or even Opici.

The programme of excavations in Region VI by Coarelli's team has demonstrated a pattern of progressive and sustained growth and development of the city from the early third century BCE.[160] This zone was certainly occupied in the archaic period, in part by a sanctuary (that from which the 'Etruscan column' survives), but seems to suffer collapse in the fifth and fourth centuries. Only in the third century BCE does a new wave of domestic construction start, occupying the city quarter with increasing density. It is precisely in the period of alliance with Rome that this growth starts: alliance brings economic prosperity, and possibly an impulse towards urbanisation in the need to supply troops for regular campaigns, and hence to reorganise the occupation of the territory to maintain the required economic and demographic base. This tendency to grow accelerates rapidly in the second century, when there are frequent signs of the restructuring of the city. The

---

[157] Fulford and Wallace-Hadrill (1999) 103–10 with previous bibliography. For further discussion, see, Guzzo and Guidobaldi (2008), 75–7, 331–3, 510–12.

[158] Zanker (1998) 32–60, Guzzo (2000).   [159] Dench (1995), Caiazza (2004).

[160] Coarelli and Pesando (2005).

Figure 3.24 Temple of Apollo, Pompeii, view to south-east (author's photo)

importance of Rome as a cultural model is specifically visible in its domestic architecture. Pompeii has long done duty as a generalised model of Roman housing, despite the fact that so much of the housing stock, and specifically the standard model of the *atrium* house with *fauces, impluvium, tablinum* and *alae*, precedes the Roman colony of 80 BCE. But that is possibly because Pompeii was indeed reflecting a standard model, as emerges dramatically from the discovery that the House of Diana in Cosa in the early second century was built to the same plan as the House of Sallust in Pompeii.[161] It must surely be the case that the underlying model is Roman.

The Pompeii of the second century has long been characterised, especially from an art-historical point of view, as hellenistic.[162] We can now point with fair confidence to a major episode of urban renewal, beginning around the middle of the second century. It is then that the temple of Apollo by the Forum receives a major restructuring, including its Doric colonnades (figure 3.24). Despite the demonstration, on the basis of a trench in the street abutting the north-western corner of the precinct, of a restructuring dating to Augustus,[163] which surely affected the western boundary, as attested epigraphically, the second-century dating of the colonnade on stylistic grounds is borne out by the detail of the inscription read by Vetter (no. 60) as

[161] Fentress (2003), see above, p. 80.   [162] Lauter (1975), Zanker (1998) 32–60.
[163] Dobbins and Ball (2005).

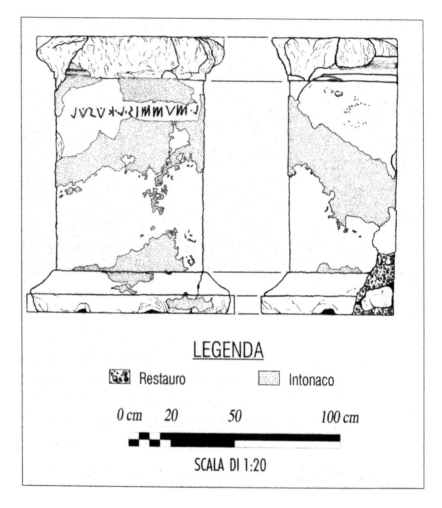

Figure 3.25 Mummius inscription, from temple of Apollo, Pompeii (drawing, after Martelli 2002, figure 4, with permission, Quasar)

'L. Mumm'. The removal of plaster from a statue base physically incorporated in the colonnade reads in Oscan letters, right to left, L. MVMMIS. L. KVSVL (figures 3.25, 3.26).[164] Lucius Mummius son of Lucius, the sacker of Corinth in 146 BCE, is Oscanised in his name form (Mummis for Mummius) and filiation form (L. for L.f. or Luci filius), but remains a recognisable Roman consul.

The dedication provides confirmation of the implicit link between urban expansion in second-century Italy and the spoils of eastern war. Mummius' numerous dedications in the cities of Italy around Rome were an

---

[164] Martelli (2002).

Figure 3.26 Mummius inscription, from temple of Apollo, Pompeii (author's photo)

acknowledgement of the obligation of Rome to its allies; in this case, the
enhancement of the temple of Apollo, the god of Corinth, implies a direct
Pompeian involvement in the campaign.[165] Some such extraordinary event
is needed to explain the sheer scale of improvement of urban amenities in
this period, all characterised by the use of the grey tufo of Nocera (Nuceria), smoothly dressed to produce the most elegant façades ever constructed
at Pompeii (figures 3.27, 3.28). It affects the nearby Basilica, built towards
the end of the century, with roof-tiles stamped in Oscan. The basilica form
has a particular claim to emblematic Roman identity, given that despite its
hellenistic architectural detail, and even its name, there has never been any
doubt that the building type evolved in early second-century Rome with the
now-lost Basilica Porcia and Basilica Sempronia. Function (administration
of justice) and form point to Rome, even if name and architectural language
point to Greece. But the roof-tiles were stamped in Oscan, Ni. Pupie, and
the builders must have been local magistrates, like the Popidius who built
the adjoining portico.

The Nocera tufo phase continues round from temple and basilica to the
Portico which gives shape and coherence to the southern end of the Forum.
It also continued around the corner into the via dell'Abbondanza, where
excavations have revealed the base of a monumental gateway linking the

[165] For an overview of Mummius' dedications, see Yarrow (2006).

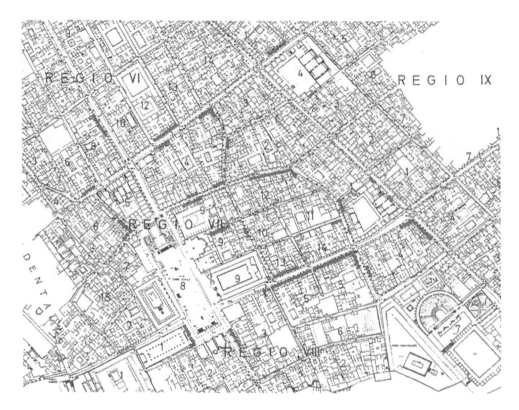

Figure 3.27 Plan of centre of Pompeii, showing distribution of Nocera tufo façades (after Hoffman 1990, with the author's permission)

street to the Forum.[166] The construction of the gateway links to the Nocera tufo façades which consistently fronted (at least until partially compromised by later seismic damage) both sides of the street, as far as the Stabian baths (figure 3.28). It is hard to propose a model whereby all the private houses simultaneously acquired façades in the same material, if it was not undertaken by decision of the local senate, and probably at public expense. The baths, too, underwent major rebuilding in this period, acquiring its new tufo façade, and restructuring the bathing facilities including a fashionable new *laconicum*, on a model developed by wealthy Romans on the north of the Bay, particularly at Baiae.[167]

The entire street from the Forum to baths evidently merited special status: its inaccessibility to traffic, cut off at the Forum end by the steps of the gateway, and at the Stabian baths end by a sharp drop in road-level, combined with the exceptional absence of bars from a busy street, points to its

---

[166] Nappo (1997).   [167] Eschebach (1979).

Figure 3.28 Via dell'Abbondanza, Pompeii, tufo façades (author's photo)

character as a processional route for religious purposes, as first suggested by
Nissen.[168] The terminus of the procession must be not so much the baths as
the complex of facilities in the area of the Triangular Forum. Here the archaic
temple to Minerva retained its archaic architecture, with the heavy entasis
of its columns and the squat *echinus* of its capitals.[169] But the surrounding area was heavily remodelled with its Doric portico and monumental
gateway (doubtless related visually to the gate into the main Forum). After
some vigorous debate occasioned by the discovery of Neronian material in
the foundations of the colonnade, it seems likely that the area underwent
reconstruction after the earthquake of 62/63 CE, but that the original construction is indeed of the second century BCE.[170]

The remodelling of the triangular Forum might be seen more closely
in association with the works on the two theatres to its east. Temple and

---

[168] Nissen (1877), Wallace-Hadrill (1995).   [169] De Waele (2001).
[170] Carandini and Carafa (1995) for the Neronian date, modified in subsequent discussion.

theatre were connected to a monumental flight of stairs, suggesting that access from one to the other was formal, not casual.[171] This is not precisely a theatre/temple complex like those of Praeneste or Pietrabbondante, since they do not form an organic architectural ensemble.[172] But the juxtaposition and interlinking of temple, and the Samnite Palaestra to its side, and two theatres, and in addition the temple of Isis, resulted in a formidable complex of public areas. It is a complex in which the citizens could define their identity, between worship, shared ritual, entertainment and surely public meetings in the theatres, and the gymnastic practices of the gymnasium, with strigils and oil-containers, that we have seen defining citizen identity at Praeneste. The close linkage of this complex to that round the Forum shows Pompeii vigorously redefining its public face, with constant reference to hellenistic idiom, but indebted to Roman models of public life.

This major series of public building works was carried out, as the numerous inscriptions inform us, by the Oscan elite. The impact of conquest and booty on second-century Italy was anything but egalitarian. The same conventions which gave Roman commanders powers to distribute booty unequally to the troops, creating substantial fortunes for themselves and the high command, and slim pickings for the troops, must also have applied in Pompeii. This is surely the implication of the House of the Faun, built in the second half of the second century to occupy the entire *insula* with one of the most splendid examples of luxury domestic architecture of any period.[173] Pesando has argued that with its vast peristyles and breathtaking vermiculate mosaics, it exceeded in luxury even the houses of the nobility in Rome.[174] For lack of evidence in Rome, we cannot be sure, but it is clear that, within terms of Pompeian society, this was a family enriched far beyond the norm, putting it on a level with eastern kings. The Alexander mosaic seems to spell out explicitly the ambition to be seen as an eastern conqueror, on a par with a Roman *imperator*. Nevertheless, the builders must have been a local family; and Pesando brilliantly associated the Oscan dedication to a Satrius associated with the family shrine at the rear of the house with the *nom parlant* of the satyr depicted in bronze in the *atrium* (the Faun) and in mosaic in the prime bedroom.[175]

We seem to have a local Oscan elite, fighting alongside Rome in eastern conquest, and presenting themselves to their fellow citizens in much the same ways as the Roman nobility aggrandised their own status at Rome: self-presentation as Alexander-like heroes, the elevation of the *domus* into

---

[171] Zanker (1998) 48.   [172] Johannowsky (2000).   [173] Zevi (1998).
[174] See p. 100 n. 91.   [175] Pesando (1996), also Meyboom (1995) 167–72.

a sort of hellenistic palace, though retaining the language of *atria* that was linked with patronal power; and dominating the local senate, ensuring that public funds were spent on major public building schemes under their direction, vastly increasing their own powers of patronage and ensuring the survival of their names on their *monumenta rerum*. The collusion with Rome is pervasive, and one might almost be lulled into inferring a loss of local identity, had not Pompeii joined the rebels of the Social War, carrying the violent marks of the Sullan siege in its pockmarked walls, and leaving the traces of the muster stations of its defensive system in the Oscan messages, painted in angry red on the street corners, referred to, after their first word, as 'Eituns' inscriptions, directing the citizens where to muster under each local commander. It is the rebellion which pulls us up with a jolt and says that no amount of cultural assimilation will eliminate the wounded pride of a loyal ally. It was the doubtless the fact that the local elite had done so well out of Roman conquest that made them so angry not to be treated as equals by the Roman elite.

Pietrabbondante

If Pompeii looks like a text-book example of urban expansion, affecting all sectors, religious, civic (basilicas, Forum, streets), ludic (baths, *palaestra*, theatres) and domestic, Pietrabbondante (figure 3.29) rates as the opposite, the non-city *par excellence*. The site consists in its sanctuary complex alone, two temples and a theatre. It is true that there is a walled circuit round the nearby hilltop of Monte Saraceno, and the local interests that protest that this is the town of Bovianum Vetus maintain that it was populated.[176] But Adriano La Regina not only failed to find any trace of urbanisation, but could justly point to the series of nearby sanctuary sites, at Schiavi d'Abruzzo, Vastogirardi, Alfedena, S. Giovanni in Galdo and elsewhere in the area, that confirm that this is a pattern.[177] His latest excavations, revealing what must be the *domus publica*, the official residence of the *medix tuticus*, still do not turn the site into a regularly inhabited centre. The continuous use of the sanctuary goes back at least to the fourth century, though this is known only from votive deposits beneath later reconstructions. But the character of those deposits, with a heavy presence of armour, including a whole sequence of cheek pieces from helmets that seem to have been nailed together on a wall, suggests that a primary function of the sanctuary was

---

[176] Di Iorio (1995).
[177] La Regina (1976); see La Regina (1989) for an overview. See also Tagliamonte (1996) 179–89.

Figure 3.29 Pietrabbondante, general view (author's photo)

to celebrate military victories. La Regina's observation that the dimensions of the original enclosure, 200 by 200 ft, correspond to Livy's description of the area demarcated for the ritual oath of the Samnite legions in 293 BCE (Livy 10.38.5), even if that passage refers to a different centre, Aquilonia, and strengthens the suggestion that it started as a highly charged Place of Memory of the struggle for independence in the Samnite Wars, marking the prime assembly place of the Pentrian Samnites. This is, he suggests, Cominium, the place where the Pentri held their *comitia*, assembling beneath the sacred space of the *templum*.[178]

However, the warlike shrine is replaced in the third century by a new Ionic temple. We have seen that in comparison with the prime temple of the Latin colony of Aesernia, it seems sophisticated and in touch with new Greek currents. This temple is sacked in the Hannibalic invasion, and replaced in the course of the second century by two new temples (distinguished only as A and B). It is temple B which forms an organic complex with the theatre at the end of the second century (figure 3.30). The new work on this temple

---

[178] La Regina (1989) 421–3. Coarelli and La Regina (1984) 230–57 is the clearest summary. Sisani (2001a) argues that Pietrabbandante is, after all, Aquilonia.

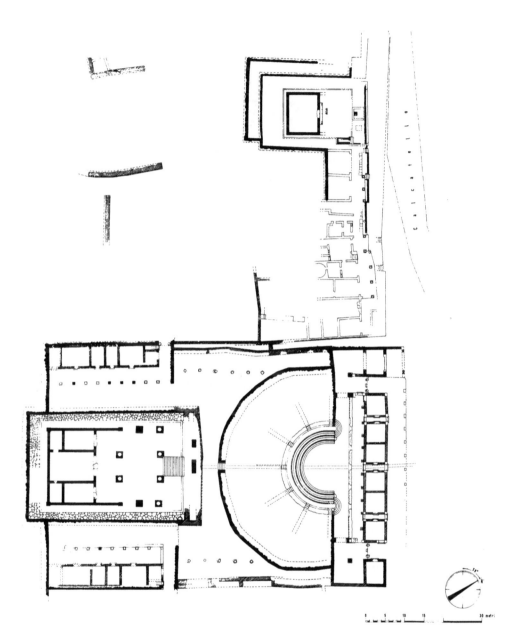

Figure 3.30 Pietrabbbondante, plan of theatre/temple complex (after La Regina 1989: 370, drawn by B. Di Marco)

Figure 3.31 Detail of corner of temple B at Pietrabbondante (author's photo)

and temple A show no signs of subsequent modification, consonant with the signs that the sanctuary simply falls out of use after the Social War.

There are several elements here to encourage the romanticised view of Pietrabbondante as the last symbol of Italic independence: the remote position in the Apennine highlands, the martial connotations, the evident role of sanctuaries in providing coherence and definition for a people (of warrior pastoralists) scattered in their villages *vicatim*, and of course the potent series of inscriptions in Oscan that show the Samnite elite at work as *medices*, the Papii and Staii and Statii and others, names familiar too from Vastogirardi and Schiavi, sites where temples are built to specifications extremely close to that of temple B at Pietrabbondante (see figures 3.31, 3.32).[179] As if to add the final touch of historic irony, one of the latest inscriptions in temple B is of one G. Staatis L. Klar, or Gaius Statius Luci f. Clarus,[180] who may (or may not) appear in the text of Appian, as Statius the Samnite who, having distinguished himself in the Social Wars, was raised to the Roman senate, yet died in his eightieth year as a victim of the proscriptions of the triumvirs in 43 BCE (Appian, *BC* 4.25[181]). He seems to stand as symbol of the end of Samnite independence, his magnificent hill-top sanctuary abandoned, sucked into the politics of the metropolis, and victim finally of Roman greed for wealth.

---

[179] Poccetti (1979) nos. 13–34.   [180] Poccetti (1979) no. 18.   [181] La Regina (1976) 233.

Figure 3.32 Detail of corner of temple at Vastogirardi (author's photo)

That economic and social structures are different in the highlands from the Campanian plain is beyond dispute. But what is so interesting for the problem of reading identity from the material culture is the astonishing similarity that ties Pietrabbondante with Pompeii. The construction and design of the theatre at Pietrabbondante, a triumph of sophistication with the elegant counter-curves of the lower seating, and the splendid finials with Atlas figures and griffin legs (figure 3.33), are most precisely paralleled in the small theatre at Pompeii (figure 3.34). The similarity of design of these two, along with the further theatre at Sarno, is so close as to lead to the assumption that the architect must be the same; or, if not, that there is a common model, most probably in Capua.[182] There is of course a chronological problem. Pompeii's small theatre has a dedicatory inscription in Latin, naming the same magistrates of the Roman colony, Quinctius Valgus and M. Porcius, who also constructed the amphitheatre. The dedication at Pompeii should belong to the 70s BCE, that of Pietrabbondante must be before 91. On the other hand, too little thought has been given to the possibility that the small theatre at Pompeii was itself projected before the Social War, and completed only in the early years of the colony, so giving the Roman magistrates the chance to put their names to an Oscan monument. The link of this theatre

---

[182] For Sarno, see Sear (2006) 138 with bibliography; for the links, see Lauter (1976).

Figure 3.33 Pietrabbondante, view of curve of *ima cavea* with Atlas support (author's photo)

Figure 3.34 Pompeii, small theatre, view of curve of *ima cavea* with Atlas support (author's photo)

to the temple of Minerva on the terrace above raises the possibility that it, too, was thought of in the context of a sanctuary complex.

The important lesson is this. The language of hellenistic architecture could be employed in quite different contexts. It could add to the sophistication of a city with centuries of experience of urbanism, and prolonged contact with the Greek world of Magna Graecia. It could also transform and modernise a Place of Memory resonant with the independent spirit of the Samnite wars. The Pentrians, short of urbanising, had changed as much as the Pompeians, and it is surely no coincidence that the Staii, the most frequently commemorated of the dedicators at Pietrabbondante, are also found on Delos. Constant fighting with the Roman armies brought to them, too, wealth and luxury, though as far as we know they expressed it only in their magnificent sanctuaries, and not in urban baths or luxurious houses. The process doubtless brought social change: we see an emergent elite of top families in Samnium as much as any city, and the entire language of benefaction with which they lay claim to public buildings echoes closely the standard Roman formulae. When a Pacius Staius takes care of the water supply, 'takes care of the construction and approves the work',[183] both the language and the supply of water is an act, just as much of that of Betilienus Varus at Alatri, that reflects Appius Claudius and his successors at Rome.

The elements are too deeply enmeshed to be disentangled. Roman, Greek and local elements work together, draw on repetitive formulae, to create quite different outcomes. The sanctuary of Fortuna at Praeneste, the temple of Juno Moneta at Signia, the temple–theatre complexes at Pompeii and at Pietrabbondante each have numerous features in common. But each of these sites creates a fundamentally different impression, because each draws on the specific location, history and character of the place. Roman power and Greek culture engender radical transformations of society and economy; but there is no reason to see them as suppressing or substituting local identity. Cultural multilingualism only enhances their power of self-expression.[184]

---

[183] Poccetti (1979) nos. 13–15.   [184] See now Bradlcy (2008).

4 | Vitruvius: building Roman identity

'Hellenisation' and 'romanisation', as we saw in chapter 3, are terms which do indeed refer to recognisable aspects of the process of cultural transformation in late republican Italy. Yet neither singly nor together do they provide an adequate interpretative framework within which to account for the process. To grasp the issues of identity at stake in the physical and architectural transformation of Rome, we have the luck to have an articulate, if sometimes frustrating, guide in Vitruvius. The author, elevated to a canonical status by the Renaissance (despite Alberti's criticisms) and by the Neo-classical movement, fell from favour in the twentieth century. In particular, historians of Roman architecture have found that he was not telling the story they expected and wanted: he appears not to appreciate the revolutionary potential of Roman concrete construction as it developed from the second century BCE, questions the reliability of *opus reticulatum* facing, the dominant type of the Augustan period, and shows little interest in the potential of vaults and domes for creating the sort of spaces we admire in the Domus Aurea or the Pantheon.[1] The disappointment of not finding in him the spokesman of the 'revolution' which we admire has led to his dismissal as a conservative. He has been depicted as a failed architect, who made up for his lack of understanding of the real practice of the profession by over-reliance on hellenistic handbooks.[2] Yet, as more recent studies have come to appreciate, it is the very fact that Vitruvius does not see things the way we expect them that makes him such a valuable guide to the conceptual world of late republican Rome.[3]

Vitruvius' complex and challenging treatise *On Architecture* illuminates three fundamental aspects of the cultural transformation of the first century BCE. First, the profound debt to the intellectual legacy of the contemporary Greek ('hellenistic') world to create a new rationale and theoretical basis for Roman practice. Second, the incorporation of that hellenistic theory into an unmistakably Roman framework by its insertion into the social and political structures of Rome. Third, the generation of a new definition of

[1] Rowland and Howe (1999) 11, Wilson Jones (2000) 33–46. [2] Tomlinson (1989).
[3] Gros, Corso and Romano (1997), McEwen (2003).

Roman identity by a process of comparison and contrast with the Greek, one that crucially involves aligning the Italic with the Roman.

Greek theory

The debt to Greek writing is paraded throughout the treatise, though most explicitly in the preface to the seventh book. Here an anecdote introduces his reading list of works consulted: the critic Aristophanes of Byzantium as judge at the games of the Muses and Apollo organised by a Ptolemy was able through his comprehensive knowledge of the library of Alexandria to convict all but one of the entrants of plagiarism (7 *preface* 4–7).[4] Vitruvius is able to cite some three dozen names of Greek authors; he can only cite three Latin authors, Fufidius, Varro and P. Septimius, who between them published four volumes (7 *preface* 14). Modern scholars should reflect rather more on the implications of the story of Aristophanes of Byzantium: it was only the creation of the major library collections of Pergamum and Alexandria that made it possible to discover who had previously written on a subject; and though after Pollio's creation of the Atrium Libertatis, Augustan Rome came to match the eastern centres, we may wonder whether Vitruvius could have possibly compiled his own bibliography without access to Pergamum and Alexandria, the centres he mentions.

We can be confident that he was not simply transcribing some Greek manual: all those he cites, so far as he indicates, wrote on specific buildings or aspects of architecture and mechanics, rather than the sort of comprehensive study he offers. As Indra McEwen has shown, the project of 'writing the body of architecture', complete in its perfect number of ten volumes, is the author's own.[5] It is one that makes sense in the context of the ferment of late republican Rome, and in this sense, though the volumes were seemingly published after the re-branding of Augustus in 27 BCE, Elizabeth Rawson was right to treat him as part of the intellectual life of the late republic.[6]

Vitruvius declares his own intellectual models in the preface to the ninth book: Lucretius' *De Rerum Natura*, Cicero on Rhetoric, and Varro on the Latin language (9 *preface* 17). It may strike us as odd (and therefore interesting) that the architect admired an exposition of Epicurean physics, a rhetorical handbook and a work on linguistics; Cicero and Varro wrote so much else that he might have singled out for admiration – in the case of

---

[4] Pfeiffer (1968) 171ff. on Aristophanes ignores the episode; his librarianship started around 200 BCE.
[5] McEwen (2003).   [6] Rawson (1985) 185–93.

Varro, the work on the Nine Disciplines among which architecture numbered. But they are works important for his intellectual project.[7] Cicero's rhetorical works represent the classic example of the transposition of the highly theoretical and rule-oriented works of hellenistic rhetorical manuals to the actualities of Roman society and politics. Varro's *On the Latin Language* was, as we saw in chapter 2, the most comprehensive treatment of the dialectic between systematic rules and usage, between *ratio* or *analogia* and *consuetudo* or *anomalia*. Lucretius was the outstanding model for a Roman doing battle with the linguistic and conceptual obscurities of Greek scientific thought, and with the challenge of transposing them into both the Latin language and a conceptual framework which made sense to the Roman political elite. Vitruvius' project, like theirs, was to marry Greek *ratio* with Roman *consuetudo*.

Consequently, Vitruvius places a high premium on Greek theory in the broadest sense. Just as Cicero urges the orator not to be a specialist, but to master all disciplines (*de Oratore* 1.187ff.), Vitruvius insists that the architect must command all disciplines (1.1.3–10), and thanks his parents for the head-start they provided in acquiring the Greek rounded education or *encyclios paideia* (6 *preface* 4). But he puts especial weight on the most abstruse aspects of Greek theory, mathematics and music. Geometric drawings in the sand are the first sign of civilised man (6 *preface* 1). When he urges that thinkers have done more for mankind than athletes, he points to Plato's explication of the Pythagorean theorem, and Archimedes' discovery of specific gravity, along with the use of optics by Archytas, by Eratosthenes and by Democritus in his *De Rerum Natura* (9 *preface* 4–14). There is the same missionary zeal in Lucretius for convincing a Roman readership resistant to the sheer excitement of Greek science. The classic example of patient exposition of difficult theory in the Lucretian mode, in the face of *patrii sermonis egestas*, the poverty of his native tongue, is his explanation of musical and acoustic theory which occupies so much of his account of theatre construction (5.4–5). He must explain to those who cannot read Greek, and apologizes for the frequency of Greek terms (5.4.1). The voice of Roman protest breaks through, and is duly suppressed:

Perhaps somebody will say that many theatres are built each year at Rome without using any such theory: but in that he errs. (5.5.7)

It is helpful to think of Vitruvius, too, as a missionary. He does not use Greek architectural writings because he is intellectually lazy, plagiarising in a

---

[7] Gros, Corso and Romano (1997) xxxii–xl, Moatti (1997), Gros (2006) 183–9.

way that could be caught by an Aristophanes of Byzantium; nor because he is lacking in real experience and understanding of the practice of architecture. He knows that there have been Roman architects more famous than himself: he names particularly Cossutius, the Roman architect of the Olympium at Athens, to him one of the four great temples, and C. Mucius, architect of Marius' temple to Honos and Virtus (7 *preface* 17): these Romans had matched Greeks as builders, but not as theorists.[8] The temple which Vitruvius is building is conceptual: the rationale upon which the practice of Roman architecture as a whole can rest. The debate whether this is a '*Handbuch*' or a '*Sachbuch*', a manual for guiding professionals, or a popularising work for the public, is wholly beside the point, trapped in the tramlines of modern thinking;[9] his mission is to persuade his Roman reader, architect or client, that architecture is no mere technical and practical field, but an expression of deep rational structures, of *ordinatio* and *dispositio*, of *eurythmia* and *symmetria*, that can give to the built environment a logic and order that is underpinned by the deeper logic and order of nature, the object of scientific study.

Roman context

In this mission, even though his thinking is formed in the context of the mid first century BCE, based upon Cicero, Varro and Lucretius, Vitruvius articulates his thought in the recognisable context of the recovery from civil war. The publication date must lie in the 20s BCE, since Augustus is named as the recipient of cult in Vitruvius' own single building, the basilica at Fanum (5.1.7). It is generally agreed that it is more likely to be in the first half of the decade, given his ignorance of much of the architecture of the reign.[10] But the date is not crucial, and the political context is the one he himself emphatically supplies. Imperator Caesar, whom he addresses in the prefaces to nine out of the ten volumes, has brought the whole world under the control of his intellect, *divina tua mens et numen* (1 *preface* 1); he has liberated it from the terror of civil war and rules it by intellectual force, *amplissimis tuis cogitationibus consiliisque* (*ibid.*). Vitruvius writes because within the Augustan scheme of rebuilding the Roman world by the divine

---

[8] See Rawson (1991a) 189–203, Gros (2006) 51–73.   [9] Gros (1994) 75f., Gros (2006) 311f.

[10] Baldwin (1990), Fleury (1990) xvi–xxiv, Corso and Romano (1997) xxviii–xxxii, Rowland and Howe (1999) 3–4, Gros, The address as 'imperator Caesar' is seen by some as proof of composition before 27; but Horace, too, continues to call him 'Caesar' after 27 (e.g. *Odes* 4. 15.4, *Epist.* 2.1.4).

nous, which for Greek philosophers underpins creation, architecture, too, plays a significant role. There is a strict parallel between the rebuilding of empire and the rebuilding of cities: the citizen state is augmented by provinces (*civitas . . . provinciis . . . aucta*), and the majesty of empire is augmented by architecture (*maiestas imperii publicorum aedificiorum . . . auctoritates*, 1 *preface* 2). The language of *auctoritas* (*aucta . . . auctoritates*) is the language of Augustus (it is hard to imagine that the word-play is not intentional despite his failure to invoke Imperator Caesar's new name), and the building of *auctoritas* is essential to Vitruvius' argument.[11]

If the universe is the rational creation of the divine mind, and the Roman empire the rational creation of Augustus' mind, the body of architecture is the rational creation of Vitruvius' mind, enriched by philosophical and scientific reading.[12] His ambition is to be useful to Augustus, not by providing a simple handbook for the construction of his public buildings, but by providing the conceptual framework within which such buildings will make sense, and will function as part of a wider order. Most modern readers would happily jettison his long and difficult thoughts on harmony and acoustics in exchange for a chapter on the construction of amphitheatres, which he is aware of and casually mentions in passing (1.7.1), but which he so egregiously fails to discuss. But we would lose more than we gained; for the principles of amphitheatre construction are amply evidenced by the surviving specimens, but without Vitruvius we might never guess that the superb sight-lines and acoustics that characterise Roman theatres and amphitheatres were the outcome of highly sophisticated scientific thought, that correctly understood the movement of sound-waves.

What Vitruvius has in common with late republican authors like Cicero and Varro is the desire to create a rational order, to underpin Roman public speech, or Latin linguistic usage. He differs from them in the chronology of being able to anchor this conceptual order to a precise political structure. He served, he tells us (1 *preface* 2), in Julius Caesar's army, whether as a *praefectus fabrum* as was once assumed, or as a *scriba armamentarius* as is now argued.[13] He passed to the service of Octavian, enjoying the patronage of his sister Octavia. Commentators forget that Octavia was married to Antony, and that consequently he may have spent some of the 30s BCE serving Antony in the east, which might explain his familiarity with the great hellenistic libraries. But his loyalty to the victor of the civil wars is emphatic, and his prefaces go far beyond ritual obeisance to the regime: Vitruvius' project, latterly at least,

---

[11] Gros (1989), Gros (2006) 263–70.   [12] McEwen (2003).
[13] Gros, Corso and Romano (1997) x–xvii, Gros (2006) 311–26.

became the Augustan one of the replacement of the old order and republican *consuetudo* by an imperial rationality. In comparing his own relationship with Augustus to that of Dinocrates with Alexander, he suggests the boldness of his ambitions (2 *preface* 1–4): unlike Dinocrates, he had no Herculean body, but the body of architecture he writes is truly Herculean, a labour to save the world.[14]

Architecture and identity

Three aspects of cultural transformation, it was suggested, are seen in Vitruvius. The transposition of hellenistic theory and its relocation in the context of Roman political and social order have been discussed. The third emerges from these, and is the forging of a new identity, that plays off Greek against Roman, and incorporates the Italic. It is here that Vitruvius provides a commentary on the issues of hellenisation and romanisation discussed in chapter 3. The issue of identity is so fundamental to Vitruvius that one could characterise his project as the rebuilding of Roman identity through architecture. This is an operation performed without a trace of disrespect for the Greek; elite Roman prejudices against music and mathematics could be severe (as Cicero reveals in his *Tusculan Disputations*), but he does not share them. Late republican authors, notably Cicero in the *Verrines*, were uncomfortable about revealing too much knowledge of Greek artists; Vitruvius regards Greek art history as necessary knowledge (1.1.13; 3 *preface* 2). But he has no doubt about Roman superiority.

He does not hesitate to argue that the Roman world empire is the result of divine providence manifested in the geographical location of Italy (6.1.11).[15] Deploying a set of arguments about the impact of geographical location on human condition and health which was developed by Greek medical science (most familiar to us from the treatise on *Airs, Waters and Places* preserved in the Hippocratic *Corpus*), he builds a set of contrasts based on north and south, that uses the simile of a stringed instrument (the *sambuca*). The northerners are the long strings, the southerners the short. Consequently northerners have deep voices and are tall, fair, and straight-haired, southerners have high voices and are short, dark and curly-haired. Northerners are physically strong, but of sluggish intelligence, southerners sharp-witted but

---

[14] McEwen (2003).
[15] 'ita divina mens civitatem populi Romani egregiam temperatamque regionem collocavit uti orbis terrarum imperii potiretur.'

physically weaker. It is thus through its balanced and temperate positioning that Italy can defeat the physically stronger northern barbarians by intelligence, and the sharp-witted southerners by superior strength (6.1.3–11). Vitruvius does not hesitate to appropriate a schematisation that evidently comes out of Greek medical theory to the confirmation of Roman rule as the natural order of things.[16]

The same schematisation that opposes north and south opposes Greek and Roman. The us/them opposition, as we have seen in chapter 2, runs through Roman writing, not least the authors Vitruvius admired, Lucretius, Cicero and Varro. At one level, it is the automatic consequence of the linguistic disjunction between Greek and Latin: the Latin author struggling to write of technical matters where Greek has gone before is constrained to make constant apologies: 'as the Greeks say' reassures a Latin readership that the use of a loan-word has done no damage to identity. Given the importance of language in defining hellenic identity (ch. 1), this is no small matter. Vitruvius' text is peppered with such apologies, one interesting effect of which is to keep a Greek/Roman opposition constantly present in the reader's mind. Occasionally, Vitruvius plays games. So he distinguishes three types of sun-dried brick: 'one, which in Greek is called "Lydian", which our people use' is distinguished from the two types the Greeks use (2.3.3). Here the Greek term for the brick displays their awareness that it is a non-Greek variety, but also their ignorance that it is 'our' type. '*Nostri*' or '*nos*' are rarely specified as Roman, not least because he often has Italic practice in mind.

Vitruvius, attentive reader of Varro, *On the Latin Language*, is sensitised to the use of loan-words. It is in discussing the Greek house that he permits himself a small excursus on mistaken Greek loan-words in Latin (6.7.5). The corridors between two courtyards and the guest suites are called '*mesauloe*' because they run between two *aulae*; nevertheless, *nostri* call them *andronas*. Amazingly, so he continues, this term fits neither Greek nor Latin, since *andron* is the Greek term for the men's dining quarters. He goes on to instantiate other terms which have entered Latin 'incorrectly', not least *xystos*, which in Greek refers to a covered promenade, but in Latin to the open promenade which Greeks actually call *paradromis*. Another good example, he adds, is the Latin description of male figures which support cornices as *telamones* rather than the Greek Atlantes. An 'Atlas' who supports the world is easily understood, whereas the Greek-derived *telamon* makes no sense at all. However, he reassuringly concludes, it is not his aim to change Latin usage, *consuetudo*, merely to draw the attention of the philologists to the point. He has Varro in mind in more ways than one. A strict 'analogist'

---

[16] See Dench (2005) 267–70.

would insist on correcting usage, but a soft 'anomalist' merely observes the error. He would not dream of allowing his knowledge of Greek theory to be construed as an attack on Roman practice.

The us/them contrasts only begin to bite when they affect architectural practice. The notion that 'Greek architecture' and 'Roman architecture' are inherently distinct (enshrined in virtually every modern handbook on ancient architecture) owes much to Vitruvius. The division is an artificial construct, with evident ideological and nationalistic underpinnings. It glosses over the degree of continuous contact between the cities of Italy (in all their variety) and Greek models from Magna Graecia to Asia Minor; underestimates how early the Roman presence in Greece impacts on hellenistic practice; let alone the continued transformations of Greek and eastern idioms under Roman rule. Even Vitruvius had difficulties in establishing a canon of 'our' practice, visible above all in his oscillation between references to the city of Rome and to the cities of Italy. Yet his project is to construct a Roman architecture no less founded in rationality than the Greek, which he constructs in opposition to it. Sometimes the same logic and rules apply to both; sometimes there are contrasts to register. The key is an underlying contrast of social practice, *consuetudo*. When 'we' do things differently, 'we' also build things differently.

The contrasts are developed subtly to begin with, in books three and four on temple construction.[17] He offers no overall contrast between Greek and Roman or Italic practice in temples: the contrasts which most modern handbooks offer, such as the frontality of the Italic temple, its high podium, and its axial emphasis, are not mentioned.[18] The rules which he offers of symmetry and proportion ('which the Greeks call *analogia*') are presented as universally applicable principles founded in nature and the human body (3.1). As he embarks on distinguishing the five types of plan, we may be struck by the way he does his best to exemplify each from the city of Rome itself: the temple *in antis* as in the temple of Fortuna by the Colline gate, prostyle as in Jupiter and Faunus on the Tiber Island, peripteral as in Jupiter Stator in the portico of Metellus or Mucius' Honos and Virtus (3.2.1–5). Only when he reaches the pseudodipteral is he forced by the lack of a Roman example to instance Hermogenes' temple of Diana at Magnesia (3.2.6). Hermogenes was a crucial source,[19] but he has taken his time to reveal his hand, reassuring the reader that these arcane categories of which he speaks are met daily in their streets. His next type is instanced both from Rome

[17] Gros (2006) 27–50.
[18] For this contrast as a false modern perspective, see Coarelli (1996c) 18–20.
[19] Tomlinson (1989), Gros (2006) 139–56.

and Greece: the dipteral, as in the temple of Quirinus and Diana at Ephesus. The last type, the hypaethral, is not present in Rome, but at the Olympium of Athens – the work of the Roman architect Cossutius.

In similar vein, the next chapter (3.3) finds Roman examples of most of the five types of spacing: the tightly spaced columns of pycnostyle in the new temple of Divus Julius, and that of Venus in Caesar's Forum, the systyle in the Fortuna Equestris by the 'stone theatre' (this the only reference to Pompey's theatre), diastyle in Apollo and Diana (not Augustus' Palatine temple),[20] and the araeostyle in Ceres on the Circus Maximus, Pompey's Hercules and the Capitolium itself. He flags up that there is something particularly 'us' not 'them' about this spacing, in specifying that it involves wooden pediments, and ornaments in terracotta or gilded bronze *Tuscanico more* (3.3.5). Yet though he might choose to elevate the Tuscan as a distinctively Roman model, especially with the authority of Jupiter Capitolinus, he makes clear that the ideal spacing is that of the eustyle, which is not instanced in Rome, but is prescribed, like pseudodipteral, by Hermogenes (3.3.6–9). There is conflict here between his Greek theoretical sources and Roman practice: Hermogenes urges the temperate balance of eustyle, mid-way between the exaggerations of pycnostyle (too close) and araeostyle (too widely spaced), but though Vitruvius has shown that Hermogenes' system of proportions or *analogia* is fully applicable to Rome, he will not elevate the national model to superior status.

He returns to the category 'Tuscanic' in book four (4.7), once he has finished with the Doric, Ionic and Corinthian types (what the Renaissance called 'orders'). He notably fails to incorporate it fully within the Doric/Ionic/Corinthian system: not only are these discussed at considerably greater length with far more mathematical precision, but he interposes chapters on aspect (4.5) and doorways (4.6) before turning to Tuscanic. Of course, this is partly the effect of tacking a local variant onto a coherent body of discussion in the Greek treatises; but the effect is to play down any sense that Roman religious identity might depend on adherence to the local 'Tuscanic'; nor does he agree with those (maybe the mysterious P. Septimius?) who would incorporate elements of Tuscanic within Corinthian and Ionic (4.8.5). Here Vitruvius is well in line with the mood of his age: Augustan building is characterised by a Roman development of the Corinthian, and not by the Tuscanic.[21] Remarkably, he seems unaware of the simple principles of proportion, based on a 6:5 ratio, that underlay the Roman Corinthian.[22] But then, he was engaged in transposing to Roman realities an earlier body of

[20] Gros (1976) 198.   [21] Gros (1976) 197–234.   [22] Wilson Jones (1989).

theory quite innocent of Rome. His very success in applying Hermogenean theory to Rome lulls us into expecting a perfect fit. His project was not to describe Roman practice, but to convert Romans to Greek theory.

Once he has finished temples, the going becomes much easier for Vitruvius. Greek theory was fixated with temples. Other buildings were remarkably undertheorised. Book five examines non-religious public buildings. He starts with the Forum, and is at once able to establish a clear us/them contrast: the Greeks build a square surrounded by closely spaced colonnades, 'but in the cities of Italy one should not follow the same rationale, because the tradition of ancestral practice is to put on gladiatorial shows in the Forum' (5.1.1). It is the convenience of spectacle, he suggests, that dictates a rectangular shape, wide spacing of columns and the use of upper balconies. We are back to the fundamental Varronian language of *ratio* versus *consuetudo*, and the invocation of *maiores* indicates that usage must win; indeed, not rejecting *ratio* as such, but rejecting the different *ratio*, equally determined by social factors, which underpins the Greek *agora*. One may suspect there was little or no Greek theory attached to *agora* construction, and no elaborate system of proportions for Vitruvius to adapt or reject.

The fundamental importance of invocation of ancestral *consuetudo* surely helps to explain the feature of his text that causes such puzzlement: the failure to discuss the amphitheatre. The first permanent amphitheatre in Rome, that of Statilius Taurus, was finished in 29 BCE, certainly before the publication of the book; the earliest examples elsewhere in Italy, notably that of Pompeii, date back to the early first century BCE. Despite the Greek formation of its name, which Vitruvius knows, it is a brand new architectural form, developed in Italy, and based on the specifically Roman promotion of gladiatorial games.[23] We cannot invoke ignorance, nor an old-fashioned resistance to new-fangled ideas. But the Forum Romanum continued as a prime location of shows into the reign of Augustus, and Vitruvius is not interested in undermining his point about Greek and Italic *consuetudo* differing. The amphitheatre would also compromise a much more elaborate set of oppositions which he constructs between Greek and Italic theatres.

Greek and 'Latin' theatres

Theatres bring Vitruvius back to a heartland of Greek theory. We have already seen his emphatic interest in Aristoxenus' theory of harmony and its application to the acoustics of the theatre (5. 4–5). The strength of the

---

[23] Welch (1994) and Welch (2007).

objection that acoustic theory is irrelevant to the wooden theatres annually constructed in Rome (5.5.7) is not to be underestimated in his terms: this is Roman *consuetudo* encountering the irrelevance of Greek theory, just as in the Forum. But he deftly parries the objection by citing the frequent use of acoustic devices in the solid theatres of *Italiae regiones* (5.5.8). This slide from Rome to Italy eventually leads to a new phrasing of his opposition: 'Latin' theatres versus Greek (5.8.2). This formulation points not so much to Latium among the regions of Italy, but to the Latin-speaking as opposed to the Greek-speaking, a linguistic distinction of clear relevance in theatrical performance.

Greek theory did not stop at acoustics. It also prescribed in considerable detail, as he explains (5.7), the geometry of the layout of the theatre. But here he encounters another series of obstacles in terms of Greek and Italic practice. The most basic distinction is the use of the circle of the orchestra in Greek drama for choral dancing, in contrast with the Italic seating of senators in the orchestra and the implications for the height of the stage (5.6.2). Yet though the contrasts may be *caused* by differing practice, he expresses the rationale of planning in much more theoretical terms.

The plan of the Roman theatre (5.6.1–6) is based on inscribing four triangles in a circle. The circle marks the edge of the orchestra, the diameter the boundary between orchestra and stage, the base of the bottom triangle the front of the scene (scaenae frons), and the points of the triangles in the upper semicircle the steps that divide the blocks of seats (figure 4.1). The Greek theatre is planned on a contrasting principle (5.7.1). Three squares are inscribed in the circle, and the orchestra extends to the baseline of the bottom square, the narrow stage only occupying the space defined by this line and a tangent to the circumference of the circle (figure 4.2).

The problem here is to know the status of Vitruvius' prescriptions. Is he saying that this is the principle on which architects *in fact* worked? Or is it the principle on which they *ought* to work? Or is it an attempt to make mathematical sense of the rule-of-thumb principles on which they really work? It has long been observed that surviving specimens of Roman theatres are far from conforming regularly to his rules: Frézouls dismissed Vitruvius' prescriptions as a flight of fancy ('*une vue de l'esprit*').[24] On the other hand, several Greek theatres follow the rules with reasonable fidelity, like that of fourth-century Priene and a number of others of that period, and it seems likely enough that hellenistic theatre architects were aware of the rules Vitruvius transmits, doubtless prescribed by one of his authorities. Oddly enough, Vitruvius is much less reliable as a guide to Roman theatres: a number of attempts have been made to reconcile his rules with surviving examples, but the enormous variety of Roman practice means that either

[24] Lepik (1949), Frézouls (1982) 356–69, Small (1983).

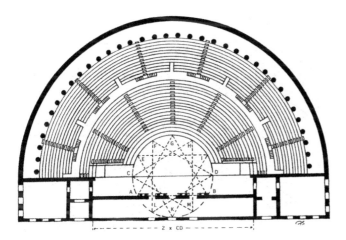

Figure 4.1 Geometry of 'Latin' theatre according to Vitruvius
(from Sear 2006, figure 3, by permission of Oxford University Press,
drawn by F. Sear)

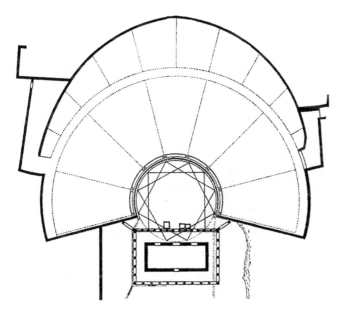

Figure 4.2 Geometry of 'Greek' theatre according to Vitruvius
(from Sear 2006, figure 3, by permission of Oxford University Press,
drawn by F. Sear)

the Vitruvian system has to be substituted with an alternative one,[25] or
a wide range of variations conceded on the basic Vitruvian idea.[26] The
best case that can be made is that two theatres do in fact conform: that

[25] Small (1983).   [26] Sear (1990), Sear (2006) 27–9, with figures 2–5.

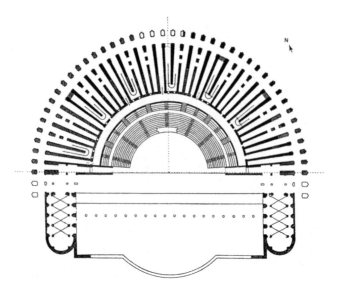

Figure 4.3 Plan of theatre of Marcellus at Rome (from Sear 2006, figure 18, after Calza Bini)

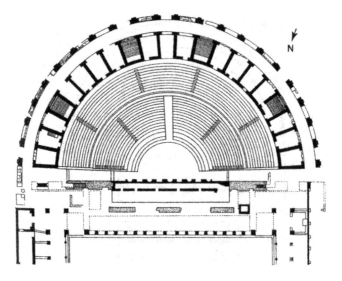

Figure 4.4 Plan of theatre at Ostia (from Sear 2006, plan 19, after Becatti)

of Marcellus in Rome (figure 4.3), dedicated between 13 and 11 BCE (of which, however, the stage building is not preserved), and that in Ostia built under Augustus, before the death of Agrippa in 12 BCE (figure 4.4).[27] On this showing, the rules for the Roman theatre are Vitruvius' own design, which bore fruit in influencing two important buildings by Augustus, the dedicatee of the treatise, shortly after its publication, but little else thereafter until the Renaissance.

This may well be right, and must serve as a warning to those tempted to treat this complex work as a sort of recipe book to explain all Roman building. But it is worth going further and asking why Vitruvius troubles to design a set of mathematical rules for building the Roman theatre, if they were in practice superfluous. The rules for the Greek theatre, we may take it, were the work of some late fifth- or fourth-century theorist, whose writings were influential in the building of a Hippodamian 'model city' like Priene. For a Roman architect to offer an alternative set of rules, based on equally mathematical principles, implies a consciousness of the 'Roman' theatre as a parallel but distinct form. This would hardly have been possible before the building of Pompey's theatre in 55 BCE; wooden theatres may have been formalised enough to have evolved their own set of rules, but it seems improbable that they were the same as for solid structures. The Italian theatres of the early first century BCE, like those of Pietrabbondante, Pompeii and Sarno, certainly observed design rules, but they were not Vitruvian so much as variants on contemporary hellenistic design.[28]

Vitruvius is concerned with something more fundamental than giving rules for building. He wants to offer a theoretical underpinning for the Roman theatre that gives it parity with the highly theorised construction of the Greek theatre.[29] He does so by a stroke of mathematical ingenuity. If the Greek theatre is based on three squares in a circle, the Roman will be based on four triangles. The ratios stand in symmetry – 3 × 4:4 × 3. The Roman is a mathematical inversion of the Greek. The difference is more apparent than real. The effect of either calculation is to produce a clock face with twelve hours (figure 4.5). The substantial difference is that the seating of a Greek theatre occupies seven hours of the face (from nine o'clock to four o'clock, with the axis set on half past twelve), and the wedges of seats divided by steps occupying the seven segments so defined. The Roman theatre occupies only six segments (from nine o'clock to three o'clock, with the axis set on twelve), and pulls the edge of the stage right forward to the diameter. For the distinction of four triangles versus three squares to work, it is crucial that the position of the *scaenae frons* be determined by the base of the triangle represented by the points 8, 12 and 4 on a clock face: it is the failure to respect this element of the rules that shows we are dealing with a mathematical game.

Vitruvius' mathematics links architecture to other disciplines. Among other examples he offers of how different disciplines regularly do overlap on matters of theory, he points to the common interest of astrologers and

[27] Isler (1989).   [28] Lauter (1976), Isler (1989).   [29] Gros (2006) 327–50.

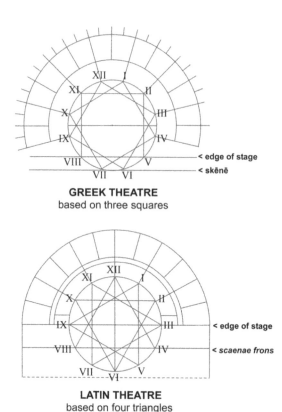

GREEK THEATRE
based on three squares

LATIN THEATRE
based on four triangles

Figure 4.5 Vitruvius' plans as mathematical game:
squares and triangles (drawn by Amy Richardson, after
Gros 2006: 332, figure 3, 333, figure 4)

musicians in the 'sympathy' of the constellations and musical harmonies in
quadrants and triangles (1.1.16). That is a helpful hint of the intellectual
context to which his analysis of the theatre belongs. He observes that laying
triangles in circles is the method by which astrologers calculate the musical
correspondences of the twelve constellations (5.6.1) (figure 4.6). Since he
is already preoccupied with the relevance of harmony to acoustics, it is no
surprise to find him extending his interest to the 'music of the spheres',
an area in which the Stoic doctrine of cosmic sympathy underpinned the
intellectual respectability of astrology and the prediction of the future from
the stars. The mathematicians who calculated the layout of the Horologium
laid out by Augustus in 9 BCE would have appreciated his method.[30]

---

[30] Gros (2006) 332–6 for the links with astrology. The analysis by Buchner (1982) has been
criticised by Schutz (1990), but the application of astrology is clear, Barton (1994) 45–7.

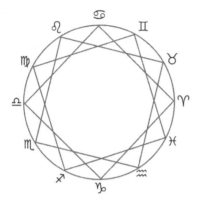

Astrological scheme of oppositions
based on three squares

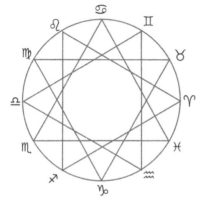

Astrological scheme of oppositions
based on four triangles

Figure 4.6 Astrological scheme of
oppositions by Geminos of Rhodes based
on three squares/four triangles (drawn by
Amy Richardson, after Gros 2006: 336,
figure 7)

By elevating the contrast of Roman and Greek architecture from custom
to theory, Vitruvius did for architecture what contemporary grammarians
were doing for the Latin language, which by the elaboration of grammatical
rules on the model of Greek was elevated from pure *consuetudo* to *consuetudo*
supported by *ratio* (ch. 5). He lays considerable stress, as we have seen, on the
intellectual context of what he is doing. Architecture, as he explains at the
beginning of book one, consists of the practical and the theoretical, *fabrica*
and *ratiocinatio*: one may be a very skilled craftsman, but without theory

one will have no *auctoritas* (1.1.1). Vitruvius seeks to make architecture worthy of the *auctoritas* of the Augustan age by producing the convergence of two systems of authority: that of social custom and ancestral practice with that of pure mathematical theory. If it is true that Augustus' architects respected the Vitruvian rules in constructing the theatre of Marcellus, it was a nice exchange of *auctoritas*: the authority of the emperor stamped upon the authority of the architect. Dinocrates and Alexander have converged in their Herculean labour of reordering the world.

Read in this way, Vitruvius much enriches our appreciation of 'hellenisation' at work. High Greek theory is essential to his strategy. It draws architecture into the ambit of contemporary intellectual preoccupations at Rome, lending it both greater interest to laymen, and greater *auctoritas*.[31] There is no sacrifice of Roman identity involved. The whole work is firmly planted in a Roman social context: the *consuetudo* that sets apart the Romans (or, as he frequently expresses it, Italians) dictates the use of architectural form. Greek-derived *ratio* does not weaken Roman *consuetudo*: on the contrary, it is the means of elevating it to a theoretical level where it becomes stronger and clearer. It elucidates the nature of 'Roman' identity, and gives it parity of esteem with Greek. Vitruvius saw Augustus as equipping the *maiestas imperii* with the authority of public buildings (1 *preface* 2): he did no less with his own theoretical contribution.

From wooden to solid theatres

Vitruvius' contribution, then, is to articulate a rationale for Roman architecture that gives it parity of standing with Greek architecture. But even without Vitruvius, the late first century BCE saw a critical moment in the remaking of the built expression of Roman identity. The most radical change of the period was the abandonment of the tradition of the wooden temporary theatres which Vitruvius mentions in favour of solid, permanent structures of 'stone' – or rather, in practice, concrete clad with stone – finally putting Rome in line not only with Greek practice but that of central Italy in general. The change is summed up in two moments: the destruction in 154–150 BCE, on the motion of Scipio Nasica, of the stone theatre on the Palatine contracted by the censors of 154, and the opening in 55 BCE by Pompey as consul of Rome's first permanent theatre on the Campus

---

[31] For the importance of *auctoritas* in Vitruvius' thought, see Gros (1989).

Martius, thinly veiled as a temple with spectators' seats below.[32] Each of these moments represents a different conception of Roman social and moral order, and the shift from the one to the other is as radical as the shift politically from republic to Empire. It is worth stepping aside from our discussion of Vitruvius to examine this critical shift.

There has been much discussion of the Roman resistance to permanent theatres: was it political (an attempt to control democratic tendencies), cultural (opposition to Hellenic influence), or, as Erich Gruen suggested, an assertion by the ruling class of their control over the cultural sphere?[33] But an attempt to separate out the cultural from the political, the social and the religious, and to give primacy to one factor against others understates the intimacy with which these aspects were intermeshed, and reduces the complexity of ideologies to conscious and overt motivations.[34] We can concede that there were real anxieties about the impact of Greek culture on Roman identity without constructing a false picture of 'pro-Hellenic' and 'anti-Hellenic' political factions; we can accept that theatrical *ludi* played a central role in public and political life, without attempting to correlate political success with the holding of the office of aedile responsible for staging the games; we can accept there was a deep debate about the nature of Roman social order without making it a tussle between *populares* and *optimates*.

Scipio Nasica's demolition of the theatre is one of a considerable list of official measures in the mid second century which have seemed to constitute a sort of campaign of resistance to Greek culture: the suppression of the cult of Bacchus of 186 BCE, and various expulsions of foreign cults in the years following, including that of astrologers and followers of Sabazius in 139, the burning of the works of Pythagoras of 181, the expulsion of philosophers and rhetors of 161, the banishment of two Epicureans in (perhaps) 154, the accelerated return of the mission of the three heads of the Athenian philosophical schools in 155, and of course the string of laws against table luxury (sumptuary laws) through the period, including the lex Orchia of 181, the lex Fannia of 161 and the lex Didia of 143. The attitudes involved are too complex to be reduced to a wave of 'anti-hellenism', let alone the workings of an 'anti-hellenic faction', yet they show a persistent concern

---

[32] The inauguration of the theatre belongs to 55 BCE; of the attached temple to 52; see Gros (1999) 35–8.

[33] Hanson (1959), Frézouls (1982) 353–56, Morgan (1990), Gruen (1992) 183–222.

[34] Cf. Gruen (1992) 197: 'A cultural rather than a political significance held primacy.'

with the impact of external and specifically Greek influence on Roman identity.[35]

Rather than using the sources to identify one among a variety of factors as a 'true cause', a Thucydidean *alēthestatē prophasis*, we can learn more by listening to the terms in which they couched the debate, and try to make sense of attitudes which in our terms seem nonsensical. Communal decisions are singularly difficult to 'explain', particularly when they do not issue from a firm consensus, but from disagreement: we must assume that the censor Cassius who was constructing the stone theatre of 154 BCE disagreed strongly with Scipio Nasica, and that the historian would need to reconstruct a series of arguments on either side, as Tacitus does on the occasion of the parallel debate on Nero's new 'Greek' festival (*Annals* 14.20–21).

The difficulty is that we only have highly abbreviated accounts of Scipio's case, presented by authors the earliest of whom was writing over a century later. Livy's history, which may well have offered a reconstruction of the debate, is lost for this period, though the surviving summary reports that Scipio urged the destruction of the theatre 'as being unbeneficial and damaging to public morals' (*Per.* 48). That *mores* featured largely in the debate is likely enough. Valerius Maximus, whose image of the 'good old Romans' is suspect enough, expands on this:

on the proposal of P. Scipio Nasica it was resolved to sell all the apparatus for the theatre's construction in public auction. In addition a ban was imposed by decree of the senate that nobody should attempt within the city or one mile of its boundaries to set up seating or to watch games seated; the purpose, that is to say, being that in standing the proper virility of the Roman race should be linked to relaxation. (Valerius Maximus 2.4.2)

The idea that the Roman people was likely to impair its virility, *virilitas*, by sitting at the games is by our standards so bizarre that we are little tempted to take it at face value. We may prefer the more political account of Appian, that the theatre 'was liable to start further civil conflict, or that it was unbeneficial for the Romans to become wholly accustomed to Greek luxuries' (*Civil Wars* 1.28). But the emphasis on standing is a persistent element in the accounts: it seems hard to get round statements that the senate did ban sitting at games within the city, and that was certainly what Romans chose to remember later. So Tacitus' traditionalists argue:

---

[35] See at length the arguments of Gruen (1990) and Gruen (1992) 223–71. On 'philhellenism', see Ferrary (1988).

In earlier times plays used to be given on makeshift seating and on a temporary stage; or if you go further back, you find that the people watched standing, lest it waste whole days on end in idleness should it sit in the theatre. (Tacitus, *Annals* 14.20)

It is pertinent to observe that the same Scipio Nasica won a triumph for the campaign against the Dalmatians which Polybius reports was undertaken for fear that the Romans should go soft from lack of fighting, and subsequently spoke against the destruction of Carthage lest the Romans go soft for lack of an enemy.[36] The rhetorical antitheses that emerge from the theatre debate fit well enough. Romans are tough; Greeks are soft. Pleasure and relaxation are bad for armies: theatres, *gymnasia*, table luxury and the like undermine the discipline and manliness of the citizen-soldier. Sitting is comfortable and soft: standing is tough and manly. Those who sit are happy to remain for hours, even days on end, and turn idle: those who stand relax briefly, then get on with their serious business. A permanent set of seats is an inducement to sit permanently. That way the army goes soft and the people is corrupted.[37] If we find some of the logical steps here involved less than cogent, we may reflect that much contemporary moralising about the corrupting effect of television (sedentary entertainment twenty-four hours a day) rests on scarcely better logic.

The weakest link in the chain of argument is the suggestion that permanent seating of solid construction is more liable to corrupt an audience than temporary wooden seating. That Roman audiences had long been seated seems implicit in the plays themselves, and in the assignment as early as 194 BCE of front-row seats to senators.[38] However, it is as well to recall the conditions of the medieval stage, for which movable wooden stages and standing audiences were normal, and it is imaginable that in the early second century temporary seating was only limited, so that the privileged sat, while the crowd milled about behind. A permanent structure might involve a considerable extension of available seating, and hence a greater moral risk to 'the people'. Be that as it may, the very illogicality of declaring stone seats unacceptable while wooden ones were acceptable is admitted, and consequent objections forestalled, by the linked *senatusconsultum* banning *any* form of seating within the city. It is that ban itself which is the securest

---

[36] Morgan (1990).

[37] On Roman concerns about softness, *mollitia*, see Edwards (1993) 63–97, and further Dench (2005) 264ff.

[38] Livy 34.44.4–5 – see below, p. 168.

argument for accepting that the moral objection to sitting was indeed at the heart of the debate.

In practice, this ban cannot have lasted long. But the moral objections to permanent seating were maintained for a century, so that by the 50s BCE the absurd situation had been reached that temporary wooden theatres were regularly erected in Rome, but on such a scale of lavish ostentation as to rate as one of the leading forms of luxury. The elder Pliny in describing the wooden theatre erected by Aemilius Scaurus in his aedileship of 58 BCE suggests that this aedileship may have done more to corrupt the Roman people than any other single event (*Natural History* 36.113). This, like that of Scribonius Curio a couple of years later, who turned the wooden stage into the ultimate in magnificence, transformed the use of temporary materials from a symbol of traditional restraint into a kind of potlatch.

In fact, what we need to make sense of is not just the decision of the 150s, and the arguments that swayed people at the time, and the effective reversal of that decision in the 50s, but more widely the attitudes of Romans over the course of a century, during which that initial decision was reinterpreted, adhered to or modified, religiously followed or opportunistically exploited. Here the literary tradition which 'explains' the decision is of particular significance, for it says something about how those who lived with its results made sense of it for themselves. Reconstruction of a century of developing attitudes is impossible on the basis of our evidence; but what is possible, thanks to Cicero, is to see how the debate presented itself at the turning point in the 50s when it was in the process of crumbling.

What in Cicero occupies the foreground is the political dimension of the theatre. According to context, he represents this political dimension as a threat and danger or as an advantage. Thus it is when, in the trial of Flaccus for extortion in 59 BCE, he is trying to discredit the value of decrees passed against his client by Greek assemblies that he elaborates the role of the theatre in Greek political decision making. 'Our ancestors' have established the fine principle (already sadly crumbling) that voting, conducted according to the proper divisions of society, should be physically separate from the assembly for debate (*contio*):

Greek states are wholly run by the rashness of a seated assembly (*sedentis contionis*). To pass over modern Greece which has long been so disturbed and afflicted by its own decision-making, even the Greece of old which flourished in wealth, power and glory, fell from this one ill, of unrestrained liberty and licence in assemblies. When completely unskilled and ignorant men without experience *sat down together in the theatre*, that was when they undertook profitless wars, put seditious men in charge of the state, and threw out their most deserving citizens. (Cicero, *pro Flacco* 16)

Cicero presents us with two models of social order. The well-ordered Roman society keeps the people under control by its hierarchical divisions of wealth, age and rank, and by its sense of respect for the men who lead it, shown through standing in their presence: the standing assembly, below the rostra on which the Roman magistrate is elevated above the people, 'stands for' order. The assembly seated in the theatre and showing no respect to its leaders symbolises the disorder which is alleged to have ruined Greece, and which implicitly now threatens Rome. Sitting symbolises social disorder: *seditio* is the standard Latin word for civil strife, *seditiosus* the favoured epithet for the disruptive tribunes of the late republic, and Cicero is here underlining its etymology (ironically the inverse of the Greek word for sedition, *stasis* or 'standing').

The use of theatres for assemblies, particularly in post-classical Greece, is well attested, and it has repeatedly been suggested, from Mommsen on, that anxieties on this score are the 'real' reason for the demolition of the stone theatre of 154.[39] It is of course possible, but unprovable, that Scipio pointed to the danger of Greek-style assemblies. What we can be more confident of is that in highlighting the morality of sitting versus standing, the debate implicitly involved notions of social order. 'Sitting in the theatre' might threaten to undermine by the same token the moral, social and political order of Rome.

In view of that identification of theatre and sedition, it is the more remarkable that Cicero, at exactly the same period in the early 50s, though in a different context, could cite with approval the expressions of political opinion in the theatre. A passage from his defence of Sestius of 56 has been repeatedly cited in evidence of the general proposition that the theatre had political importance;[40] what has not been brought out is that it represents a complete reversal of the attitudes of the *pro Flacco*. The context is an ingenious argument that seeks to redefine the contrast of '*optimates*' and '*populares*' in such a way as to represent the '*optimates*' as the true voice of grass-roots opinion, and the 'populares' as a minority voice that only makes itself heard through the use of violence. At stake is the standing of his enemy Clodius: Cicero wants to show that, far from being the popular hero he tries to

---

[39] For the debate, Gruen (1992) 205–10, with references to earlier debate, esp. Frézouls (1982), Nicolet (1980) 363. For the context, see Millar (1998) 220–6.

[40] E.g. Hopkins (1983) 14, Nicolet (1980) 363f.

represent himself as, he is a thug who prevails by the abuse of organ-ised violence. He therefore distinguishes Clodius from the *populares* of old, the Gracchi or Saturninus, whose handouts made them genuinely popular:

And so in those days, the people who were 'popular' caused offence to serious and honourable men, but flourished on every indication of popular judgement. It was they who received applause in the theatre; it was their leading in the voting that was followed in any issue; it was their reputation, style of speaking, expression and gait which men loved. (*pro Sestio* 105)

With a brief to demonstrate that, unlike them, Clodius is not genuinely popular, Cicero proceeds to distinguish 'the three places in which the judge-ment and will of the Roman people is best indicated, in the *contio*, in voting assemblies and in the audience of shows and games, *ludorum gladiatorumque consessu*' (106). But the *contiones* and *comitia* in which Clodius humiliated Cicero and drove him into exile can be discredited as the work of hired bands of thugs and desperadoes. Only the theatre represents the voice of the people reliably:

Indications (of popular opinion) in the *comitia* and *contiones* are occasionally gen-uine, but frequently are vitiated and corrupted: theatrical and gladiatorial audiences (*consessus*) where support has been bought by irresponsible parties are said to stir at worst thin and spasmodic applause. (*pro Sestio* 115)

Since you cannot really purchase a theatrical audience, so the argument runs, you can trust its expression of opinion, and it thus is highly signif-icant that Clodius failed to show his face at the spectacular shows staged by Scaurus in 58 (116), and that they showed wholehearted support for Cicero and repudiated Clodius (117). He launches into a long account of cheers and whistlings in the theatre designed to prove 'the indica-tion of universal feelings, the demonstration of will of the whole Roman people' (122).

The situation is thus turned on its head. There is still a contrast between the traditional and formal expression of the will of the people in *comitia* and *contiones* (in which citizens stood) and the informal voice of the seated audience (*consessus*) of the theatre. But the same political disorder and cor-ruption that discredits the traditional assemblies now gives legitimacy to the seated theatre. Because Clodius (and tacitly others like Caesar) have turned Roman politics upside down by turbulence and violence, the alternative order is now preferable and more Roman. In the same year (56), Cicero attacked Clodius again for misconduct at the theatre, in his conduct of the *ludi Megalenses* in April, an occasion which Cicero represents as an invasion of slaves, outraging the audience.[41] It was in the next year following this speech, 55 BCE, that Pompey inaugurated his new theatre on the Campus Martius; the final touch was marked by his inauguration of the attached temple in 52, holding the sole consulship for the purpose of bringing the rioting and political violence of the city under control. Cicero's disingenuous rhetoric veils the vital point that the theatre was now desirable not because it was (as he claims) a spontaneous expression of popular sentiment, but rather one that could be effectively manipulated as a weapon against 'the mob'.

It is to this extent misleading to represent Pompey's theatre as a victory for the *populares* against traditionalist opinion.[42] On the contrary, it reflects a reversal of symbolical polarities. Temporary wooden theatres, reaching a climax in this decade thanks to Scaurus and Curio, now stood for luxury and corruption. Pompey's theatre stood for order and control, a better and more 'Roman' order than that now offered by the chaotic political system. He presented the theatre as a temple with steps for the audience below. One can, with Tertullian, think of that as a ploy to evade censorial disapproval; but another and more positive way of expressing it is to say that he gave his theatre the religious solemnity which contemporary analysis identified as a prime method of social control, and guaranteed the 'Roman-ness' of his construction by inserting it in a long and venerable Italic tradition of theatre–temple complexes.[43] The authority of Pompey converted the permanent theatre from a symbol of corruption to one of a new and better Roman order, and his lead was followed by Augustus and his successors. As Claude Nicolet well observed, the shift of the popular voice from assemblies to theatres encapsulates the shift from the republican to the imperial order.[44] But both orders are Roman.

Two changes underlie this paradigm shift. One is the progressive collapse in belief in political assemblies as the authentic expression of the identity of the citizen body, as a direct result of the political turbulence of the last century of the republic. The other is the progressive transformation of the theatre into an image of the citizen body by seating regulations. The entire history of these *leges theatrales* can be read in the context of the debate about

---

[41] Cicero, *de Haruspicum Responso* 22; see Wiseman (1974) 159–69.
[42] So Frézouls (1982), following Rumpf (1950).   [43] Hanson (1959).
[44] Nicolet (1980) 361–73.

seating and standing, and the determination to avoid the false constitution of the citizen body in a seated theatre.[45]

Part of Cicero's objection to political decision making by men seated in theatres is that the citizen body needs to be divided up into its parts by rank to vote properly. It is of course a misperception of the Greek theatre to represent it as a disorganised mass of people: the Athenian theatre had its own hierarchies, with divisions by tribes, and front ranks for priesthoods, that constituted the audience as a citizen body for ceremonial purposes.[46] But if an imagined objection to the Greek theatre was a 'promiscuous' social mix, it was a major Roman preoccupation from an early stage to ensure that the Roman audience did indeed reflect its social hierarchy. Senators were divided from the rest, as we have seen, as early as 194 – Livy reports that the division was initially very unpopular, and that Scipio Africanus endured odium for it (34.44.4).

But separation of seating not only reflected the existing social order: it actually played an important part in defining it. This is strikingly so in the case of the *equites*, the 'second order' in Roman society, one so notoriously difficult to define. Their separate political identity was above all the work of Gaius Gracchus, who assigned them separate seating, so visibly displaying their common identity. This privilege was apparently abolished by Sulla, who wished to eliminate their separate political identity, but restored in 67 by L. Roscius, who established the 'fourteen rows'. Cicero, so vocal a supporter of the *equites*, rallied to the defence of Roscius when he was booed, and delivered a harangue (from the steps of the temple of Bellona, symbolically, since the theatre was no place for a *contio* by a magistrate) persuading them to cheer Roscius in future (Plutarch, *Cicero* 13). Seating regulations were probably further refined by Pompey himself as part of his extensive legislation of 52, the year of the completion of his theatre complex; but the definitive *lex theatralis* was to be that of Augustus, who much extended distinctions, between citizen and foreigner, free and slave, soldier and civilian, married and unmarried, *togati* and *pullati* (wearers of togas and wearers of cloaks), and men and women. From 194 to 17 BCE we see a gradual shift of relationship: as the seating arrangements are refined, the theatre becomes not merely compatible with the social order, but a prime way of defining it.

Simultaneously we see a convergence between Rome itself and the regions of Italy, which had not shared Roman scruples about solid theatres and for

---

[45] Bollinger (1969), Rawson (1987), reprinted as Rawson (1991b) 508–45.
[46] Rawson (1991a) 521.

over a century had evolved forms with strong hellenistic influences. We have seen Vitruvius refer to them to substantiate his vision of a 'Latin' theatre. We have seen formal links between Pompey's theatre and Italic theatre–temple complexes. It is significant that the Augustan reforms of seating laws were provoked by an incident not at Rome but at Puteoli, when a senator was unable to find a seat; Augustus' regulation addressed 'the most confused and lax custom of spectating' not just in Rome but 'everywhere' (Suetonius, *Augustus* 44). The convergence of architectural form envisaged by Vitruvius is the consequence of the transformation of Italy that makes any assembly of Roman citizens in *any* Roman city an image of Roman social order. It is because the theatre is such a potent expression of Roman identity that Vitruvius needed to construct it at a theoretical level in contrast to the Greek theatre.

Baths and *gymnasia*

The urgency to construct the Roman in antithesis to the Greek emerges again in the following chapters of Vitruvius' book five on baths (5.10). But whereas for theatres Vitruvius constructs his Greek/Roman opposition by an inversion of mathematical formulas, with baths he uses a different distancing technique. Baths are set against the *palaestra*, a form which, so the author is anxious to reassure us, the Italic tradition simply does not have (5.11). 'They do things differently there' is a sort of alibi, a reassurance that we are here not there, and one that conceals a complex dialectic.

The prescriptions for baths (*balineae*, rather than *thermae*, the word which became standard under the Empire)[47] evoke a world of Roman engineering, rather than Greek theory. Arrangements are driven by practicalities, not mathematics: positioning to take advantage of the sun, efficient juxtaposition of male and female baths, sequences of hypocausts graded from cold to hot to optimise heating efficiency, practical arrangements for setting tiles to make the suspended floors of *suspensurae*, and methods of constructing vaulted ceilings, whether of solid concrete, or false vaults in tile hung from wooden beams (5.10.1–3). Little here overtly suggests the influence of Greek architecture, except perhaps the use of the word *hypocausis* for underfloor

---

[47] Nielsen (1990) 3 distinguishes *balnea* as bath complexes from *thermae* as complexes which include a *palaestra*. This distinction is incompatible with the usage of Vitruvius, which coincides with that of Varro, *De Lingua Latina* 9.68, in distinguishing the small private bath as the neuter single *balneum* and public baths as the feminine plural *balneae*. *Thermae* are not typologically distinct, but a later usage associated with imperial baths, see also Yegül (1992) 43.

heating (hypocaust), and even this is not flagged as a Greek usage. Only in the last paragraph when he turns to the domed sweating room or *Laconicum* does Vitruvius invoke a characteristically Greek proportion: the height of the walls to the spring of the dome should be equal to its diameter (5.10.5).

The mention of this feature with a recognizably Greek name ('the Spartan bath') appropriately leads to discussion of the corresponding Greek institution, which Vitruvius terms *palaestra* rather than the more familiar gymnasium.[48] He thinks it worthwhile to show how the Greeks do things, even if it is not part of the Italic tradition (*Italicae consuetudinis*). We find ourselves in a world of proportions (the four porticoes of the peristyle whether square or rectangular to total two stades, and one portico to be twice the depth of the other three) and technical terms (*ephebeum, coryceum, conisterium, loutron, elaeothesium, propigneum,* etc.) all of which evoke a foreign world with foreign customs – the philosophers and rhetors who dispute here, and the educational institutions connected with ephebes and athletics (5.11.1–2). Vitruvius' exposition of the main peristyle of the *palaestra* culminates with the *Laconicum*, and cross-reference is made to the proportions already prescribed for this space (5.11.2). Crossover between Italic baths and Greek *palaestrae* is thereby conceded, as it is in the next section where prescriptions are given for the covered and open walkways that should stretch beyond the palaestra, 'which the Greeks call *paradromidas*, but our people call *xysta*' (5.11.4). If the Italians do not have such buildings, why, we may enquire, do they have a vocabulary for them?

The answer is that it was only in a quite specific sense that the *palaestra* or gymnasium was *not* an Italic tradition. It was a source of major influence on building in Italy in the last two centuries BCE in both private and public spheres. One only needs to turn to Varro and Cicero, Vitruvius' masters in linguistic sensibility. Varro, who in his *Res Rusticae* plays up the antithesis of tough old-fashioned Roman rustic ways versus contemporary luxury villas, waxes sarcastic about the 'citified *gymnasia* of the Greeks' which constitute the farmsteads of his day:

These days one gymnasium each is scarcely enough, and they don't believe they have a real villa unless it positively tinkles with Greek names: *procoeton, palaestra, apodyterion, peristylon, ornithon, peripteron, oporothece.* (*de Re Rustica* 2.1)

As Varro represents it, the use of Greek names is a way of flaunting the importation of the Greek city into the Roman countryside. A form that is not merely 'borrowed' or 'imitated' but flaunted provokes a response. Cicero

---

[48] For the distinction, Ginouvès (1998) 126–7.

points to the associations evoked in a sequence of letters to Atticus in the early 60s, when he is doing work on his villa at Tusculum, and enquires anxiously after Atticus' efforts to acquire statuary from Greece such as a Hermathena that will be as suitable as possible for a gymnasium (*gymnasiodē* as he suitably says in Greek).[49] Suitable statuary reinforces the effect of architectural form, the four-sided colonnade, in evoking a Greek context.

The effect of such evocation is illustrated by Cicero's philosophical dialogues, which are almost without exception set in country villas, at Tusculum and elsewhere, in areas that are implicitly or explicitly 'gymnasia'. These show how architectural setting meshed with patterns of behaviour in generating a set of associations. To philosophise in proper Greek fashion, one must follow a sequence of actions: first to stroll with one's friends in the walks (*ambulationes, xysti*) of a gymnasium, then to sit down either under cover (in an *exedra* or *bibliotheca*, say) or in mild weather out in the open on the grass, under a plane tree perhaps:

> Then Scipio, taking his shoes and clothes, left his *cubiculum*; and after strolling a little in the portico, greeted the arrival of Laelius and his companions . . . After greeting them, he turned to the portico and put Laelius in the middle. They took one or two turns chatting together . . . then decided to sit down together in the warmest part of the lawn, since it was winter. (*de Republica* 1.18)

The use of Cicero's own Tusculan villa is anything but casual, since it had two *gymnasia*, the Lyceum and the Academy, ideal for philosophical discourse. The Tusculans are five successive 'schools', *Graeco more*, held on five successive afternoons (1.7–8); in the morning they practice declamation; 'in the afternoon we went down to the Academy' (2.9). The naming of these *gymnasia* of course reflects Cicero's own preference for philosophical schools; and it allows a touch of variety. Cicero had often discussed the question of divination with his brother, including their recent disputation at his Tusculan villa. So in his dialogue *On Divination*: 'When we had gone to the Lyceum for a stroll (so the upper gymnasium is called)', then brother Quintus put forward his point of view (*de Divinatione* 1.8); 'when brother Quintus had finished his argument, and the stroll seemed long enough, then we sat down in the library in the Lyceum' for Marcus to refute him (2.8).

The architectural form of the gymnasium is thus valued by Cicero and his friends as the appropriate setting for the intellectual activities, and the sequence of physical movements, felt to belong to it. It may seem ironical that it is precisely in these settings that attacks are launched on *gymnasia* as

---

[49] *ad Atticum* 1.6–10.

a source of debasement and sexual corruption. But the irony is conscious: the dialogues display what is for Cicero the proper use of the gymnasium by a Roman. Even philosophy is problematic for a Roman, and Cicero is out to resolve that problem. The *de Oratore*, too, is set in a Tusculan villa, that of Crassus a generation before. The aged Catulus arrives on the second day, delighted and surprised to hear that Crassus has been holding forth on rhetoric, 'disputing as if in a school, virtually in Greek fashion' (1.13). Crassus feels a touch embarrassed to have engaged in disputation, a practice he has always avoided, and blames the younger men for egging him on (1.15). When pressure is put on him to resume, he points out the undesirability of disputing out of season. The word '*ineptus*', 'out of place', a concept which does not even exist in Greek, characterises the worst fault of the Greeks who are forever disputing, out of place and out of season, on extremely difficult and superfluous questions (1.17–18). But how, rejoins Catulus, could disputation be out of place where they now are?

Doesn't this place seem ideal, in which the very portico in which we are walking, and the palaestra, and choice of sitting areas, stir some sort of memory of *gymnasia* and Greek disputations? (1.20)

Crassus begs to differ: the *palaestra* and sitting areas and walks were thought up long ago by the Greeks for exercise and enjoyment, not for philosophical disputations. 'Gymnasia were invented many centuries before philosophers began to prattle in them' (1.21). Crassus prefers to use his gymnasium for the perfectly proper purpose of relaxation, like Scipio who used to go to the seaside and play with shells. By the end of the conversation, they agree that this disputation about disputations was as good as the disputation originally requested (1.26).

The passage illuminates the high degree of subtlety with which architectural evocation could work. The gymnasium could evoke different things for different Romans, physical exercise and relaxation for some, philosophising for others. We may suspect that more Romans reacted like Crassus, and that Cicero is trying to use the already widespread architectural form to smuggle in the less popular philosophy. Cicero is attempting to disengage the gymnasium from a set of associations which many Romans may have been only too happy to acknowledge, in the cultivation of physical well-being and enjoyment. And could they not invoke precisely the doctrine of 'proper season' deployed by Crassus? It was not right for a Roman to dispute about philosophical trivia – except in a gymnasium. By the same token, it was not right to strip and oil – except in a gymnasium. In this way, the imitation of architectural form is not a question of derivation, but of purposeful evocation of the alien. The very Greekness that adhered to the form in its Roman – and private – context of a villa enabled the Roman to act in Greek ways without compromising Roman public identity.

The physical remains are as eloquent as the written texts. They parade features that invite the viewer to see them as *gymnasiōdai*. The Villa of the Papyri is the classic example: the mood of the breathtaking double peristyle is reinforced both by the great collection of 'suitable' Greek statuary, complete with ephebes and Herms, and by the Epicurean texts found in the library.[50] The expectation to discover general libraries of Latin as well as Greek literature still buried in this villa overlooks the context evoked by Ciceronian dialogues almost precisely contemporaneous with the villa (mid first century BCE). If it did belong to a leading Roman noble, Calpurnius Piso, it was not the place for him to display his Roman credentials, but to stroll in his *xysti* accompanied by Philodemus and his other Greek *amici*.[51]

Town houses as well as country villas have their *gymnasia*. The handsome double peristyle of the House of the Faun at Pompeii (figure 4.7a, 4.7b), which occupies more than half the surface area of the house, far from acting like the peristyle of a Greek house, as the centre round which rooms can be arranged, is so large as to exclude all but a narrow file of rooms. These include a small bath suite. That, and the *exedra* carpeted with the stunning Alexander mosaic, combine to evoke a double gymnasium like Cicero's, with porticoes for *ambulatio*, lawns and *sessiones* for sitting and discussing and space for oiling, exercise and washing.[52] Somewhat later in date, the House of the Menander (figure 4.8) spells out its gymnastic associations by its symmetrical set of semicircular and rectangular *exedrae* that invite by position and decoration sitting, discussion and reading (facilitated by the nearby library). The baths in the corner of the peristyle point to gymnastic exercise and, in case there should be doubt, the painted figures of wrestlers and athletes on the walls of the *calidarium* spell out the associations (figure 4.9).

The only problem is to know where to draw the line. While we may be happy to see a gymnasium in the Villa of the Papyri, should we do so in every little Pompeian house that has a peristyle garden? Of these there are hundreds, many of them tiny plots with only a rudimentary colonnade on a single side. Naturally, the references to Greek form are least distinct in the most modest houses, and will have been so for the owners themselves. Social diffusion banalizes and thereby transforms connotations. We can say no more than that there is a continuum between the villas of the high

---

[50] Neudecker (1988), Neudecker (1998).
[51] D'Arms (1970) 57–60.   [52] Dickmann (1997), Dickmann (1999) 127–58.

Figure 4.7a View of peristyle of the House of the Faun, Pompeii (author's photo)

Figure 4.7b View of *atrium* of the House of the Faun,
Pompeii, with eponymous 'Faun' or 'Satyr' (author's photo)

Ciceronian aristocracy and modest town houses, a spectrum along which insensibly the aristocratic evocation of the Greek turns into a lifestyle that signals comfort and conformity with 'Roman' norms.[53]

While allusion to the gymnasium-form may be explicit in the private sphere, in the public it is relatively masked. The porticoes of the city of Rome are one form of transformation of the gymnasium.[54] In the mid second century BCE, starting with the Porticus Octavia of 168 and the Porticus Metelli of 146, a series of four-sided marble colonnades were erected on the Campus Martius. They were the earliest marble structures in the city, and were treated by some as an importation of foreign luxury that spread decadence.[55] Culminating in Pompey's Porticus of 55 (figure 4.10), they transformed the urban face of Rome, making the Campus Martius by Strabo's day one of the most magnificent sites in the world. The *porticus* has no single parentage, since colonnades might be found in Greek cities in a variety of contexts, including the Stoa and temple precincts. Vitruvius indeed dedicates a chapter to the *porticus* immediately between theatres and baths, and refers to the *porticus Pompeianae* (5.9.1). But though the colonnade-form in itself would not point specifically to the gymnasium, the way in which these porticoes were fitted out created a visible analogy.[56] Decorated with looted statues and paintings, they became the main art galleries and cultural centres of the city. Augustus' porticoes, the Porticus Octaviae and that of the Danaids by Palatine Apollo, provided the first public libraries. Pompey's portico boasted shaded walks planted with rows of plane trees, pleasant venues for strolling and discussion. When we take into account that this and the others on the Campus Martius stood on the edge of the traditional area for physical exercise, they provided Rome with most of the amenities that a gymnasium offered a hellenistic city. Until the fashion moved to *thermae*, porticoes offered the finest monumental building in the city.

It is the baths themselves, however, which came in the Roman mind to represent the Roman 'answer' to the gymnasium.[57] Public bath buildings mark Roman urban culture in the western cities, just as *gymnasia* mark Greek urban culture in the east.[58] The first imperial baths, those of Agrippa and subsequently of Nero on the Campus Martius, seem to have been referred to as *gymnasia*, and provided facilities for oiling and exercise;

---

[53] Zanker (1979), Wallace-Hadrill (1994) 82–7.

[54] Nielsen (1990) 36 for the link between porticoes and *gymnasia*.

[55] Velleius Paterculus 2.1.   [56] See Sauron (1987).

[57] For work on Roman baths, see DeLaine (1988), DeLaine and Johnston (1999), Manderscheid (2004).

[58] See Macdonald (1986) 111ff. for the urban picture. See Nielsen (1990) for a full catalogue.

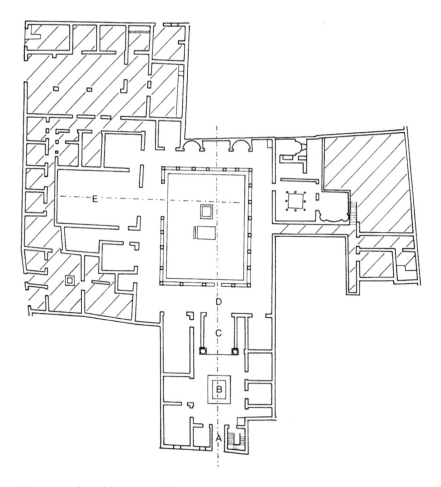

Figure 4.8 Plan of the House of the Menander, Pompeii (after Wallace-Hadrill 1994, figure 3.1)

both Agrippa and Nero celebrated their buildings with a typically Greek form of benefaction, a free distribution of oil.[59] Indeed, the flow of influence is two-way, and the characteristic transformation of *gymnasia* in the imperial period is the addition of extensive bath complexes in the Roman style, such as are strictly excluded by Vitruvius in his account of the *palaestra* (figure 4.11).[60]

The relationship between Roman baths and Greek *gymnasia* has been much discussed, with results that are less than clear.[61] Vitruvius' account

[59] See Tamm (1970).

[60] Delorme (1960) 245ff., Yegül (1992) 250–313 for the transformation in the imperial period.

[61] See Brödner (1983) 75–85, Nielsen (1990) 6–35, Yegül (1992) 6–29. See Thébert (2003) 45–74 for the Mediterranean context.

Figure 4.9 Wrestlers from the *calidarium* of the House of the Menander, Pompeii (author's photo)

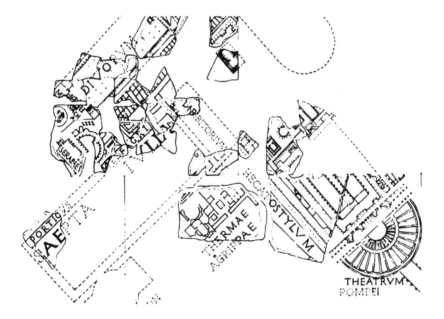

Figure 4.10 Plan of the Porticus of Pompey ('Hecatostylum') from Forma Urbis (after Gatti)

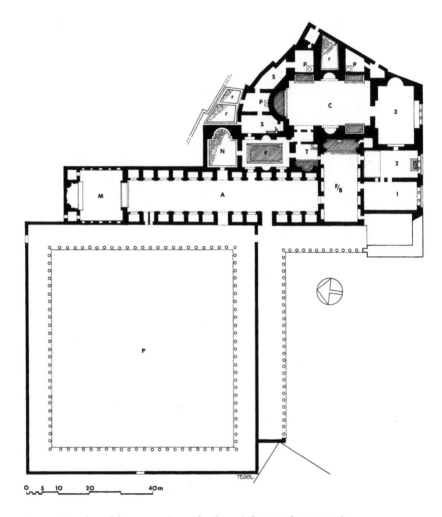

Figure 4.11 Plan of the gymnasium of Miletus (after Yegül 1992, 292)

of the contrast between baths and *palaestrae* reveals that each had similar components: porticoed areas for walking and exercising and rooms for bathing. We can polarise this contrast: the *palaestra* was a place for exercise in which washing was simple and played a subordinate role; the Roman bath was a place for bathing in which exercise played a subordinate role. But a more historical account would see it as no more than a shift of emphasis: the public bath complex is a Roman modification and development of the gymnasium, which in its turn results in significant modifications or 'romanisation' of the Greek gymnasium in the first century CE.[62]

[62] Farrington (1999).

This point of view is encouraged by the one careful investigation of a bath developing over the last two centuries BCE, the Stabian Baths at Pompeii. The first three phases distinguished by Hans Eschebach, dated to the fifth–third centuries BCE, show a large *palaestra* area to which is attached on the north-western corner a small set of washrooms (figure 4.12). These follow a well-established Greek pattern of '*Sitzbäder*' or hip-baths, recessed niches in which the bather sat to be doused with water, typical not of *gymnasia* but of *balaneia*, specific bathing institutions.[63] But in the fourth to sixth phases, belonging to the last two centuries BCE, the *palaestra* is dramatically reduced by the development along the east side of a double sequence of heated baths, with a separate set of hot and warm rooms for men and women. Eschebach's phases thus illustrate both the contrast of gymnasium and baths, and the sense in which the one is a development of the other.

The most vexed issue in all this is of the development of the hypocaust.[64] Since it was this technological feature, coupled with techniques of concrete construction, that allowed the elaboration of the Roman bath into its familiar imperial form, it is convenient if we can call it a Roman invention, and contrast it with the much more restricted hip-baths of the Greeks. This is encouraged by the attribution by the sources of 'suspended' baths to Sergius Orata, who made a large profit in the period preceding the Social War (i.e. early first century BCE) by developing both heated baths and heated oyster beds at Baiae. But the neatness of this picture was spoilt by the discovery of rudimentary hypocaust systems in third-century baths at Gortys in Crete, and in the late-second-century phase of the bath at Olympia. Recent excavations at Fregellae have shown that this Latin colony also had a public bath with hypocaust heating at the time of its destruction in 125 BCE.[65] Orata can no longer be said to have 'invented' the hypocaust, and the possibility arises that the development is a gradual Mediterranean-wide evolution, with the cities of Sicily and South Italy playing an important mediating role.[66]

Roman baths thus emerge not as a contrast to, but an evolution from, Greek *gymnasia*. Moreover, the Romans valued and indeed advertised the associations with Greek gymnastics. The neatest illustration of this is the *laconicum*. It is the one element which Vitruvius prescribes for both the Roman baths and the Greek *palaestra*. In fact it represents a temporary

---

[63] See Ginouvès (1962) for the distinction; Hoffmann (1999).
[64] Brödner (1983) 6–23, Nielsen (1990) 14–24, Yegül (1992) 48–66.   [65] Thébert (2003) 82–85.
[66] DeLaine (1990); Nielsen (1990) 25–37; Nielsen (1985) questions Eschebach's dating of the phases of the Stabian baths and supports Orata's originality. Thébert (2003) 73–4 warns against overestimating the role of Campania.

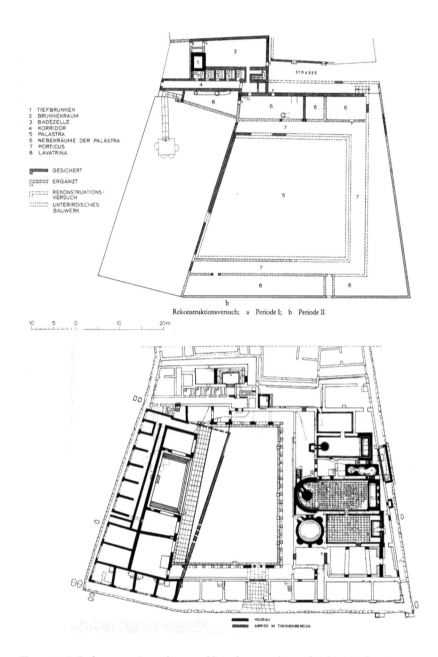

1 TIEFBRUNNEN
2 BRUNNENRAUM
3 BADEZELLE
4 KORRIDOR
5 PALASTRA
6 NEBENRÄUME DER PALASTRA
7 PORTICUS
8 LAVATRINA

GESICHERT

ERGÄNZT

REKONSTRUKTIONS-
VERSUCH

UNTERIRDISCHES
BAUWERK

Rekonstruktionsversuch;   a   Periode I;   b   Periode II

NEUBAU
ABRISS IM THERMENBEREICH

Figure 4.12 Early gymnasium phase, and late *thermae* phase of Stabian Baths at Pompeii (after Eschebach 1979)

phase in bathing fashion, belonging particularly to the last two centuries BCE. There is remarkably little evidence for it from the Greek side, whether archaeologically for the characteristic circular domed room which is found in Roman contexts, or epigraphically for the word '*lakōnikon*' (the Greek word attested is *pyratērion*).[67] But it is clear that it was thought of as representing an especially Spartan mode of bathing, a point most explicit in Strabo's account of a Lusitanian tribe, 'who are said to behave in Laconian fashion, using double oilings and hot rooms heated by stones, washing in cold water and eating pure and simple diets' (3.3.6). The *laconicum*, that is to say, is part of a regime of oiling, sweating in a hot dry space, then washing in cold water, that was thought of as tough and 'Spartan' like their diet.[68]

Whether or not the regime actually was Spartan, its reputation as such gave it considerable *cachet*. The label itself is no neutral technical term, but an attempt to capture prestige by association. It was paraded in public dedications. The one building-inscription from the Stabian baths at Pompeii records the duumviri, probably from the early years of the Sullan colony, dedicating a *laconicum* and *destrictarium* – the latter too a rare word, presumably for the oiling practices linked with the sweating (*Corpus Inscriptionum Latinarum* X 829). Ironically, within a century fashion had moved on, and the *laconicum* was converted into a cold dip. Agrippa, too, labelled his baths in Rome (or part of them) as a *laconicum*, according to Dio, who by the Severan period needs to explain that 'he called the gymnasium Laconic because in those days the Lacedaemonians had the best reputation for exercising naked and oiling' (53.27.1).

Whatever the misgivings about Greek gymnastics, Romans were not embarrassed to advertise their imitation. Even Cicero had a *laconicum* made by his architect Cyrus, which he was anxious for Atticus to keep an eye on (*ad Atticum* 4.10.2). And it is likely that in other respects, too, they thought of their baths as an attempt to capture something Greek. We may like to construct a contrast between the austerity of the Greeks and the luxurious indulgence of Roman bathing practice; but the Romans thought of the luxury, too, as something they were imitating from the Greeks. Luxury was a focus of contemporary Greek moralisation about *gymnasia*. Posidonius speaks of the luxury of second-century Seleucid Syria:

[67] See Delorme (1960) 312ff., Nielsen (1990) 158–9, Ginouvès (1998) 104.

[68] Cartledge and Spawforth (1989) 129–35 make no mention of it, but do discuss the transformation of bathing in Sparta under Roman influence. See now Bürge (2001).

All the people of Syria, because of the great plenty which their land afforded were free from worry about the basics of life, and met frequently to feast, using the gymnasia as baths in which they anointed themselves with expensive oils and perfumes.[69]

Distributions of scented oil were a feature of the extravaganzas put on by Antiochus IV, and the users of *gymnasia* were treated on successive days to oil scented with saffron, cinnamon, nard, fenugreek, marjoram and orris, served in golden bowls.[70] The *gymnasia* of the hellenistic world offered the Romans not one model, but a range of possibilities from 'Spartan austerity' to 'Asian luxury'. The Roman baths seek to imitate and outdo all possibilities.

Medicinal considerations played an important part, and here too it was Greek knowledge which Romans turned to their own uses.[71] The thermal springs at Baiae were the magnet that from the beginning of the second century drew the Romans to the Bay of Naples, and provided the spur to innovation in bath construction.[72] It seems likely that Sergius Orata's *suspensurae* involved using the naturally hot vapours of the area to create a heated room.[73] The effect was very similar to that of the *laconicum*, and both were put to medicinal use: Celsus notes the medicinal use of dry (as of wet) heat, as in the *laconicum* 'and certain natural sweating-baths, in which the hot vapour issuing from the ground is closed in, as we find in the myrtle groves above Baiae', and adds that sunshine and exercise achieve the same effect (*de Medicina* ii.17.1). The use of hot sweating was particularly promoted by the Greek doctor Asclepiades of Bithynia, who enjoyed high vogue in Rome in the first part of the first century.[74] The elder Pliny, who regards Asclepiades as a charlatan who exploited his skill in the lecture-hall to make vast profits, says that it was no wonder that people preferred the 'hanging' baths he recommended to the previous medical fashion of smothering sufferers in clothes (*Natural History* 26.8).

The power of medical opinion in shaping bathing fashion, and consequently architectural form, should not be underestimated. It was the medical advice of a certain Dr Russell of Lewes in 1753 to take seawater (internally) at the unknown village of Brighthelmstone that led to the development of Brighton (as it was renamed) and the English seaside resorts.[75] Asclepiades' advocacy of the hot cure suffered a dramatic reversal when Antonius Musa

---

[69] Posidonius F62 (Edelstein and Kidd), cited by Athenaeus, *Deipnosophistae* 5.210f = 12.527e.

[70] Polybius, *Histories* 30.26.1–3, cited by Athenaeus, *Deipnosophistae* 5.195c–d. Cf. Polybius 26.1.12–14 for an anecdote of Antiochus at the public baths, also related by Ptolemy VIII in his *Memoirs*, Athenaeus 10.438.

[71] Fagan (1999) 85–103, Jackson (1999).   [72] D'Arms (1970) 139–42.

[73] Nielsen (1985), Nielsen (1990) 20–2.   [74] Rawson (1985) 170–7, Rawson (1991a) 427–43.

[75] Walton (1983).

saved the life of Augustus in 23 BCE by using cold baths in place of hot. Cold water cures became the vogue, and Horace speaks of deserting the myrtle groves and sulphur springs of Baiae for Clusium, Gabii and cold springs (*Epistles* 1.15.2–11). The precipitous collapse in fashion of the *laconicum* (and the conversion of the Stabian Baths) were surely the direct result of Musa's success. The sequence of *frigidarium–tepidarium–calidarium* that established itself as the predictable formula of baths across the empire had the advantage of full medical flexibility. The sufferer could, as Celsus recommends, try out the temperatures gradually, feeling his temples to see if he was able to take the heat; and try cold regimes or hot regimes to suit his fitness (*de Medicina* 2.17.2). Baths pandered to medical neurosis, and allowed the Roman to indulge in 'the care of the self'.[76]

What emerges, then, is a highly complex interaction of cultures. Roman baths drew on Greek inspiration in a variety of ways. There was the 'pure' form of the gymnasium which presents itself as a high cultural ideal: Sparta may have seemed to offer the paradigm. But there were 'contaminated' forms too: Asiatic or South Italian *gymnasia*, more tempting in their luxury, and less anxious to maintain the distinction between *gymnasia* and baths. *Balaneia* themselves offered models, as a rudimentary underfloor heating system emerged. South Italian cities like Pompeii, which were not Greek in their social structures and institutions, and yet were in close enough contact with Greek cities like Naples to be constantly adapting Greek forms, offered important paradigms for transference. At the same time, Roman reactions were formed of numerous and conflicting elements: admiration for high cultural ideals, and eagerness to measure up to them; suspicion of alien social structures and different *mores*; desire for luxury and the cult of leisure that marked success; anxiety about physical well-being and susceptibility to impressive medical theorising. New forms emerge from this unpredictable cocktail of influences and reactions within a specific geographical and historical context, in which the geographical proximity of the hot springs of Baiae, the potential of the local sand, pozzolana, to make water-resistant concrete, and the availability thanks to rapid imperial expansion of massive sums of money for investment in villas in Campania and elsewhere are all significant factors.

The Greek gymnasium thus proves to have been, far from a form that was as Vitruvius claims *non Italicae consuetudinis*, one of the most potent sources of inspiration in the development of late republican architecture. Why, then, is Vitruvius so anxious to establish a distance between the two?

---

[76] Foucault (1986).

The answer lies in the consistent thread of Roman moralisation that rejects Greek *gymnasia* as a major threat to Roman morality.[77]

Already in the late third century, Scipio Africanus was criticised on the eve of his invasion of Africa because, far from training the troops in preparation for their assault, he was allowing them to go soft on the urban enticements of Greek Sicily. Scipio himself set the worst example by attending the gymnasium in Syracuse, and by strolling there in a Greek cloak and Greek sandals (*crepidae*) reading Greek books, and giving his attention to wrestling instead of war (Livy 29.19.12, cf. Valerius Maximus 3.6.1). As we have seen (ch. 1), dress played a central role in defining Roman identity. But the central focus of the Scipio episode is not the wearing of Greek clothes, but the context in which he does so, of the gymnasium.

Across three centuries, Romans persist in identifying the gymnasium as a core feature of Greek culture, and treating it with hostility or suspicion, or at least distance, as being incompatible with Roman ways: *gymnasia* are a weakness of the little Greeks, 'gymnasiis indulgent Graeculi', is Trajan's condescending response when Pliny outlines the problems caused by an overambitious reconstruction of the gymnasium at Nicaea (*Letters* 10.40). Yet hostility is mixed with fascination. This ambivalence does not allow itself to be resolved as a chronological progression: we cannot chart a movement from hostility and rejection through acceptance to enthusiasm. Here, as in many other spheres, there is remarkably little development in Roman moralisation, and viewpoints voiced by Cato in the early second century BCE are still endorsed in the late first century CE. Rather there is a refinement and modification of positions as what has once been identified as 'un-Roman' is negotiated, and the limits of its acceptability within Roman contexts are explored and tested.

Roman anxieties about the gymnasium focused on its physical side: on nakedness, oiling, and the attitudes to sexuality supposedly bound up in these activities. Cicero twice draws the link between *gymnasia* and pederasty in his philosophical dialogues, despite, as we have seen, giving them consciously 'gymnastic' settings. In a fragment of the *de Republica* Scipio Aemilianus is discussing a traditional Roman ban on adolescents stripping:

So far back do the foundations of modesty go. Yet how absurd is the exercise of young men in gymnasia! How trivial the military training of 'ephebes'! How free and easy are gropings and passions! Forget about the Elis or Thebes, where there is free permissive licence for lust in the love of freeborn men. Take Sparta, where they allow anything in the love of young men except the sexual act. How narrow is the

---

[77] See the discussion of Hallett (2005b) 68–87.

line they draw in banning intercourse: embraces and sleeping together are allowed, but there must be 'cloaks between breasts'. (*de Republica* 4.4.4)

By a familiar rhetorical trick, Cicero suggests the prevalence of pederasty in *gymnasia* despite conceding that it was only exceptionally permitted. It is likely enough that the majority of *gymnasia* had detailed regulations, like those that have survived from Beroea in Macedonia, where undesirables were excluded under penalty of a considerable fine:

No one may enter the gymnasium and take off his clothes if he is a slave, a freedman, or the son of a slave or freeman, if he has not been to wrestling school, if he is a pederast, or has practised a trade in the market place, or is drunk, or mad.[78]

Cicero's (or Scipio's) protests mean neither that Romans did not in fact widely practise pederasty themselves, nor that all Greeks were willing to associate sexual licence with the gymnasium. What is significant is that the Romans represented the gymnasium as incompatible with supposed traditional morality.[79]

Similarly in the *Tusculan Disputations* Cicero elaborates a contrast between Greek philosophy and Roman morality:

What is this passion for 'friendship'? Why do none of them love an ugly young man or a handsome old one? This is a practice which seems to me to have started in the *gymnasia* of the Greeks, in which this sort of love is freely permitted. Ennius put it well:

> Flagitii principium est nudare [inter] cives corpora.
> The beginning of outrage is for citizens to strip.
> [*Tusculan Disputations* 4.70]

We cannot tell whether the Ennian line was in fact an expression of Roman morality or was simply a translation of a line of Greek drama: but Cicero likes to represent Ennius as the authentic voice of Roman tradition.

Disapproval of nudity is a significant factor in the Roman response to the gymnasium. Cicero argues (*de Officiis* 1.126–9) that physical modesty, *verecundia*, is a Roman tradition which follows nature, which hides away the 'obscene' parts of the body, and asserts in evidence of Roman behaviour that by Roman tradition (*nostro more*), parents do not bathe with their sons after puberty, nor fathers-in-law with sons-in-law. The same *mos* is attributed by Plutarch to the elder Cato, and the biographer goes on to comment that the gymnasium had brought about a change:

---

[78] Trans. Austin (1981) 203ff.   [79] MacMullen (1991), Hallett (2005b) 71–6.

This seems to have been the general custom among the Romans, and even fathers-in-law avoided bathing with sons-in-law, because they were ashamed to show themselves naked. In later times, however, the Romans adopted from the Greeks the practice of stripping in front of other men, and they in turn taught the Greeks to strip even in the presence of women. (Plutarch, *Cato the Elder* 21)

The retrospective invention of tradition seems to be at work. Plutarch's inference seems extremely perilous: a convention that fathers- and sons-in-law should not bathe together, far from pointing to a general avoidance of nudity, might argue that outside the case of close family links naked bathing together was normal. By Cicero's day, let alone by Plutarch's a century later, naked bathing in public baths at Rome was quite normal – so in the *pro Caelio* Cicero assumes that men in clothes and shoes would be excluded from the baths by the attendant.[80] As often, when the Romans present us with an 'authentic' Roman tradition, we fall for it too readily.[81] But for our understanding of attitudes to *gymnasia*, the important point is that the Romans of Cicero's age had indeed persuaded themselves that nudity was a regrettable novelty at Rome, and attributed it to the influence of the gymnasium.

By the early empire the antithesis had established itself as a commonplace that Roman exercise was a tough form of military training that enhanced virility, while the Greek *gymnasia* were a form of soft indulgence that led to effeminacy. On these grounds Seneca excludes gymnastic exercise from the elements of a liberal education, linking it to perfume, cookery and the service of pleasure, and contrasting it with traditional javelin-throwing and riding (*Moral Letters* 114). The elder Pliny castigates the use of oil in *gymnasia* as a luxury invented by 'those parents of all vices, the Greeks' (*Natural History* xv.19). Lucan depicts Caesar belittling Pompey's troops before Pharsalus as 'youth picked from Greek *gymnasia*, idle with the pursuit of the *palaestra* and hardly capable of bearing arms' (*Pharsalia* 7.270–2). Tacitus reports the objections to the introduction of a Greek-style competitive festival by Nero: traditional ways were being overthrown by imported wantonness, 'and the youth was degenerating with foreign pursuits, by practising *gymnasia* and leisure and disgraceful loves' (*Annals* 14.20). That is only one side of the debate which Tacitus reports: the majority were not convinced that wantonness and corruption would result from the festival, and the historian implies that they were right. Yet, for the purposes of the rhetoric of protest, the close associations of *gymnasia*, pederasty, foreign corruption and effeminacy persist.

---

[80] Nielsen (1990) 140f.   [81] Zanker (1988) 5–8 takes it literally, cf. Gruen (1992) 75.

The very incoherence of the Roman protest against *gymnasia*, this rejection of aspects like nudity, pederasty and luxury which in practice they embraced, betrays a deeper set of issues that concern identity. What made the gymnasium a challenge to Roman identity was the core role it played in the hellenistic world in Greek constructions of their own identity. The gymnasium is a conspicuous feature of the Greek urban landscape. Pausanias could question whether Panopeus in Phocis deserved the name of a *polis* when it lacked a gymnasium and other urban amenities: *gymnasia* are indeed attested in hundreds of hellenised cities, both archaeologically and in the inscriptions which reveal them as a major focus for benefactions.[82] They are for us, and were for the Greeks, a major index of the spread of hellenism, as was dramatically illustrated by the discovery at Ai-Khanoum, on the banks of the Oxus in Afghanistan, of a gymnasium complete with Greek inscriptions of a collection of maxims brought from Delphi.[83] The gymnasium was treated as the crucial marker of the arrival of hellenism in non-Greek areas, whether Commagene, Egypt, or Judaea. The educated Greeks of Ptolemaic Egypt described themselves as 'those from the gymnasium'.[84]

The gymnasium is so loaded with significance because it is the focus of so much that was held to distinguish Greek and barbarian. This is true even of its etymological sense as a place of nakedness, of stripping and oiling and exercise. Awareness that the Greeks are set apart from barbarians by the pride in nakedness is already explicit in Herodotus (2.91). Greek art, in which the athlete or hero in nakedness reaches his ideal form, played an important role in parading this awareness: it incorporated, in its high artistic expressions male beauty and prowess, cultural assumptions which were alien to a barbarian who had no experience of the gymnasium. Greek art thus confronts the viewer with a challenge: to share the ideals on which it is premised, or to be excluded from appreciation.[85]

The gymnasium did not merely exemplify cultural ideals: it transmitted them. It was the place of *paideia*, where not only athletic but intellectual and cultural skills were taught and exercised.[86] *Paideia* was an essential part of Greek self-definition. The link with citizenship was more than casual, since many cities required young men to pass, as at Athens, through the *ephebeia* which prepared them for military service and the duties of the citizen. The gymnasium was thus implicated in the process which made and

---

[82] Delorme (1960), and Delorme (1986).   [83] Robert (1968), Colledge (1987), Veuve (1987).

[84] Jones (1940) 220–6, Walbank (1981) 60–71.

[85] Hallett (2005b) 5–19 for the considerable debate on the symbolism of Greek nudity; see above pp. 51–4.

[86] Marrou (1956) (pt. 2 ch.1).

marked a citizen. The structural contrast with the making and marking of the Roman citizen is significant. In Greek cities, citizenship was normally acquired by right of birth, and outside honorific circumstances could rarely be acquired. A citizenship acquired by birth is marked by upbringing and the socialisation ritual of the *ephebeia*. Roman citizenship was a legal status regularly extended to freed slaves and foreigners. There is no *rite de passage* comparable to the *ephebeia*.

The gymnasium also had a significance in transmitting hellenism to outsiders as well as to born citizens, and it was this that could raise the most acute problems for other cultures. Here the story of accommodation and tensions between Judaism and hellenism offers a valuable parallel. The disputed role of the gymnasium is most powerfully dramatised in the account of the second-century BCE revolt of the Maccabees against Antiochus IV of Syria. According to this (probably fictionalised) account, the high priest Jason had bargained with Antiochus to hellenise the Jews, abolishing their ancestral ways:

He lost no time in establishing a sports stadium [i.e. a *palaestra*] at the foot of the citadel itself, and he made the most outstanding of the young men assume the Greek athlete's hat [*petasos*]. So Hellenism reached a high point with the introduction of foreign customs through the boundless wickedness of the impious Jason, no true high priest. As a result, the priests no longer had any enthusiasm for their duties at the altar, but despised the temple and neglected the sacrifices; and in defiance of the law, they eagerly contributed to the expenses of the wrestling school whenever the opening gong called them. They placed no value on their hereditary dignities, but cared above everything for hellenic honours. (II *Maccabees* 4.12–15)

However distorted, this passage set out clearly the terms of the cultural antithesis. Judaism consists in ancestral tradition, observation of the law and religious practice. Hellenism consists of a set of cultural practices centred on the gymnasium. Hellenism did not of itself demand the abandonment of Jewish ancestral ways, and many Jews, notably in Alexandria, vigorously contested their right to participate in the gymnasium. Yet it is precisely because the gymnasium is so central in the construction of a cultural identity that it may present itself as a challenge to existing identity.[87]

Both Greek *gymnasia* and Roman baths were about constructing social identities. Yet they constructed society differently. The gymnasium trained and marked the citizen as Greek. Roman baths trained nobody, but made a lot of difference: they made the difference between work and leisure;

---

[87] See Harris (1976) 29ff., Hengel (1980) 55ff., Millar (1987), Gruen (1998) 1–40.

between suffering and health; and perhaps above all between the smelly and unwashed barbarian or rustic, and the sweet-smelling, urbane and polished citizen (*lautus*, washed, is the word which summons up the essence of elegance, taste and civilised polish). To allow the gymnasium to define Roman civic identity as in the hellenic world would run up against other core institutions, legal and educational, by which citizenship was defined. Vitruvius' careful distinction of *balineae* and *palaestra* was an important alibi: even in defining baths as not-*gymnasia* it opened the doors to the incorporation of the gymnasium within Roman structures. One of the first buildings created by the Augustan regime were Agrippa's baths, the first in the series of imperial *thermae* to dominate the landscape of the imperial city. Baths could become a marker of Roman civilisation at the moment that it could be shown that they were not a marker of Greek culture at Rome.

Roman moralisation characterised the gymnasium as making men soft, effeminate and sexually depraved. But this rhetoric did not act as a filter to purify the gymnasium of its unacceptable elements – indeed, the rhetoric which Christian polemic levelled against the depravities of the baths was the lineal descendant of pagan Roman rhetoric against *gymnasia*.[88] On the contrary, it pointed to a source of power, power which could be extricated from its original contexts and appropriated. The baths purveyed sensuous pleasure: the cultivation of the body, its health, beauty and comfort. Peripheral services abounded, from prostitutes to hair-pluckers.[89] Pleasures generate power. Baths attracted, on a daily basis, crowds of extraordinary size. That is visible archaeologically in the stupendous magnificence of the public baths constructed by a series of emperors in Rome. Vitruvius' simple observation that the size of baths must be proportional to the number of users (5.10.4) means that gigantic constructions like the baths of Caracalla and Diocletian need to be translated not only into man-hours of labour, as a measure of the mobilisation of resources,[90] but into a headcount of users. Such *thermae* acted as a monumental display of the power of the emperors who built them; that power was advertised by the physical mass, by the feats of architecture, and by the capacity to pull crowds. If baths, through purveying pleasure, could display power, whether of the villa-owner, or the provincial city magistrate, or of the Roman emperor, then it was successful as a construction of a social identity that was unmistakably Roman. In civilisation, power and pleasure advance hand in hand, as Agricola taught the Britons:

[88] Nielsen (1990) 147.   [89] Nielsen (1990) 144ff., Fagan (1999) 75ff.   [90] DeLaine (1997).

Hence respect also spread for our dress and the toga became common; and by a gradual spread, they came to be softened by the vices – porticoes, baths and elegant parties. But what the inexperienced called humanity was in truth an instrument of their enslavement.[91]

Private space: the town house

Vitruvius approaches private buildings on the same principles that he uses for public buildings. He sees buildings as determined by underlying social practices, which lead to basic differences between the Greek and Roman versions, and the role of the architect as being the imposition of rational disposition and symmetry. He distinguishes craftsmanship, which reflects credit on the builder, magnificence, which reflects on the pocket of the patron, and the proportion and symmetry, which reflect on the architect (6.8.9–10). The vital challenge, even for the amateur architect, is to introduce the theoretical principles, *ratiocinationes et commensus symmetriarum* (6 *preface* 7). The 'rationalisation' of the house by the introduction of principles of proportion and symmetry lies at the heart of his enterprise, and it should occasion no surprise if surviving houses do not always conform to his rules.

What, for Vitruvius, sets apart the Roman from the Greek house? It is helpful to start by looking at his prescription for the Greek house for, though it may not be a useful guide for understanding Greek houses, it constitutes a mirror image of what the Roman house was not supposed to be. 'Because the Greeks do not use *atria*, they do not build them', it opens.[92] That establishes at the outset that the house is driven by social usage, and it instantly turns the *atrium*, and the social practices that adhere to it, because it is not-Greek, into a symbol of the Roman. What are Greek practices, for should these not prove the principle of the not-Roman? One passes directly from the entrance-passageway (*thyroron*) into a peristyle, with colonnades on three sides, including the south-facing *pastas* or *prostas*; and inside these colonnades are the great *oeci* where the *matres familiarum* do their spinning, and the slave family resides. This part of the house is called the *gynaeconitis* (7.1–2). Vitruvius has moved us straight into the territory which every Roman knew was different from their own practice, the land of women's quarters. In doing so, he constructs a somewhat quaint Greek house, for the

---

[91] Tacitus, *Agricola* 21 (cf. ch.1, n.112): 'Inde etiam habitus nostri honor et frequens toga; paulatimque discessum ad delenimenta vitiorum, porticus et balinea et conviviorum elegantiam. Idque apud imperitos humanitas vocabatur, cum pars servitutis esset.'

[92] 6.7.1: 'Atriis Graeci quia non utuntur neque aedificant.'

seclusion of women demands that they be remote from the front entrance, not immediately by it and acting as a passageway through to the men's quarters.

Adjoining his *gynaeconitis*, he sets a finer peristyle, with colonnades on four sides, including one side more elevated than the others in the 'Rhodiac' style. Here are fine rooms with plasterwork and stucco and inlaid ceilings, and a careful arrangement of rooms on each side: on the north aspect, 'Cyzicene' *triclinia* and *pinacothecae* (picture-galleries); on the east aspect libraries; on the west aspect *exedrae*; on the south aspect, large *oeci* with wide doors that can fit four sets of sittings and entertainers. These are the men's quarters, *andronitis*, where men are entertained alone: 'for it is not a practice under their *mores* for *matres familiarum* to lie down to dinner with men' (6.3–4).

Here again, Vitruvius' account is driven by a Roman construction of the fundamental contrast of Greek and Roman *mores*.[93] It has proved notoriously difficult to reconcile with surviving archaeological evidence, and some have dismissed Vitruvius' account as pure fiction.[94] Certainly the pattern familiar from sites like Olynthos is of the *andron* as a dining room which can be reached by male visitors from the front door without passing into the heart of the house, set aside for family and female activity (figure 4.13).[95] This is very different from setting aside a whole peristyle, complete with libraries and picture galleries, for the men. But this is exactly the pattern that has been found at Eretria and a number of other sites with double-courtyard houses, where the front lobby leads alternatively to a grand peristyle court, with well-decorated reception rooms, often with mosaic floors, and dining rooms specially designed for a number of couch settings, and on the other side to a simpler courtyard around which the family and service rooms are arranged (figure 4.14).[96] As more attention is paid to Greek domestic architecture, we may expect further examples to emerge, though it is clear that there was a great variety of spatial arrangements, both regionally and chronologically.[97]

But the most striking observation is that Vitruvius' prescriptions, whatever their relation to Greek houses, reflect patterns observable in Italic houses of the second century BCE.[98] Most strikingly, the house of the Faun at Pompeii (figure 4.7) with its double *atria* can be read, as it was by Maiuri, as a

---

[93] Milnor (2005) 94–139.   [94] Kreeb (1985), Raeder 1988 ('eine Fiktion').

[95] Nevett (1999) 68–74.   [96] Reber (1988), Nevett (1999) 107–23.

[97] Fentress (1998) suggests that the second-century BCE villa of Contrada Mirabile near Lilybaeum in Sicily fits Vitruvius' prescription; if so, it lacks the crucial 'men's quarters'.

[98] Pesando (1987) 175–97.

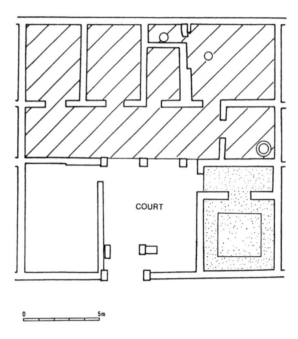

Figure 4.13 Example of house plan from Olynthos (after Wallace-Hadrill 1994, figure 1)

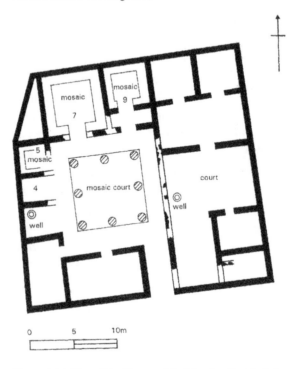

Figure 4.14 Plan of the House of the Mosaics, Eretria (after Nevett 1999, figure 32)

Vitruvian Greek house, with the *hospitalia* in a separate quarter in the secondary *atrium*, linked by *mesauloe* (defined by Vitruvius as corridors between halls); other second-century houses with double *atria*, like those of the Labyrinth and the Centenary, follow this pattern.[99] Indeed, the rooms of the Greek 'men's quarters', and the aspects he prescribes, are just those proposed for the Roman house, with its winter *triclinia* looking south to catch the sun, its libraries east to catch morning light and to avoid the wet winds which cause book-rot, and its *pinacothecae* north to avoid sunlight and fading (4.1–2).

On this showing, Vitruvius has signally failed to distance the Greek house from the Roman. But that is surely the point. The Roman house is imagined in numerous respects as drawing by imitation on the Greek house, with its parade of names like *oecus, exedra, bibliotheca, pinacotheca*, even *peristylon*. It becomes necessary to construct, even if none such existed, a hypothetical 'Greek house' from which these elements are derived. Its foreignness and distance are guaranteed by underlining a (partly misapprehended) pattern of male/female separation. In reality, the separation may be closer to that of the Roman house: between a less accessible area of low status where slaves and women operate, and a high-status peristyle suitable for reception of guests, with elegant decoration and impressive Greek-named rooms.

In the light of this account of the Greek house, we may return to Vitruvius' account of the Roman house (6.3–5), and ask what he does to establish its Roman identity and to reconcile that with its Greek elements.[100] The organisation of the section is careful. The separate parts of the house are introduced in a deliberate sequence. We start with the quintessentially Roman, the *atrium* (which he also terms *cava aedium*, the 'hollow' of the house), and its associated structures, the *alae, tablinum, fauces* and *compluvium* (3.1–6).[101] Then we move away to rooms in which the names and discussion indicate a progressive degree of foreignness: *peristylia* (in the Doric fashion, for instance), *triclinia* (Roman enough, but the word was of Greek derivation), *oeci* and *exedrae*, and *pinacothecae* (3.8); next some varieties of *oeci*, the labels of which point more specifically to foreign 'origin', Corinthian and Egyptian (3.9); and finally, with an explicit comment that this, too, is not *Italicae consuetudinis*, the Cyzicene *oecus* (3.10).

The Roman-ness of the Roman house is thus concentrated in its *atrium*. This is the first thing you see when you stand at the door; and it is the first thing you talk about as an architect. There is a further contrast in Vitruvius'

---

[99] Pesando (1987) 181.   [100] See Hales (2003) 25–39.   [101] Gros (2001) 27–9.

treatment. His rules for the *atrium* and its surrounds bristle with exact proportions and measurements, with slightly different rules, for instance, depending on whether the *atrium* has a length of 30–40, 40–50, 50–60, 60–80, or 80–100 feet (4). The proportions of the 'Greek' rooms are at best sketchy, and the differences between the *oeci* lie rather in design. But this is because he is doing different things. With the 'imported' rooms what is needed is definition of the form: just what is the distinction between Corinthian, Egyptian and Cyzicene? The Roman rooms need no definition, but they do need 'rationalisation' – that is, reduction to a system of rational proportions based on the laws of symmetry. Because Vitruvius spells out these rules, it is generally assumed that they were always there.[102] It might be that, as with the rules for the Roman theatre, they represent his own attempt to add authority to Roman *consuetudo* by giving it *ratio*.

How compromised is the identity of the Roman house by its Greek rooms? Not at all, it would seem. Not only does Vitruvius allow rooms of non-Italic usage, and use Greek rules of symmetry to bring proportion to Roman spaces, but we may observe with surprise that two of the five varieties of *atrium* are apparently Greek, the Corinthian and the tetrastyle (3.1). If the Greeks built no *atria*, how could there be a Corinthian one?[103] The problem seems not to occur to him. But we may note that an effect of opening his list of five *atrium* types with Tuscanic and Corinthian is to establish a form of correspondence with the types or 'orders' of architecture as he has defined them in book four: Doric, Ionic, Corinthian (4.1–6) and Tuscanic (4.7). Paradoxically, the presence of a Greek variant helps to lend a 'canonical' status to his analysis of the *atrium* (which has been taken for granted ever since). 'Tuscanic' is the guarantee of Roman-ness, or, as he puts it, *Italica consuetudo*.

What makes this sense of identity so robust is the perceived presence of social custom that informs it. Vitruvius' discussion of the link between social rank and the architecture of the house is one of his most famous (6.5). He picks up the distinction of public (*communia*) and private (*privata*) which structures the division of books five and six (6 *preface* 7). But the house itself is divided into *privata*, the territory of the *pater familias*, where no guest may approach uninvited, and *communia*, to which the public has free access, '*vestibula, cava aedium, peristylia*' and the like. It is these public spaces which are distinctive of men of high rank; the members of the public themselves (*communi fortuna*) will have no need of magnificent *vestibula*, *tabulina* and *atria*; but noblemen, who in the execution of public office must

---

[102] See Hallier (1989) for the difficulties.
[103] See Pesando (1997) 249–63 on Greek elements in second-century BCE Pompeian *atria*.

serve the citizens, need *vestibula* that are lofty and regal, the most ample *atria* and peristyles, woods, walks, libraries and basilicas on the scale of public buildings.[104]

Although the overlap of private/public with Greek/Roman is not complete (peristyles and libraries are public), it is enough to establish a firm correlation between the *consuetudo* of Roman social life and the office-holding class, and the architectural features that make the house most Roman. Indeed, these features, far from being an Italic universal, are represented as superfluous to men of 'common fortune'; even if they are extended to some below the top rank, to money-lenders, *publicani*, advocates and *forenses*, these are all, more or less explicitly, involved in public life and the forum, the world *foris*, outside the doors. Activity outside brings outsiders inside, and makes the domestic sphere suitable for the architect with his symmetries. The features which guarantee the sense of the Roman are those which stand for the sense of rank and social order. Consequently, if Greek features like peristyles also enhance that sense of rank, they enhance rather than compromise the 'Roman-ness' of the house.

Vitruvius' presentation of the house, with all its contradictions and implausibilities, gives us a powerful model for interpreting the transformation of Roman domestic architecture. If we had to rely on the archaeological material on its own, we might only see a progressive 'hellenisation'.[105] The traditional Italic house built round an *atrium* is modified throughout the last two centuries BCE by the addition of peristyles and associated Greek room-types, by the use of columns, by room decoration in marbles, painted plaster and mosaics, and further embellishment through statuary, that are either directly imported from the east, or made to look as if they were. By the first century CE these Greek-derived forms have become the dominant idiom, and the original 'Roman' elements start to slip away; the *atrium* becomes superfluous, and the house is fully 'hellenised'. But this picture confuses cultural myths with realities. What is 'borrowed' is transformed, and the 'hellenised' Roman house emerges at the end of its development no less distinctive and powerful as an expression of Roman identity.

The 'imitation' of Greek idiom is a historical phase, reaching its climax in the late republic and under Augustus. Innovation continues thereafter, in its own developing idiom of vaults and domes and volumes of space sculpted by curvilinear design in which the distinction of Greek and Roman becomes meaningless. The sheer rarity of Vitruvian *atria* in the provincial context,

---

[104] Wallace-Hadrill (1994) 10–14, Coarelli (1996c) 344–59.
[105] So, e.g., Pesando (1997b), Dickmann (1999). See further Wallace-Hadrill (1997b).

including South Gaul, Spain and North Africa, makes it clear that this feature was no longer seen as definitive of Roman identity.[106] Curiously enough, it is in Greece and Asia Minor that a vestigial '*atrium*' seems to serve in particularly 'Romanised' contexts as a marker of a partially Roman identity.[107] There is still a reciprocity between public and private, even if Vitruvian rules cease to apply: sequences of spaces, axial vistas, large reception rooms with lavish decoration in dominant positions, and many other features emerging in the last two centuries BCE generated a recognizably 'Roman' set of formulae. What has emerged from the process of cultural borrowing is not a Greco-Roman house, nor a hellenised house, but a house with new powers to impose a Roman order on the environment. Vitruvius' contribution is not to define the rules of Roman-ness, but to create a flexible structure within which the Roman can embrace innovations perceived initially to be Greek.[108]

Private space: the country villa[109]

The Roman villa might seem to us one of the most important contributions of the Romans to architectural history.[110] Certainly, villas are one of the dominant features of the landscape of 'romanisation' empire-wide, a hallmark of Roman power-relations and the control of terrain through rich landowners. Nor is there any suggestion here of Roman indebtedness to Greek models: the pursuit of Greek antecedents for the villa is remarkably frustrating.[111] Here Vitruvius might be expected to expatiate on an authentically Roman form, and take pride in structures like the Villa of the Papyri at Herculaneum or the Villa of the Mysteries at Pompeii which by his day set new standards of magnificent living. Any such expectations, however, are confounded.

Roman discussion of villas in the republican period is wrapped up in a strongly moralising discourse: one that opposes country to town, luxury to ancestral virtue, productivity to consumption. Agricultural writing, from Cato to Varro, is consistent on the issue. Cato urges the young landowner to focus his resources on securing good returns rather than comfort:

---

[106] Gros (2001) 136–213, Hales (2003) 167–206.

[107] Gros (2001) 214–30. The use of *atria* in Greek houses to mark Roman affinities, especially in Roman colonies, has been underestimated: see the studies of Maria Papaioannou (forthcoming).

[108] Cf. Hales (2003) 244–7.   [109] This section draws on the discussion in Wallace-Hadrill (1998).

[110] In general, see Percival (1976), Mielsch (1989), Frazer (1998).   [111] Lauter (1998).

(3) In his youth a head of household should concentrate on planting. He should think long before starting building work, but get on with planting without further thought. When you reach the age of 36, then finally, once the estate is planted, you should put up buildings . . . A head of household should have a well built working farmstead (*villa rustica*), cellars for oil and wine, plenty of vats . . . (details follow) (4) You need good cowbyres, good sheep pens, and latticed feed racks with bars one foot apart (if you do this, the cattle will not scatter their feed). As for residential buildings (*villa urbana*), build them to suit your resources. If you build a good residence on a good estate, and site it in a good position, the result of living comfortably in the country is that you will come more willingly and more often. That way, the estate will improve, less will go wrong, and your profits will rise: the forehead leads the backhead, as they say. (Cato, *de Agricultura* 3–4)

We hear from elsewhere of Cato's attacks on the *villae expolitae* of his contemporaries, villas elaborate with citrus wood and ivory and Punic pavements, and his boasts that no stucco was to be found on the walls of his own farm buildings (the moulded stucco of the 'incrustation' style being the fashionable decoration of the day).[112] In this context, we may note, he concedes a logic to investment in a more luxurious residence: the landowner who visits his estate more willingly and frequently will help to maximise his returns. But that concession embeds the rationale of villa-building in a context of profitable production, rather than wasteful consumption.

Varro follows the Catonian lead in neglecting to offer prescriptions for the villa buildings. Even so, by a series of ironical contrasts, he keeps the luxury features of the villa before the reader's eyes, and establishes a moral counterpoint between the 'rustic' spaces he invests with value, and the 'urban' spaces that are ironically divested:

Certainly a farm derives more profit from its buildings if you construct them on the model of the diligence of the ancients rather than the luxury of the moderns . . . In those days a villa was praised if it had a good country kitchen, ample stables, and wine and oil storage to suit the size of the estate . . . Nowadays they concentrate their efforts on having an urban villa as large and polished as possible, and they compete with the villas of Metellus and Lucullus built to public ruin. Hence their preoccupation is with the aspect of summer *triclinia* towards the cool east, and of winter ones towards the sunny west, while the ancients cared about the side the wine and oil cellars had their windows, since wine production requires cooler air on the vats, oil production warmer air. (*Rerum Rusticarum* 1.6–7)

Aspect is indeed, as we see from Vitruvius, a preoccupation of first-century construction: Varro manages to construct rustic aspect and urban aspect

---

[112] D'Arms (1970) 10, citing Cato in Malcovati (1955) fr. 174 and 185; Plutarch, *Cato maior* 4.4.

as parallel and alternative systems. Such parallelisms are developed with considerable ingenuity. Lucullus is again held up to criticism for his picture-galleries: people prefer to dine in his *pinacothecae* than in *oporothecae*, the produce-stores of old. But not only is dinner in the barn a fantasy generated by moral antithesis: the Greek pseudo-formation *oporotheca*, found only here, shadows and mocks the fashionable Greek label of *pinacotheca*.

Varro's sense of irony affects our reading of his moralisation. Here is an author with *villae urbanae* of his own, writing a dialogue in which none of the participants are exemplars of ancient Roman rusticity. It is an issue on which they tease each other. The third book is dedicated to Pinnius, who has a villa 'spectacular for its plaster-work and inlay and noble pavements of *lithostroton*' which Pinnius further adorned with his own writings, and Varro now complements with further produce, a discussion *de villa perfecta* (3.1.10). The participants sit down for their discussion in the Villa Publica on the Campus Martius. The setting is used to form the pole of two separate contrasts. First Appius compares it favourably, being constructed by *maiores nostri* and frugal, to Axius' polished villa at Reate, with its citrus wood and gold, rich pigments of minium and armenium, its mosaic and marble inlay (*emblema* and *lithostroton*). But Axius hits back by contrasting the paintings and statues (works of Lysippus and Antiphilus) of the Villa Publica with the works of the hoer and shepherd to be found in his own. Hay in the loft, wine in the cellar, grain in the granary are the real ancestral marks of a villa (3.2.3–6). The banter continues, as the speakers produce further examples of villas that are or are not decorated, do or do not have agricultural produce. The moral contrasts fold in on themselves as it emerges that the ass which is the proudest rustic boast of Axius' villa cost a staggering 40,000 sesterces (2.7), and that the best way to make profit from a villa may be '*villatica pastio*', the breeding of bees or birds or fish, which directly serve the luxury of the city (2.16). In the end, rustic and urban, fruitful production and luxury consumption, feed off each other.

The problem, then, is to relate the moral antitheses in terms of which such discussions structure the whole idea of the villa with the practices to which the archaeological remains so abundantly testify. The trap into which we fall is to swallow the antithesis while stripping out its moral evaluation. The rustic elements are assumed to be genuinely 'Roman' and in some sense a static heritage of tradition; while the luxurious urban elements are seen as the product of 'hellenisation'. It is assumed that the villa-owners them-selves did not share the moral qualms of a Varro, and that they saw the luxury appurtenances of their properties as a form of desirable modernisa-tion in line with the fashion for the Greek. But Varro and his friends *are* the villa-building class: we risk misunderstanding by blinding ourselves to the moral values which they attribute to their structures.

Vitruvius again proves a revealing witness. He proves himself an orthodox Catonian. His account of the villa (6.6), which immediately follows that of the town house, is a purist discussion of 'rustic practicalities', of barns and vats and stables, and of the very down-to-earth considerations that govern their disposition. There is nothing here to which Varro could take exception: in stressing again the importance of aspect, it is certainly not the orientation of winter *triclinia* with which he concerns himself:

Similarly cowbyres will be not impractical if situated outside the kitchen in the open facing the east: for when in winter in clear weather the cows are brought across to them in the morning, their condition improves from taking fodder in the sunshine. (6.6.5)

Vitruvius has not forgotten the *villa urbana*: it is a question of strict categories. The urbanity of the luxurious features of the villa is their defining characteristic; they can only therefore be discussed as part of the town house. At the end of his authentically 'rustic' winter cowbyres, the architect notes another side to the villa:

If anything needs to be made of a more delicate sort in villas, they should be constructed according to the rules of symmetry given above for urban buildings, but in such a way that no obstruction is caused to rustic practicalities. (6.6.5)

The *villa urbana* is thus presented not as an organic part of the estate, but as the transposition of an alternative and contrary set of considerations from town into country. The countryside is the place of production, *fructus*, and the dominant considerations must be the practical ones of maximising returns. The town is, except for the humble tradesmen also concerned with practicalities, a place of social display, of decorum, the dignity imparted by elegance. Its symmetries can indeed be transposed into the countryside, provided that production does not suffer thereby.

This principle may seem to leave the owner rather at a loss as to how to shape the rustic and urban parts of his villa. But indeed he will find all the necessary prescriptions in his Vitruvius, not only in the rules for the town house, but in the ensuing discussion of the Greek house, and then in book seven with its instructions on decoration, on pavements and wall-plaster, and on the use of expensive pigments like minium and armenium, which Vitruvius, like Varro, sees as luxuries (7.5.7–8), but nevertheless details (7.8–9). As for overall planning, he offers a single, but illuminating, hint:

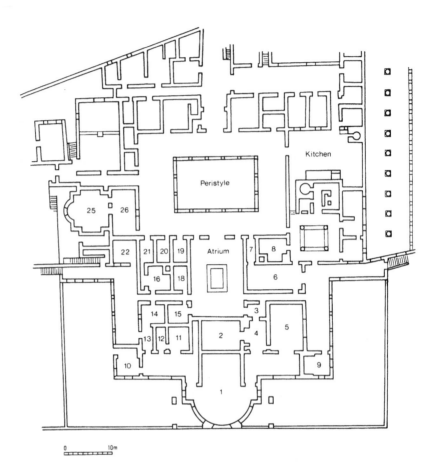

Figure 4.15 Plan of the Villa of the Mysteries, Pompeii (after Wallace-Hadrill 1994, figure 3.19)

These principles (*rationes*) will apply not only to buildings in the city, but also in the country, except that in the city atria are normally next to the entrance, whereas in the country pseudourban villas have peristyles immediately at the entrance, then atria with paved porticoes around them looking out to palaestras and walks. (6.5.3–4)

At a single, brilliant stroke, Vitruvius turns the villa into the mirror image of the town house. In town you move from *atrium* to peristyle, in country from peristyle to *atrium*. To 'urbanize' the country is to stand the town on its head.

The actual diversity of plans of excavated villas shows that Vitruvius' principle of inversion was not universally respected. But, as has already been suggested, Vitruvius is not in the business of describing how the Romans do things, but of imposing *ratio* on *consuetudo*. His rationality is an attempt to create order, giving a more secure basis to the sometimes messy or contradictory tendencies in Roman usage. There is, however, one villa that follows his principle of inversion precisely, the Villa of the Mysteries at Pompeii. This is an illuminating example to consider, both because it makes explicit the rationale of the town/country antithesis, and because it exposes modern incomprehension of that rationale (figure 4.15).

The villa is a model Vitruvian exercise in symmetry and aspect. Its entrance, which lies to the east on the road from Pompeii, is set on a strongly marked east/west axis which defines the symmetries of the building, passing from the entrance through the centre of the peristyle, through the *atrium* with its *impluvium*, to the so-called *tablinum* and the semi-circular room called the *exedra*. This axis corresponds to the characteristic sight-line of the town house, but visibly inverts the usual sequence. It is perhaps no coincidence that modern publications frequently offer pictures of the sight-line in reverse, from *atrium* back to peristyle and entrance (figure 4.16), and not the view presented to the ancient visitor (figure 4.17), a tendency much encouraged by the modern construction of an approach road and entrance at the western façade (i.e. the back) of the villa.

The east/west axis is crosscut by a north/south axis which is invisible to the visitor, but basic to the plan. Running along the wall between peristyle and *atrium*, it divides the building into two contrasting areas. The plan is inscribed in a square which has as its centre the point on the central visual axis of crossing between *atrium* and peristyle (figure 4.18). The two halves of the square, eastern and western, are contrasted in architecture and types of room. The eastern half is the *pars rustica*, with a string of service rooms, decorated simply if at all, along the eastern side, the kitchen area to the south, and to the north the handsomely constructed pressing room and storage vat area beyond. There are no finely decorated reception rooms opening on to the peristyle, though to the south the bath complex (including a small but beautifully constructed *laconicum*), approached through its own 'tetrastyle' *atrium*, adjoins the kitchen, and to the north an impressive room with an apsidal end was under construction in the final phase of the villa, perhaps as a new bath suite.

The western half forms the *pars urbana*. Several phases of highly elaborate decoration are apparent. The *atrium*, though of the usual rectangular shape around a central *impluvium*, lacks the canonical *tablinum* and *alae*. The room (2) referred to as a '*tablinum*' appears to have been cut off visually from the *atrium* by a solid wall. The *atrium* acts as distribution centre for access to four sets of rooms, each of them forming a neat square, symmetrically disposed around *atrium* and '*tablinum*'. The arrangement of this central

Figure 4.16 View from the rear of the Villa of the Mysteries, Pompeii, towards front (author's photo)

Figure 4.17 View from the entrance of the Villa of the Mysteries, Pompeii (author's photo)

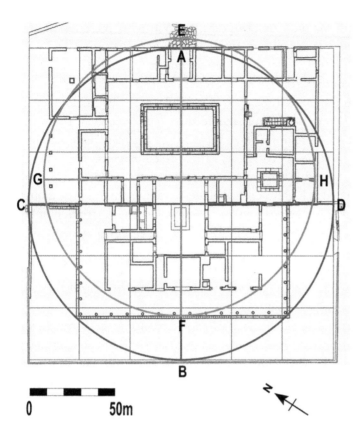

Figure 4.18 Analysis of the geometry of the Villa of the Mysteries, Pompeii, based on hypothetical original layout of villa (plan drawn by S. Hay, based on Esposito 2007, fig. 8)

block replicates the symmetries of the villa as a whole: its east/west axis is cut by a north/south axis which divides the sets of rooms, though this time the north/south axis is visually demarcated by the two corridors that open to right and left of the west end of the *atrium*.

The excavator of the villa, Amedeo Maiuri, posited an earlier phase in which the four suites of rooms had a somewhat simpler internal arrangement (questioned, however, by Esposito 2007). This makes clearer a pattern still detectable in the later arrangement: each set has a large reception room (*triclinium*) with a different orientation, and a *cubiculum* beside it with a double alcove for two beds. In the final phase, two of these 'sets' survive, those with the sunniest and most visually spectacular orientations, to south and west, and these also contain the most spectacular decoration. Outside the four sets are linked by a double 'walk': beside the rooms a handsomely paved colonnade, and beyond this the open walk of the garden that runs above the *cryptoporticus*.

The *pars urbana* thus conforms exactly to Vitruvius' prescription. Here is the '*atrium* with paved porticoes looking out to palaestras and walks (*ambulationes*)' (6.5.3). But there are also numerous elements which fit his prescription for the Greek house. The walks recall his discussion of *xysti* and *paradromides*, the covered and open promenades of the gymnasium (6.7.5). The 'Greek' house, as we have seen, features *hospitalia*, guest suites with independent access, and their own *cubicula* and *triclinia*. These are linked to the main peristyles by corridors, strictly called *mesauloe*, but 'wrongly' Latinised as *andrones*. There is a good chance that the corridors here, handsomely decorated in highly polished plasterwork, were meant to be thought of as '*andrones*' and the room suites as '*hospitalia*'. The description of how 'when the Greeks were more delicate and opulent', they provided visitors with their own bedroom/dining room suites (6.7.4) maps so neatly onto the first-century BCE fashion for such suites, met also for instance in the Villa of the Papyri and the Settefinestre villa,[113] that it is hard to imagine they were not a consciously hellenising feature.

The important point in this analysis is not so much that the plan of the villa conforms in detail to Vitruvian prescriptions, but that it embodies the moral dichotomies which the literary sources offer so insistently. The *pars rustica* parades the 'practicalities' and productivity that the 'true' villa is all about. The *pars urbana* is a supplement, not obstructing the rustic practicalities, but adding 'something more delicate', urbanity in a rustic setting. The urbanity is 'Greek', a potential repertory of the sort of 'Greek' names with which the luxury villa tinkles. The two parts stand counterpoised in symmetrical antithesis.

Seen from the sightline of the visitor, this villa organizes its constituent antitheses, of rustic and urban, Roman and Greek, practical and luxurious, in careful sequence. The entrance presents the visitor with what he should expect of the Roman countryside: traditional Roman rusticity. As he steps over the threshold from peristyle to *atrium*, he moves from rustic to urban, from production to luxury. He also begins to cross a threshold from Roman to Greek, except that the *atrium* is itself reassuringly Roman, as the piles of arms depicted in the decoration underline. But as he passes down the *andrones* to the *hospitalia* with their views of *porticus* and *xysta*, and gazes in the climactic west-facing suite at scenes of Dionysus and Ariadne and the exotic mysteries of Bacchic initiation, he knows he has moved into another world.

---

[113] Wallace-Hadrill (1994) 57.

The significance of this sequential arrangement becomes more marked if we return to the urban axial vista which, in accordance with Vitruvian rules, it inverts. In the town, to enter the *atrium* is to be confronted with an assertion of Roman identity, with the image, if not the practice, of patronal power; to pass through to the peristyle is to cross the threshold from urban to rural (gardens and fountains), from the practical to the luxurious, and from the Roman to the Greek (statuary, Rhodian peristyles and Corinthian *oeci*). In both city and country, then, despite or rather because of the inversion of *atrium* and peristyle, the Greek represents a level of privilege, less accessible but more desirable than the Roman. That can be translated into the inclusion and exclusion of visitors according to their status. In the town, the humble townsman may be received in the *atrium*, so close to visible reminders of the humble practicalities of the town (shops flank the entrance); to pass through to the Greek and rural is a privilege. In the country, the opposite sequence of town and country is required: it is the rustic peristyle in which the countrymen can do their humble business, and the privilege consists in advancing to the *pars urbana*.

Modern incomprehension of the way the rustic and the urban play off each other in the villa is seen most clearly in Maiuri's strange hypothesis that the great wine pressing room was originally a dining room, and only debased to rustic usage by the later, tasteless, owners of the villa (figure 4.19).[114] Archaeological evidence for this supposed conversion and degradation is wholly lacking: the rough walls show no trace of earlier window openings or decoration to grace a fine reception room. On the contrary, it is perfectly shaped and decorated for its purpose as pressing room. Nor is there the slightest architectural sense in placing a grand reception room so close to the roadway, and on a northern aspect. No decorator's ingenuity could elevate this room above the 'room of the Mysteries' with its views west and south through broad windows past the columns of the porticoes and out over the panorama of the Bay (figure 4.20).

The deep implausibility of Maiuri's construction (which he so successfully wished on the modern visitor) flows from the refusal to accept the *morality* of the Roman villa, the value system which agricultural writers set out. The *torcularium*, fascinating to any reader of Cato and Varro, must be allowed to recover its positive moral connotations, a conspicuous centre of fruitful production and rustic virtue (figure 4.19). It stands in moral (as well as aesthetic) antithesis to the 'room of the Mysteries' at the diagonally opposite corner of the villa. Here Roman-ness, rusticity, productivity and virtue;

---

[114] Maiuri (1931) esp. 93 and 100.

Figure 4.19 View of *torcularium* of the Villa of the Mysteries, Pompeii (author's photo)

Figure 4.20 View of 'mysteries' frieze in the principal *triclinium* (author's photo)

there foreignness, an exotic oriental cult once driven by the senate from the land, the corruption of hellenistic luxuries. The architecture 'moralizes' no less than Varro. But the antithesis that separates also binds together, and the connection should not be missed: for here the fruits of the vine gush richly out to flow into the vats, while there the orgiastic mysteries of Bacchus, the god of the vine, are celebrated.

We must abandon the cherished delusion that the '*villa rustica*' and the '*villa urbana*' are separate types.[115] The achievement of Carandini's handsome publication of the villa at Settefinestre was to show, with constant reference to agricultural writers, how the two hang together.[116] The power of the *dominus* is expressed by the complementary messages of the *pars rustica* and the *pars urbana*, in the rustic quarters by the control over manpower manifested in slave gangs and the control over the land manifested in the vintage and the oil pressing, and in the urban quarters by the control of wealth and the ability to impose on the countryside an alien cultural language. Neither part diminishes the other, since together they express an embracing dominance, of country and town, production and consumption, moral rectitude and transgression, the Roman and the non-Roman.

It may seem strange that the Roman ruling class chose to advertise its dominance in language so ambivalent and risky. But the ambivalence is itself the source of power. In Horace's fable (*Satires* 2.6.77ff.), the Roman does not know whether he wants to be a town mouse or a country mouse; when in one, he longs to be in the other. The hesitation was natural for men who had an equal ideological investment in both, and whose superior status was bound up in the ability to play off one against the other. As landowner and rural patron, the villa owner derived authority from his links with the city, from the wealth and political power he could generate there; he was the broker between country and town. But as politician in the city, he owed his clout also to the strength of his country backing, the wealth of his acres and the support of the countrymen who turned up to vote for him or his candidate on polling day. The double face presented by both his villa and his town house reflects this duality. He must be able at once to impress the townsman by the ideological force of his rustic credentials, and the countryman by the sophistication of his urbanity. The villa thus asserts urban values in the middle of the countryside, but on condition that the town house asserts rural values in the midst of the town. This sense

---

[115] Carandini (1985) vol.1 126: the non-agricultural villa is the product of selective excavation.
[116] Carandini (1985) 107–37.

of reciprocity is elegantly encapsulated in Vitruvius' vision of the villa as inversion of the town house.

Identity rebuilt

The text of Vitruvius belongs to a quite specific historic moment, on the cusp between political systems, one that is of critical importance for the transformation of Roman culture. Too often, it has been read as a timeless expression of quintessential realities: as if 'Roman identity' were always there to define and inform the Romans, with the natural result that there was always a 'Roman architecture' to be built by the Romans. The 'rules' of Roman architecture, on this thesis, must always have been there, because Roman architecture must always have been different from Greek; and even if they had not been articulated so clearly before, Vitruvius had but to draw on a body of common assumption and common practice. This chapter has argued that, on the contrary, the Roman-ness of Roman architecture is something elaborately constructed by Vitruvius, a specific product of a specific historical juncture. His project is to create a new marriage of *ratio* with *consuetudo*, of a rational set of principles derived from, but not identical to, those elaborated by Greek architectural theory, together with a set of 'traditional' practices that are themselves a new invention, a new amalgam derived from selective observation of both metropolitan Rome and of the cities of Italy.

Had Vitruvius been the 'traditionalist' he is often taken for, his Roman architecture might have looked very different. His theatre would be constructed temporarily of timber, and would have no need of the elaborate rules of acoustics; he comes close to admitting as much. His baths might not even appear as a public building, for baths at Rome up to Agrippa were private institutions; the world of nudity and indulgence and athletics they represented were altogether too foreign. His town house would stretch no further than the *atrium*, and his country villa would have been limited to agricultural necessities. Roman 'ancestral practice', whatever that might be, was too implicated in a myth of rustic simplicity to form a basis for an Augustan architecture.

At the same time he has no perception of the 'revolution' which twentieth-century architectural history sees in Roman architecture. He knows all about the properties of *pozzolana* sand, but shows no sign of excitement about the possibilities for new volumes and spaces it opened up. He tells us coolly about the proper proportions for a temple without hinting that it might form part of a magnificent sanctuary complex like that of Palestrina, with its bold succession of ramps and terraces, its rhythms of rectilinear and curved, and the anular vaulting of the hemicyclical *exedrae* which is an exercise in mathematical calculation worthy of the highest Greek theory. He goes on about the proportions of the theatre without mentioning that the amphitheatre was already established as an outstanding feat of design and engineering. He talks about the vaults of baths without indicating that by his day at Baiae they had concrete domes of a size never dreamed of by Greek builders of *laconica*, domes which would pass to palatial architecture, and eventually in the Pantheon to religious buildings, and would linger in the city of Rome as the distinctive feature of its skyline. It is not that Vitruvius was completely blind or obstinate: simply that his perspective and his revolution were not ours.

Vitruvius' revolution lay in the demonstration that Greek theory could be reconciled with current practice in Italy without compromising identity. Whence the urge to impose at all costs *ratio*? His project is exactly parallel with those of the Latin intellectual figures he admired, Cicero and Varro. In oratory, Cicero had shown that Greek rhetorical theory could empower a public speaking rooted in the conditions of Roman public life; in language, Varro had shown that rational grammatical systems could be reconciled with the vagaries of current usage. To Vitruvius' mind Roman architecture could have no real authority unless underpinned by a systematic grammar; and yet it must acknowledge that 'we' do things differently here.

The 'we' he constructs is remarkable, and the product of a specific moment, an Italy transformed by the trauma of the Social and civil wars and brought together in the new Italo-Roman identity which Syme recognised as a key to the Augustan revolution. The *Italica consuetudo* which Vitruvius repeatedly sets against the Greek is a bold conception scarcely imaginable before Augustus.[117] It takes some courage to trump Roman *maiores* like Scipio Nasica, who insisted on wooden theatres, with the local elites of Oscan Pompeii, or Samnite Pietrabbondante, who built fine stone theatres in the best hellenistic style. Only in the later first century BCE could a Roman comfortably recognise *maiores* in such non-Romans. Vitruvius' ancestors are an elastic concept: when he starts the preface of his book seven by reference to 'the wise and useful institution of our *maiores*' in leaving commentaries, it is natural to assume that with such language he is referring to Roman

---

[117] Boethius and Ward-Perkins (1970) 115–80, von Hesberg (1984), Wallace-Hadrill (2000b).

ancestral practice; but he goes on to cite the luminaries of Greek philosophy and science.[118]

Vitruvius' text consequently illuminates the questions of identity posed in chapter 3. Did the Praenestines in constructing their great sanctuary at the end of the second century feel less Latin and more Greek for 'hellenising', or more Roman for sharing in the 'concrete revolution'? We can only speculate. What Vitruvius, a century later, allows us to say is that building did indeed raise issues of identity, and that he wants simultaneously to say that the Greek is different and that it can be embraced provided that difference is respected. Over a century of frenetic building work across Italy, in the public and the private sphere, unleashed an extraordinary creativity, but also a debate about identity that was implicit in the debate about citizenship and the distribution of power within the citizen body. Vitruvius, from the viewpoint of the new Augustan order, can resolve that debate, and enfold the Greek and Italic within the Roman.

---

[118] A connection missed by Granger (1970), commenting on the passage.

Plate I Cista Ficoroni, Villa Giulia Museum, Rome (courtesy Soprintendenza per i Beni Archeologici dell'Etruria Meridionale, foto n. 9152D) (fig. 3.8)

Plate II Ferentinum, substructure and citadel erected by Hirtius and Lollius (author's photo) (fig. 3.16)

Plate III Ferentinum citadel, detail of dedicatory inscription (author's photo) (fig. 3.17)

Plate IV Temple of Apollo, Pompeii, view to south-east (author's photo) (fig. 3.24)

Plate V Mummius inscription, from temple of Apollo, Pompeii (author's photo) (fig. 3.26)

Plate VI Via dell'Abbondanza, Pompeii, tufo façades (author's photo) (fig. 3.28)

Plate VII Pietrabbondante, general view (author's photo) (fig. 3.29)

Plate VIII Detail of corner of temple B at Pietrabbondante (author's photo) (fig. 3.31)

Plate IX Detail of corner of temple at Vastogirardi (author's photo) (fig. 3.32)

Plate X Pietrabbondante, view of curve of *ima cavea* with Atlas support (author's photo) (fig. 3.33)

Plate XI Pompeii, small theatre, view of curve of *ima cavea* with Atlas support (author's photo) (fig. 3.34)

Plate XII Street scene from the Via dell'Abbondanza, Pompeii (from Spinazzola 1953, plate I) (fig. 6.7)

Plate XIII Altar to neighbourhood *lares* from Via dell'Abbondanza, Pompeii (Spinazzola 1953, plate XVIII) (fig. 6.8)

Plate XIV House of Chaste Lovers, Pompeii, scene from west wall of *triclinium* (photo Michael Harvey (fig. 7.1)

Plate XV House of Chaste Lovers, Pompeii, scene from centre wall of *triclinium* (photo Michael Harvey) (fig. 7.2)

Plate XVI House of Chaste Lovers, Pompeii, scene from east wall of *triclinium* (photo Michael Harvey) (fig. 7.3)

Plate XVII South Italian fish plate from Paestum (photo courtesy Soprintendenza di Salerno, Museo di Paestum) (fig. 7.4)

Plate XVIII Mosaic from the House of the Faun, Pompeii illustrating varieties of fish (Naples Museum inv. 9997, photo Alfredo Foglia) (fig. 7.5)

Plate XIX Third-style decoration with Egyptianizing motifs, the House of the Fruit Orchard, Pompeii (watercolour Nicholas Wood, courtesy British School at Rome) (fig. 8.1)

Plate XX The Boethus Herm of Dionysus from the Mahdia wreck (photo Rheinisches Landesmusem Bonn, courtesy Musée Nationale du Bardo, Tunis) (fig. 8.3)

Plate XXI The Boethus Herm of Dionysus from the Getty Museum (79.AB.138, courtesy the J. Paul Getty Museum) (fig. 8.4)

Plate XXII Marble Herm of Dionysus from Pompeii, inv. 2914 (photo Alfredo Foglia, courtesy Soprintendenza Archeologica di Pompei) (fig. 8.5)

Plate XXIII Example of 'Corinthian bronze': inlaid bronze statuette base from Herculaneum, inv. 77281 (photo Soprintendenza Archeologica di Napoli e Pompei) (fig. 8.14)

Plate XXIV Bronze lamp-stand from the House of Amarantus (I.9.12), Pompeii, inv. 10026 (photo Hay/Sibthorpe, courtesy British School at Rome) (fig. 8.15)

Plate XXV Calyx *crater* from the House of Julius Polybius, Pompeii (courtesy Soprintendenza Archeologica di Napoli e Pompei) (fig. 8.24)

Plate XXVI Bronze boiler from Pompeii (photo Alfredo Foglia, courtesy Soprintendenza Archeologica di Napoli e Pompei (fig. 8.32)

Plate XXVII Examples of Campanian black-glaze wares from Pompeii (photo Hay/Sibthorpe, courtesy British School at Rome) (fig. 8.36)

Plate XXVIII Examples of Arretine wares from Pompeii (photo Hay/Sibthorpe, courtesy British School at Rome) (fig. 8.37)

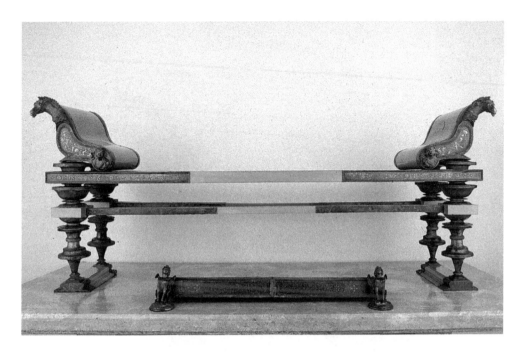

Plate XXIX Amiternum couch, Capitoline Museum (photo Araldo De Luca, courtesy Musei Capitolini) (fig. 8.42)

Plate XXX Amiternum couch, Capitoline Museum, detail of leg (photo Araldo De Luca, courtesy Musei Capitolini) (fig. 8.43)

Plate XXXI Amiternum couch, Capitoline Museum, detail of *fulcrum* (photo Zeno Colantoni, courtesy Musei Capitolini) (fig. 8.44)

PART III

Knowledge and power

Knowledge and power

> He [Gibbs] knew that the Orient in general and Islam in particular were systems of information, behaviour and belief, that to be an Oriental or a Muslim was to know certain things in a certain way, and that those were of course subject to history, geography and the development of society in circumstances specific to itself.
>
> (Edward Said, *Orientalism* 195)

Central to the thesis of Said's *Orientalism* is the assumption that structures of knowledge and power depend on each other. 'Orientalism' is the body of knowledge that constructs the 'Orient' as something the west can know and thereby control. Western 'knowledge' stands in tension with the self-knowledge of the Orient. Said endorses the western scholar who sees that the East is not simply an object of external 'scholarly' knowledge, but owes such identity as it has to its knowledge of itself. So Gibbs perceives 'that Islam was a coherent system of life, a system made coherent not so much by the people who led that life as by virtue of some body of doctrine, method of religious practice, idea of order, in which all the Muslim people participated'.[1] With equal force, we can say that the system of knowledge of the Greek or 'hellenistic' world was a system of power, and that in appropriating the one, the Romans necessarily transformed the other.

The perception that power and knowledge are mutually involved in complex and reciprocal ways is above all associated with Michel Foucault:

The exercise of power perpetually creates knowledge and, conversely, knowledge constantly induces effects of power . . . Modern humanism is therefore mistaken in drawing this line between knowledge and power. Knowledge and power are integrated with one another.[2]

The theme runs through a life's writings that are too rich, and at the same time shifting and evasive, to allow any easy summary, but certain of his

---

[1] Said (1978) 276.   [2] Foucault (1980) 51f.

central concerns remain constant, and have led to fundamental rethinking of what 'power' and 'knowledge' are each about and where the boundaries between them are to be drawn. Foucault preferred not to look for power in the authorities and agencies in which it is normally located, but in the tactics and strategies of what he terms a 'discourse'. Not so much in the *The History of Sexuality* (1979), more familiar to classical scholarship,[3] but in *The Order of Things* (1970), the history of western science was seen as a succession of archaeological layers, each characterised by its own *epistēmē* or discourse, a fundamental reordering of 'configurations within the space of knowledge'.[4] The sixteenth century, the classical age of the seventeenth and eighteenth centuries, and the modern age of the post-industrial era are each seen as patterned by their own *epistēmē* (the similitudes of the sixteenth century, the taxonomy of the classical age) which transcends individual sciences. In his studies of madness, prison and sexuality the emphasis on academic forms of knowledge remains, but the question is rather of how the 'ways of knowing' of a discourse create fields of power. The most vivid image perhaps is Bentham's Panopticon, the ideal prison which enables the warder to survey and know in detail the life of each prisoner. Whereas the power of the state made itself felt under the *ancien régime* by the public exhibition of the exercise of violence on the body of the criminal, the power of the modern state consisted in subjecting the criminal to its minute knowledge.[5] The same discipline of minute knowledge could be seen in education or factories; and, as *The History of Sexuality* later suggested, in the post-Freudian construction of sexual behaviour as a field of knowledge.

Foucault exercised a deep influence on a number of fields, including the 'New Cultural History' of the 1980s.[6] A significant role in transposing his ideas into the historical field was played by Roger Chartier, whose *The Cultural Origins of the French Revolution* (1991) re-examined the relationship of cultural and political change in the French Enlightenment and Revolution.[7] Challenging the approach that saw in the Enlightenment an intellectual revolution that in some sense was the 'origin' of the political revolution, he suggested that Enlightenment and Revolution were rather part of a single greater transformation of French society. He mirrors Lawrence Stone's analysis of the English Revolution of the seventeenth century, which had pointed to a range of intellectual and cultural preconditions which undermined

---

[3] Cameron (1986), Golden and Toohey (1997) 5–7.
[4] Foucault (1970), Dreyfus and Rabinow (1982) 16–43.   [5] Foucault (1977).
[6] See Hunt (1989) for the influence of Geertz, Foucault and others on the practice of modern history. On the new historicism, see further Vesser (1989).
[7] Chartier (1991) esp. 169–92. See also Chartier (1988) 19–52.

adherence to the old political and religious order, in religion, legal practice, relations of court and country, the erosion of authority and the growth of an educated class. All five factors could be pursued with equal plausibility in an analysis of the collapse of credibility of the old social, religious and political order represented by the Roman Republic, preparing the way for radical political change. This chapter and chapter 6, rather than follow these headings, pursue the idea of a fundamental shift in the location of authority. Here it is not a royal court that collapses, but the dominance of an elite which, albeit subject to constant competition, sought to stabilise and shore up its own power by control of social knowledge. The Augustan revolution, it is proposed, is a revolution in structures of knowledge.

Ancestral ways

Cornelius Nepos prefaces his series of biographical sketches of Greek generals, written in the triumviral period, with some reflections on the differences between Greek and Roman cultural values which a Roman readership needs to appreciate in order to avoid misjudging the Greeks:[8]

> I do not doubt, Atticus, that there will be several who judge this branch of writing trivial and beneath the dignity of men of the highest rank, when they read an account of who taught Epaminondas music, and find listed among his virtues his skill at dancing and his mastery of singing to the pipes. But these will be people who, for lack of knowledge of Greek literature, think nothing right unless it conforms to their own society's *mores*. If they learnt that standards of respect and shame are not universal, but that everything is judged in terms of traditional practice (*maiorum institutis*), they would be less surprised that in expounding the virtues of Greeks, I have subscribed to their *mores*. (Nepos, *de Excellentibus ducibus* 1–4)

Just as Vitruvius, writing around the same time, Nepos sets up a basic 'us/them' contrast between Roman and Greek. 'We' do things differently because our ancestors taught us to do so. The key to understanding difference lies in ancestral tradition. The example Nepos picks, of the Theban general Epaminondas, had been used not long before by Cicero, writing under Caesar's dictatorship. In the preface to his *Tusculan Disputations*, he makes the same point about Epaminondas and music, though he lays the emphasis on different standards of social esteem, *honos*, rather than *mores*:

---

[8] See on Nepos and his context, Geiger (1985), Horsfall (1989), Millar (2002) 183–99, Anselm (2004).

It is social esteem that feeds the arts, and all are fired to their pursuits by public recognition, while pursuits that meet disapproval in some quarters languish. The Greeks regard the highest cultural attainment as located in string and vocal music: hence Epaminondas, in my view the greatest statesman of Greece, is said to have sung outstandingly to the lyre, whereas Themistocles some time before is held to be less cultured (*indoctior*) because he refused the lyre at a party. (*Tusculan Disputations* 1.2.4)

The context of Cicero's argument is an assertion of the superiority of Roman *mores*; he contains the advantage of Greece to the sphere of *doctrina* (i.e. *paideia*), and the theory of social esteem seeks to establish that the Roman achievement in the same sphere could be equal if not greater were the Romans to learn to esteem such things. Greek superiority is limited to those areas where the Roman has not seen fit to compete. Romans are not merely different, but inherently superior:

Our ways and practices of living, our domestic and private affairs are both better conducted and more polished; our public life has been regulated by our ancestors through institutions and laws that are clearly superior. Need I mention military life, in which we have always been strong both in virtue and even more in discipline? (*Tusculan Disputations* 1.1.2)

Ancestors, *nostri maiores*, are invoked to authenticate the Roman-ness of 'our' ways; and what Roman could doubt that ancestral *mores* were better than those of the Greeks? But this sense of superiority did not prevent the Roman acknowledging that Greek difference deserved respect. Another example Nepos gives is the position of women in the house. In a passage closely parallel to Vitruvius, he explains:

By contrast, several things which by our own standards (*mores*) are respectable are held shameful by them. What Roman is ashamed to take his wife to a dinner party? Or whose *materfamilias* does not hold a prominent position in the household and move freely in company? In Greece things are quite different. She is neither invited out to dinner, except by close relatives, nor takes a seat except in that inner part of the house, called the 'gynaeconitis', which nobody except close members of the family approaches. (Nepos, *de Excellentibus ducibus*, preface 6–7)

Awareness of different practices in the treatment of women in Greek areas was particularly well established in first-century BCE Rome. One of Cicero's charges against Verres in 70 BCE was that while on duty in Lampsacus, he had billeted one of his staff on a leading citizen of the town, who on entertaining his Roman guests was outraged by the demand to produce his unmarried daughter at dinner (*Verrines* 2.1.25.66). The significant point is not simply that Cicero himself knew that such a request was highly offensive to Greek (in contrast to Roman) *mores*, but that he could expect Verres and his staff, and indeed the trial jury and the Roman readership, to be equally aware of the point.

The central importance of ancestral practice, *mos maiorum*, in Roman ideology has long been observed. It is rather too easy to fall for the Roman line that such values were a quintessential part of Roman identity, as did the German scholars in the early twentieth century who were as keen to map out Roman *Wertbegriffe* as were their archaeological colleagues to use material culture to establish ethnic identity.[9] But tradition is peculiarly subject to invention.[10] The distinction of Scottish clans by tartan plaids seems so authentically ancestral, it is a shock to discover that they are a modern invention.[11] A 'shared history, or myth of origin' is a key ingredient in defining a sense of ethnic identity.[12] Work on a wide variety of societies, from African tribes to modern nation-states, has shown both the vital role played by such shared histories, and the way in which tradition is constantly reinvented, above all at times of radical social and political change.[13] To invoke the ancestors is to invoke a stable model of legitimacy: they are most invoked when legitimacy is most at issue, and the winners are those who succeed in imposing their model of legitimate behaviour on the ancestral past.

From this perspective, our own image of the Romans as a highly conventional and tradition-bound people demands reassessment. The question could be approached from many angles, including examination of the historiographical tradition of the late republic which actively and continuously rewrote the Roman past in the light of contemporary political debate, a theme that has been much discussed. This chapter, however, will focus on the group of writers we choose to call 'antiquarians', particularly those of the first century BCE. It is they who focus most explicitly on the issue of what the *mos maiorum*, the accepted 'Roman way' is, and confront most clearly the issues of identity at stake. It is our reading of them that has fed a sense that Roman identity was fixed and known. Here a different reading will be offered of antiquarian writers, as major players in the redefinition of identity that reaches its climax in the Augustan political revolution.

---

[9] Above all Heinze (1930), Heinze (1938), Pöschl (1940); see also Earl (1967), Oppermann (1967).

[10] See the classic collection of essays by Hobsbawm and Ranger (1983), with Dench (2005) 15.

[11] Trevor-Roper (1983); and see p. 40, n. 7.

[12] Renfrew (1996) in Graves-Brown, Jones and Gamble (1996) 130; Hall (1997).

[13] Graves-Brown, Jones and Gamble (1996) 1; for Rome see Bettini (1986).

Once we start to look at how the Romans used their *maiores*, it emerges that there are a number of important contrasts, and that they were used in different ways in different contexts. At once we can distinguish three broad uses. One (characteristically aristocratic) deployment draws attention to what 'my ancestors' did or were. Essentially competitive, it contrasts the achievements and merits of the ancestors of one individual with those of others, and it is on this that the Roman noble's claim to priority depends. The second, by contrast, amalgamates everybody's ancestors, and blurs all periods: 'our ancestors have always done so.' That claim implies a seamless web between past and present: only if we fail to act as our ancestors have always done will we betray the Roman tradition. The third postulates a gap: 'in the good old days our ancestors used to do one thing; but we of the present age do another.' The three ways of using ancestors are closely linked, in that all assume a special status of authority for the *maiores*: and a defining feature of the Roman is to recognise this authority in whichever context. But even if they rely on a common assumption, the ways in which they are deployed to persuade lead to radically different results.

Ancestors and nobility

That the achievements of a man's ancestors gave him respect and made him 'noble' was once one of the cardinal 'knowns' about Roman history.[14] Familiar texts include Polybius' vivid description of the noble funeral, with its parade of ancestral images and its funeral oration delivered from the Rostra by a young member of the family (6.53–4). Not only does the Roman noble ritually parade the wax images of the family, and recount the achievements of each ancestor on the occasion of each funeral, but he displays the *stemma* or lineage permanently in his *atrium*.[15] Such a display of ancestry was the prerogative of the nobility. Mommsen's attempt to make the *ius imaginum* a legal privilege misinterprets the social and customary basis on which power was constructed: 'nobility' was not a legal category, but was defined by social expectations that go back to the emergence of a new power-class in Rome after the fourth-century BCE struggle of the orders.[16] The display of *imagines* was the ritual by which a group constructed its own exclusivity; the converse was men without ancestors or nobility, who

---

[14] See esp. Gelzer (1969), with the critiques of Brunt (1988) 28–32, 385ff. and Millar (2002) 124–32.

[15] Pliny, *Natural History* 35.4–14. See Flower (1996) for texts and discussion.

[16] Hölkeskamp (1987), Flower (1996) 53–9.

as Cicero puts it, could not speak before the Roman people of their *maiores* because they had not had the people's praise and the illumination of their honour (*de Lege Agraria* 2.1).

This aristocratic ideal is closely linked by historians to their own activity in writing: Sallust specifically cites the sense of moral spur provided to nobles like Scipio and Fabius by the contemplation of their ancestors' achievements as a model for the sort of benefit which history writing itself can provide (*Jugurtha* 4). The temptation, therefore, is to regard this tradition of respect for and emulation of noble ancestors as one of the 'givens' of Roman history, part of the genetic programming, so to speak, of their culture. But things are a great deal less straightforward when we consider how this tradition is actually being *used* by the authors who feed it to us. The case of Sallust is particularly striking: he invokes the positive moral effect of the contemplation of noble ancestors in the preface to a monograph of which the central theme is the decline in inherited Roman *virtus*, and the conflict between the narrow group (*factio paucorum*) who used the claims of ancestry to justify their monopoly of power, and the Roman people whose liberties and sovereignty were consequently infringed. For Sallust, the use of *maiores* is only acceptable as a spur to actual virtue, whereas the contemporary reality is their abuse as a route to illegitimate power.[17]

This point comes out more sharply if we consider the specific nobles whose view on the matter Sallust invoked: Scipio and Fabius Maximus. Both belong to families which were at the time active in pushing 'tradition' well beyond the images, funerals and orations described by Polybius and Sallust. The *imagines* of tradition were wax masks kept within the private household of the noble, and only publicly displayed on the occasion of a funeral. Both Scipiones and Fabii were active in erecting statues and monuments in prominent positions in the city of Rome which made a permanent public display of their ancestors.

The Fabii Maximi were made conspicuous by the arch at the point where the Via Sacra entered the Forum, known as the Fornix Fabianus.[18] Arches, though they may appear to us the quintessence of Roman tradition, only became so thanks to their use under the Empire as a status-marker for emperors and members of their families.[19] Republican arches were irregular and experimental, and only one of a variety of ways in which the powerful attempted to cash in on their success. The Fornix Fabianus was erected

---

[17] Pöschl (1940), Earl (1961), Syme (2002).
[18] Chioffi (1995) (*Lexicon Topographicum Urbis Romae*, ed. E. M. Steinby, Rome, 2: 264–6).
[19] Wallace-Hadrill (1990b).

by the conqueror of the Gallic Allobroges in 121 BCE, then renewed in 56
by his grandson, who put up a portrait-gallery of family statues, as we
learn from its inscription.[20] His gallery was something of a bluff, including
Aemilius Paullus and Scipio Aemilianus, whose 'ancestral' link was remote
and through adoption.[21] The sentiments it incorporated, of the linkage
between the military glories of an ancestor and the fame of his descendants
may have been traditional, but the expression given to them was creative,
and politically charged. It made the required impression, as Cicero attests:

> Maximus did nothing incompatible either with his virtue or that of those most
> famous Paulli, Maximi and Africani whose glory we not only hope to be renewed
> in him, but we now see with our own eyes. (*in Vatinium* 28)

The Scipiones, too, had an arch straddling the Clivus Capitolinus.[22] They
also had a large collection of gilded statues in the central piazza of the Capitoline, several of them 'equestrian' – with the subject depicted on horseback –
which went back to the brothers Africanus and Asiaticus (or Asiagenus).
Metellus Scipio, the consul of 52 BCE, was busy in the 50s installing what
Cicero with amusement called his 'squadron' of statues, and indeed revealed
his ignorance of his own ancestry by attaching the label 'Sarapio' to the wrong
Scipio, and falsely attributing a censorship to Africanus (i.e. Scipio Aemilianus).[23] An attempt by a noble to make maximum political capital out of
his ancestry is met by mockery.

The same family is responsible for the most famous example of a republican family tomb which survives, the inscriptions from which offer us some
of the earliest and most vivid articulations of the noble ideals of *virtus*.[24] But
though we like to use these as 'typical examples' of the ethos of the nobility
(particularly for lack of alternative republican tombs at this level), the Scipiones were far from typical: their method of burying the dead rather than
cremating was noted as exceptional.[25] In its original form, going back to the
early third century BCE, the tomb of the Scipiones was closely comparable
to Etruscan family tombs, characterised by the location of inhumed bodies
in sarcophagi, and the use of inscriptions to distinguish family members,

---

[20] *Corpus Inscriptionum Latinarum* VI 1303–4, 31593 = 1^2 762–3. See Coarelli (1985) 172–80,
Lexicon Topographicum Urbis Romae, ed. E. M. Steinby. Rome, 2 (1995) 264–6 ('Fornix
Fabianus').

[21] Flower (1996) 72–3.

[22] *Lexicon Topographicum Urbis Romae*, ed. E. M. Steinby. Rome, 2, 266–7.

[23] Cicero, *ad Atticum* 6.1.17, Flower (1996) 73–4. Coarelli (1996b) 68–9 sees in the squadron a
reprise of the Lysippan squadron of Alexander in the porticus Metelli.

[24] Wachter (1987) 333–37, Coarelli (1996a) 179–238, Flower (1996) 166–80.

[25] Cicero, *de Legibus* 2.56; Pliny, *Natural History* 7.187.

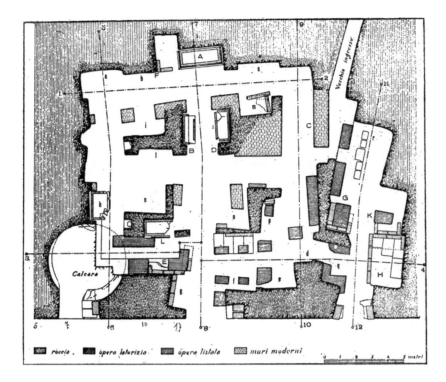

Figure 5.1 Plan of the tomb of the Scipiones (drawing by I. Gismondi)

hierarchically arranged around the founding figure of Barbatus (figure 5.1). The earlier inscriptions are in Latin verse, in the archaic form called Saturnians, which is also attested for other mid-third-century funerary inscriptions.[26] But the tomb received a major makeover in the mid-second century, surely by Scipio Aemilianus, who gave it an elaborate architectural façade in hellenistic idiom (figure 5.2), and added a number of portrait statues, including Publius and Lucius Scipio (i.e. Africanus and Asiaticus) and the poet Ennius (Livy 38.56). There is a strong likelihood that the portraits of the Scipiones are the pair excavated in the early seventeenth century, which became part of the Barberini collection, to be dispersed to Munich (figure 5.3) and Copenhagen (figure 5.4), and mislabelled as Marius and Sulla, while Ennius survives only in a later copy (figure 5.5).[27] The ostentatious façade helps to set a new fashion in burial practice, of monuments designed to impress the passer-by and not merely serve the internal needs of the family. At the same time, the verse inscriptions within shift from Saturnians to

---

[26] Cicero, *Cato* 61 cites that of Atilius Calatinus, censor in 247; Morel (1927) 7.
[27] Coarelli (2002).

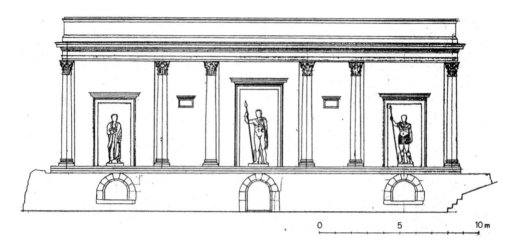

Figure 5.2 Tomb of the Scipiones, reconstruction of façade (from Coarelli 1972, figure E)

Figure 5.3 Portrait identified as Scipio Africanus, so-called 'Sulla' (from Ny Carlsberg Glyptotek, Copenhagen)

Figure 5.4 Portrait identified as Scipio Asiagenus, so-called 'Marius' (photo Munich, Photothek des Museums für Abgüsse Klassischer Bildwerke)

Figure 5.5 Portrait identified as Ennius, so-called 'Virgil' (photo Ny Carlsberg Glyptotek, Copenhagen)

elegiac couplets on the new hellenistic model – at a date when Ennius himself could describe Saturnians as 'sung by the fauns and bards of old'.[28]

Perhaps the most remarkable innovation of the Scipiones was that they kept the *imago* of Africanus in the *cella* of the temple of Jupiter on the

---

[28] Ennius, *Annales* 207 (Skutsch).

Capitoline, so that family processions had to take a route via the temple. How this was possible, the sources do not explain, though they emphasise the frequency of his visits to the temple. But this substitution of public for private, of religious shrine for domestic hall, was a startling inversion of the theme that a noble *atrium* was open to the public.[29] It also (since triumphs processed to this temple) converted each funerary procession of the family into a shadow triumph, a point underlined by the erection in 190 BCE of a triumphal arch with seven gilded statues on the Clivus Capitolinus, through which the family processions passed. What the Scipiones, then, exemplify is not so much the standard behaviour of the nobility, but Roman ability to adapt and exploit to advantage in imaginative ways standard conceptions of tradition.

Nor should we imagine the Scipiones were unique in their redeployment of the tradition of wax images as the basis for invention. Pliny complains about the substitution of simple wax images by costly *imagines clipeatae*, portraits on silver-plated shields, and identifies as the innovators Appius Claudius Pulcher (consul of 79 BCE) in the temple of Bellona, and Aemilius Lepidus (consul of 78 BCE) in the Basilica Aemilia in the Forum.[30] These 'nobles' were, like the Scipiones, maximizing the crossover between the private/domestic context and the public/religious. Lepidus placed shield portraits *both* in his *atrium and* on the façade of a major public building facing the centre of the Forum. 'Nobility' is an illusion generated by the aggressive appropriation of the public sphere by private families and their domestic rituals.

We see the same in the outbreak of ancestor-references placed on Roman coinage from the 130s BCE.[31] Images of the Roman state are partially displaced on the reverse by references to the supposed origins and exploits of the family of the young magistrates responsible for minting, such as the coins of Minucius Augurinus of 135 BCE, celebrating of the column put up in honour of his ancestor (figure 5.6). Such ancestral themes typically occupy the reverse of the coin.[32] The obverse, however, long reserved for images of the gods, only starts to host ancestor portraits in the final years of the republic. Ironically, it is Brutus, the future assassin of Caesar, who in 54 BCE celebrates his ancestral commitment to tyrannicide by placing the portraits of Brutus and Ahala on a double-headed coin, and so breaks this ultimate taboo (figure 5.7). A gesture designed to proclaim traditional

[29] Flower (1996) 48–52.   [30] Pliny, *Natural History* 35.12–14; Flower (1996) 75–7.
[31] Flower (1996) 79–88.
[32] Crawford (1974) 242; Flower (1996) 333–8 assembles a full list of such ancestral themes, but it should be underlined that only a minority of these are portraits.

Figure 5.6 Denarius of Minucius Augurinus (© Copyright the Trustees of the British Museum, BMCRR 1005)

Figure 5.7 Denarius of Brutus, with heads of Brutus and Ahala (© Copyright the Trustees of the British Museum, BMCRR 3866)

republican values is expressed in an innovative form, in a hellenistic language that points the way to monarchy.[33] The coin neatly encapsulates the Gattopardo-like paradox, that to express ancestral tradition, even using the traditional language of *imagines maiorum*, it is necessary to innovate.

To this aggressive exploitation of *maiores* by the self-styled nobility there is a reverse side. Their assertions were not accepted automatically, but were on the contrary subject to vigorous challenge. The classic conflict is between the *nobilis* whose virtues are hereditary and the *novus homo* who owes his advancement to his own virtues. In Sallust's *Bellum Jugurthinum*, Marius, fighting for the consulship and the displacement of his own commander,

---

[33] Crawford (1974) 433; Wallace-Hadrill (1986) 74–5; Flower (1996) 88–9.

the noble Metellus Numidicus, symbolises the conflict and the hostility to the pretensions of the aristocracy.[34] The same antithesis is repeatedly rehearsed by Cicero. He is, as he tells the popular assembly, a man 'without the faculty of addressing you about my ancestors', because, despite their local distinction in Arpinum, 'they lacked the illumination of honour from you' (i.e. of holding office at Rome).[35] At the opening of a speech before the assembly in which he wants to dissuade them from passing a land law that might appear to be to their advantage, it is not a complaint, but a play for the sympathy of the audience, as he establishes himself as a favourite of the people, not an arrogant aristocrat. Images of ancestors can, in context, be as readily turned to a man's disadvantage as to his advantage:

You crept into office because men were fooled, fooled by the commendation of smoke-stained images with which you had nothing in common but colour. (*in Pisonem* 1)

The late republican authors who feed us the notion that Romans revered a noble's ancestors in fact offer not a single 'given', but a triangular relationship. At the summit of the triangle is an ideal: that the *virtus* of a great man is transmitted to his descendants who will equal his achievements. That ideal is set in a past separate from the unsatisfactory present. At the base of the triangle are the two competing deployments of the ideal which constitute the reality of the present: the noble exploits his smoke-stained *imagines* for political advantage, and his opponents counter by representing him as degenerate scion who has let down his forefathers. The ideal itself is not contested, since both sides need to play off it for their opposing rhetorics; and thus they conspire to construct an image of the past when ideal was reality, and without the contestation that in fact typifies the present. The essence, then, of the *use* of ancestors is as a means of persuasion within a situation of conflict.

Ancestors in rhetoric

The same analysis applies to the second category of use of ancestors, the generalised appeal to *nostri maiores*, the ancestors of the Romans at large, not of individual nobles. Instances of this appeal are, as a group of German studies in the 1930s showed, almost universal in Cicero's oratory.[36] That is natural,

---

[34] Sallust, *Jugurtha* 84–5; Flower (1996) 16–23.
[35] Cicero, *de Lege Agraria* 2.1.   [36] Plumpe (1932), Rech (1936), Roloff (1937).

for where an irreproachable authority is vested in ancestors, the appeal to ancestral precedent must be a central feature of persuasive argument. Nor is there the remotest plausibility in the view that the appeal to ancestors is limited to those of one political persuasion ('conservatives'), while another tendency ('progressives') spurned it.[37] As emerges in the theoretical treatises on rhetoric, whichever side you took, you needed the appeal to ancestors to persuade a Roman audience.[38]

One of the earliest of these, the anonymous *Rhetorica ad Herennium*, a manual dating from the mid-80s BCE, well illustrates the flexibility of such arguments, to support or, conversely, to undermine an argument:

> We may speak *in support of* the use of torture by demonstrating that our ancestors, for the sake of discovering the truth, wished inquisition to be made by torments and crucifixion, and men to be compelled under extreme pain to reveal what they know . . . We may speak *against* inquisition by torture as follows: first our ancestors wished torture to be used only in certain circumstances, when they could know what was said truthfully, and refute what was made up in a false inquisition. (*Rhetorica ad Herennium* 2.10)

Cicero, who knows the same principle,[39] twice puts it into practice in surviving speeches:

> But our ancestors did not wish torture to be applied to a slave to give evidence against his master, not because the truth could not be extracted, but because it seemed shocking to do so, and worse than killing the master.[40]

Characteristic in these passages is the studied vagueness of the reference to the *maiores*, who either did or did not 'wish' torture to be used. Which ancestors, at which period, and how did they make their wish plain? The word 'wish' (*velle*), which is common in such contexts, hints at the language of the assembly in legislating (*velitis iubetis?*). But no law is being cited, since the nature of the *mos maiorum* is to stand alongside formal written law in the pair of *mos/lex* which together constitute *ius*. Custom is 'willed' by the Roman people just as much as a law, but not at a particular time in a particular place.

This way of thinking leads to a conception of custom that is seen not as the accidental product of history ('this is how we happen to have done it in the past'), but as a consciously willed creation. 'Our ancestors' are always possessed of endless wisdom and prudence: they have deliberately

---

[37] Thus Roloff (1937) 72f. contrasts the conservative Cicero to Caesar and his supporters.
[38] So Cicero, *de Inventione* 1.101, 2.113f.; *de Oratore* 2.335; *Partitiones Oratioriae* 118.
[39] *Partitiones Oratoriae* 118.   [40] *pro Milone* 59, cf. *pro Rege Deiotaro* 3.

designed or 'instituted' each and every feature of Roman life, public or private, political, legal, religious, military, domestic, and to question any aspect of tradition is to insult their intelligence:

The one legal action available is that by interdict, which we used. If it is not valid, or if it does not apply in this case, what could be more foolish or negligent than our ancestors . . . ? But honestly, it is quite shameful to condemn men of the greatest wisdom of such stupidity, as you do in suggesting that it never occurred to our ancestors to provide for this charge and action. (*pro Caecina* 40)

The possibility of errors or oversights by the ancestors is so absurd that it can be rubbished. Just as the design of the Universe may be used to argue the existence of a perfect creator, so the perfection of Roman life argues a conscious design by ancestors endowed with a divine intelligence. The orator not only can assert what they willed, but why, given this wisdom, they willed it. Ancestral custom is therefore always simultaneously right because it is traditional, and because it is absolutely wiser. That means that, inversely, ancestral custom can be inferred, since whatever course of action is wiser must also be traditional.

This sort of rhetorical deployment of the *maiores* generates a picture of the past that is fluid and without boundaries. There can be no sense that the Romans at different periods behaved in fundamentally different ways, nor of any conflict of opinion and interest between different individuals and groups (and this despite the historical tradition of the conflict of the orders). Historical awareness becomes half-suspended, in order to sustain the image of internal coherence, of prudent and virtuous ancestors in unison calling the present to follow their perfection. Yet this anti-historical picture can be and is reconciled with a sense of historical development. The classic example of this reconciliation is attributed by Cicero, in his transformation of Plato's *Republic*, to the elder Cato: the reason for the superiority of Rome to all other states was that they depended on single individual lawgivers (Minos, Lycurgus), or on lawgivers who in succession founded different constitutions (Theseus, Draco, Solon, Cleisthenes), whereas 'our republic is the product not of one mind, but of many, and has been established not by a single lifetime, but by many centuries and ages' (*Republic* 2.2). That leads to an account of the evolution of the Roman constitution that is radically opposed to the Platonic theory of different types of constitution displacing each other in succession; the Roman constitution is cumulative, and however great the differences, between individual kings, and between them and the republic that displaced them, they work together to form a common pool of shared wisdom on which the present draws (*Republic* 2.17ff).

This construction of ancestors elides the gap between past and present. Although the orator by definition speaks at a moment when there is dispute over how to act, his persuasion asserts that in following the course of action he recommends, the continuity between ancestral wisdom and current practice will be preserved. Here there is a striking contrast with the use of ancestors in Greek oratory. Attic speakers, too, praised the virtues of their ancestors, but in significantly different contexts and ways. Praise of *progonoi* is one of the commonplaces of fourth-century Athenian rhetoric, and extended passages sing the merits of 'our ancestors who fought at Marathon'. But these set pieces are highly generalised, rather than offering a series of specific models for action in the present; they occur in public speeches, in 'epideictic' or display oratory like funeral orations or in Isocrates' show pieces, and never in court speeches on matters of private law; and they set the ancestors in the rosy glow of a past that is essentially distant from the present, to be remembered and revered, not of a living tradition to be preserved and maintained.[41] Just as Greek political theory (unlike Roman) posits a rupture between different constitutional phases, Attic oratory nostalgically posits a rupture between their ancestors and themselves. It is characteristic of the viewpoint that the idea of 'the ancestral constitution', *patrios politeia*, becomes significant in Athenian politics in the context of oligarchic attempts to subvert democracy and to 'return' to a supposedly 'traditional' constitution of the past.[42]

The second use of the *maiores*, then, can be seen, like the first, as a triangular relationship. At the base is the present reality of dispute over how to act; at the apex is the pattern of the conduct established by the cumulative wisdom of the past. Although the competing parties in the present may attribute diametrically opposed models of action to the *maiores*, that implies neither conflict within the tradition, nor rupture between past and present. The dispute is rather how, in the precise and novel circumstances of the present, our ancestors would have acted. If, as Sahlins puts it, the transformation of a culture is a mode of its reproduction, then it is precisely by the innovative adaptation of received, or rather perceived, tradition to the unpredictable circumstances of the present that the continuity with the past is preserved.

We can see the process depicted vividly at work by Sallust in his account of the senatorial debate of 63 BCE over the fate of the fellow-conspirators of Catiline.[43] The circumstances of the conspiracy have presented the senate

---

[41] See Plumpe (1932) 20ff. for all these contrasts, borne out by the detailed study of Jost (1936).
[42] Finley (1971).
[43] Sallust, *Catilina* 51–2. On the debate, see Earl (1961), Syme (2002) 103–20, Kraus and Woodman (1997).

and Cicero as consul with an unprecedented threat. Caesar points to models of ancestral *clementia* in urging that their lives be spared; Cato to models of ancestral *severitas* in urging their instant execution. Cato's reading of true Roman tradition prevails in the senate; but the reader knows that Caesar's reading will be reasserted shortly after, and Cicero driven into exile, then, after further dispute, recalled.

Ancestors betrayed

Alongside this idea of ancestors as living tradition sits the third, and quite different, picture of the past as a lost ideal. The *maiores* remain, as before, models of virtue and wisdom, whom the present should imitate; but far from marking and giving authority to a continuity ('this is the Roman way'), they mark a rupture. They belong to a different world, of an idealised past; and though they ought to be imitated, the present world is either rapidly slipping away, or already so deeply corrupted that imitation must involve a major effort of revival.

So, as we have seen (above, p. 164), Cicero contrasts the Roman tradition of assemblies conducted standing on foot, and organised on the principles of military rank, with the supposed disorder of a Greek assembly, conducted seated in the theatre:

What a fine custom and discipline we inherited from our ancestors! If only we could stick to it! But somehow or other it is already slipping from our hands . . . But with the Greeks whole states are run by the rash decisions of a seated assembly. (Cicero, *pro Flacco* 15)

Here there is slippage rather than rupture, and in general it is the case in Cicero's speeches that ancestral tradition is not seen as completely out of touch with the present.

It is in his philosophical works that the sense of rupture becomes uppermost. This is partly because most were written in the period of Caesar's dictatorship, when Cicero felt strongly that the world he knew had been lost, but it applies also to the *Republic*, written in the 50s BCE. Context is significant here, for while speeches depend on the myth of living tradition in order to persuade, philosophical works are concerned with ideals which can be located in a remote past without harm to the argument. The opening of the fifth book of the *Republic* sets the tone. The idea that the greatness of Rome derives from its respect towards ancestral custom is epitomised in the Ennian line,

Moribus antiquis res stat Romana virisque.
By ancient customs the state of Rome stands and by its men.

The men made the *mores*, and the *mores* made the men. But now, all is changed:

> And so before living memory traditional custom by itself made men outstanding, and excellent men preserved the old ways and practices of their ancestors. But our age, having inherited the *res publica* like a masterpiece of painting that was already fading with age, has not only neglected to restore the old colours that were there, but has not even troubled to preserve its shape and outlines . . . It is by our own faults, not by accident, that we keep the *res publica* in name only, and have long since lost its substance. (*de Republica* 5.1–2)

The image of the 'old master' allows for the constant process of 'retouching' that imitation of the *mos maiorum* implies; but the loss even of outlines is a perversely deliberate rupture.

This attitude is recurrent in the philosophical works. Two areas are particularly closely associated with the heart of Roman tradition, civil law and religion. But both traditions have collapsed:

> Our ancestors wished to distinguish civil law from *ius gentium*, universal law . . . But we have lost the solid figure set in the mould of true law and its twin, justice; instead we use a shadow and reflections. (*de Officiis* 3.69)

Again, Cicero turns to the world of art to express the sense of loss of genuine substance. The present follows the past, but falsely, only in name, a shadowy reflection not a solid reproduction.

In religion, the sense of loss is even more acute. Tradition is not only the reference point for resolving disputes involving religious matters, as Cicero uses it in his disputes with Clodius,[44] but is itself the philosophical justification for religious belief. The famous words which Cicero puts in the mouth of Cotta, with twin role as Roman pontifex and Greek Stoic philosopher, rests on the commonplace that the *maiores* are wiser than any philosopher, and imitation of their practice is more potent than any amount of philosophising:[45]

> I was much moved, Balbus, by your authority, and your encouragement to recall that I was a Cotta and a Pontifex. The implication, I believe, was that I should defend the opinions which we have received from our ancestors about the immortal gods, their rites, ceremonies and religions. In truth, I have always defended them, and shall always do so: no speech of any man, however learned or otherwise, will shake me

---

[44] E.g. *de Haruspicum Responso* 18.

[45] So *de Oratore* 2.1 prefers Roman practice to Greek rhetorical theory; *de Republica* 3.5 prefers Roman custom to Socratic ethics.

in the opinion which I received from my ancestors about the cult of the immortal gods. (*de Natura Deorum* 3.5)

Yet the same work laments the demise of this tradition:

But by the negligence of the nobility the discipline of augury has been dropped, and the true practice of auspices is spurned, and only its appearance retained. And so most functions of the state, including warfare on which its safety depends, are administered without auspices. By contrast, religion had such force for our ancestors, that some of them ritually veiled their heads and vowed their lives to the immortal gods for the republic. (*de Natura Deorum* 2.9–10)

The juxtaposition of the view that a Roman noble and priest ought to remain true to his ancestral religion with the assertion that the nobility now neglect that tradition except in name has led to the modern view that Roman traditional religion was in actual decline in the late republic. But that reading underestimates the ambivalence of the Roman construction of the past: on the one hand tradition is a living force that defines action in the present; but, on the other, it is a remote ideal which reproaches the present with its inadequacy. Where does this ambivalence come from?

Antiquarian study and the rupture of tradition

The three ways of using ancestors which I have here distinguished coexist chronologically, and are linked to each other logically. Noble ancestors are the specific individual manifestation of the general respect for all ancestors; and the nobility above all, like Cotta, because they are the men with visible ancestors, are seen as guardians of the Roman tradition. The same assumption of the unquestionable wisdom of the ancestors which leads to competitive assertions of ancestral practice in situations of dispute, also leads to lamentations about the decline of tradition in contexts which encourage criticism of the present.

But though these attitudes may coexist, and even reinforce each other, there is a distinction to be drawn which corresponds to the supposed difference between oral and literate modes of constructing the past. To treat ancestors, whether of the individual noble, or of the Romans in general, as a living tradition coheres with the use of tradition characteristic of 'oral' or 'pre-literate' societies. Memories of the past transmitted by word of mouth survive only to serve the present, and can be constantly discarded, shuffled and adapted to fit changing circumstances. The very vagueness of the usage of *maiores nostri* and the homogeneity it implies cohere with an essentially oral usage. The temptation is to posit this as the 'original' Roman concept of ancestors, surviving from a period of 'orality' before the spread of literary culture at Rome. Yet orality is not extinguished by literacy, but enters a dialectical relationship with it;[46] and it may be more apposite to draw attention to the continuing oral context of persuasion in the Forum. The best parallel to this type of oral tradition may be not the 'pre-literate' societies studied by anthropologists, but that of high medieval Europe, in which oral modes continued to dominate the courts, despite the use of writing within the church and the central administration.[47]

The contrasting sense of rupture between present and past is closely allied to developed literate modes of thought. Once recording intervenes to disrupt the continuous adjustments of oral memory, the past emerges as strange and other. This is not to say that a nostalgic sense that ancestors did things better is incompatible with an oral tradition; as we have seen, Greek orators tended to cast their *progonoi* in this light. But it is demonstrable that, as developed in the late republic, the Roman sense of a tradition neglected, abandoned and in urgent need of restoration has much to do with scholarly reconstruction and book-learning. Roman antiquarianism developed a powerful discourse about the past that relied on scholarly research.[48] But it did so in the context of a period of radical political and social upheaval. It had the effect of unhooking the present, so to speak, from the obligation to follow the recent past. By relocating the legitimising authority of the ancestors in a remote past, it gave the present a greater freedom to innovate.

Varro was the dominant figure of Cicero's lifetime, and though scarcely anything of his *Antiquities* survives,[49] the mood of that massive work is captured by Cicero and Augustine. The sense of otherness of the past is highlighted by Cicero:[50]

When we were like strangers abroad and lost in our own city, your books led us back home, so to speak, so that at last we were able to recognise who and where we were. You revealed the age of our native land, its divisions of time, the rules of sacrifice and priesthoods; discipline at home and at war; the location of regions and places; and the names, types, functions and causes of all matters divine and human. (*Academica Posteriora* 9)

---

[46] On the interpenetration of orality and literacy, see Ong (1982), Thomas (1992).
[47] Clanchy (1979); McKitterick (1989).
[48] Rawson (1985) 233–49 is fundamental on Roman antiquarianism; Momigliano (1966) on antiquarianism versus historiography.
[49] For the text, Cardauns (1976); in general Dahlmann (1935) 1229–47, Cardauns (2001).
[50] *Academica Posteriora* 9 = Cardauns (1976) T1.

The image Cicero offers is an astonishing inversion. Where Roman legal language divides the world into Roman citizens and *peregrini*, outsiders, the Romans now emerge as outsiders in their own city who have wholly lost their sense of identity (*qui aut ubi essemus*) and need showing their way home. This is not simply Ciceronian hyperbole, since Augustine makes it plain that it was Varro's own purpose to drive home to his Roman audience this sense of being lost:

He feared that the gods should perish, not by enemy invasion, but by the negligence of citizens, and he claimed that this was the doom from which he was rescuing them, and that it was a more useful service that things should be stored away and preserved in the memory of good men through books of this type, than when Metellus is said to have rescued the sacred objects of the Vestals from burning, or Aeneas to have saved the *penates* from the sack of Troy.[51]

Varro's claim is no modest one. Aeneas' rescue of the Trojan *penates* is the act of preservation of the past upon which the continuity of the foundation of the Roman state is based. Varro is Rome's second founder, preserving it from the ruin of forgetfulness. Books are his essential instrument, and they ensure that the essential information will return to the mainstream of living tradition, to the 'memory of good men'. He will, in fact, reintegrate the continuity of living tradition with a past that has become discontinuous through neglect. His book serves a purpose as practical and salutary as any medical text, for knowing which gods should be invoked when and for what purpose is like knowing which medicines to use and how.[52]

Such reconstruction of the lost past necessarily involves going back behind living memory. The techniques were pioneered at the end of the second century by Varro's model, Aelius Stilo. He ranks as one of Rome's first men of learning: rated by Cicero as 'most erudite in both Greek and Roman letters', Stilo is placed by Suetonius at the head of his biographical account of the study of grammar and rhetoric at Rome.[53] With a proclaimed interest in Stoic philosophy, he studied in Rhodes, perhaps the leading Greek scholarly centre of the day. As we have seen (p. 68), his work on the Latin language (in which he was also followed by Varro) transposed the dominant controversies about the nature of the Greek language to the study of Latin. His antiquarian studies, too, seem to have relied on Greek methodology, based on the critical exposition of texts:[54]

---

[51] Fr. 2A = Augustine, *de Civitate Dei* 6.2.248.   [52] Fr. 3 = Aug. *de Civitate Dei* 4.22.172.

[53] Cicero, *Brutus* 205; Suetonius, *de Grammaticis et Rhetoribus* 2.

[54] For the methods of Greek antiquarianism, see Pfeiffer (1968) esp. 234–51.

Whoever enjoys the studies of Aelius will find in the civil law and in the pontifical records and in the Twelve Tables a rich source of images of antiquity, both in the archaic style of language and in the picture suggested by certain procedures of the ways and life-style of our ancestors. (Cicero, *de Oratore* 1.193)

The association of scholarly interest in language with that in ways of life, *consuetudo vitaque*, is not casual, since a prime method of reconstructing ancient ways was through the exposition of difficult 'glosses' in such texts. This can be seen throughout the three books of Varro's *De Lingua Latina* (5–7) devoted to etymologies, in which reference to 'Aelius' is repeatedly made. Antiquarian concerns surface constantly, and in the absence of the *Antiquities* themselves, these books have become a prime source for Varro's views on matters like the topography of Rome and the calendar. The link is founded on one of the core assumptions of the Greek science of etymology, that the 'true' meaning of a word can be uncovered from the words which go to make it up. Thus *panis*, bread, is explained as a derivative of *panus*, sheet, on the grounds that originally bread was made in sheets, and later in other shapes (*De Lingua Latina* 5.105). A bogus etymology thus generates a bogus 'fact' about how the Romans used to live.

Not all was based on this type of random conjecture. Critical analysis of genuinely ancient documents revealed a language and a world that differed palpably from those of the present. Varro praises Aelius for his painstakingly scholarly work on the Salian Hymn, which they allowed might date back 700 years to the reign of Numa: such was its obscurity that attention to an individual letter might make all the difference (*De Lingua Latina* 7.2–3). One of Varro's own most impressive passages is his analysis of the archaic term *inlicium*, invitation, which he traces in the records of the censors, the consuls and an ancient formula for summonsing a defendant (6.86–95). What for him emerges from these passages is not only the sense of the word, but documentation of the changes in the ways Romans conducted their public life:

The procedure nowadays is different from what it once was, since it is the augur who attends on the consul when he summons the army and who dictates the words he should speak. Usage now is for the augur, not an 'accensus' or 'praeco' [these are named in the documents] to be instructed by the consul to issue an *inlicium*. (Varro, *De Lingua Latina* 6.95)

Confrontation with such documents explains how, for all the tenacious loyalty of a noble like Cotta to what he saw as ancestral tradition, Varro could regard 'true' Roman tradition as perishing by neglect. Study of old documents produced a double sense of awareness of the gap between the *maiores* and the present: the old ways were different, and the Latin language itself in which they were described was different. The antiquarian's enterprise was premised on this awareness:

These matters are the more obscure because not all words coined remain extant, as age makes many obsolete, and not all extant words are without error (many words have letters interpolated or changed). (Varro, *De Lingua Latina* 5.3)

If the Latin language itself, which lies at the heart of Roman identity,[55] is subject to constant change, indeed deterioration, over time, the change of customs is part of the same process:

Have not shapes of pots of unprecedented type, recently imported from Greece, obliterated those of traditional custom, called *sini* and *capulae*? . . .

How many people still have slaves with the old-fashioned style of name? What woman calls her clothes and jewellery by the old names? (Varro, *De Lingua Latina* 9.21–2)

The same irresistible movement that changes daily life, housing, furniture, clothes and jewellery, changes language: 'the practice of language is in motion', *consuetudo loquendi est in motu* (*De Lingua Latina* 9.17). However, for language at least, Varro does not draw the conclusion that all change must be resisted; some words, he continues, that were wrongly formed by the ancients are now corrected, while some that were correct have been corrupted (*De Lingua Latina* 9.17).

The emergence of a discourse of antiquarianism had a radical effect on Roman perceptions of tradition and on their sense of identity. Scholars have tended to underestimate this impact, because of the assumption that it was merely a reflection of a long-established traditionalism that could only be conservative in its impact. Since Rome was in fact changing profoundly at this period, the antiquarians are seen as moralists vainly and irrelevantly hankering after the old days. They might have an impact at a purely literary level (for instance, in shaping Virgil's picture of early Rome), but little in the shaping of a new identity for Rome.

Such a point of view misconstrues the Roman use of ancestors. It is doubtful whether even the 'oral' tradition of reference to the authority of ancestral practice could be purely conservative in its effect. Of course it might act as a brake on innovation, as in the notorious expulsion of Latin rhetors in 92 BCE, when 'our ancestors' were invoked as wishing other types of schools. But the very fluidity of oral memories of tradition, and the contexts

---

[55] Cf. Dench (2005) 316–21.

of contestation in which they were characteristically invoked, made genuine adherence to tradition unachievable. An alternative analysis would be that reference to the *maiores* enabled the Romans to legitimate the constantly innovative responses to new circumstances demanded by an ambitiously expanding society, and to regain a sense of continuity of identity in the face of change.[56]

Antiquarianism, far from enhancing the reassuring sense of continuity provided by traditionalism, subverted it. First, we should consider its impact on the traditional authority of the nobility. The republican elite, as we have seen, constructed its superior status (*nobilitas*) by reference to *maiores*. The noble by definition possessed ancestors, and with them a memory of the past and the obligation to parade and reproduce it. If there was question of what the *mos maiorum* actually was, those with *maiores* might be expected speak on the issue with peculiar authority. That authority was certainly not unchallenged; but the concentration of the two vital functions of priestly office and knowledge of the law in the hands of the nobility underpinned their authority in precisely those areas that were regarded as the heart of the *mos maiorum*.

Antiquarianism presented a frontal challenge to that authority. The claim that traditional rites had fallen into disuse by the negligence of the very priests obliged to preserve them struck at the heart of their authority, and raised up an alternative structure of authority. It was now the antiquarian, by his laborious study of obscurely worded documents, and displaying the credentials of Greek academic learning, who 'knew' what the 'real' Roman tradition was. The 'memory of good men', as Varro put it, now started from books, not oral tradition. The noble priest and jurisprudent not only finds his authority subverted, but is subjected to contumely as the man who has betrayed his own ancestors. Here Cicero in his philosophic works stands close to Varro: if the *res publica* is a masterpiece whose very structure and substance has been lost, the nobility have nothing to offer, and much to answer for.

Antiquarian research undermined both the claim of the self-constructed nobility to define true Roman ways (and hence identity), but even, devastatingly, their claim to know their own *maiores*. Cicero, we have seen, was amused by the inability of Scipio Metellus to identify his own ancestors and know their careers. Elsewhere he gives his friend Papirius Paetus an extensive lesson in the ancestry of the Papirii, to correct his mistaken claim that they were an exclusively plebeian family.[57] It was a commonplace that false

---

[56] Cf. North (1976).   [57] Cicero *ad Familiares* 9.21.2–3; Flower (1996) 290–1.

family histories confused the record of the Roman annalists. The notion that the nobles were neglectful of their own ancestors was fed by the production both by Varro and by Cicero's friend Atticus of books called *Imagines*, in Varro's case including, so Pliny tells us, 700 portraits, though these were not of Romans only.[58] Such antiquarian studies acquired a new authority in identifying the ancestors for whom the reference point was supposed to be the wax masks stored in noble *atria*. But take knowledge of his ancestors away from him, and what authority is left to the noble?

Greek models

We may be struck by the complexity of the role played by Greek culture in the construction of Roman identity. Cicero in the *Tusculan Disputations* offers us an apparently unproblematic contrast between the *mores* inherited from their ancestors which give the Romans their superiority and the arts in which the Greeks are stronger (but only so long as the Romans do not compete). Such passages create the impression that the contribution of Greek culture to Rome lies purely in the artistic and the intellectual sphere, and that *mores maiorum* constitute the pure and authentic Roman strand in Roman culture. The analysis above has tended to dissolve this opposition. The *maiores* emerge as a complex construct; and in the articulation of this tradition as we meet it in authors of the first century BCE, from Nepos, Cicero, Aelius and Varro to Virgil and Ovid, Greek learning has a vital part to play.

We may observe, first, that Greek authors like Polybius and Posidonius were themselves anxious to affirm the Roman claim that their ancestors set a model of moral superiority. Second, that the Roman authors who present us with the image of the *maiores* were steeped in Greek literary tradition, and actually employed in the process of construction sophisticated techniques, such as etymology and the criticism of documents, which they took directly from contemporary Greek scholarship. And we may add a third suggestion, that Greek culture itself offered a model around which a Roman culture could be reconstructed. We have already seen that fourth-century Attic oratory set its ancestors in a nostalgic haze in the past, the fighters of Marathon who won Athens her glory. The Roman construction of their own *maiores* as men of incomparable *virtus* who by industry and parsimonious ways won the Roman empire is analogous in that it locates the core moral values in the past.

---

[58] Pliny, *Natural History* 35.11; Nepos, *Atticus* 18.5–6; Rawson (1985) 198–9; Flower (1996) 182–3.

Greek idealisation of the past and antiquarianism were specifically stimulated in response to Roman conquest. It was a natural response to defeat and humiliation to locate the core values and enduring superiority of Greek culture in the classical past.[59] That made it easier to deplore the corruption and degeneracy of the contemporary world: Polybius and Posidonius not only warn the Romans of the dangers of falling from ancestral standards, but point to the luxury and degeneracy of the contemporary Greek world as a source of corruption.

Sparta offers a particularly clear example of this response.[60] 'Lycurgan' institutions, which had long since become obsolete in the hellenistic world, were formally abolished as part of the incorporation of Sparta in the Achaean League in 188 BCE. Yet soon after, probably after the Roman settlement of 146/145 BCE, those institutions underwent a massive 'revival'. The 'restored' Lycurgan constitution was significantly different from the archaic and classical pattern: the *agoge* no longer trained boys from age seven onwards, but became an extended *ephebeia* for teenagers; completely new institutions with a false patina of antiquity, like a priesthood of Urania, were introduced; and, by an ironic symbolism, the face of Lycurgus himself, who had forbidden the use of coinage, appeared on Spartan coins.

The recreation of a 'traditional' Sparta was of great importance, not just for attracting the tourist trade, though there is a strong element of that too,[61] but for recreating a sense of identity in the face of Roman conquest. Under such circumstances, continuity with the immediate past was inadequate, and it became necessary to reach back to a perceived past to recreate identity. Just as Varro saw his own antiquarian works becoming the foundation for living tradition, the Spartans depended on antiquarian writings for their image of the past. The study of the Spartan constitution by Dicaearchus of Messene, whose *Bios Hellados* Cicero so admired, was read annually by the ephors to the Spartan youth, and a batch of other Spartan antiquarians, like Sosibius, studied Spartan cults and customs, and the poetry of the Spartan Alcman.[62]

What emerges is a complex interaction of Greek and Roman.[63] Roman conquest had the effect of throwing the Greeks back on their past and

---

[59] The point has been made especially for a later period by Bowie (1970); Swain (1996), Whitmarsh (2001b).

[60] See Cartledge and Spawforth (1989) esp. 190ff.

[61] Stressed by Cartledge and Spawforth (1989) 210f.

[62] Cartledge and Spawforth (1989) 176 (Sosibius), 198 (Dicaearchus). Note that the antiquarians predate 146. On Dicaearchus' influence, see Ax (2000).

[63] For closely comparable interactions in the imperial period, see Swain (1996).

bringing out an already developed sense of heritage. The sense of gap between glorious past and degenerate present was heightened. But if Greeks located identity and pride in the past, they provided the Romans with both encouragement and, through learned studies, the technical means, to do the same. By a parallel, indeed collusive, movement the definitions of 'the Greek' and 'the Roman' were unhitched from contemporary realities. For both sides, 'traditionalism' brought not inflexibility, but the basis for creative adaptation. Cultural identity invested in a remote past becomes not so much a programme as an alibi.

Calendars and time[64]

What implications did antiquarianism carry for action in the present in the context of radical political change? In proclaiming the discontinuity between the present and tradition, it could hardly serve as a force for conservatism. By fostering the sense of the inadequacy of the present, it generated the demand for change. The change, true, should be the recovery of the 'true' Roman tradition, but one so located in a past when circumstances were fundamentally different, and so fragmentarily reconstructed by book learning, that the scope for representing radical change as 'return to tradition' was enormous.

This is exactly what happens with Augustus. In his radical realignment of the structures of power and authority around his own person, Augustus brought about a sharp hiatus with the traditions of the recent past. Yet he was able to represent this discontinuity as a continuity at a deeper level, a return to older and more authentic Roman traditions, a 'restoration of the *res publica*'. This 'deeper' continuity was elaborately paraded: in monuments, like the new Forum Augustum, with its statues of heroes of Roman history whose example Augustus claimed to perpetuate (in his own words, 'he had designed it so that they should provide an exemplar for himself while he lived and the *principes* of future ages to be measured against by the citizens');[65] in religious ceremonial, by the restoration of sacred buildings, priesthoods and rites, in which, thanks to Varro, the resuscitation of rituals supposed to have fallen into neglect had particular symbolic force; and in literary presentations of his reign and its relation to the past, from the *Aeneid*, through Propertius' fourth book with its antiquarian themes, to Ovid.[66]

---

[64] See now the stimulating discussion of Feeney (2007) esp. 167–211.
[65] Suetonius, *Augustus* 31.5; see Zanker (1988) 210–15.
[66] Scheid (1992); Beard, North and Price (1998) 167–210.

Ways of marking time are also powerful ways of marking identity. The French Revolution, for instance, within a year imposed a radical new calendar, numbering the years of the Revolution from 22 September 1792, renaming all months, decimalizing them as thirty days in length, and substituting weeks with ten-day cycles. The experiment lasted fourteen years, and collapsed in the face of popular resistance. The subtlety (and durability) of the Caesarian/Augustan metamorphosis lies in the perpetuation of most features of the republican calendar, combined with a pervasive incorporation of the imperial presence.[67] The Roman calendar reform is therefore of a quite different order from that of the French Revolution, which sought to mark republican time in every possible way as an abandonment of the time of the *ancien régime*. Rather than parading change, it masks it, or re-presents republican time in such a way that imperial time seems its natural and organic extension. But the rupture is there.

Roman accounts of Caesar's calendar reform of 46 BCE locate the need for change in the corruption of the pontifical college: so explicitly Suetonius, almost certainly recycling in his life of Caesar the results of his antiquarian compilation *On the Roman Year*:

Turning then to bringing order to the state of public affairs, he corrected the calendar long since confused by the fault of the *pontifices* thanks to arbitrariness in intercalation, so much so that harvest festivals no longer fell in the summer, nor vintage festivals in the autumn.[68]

The corrupting influence brought to bear on the pontifical college is elaborated in the parallel accounts in the numerous writings of the antiquarian tradition that discuss the question as both political and financial:

Many of them [the *pontifices*] through hatred or favour, in order to extend or contract the term of office of a particular magistrate, or to increase or decrease the profit of a public contractor by the length of the year, by intercalating more or less at will had the effect of further depraving what it was their mandate to correct.[69]

The rhetoric of these accounts is consistent: order and reason versus confusion and arbitrary power, observation of tradition versus favouritism and corruption. The rhetoric demolishes the claims of the *pontifices* to the legitimacy derived from observation of long-standing ancestral practice. This

---

[67] Meinzer (1992), Rüpke (1995) 379–80.

[68] Suetonius, *Julius* 40: the passages are conveniently assembled in Michels (1967) 146–60. On the reforms, see Rüpke (1995) 369–91, Hannah (2005) 106–22.

[69] Censorinus, *De die natali* 20.7; cf Solinus 1.45 (?); Ammianus 26.1.12; Macrobius, *Saturnalia* 1.14.1. On intercalation, see Warrior (1992).

rhetoric, which is of a piece with the entire late republican rhetoric of the 'corruption of the few', is surely contemporary with the reforms. Already Cicero, though his letters reveal him intervening with all the influence at his disposal to prevent intercalation and so the extension of his tenure of office in Cicilia,[70] voices the theme of the negligence of the pontifices in this sphere, too:

The calculations of intercalation should be carefully observed, a practice wisely instituted by Numa but dissolved by the negligence of later pontifices.[71]

Since the matter was an issue of contemporary political debate of the 50s BCE, including the failed attempt of Curio to pass a law on intercalation,[72] and the law of Clodius of 58,[73] it might be enough to refer the rhetoric to political debate itself. But behind the rhetoric lies a perception of what the proper role of the pontifices was, and how generally they had abandoned tradition, from which Varro's researches cannot be dissociated. Caesar's reforms prove to have a sort of foreshadowing in earlier history, in the publication of the *fasti*, apparently at the end of the fourth century BCE, by the freeman's son and scribe Cn. Flavius:

There were once only few who knew whether legal actions were permitted on any day; the calendar of permitted days (*fasti*) was not yet published. The people who were consulted on the matter enjoyed vast power; it was like approaching the Chaldaeans to get information from them about days. A certain scribe, one Cn Flavius, was found to peck out the proverbial crows' eyes, and by working out each and every day, displayed the calendar before the people and on the basis of these very legal experts with all their caution made a compilation of their learning. (Cicero, *pro Murena* 25)

Cicero's language cannot be taken as a reliable historical account of whatever happened in the fourth century, which is far from clear. Since tradition maintained that the decemvirs themselves, as part of the exercise of codifying Roman law in the Twelve Tables, had already published the calendar, a contradiction that struck Cicero himself,[74] it has always taken the ingenuity of specialists on the calendar to explain the nature of the Flavian 'publication'.[75] There is no need to solve this mystery (which surely points to an unreliable tradition), only to observe the language in which the issue was represented in the late republic. It is seen as a battle between '*pauci*', the few who use

---

[70] Michels (1967) 146, passages 2–7.   [71] Cicero, *de Legibus* 2.29.

[72] Cicero, *ad Familiares* 8.6.5.   [73] Michels (1967) 94f.

[74] Cicero, *ad Atticum* 6.1.8 confesses his puzzlement.

[75] Michels (1967) 106ff., Rüpke (1995) 244–74.

their privileged access to knowledge, and the low-born hero who benefits the entire Roman people by publishing the arcane knowledge. The reference to Chaldaeans, precisely experts who wield power through access to astrological lore, adds to the rhetorical subversion of traditional priestly wisdom.

We need not assert that the rhetoric comes from Varro (though it runs close to his general representation of the nobles as those who have betrayed the knowledge of the past) in order to see how Varronian *sapientia* offers a plausible alternative structure of knowledge. Varronian calendrical learning naturally went far beyond identifying which days were *fasti* and which *nefasti* – so much by the first century was certainly well known. Rather, he was interested in matters of etymology, of just what '*fasti*' meant: a word he saw as derived from *fari*, 'speak', because on these days it was allowed for the praetor to utter the three words, '*do, dico, addico*' which indicated that he could give justice, and so pronounce on legal cases.[76] That etymology, as many of Varro's etymologies, seems unconvincing to modern experts, who would rather focus on what was *fas* or *nefas* to do on those days, namely to hold legal actions.[77] What matters is that he persuaded all subsequent commentators that this was the sort of thing one should be saying. He defined a discourse of learning, a way of thinking and speaking about the calendar, that offered a *sapientia* infinitely more convincing than the Chaldaean wisdom of *pontifices* who played their cards so close to their chest, and used bogus learning as a screen for bribery and political corruption. It is still to his brief summary of his conclusions in the *De Lingua Latina* (6.27–34) of the names for parts of the calendar that scholars turn for understanding of the arcane terms and abbreviations: if only his explanation of the ligatured letters NP had survived, endless discussion could have been spared.[78]

The verse calendar Ovid conjures up in the *Fasti* well exemplifies the closeness of Augustus' links with antiquarianism. Behind Ovid's poem lies the scholarly edition and exposition of the Roman calendar by the grammarian Verrius Flaccus, who will have drawn on Varro's *Antiquities*. Verrius had close links with the palace, acting as tutor to Augustus' grandsons, as Suetonius explains in his brief biography. His publication of the *fasti*, which survives in part on stone from the Forum at Praeneste, doubly serves Augustus' purpose: by setting out the proper cycle of Roman festivals with appropriate exegesis it advertises the fact that ancient religious traditions are no longer neglected; and by incorporating the numerous thanksgivings

---

[76] Varro, *De Lingua Latina* 6.29–30.

[77] Extensively discussed by Michels (1967) 48–54, Rüpke (1995) 251–8.

[78] Michels (1967) 61–83. Rüpke (1995) 258–60 offers the new solution of the abbreviation 'NP' as Nefas Piaculum.

and celebrations for Augustus himself, it displays Augustus' status as part of the fabric of Roman tradition itself.[79] Ovid's *Fasti* elaborate and popularise the antiquarian's message, not simply using the calendar as a springboard to praise Augustus, but redefining Roman tradition to give him the key role.[80]

Ovid's *Fasti* celebrate ceaselessly the triumph of an antiquarian discourse. We are offered festivals 'annalibus eruta priscis', 'dug out of ancient records' (1.7). We are offered etymologies of classic Varronian stamp: 'that day will be *nefastus* on which three words are not spoken' alludes to Varro's praetorian formula of '*do, dico, addico*' – but how many readers knew?[81] The game is to explicate the obscure origins of strange words and practices, and to relish scholarly dispute in all its indecisive glory. On the doctrine of the ten-month year, the idea that March was originally the first month and December the tenth and last, Ovid stands firm to the canonical version – according to Censorinus, the line-up was Junius Gracchanus, Fulvius Nobilior, Varro and Suetonius, against Licinius Macer and Fenestella who maintained the view the year was always of twelve months.[82] But elsewhere, he relishes the controversy: why are 'May' or 'June' so called? There are at least three explanations for each name, and Ovid takes pleasure in calling a dead heat in the debate, as if the purpose was not so much to know the answer, as to know the dispute.[83] One might almost think of the dispute as Varro's new Chaldaeanism: now you have to be a skilled grammarian, read in obscure texts, offer variant hermeneutics, to impress anyone with your control of the calendar.

Scholarly discourse by itself is not enough to refashion Roman time in the image of Augustus; political gestures and decrees of the senate play their role too. The function of antiquarianism is to lend legitimacy by aligning the most credible form of knowledge about Roman tradition and identity with the activities of the reformer. We may be struck by the ideological capital which Augustus derives from calendar reform.[84] The essence of the Julian reform is to abolish the intercalary month, designed to reconcile the eleven-day shortfall of the Roman pseudo-lunar calendar with the solar

[79] On Verrius' *fasti*, see Degrassi (1963) xxii ff. On Verrius, see Kaster (1995) 190–6, on his Praenestine *fasti*, see Coarelli (1996b) 455–69. On the key role of exegesis for the calendar, see Beard (1987).

[80] Wallace-Hadrill (1987). For the growing bibliography on the *fasti*, see Barchiesi (1992), Scheid (1992) 118–31, Herbert-Brown (1994), Feeney (1998, Myres (1999) 198–200. On Ovid and Varro, see Cole (2004).

[81] *Fasti* 1.47: 'ille nefastus erit, per quem tria verba silentur.'

[82] *Fasti* 1.27–44; cf. Censorinus 20.2–3; Samuel (1972) 167ff.

[83] *Fasti* 5.1–110 – over a hundred lines on the name of May; similarly 6.1–100 on June.

[84] See more broadly Feeney (2007) 167–211.

cycle, and to substitute the system with which we are familiar, of the regular four-yearly leap year. That reform, which must have been undertaken on the advice of Greek astronomers who understood the mathematics perfectly well, was incautiously phrased: the additional day to be inserted *quarto anno*, 'every fourth year'. But since on Roman inclusive reckoning, the 'fourth' year includes the year you are counting from, for thirty-six years, between 46 and 9 BCE, leap years were inserted on a three-yearly rhythm. Vitruvius might have noted with amusement the inept hellenisation: a Greek expert says '*tetartō/τετάρτῳ*', but the Roman misinterprets 'fourth' and gets it wrong. Augustus' 'reform' of 9 BCE is merely to note the error, and correct it by suspending leap-years for the next twelve years, until the calendar was in synch again for a four-yearly cycle.

This minor correction is greeted with a major fanfare. The month Sextilis is renamed Augustus, just as Quinctilis had been named for the calendar-reforming Caesar.[85] The year of the reform is marked by a parallel reform in Asia Minor, where on the proposal of the proconsul, cities which traditionally had a wide diversity of local calendars agreed to adopt a common calendar – not, interestingly, that of Rome, but a Macedonian calendar with modifications to make it coincide with the Roman, and a celebration of New Year's day on 23 September, the birthday of Augustus, the day of the 'good news', in the remarkable messianic language that embellishes the decree, on which 'we ceased to regret being born'.[86] 9 BCE is also the date of the dedication of that astonishing architectural complex in Rome, the Horologium Augusti which, with a 100-ft obelisk as its *gnomon*, marked the day of the year if not the hour of the day, with Augustus' birthday on the equinox as a critical point, possibly aligned with the Ara Pacis, dedicated in this year.[87]

The reforms take place only when he takes over the role of Pontifex Maximus on the death of his old triumviral colleague, Aemilius Lepidus, whose life he had ostentatiously spared. The fact that the pontifical college under Lepidus' presidency had contrived to misread and vitiate Caesar's reform can only underline the lack of legitimacy of the old pontifical aristocracy. The matter could not be underlined often enough: whether the Chaldaean pontifices whose knowledge Cn. Flavius published, or the bribe-taking pontifices who had allowed the year to fall ninety days out of true by 46 BCE,

---

[85] 'August' was renamed from 8 BCE onwards: Censorinus 22.16; Macrobius, *Saturnalia* 1.12.34–5; Suetonius, *Augustus* 31; Scott (1931) 241–63.

[86] For the text of the decree, see Laffi (1967); for details of the reception of the reform, see Samuel (1972) 171–88.

[87] Buchner (1982); the important criticisms of Schutz (1990) 432–57 are partly accepted by Barton (1995) 33–51.

or Lepidus' college, which could not even apply correctly the reform which brought *ratio* in place of *consuetudo*, an old form of knowledge had collapsed. In that case, the Ara Pacis, dedicated in 9 BCE, with its long line of priestly figures around Augustus as Pontifex Maximus, *capite velato*, refers closely to the calendar of the Horologium, in promoting the sanctity of the new priestly order against their predecessors under Lepidus.

The range of Augustus' attempts to make all time revolve around himself is breathtaking: he penetrates all corners of the calendar of festivals around which the Roman religious and legal year is structured, he provides the evangelistic hinge of a new common calendar for the cities of the east, and he sets himself at the heart of a representation of cosmic order of which his natal sign, the Capricorn, becomes the teasing and elliptical signal. Of forty-eight different versions of the *fasti* found inscribed on stone or painted in Italy, forty-four belong to the reigns of Augustus or of Tiberius.[88] To publish the Augustan *fasti*, town by town, was to celebrate the new order, reflected in 'the power of dates'.[89]

These '*fasti*' consist of two types of list: the first is that of the high officials who mark the years, the consuls, supplemented by *triumphatores*, dictators and others, the second is the calendar of months and days. Many monuments combine the two types.[90] Behind the Augustan proliferation of monthly calendars, above all in marble, lies not only the confidence that the cycle of the year and its festivals is completely predictable, but the opportunity it offers for displaying the festivals and anniversaries of the imperial house. The mechanism is not of a centralised propaganda machine, but of competitive flattery: senators, local town councillors, members of colleges and corporations competed in their zeal to display their loyalty.[91] To inscribe the Roman calendar was a statement of loyalty to the Roman system, and the acknowledgement of the Emperor as the central feature of that system. That was why Ovid could not embark on a poetic *fasti* without knowing that his own zeal would be at every point under scrutiny.[92]

The enormous success of this imperial appropriation of Roman time can be illustrated by its wide diffusion beyond the inner circles of power. The *fasti* of Praeneste, despite their 'official' appearance, must have been a

---

[88] Salzman (1990) 7.　　[89] Rüpke (1995) 174–86.

[90] The classic edition is that of A. Degrassi in *Inscriptiones Italiae* vol. XIII. It is unfortunate for the understanding of how the two types of *fasti* relate that he splits into two volumes the *fasti* of the magistrates (Degrassi 1947, fasc.1), and the calendars (Degrassi 1963 fasc.2). On the connection, see Rüpke (1995); on the unity of '*fasti*', see Feeney (2007) 167–70.

[91] Cf. Wallace-Hadrill (1986).

[92] See the discussions of the *fasti* in Hardie (2002), esp. Schiesaro (2002) 62–75, Newlands (2002) 200–16; also Boyd (2000) 64–98.

local commission. The lists of consuls, of which only two small fragments survive, were found together with lists of the local magistrates of Praeneste, inscribed in the same style, and it surely follows that the monument was locally commissioned, mirroring a metropolitan model.[93] At a local level, Roman time becomes local time by the juxtaposition of Roman magistrates with local ones. The same phenomenon is seen in the *fasti* of Venusia and of several other Italian towns, where the lists interleaf Roman magistrates and local magistrates under each year.[94]

The monthly calendar of Praeneste is likely to be part of the same commission.[95] We learn from Suetonius' *Lives of Grammarians* that it was Verrius Flaccus, the most distinguished grammarian/antiquarian of the Augustan age, and tutor to Augustus' own grandchildren, who was responsible for their publication, and who was celebrated by an honorific statue nearby.[96] Verrius Flaccus encapsulates to perfection the process by which Augustus made Roman time his own. We need not think in terms of the emperor distributing copies of the 'official' calendar to local centres like Praeneste. They are willing enough to do it under their own impulse, and buy into the system by synchronizing Roman time with Praenestine time (and local festivals, especially that of Fortuna Primigenia, are registered on the calendar along with Roman ones, just as are local magistrates). But who better to turn to for an authoritative version of the calendar than the great expert of the age, Verrius Flaccus, whose tutorship on the Palatine gave the ultimate stamp of approval to his scholarly learning? What substitute in terms of authority could the college of the *pontifices* now offer? Roman time has definitively slipped beyond the grasp of the nobility.

In slipping from the nobility, Roman time becomes the common property of all Romans. It is not only town councils through Italy which enthusiastically inscribe the *fasti*. Two remarkable examples illustrate the habit reaching the level of freedmen and slaves. One is the calendar of the local magistrates of a *vicus*, a city ward, in the Testaccio area of Rome near the Via Marmorata.[97] Here the monthly calendar was inscribed on two faces of a marble panel, the six months in six vertical columns on each side (see below,

---

[93] Degrassi observes the relationship, but does not print names of local magistrates, which are published in *Corpus Inscriptionum Latinarum* XIV, 2964–9.

[94] Venusia, Degrassi (1963) no. 8 (249–56), compare no. 5 (173–241) Ostia, no. 7 (243–8) Cupra Maritima, no. 10 (259) Luceria, no. 12 (261) Nola, no. 13 (263) Volsinii, no. 14 (264–5) Teanum, no. 15 (266–8) Interamnia, no. 16 (269–70) Cales.

[95] Degrassi (1963), no. 17 (107–45). His publication separates the two lists between two volumes while admitting the link.

[96] Suetonius, *de Grammaticis et Rhetoribus* 17, with the commentary of Kaster (1995) 190–6.

[97] Degrassi (1947) no. 20 (279–90) and Degrassi (1963) no. 12 (90–8); discussed by Rüpke (1995) 58–63, Rüpke (1998).

figs. 6.15 and 6.16). Beneath the first six months are listed the *fasti* of the consuls from 43 BCE, the year of Augustus' first consulship (Hirtius and Pansa are passed over in silence) down to the end of his reign and slightly beyond. Beneath the second are listed, after the names of the consuls, the four *vicomagistri* of each year, from the first year when Augustus presented to them the 'Lares Augusti'; that year (7 BCE) is dated by Augustus' eleven consulships and the seventeenth year of tribunician power. The adulation of Augustus is unconcealed, but the important point is that, at the level of the parish pump, local officials of freeman status could also make Roman time their own. Trimalchio, too, had a calendar painted on his walls.[98]

Equally remarkable are the *fasti* from Antium, put up by the slaves of the imperial household.[99] The inscription comes almost certainly from the imperial villa at Antium, beloved of Nero, where the household slaves have set up a *collegium*, apparently with the approval of the local council which periodically requests a contribution, made by one of the officers of that year. The inscription has the familiar combination of monthly calendar and lists of magistrates. Spanning a period from the 30s to the 50s CE, for each year are given the names of the two consuls, followed by the slaves who held office that year: Eros glutinator (the man who glued together papyrus rolls), Dorus atriensis (the doorman), Anthus topiarius ('Flower the gardener'), Primus subvilicus (the sub-bailiff), Claudius Atimetus a bybliothece (the librarian, a freedman), take their proud places in the roll of annual honour. On the one hand, the wealth, power and self-confidence of the imperial court and its staff are evident; on the other, the success of Augustus in opening access to Roman time to all those who would be loyal to himself.

There is perhaps one final point to make about calendars and time. If in one sense the Varronian antiquarian learning is the official *epistēmē* which displaces the *sapientia* of the old nobility, both rendering their authority hollow and the authority of the new regime solid, it is actually inadequate as a discourse about time and the relationship of Roman life to cosmic order. Impressive as the learning may be, it is of little practical consequence. Far weightier is the form of counter-knowledge offered by the *mathematici*, the astrologers who from the precise moment of your birth and the conjunction of the stars can offer practical advise about your future. The dramatic rise in significance of astrology in precisely this period has long been remarked,

[98] Petronius, *Satyricon* 30, noted by Degrassi (1963) 217. Note also the *fasti* of the *vicomagistri* of Pompeii, dating back to Caesar's dictatorship: Degrassi (1947) no. 17 (271–2).

[99] Degrassi (1947) no. 31 (320–34); Rüpke (1995) 139–45. Cf. no. 23 (294–5), the *fasti* of a burial college of Augustan date, with freedmen and slaves as officers, no. 25 (302) from Tusculum, of Augustan date with slave *magistri*, and no. 28 (309–10), Fasti Lunenses, of a servile college of Tiberian date. Rüpke (1995) 391–6 discusses the appeal to 'the little man'.

more notable because it is admitted from the very top in Augustus' publication of his own forecast, and seemingly a subtext to his Horologium.[100] The point to make here is that it is in some sense a correlate of antiquarianism in displacing pontifical knowledge. Cicero's very description of the pontifices as Chaldaeans points to what is lacking: high mathematical skill with a system of knowledge that allows the individual to draw real benefit from the expert. The nobility were neither the transmitters of ancient lore, *mos maiorum*, nor able to offer any new lore in its place. The perception of corruption, or voided authority, hangs from the observation that they had no special knowledge to offer, when others did. Collapse of authority, and the role of changing forms of knowledge in that collapse, will also be the theme of the following sections.

Religion and tradition

On the model here proposed, calendar reform, while on the surface a technical matter of sorting out a confused traditional practice, entailed a far deeper shift of social authority and control of knowledge: from a republican society in which a 'nobility' maintained its pre-eminence by a superior knowledge of Roman discourse, in this case, through the right of the pontifical college to 'know' the year, to a court society in which knowledge, far from being concentrated in a single power group, was diffused among experts, whose authority was endorsed by the ruler.

One way to interpret this transformation is as a process of structural differentiation. A ruling elite upon which are concentrated the functions of priests, politicians, legal authorities, advocates and military leaders is replaced in a larger and more complex society by a broader elite in which functions are more specialised.[101] It is part of a much larger and slower transformation of the Roman world. But though it is true that a long-term tendency is at work, we may be struck by the success with which the nobility clung on to their monopoly of functions until the very last stages of the republic. The *pontifices* of Cicero's day may have been partly discredited, but they retained control of the calendar, and used it as vigorously as ever. It took a violent act of political change, the establishment of Caesar as dictator, to wrest the control from them.

Time is no more than an instance of a far-reaching sea-change affecting all aspects of Roman custom, religion and tradition. I wish to underline the

---

[100] Barton (1994).   [101] So, e.g., Beard, North and Price (1998) 149.

common theme that affects diverse areas: the perception by late republican Romans, including many nobles, that the nobility has lost its grip of matters for which it was supposed to be responsible, and that this is part of a deep malaise affecting the state, and the representation of the Augustan regime as having addressed these issues in setting up a new order.

Religion

Perhaps the most familiar example is the picture of 'decline' of Roman religion in the late republic, followed by Augustan 'revival'. To translate the laments of Cicero and Varro of negligence and the celebrations by Augustan authors of the revival of neglected practices into a story of a profound decline of a religious system may be to fall too naively for the rhetoric of the sources: religion was as central as ever to Roman public discourse in the late republic. But, leaving aside the intractable question of what identifies a religion in true 'decline', we can focus on the issue of the authority of the priesthood.

When Polybius identified religion as the single element which most contributed to the superiority of the Roman constitution (6.56), it was an instrument of social control, a means of keeping the unruly desires of the populace (*plēthos*) under control by fear. Fear of the gods is exactly what the Epicurean Lucretius sought to dispel, but Polybius (who acknowledges the philosophical arguments) asserts its social utility. In the same spirit, Cicero justified the practice of augury in terms of the benefit of the state. The thesis that religion and control of priesthoods was as much a foundation of the social dominance of the nobility as patronage is indeed attractive. As Cicero put it (albeit addressing the college of *pontifices* in flattering terms):

Among the many things, gentlemen of the pontifical college, that our ancestors created and established under divine inspiration, nothing is more renowned than their decision to entrust the worship of the gods and the highest interests of the state to the same men – so that the most eminent and illustrious citizens might ensure the maintenance of religion by the proper administration of the state, and the maintenance of the state by the prudent interpretation of religion.[102]

The great importance of priesthood to the nobility is underlined by the scrupulous care with which families shared out this privilege, ensuring both that no more than one member of any *gens* was member of any priestly college, and that nobody held more than one priesthood.[103]

---

[102] Cicero, *de Domo Sua* 1, see Beard, North and Price (1998) 1,115; 2,197f.
[103] North (1990) 527–43, Beard, North and Price (1998) 99–108.

But if it is plausible that the tenure of priestly office was one of the means by which a group of families shored up their social dominance, it follows that doubts about their competence must have eroded that respect. Cicero, himself an augur, and a sceptic about the philosophical underpinnings of the practice of augury, is the more damaging when he suggests that the nobility are culpable of a deep negligence:

> But by the negligence of the nobility (*negligentia nobilitatis*) the discipline of augury has been dropped, and the true practice of auspices spurned, and only its appearance retained. And so most functions of the state, including warfare on which its safety depends, are administered without auspices . . . By contrast, religion had such force for our ancestors, that some of them ritually veiled their heads and vowed their lives to the immortal gods for the republic. (*de Natura Deorum* 2.9–10)

That claim of neglect parallels the complaint that the calendar had fallen into confusion through neglect; that neglect had allowed temples to fall into decay, and priesthoods into desuetude, and set the stage for Augustus' claim to reverse the neglect. Such allegations deliberately overlooked the historical record of Roman religion for constant innovation and self-renewal, and attributed to much significance to the antiquarian unearthing of obscure rituals. But the crucial point is that such allegations were made, and were potentially devastating not for the practice of religion, but for the credibility of the *nobiles*.[104]

Divination

One area of religious practice in which the shift from traditional to scientific discourse is especially marked is the set of practices by which the will of the gods was 'known'.[105] To simplify a complex story, the republic is characterised by forms of divination aimed at establishing the will of the gods with regard to the state, as opposed to the prediction of the future with regard to the individual. The traditional forms of divination were under the control of the priestly colleges: the *augures* as authorities in reading the flight of birds, the *XVviri sacris faciundis* authorities on the Sibylline books and prodigies and portents, while the *haruspices* stand slightly apart as Etruscan (hence non-Roman) experts in the reading of entrails whom the *pontifices* called in for advice. The forms of 'knowledge' of divine will are firmly under the control of the political class, and are essentially non-scientific,

---

[104] Similarly Moatti (1997) 30–44.
[105] Liebeschuetz (1979) 7–29, North (1990) 49–72, Barton (1994) 27ff.

though there is evidence that haruspicy, distinctive in depending on a class of experts, developed under the influence of hellenistic astrology, and came in the first century BCE increasingly to play a role as offering individuals a way of foreseeing the future.

In the course of the first century, the emphasis shifts dramatically towards predictive sciences. The central argument of Cicero's *de Divinatione*, over whether it is philosophically tenable to hold that the future can be predicted, is interesting not for its implications about belief in traditional religion (the arguments for and against are, after all, carefully balanced), but for its implications about the expectations for divination.[106] Cicero can maintain that the debate does not affect the function of augury as a powerful mechanism for keeping the Roman state in balance. The opponent, however, with which Cicero does not openly engage, is astrology, with its offer of rational predictions of the future of each individual derived from the inherent logic and order of the universe. It was exactly in this period that astrology established widespread credibility among leading Romans, and that Roman experts emerged alongside the Greek practitioners, like Cicero's friend Nigidius Figulus.

The triumph of Augustus is also the triumph of astrology: his own publication of his horoscope and the widespread diffusion of his sign of the Capricorn already imply acknowledgement of its validity, despite continued bans; and the Horologium erected in the Campus Martius, even if Buchner was overoptimistic in some of his hypotheses, was a monumental expression of the victory of Augustus as the will of a divine universe, written in the stars. From Augustus onwards, astrology and other predictive sciences (including physiogonomics and the interpretation of dreams) flourish, and traditional divination disappears below the horizon. A form of knowledge predicated on the application of rational principles to a highly complex body of material by professionals displaces the traditional forms of knowledge embedded in the ruling class.[107]

Public speech

If knowledge of religious and secular tradition and morality may appear to us to impact only tangentially on political life, other areas of knowledge were manifestly at the core of the public activity of the ruling class. What has

---

[106] Beard (1986) 33–46.
[107] On the evidence of Suetonius, in striking contrast with republican historiography, see Wallace-Hadrill (1983) 189–97.

been taken as the classic image of patronal power is the description placed by Cicero in the mouth of the orator Crassus of the nobles, who

> in the old days either strolling thus (i.e. across the Forum) or sitting at home on the chair of state, were approached to be consulted not only on matters of civil law, but also about marrying off a daughter, buying a farm, cultivating the land, in fact on any matter of duty or business. (*de Oratore* 3.133)

Interestingly, however, it is not a norm but a lost ideal that he describes. The discussion, already distanced by being placed in the mouths of a previous generation, addresses precisely the issue of the knowledge (*scientia*) of a Roman public figure, and the impact on it of Greek learning and its tendency to specialisation. Crassus is sustaining the unity of knowledge, and holding up as a model the men of a generation before himself whose knowledge was not specialised but wide-ranging. He cites the memories of his own father and his father-in-law Sex. Aelius, and his own observation of Manius Manilius, whom he had seen so wandering in the Forum and offering advice to all comers.

Crassus makes clear that the ideal has not survived the importation of sophisticated foreign learning ('hanc politissimam doctrinam transmarinam atque adventiciam'). He draws a contrast between Cato as the universal man, equally adept at civil law, at oratory, at political life and military action, as one who 'knew everything which in those days could be known or learnt' (3.135), with the young men of today who approach public life naked and unarmed, and think themselves clever if the have mastered a single area of knowledge – military, legal (let alone pontifical law), and rhetorical, little knowing the kinship between all the skills and virtues (3.136).

This Crassus would certainly agree that knowledge (*scientia*) should lie at the basis of the power of the ruling class, and believes that at some point in the past the various forms of knowledge were united in practice in a social elite. He also sees Greek learning as making a fundamental impact in its tendency to make knowledge more complex and hence specialist. Even so, Cicero must have been conscious of his exaggeration: Caesar proved every bit as successful as Cato in uniting the diverse forms of *scientia*, and doubtless Cicero would like us to think of himself. But the discussion makes clear that certain forms of *scientia* were fundamental to Roman public life – namely, law, oratory and military science. The claim that each of these became more specialised and restricted can be substantiated.[108]

---

[108] For what follows, cf. Hopkins (1978) 74–96, who looks at the army, education and law from the point of view of structural differentiation. My emphasis on an epistemological paradigm shift does not contradict or substitute the thesis of differentiation.

Law

Knowledge of the civil law was essential for a public figure. Servius Sulpicius Rufus, the dominant jurist of Cicero's generation, was told by Mucius Scaevola the pontifex that ignorance of the law was disgraceful in one who was a patrician, a noble and an advocate (Pomponius, *Digest* 1.2.2.43). True, the same Servius was beaten to the consulship by Licinius Murena, and when Cicero defended Murena against the charge of bribery, he took the opportunity to downplay the importance of jurisprudence: the two skills that paved the road to the consulship were military and oratorical: the jurist was too much of a backroom boy, an orator manqué (Cicero, *pro Murena* 29). He can mock the pettifogging nature of jurisprudence, and suggest that the profound obscurity of legal language is a plot to make lawyers powerful, frustrated that their old ploy of ruling on which days public business could or could not be done had been foiled by the scribe Cn. Flavius in his publication of the *fasti* (*pro Murena* 25). But this is only to express in a different way the shared awareness that legal, just like religious, knowledge (the calendar) was a pillar of the power of the ruling class.

In a different context, at a different time, Cicero expressed the profoundest respect for Servius' knowledge, and lamented the passing of an era:

Among the many excellent practices of our ancestors was the high respect they always accorded to knowledge and interpretation of the corpus of civil law. Until the present age of confusion (*hanc confusionem temporum*), the *principes* kept this profession exclusively in their hands; but now, with the collapse of every other grade of social distinction, the prestige of this science has been destroyed – and that in the lifetime of one (Servius) who equals all his predecessors in social standing, and excels them all in science. Cicero, *de Officiis* 2.19.65

This squares exactly with what Crassus says about Greek learning and specialisation, and even with Cicero's own mockery in the *pro Murena*. Jurisprudence has shifted its social location, from a necessary skill of a nobility which dominates all forms of knowledge, war, law, religion and public speaking, to the specialist activity of a subset, who talk a legal language that seems obscurantist to the ordinary Roman.

As Bruce Frier has shown, it was precisely Mucius Scaevola the Pontifex and Servius Sulpicius who transformed Roman jurisprudence into a legal science and a distinct profession.[109] Their voluminous publications made it what Crassus would call a *politissima doctrina*. But that in turn put a premium

---

[109] Frier (1985).

not on noble birth but mental agility, the ability to master a complex discipline; as the complexity of the discipline rises, so the social status of its practitioners drops.

Jurisprudence happens to be an especially sharp example of the transformation, completed, as Cicero observes, within his own lifetime. Chronologically, it stretches back at least to Mucius the Pontifex, to the generation of Crassus at the turn of the second and first centuries BCE. The last great proponent of the 'patrician-noble' style, Servius, dies at the very end of the republic, on the verge of the final civil war. Caesar and Augustus did nothing to engineer the change, but their new order exploited it: Caesar's plan to publish a code of Roman law would have been, in Cicero's vivid description of the publication of the *fasti*, 'to poke out the eyes of the crow', in ensuring that no social group had a monopoly of knowledge. Augustus' approach was not codification, but continuous modification. Under Augustus and his successors, the profession of jurist flourished as never before, and the deep imperial involvement in ruling on the law gave jurists a key role in the imperial *consilium*. The court of Augustus relied on the authority of experts like Capito and Labeo, but their authority was unconnected with high social standing.[110]

Rhetoric

Similar processes are surely at work with oratory, which was, at least from Cicero's perspective, the key tool of public life. The *de Oratore*, and several of Cicero's other rhetorical treatises, like the *Brutus*, are centrally concerned with the issue of whether oratory should be seen as a specialised technique of speaking, or as a much broader set of social skills. Cicero's tendency is to argue for the broad vision, the Catonian *vir bonus dicendi peritus*, a 'good man' in the broad sense of one with all the social skills of the citizen, with a specific skill in speaking. That is also the ideal of the *Brutus*, which sees the history of Roman speaking as coterminous with the history of Roman politics: the orators are the leading politicians, because public speaking is the vital tool of politics.

But the pressures in the direction of highly specialised skills of rhetoric are obvious, and Cicero himself has a responsibility exactly parallel to that of Servius in the law for being the practitioner whose example (in his published speeches), and whose detailed contributions to the theory of rhetoric

---

[110] Cf. Moatti (1991) and Moatti (1997) 137–9, 186–8.

transformed the practice of oratory at Rome. The easiest way to see the transformation is in the history of its teachers. Here we have the particularly helpful insight offered by Suetonius' *Lives of the Grammarians and Rhetors.*[111] The theme is the professional teaching of grammar (i.e. Latin language and literature) and rhetoric, and the dramatic rise in social significance of these disciplines. Both are seen by Suetonius as late-comers, and make a tentative appearance in the mid second century BCE. The teaching of rhetoric, he maintains, arrived late and in the teeth of opposition, and he cites a senatorial decree of 161 BCE expelling philosophers and rhetors from Rome.

He then cites the edict of the censors Domitius Ahenobarbus and Licinius Crassus (92 BCE) which the laments the arrival of men calling themselves 'Latini rhetores', and the way young men waste whole days hanging around listening to them. They are banned in a memorable assertion of traditional values:

Our ancestors established what manner of things they wished their children to learn and what manner of schools they wished them to attend. These novelties, which do not accord with received and traditional practice (*consuetudinem et morem maiorum*), neither meet our approval nor seem right. (*de Grammaticis et Rhetoribus.* 25)

The same edict is cited by Cicero in the work already discussed, for the censor Crassus is the great orator whom Cicero portrays as enemy of Greek specialisation. Cicero had to deal with the fact that one of his greatest predecessors was author of this remarkable ban, and he embraces the paradox by setting his dialogue in the year after Crassus' censorship. He has Crassus grudgingly admit that Greek teachers of rhetoric at least had some learning, whereas the Latin teachers contributed nothing but daring, a 'school for impudence' (*de Oratore* 3.70).

The motives for the edict, political or otherwise, have been much debated. What is clear is that the Roman traditional practice, by no means so fixed as the censors suggest, was based on the system still advocated by Cicero of *tirocinium fori*, of following an established speaker and learning by example in practice. It therefore favoured a pattern of transmission of knowledge within the ruling class. Greek rhetorical instruction was probably well established by 92 BCE (though scarcely a 'school established by our ancestors'), and by definition was limited in access. The arrival of rhetorical instruction in Latin offered the potential of greater accessibility, and the *impudentia* threatened is that of pushy newcomers.[112]

---

[111] Kaster (1995).   [112] Corbeill (2001).

The motivation of the censors scarcely matters. The real question is the effect of the availability of teachers of rhetoric in Latin. The most palpable effect was the rise of the practice of declamation, not only in the use of the declamatory exercises of *controversiae* and *suasoriae* in training young orators, but the use of these exercises as performances. Suetonius demonstrates the rising prestige of rhetoric from the prestige of those who declaimed. The real take-off of the practice is in the 40s BCE, and the remarkable compilation by the elder Seneca of *Controversiae* shows the new phenomenon at the heyday of its fashion under Augustus. Already under the early Empire, it became a topic to blame declamation for the decline of true oratory, and Tacitus in the *Dialogus* is the heir of Crassus, the orator who blames the teaching of rhetoric for a supposed crisis in oratory.[113]

The point is that oratory follows the same paradigm as other branches of knowledge. The republican model, or at least the model which Cicero projects on the past, is of public speaking transmitted as part of a bundle of knowledge of Roman ways (with law and religious law in close association) within a relatively closed ruling class. Specialisation gathers pace throughout the first century BCE, with Cicero himself as the outstanding example of the potential of oratory as a special skill to bring rapid social promotion to a new man. Once declamation settles in as a standard practice, especially under Augustus, the nature of public speaking has changed.

Declamation becomes a language in its own right, a specialised discourse, with its own extensive complex of rules and tricks and 'colours'. It is a discourse accessible only to those who have undergone the demanding training. They do indeed constitute an elite, but an elite defined and constituted by the process of education itself. That is a different *sort* of elite from a hereditary nobility that maintains its social advantage by keeping knowledge, as far as it can, within itself. Such an elite suits a court society, which constantly recruits to its ranks from outside: enough to recall the success of the elder Seneca from Corduba, who documents the fashion for declamation, and whose son's skill in rhetoric carried him to the inmost circle of the court.

Language[114]

The teacher of rhetoric comes as a package deal, as Suetonius documents, with the grammarian. The 'guardian of the language' (*custos Latini sermonis*)

---

[113] Bonner (1969) 71–83.
[114] Cf. ch. 2, pp. 64–70. This section for convenience summarises the earlier discussion.

also has a vital social role.[115] As Suetonius shows, the learned study and teaching of the Latin language arrives late, taking its impulse from Greek exemplars in the mid second century. But it leads to a decisive shift of authority over the language of the public life. The public speaker, to carry conviction, must speak good Latin. But how can you tell what proper, correct Latin is? The debate was launched at the end of the second century by Aelius Stilo, who got his name for his 'stylistic' support to his noble patrons in their speech writing. As Greek theory taught, there was a choice between the principles of anomaly, based on standard usage, *consuetudo*, however illogical or anomalous that might be, and that of analogy, that assumed usage should be dictated by *ratio*, the set of logical rules ensuring that words of similar formation behaved in similar ways in similar circumstances. Neither Stilo, nor more importantly Varro, whose *De Lingua Latina* preserves much of this debate, ever fully came down on one side or other: they knew that it must be a continuous tussle between received usage and systematic rules. But in the very process of launching the debate, they constituted the grammarian as the new figure of authority.

Here, too, as we have seen, Cicero proves a key witness of the shift:

Hitherto, pure Latin was not a matter of reason and science (*rationis et scientiae*) but of good usage (*bonae consuetudinis*). I pass over Laelius and Scipio; in that period men were praised for their pure Latin as for their innocence (though there were those who spoke badly). But virtually everyone in those days who neither lived outside this city, nor was tainted with domestic barbarity, used to speak correctly. But this has been corrupted in Rome as in Greece. Both Athens and this city have received a flood of people from a diversity of origins whose language is polluted (*inquinate loquentes*). This is why our talk needs purging, and some sort of rationality needs to be applied by a touchstone, which cannot be changed, nor are we to go by the perverted rule of usage.[116]

This revealing passage exposes the link between demographic and linguistic change. Of course, second-century Rome was not a haven of true-born native Romans, all speaking a consistently pure tongue. What is more probable is that the elite from which the speakers were drawn was small and homogeneous enough to be able to impose its own linguistic authority. To revert to our paradigm, a nobility which gave itself the authority to 'know' the Roman way, 'knew' the Latin language as the rest of Roman usage

---

[115] Seneca, *Epistulae Morales* 95.65 for the expression, taken up in the title of the perceptive study of Kaster (1988).

[116] Cicero, *Brutus* 258. The reference to Athens evokes the parallel debate on pure Attic, which goes back at least to Ps-Xenophon, *Constitution of Athens* ii.8.

(*consuetudo*). What Cicero is observing is that this authority had collapsed. A flood of 'outsiders' in Rome, and not just servile immigrants, but members of the municipal elites like Cicero himself, wanted to make the Latin language their own, and turned to Varro and to the growing profession of grammarian to get clear rulings.[117]

The Augustan revolution

In a wide range of fields, we have seen, a profound shift can be traced between republic and Empire in the location of authority. The pace of change is simultaneously slow and swift. There is a slow process of disintegration of credibility in an older system of authority, an *ancien régime*, whereby a nobility, which is a great deal less ancient and traditional than it claimed, even as it attempts to assert a monopoly of power in new ways, lost its grip on its ability to define what constituted being a Roman. Cicero and Varro were key figures in articulating this sense of disintegration; but though they implied that the nobility *ought* to be successfully preserving the ways of their *maiores*, they were actively engaged in dismantling their authority. Then there is a swifter pace of change, a crisis that comes to a head with the civil wars, and is seen to resolve itself in the new order of the rebranded Augustus. But if his seizure of power is the definitive moment in this 'revolution', he is far from wanting to present it as a revolution. He is recovering the lost traditions of the *maiores* which others had let slip, and allowing the Romans to be themselves again after their traumatic moment of identity crisis. In demolishing and substituting the authority of the *nobiles*, he can draw on the authority of the dominant voices of a century of debate about what the Roman way should be. He draws his own authority from Cicero and Varro, and feeds it back into the system by giving his own authority to their successors. It is the perfect revolution, which in changing everything changes also the perception of what is normal and traditional, and so erases its own revolutionary status.

[117] Cf. Dench (2005) 314–15.

6 | Knowing the city[1]

The city of Rome, along with Roman citizenship, lay at the core of Roman identity. We have already met Cicero's comment on Varro's *Antiquities*: 'When we were like strangers abroad and lost in our own city, your books led us back home, so to speak, so that at last we were able to recognise who and where we were.'[2] For Cicero, the sense of being outsiders, *peregrini*, lost in their own city, is the physical correlate of the sense of loss of traditions that defined the Roman way, and the disintegration of the Roman state. That strong identification of the city with Roman identity is forcibly expressed by Livy in his representation of the debate after the Gallic sack of Rome in 386 BCE. It is the hero Camillus, conqueror of Veii, who opposes a transfer of the city to Veii, objecting that every feature of Roman religious ritual is associated with the specific topography of the city:

We have a city founded with all due rites of auspice and augury; not a stone of her streets but is permeated with our sense of the divine; for our annual sacrifices not the days only are fixed, but the places too, where they may be performed. (Livy 5.51)

These passages are familiar, especially to any discussion of the Augustan 'revival' of Roman religious ritual. Camillus' speech in Livy depends heavily on the publication of Varro's *Antiquities*, which heightened Roman awareness of the rites, both practised and forgotten, associated with 'each stone', and on the mood of 'restoration' of Augustan Rome. In this sense, it would appear, Varro's *Antiquities* offered a map of the city: its topography was synonymous with the specificities of its ritual practice. Consequently, modern topographical study of the city, a tradition of intense study stretching back to the mid-nineteenth century, sometimes may seem like a commentary on the missing books of Varro.[3] But what this tradition masks is the transformation of ways of knowing the city that is represented by Varro and the Augustan reforms. Just at the moment when Rome presents itself to us in its

---

[1] This chapter develops ideas previously aired in Wallace-Hadrill (2000b), Wallace-Hadrill (2001a), Wallace-Hadrill (2003).

[2] Cicero, *Academica Posteriora* 9 = Cardauns (1976) T1. See ch. 5.

[3] E.g. Coarelli (1997a), index s.v. 'Varrone': with thirty-five citations, the most quoted ancient source in the volume.

most classic and definitive form, it is in fact caught up in its most remarkable metamorphosis.

Let us put ourselves in the shoes of Cicero, despite his long knowledge of Rome still conscious of his Arpinate origins, and ask how the outsider orients himself and knows this city. Could he buy a map, or go to some central information point from which to orient himself? So far as we know, there is no reference to any sort of plan of the city from the republican period. It is hard to imagine that no plan existed, but of a version that was generally available, displayed to the public, there is no surviving trace. It is worth reflecting briefly on the implications of this absence. The Rome we know today is one of the most intensely mapped cities in the world, with surviving plans in large numbers stretching back into the fifteenth century and beyond.[4] Even antique Rome as we know it is densely mapped: Lanciani's achievement in mapping the remains of antiquity onto the plan of the late-nineteenth-century city at a scale of 1:1,000 is the basis for a precision of topographical knowledge that allows (for example) the detailed mapping of Augustan Rome,[5] and for the six splendid volumes of the *Lexicon Topographicum Urbis Romae* which is an extended alphabetical commentary on the entries on such maps.[6] It is therefore easy for us to imagine a stranger in ancient Rome overwhelmed by the sheer density of information available about the city, a feature aggravated by the extent of scholarly dispute on almost every item; it is much harder to imagine a republican Rome in which such information was only available orally, and Varro's writings could be a revelation.

The Seven Hills: *montes* and the shrines of the *Argei*

Despite the loss of the *Antiquities*, something of Varro's picture of Rome survives in the *De Lingua Latina*: his interest here in explaining the origins and meanings of names for places gave him the opportunity to summarise much material from the longer work. A substantial section offers a valuable insight not only into how Rome mapped onto contemporary minds in the mid first century BCE, but also into the way in which his learned research exposed how little Romans understood of the elements of a forgotten past

---

[4] Frutaz (1962) is the classic repertory, now supplemented by a range of digital initiatives.
[5] Lanciani (1893–1901, 1988), Haselberger and Romano (2002).
[6] Steinby (1993–2000); on the relationship of the alphabetised lexicon to maps, see Wallace-Hadrill (2001b).

embedded in their ways of talking about the city.[7] He presents us with a Rome of seven hills, four quarters, and twenty-seven local shrines or *Argei*.

Varro starts (5.41) by linking the seven hills with the festival of the Septimontium, which, as he later points out (6.24), was strictly celebrated not by the whole population, but by the inhabitants of those hills, the *montani* – just as, he adds, the *Paganalia* were celebrated only by inhabitants of the *pagi*. But here he runs into deep waters, deeper than he cares to admit. Which were the seven hills? As the fourth-century Virgilian commentator Servius was to observe, it was a matter on which none could agree.[8] Varro, who never in the surviving texts spells out his full list, took them to be the hills within the Servian walls of the city: as he quaintly puts it, 'where Rome now is, was called Septimontium after the number of hills which subsequently the city embraced within its walls'. If the Rome of Romulus was limited to the Palatine hill, he implies, then the area of seven hills within the later walls was not yet 'Rome'; but he fails to explain how a festival of seven hills could have anticipated the later walled area.

However, the area of the *montani* who celebrated the festival was not at all coextensive with that of the walls of Rome: most obviously the Aventine, which long stood outside the *pomerium*, was no part of the festival, though Varro proceeds to offer a number of explanations for its name (after birds, '*aves*', or the arrival of newcomers, '*adventus*', or from an eponymous king). Modern scholarship tends to see in the Septimontium a fossil of a festival long predating the sixth-century wall-circuit, including a much smaller group of hills. It is not even clear there were seven of them (the list of the Augustan legal scholar Labeo gives eight), and it has been suggested that the true etymology is to do with enclosed areas (*saepti-montes*) and not the number seven.[9] Nor does the Latin *montes* mean 'hills' (the normal equivalent is 'mountains'); it refers rather to areas, as inhabited by the *montani*, including indeed the Subura, which was scarcely hilly, let alone mountainous.

The apparent clarity of Varro's picture rapidly dissolves before our eyes. This scholar, who loved careful divisions and distinctions, and a philosophical rationality, finds the presentation of his city a challenge. He now moves on to the detailed articulation of the city of seven hills (45). Rome, he says, was long ago divided into four parts or regions, the Suburan, the Esquiline, the Colline, and the Palatine (figure 6.1). The four regions, he explains further on (55–6), correspond to the four tribes which replaced Romulus' original system of three tribes. The four urban tribes were of course a feature

[7] Varro, *De Lingua Latina* 5.41–56, with the detailed discussion of Fraschetti (1990) 132–203.
[8] Servius on *Aeneid* 6,784.   [9] See Fraschetti (1996), Gelsomino (1975).

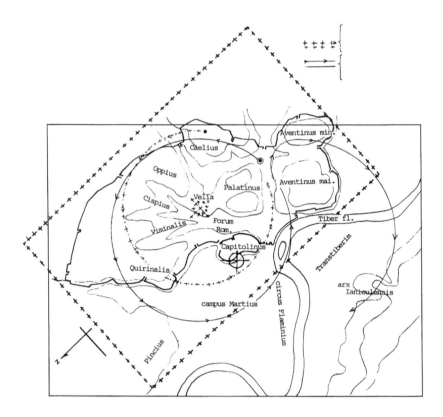

Figure 6.1 Ideal plan of Republican Rome, drawing from Rodríguez-Almeida (2002, figure 8)

of the political system familiar to Varro's contemporaries, used in the late republic as a mechanism for limiting the voting power of the urban plebs, and particularly of freedmen: only in 67 BCE did a law of the tribune Manilius break this limitation and permit freedmen to be attributed also to the thirty-one rural tribes (see p. 267). Tribal affiliation was an essential part of how Roman citizenship worked, and its importance for citizen identity is displayed in the custom of stating it after the patronymic in the most formal listings of names. But any overlap between membership of the four urban tribes and residence in the four urban regions with the same names had long since disappeared. We do not even know how far the regions survived in practice and popular awareness. Thus while the Subura was a well-known, and indeed ill-famed, area of the city, the *regio Suburana* as described by Varro extended far beyond the Subura to include the Caelian hill.[10]

[10] Welch (1999).

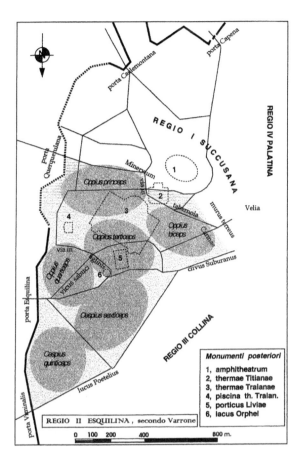

Figure 6.2 Varro's subdivision of the Esquiline into districts, according to Rodríguez-Almeida (2002, figure 6)

Whether Varro's four regions were perceived as a reality on the ground depends on how far the rituals he associates with them were in fact still observed. Among the four regions were distributed the twenty-seven shrines of the *Argei*. He goes into considerable (yet, frustratingly, incomplete) detail in illustrating the locations of these shrines. In doing so, he repeatedly cites a text which he calls the *Sacra Argeorum*, which lists the location of each shrine within the region. The text was apparently a book of priestly ritual, and the language suggests that it is either of considerable antiquity, or at least heavily archaising. Most strikingly, the shrines are listed with serial numbers such as 'terticeps', 'quarticeps', 'quinticeps' ('thirdmost', 'fourthmost', 'fifthmost'), terms which had long since fallen out of standard Latin usage – indeed, they are not met elsewhere in Latin literature, with the exception of the first in the series, *princeps* (figure 6.2).

Of the antiquity of this system of four regions (or *montes*) there can be little doubt. We seem to have the fossilised remains, probably of several layers of deep past.[11] The very fact that the regions are not, despite Varro's opening remarks, coextensive with the area within the Servian walls, and that they seem to include an alternative system of 'hills' which excludes obvious hills like the Capitoline and Aventine, may point to an origin of the rituals in the pre-Servian city. Another sign of antiquity may be the number 27, not so much an odd number, to be corrected to a multiple of 4 (like 28) or a decimal system (30), but a reflection of a ternary system ($3 \times 3 \times 3$ or thrice nine), compatible with the Romulean three tribes.[12] Such questions are highly speculative and obscure, and while attracting much scholarly debate, leave us in the dark over the realities of first-century BCE Rome. Were the twenty-seven shrines of the *Argei* familiar features of the cityscape of republican Rome, and did they offer a way of orienting the visitor's itinerary, or were they no more than a dim memory of obscure rites which only the learning of a Varro could revive?

Our uncertainty throws into relief just how hard a city republican Rome was to know. No sign of a map, and no sign of a system of urban organisation which could be readily comprehensible to the visitor, or even to the native. With Varro as our guide, from an initially promising start of the division of the walled city into seven hills in four regions, we are plunged into dismaying obscurities: just which are the seven hills, and what is a hill (or 'mountain'), what does it mean to call the valley bottom of the Subura a 'mountain', and was the area everyone called the Subura anything to do with the region or mountain described by priestly ritual? It is worth underlining this degree of uncertainty in order to grasp better the contrast offered by the reforms of Augustus.

Vici in republican Rome

Was there any alternative system of organisation apart from Varro's Septimontium? The key to the Augustan system, as we shall see, was the neighbourhood or *vicus*, the local organisation with its own magistrates and rituals. That neighbourhoods existed in some form under the republic, too, seems certain; what role they played in the organisation and cognitive mapping of the city is highly controversial. Augusto Fraschetti, underlining the radical nature of the Augustan reforms, argued in detail that *vici* played

---

[11] Fraschetti (1990) 134ff., Carandini (1997) 267–456.   [12] Coarelli (1993).

no part in the formal organisation of the city under the republic, even if by the late republic they certainly existed informally. For Fraschetti, the Varronian system remained formally in force, with the area of the four urban tribes divided into its constituent *montes*, and zones outside the *montes* described as *pagi*. So in two passages in which Cicero describes efforts to reach the urban electorate at grass-roots level, he talks of *montani* and *pagani*, the groups which Varro mentions in the same breath (above) as celebrating the Septimontium and the Paganalia, respectively. Most strikingly in his speech *de Domo Sua*, he asserts that these were the only urban subdivisions acknowledged by tradition:

No college in this city, none of the *pagani* or *montani* – since our ancestors wished the urban plebs too to have gatherings and a sort of a council – failed to make decrees in the most ample terms not only about my health and safety, but also about my dignity.[13]

For Fraschetti, these remained to Cicero's day the only institutionally acknowledged subdivisions of the city. The Augustan reform was a radical break with the past, even if the components had their own historical precedents.

Fraschetti's black-and-white contrast between republican and imperial systems has come under question in two recent studies.[14] *Vici*, too, had good claim to be regarded as an ancestral institution. The antiquity of *vici* at Rome is supported by their attestation as early as the third century BCE in the Latin colonies of Cales and Ariminium; they even echoed Roman topography, as in the *Vicus Esquilinus* at Cales, the Cermalus, Velabrum and Aventinus at Arminium.[15] Most explicitly, the Augustan antiquarian Dionysius of Halicarnassus explains in detail that they were created by Servius Tullius, when he divided Rome into its four urban tribes. Indeed, Dionysius says nothing of the Varronian *montes*, and regards *vici* as the only subdivision of the city, and goes further to assert that Servius banned transfer of residence between the four tribal regions, a claim that fits in with claims elsewhere that he banned patricians from residence on the Capitoline, and created

---

[13] *de Domo Sua* 73–4: 'nullum est in hac urbe collegium, nulli pagani aut montani – quoniam plebei quoque urbanae maiores nostri conventicula et quasi concilia quaedam esse voluerunt – qui non amplissime non modo de salute mea, sed etiam de dignitate decreverint.' Also see the *Commentariolum Petitionis* 30, 'deinde habeto rationem urbis totius, collegiorum, montium (Mommsen, cod. omnium), pagorum, vicinitatum': the reference here to *montes* depends on Mommsen's emendation.

[14] Lott (2004), Tarpin (2002).

[15] Tarpin (2002) 330 and 347–8; the point has been made to me by Filippo Coarelli, and is the subject of a forthcoming study.

the *vicus patricius* as a sort of ghetto where suspect patricians were kept under control. Dionysius goes on to say that each neighbourhood was given its own shrine, called *compitum*, and that the festival of the Compitalia was instituted shortly after the Saturnalia, at which sacrifice was made to the 'heroes', evidently Greek for *lares*.[16]

Dionysius' account is suspect, in the same degree that any Augustan account of ancestral tradition risks being a deliberate retrojection of the present. If Augustus wanted to make his reform acceptable by representing it as a revival of the true Roman tradition, king Servius was the ideal figure onto whom to project the invention of *vici*. Moreover, we may ask how it can be that a Greek scholar writing under Augustus knows about a Servian reform of which the great Roman antiquarian Varro had nothing to say? For Varro certainly knows the word *vicus*, for which he supplies an improbable etymology (from *via*, rather than the Indo-European root for 'house' as in Greek Ϝοῖκος),[17] but he gives no hint of a Servian origin, and discusses it in a wholly different context from the Septimontium. This may be the product of the chances of survival of limited parts of his text, yet it is notable that he does nothing to elucidate the relationship of *vici* to the *montes*, which he does discuss.

Yet this scholarly discussion has underestimated the capacity of both sides in a Roman debate of laying claims to knowledge of ancestral tradition. Cicero at least had an evident political agenda in underlining the traditional legitimacy of *montes* and *pagi* at the expense of *vici*, for it was these neighbourhoods which played a crucial part in the urban disorders of the 60s and 50s BCE. Cicero's assertions about which groupings expressed the 'true' will of the urban plebs are particularly suspect in the context of his polemic against Clodius: for it was Clodius who pushed the political potential of *vici* to their utmost, to Cicero's personal cost. Varro was writing the *De Lingua Latina* in the aftermath of the Clodian troubles, in the 40s BCE, and shared Cicero's political sympathies (he was a long-term supporter of Pompey). It is surely no coincidence that Servius was presented as the inventor of the *montes* at the time that *vici* were proving most troublesome, and conversely that he was presented as inventor of *vici* at the time, under the new Augustan regime, when it was politically expedient to revive them.

We can therefore attempt to escape the controversy about the origins of the *vici* by shifting focus. Rather than asking about their origins, an issue entangled with questions of political legitimacy, we can focus on their

---

[16] Discussed by Fraschetti (1990) 204–10, Tarpin (2002) 101–11, Lott (2004) 30–7.
[17] *De Lingua Latina* 5,145, 'purement fantaisiste' according to Tarpin (2002) 7–14.

well-attested function as a site of contestation in the late republic. *Vici* feature, unlike the *montes*, with some frequency in the historical narratives of the period. Livy repeatedly describes activities taking place across the city as 'by neighbourhood, '*vicatim*' or '*per vicos*'; whether heralds calling an assembly in 421 BCE, guards for the watch being raised in 302 and 198, free oil being distributed by the aediles in 213, or cheap grain in 203.[18] On each occasion, he may, of course, be using the language of the late first century BCE, rather than contemporary terminology. But by the late republic, *vici* play a more active role, typically as groupings of the urban plebs, and usually in situations of conflict, spurred on by radical politicians; they acquire 'revolutionary' associations not detectable in the earlier passages.[19]

So much is already clear in the response to the currency reform of Marius Gratidianus of 85 BCE, celebrated by the erection of statues to him by the *vici*, before which, as before the *Lares* of the Compita, they burned incense and candles, a story told by Cicero, Seneca and the elder Pliny.[20] Not only are the *vici* the geographical articulation of popular sentiment, but the association of Gratidianus with a compital cult foreshadows the cult of the Genius Augusti. With the victory of Sulla, Gratidianus' statues were overthrown, and new statues erected to the dictator; the dedication plaque of such a statue from the Vicus Laci Fundani survives.[21] The *vici* were also implicated in the passage of the law to distribute freedmen to non-urban tribes proposed by the tribune Manilius in December 67, on the day of the Compitalia: the close involvement of the slave and freed-slave population in the neighbourhoods makes it likely that the Compitalia was chosen for its suitability for mobilising the *vici*.[22] The subsequent suppression of the Compitalia by a *senatus consultum* in 64, linked to a ban of *collegia*, shows how this festival had now become closely associated in the minds of the senatorial class with popular dissent.

The *vici* feature again in Sallust's narrative of the Catilinarian conspiracy, when the freedmen and clients of Lentulus go around the craftsmen and servile population of the *vici* trying to recruit popular support and bribe people to start a fire (*Catilina* 50). The corresponding passage in Cicero's speech against Catiline is one of the few vivid insights into the conditions of the urban plebs: he depicts Lentulus' agents as going around the shops and workshops (*tabernae*) appealing to the poor and needy, and dismisses

---

[18] Tarpin (2002) 94, and Lott (2004) 37–41 for the references.

[19] Flambard (1977), Fraschetti (1990) 213–86, Tarpin (2002) 95–7, Lott (2004) 45–60.

[20] Cicero, *de Officiis* 3.80, Seneca, *de Ira* 3.18, Pliny, *Natural History* 33.132 and 34.27.

[21] *Corpus Inscriptionum Latinarum* 6.1297 = *Inscriptiones Latinae Selectae* 872; Tarpin (2002) 325 (R77).

[22] So Lott (2004) 49–51.

as absurd the idea that the poor would burn not only their only sleeping quarters, but the place they make their daily income (*in Catilinam* 4.17). In identifying the shopkeepers as a class devoted to peace, Cicero shows an ambivalent perception of such grass-roots neighbourhoods as both seats of popular unrest and of stable plebeian subsistence.[23]

It is with the deep urban unrest associated with Clodius that the negative connotations of the *vicus* and the festival of the Compitalia become most acute. Cicero attacks Piso as consul for 58 for allowing the celebration of the *ludi Compitalicii*, banned since 64, and so letting Sextus Cloelius, the Clodian gang-leader, put on the *toga praetexta*, that is as magistrate celebrating the games.[24] Passing over the endless debate around this incident and its implications, we soon find Cicero inveighing against Clodius and his recruitment of gangs (*operae*) by some sort of act of formal enrolment *vicatim*, carried out on the Aurelian tribunal in the Forum.[25] The common thread here is that the *vici* act as potentially subversive formations which empower the *plebs infima*, craftsmen and artisans, including people of servile origin, and act as a potential reservoir of alternative power into which the revolutionary can tap.[26] The model, in a word, is the street gang not the parish.

It is not clear whether, on our present state of evidence, we can extrapolate a reliable picture of what the traditional republican *vicus* was supposed to be, what sort of administrative structure and role it had, above all whether each *vicus* had its officials, *vicomagistri*, and how such structures related to others like *montes* and *pagi*. There seems no reason to doubt that the Compitalia was an ancient festival, and that it was celebrated in neighbourhood shrines at the crossroads (where, so Varro etymologizes it, the roads 'head together', *competunt*). These shrines were identified with neighbourhoods, however organised. If they once in the past had played any significant role in the organisation of the city, by the last century of the republic the ruling class were in denial over the matter; either, like Cicero and Varro, pointing to other forms of local ritual association as the 'true' Roman tradition or, like Clodius and other *populares*, pushing to new levels their potential for articulating popular support. From the Augustan perspective, they represented another aspect of Roman tradition that had become corrupted, and needed revival.

---

[23] For the key role of the *taberna* in the city population, see Purcell (1994) 659–73.

[24] On Clodius and Sex. Cloelius, Cicero, *in Pisonem* 8 and 23, Asconius *ad loc.* p. 7, ll. 9–26 Clark; for the debate, see Fraschetti (1990), Lott (2004) 51–5.

[25] On Clodius and the Aurelian steps, see Cicero *pro Sestio* 34, 'servorum dilectus habebatur pro tribunali Aurelio nomine collegiorum, cum vicatim homines conscriberentur, decuriarentur.' See Fraschetti (1990) 210–50, Nippel (1995) 70–84; Millar (1998) for the background.

[26] The importance of the *populares* for the Augustan reform is stressed by Laurence (1991).

If we return to our initial question about Roman identity, of how republican Rome could be known, whether to the outsider or the native, the answer appears to be that, by the first century BCE at least, it was a hotly contested territory, and the very contest rendered it harder to know and map. Divisions and articulations of the space of the city there were; but there was no real consensus among the population about how to apply them. One may guess that Varro's system of *montes* and shrines of *Argei* must have seemed as obscure to the majority of the shopkeepers and craftsmen of the city as to the modern reader. Equally, the divisions of grass-roots neighbourhoods, which they would have been more prone to embrace, were rejected with contempt and suspicion by many authority figures; only the radicals learned to speak their language. If this is right, the city as an image of Roman identity was in a deeper sense unmappable, for lack of a common language and consensus about its articulation.

Streets and order

The absence of an agreed system of local subdivision fits in with the perception of republican Rome as chaotic and disordered in terms of urban design. It is a commonplace complaint that late republican Rome failed to rise to the standards of urbanism set by the cities of the hellenistic world.[27] In the early second century BCE, Rome was thought to be an object of mockery in the Macedonian court, thanks to the 'appearance of the city itself, which was still undeveloped in its public and private spaces'.[28] It was not only those from the eastern Mediterranean who looked down their noses at Rome: in the 60s, Cicero evokes the arrogance of the Campanians, conditioned by the wealth of their plain:

They will mock and despise Rome, set on its mountains and valleys, with its tenements raised and suspended in the air, its substandard streets and its extremely narrow alleys, in comparison to their own Capua, spread out in the flattest of plains and superbly situated.[29]

The image of the ideal city is the classic 'Hippodamian' layout of a well-ordered grid on a plain, with broad *plateae* crossed with narrower, but not too narrow, *stenopoi* or *angiportus*, doubtless set, as Vitruvius prescribes

---

[27] Zanker (1988) 19, Favro (1996) 50ff.

[28] Livy 40.5.7: 'speciem ipsius urbis nondum exornatae neque publicis neque privatis locis.'

[29] Cicero, *de Lege Agraria* 2.96: 'Romam in montibus positam et convallibus, cenaculis sublatam atque suspensam, non optimis viis, angustissimis semitis, prae sua Capua planissimo in loco explicata ac praeclarissime sita inridebunt atque contemnent.'

(1.6), at an angle to the prevailing winds. The image was perfectly familiar to the Romans, who indeed frequently applied it to their own colonies, let alone the well-ordered camps which aroused Polybius' admiration. Their very consciousness of this 'ideal' led both to an apologetic tone, and to 'explanations' of why Rome, too, was not an ideal city.

The 'explanation' given by Livy locates the causes in the deep past, with the reconstruction of Rome after the Gallic sack of 396:

All work was hurried and nobody bothered to see the streets were straight; individual property rights were ignored, and buildings went up wherever there was room for them. This explains why the ancient sewers, which originally followed the lines of the streets, now run in many places under private houses, and why the general layout of Rome is more like a squatters' settlement than a properly planned city.[30]

Livy's image of a chaotic city applies to his contemporary, Augustan, Rome, as is made clear by the echo of his account in Tacitus, who depicts the Neronian fire of 64 CE as the first chance to put to rights the errors of the fourth-century city:

The rest of the city was not, as after the Gallic fire, put up indiscriminately and all over the place, but districts (*vici*) were measured and laid out, streets were broad, heights of houses were limited, with wide open spaces, and porticoes added to protect the frontages of insulae.[31]

The ramshackle settlement of high tenements on narrow, winding roads is still seen as the opposite of the well-ordered city.

It is tempting to subscribe to these contrasts as self-explanatory, especially in a Europe that is heir to a long history of urban design predicated on a Hippodamian model. The current western city is the outcome of a long struggle to reverse the heritage of the medieval city, often similarly characterised by narrow, winding roads, and fire-prone wooden houses built too high and too close; the 'slum-clearances' of the late nineteenth and twentieth centuries, and Mussolini's *sventramenti*, stand in line with Baron Haussmann's reshaping of post-revolutionary Paris. As Spiro Kostof vividly showed, the long-standing battle between two images of the city is deeply implicated in ideology and the attempt to impose a particular type of social

---

[30] Livy 5.55: 'Festinatio curam exemit vicos dirigendi, dum omisso sui alienique discrimine in vacuo aedificant. Ea est causa ut veteres cloacae, primo per publicum ductae, nunc privata passim subeant tecta, formaque urbis sit occupatae magis quam divisae similis.'

[31] Tacitus, *Annals* 15.43: 'Ceterum urbis quae domui supererant non, ut post Gallica incendia, nulla distinctione nec passim erecta, sed dimensis vicorum ordinibus et latis viarum spatiis cohibitaque aedificiorum altitudine ac patefactis areis additisque porticibus, quae frontem insularum protegerent.'

order.[32] The alternative to the 'rationalism' of the grid-design is not irrational chaos, but systems that follow their own logic. The cellular structure typical of the Islamic city, which in cases like Damascus or Mérida transformed the Roman grid, breaking down its broad throughways and central spaces, replacing them with a maze of narrow, winding lanes and blind alleys, is not the result of 'confusion' but of social structure, of the division of the city into neighbourhoods controlled by kinship, tribal or ethnic groupings.[33]

If late republican Rome did not strike its inhabitants as a well-ordered city, it may be that they had become blind to the earlier logic which underpinned it. Even a squatter-settlement, which strikes the inhabitants of the modern city as chaotic, can be shown to have its own coherence:

Beneath the apparent chaos of the modern squatter settlement, there is often a clear consistency of form and urban structure which varies from place to place. Such consistencies derive at the local level from the relationship between urban form and social processes. Local spatial customs and unwritten social codes determine the layout, spacing and growth of houses, and the development of plots and settlement form.[34]

It is striking that even in the squatter-towns that are the informal outgrowth of some third-world cities, like Manila, tightly organised neighbourhood groups emerge to play a critical function in helping inhabitants orient themselves in the wider urban environment, carefully policing intruders, and providing mutual support for families knit together by links of patronage.[35]

The logic that underpins the squatter-town or the Islamic city is one of social nucleation: the creation of tightly controlled neighbourhoods which defy the outsider, and limit freedom of movement around the city as a whole. The same principles apply to early medieval Italy: as in the *Roma turrita* of baronial families with their strongholds, like the Orsini in Pompey's theatre, or the Savelli in that of Marcellus.[36] Genoa is a particularly well-documented case, where the streets of the centre, based on the grid pattern of the Roman colony, are still now a maze in which the cellular structure is clear.[37] Medieval Genoa was built, and run, by its family clans, its *consorterie* or *alberghi* (figure 6.3). The city had no public piazza, and no seat of government. The only piazzas were the slight widenings in the street network around which the houses of a clan were grouped. The *albergo* is a quasi-kin group, of many heads of family who, if not by birth, then by legal pact, agree to

[32] Kostof (1991), Kostof (1992).   [33] Kostof (1991) 47–9.

[34] Erickson and Lloyd-Jones (1997), cited by Kemp in Carl, Kemp and Lawrence (2000) 342.

[35] Hollnsteiner-Racelis (1988).   [36] See Brentano (1974), Mairie-Vigueur (1989).

[37] See Grossi Bianchi and Poleggi (1980); on family clans, see Heers (1977).

Scala 1:5.000

Figure 6.3 Genoa of the medieval consorterie, with roads terminating in clan strongholds (after Grossi Bianchi and Poleggi 1980, figure 100)

share the same name and hold property and interests in common. Fiercely competitive, they needed their defences; the tower is the symbol of this family power. The central places, called *contrate* or *curie*, of which the Doria stronghold in the piazza S. Matteo is the classic example, were the meeting places of the clan. Round it clustered the multiple family units: the *domus magna* of the head of the *albergo*, the lesser *domus* and *domunculae* of the other members. When the monopoly of the clans was broken in the early sixteenth century by the reform of Andrea Doria, there was a marked rupture simultaneously in the aspect of the street plan and of the architecture of the houses of the nobility. The Strada Nuova, now via Garibaldi, is the symbol of this new order. Broad and straight, it is lined with the renaissance palazzi of the new nobility. This is a nobility of property, not of clan-control: so there are no shops, no clutter of lesser dwellings. The broad street spells accessibility: what matters now is to be in the first *rollo* of houses suitable for entertainment of public visitors, princes, cardinals and ambassadors (figure 6.4).

We know too little about the street-plan of republican Rome to say whether it followed the model of cities like medieval Genoa or Islamic Mérida. These parallels simply enable us to think in terms of alternative models to the rationality of the grid-pattern. The narrow, winding streets of republican

Palazzo Ducale

Palazzi del primo rollo, 1599

Palazzi del secondo rollo

Palazzi del terzo rollo

Figure 6.4 Renaissance Genoa, with hierarchy of important houses, now concentrating on the Strada Nuova not the medieval centre (after Grossi Bianchi and Poleggi 1980, figure 276)

Rome were the fossilised outcome not only of the complex topography of the site, what Cicero called its 'mountains and valleys', and of historical accident (the Gallic sack may or may not have played its role), but of social formations. It would be particularly valuable to understand how the topographic location of the middle republican *gentes* related to the street plan. It is conceivable that they exercised local control of their areas as the clans of Genoa did over their *contrate*. By the late republic, the houses of the aristocracy were heavily concentrated around the Palatine and Forum;[38] and the reconstruction by Carandini of the houses at the foot of the Palatine of the sixth-century 'Rome of the Tarquins' can be used as an argument for the antiquity of that concentration.[39] But the division of the city into four regions identified with

[38] See Guilhembet (1995).   [39] Carandini and Carafa (1995).

the urban tribes might suggest a different, more dispersed pattern of kinship groups.

We can only speculate about what made Rome grow as a settlement in the way it did. What is evident is that, by the late republic, it no longer made sense. Rome underwent a great shift in its self-image. One approach is to attribute this to 'hellenisation' – that is, the spread of an image of the ideal city based on knowledge of the cities of the Greek east. We have already seen how a new image of urban pride spreads through the cities of central Italy in the second and early first centuries BCE (ch. 3). Yet it would be absurd to suggest that this Greek model was a novelty. The grid plan was known in Italy from the seventh century on, and even without moving into the Greek sphere, Etruscan foundations like Marzabotto from the late sixth century offered Rome a model for the taking. Foundations like Cosa, Alba Fucens, Falerii Novi, Fregellae and Paestum show Rome adopting this model for its colonies from the late fourth century onwards.[40] If a new image of urban magnificence was spreading in the second century, it was not due to a sudden new discovery of Hippodamian principles, but to the encounter with new models of urban magnificence, as set by Alexandria, Antioch or Pergamum, the *luxuria Asiatica* brought back by eastern conquest.[41]

The effect of the new model produced a rupture with the past as profound as the new ideal-city of Renaissance Italy. The Renaissance ideal required perspectival vistas with vanishing points: from Pope Julius II's via Giulia, cutting through the medieval mess of the southern Campus Martius towards the Vatican, to Paul III Farnese's 'Tridente', to Sixtus V's long vistas marked by obelisks. These powerful interventions in the medieval fabric were not driven by pure aesthetics, but by the need to demonstrate and assert papal power and control.[42] Equally profound was Baron Haussmann's transformation of post-revolutionary Paris. His broad boulevards smashed through the tangle of medieval housing for reasons that could be expressed in terms of hygiene, thanks to the magnificent system of sewers, but which were also intimately connected with the need for riot control. The sheer success of his project could be seen in the ease with which the troops put down the rising of the Commune of 1871 in all areas affected by his new planning.[43]

The perceived need in the late republic to refashion Rome, we may suggest, was not simply to do with aesthetic models arriving from the east, but with the perception of a city tormented by rioting mobs, no longer controllable by

---

[40] Gros (1988) 127ff.   [41] Gros (1988) 104–16; see further ch. 9.

[42] On the military and social considerations underpinning such schemes, see Burroughs (1994), Ingersoll (1994).

[43] Kostof (1991) 249–55, Kostof (1992) 266–75.

traditional mechanisms. Republican Rome, it has been well argued, lacked a police force because it had long relied on mechanisms of social respect and authority to maintain order.[44] Indeed, there were the junior magistrates, the *tresviri capitales*, who had a function of fire-control, attested in 241 BCE when they were punished for failure, and a handful of men to help them arrest runaway slaves; but this scarcely amounted to a police force and fire-brigade.[45] By the same argument, the lack of organisation in the street grid, and the lack of effective administrative subdivisions at neighbourhood level, were the outcome of alternative methods of social control. At the point at which social order was seen to break down, so the need for new 'rational' systems of urban control became pressing.

The knowable city

On the eve of civil war in 49 BCE, the city was still disorganised and out of control, a tangle of streets and monuments that preserved as fossils many levels of the city's development, but for lack of consensus impossible to present coherently. In this sense, so the argument has run, it was unmappable, beyond cognitive grasp. Over the following decades, the situation was radically transformed: the city comes to be organised, known, mapped and catalogued to a remarkable extent. Three bodies of evidence are basic to our knowledge of imperial Rome: the numerous inscriptions celebrating the *vici*, the fourth-century Regionary catalogues, and the fragments of the Severan marble map of Rome. Each has attracted a considerable body of discussion. What is argued here is that each of the three is the outcome of a common project, to render Rome known and controllable at a micro-level.

The Augustan reorganisation of Rome created a city that was defined and knowable in a fundamentally different way. The division into fourteen *regiones*, with the subdivision into an expandable number of *vici* (265 by the late first century CE, perhaps 320 by late antiquity), was systematic and comprehensive, resolving the old conflict between the regions of the Varronian Septimontium, and the *vici* of popular practice. Every corner of the city could be defined and listed in terms of *regio* and *vicus*. The *vici* provided the framework for census-taking, and the census of inhabitants *vicatim* by *domus* and *insula*, introduced by Caesar in his dictatorship, provided a detailed knowledge of the inhabitants of the city unimaginable to previous

---

[44] Nippel (1984).

[45] Nippel (1995) 22–6. Filippo Coarelli points out to me that some of the imperial *excubitoria* seem to have republican predecessors.

censors. The extensiveness of the imperial knowledge of the capital is evidenced by the fourth-century Regionary catalogues: though they present problems of detail, they reflect the possibility of establishing the detailed statistics of the housing stock of the city. A vital tool of such knowledge was cartography. The plan of the city inscribed on marble at the beginning of the third century CE, fragmentary though it is, bears witness to the same capacity to document all aspects of the urban fabric, not just public monuments and public property. The knowledge goes down to the level of the individual private property, and the individual shop.[46] The city known and displayed, measured by professional surveyors, listed by census-officials, is a city (unlike that of the late republic) under control. Let us examine the component elements in turn.

Regions and neighbourhoods

The reorganisation of Rome into fourteen *regiones* and several hundred *vici* seems not to have been finally carried out in its definitive form until the last decade of the first century BCE, probably 7 BCE. The date depends on a convergence between the historical narrative of Cassius Dio and the implicit foundation date of 1 August 7 BCE given by numerous dedications by *vicomagistri* (a couple of exceptions seem to point to the years between 12 and 7).[47] As Dio tells the story, the reorganisation was occasioned by a major fire, started by debtors; the response was to divide Rome into regions and put each under state magistrates (aediles, tribunes or praetors), and to give responsibility for the fire-brigade to the local magistrates of the neighbourhoods, who were allowed to wear the dress of magistrates (i.e. the *toga praetexta*) and be preceded by lictors within their own wards. His highly abbreviated account is puzzling: there must have been considerably more to the reform than concern for fire-control, not least because the system was replaced within a few years by the creation of a new fire-brigade of seven cohorts of *vigiles*, commanded on military lines by a prefect, distributed systematically across the regions. Those barracks became an important part of the new urban landscape.[48] Yet the function of the

---

[46] On marble plans before the Severan one, see Coarelli (1991), and now Rodríguez-Almeida (2002).

[47] Dio Cassius 55.8.6–7; on Dio's account, see Swan (2004) 78–82. Fraschetti (1990) 250–68 points to the discrepancies; Lott (2004) 84–9 defends the idea of a single foundation date. See also Galinsky (1996) 300–12.

[48] Rainbird (1986), Ramieri (1990) and *Lexicon Topographicum urbis Romae*, ed. E .M. Steinby. Rome, 1 (1993), 292–4.

Figure 6.5 The Belvedere altar, Vatican Museums: Augustus
presented with the *lares* (DAI Neg. 75.1290)

vicomagistri continued. Control of fire was at best a single aspect of care for
order in the city that was delegated to neighbourhood level in a hierarchically ordered system. But the *vici* were not simply administrative units: ritual
and symbolic aspects are prominent in all the evidence, and central to their
conception.

The monuments themselves, especially the rich harvest of dedicatory
altars from the *vici*, foreground the religious functions.[49] Augustus, as on
the Belvedere altar, hands over the Lares for worship (figure 6.5). As Ovid
puts it, the Lares Praestites dedicated by Curius have crumbled away with

[49] The evidence for compital shrines is pulled together by Pisani Sartorio (1988).

time, but now the city has a thousand Lares and the Genius of the leader who handed them over, and the neighbourhoods have triple divinities.[50] The founding moment of 1 August 7 BCE is one of the creation, or re-creation, of a cult. Hence, despite the facts that *vici* certainly existed before, that Augustus himself earlier gave cult images to them, that *vicomagistri* had existed before, and that the Compitalia was a long-standing festival, this moment is presented as a sort of zero point, which resets the clocks, and launches a new era. For centuries, the cult magistrates consistently present themselves as the 'magistrates of year x': not only close to the time, like the *magistri* or *ministri* 'of the first year' responsible for half a dozen surviving dedications, but even into the early third century, when the *magistri* of the 214th and 230th years were still keeping count of the new era.[51]

The New Age ideology is the same spirit as that met in the calendar reforms (ch. 5). The correction to the leap-year cycle made in 9 BCE was celebrated by the naming of the month Sextilis as August; inspired a new era in the province of Asia, taking Augustus' birth on 23 September as the first day of the year; was monumentalised in the Horologium Augusti with its tribute to his birth on the equinox. The New Age for the *vici* took its birth from the first of the month renamed in the previous year.

One aspect which strikes us forcibly is the incorporation of some sort of cult of the Emperor at a pervasive, street-corner level. Standard domestic *lararia*, abundantly exemplified in Pompeii, show the figure of the Genius of the master, veiled for sacrifice, between the two dancing figures of the Lares; the typical position of the *lararium* in the kitchen or service area underlines the role of this cult in the control of the servile household (figure 6.6).[52] The Genius Augusti between two Lares Augusti at the Compitum is directed by analogy at the slaves and freedmen who made up the overwhelming major-ity of the craftsman/shopkeeper population met in literary descriptions and gravestones. There is no need to push this as far as a claim that Augustus stood now in master/slave relationship with the population of Rome; but he was tapping into a familiar language of ritual which made such cele-brations a natural expression of respect and good order.[53] That the Genius Augusti formed part of the compital cult has recently been questioned; but

---

[50] Ovid, *Fasti* 5.145–6: 'mille *Lares* Geniumque ducis qui tradidit illos/ urbs habet et *vici* numina tria colunt.'

[51] Lott (2004) 180ff. lists all Augustan compital dedications by year; Tarpin (2002) 307–26 catalogues all periods. See Lott (2004) nos. 5–10 for the first year, no. 22 for the via Marmorata album, Tarpin (2002) 314, R15 and R16 for the third-century examples.

[52] Fröhlich (1991).   [53] See e.g. Fraschetti (1990) 374; Beard, North and Price (1998) 184–6.

the explicit evidence of Ovid about the *numina trina*, the trinity of Lares and Genius, is confirmed by at least one Augustan altar, and by the long series of post-Augustan dedications to the Lares Augusti and Genii of the Caesars, which make explicit that after Augustus' death the cult passed to his successors.[54] We can point also to the compital shrines on the street corners of Pompeii, which use exactly the same iconography of the trinity of Genius between Lares as do domestic shrines: these are surely a reflection of metropolitan practice (figures 6.7, 6.8).[55]

The cult of the Genius Augusti is no more (or less) problematic than the numerous manifestations of an imperial cult across the empire. The revealing question is not what it tells us about the belief or faith of those involved, but how it operated in producing social hierarchy and order. There is a close analogy with the vital role played by the Augustales, the college of priests of the imperial cult, in numerous cities of the western empire in providing a second order of dignity after the decurions to which well-off citizens, overwhelmingly of slave origin, could belong.[56] Indeed, the two groups, *vicomagistri* in Rome and Augustales outside, are linked by the symbolism they display on their monuments: the dedicatory altars in Rome carry the symbols linked with the name Augustus, the laurels, oak wreath and 'shield of virtue' (figure 6.9), which equally mark the tombs and houses of Augustales (figure 6.10).[57]

What the compital altars and dedications attest most eloquently is the potential of the neighbourhood organisations to confer dignity on the participants. Dio's account of the reorganisation of the *vici* mentions the privileges extended to the *magistri* of wearing the dress of state magistrates and being preceded by lictors (see p. 276). This cannot have been a complete novelty, since Cicero criticises Sex. Cloelius for wearing the *toga praetexta* in his controversial celebration of the Compitalia (see p. 268). Livy implies that the practice went back to the early days by an argument put in the mouth of a tribune of 195 BCE, L. Valerius, contrasting the widespread use of purple as a status symbol for magistrates, priests, children and local magistrates, to the exclusion of women from the use of purple:

---

[54] Lott (2004) 110–14 denies the standard picture; see Tarpin (2002) 312–14, R7–17 for the repeated formula *laribus Augustis et Geniis Caesarum* in post-Augustan dedications.

[55] Van Andringa (2000).

[56] Duthoy (1978), Ostrow (1985), Abramenko (1993), Camodeca (2001), Pesando (2003), Wallace-Hadrill (2004).

[57] On the iconography of the Roman altars, see Hano (1986), von Hesberg (1986), Hölscher (1988); on the links between these Augustan symbols, see Zanker (1988) 319–20.

Figure 6.6 Domestic *lares* from Pompeii, the House of the Vettii (author's photo)

Can we allow the right, here in Rome, to men of the lowest sort, *magistri vicorum*, of wearing the *toga praetexta*, and not only to wear this status symbol in life but even to be cremated with it in death, and not allow the use of purple to women?[58]

Such a speech is not reliable evidence for second-century practice; but it is indicative of Augustan attitudes, both as to the low social position of

[58] Livy 34, 7, 2–3: 'purpura viri utemur, praetextati in magistratibus, in sacerdotiis; liberi nostri praetextis purpura togis utentur; magistratibus in coloniis municipiisque, hic Romae infimo genere, magistris vicorum, togae praetextae habendae ius permittemus, nec ut vivi solum habeant tantum insigne sed etiam ut cum eo crementur mortui: feminis dumtaxat purpurae usu interdicemus.' On the Augustan stamp of the entire passage, see Purcell (1986) 83f.

Figure 6.7 Street scene from the Via dell'Abbondanza, Pompeii (from Spinazzola 1953, plate I)

Figure 6.8 Altar to neighbourhood *lares* from the Via dell'Abbondanza, Pompeii (Spinazzola 1953, plate XVIII)

Figure 6.9 Altar of Vicus Sandalarius, Rome, showing
Augustan symbols of laurels and oak wreath (DAI Neg.
59.68)

vicomagistri, men of the lowest status (*infimo genere*), and of the importance
to them of this privilege.

About the fulfilment of this respect, the Augustan and post-Augustan
monuments are eloquent.[59] The scenes depicted on the altars, like that of
the Vicus Aesculeti, at once make the tribune Valerius' point: the freedmen
vicomagistri in their purple-bordered *togas*, caught in mid-ritual like the
best of Roman magistrates, glow with local pride (figure 6.11).[60] The great
frieze in the Vatican, depicting a sacrificial procession of the *vicomagistri*,
shows a striking crossover between state ritual and neighbourhood cult: the
head of the procession, with trumpet players, and a cow and two bulls as
sacrificial offerings, goes beyond the level of the offerings of incense and
cakes of the Compitalia, or even the swine depicted on the Vicus Aesculeti
altar; but behind them, four figures in short cloaks must be slave *ministri*,
carrying the Lares Augusti, and they are followed by the togate figures of four

[59] For detailed discussion, see Zanker (1970/1).
[60] Zanker (1988) 133, figure 108, Gregori and Mattei (1999) 32–3, no. 6.

Figure 6.10 Tomb of Calventius Quietus Augustalis, Herculaneum Gate, Pompeii (author's photo)

magistri (figure 6.12). The dignity of the slave *ministri* is most explicit in the simple but exquisitely elegant carving of the altar of the Vicus Statae Matris (figure 6.13).[61] The symbol of what made Augustus august, the oak wreath for saving the lives of citizens (*cives*, we note), surrounds the names of four slaves, the *ministri* of year VI. We should not too easily take for granted the capacity of Roman visual expression not merely to mirror the Roman social hierarchy, but to push its language to the limits, investing the slave with the dignity of the citizen in a reference that goes to the symbolic heart of the Augustan principate.

Just as the iconography of the altars evokes pride, so the recording and display of names elevates local participants to a level of self-memorialisation conventionally associated with the elite. The most sophisticated Augustan example is offered by the long inscription from an anonymous *vicus* in

[61] Gregori and Mattei (1999) 30–1, no. 5.

Figure 6.11 Altar of the Vicus Aesculeti, sacrifice by four
magistri (Vatican Museums inv. 855, DAI Neg. 60.1472)

Testaccio behind the '*Porticus Aemilia*' (now identified as Navalia), termed
the Fasti Magistrorum Vici, and included by Degrassi in his publication of
the *fasti* (figure 6.14).[62] The inscription is split between the two faces of the
same stone. Each side parades in its upper half six months of the calendar,
and in its lower part one of two lists of magistrates, an arrangement that
implies that the two are mirror images. The first list is of the consuls and
censors, starting from Augustus' first consulship (figure 6.15). The second is
the *fasti* of the *magistri* of this particular *vicus*, dating back to their inaugural
year, 7 BCE (figure 6.16). The statement that *vicomagistri* are worthy of
fasti just like consuls could hardly be more pointed. Ironically, the lists

---

[62] Mancini (1935), Degrassi (1947) 173–8, 279–90, thoroughly discussed by Lott (2004) 152–61.
See also above, p. 246.

Figure 6.12 Altar of the *vicomagistri*, Vatican Museum (DAI Neg. 57.1004)

Figure 6.13 Altar of the Vicus Statae Matris (Vatican
Museums inv. 2144, DAI Neg. 35.210)

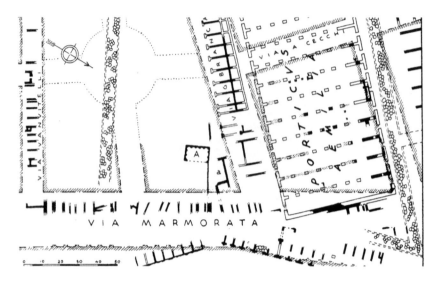

Figure 6.14 Plan of location of Fasti Magistrorum *Vici* (drawing by G. Gatti, from Mancini 1935, figure 7)

Figure 6.15 Fasti Magistrorum *Vici*, general view of first panel (DAI Neg. 2001.1481)

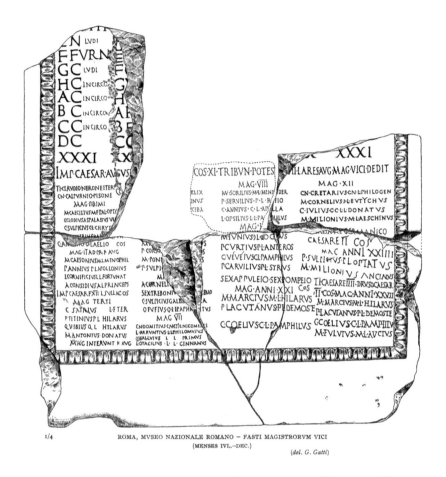

Figure 6.16 Fasti Magistrorum *Vici*, detail of lists of *vicomagistri* (Degrassi 1963)

are incomplete: starting from the four magistrates of year 1, they continue through the next eight years to 2/3 CE, only to break down. Suddenly the college of 14 CE intervenes; the list returns to 5/6, then back to 18, then to 21. By no coincidence, the magistrates of 14 and 21 were the same people, and they enthusiastically filled up any spare gap on the stone. But the very demonstration that the recording of names was not automatic underlines the positive choice and the pride involved. It was presumably up to the initiative of the individual colleges to cover the costs of adding their own names to the monument, and not all were as enthusiastic at this self-promotion as others.[63] The fact that the same *vicus* produced no less than ten dedications in addition to these panels, the majority Augustan, shows that, haphazard though they may have been, the local magistrates were enthusiastic.[64]

---

[63] Rüpke (1998) 27–44.   [64] Lott (2004) 159–60.

Figure 6.17 Dedication by *vicomagistri* of fourteen *regiones*
from the Capitoline (*Corpus Inscriptionum Latinarum*
VI.975, photo Musei Capitolini)

Possibly something similar is at work on the greatest of all *vicus* monuments, the honorific altar from the Capitoline dedicated to Hadrian in 136 CE
'by the *magistri vicorum* of the 14 regions of the city' (figure 6.17).[65] That
is what the inscription says, yet what we have is at best a fraction, some 66
of the 265-plus *vici*. For once it is not because the inscription is fragmentary. It starts, on the left side, with nine *vici* from Regio I (only a selection)
(figure 6.18), goes on to six from Regio X (a smaller selection), then to seventeen from Regio XIII (this could be the full list). The right side jumps
back to Regio XII, with twelve *vici*, and finishes with twenty-two from
Regio XIV (making Trastevere easily the best-known Region). Only five
of the fourteen Regions are represented, and none of them necessarily completely. The back of the monument is blank, leaving space for more, which
makes it unlikely that the other Regions ever featured. It was seemingly
up to each Region and *vicus* to decide whether to finance the extra stone
cutting.[66] The names we see are the result of local pride and the desire
for self-advertisement. It may be no coincidence that it is in the peripheral

---

[65] *Corpus Inscriptionum Latinarum* VI, 975 with 31218; *Inscriptiones Latinae Selectae* 6073;
Gregori and Mattei (1999) 112–15, no. 169.
[66] So Rüpke (1998), 33–36.

Figure 6.18 Detail of Capitoline altar (*Corpus Inscriptionum Latinarum* VI.975, photo Musei Capitolini)

Trastevere that the local *magistri* show most competitive zeal to memorialise themselves.

The voluntary nature of these neighbourhood inscriptions makes their frequency the more remarkable. Lott catalogues sixty-eight examples, relevant to Augustan Rome; Tarpin's list, up to the fourth century, rises to eighty-four.[67] Yet all of these have survived by chance, and none of them from key areas like the Forum, where ancient monuments are expected and hunted, but from casual finds scattered across the city. The ancient Roman street level is often 6–8 m below modern Rome, and it is by the chance

---

[67] Tarpin (2002) 307–26, Lott (2004) 180–217.

of modern urban development that *vicus* monuments emerge: the Vicus Aesculeti during the reshaping of the via Arenula in 1887, the Compitum Acili near the Colosseum during Mussolini's construction of the Via dell'Impero, or the Aventine Fasti during the enlargement of the Via Marmorata.[68] We are looking at the tip of an iceberg: each year, between the 265-plus *vici*, over a thousand freeborn and freed-slave *magistri*, and over a thousand slave *ministri* were appointed; and even if only a minority took the opportunity to commemorate themselves, the impact on the urban fabric was significant.

In ceremonial and symbolic terms, Augustus' reform had a major impact. If Varro tried, and failed, to map the divisions of Rome, and Clodius tried, and was prevented, from giving neighbourhood organisations more say, Augustus reconciled the conflict and made Rome eminently mappable. His *XIV regiones* picked up both the tradition of four tribal regions, and the magic seven of the Septimontium: the new Rome is twice the Septimontium, with seven regions within the *pomerium*, and seven outside it (figure 6.19).[69] If the old regions had been articulated by shrines, those of the *Argei*, the new regions were articulated by the *compita* of the cross-roads. Two, seemingly conflicting, republican traditions are merged into one, comprehensive system, recognisable by all. The common people who identify themselves on their tombstones as being from a particular *vicus* show how Cicero's city of shopkeepers who did not wish to lose their livelihood to riot and conflagration have got what they wanted: Nostia Daphne the hairdresser, with her freedwoman Cleopatra, and her husband M. Nerius Quadratus, all from the Vicus Longus; Curtilius Hermeros, silversmith and magister of the Vicus ab Cyclopis; the brothers Lucretius Pamphilus, dyers from the Vicus Lorarius; Petronius Philomusus, barber, from the Vicus Scauri; Sulpicius Menophilus, doctor from the Vicus Victoriae; and the cluster of clothes-makers and purple dyers from the Vicus Tuscus.[70]

Cataloguing Rome

The New Age of the Roman neighbourhood, as we have seen, dates to 1 August 7 BCE. But the use of the *vicus* to give formal articulation to the city goes back to Caesar's dictatorship. We have a single notice, typically compact, in Suetonius' *Life*:

---

[68] On the Vicus Aesculeti, see Pisani Sartorio (1993b), on the Compitum Acilium, see Dondrin-Payre (1987), Pisani Sartorio (1993a) and on the via Marmorata, see Mancini (1935).
[69] Favro (1996) 137.   [70] For the references, see Tarpin (2002) 323–4.

Figure 6.19 Map of fourteen Augustan *regiones* (after Favro 1996, figure 59)

He conducted a review of the population, not in the customary fashion or place, but by neighbourhood (*vicatim*) through the owners of blocks (*insulae*), and so reduce the 320,000 recipients of grain at public cost to 150,000. To avoid disturbances at any future time over the review, he arranged that annually, in place of the deceased, the praetor should draw lots among those not included in the review.[71]

As far as we know, the only traditional mechanism for listing the citizen population was the census conducted by the censors in the Campus Martius. The failure to complete this operation between 70 BCE and Augustus' revival of the census in 28 BCE constituted a major obstacle to the knowledge of the citizen body. Caesar's *recensus* abandons the categories traditionally

---

[71] Suetonius, *Iulius* 41.3: 'recensum populi nec more nec loco solito, sed vicatim per dominos insularum egit atque ex viginti trecentisque milibus accipientium frumentum e publico ad centum quinquagintaque retraxit; ac ne qui novi coetus recensionis causa moveri quandoque possent, instituit, quotannis in demortuorum locum ex iis, qui recensi non essent, subsortitio a praetore fieret.'

examined by the censors (tribe and property qualification) and instead lists the citizen inhabitants of the capital locally, area by area, block by block. There is good reason for thinking that Caesar's interest went far beyond the issue of entitlement to free grain: the principle of constantly updating the list of inhabitants through householders seems to have applied to other Roman cities, in the procedure of *professio* set out by the bronze tablets of Heraclea; and is later met as an innovation in Roman Egypt.[72]

Caesar's dramatic reduction of the list of those entitled to support illustrates again the difficulty of knowing republican Rome. The census mechanisms of the republic were set up to answer the requirements of a state which needed to know which citizens were entitled to vote, and who was obligated to military service.[73] They were not designed to determine who were the inhabitants of the city entitled to support in the form of cheap or free grain. For such purposes, different and more accurate information was needed: was the citizen resident within the city of Rome, whether the area defined by the walls, or by the area of continuous building, *continentia*, which better described the city? Was the citizen of an age to qualify (typically seventeen)? Implicit in the scale of Caesar's reduction is that a great number of unentitled persons had been drawing support: these would include non-citizen immigrants to the city, and slaves freed without proper process who did not have citizen status.[74] The inescapable effect of the generosity of Clodius' new regulations was to attract an influx of needy people to the city; and, as Cicero complained, by burning down the temple of the Nymphs on the Campus Martius in which the citizen records were stored, Clodius deliberately made it impossible to answer questions about entitlement.[75]

Caesar's district-by-district, house-to-house census review was, as Claude Nicolet has shown, a new way of knowing the citizen body.[76] Caesar was close enough to Clodius to understand the effectiveness of reaching the population at *vicus* level, and also the enormous popular resentment against official census lists that were desperately out of date, and deprived the needy of their entitlement. By introducing a new, locally based, listing of citizens, he was able both to reduce the cost to the state of distributions, and to remove the resentment of the citizens who found themselves deprived – hence Suetonius' reference to the avoidance of 'future disturbances' by introducing an annual mechanism for updating the lists.

---

[72] Lo Cascio (1997).   [73] Nicolet (1980) 49ff. *et passim* on the republican census.
[74] Rickman (1980) 176f.
[75] Cicero, *pro Caelio* 78 and *pro Milone* 73, discussed by Nicolet (1976), Manacorda (1996)
[76] Nicolet (1991) 123ff.

In the process, Caesar's reform transformed knowledge of the space of the city. Augustus continued and expanded on the Caesarian initiative. Again, it is Suetonius who notices:

He held a review of the population by neighbourhood (*vicatim*), and to avoid the plebs being called away more often from their business for the grain distributions, planned to give tokens for three four-monthly rations a year, but since they wanted the old practice restored, he conceded that everyone should receive monthly rations.[77]

Suetonius does not link this information to the reorganisation of the city into regions and *vici* (though in any case his practice is to split up information thematically);[78] and it is likely that long before the reform of 7 BCE, Augustus was using the *vici* as the administrative basis for his repeated revisions of the citizen lists, which eventually raised the number entitled to support to 200,000. Another clear sign that he was encouraging *vici* before 7 BCE is the practice, reported by Suetonius, and illustrated by no less than three inscriptions, of using the New Year's 'tips' (*stipes*) offered to him by the people to endow individual *vici* with new cult statues.[79] The surviving examples are dated by their inscriptions to between 10 and 8 BCE.[80]

Long, then, before the symbolic transformation of the city into one of regions and *vici*, the neighbourhood had become the key element in the articulation of the city and the control of its population. It must also be the case that Caesar restored the worship of the Compitalia and the colleges of four *magistri* for each *vicus*. The clearest evidence is that from Pompeii, where in two successive years of Caesar's dictatorship, 47 and 46 BCE, two groups describing themselves as *mag(istri) vici et compiti* listed their names in red paint on tufo blocks, later reused.[81] Pompeii must be imitating Rome, and it is hard to imagine *vicomagistri* banned in Rome while they continued in Pompeii.

---

[77] Suetonius, *Augustus* 40.2: 'Populi recensum vicatim egit, ac ne plebs frumentationum causa frequentius ab negotiis avocaretur, ter in annum quaternum mensium tesseras dare destinavit; sed desideranti consuetudinem veterem concessit rursus, ut sui cuiusque mensis acciperet.'

[78] The reform is described at Suetonius, *Augustus* 30.1 (under *urbs* rather than *populus*): 'spatium urbis in regiones vicosque divisit instituitque, ut illas annui magistratus sortito tuerentur, hos magistri e plebe cuiusque viciniae lecti.' The religious elements are discussed with other religious revivals at 31.5: 'nonnulla etiam ex antiquis caerimoniis paulatim abolita restituit, ut Salutis augurium, Diale flamonium, sacrum Lupercale, ludos Saeculares et Compitalicios.'

[79] Suetonius, *Augustus* 57.1: 'omnes ordines in lacum Curti quotannis ex voto pro salute eius stipem iacebant, item Kal. Ian. strenam in Capitolio etiam absenti, ex qua summa pretiosissima deorum simulacra mercatus vicatim dedicabat, ut Apollinem Sandaliarium et Iovem Tragoedum aliaque.'

[80] Lott (2004) 181–3, nos 2–4.　　[81] *Corpus Inscriptionum Latinarum* IV.60; Tarpin (2002) 333.

We cannot throw further light on how the *vici* may have operated in Rome between Caesar and 7 BCE. When Suetonius says Caesar reviewed the citizen lists 'by neighbourhood through the owners of blocks (*insulae*)', we cannot tell whether that means that lists were kept at *vicus* level of all owners of property in the area, or whether the *vicomagistri* had any hand in requesting, transmitting, or verifying the information.

Without a dramatic new discovery of citizen-lists at Rome, we are unlikely ever to be the wiser. But what we can say is that the hierarchy, region by region, *vicus* by *vicus*, *insula* by *insula*, still underpins the way the city was listed in the fourth century CE in the two surviving versions ('*Curiosum*' and '*Notitia*') of the 'Regionary catalogue'.

Debate still rages over what relationship these 'Regionary' catalogues bear to official lists: positions range from the optimistic belief in a virtual transcript of an official document to the sceptical dismissal of the documents as a product of hyperbolic rhetoric, intent on magnifying the importance of the city through bogus statistics.[82] The debate fails to acknowledge that on the one hand the production of a Regionary catalogue would be inconceivable were it not for the generation of the information through official census-taking at local level, and on the other that the information available officially must have been very much more extensive and detailed, and constantly changing over the course of time. What we have is at best a summary, with all the inaccuracies to which such a summary is subject.

A glance at the figures is enough to reveal the limits on their reliability (see table 6.1). After listing for each region the principal public buildings and notable features, it offers a list of basic statistics, always under the same headings in the same order. These start with the number of *vici*, followed by the number of shrines (*aediculae*), which is always identical, and the number of *vicomagistri* and of *curatores*. The main surprise here is to discover that the number of *vicomagistri* is a stable forty-eight per region, supported in all regions except the last by two curators. The one exception is Regio XIV, Transtiberim, which shows up on nearly every other statistic as significantly bigger, but the only concession is three instead of two curators. This is such a fundamental contrast of principle with the Augustan pattern of four *magistri* per *vicus* that one must infer a significant administrative reform in late antiquity. This contrast apart, it remains clear that the *vicus* is still in the fourth century the main building block of the Regio, given pride of place in the listings, and even a superfluity of information, given that the numbers

---

[82] Text, Nordh (1949). For the link with official statistics see Nicolet (1987); in favour of accuracy, Coarelli (1997b); more sceptical, Hermansen (1978), Arce (1999).

Table 6.1 Statistics for Rome from the fourth-century Regionary catalogues

NOTITIA	*vici*	*vicomag.*	*curatores*	*insulae*	*domus*	*horrea*	*balinea*	*lacus*	*pistrinae*
Regio I	10	48	2	3250	120	16	86	**87**	20
Regio II	7	48	2	**3600**	127	27	85	65	15
Regio III	12	48	2	2757	60	**17**	80	65	16
Regio IV	8	48	2	2757	88	18	**75**	**78**	15
Regio V	15	48	2	3850	180	**26**	75	74	15
Regio VI	17	48	2	3403	146	18	75	73	16
Regio VII	15	48	2	3805	120	25	75	76	15
Regio VIII	34	48	2	3480	130	18	86	120	20
Regio IX	35	48	2	2777	140	25	63	120	20
Regio X	20	48	2	2643	**89**	48	44	89	20
Regio XI	**19**	48	2	**2600**	**89**	16	15	20	16
Regio XII	17	48	2	2437	113	27	63	**81**	**20**
Regio XIII	**17**	48	2	2487	130	35	**64**	**88**	20
Regio XIV	78	48	3	4405	150	22	86	180	23
(**Totals**)	**304**	672	29	**44,251**	1682	**338**	972	1216	**251**
Summary	424	672	29	46,602	1790	290	856	1352	254
CURIOSUM	*vici*	*vicomag.*	*curatores*	*insulae*	*domus*	*horrea*	*balinea*	*lacus*	*pistrinae*
Regio I	10	48	2	3250	120	16	86	**81**	20
Regio II	7	48	2	**4600**	127	27	85	65	15
Regio III	12	48	2	2757	60	**18**	80	65	16
Regio IV	8	48	2	2757	88	18	**65**	**71**	15
Regio V	15	48	2	3850	180	**22**	75	74	15
Regio VI	17	48	2	*3403*	*146*	*18*	75	73	16
Regio VII	15	48	2	3805	120	25	75	76	15
Regio VIII	34	48	2	3480	130	18	86	120	20
Regio IX	35	48	2	2777	140	25	63	120	20
Regio X	20	48	2	2643	**90**	48	44	89	20
Regio XI	**21**	48	2	**2500**	**88**	16	15	20	16
Regio XII	17	48	2	2437	113	27	63	**80**	**25**
Regio XIII	**18**	48	2	2487	130	35	**44**	**89**	20
Regio XIV	78	48	3	4405	150	22	86	180	23
(**Totals**)	**307**	672	29	**45,151**	1682	**335**	942	1203	**256**
Summary	424	672	29	46,602	1790	290	856	1352	254

for shrines are given separately though identical to those of *vici*. Indeed, this is the one point on which the two versions, the *Notitia* and the *Curiosum*, show no variation, and at which their summary of total numbers actually agrees with the mathematical total of the individual entries.

Otherwise, as table 6.1 shows, there are numerous discrepancies, though none of them is particularly significant. The two versions give variant numbers at sixteen points (emboldened in table 6.1): these are evidently minor slips in copying from the same source. More worrying are the discrepancies between the totals of the individual entries and the summary total statistics given at the end. Since the two versions agree completely on the figures for totals, we are left with the problem that neither version, nor any possible combination of the variant readings, will give us a completely consistent set of figures. Evidently, the source from which they were working already had the discrepancies. This is frustrating to us; but it does not mean that the ultimate source of the information had inaccurate figures. That ultimate source must necessarily be some sort of official list, and its entire character shows more concern with matters of public administration than of curiosity to the tourist.

Despite all their inadequacy, the Regionary lists give us a feel for the texture of the city not possible for any other centre in antiquity. Descend to the level of detailed numbers, and the Regionaries may indeed let us down: thus they give the total for numbers of *vici* as 423 or 424, whereas adding up the lists of *vici* for individual regions gives a total of 303 or 307. The elder Pliny gives a total under Vespasian of 265 *vici*; inscriptions of various dates from individual regions point to consistent increase, though at different rates in different areas; a plausible correction of the total for the fourth-century lists is 323, coinciding with the figure given by a Byzantine source.[83] The *vicus* is the building block of the expansion of the city. Whereas the number of regions remains constant at fourteen from Augustus to late antiquity, together with the distribution of *vigiles* at one cohort per two regions, and one *excubitorium* per region, the *vici* themselves are distributed unevenly across the regions, and their numbers change over time, surely reflecting changing population density.

After the *vici* are listed the various buildings and facilities of the region. Private houses predominate: *insulae* in their tens of thousands, and a far lower figure, below 2,000, of *domus* (to the definition of '*insulae*' and '*domus*' we will return). *Horrea*, warehouses for the storage of grain or other commodities, are enumerated separately: the numbers are fairly low, on average less than one per *vicus*. Bakeries, *pistrinae*, run at similar levels. Facilities to do with water are commoner: over a thousand *lacus* represent the main distribution points of water at local level, while the high figures, not far short of a thousand, for baths, *balinea*, remind us that the monumental imperial *thermae* formed only part of a dense provision, largely privately owned, of bathing facilities. To these details, repeated region by region, the summaries

[83] Coarelli (1997b).

add two further global totals, whether reliably or not, for public latrines (*latrinae*) and for brothels (*lupanaria*).

A comparable list for a modern London or Rome might be expected to give all sorts of details we miss here: the number of public houses or bars and the number of churches are often regarded as vital statistics; and then one might expect to learn how many shops, businesses and factories or places of manufacture there were. It is certainly not that Rome was short of shops and bars: wherever one looks on the marble plan, the streets are lined with single-room units opening directly on the streets, the clear sign of commercial premises. But the Roman category system is different. The point is not an analysis of use of space, but of units of property.[84] The principle of Roman law that ownership of the soil implies ownership of everything above it is the condition that makes it unlikely that the shop by itself is ever a unit of property.[85] The failure to enumerate businesses and places of manufacture equally implies the situation we meet in Pompeii or Ostia that commerce and production are integrated with the housing stock, not a distinguishable category. If exception is made for warehouses and bakeries, this is because they are structurally distinctive units; though it is also of course relevant that the state interested itself directly in grain stores and bakeries in order to maintain the food supply of the city.[86] Brothels may also reflect an official interest, since the state imposed taxes on prostitutes and required their registration before the aediles.[87] *Latrinae*, after Vespasian's introduction of tax on urine, fall into the same category.[88]

We are dealing, then, with the units of property as declared by the owner to the administrative apparatus of the state. That is important to bear in mind when considering the most vexed feature of the lists, the numbers of *domus* and *insulae*. Numerous passages in the sources make clear that '*domus* and *insulae*' represent an exhaustive expression that covers the housing stock, all types of residential property: so in the great fire of 64 CE, Tacitus declares that an incalculable number of *domus*, *insulae* and temples were burned (*Annales*. 15.41), while Suetonius, more precisely, says that apart from an immense number of *insulae*, many *domus* of republican heroes with their attached spoils of war were lost (*Nero* 38.2). Every private dwelling, then, is either a *domus* or an *insula*, and each had an identifiable *dominus*, who could declare the residents to the census or, as Tacitus goes on to explain, collect the subsidies for rebuilding offered by Nero.[89]

[84] So Coarelli (1997b) and Lo Cascio (1997).   [85] Rainer (1987), Saliou (1994).
[86] Rickman (1980) 134ff., 204ff.   [87] Robinson (1992) 137ff.
[88] Robinson (1992) 119ff., Neudecker (1994) 92ff.   [89] Calza (1941).

Vast difficulties have been caused by the definition of *insula*. The reason is simple: the order of numbers given by the lists both for Rome as a whole (the summary gives 46,602, the totals of individual entries are 44,251 and 45,151), or even the numbers for individual regions, when divided into the available ground area, give plots so small that they are impossible to reconcile with the original meaning of the term, an 'island' of construction standing free of any other building. On the various calculations of total area available for private building, the average *insula* of the lists cannot have been much larger than 200 m², while some regions (especially VIII and X) are so densely packed that the average falls to as little as 75 m².[90] The marble plan is enough to confirm that the average free-standing block of construction was very much larger. But equally, it is no solution to suggest that the units counted must have been individual apartments, or entrance doors, for this conflicts with any known meaning of the word *insula*. The solution must be that *insula* carries precisely the meaning of a unit of property seen in the passages above, and constantly met in the legal texts of the *Digest*.[91]

Whether that is enough to rescue the reliability of these figures as an official census of property in Rome in the fourth century CE is another matter. But too many hopes have been hung on these figures. If the aim is, as it has been for many scholars, to calculate the number of inhabitants of the city, then it must be said that since there is no way of calculating the number of inhabitants per unit of property without access to those statistics which Caesar generated, we can learn nothing. Perhaps more significantly, we can learn something about the texture of the city in its aspect of a series of properties. By comparing the blocks of property mapped on the Marble Plan (see pp. 301ff.), or those actually excavated, with the implied high number of units of property, we can see that holdings must have been progressively subdivided from the moment of their unitary construction: that, from the known patterns of Roman inheritance, and the strong instinct to spread legacies wide, is probable enough.[92]

The Regionary catalogues leave us longing for something better. Almost certainly inaccurate in many of their figures, they give no more than a reflection of the type of information which Roman imperial officials might have at their disposal. It is a reasonable assumption that, from the creation of this new office in 26 BCE, the city prefect (*praefectus urbi*) had responsibility for maintaining the statistics of the city: region by region, *vicus* by *vicus*, to understand the properties, their owners, and their inhabitants, especially

---

[90] Guilhembet (1996).   [91] So Coarelli (1997b).
[92] Lugli (1941–2) attempts to identify units on the Marble Plan, with multiple subdivisions.

where these were citizens entitled to state support and benefactions. But even if this is right, it cannot be the whole story, for the information was of equal importance to a range of officials upon whose collaboration the effective running of the city relied. Perhaps the most revealing question is not who assembled the information, but who used it?

Certainly these included those in charge of the distribution of grain (or, later, bread), money, or the other rations available under the later empire, including oil, wine and pork. It was the problem of grain distribution that first spurred Caesar to conduct his review *vicatim* through owners of *insulae*, and it is surely the case that the lists of the entitled, neighbourhood by neighbourhood, remained a vital tool in distributions. The mechanics of these distributions are obscure to us, and certainly changed through time; but at all stages they inherently hinged on bureaucratic processes and knowledge. The recipient had to be incised on a bronze list, *incisus* (i.e. not just on papyrus), and would be given a token, *tessera*, as proof of his entitlement: a rare illustration is the imperial freedman Tiberius Claudius Januarius who recorded on his tombstone his right to draw his ration at entrance (*ostium*) 42 on day 14 at the Porticus Minucia.[93] As Seneca put it, to register for grain required bureaucratic process, not moral judgement:

the thief no less than the perjurer and the adulterer and everyone, without distinction of character, whose name appears incised on the register (*incisus*) receives grain from the state; whatever else a man may be, he gets that, not because he is good, but because he is a citizen, and the good and bad share alike.[94]

By the fourth century, when these lists were finalised, the *praefectus annonae* was a senatorial official of great importance, albeit subordinate to the *praefectus urbi*. He will have needed to control not merely the lists of the entitled (and, by implication, each *domus* and *insula* in each *vicus* in each *region*), but also the official lists of bakers, *pistores*, and the warehouses, *horrea*, where grain was stored.

Then the official responsible for fire-control needed the lists. We recall that Dio regarded the regional reform of 7 BCE as a response to the problem of fires. *Vicomagistri* appear to have remained involved, even if the *praefectus vigilum* was the responsible official, with his cohorts and barracks (*excubitoria*) carefully distributed around the fourteen regions, as the Regionary lists note. With the barracks goes knowledge on the part of the local commanders of the *vigiles*, who have legal power of entry into every

---

[93] See Rickman (1980) 192 *et passim* for the complex evidence; Virlouvet (1995) for a full discussion.
[94] Seneca, *de Beneficiis* 4.28.2, trans. Rickman (1980) 182.

apartment in their zone, to ensure that the inhabitants are maintaining the requisite buckets and fire-fighting equipment (*Digest* 1.15.3.4).[95] Power to enter implies knowledge of the housing stock: not just *vicus* by *vicus*, or *insula* by *insula*, but *cenaculum* by *cenaculum*. This whole need for knowledge instantly converts the *dominus insulae*, and with him his agent, doubtless a freedman or slave, the *insularius*, into a key figure: not a mere landlord, but the person responsible for keeping the local administration informed about who was living on his property, and responsible to a measure for their conduct and security – the negligence of the *insularius* was punishable by severe flogging (*Digest, ibid.*).

Other officials, too, may have found the lists of great use. The aediles, as we learn in detail from the tablets from Heraclea, were responsible for the upkeep of the roads and pavements. Each householder was responsible for maintaining the road and pavement outside his property, and for ensuring that the water falling from his roofs did not cause pooling and obstruction in the public thoroughfare. Where the owner of the frontage failed in his obligations, the aedile had the right, with ten days' public notice, to contract the work himself, and pass the bill to the householder for payment within thirty days.[96] After the regional reform of 7 BCE, this responsibility presumably passed to the magistrates responsible for each region. And whether or not householders continued to shoulder the costs (as is likely), the magistrates necessarily needed the lists of householders, the same *domini insularum* who were critical in the lists drawn up *vicatim*. Aediles also had responsibility for controlling the markets, which included the activities of bars, *cauponae*, which the early emperors regulated neurotically; for that purpose, a listing of *cauponae* would also be returned by the property-owners within whose *insulae* bars were normally incorporated.[97] Aediles, too, were initially responsible under Augustan legislation for maintaining a register of prostitutes; and even if that register was dropped, the taxation of prostitution introduced by Caligula caused a continued need for control; here, too, the administration needed lists, and to judge from the Regionary catalogues, *lupanaria* were part of the public register.[98]

Equally, the *curatores aquarum*, responsible for the water-supply, needed detailed listing not only of the householders who had paid for the privilege of a private supply, and who took such care to mark their names on the leaden water-pipes,[99] but also surely of the private as well as public baths

[95] Robinson (1992) 105ff.   [96] Robinson (1992) 59ff.
[97] Hermansen (1982) 185–205, Robinson (1992) 135–7.
[98] McGinn (1998) 201–2, 248ff. Robinson (1992) 137–9.   [99] Bruun (1991).

(*balinea*) that were such an important destination of the water supply, and the *lacus* which ensured distribution of water throughout the city, both of which are duly listed in the Regionaries.

Finally we might recall the policing needs bound up with the administration of the city. It was the *praefectus urbi*, whose office may well have been responsible for keeping these lists and records, whose first duty was to ensure order in the streets of the city, as Tacitus put it 'to keep in order the servile and unruly element of the population' (*Annales* 3.34). With the backing of the three (later, four) urban cohorts, he could doubtless put lists of owners and inhabitants to good use. But these cohorts came to collaborate closely with the Praetorian Guard in policing the city, and the praetorian prefects doubtless had an equal interest in the lists.[100] Theatres, amphitheatres and circuses which attracted large crowds were typical seats of disorder; it may be no coincidence that the Regionaries give figures, however unreliable, for the number of seats in each place of public spectacle.

In none of these cases have we direct evidence of the existence and use of a single set of official records. The point is simply that extensive and detailed records on a regional and neighbourhood basis were potentially an instrument of vast utility in the control of the city. The republic could be seen as having been brought down by the disorder in the city. Even the reign of Augustus was tormented by fires, floods, famines and riots. By a long process, that lasted throughout his reign, he gradually put in place the mechanisms to minimise their occurrence and impact. The need to know the city in miscroscopic detail was grasped by Caesar and followed up by Augustus. They also understood, with more debt to Clodius than to Cicero, the importance of recruiting the support of the local figures of respect at neighbourhood level. The regional reform of 7 BCE was a single moment in a complex process; but it made explicit the importance not only of articulating but of knowing the city.

The city mapped

The fragmentary state in which the great marble map of Rome survives, in battered pieces that cover no more than 10–15 per cent of the original extent, does nothing to diminish our awe at its magnificence.[101] This, as much as the Colosseum or the Baths of Caracalla, is an expression of the

---

[100] Robinson (1992) 173–95.
[101] The modern study of the map starts from Carettoni *et al.* (1960) with the fundamental update by Rodríguez-Almeida (1981).

Figure 6.20 Wall of SS. Cosma e Damiano, location of Severan marble plan of Rome (author's photo)

monumentality of the imperial city. Thanks to the survival of the wall to which it was originally affixed in the Templum Pacis, reused as the outer wall of the Church of Saints Cosmas and Damian, we have a visual record of its extraordinary extent: 150 marble plaques, together measuring 18 m wide by 15 m high, represented the 4,000 ha of the city at the generous scale of 1:240, or one inch to 20 feet (figure 6.20). The plan that survives is firmly dated to the reign of Septimius Severus: by the mention of the names of the

Emperor and his elder son ('Severi et Antonini Augg.'), and by the inclusion of the Severan Septizodium, erected in CE 203, coupled with the absence of post-Severan buildings.[102]

The immediate circumstances of its creation are also fairly clear. The Flavian Templum Pacis is recorded as suffering a catastrophic fire under Commodus in CE 192 (Cassius Dio 72.24.1–2); reconstruction of this important segment of the complex of imperial *fora* was part of the restoration of order after the civil wars undertaken by Septimius. By a fairly plausible set of conjectures, we can suggest that the responsibility for the map was that of L. Fabius Cilo, Septimius' close friend and ally, who became *praefectus urbi* in CE 203, and remained so till after the Emperor's death in 211. As we have seen, it is widely accepted that the City Prefect was responsible for surveying the city, though whether the Templum Pacis was his headquarters is disputed. Cilo's involvement seems to be confirmed by the circumstance that his house on the slopes of the Aventine is, exceptionally for this plan, given its owner's name, [C]ILONIS.[103] The marble plan thus stands as a symbol of the imperial knowledge of the city invested in the City Prefect, and of the importance which the Severan regime attached to this office and function.

The suggestion that a major office of the city administration should be housed in a temple complex may seem strange to modern expectations. Yet it is one of the most striking differences between the ancient and modern cities that imperial Rome lacked the vast buildings of ministries and public administration which characterise the modern centre, and contribute so much to its congestion. Ancient sources scarcely refer to administrative structures, and the tradition of locating offices and archives in temples is well attested, from the Aerarium Saturni (treasury) to the temple of the Nymphs (grain distribution).[104] Locating the City Prefect under his great marble plan in the Templum Pacis is highly plausible, though it has to be admitted that the only sources who state where he operated place him in a Basilica under Augustus, and in the Templum Telluris on the Carinae in the later empire.[105]

Whether or not the marble plan decorated the office of the great Cilo, we can be confident of two points: that this was *not* the first time such a plan had been incised, and that this was *not* the base administrative document for the administration of the city. It is generally assumed that the Severan plan had predecessors going back to Augustus, and this is confirmed by new

---

[102] The most convenient source is now the website of the Stanford Digital Forma Urbis Romae Project, at http://formaurbis.stanford.edu/. See in print Koller *et al.* (2006).
[103] See Guidobaldi, F (1995).   [104] A point well made by Coarelli (2000).   [105] Coarelli (1999).

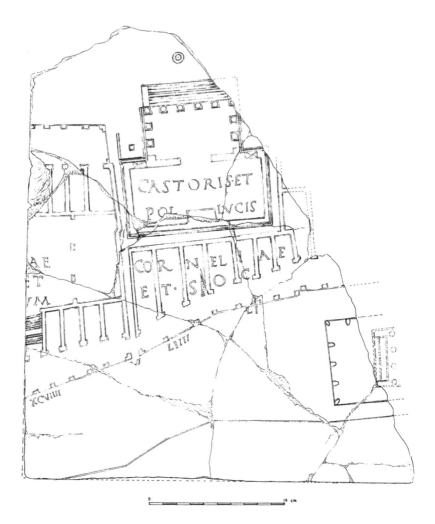

Figure 6.21 Fragment of non-Severan plan from the via Anicia (drawing from Rodríguez-Almeida 2002, figure 25, courtesy Sovraintendenza ai Beni Culturali del Comune di Roma)

fragments.[106] The need for such a plan, as we have seen, goes back to the Augustan reforms of the city, and above all to the decision to monitor the citizen population entitled to distributions of grain and other benefits *vicus* by *vicus*, and *insula* by *insula* through the owners of the *insulae*. Already in Caesar's dictatorship the surveyors must have got to work, for the procedure would demand detailed records.

That the results were inscribed on a marble plan from an early stage is confirmed by the occasional, but exciting, discovery, of a fragment of a marble plan that is evidently not the Severan one. Of particular importance

---

[106] See Rodríguez-Almeida (2002); Meneghini and Valenzani (2006).

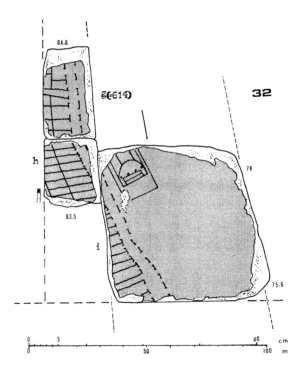

Figure 6.22 Detail of Severan marble plan for area of
Castor and Pollux (drawing from Rodríguez-Almeida 2002,
figure 16)

was the discovery in 1983 in the via Anicia in Trastevere of a group of
fragments representing the area around the temple of Castor and Pollux
on the north bank of the Tiber near the Tiber Island (figure 6.21).[107] It is
certainly not part of the Severan plan, though drawn to exactly the same
scale, 1:240, since it overlaps with surviving fragments of the Severan plan
covering the same area (figure 6.22). There are other notable differences.
Walls in the Severan plan are normally represented by a single line; the via
Anicia fragment follows the convention, which remains normal practice in
architectural drawing, of using two lines to indicate the thickness of the walls.
The use of the double line is seen in other surviving fragments of pre-Severan
plans, and the conclusion is inescapable that the Severan plan does not
represent the full knowledge available from the surveyors, but a short-cut.

The other striking difference of the via Anicia fragment is that it names
not only the public building (CASTORIS.ET/POLLVCIS), just as the Severan plan does, but the names of the owners of the neighbouring private
properties. So below the temple we see a series of shops or warehouses

---

[107] Coarelli (1991), Rodríguez-Almeida (1988), Tucci (1994), Rodríguez-Almeida (2002) 43–9.

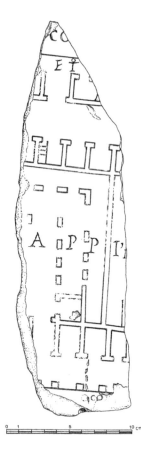

Figure 6.23 New fragment of Severan marble plan from the via dei Fori Imperiali (drawing, from Rodríguez-Almeida 2002, figure 20, courtesy Sovraintendenza ai Beni Culturali del Comune di Roma)

marked CORNELIAE/ET.SOC[iorum] – Cornelia and associates – and to its side a large warehouse complex owned by a similar group, interestingly also a woman and associates, ... AE/ ET/ [socior]VM. The same can be said of other early fragments. Excavations in the via dei Fori Imperiali in 1995 uncovered a fragment of a marble plan beneath the Domitianic paving of the Forum Transitorium, so guaranteeing a first-century CE date (figure 6.23). A large building, surrounded externally by shops, with a porticoed courtyard within, is identified by the letters APPI', indicating a member of the noble family of the Appii Claudii as proprietor. Above it is visible a slice of another building. The fragmentary letters . . . CO . . ./ ET . . . are enough to suggest a group like Cornelia and her associates. This fragment too respects the 1:240 scale.[108]

Another fragment oddly survives in the Umbrian city of Amelia (figure 6.24).[109] By a coincidence almost too good to be true, it, too, shows

---

[108] Rodríguez-Almeida (2002) 61–6.   [109] Rodríguez-Almeida (2002) 51–6.

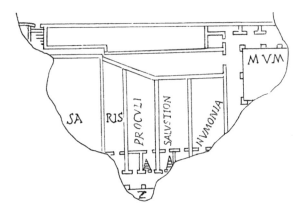

Figure 6.24 Fragment of non-Severan plan of Rome found in Amelia (Umbria)(drawing from Rodríguez-Almeida 2002, figure 17)

a series of warehouses along the north bank of the Tiber, quite possibly just to the west of the temple of Castor and Pollux. Here too, the names of the owners of each unit are provided: the largest, appropriately, is imperial property, [CAE]SARIS; it is followed by three similar properties, each with a shop in the front, together with a set of stairs to upper floors, labelled PROCVLI, SALVSTION, NVMONIA. Errors excepted (Numonia for Numoniae, Salustion for Sallustiorum), this seems to be part of a record both of properties and their owners.

At the risk of labouring the point, the presence of the names of property-owners is highly significant. If the purpose of surveying was to have an accurate record of property-owners, in their turn responsible for providing the names of citizens living in their houses, then it is the pre-Severan fragments that fit the bill. The great Severan marble plan was not fit for this purpose, whatever other purpose it may have served. Indeed, consideration of the sheer impracticality of consulting a document that rose 15 m above the ground level (did they provide a set of steps, perilous as they would be at that height?), has long led scholars to the conclusion that there must have been another version, possibly on a series of papyrus sheets, possibly on bronze, the standard Roman material for records, which served practical, administrative purposes.[110]

The conclusion is clear. Impressive though it seems to us, and doubtless was intended to seem to the Roman viewer, it is only a reflection of an

[110] See the introduction by Tina Najbjerg to the Stanford website (see n. 102), with reference to the unpublished dissertation of Reynolds (1996).

administrative reality that went back to Augustus. The Severan plan was not cut to the highest graphic standards possible, or even normal, and saved much labour by representing walls by single lines. And it omitted the most important information, from the administrative point of view – that is, the names of proprietors. But of course on a show wall, intended to last for generations and to impress, the names would have been an embarrassment, requiring constant recutting as property changed hands (and, from the point of view of the hapless lapidicide, balanced on a perilous 15 m ladder, a tall order indeed). This is why it is the public buildings are privileged with labels, with the consequence that, for long, discussion of the plan has focused on the location of public monuments, at the expense of discussion of private properties.

This may lead to another reflection. If the Severan marble plan is only a fragment of the richness of the administrative records, just as arguably the Regionary catalogues are a fragment of the same set of materials, we may be struck at the extent and density of the information required to record not only the physical layout of a city of as many as a million inhabitants, but to keep an accurate record of the innumerable owners of properties. Behind the documents lies a ceaseless task of census-taking (establishing the names of owners) and surveying. Presumably owners were required to register changes of property before the City Prefect; similarly, there must have been a procedure for reporting building work, and for resurveying ground plans. But the scale of this administrative task is truly daunting, and it would not be surprising to discover that it was pursued more energetically under some regimes (Augustus, Vespasian, Septimius Severus maybe) than others. The suggestion that the Severan plan is not so much an accurate survey of Rome in the first decade of the third century, but rather a palimpsest of information, and errors, accumulated over centuries, is more than likely.[111]

However daunting the task, and whatever the delays and slips the city administration may have committed from time to time, the base information was extraordinarily rich, and remarkably accurate. This emerges most forcefully from the comparison of the fragments to modern plans of Rome. The city, as we have seen, has been intensively mapped from the Renaissance on. Yet no city map (as opposed to a cadastral register of properties) attempts to go beyond the representation of property boundaries to that of individual rooms. Archaeologists are so habituated to providing floor plans representing internal divisions that the element of surprise in finding such divisions on the Severan plan is blunted. Yet the convention of the

---

[111] So Trimble (2008).

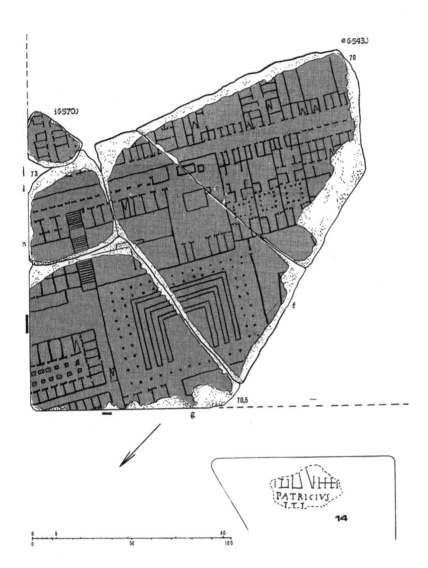

Figure 6.25 Fragment of Severan plan of Rome showing Vicus Patricius (drawing from Rodríguez-Almeida 1981, tav. X)

Roman marble plans, whenever a series of shops or warehouses lines a road, is to represent each unit separately, even when, as is made plain by the via Anicia fragment, they were jointly owned, and surely, as so often at Ostia, part of a single construction. Similarly, as in the case of the row of *atrium* houses along the Vicus Patricius, we can make out the divisions between front rooms, the *atrium* space and the columned *peristyle* at the rear, even if it is fairly clear that the cutter has taken a number of shortcuts, and the full archaeological detail is not revealed (figure 6.25).

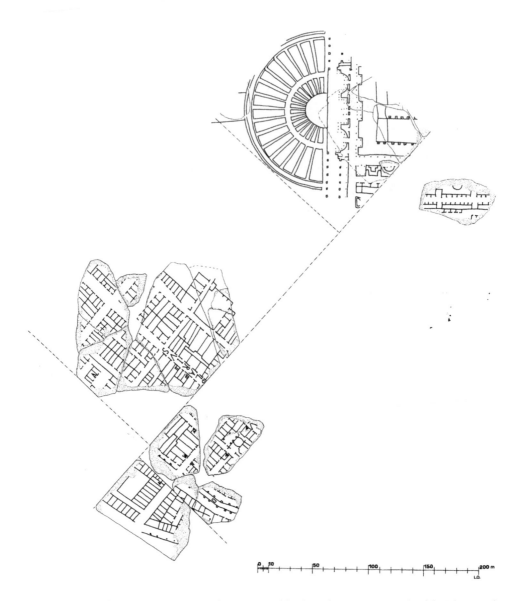

Figure 6.26 Fragments of Severan marble plan of Rome, area south of the Theatre of Pompey (Vicus Stablarius) (after Quilici 1983, figure 3)

The enterprise of surveying the housing stock of a city, *including its principal internal division walls*, is a truly remarkable one, underlining the degree of microscopic local knowledge which the imperial administration achieved. The other striking feature is the degree of accuracy. One of the clearest testimonies of this is the possibility to locate fragments by reference to the modern street plan. Here, the most conspicuous example of matching was Emilio Rodríguez-Almeida's success in reconstructing the zone to the south

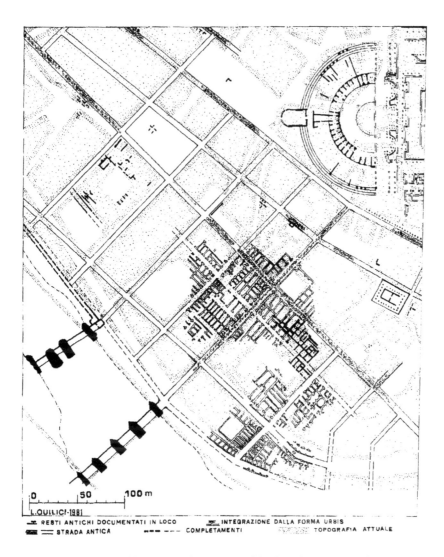

Figure 6.27 Relation of fragments of Severan marble plan of Rome to modern street plan of area south of the Theatre of Pompey (after Quilici 1983, figure 4)

of the theatre of Pompey in the Campus Martius.[112] It was his observation that a bend in a road on a marble fragment corresponded closely to the bend in the modern via delle Zoccolette that allowed him to locate the entire set of fragments (figure 6.26). The correspondence is remarkable, for not only that road, but the other roads of the area labelled [Vicus Sta]blarius, lock in tightly to the modern layout (figure 6.27). It is testimony to the remarkable

---

[112] Rodríguez-Almeida (1983). The relation of the ancient to the modern street plan of the southern Campus Martius was studied in the same issue by Quilici (1983), building on Coarelli (1977a).

persistence of the road network from antiquity to the present; but the point could not be established except in the context of the overall accuracy of the surveying. Even when there appears to be misfit, as in the Aventine area, where a nodal set of roads is skewed by 21 degrees, it may be an error not of surveying but of inscription.[113]

Had we only a sample of the records available to imperial officials, naming owner after owner against accurately mapped properties in a city of some million inhabitants, it would offer an incomparable insight into Roman society. Instead we operate, as ever, in a twilight of knowledge caught in occasional glimpses. But at least we can appreciate the importance of the knowledge revolution that allowed the city administration to control its social fabric in such intimate detail. That republican Rome was completely without maps is perhaps too much to ask us to believe. It is reasonable enough to suppose, with Emilio Rodríguez-Almeida, that Varro had access to a map setting out his seven *montes* with their twenty-seven shrines.[114] The census required declaration of property to the censors, and it would have been convenient to generate a map of property in the city; though the spectacular disorder of public records in the first century BCE, and the intermission of the census, would have made a reliable map extraordinarily hard to achieve in that period.[115] There is no sign of a detailed republican street map, let alone one identifying individual properties. Lack of maps puts the visitor at a disadvantage, empowering the local knowledge of the inhabitants. The open display by the emperors of a detailed map of their capital was more than a boast of monumental scale. It advertised their own knowledge and control of that dangerous capital, advertised the expertise of the officials, surveyors, census-takers and City Prefects, on whom they relied; and proclaimed to the stranger that the city was open to all citizens, wherever in the empire they came from, and not under the control of the local power-brokers. Just as Cicero commented on Varro's *Antiquities*, the maps allowed the Roman citizens, strangers in their own city, to recognise who and where they were.

[113] Insalaco (2003).   [114] Rodríguez-Almeida (2002) 13–21.   [115] Nicolet (1991) 124–5.

PART IV

The consumer revolution

7 | Luxury and the consumer revolution

Discourses of luxury

On 5 March, 186 BCE, Gnaeus Manlius Vulso and his troops entered Rome in triumph to celebrate victory over the Gauls in Asia Minor. Vulso was not a particularly important figure, nor was his success in Asia the first or the most spectacular: he had taken over from Lucius Scipio, the brother of Africanus, whose fame and successes were far greater, and whose conviction for misconduct in Asia in the previous year caused Vulso to delay his triumph. Scipio's triumph had brought spectacular levels of precious metal to Rome, and with it the accusation of corruption; some said it was the beginning of the end.[1] Nevertheless, some Roman historians decided to mark Vulso's triumph as a significant turning point. In Livy's (clearly derivative) account, the beginnings of overseas luxury (*luxuriae peregrinae origo*) were brought to Rome by his ill-disciplined and licentious army. Rome now for the first time saw the apparatus of high living:

bronze couches, costly cloth spreads, tapestries, and what was then regarded as magnificent furniture, tables with single pedestals and side-tables (*lectos aeratos, vestem stragulam pretiosam, plagulas et alia textilia, et quae tum magnificae suppellectilis habebantur, monopodia et abacos*).

Female musicians, playing psaltries and sambucas became part of the entertainment at feasts, and the cost of feasting rose. Cooks rose in status from the lowest to the most expensive of domestics. Yet these were but the seeds of the luxury to come, *semina futurae luxuriae*.[2]

A probable candidate for the source of this apocalyptic vision of decadence is the historian Calpurnius Piso, whose frugal ways earned him his nickname of Frugi. According to the elder Pliny, who scoured such sources repeatedly for evidence of his favourite theme, the advance of luxury, it was Piso who recorded that Gnaeus Manlius in his triumph over Asia was the first to bring into the city *triclinia aerata, abacosque et monopodia*.[3] The verbal echoes here might suggest that the whole thesis of seeds of luxury was Piso's. That

---

[1] Pliny, *Natural History* 33.148.   [2] Livy 39.6.7–9.   [3] Pliny, *Natural History* 34.14.

Figure 7.1 House of Chaste Lovers, Pompeii, scene from west wall of *triclinium* (photo Michael Harvey)

Figure 7.2 House of Chaste Lovers, Pompeii, scene from centre wall of *triclinium* (photo Michael Harvey)

Figure 7.3 House of Chaste Lovers, Pompeii, scene from east wall of *triclinium* (photo Michael Harvey)

would not be incompatible with his view, cited elsewhere by Pliny, that the year 154 BCE was a turning point, marking the end of Roman sexual modesty, *pudicitia*.[4] Cicero, too, relished the moralising of Piso, who complained that young men were obsessed with the penis.[5] Of course, we can no longer tell what event occasioned this fall from grace in 154, but we may hazard a guess that it was linked to the theatre, so often seen as the font of immorality, since it was at this time that the senate had the first solid theatre in Rome torn down.[6] Piso was writing towards the end of the second century BCE; but the debates he reflected were contemporary ones, stretching throughout the century. Indeed, the very observation that the collapse of Roman morals was so often announced reflects the recurrent nature of the preoccupations and anxieties of contemporaries.

[4] Pliny, *Natural History* 17.244.   [5] Cicero, *ad Familiares* 9.22.2.
[6] Edwards (1993) 98ff.; see ch. 4, pp. 160ff.

We may juxtapose the Pisonian image of the apparatus of luxury and feasting with an image from Pompeii over two centuries later (figure 7.1). In the House of the Chaste Lovers, the *triclinium* offers a sequence of three images of feasting. In each, two couples recline on couches to eat and drink. Whether the couches had legs made of fashionable bronze we cannot tell, because the richly coloured drapes that cover them reach the floor. Above the heads of the couples in the central scene is stretched a richly embroidered tapestry. Beside the couches are side-tables, *abaci*, with finely carved legs terminating in deer's hooves. On the tables are silver drinking vessels, scoops and strainers, while in the foreground, a slave-boy pours wine from an amphora into a silver mixing bowl (figure 7.2). In the last of the scenes, a girl is seductively represented as wearing a diaphanous silk dress, presumably what contemporaries referred to as 'Coan silk' (figure 7.3). Piso would doubtless have recognised in the details many more seeds of corruption. Part of the joy of luxury lies in the fine detail, the ability to recognise in the precise stage-props the significant and meaningful elements of this system of knowledge they represent. This is connoisseur's territory. Frankly, we are not so certain what *plagulae* or *abaci* were; but the vocabulary of fashion is always rich in technicalities, and recognition, of rarity, origin, connotation and status of the object, is essential in the attachment of meaning to the commodity,[7] of making these goods good for thinking.[8]

The Pompeian scenes are not snapshots from daily life. They are something more complex: at once 'reproductions' of stereotypical scenes embedded in a long Mediterranean-wide artistic tradition, and symbolic representations that carried instantly recognisable meaning for the Pompeian baker whose house they graced. This chapter attempts to bridge the gap between two discourses: on the one hand a Roman moralising discourse which saw in the lush details of luxury a threat to the fabric of Roman social order; on the other a contemporary anthropological discourse that sees in material culture a language or semiotic system out of which social meaning and order can be constructed. Nor is it a matter of choosing between them. Piso's way of thinking is not ours, but that does not affect its validity. What has been said about the debate about luxury in the eighteenth century is equally valid for the second century BCE:

Debate over luxury laws was thus both a debate about the character of contemporary society, and itself a characteristic of that society.[9]

The goods brought home by marauding Roman armies proved extraordinarily good for talking about. They would have lost their effect as luxuries had

[7] Appadurai (1986).   [8] Douglas (1979).   [9] Berry (1994) 142.

they attracted no attention, no comment, no criticism. Whatever the mean-ing of these objects in their country of origin, they acquired new meaning as they crossed the waters and entered new contexts, as is the way of cultural goods in transit.[10] It was the debate that determined that new meaning. What was at issue was not the objects themselves, but their use in Roman society. They were consequently an important way of talking about Roman society. The argument of this chapter is that this discourse was not inciden-tal, but fundamental, and played a central role in the reconceptualising of Roman society itself.

Sumptuary laws and the consumer revolution

Perhaps the first issue to address is why it is so self-evident to us that Roman moralising discourse was misplaced. Modern historians of Rome have found little attraction in the theme of luxury and moral decline.[11] It is a familiar fact of the last two centuries BCE that a stream of laws were passed to control luxury; but though these have been studied more than once, the discussion rises rarely above the technical, and never has entered the mainstream of debate about republican history.[12] Equally, it is well-known that the con-temporary historians of the late republic, from Piso to Sallust, including the Greek philosophically inspired historians Polybius and Posidonius, put luxury at the heart of their explanation of the crisis of the Roman state. But while that is regarded as of historiographical interest, notably for discussion of Sallust, no modern historian would put it at the heart of their own explana-tory framework. For that, we must probably go back to Montesquieu's essay *De la grandeur des Romains et de leur décadence* of 1734, which still puts a Sallustian account of corruption at the turning point between the strengths that explained Roman greatness and the flaws that explained decline.[13]

But for this there are good reasons, more to do with the modern world than the ancient. When a set of thoughts and a way of thinking that appears self-evidently true to one society then seems self-evidently false to another, it becomes interesting to enquire into what has changed at such a deep layer within the culture and the assumptions on which it rests that the rejection becomes automatic and unthinking. Passionate argu-ments about the ill effects of luxury, and repeated attempts to control it in hundreds of legislative acts in numerous states right across Europe extend from the twelfth to the eighteenth century.[14] In England, Scotland,

[10] Kopytoff (1986).   [11] Lintott (1982), Lintott (1990).
[12] Sauerwein (1970), Clemente (1981), Baltrusch (1989), Bottiglieri (2002).
[13] Ch. X, see Lowenthal (1965).   [14] Hunt (1996).

France, Spain, Germany and Switzerland the legislation is recurrent; in Italy alone over forty independent Italian cities enacted over 300 sumptuary laws between 1200 and 1500.[15] There is no doubt that the entire discourse of luxury was taken seriously in Europe for some six centuries. Why, then, do we assume so readily that sumptuary laws were absurd, pointless and ineffective?

The answer lies in a great shift of discourse in the eighteenth century that underpins 'modernism', one which produces new couplings and uncouplings.[16] The rise of the new discourse of 'the economy' is fundamental; the new focus of attention is economic prosperity as a national interest. How directly that clashed with 'luxury' thinking was first, at the time scandalously, exposed by Bernard Mandeville in his *Fable of the Bees or Private Vices, Publick Benefits*, first printed in 1714, but known from the enlarged and definitive edition of 1723.[17] He quite deliberately made his case provocatively and paradoxically:

The root of Evil, Avarice,
That damn'd ill natur'd baneful Vice,
Was slave to Prodigality
That noble sin; whilst Luxury
Employ'd a Million of the poor
And odious Pride a Million more.

The luxurious spending of the rich spelled employment for the poor. Morality as a discourse was in conflict with economic prosperity. For the first time, we are offered the modernist discourse of trade and industry in direct clash with the old morality of vice and luxury:

Envy itself, and Vanity,
Were Ministers of Industry;
Their darling Folly, Fickleness
In Diet, Furniture and Dress,
That strange ridic'lous Vice, was made
The very Wheel that turn'd the Trade.

The satirical exposition of the verse was amplified by a series of essays or Remarks. Remark (L), on Luxury, spelled out in considerable detail the arguments for supposing the balance of trade to be of national concern, and the patterns of fashion and purchase decried as luxury to be fundamental for the economy, for creating work for the poor and wealth for the nation.

---

[15] Killerby (2002).   [16] So Hunt (1996) 97f.   [17] For edited and commentary, see Kaye (1924).

Mandeville went out of his way to point the issue by taking provocative examples: prostitution too was good for the economy:

A poor common harlot . . . must have Shoes and Stockings, Gloves . . . the Stay and Mantua-maker, the Sempstress, the Linnen-draper, all must get something by her, and a hundred different tradesmen dependent on those she laid her money out with, may touch part of it before a month is at an end.[18]

Mandeville made a deep impression. Denounced by clerics from Bishop Berkeley to John Wesley, his books condemned to burning in France, he was read and admired by some of the mainstream thinkers of the century, from Voltaire (in his *Défense du Mondain ou l'Apologie du Luxe* of 1736) to David Hume to Adam Smith to Samuel Johnson. Even Montesquieu came to think him right on luxury.[19] Voltaire built on Mandeville's argument, and ridiculed sumptuary legislation:

History has proved that all sumptuary laws have been everywhere, after a brief time, abolished, evaded or ignored. Vanity will always invent more ways of distinguishing itself than the laws are able to forbid.

David Hume's essay *Of Luxury* (1752) argued that Spartan austerity was a function of their lack of trade, and that Sallust was wrong about Roman luxury, since the crisis of the Roman republic was rather one of bad government. Adam Smith's *Wealth of Nations* (1776) put the economy at the centre of the national debate, and borrowed from Mandeville at some points word for word, a debt he himself did not openly acknowledge, something for which Karl Marx took him to task.[20] Samuel Johnson, by contrast, is reported by Boswell as openly avowing his debt to Mandeville in his constant defence of luxury:

He as usual defended luxury: 'You cannot spend money in luxury without doing good to the poor.'[21]

Concern for the moral effects of luxury does not of course die with the eighteenth century, and it can be argued that many of the old preoccupations of luxury legislation have shifted their location rather than disappearing: states still regulate gambling and recreational drug consumption, and place higher taxes on 'luxuries' like tobacco and alcohol.[22] But luxury no longer functions as an overarching framework for the state's control of the behaviour of individuals. The eighteenth century brings such a

---

[18] Cited by McKendrick, Brewer and Plumb (1982).   [19] Kaye (1924), Hundert (1994).

[20] Hundert (1994) 220.   [21] Boswell, *Life of Johnson* iii, 291.   [22] Cf. Hunt (1996) 357ff.

sea-change in ways of thinking that we can unquestioningly follow David Hume, and part with Montesquieu, in dismissing Sallust's entire approach. The concept of luxury had irrevocably shifted.[23]

The reasons for this sea-change clearly lie not in Mandeville's articulation of the issue, but in the transformation of the economy itself that characterises the seventeenth and eighteenth centuries. In the last two decades, historians of the period have given increasing attention to patterns of consumer behaviour. It is now common to speak of a 'consumer revolution', especially in England and France. It was, as McKendrick puts it,

the necessary analog to the industrial revolution, the necessary convulsion on the demand side of the equation to match the convulsion on the supply side.[24]

It is characterised by a dramatic rise in both the number of consumer goods and the social diffusion of their consumption.[25] The consumer boom affects a large range of familiar, everyday items. In France, after the collapse of sumptuary legislation in 1720, there is a boom in ownership of items like gold watches (rising from 5 per cent to 55 per cent of the population), jewellery, furniture, tea and coffee sets, snuffboxes, fans and umbrella, documented in probate inventories from 1725 to 1785. The umbrella first appears in Paris in 1705, based on Chinese imports. After some competition between the guilds for the right to produce them, sales rise to from 10 per cent to 31 per cent of the population between 1725 and 1785. The umbrella crossed the water to England to initial cries of dismay, to spread widely, and become a standard item in both England and France by the nineteenth century.[26]

Among comestibles, the arrival of sugar, as Werner Sombart observed in his *Luxus und Capitalismus*,[27] spells a major change, encouraging the spread of tea, coffee and cocoa which depend on sugar as an additive. Just how important tea consumption could be for eighteenth-century society has been brought out by Breen's challenging rereading of the American Revolution.[28] It was by no coincidence that the Revolution was triggered by the Boston Tea Party. He demonstrates the enormous volume of consumer goods imported from Britain to the American colonies in the course of the century, so high that Edmund Burke could warn Parliament in 1772 that the total value of exports to America was equivalent to the total value of British exports to the entire world at the beginning of the century.

---

[23] Sekora (1977), Berry (1994).   [24] McKendrick, Brewer and Plumb (1982) 9.

[25] Weatherill (1988), Brewer and Porter (1993), Bermingham and Brewer (1995), Roche (2000), Stearns (2001).

[26] Fairchilds (1993).   [27] 1913; see Sombart (1967).   [28] Breen (2004).

The latest fashions from London were a matter of obsessive concern to the colonists, whether in clothing, or in the consumption of tea and the entire apparatus of consumption, tea-kettles and crockery, that surrounded it, notably the high-fired pottery from Staffordshire in which Wedgwood made his name. Consumption of tea had reached 'the most remote cabins' of Delaware by the 1760s; such was the urge to consume tea that the ignorant prepared it as a sort of porridge.[29] What the Americans objected to was the imposition of arbitrary taxes on their consumer goods: the symbolic gesture of Boston underlined simultaneously the dependence of American fashion on Britain, and its desire for freedom from British arbitrary government.

On Breen's argument, consumption of British luxuries, 'the Baubles of Britain', played an essential role in defining American identity and social order. For understanding the power of luxury, and the nature of the objections to it, within Roman society, the greatest illumination which luxury and consumerism in the early modern period can cast is on the social mechanisms which are implicit in it. Luxury may have an economic impact, but the mechanisms which drive it, as contemporaries repeatedly observed, were social. The thesis most frequently put forward was that of social emulation. As Henry Fielding put it in his *Enquiry into the Causes of the Late Increase of Robbers* of 1750 (p. 7):

While the Nobleman will emulate the Grandeur of a Prince and the Gentleman will aspire to the proper state of a Nobleman, the Tradesman steps from behind his Counter into the vacant place of this Gentleman. Nor doth the confusion end there: it reaches to the very Dregs of the People, who aspire still to a degree beyond that which belongs to them.

That is, the motor behind purchase of luxuries was seen as aspiration to social status in a hierarchically ordered society, and the objections to the phenomenon lay in the perceived challenge to the hierarchy.

There are several objections to 'emulation theory', familiar also as 'trickle-down'. To accept it is to buy into the hierarchical structure of society which its critics saw as endangered, and to assume that hierarchy was stable at the very point at which it reveals itself fluid.[30] The explanatory model is most effective with two further provisions. The first is that imitation is only effective as the counterpart of differentiation: the urge to mimic social superiors goes hand in hand with the urge to be seen as different from social inferiors.

---

[29] Breen (2004) 170ff.

[30] Fine and Ellen (1993) 120ff., Bermingham and Brewer (1995) 12ff., Hunt (1996) 49ff.

The process is driven as much by anxieties about visibly maintaining social standing in a society where appearances count, as by aspirations to rise. Mandeville captured the contradiction with his usual pointed satire. In his vision, the Labourer's wife buys gown and petticoat rather than a sensible better-lasting 'Frise' because 'it is genteel'. The working people spend their money to look like merchants:

> The Merchant's Lady, who cannot bear the assurance of those Mechanicks, flies for refuge to the other end of the Town, and scorns to follow any Fashion but what she takes from thence. This Haughtiness alarms the Court, the Women of Quality are frighten'd to see Merchants Wives and Daughters dress'd like themselves: this Impudence of the City, they cry, is intolerable; Mantua-Makers are sent for, and the contrivance of Fashions becomes all their study, that they may always have new Modes ready to take up, as soon as those saucy Cits shall begin to imitate those in being.[31]

His satire captures not only the constant anxiety that underlies the maintenance of difference, but the second essential feature of the emulation mechanism: that the social hierarchy itself is anything but stable, and is specifically threatened by the rising class of the merchants. Quentin Bell proposed the rule that fashion depends not on the ruling class, but on a rising class beneath it that has the financial power to challenge it.[32] Both spending on luxuries and the attempts to control it flow from the perception that the social order is open to challenge.

The eighteenth-century commentators were looking at these phenomena from the perspective of a period when attempts to control them legislatively had been abandoned by most states. The French crown, which had passed sumptuary regulations repeatedly through the seventeenth century (in 1621, 1629, 1636, 1644, 1672 and 1708), abandoned the unequal struggle in 1720. England, where sumptuary legislation went back to 1363, after a flurry of ever-more-tightly defined regulations in the sixteenth century up to 1597, repealed the law in 1604 on the accession of James I, and agreed no further laws, not so much because of disagreement with the principle, but of failure to negotiate the distribution of authority in the matter between King and Parliament.[33] Despite the scepticism of modern commentators over the effectiveness and enforceability of such legislation, its repeal seems to have removed a significant break on the economy,

---

[31] Mandeville, *Fable*, Remark M.
[32] Q. Bell, *On Human Finery* (London 1947), cited by Berry (1994) 80.
[33] Hunt (1996) 320ff.

and the consumer boom of the seventeenth and eighteenth centuries, and the new attitudes to luxury it engenders, take place in the absence of sumptuary control.

That English sumptuary laws were directed at protecting the distinctions of a hierarchical social order is explicit in their wording and details. The Statute of 1363 was given in response to a petition that complained that

Labourers use the apparel of craftsmen, and craftsmen the apparel of valets, and valets the apparel of squires, and squires the apparel of knights.

The effect of excessive spending on diet and clothing was seen as equally damaging to their nobility and their feudal dependants:

For the great men by these excesses have been sore grieved, and the lesser people who only endeavour to imitate the great ones in such sorts of meats are much impoverished; whereby they are not able to aid themselves nor their liege lords in times of need as they ought.[34]

The form this legislation takes is to restrict the use of specific foodstuffs (including game, swans, fish, etc.) and specific clothing (especially furs, ermine, silk, cloth of gold, etc.) to specific ranks. The effect of the laws is to spell out ever more clearly the social hierarchy envisaged. In 1363 this extends from servants to ploughmen, handicraftsmen, yeomen, squires, substantial merchants to knights. By 1533 the attempt to specify the lower ranks by occupation has been abandoned, in favour of ranking by annual income (under 20 pounds, over 20, 40, 100, 200), while the upper ranks are more precisely defined (Knights of the Garter, Barons, Viscounts and Earls, Dukes and Marquises, and Royalty). There is always a tension, or compromise, between ascriptive status, based on rank (nobility) or occupation, and wealth, defined by income or value of goods, that allows the merchants to map comfortably into the hierarchy.

Sumptuary law was thus not only a way of policing social behaviour, but a discourse that defined the social order itself. The repetitive nature of the enactments shows not so much that they were ineffective, as that they had the paradoxical effect of reinforcing consumption as the definitive discourse. The more precisely specific fashions were subjected to restrictions, the more ingenious became the devices for evasion: legislation creates its own loopholes. Restricting silver buttons could lead to a fashion in silver hooks. For Mandeville, it was a fundamental flaw of legislation:

---

[34] Preamble to the Statute of 1336, cited by Hunt (1996) 299.

Their Laws and Clothes were equally
Objects of Mutability;
For, what was done well for a time,
In half a Year became a Crime;
Yet while they alter'd thus their laws,
Still finding and correcting Flaws,
They mended by Inconstancy
Faults, which no Prudence could foresee.

At the same time, the constant definition and redefinition of restricted expenses automatically enhanced their social desirability. Montaigne put his finger on the inherent contradiction:

To say that none but princes shall eat turbot, or shall be allowed to wear velvet and gold braid, and forbid them to the people, what else is this but to give prestige to these things and increase everyone's desire to have them?[35]

In a society characterised by rising prosperity, and potential social fluidity, the effect of sumptuary control was not to eliminate or suppress luxurious behaviour, but to make it the dominant social discourse:

The result is that far from clarifying social differences, sumptuary law actually provokes increasing competition and imitation since it is 'cheaper' (economically and politically) for all parties to compete over the symbols than over what those symbols represent.[36]

We thus find two models of society in which consumer spending serves to define a social order reliant on appearances. In the late medieval and renaissance model, sumptuary legislation, far from blocking a shift away from feudal values, helps to redefine an order in which trade and wealth have an acknowledged place; in the early-modern model, the removal of sumptuary control allows a sort of free market of social self-definition, since each may consume and dress what they can afford.

But that free market also produced a shift away from reliance on the 'appearential' model. It is towards the end of the eighteenth century that the concepts of 'class' and 'culture' start to be articulated.[37] The critique of luxury goes hand in hand with a society of rank and hierarchy formally defined by the state. Abandonment of that critique also spells abandonment of a society defined by rank. Class, though like rank partly defined by wealth, is also defined by taste, the 'distinction' which Bourdieu examines. It is closely

---

[35] Essays 1572, cited by Hunt (1996) 102.   [36] Hunt (1996) 105.   [37] Williams (1983).

linked to ideas of high, versus popular, culture, and to the emergence of education and accent as signifiers of standing. In the city, appearential ordering gives way to spatial ordering: which street you live in can define standing, whereas the pre-industrial city is characterised by the intermingling of rich and poor, whose clothing and appearance was enough to distinguish them.[38]

Before turning to the case of Rome, one further model is relevant. The Italian states, between the twelfth century and the Renaissance, provide one of the most extensively documented examples of sumptuary control.[39] To some extent, it may be felt that the Italian case was different, more democratic and egalitarian than the model of the northern monarchies, more concerned with the cohesion of the citizen body than the hierarchical differentiation of rank. Some contrast there certainly is: only 7 of 300 laws spell out a detailed class structure in the manner of the English statutes.[40] But it is far from true that sumptuary laws in Italy were restricted to the republican states of the north. On the contrary, they are imposed in Sicily and Puglia by the Angevin and Spanish rulers, and are as common in the northern states under despotic regimes: indeed, the despotic regimes can be said to be more interested in fettering the luxury of the local aristocracies than were the republican ones.[41] There is much concern with safeguarding capital from erosion by 'useless' expenses, especially on dowries, weddings and funerals.[42] There is a degree of misogynistic urge to control the behaviour of women that goes beyond the northern states.[43]

But above all there is concern with social order and perceived threats to it:

The endless ordinances (*ordini*) to right the disorders (*desordini*) of dress seem to be ways of talking about a society which had lost its right order, a society in which (by Simmel's definition) differentiation had got out of hand.[44]

There is a clear urge to repress social mobility. Cosimo de' Medici complained that 'a gentleman can be made with two yards of silk'.[45] In Brescia in 1439, protests were registered that 'builders, blacksmiths, pork butchers, shoemakers and weavers dressed their wives in crimson velvet, in silk, in damask . . . I myself saw wives of shoemakers wearing stockings of cloth of gold.'[46] Frequent categories of exemption were created, for doctors of medicine and law, judges, nobles, magistrates, etc. The 1474 Bologna law allowed you to tell rank from the mere colour of dress:

---

[38] Hunt (1996) 111ff.   [39] Owen Hughes (1983), Killerby (2002).   [40] Killerby (2002) 85.
[41] Killerby (2002) 83.   [42] Killerby (2002) 39ff.   [43] Owen Hughes (1983) 99.
[44] Owen Hughes (1983) 90.   [45] Killerby (2002) 61.   [46] Killerby (2002) 82.

Colour alone would have placed a woman: gold for wives and daughters of knights, sleeves of gold for those of notaries, bankers and similar grandees, crimson for those of important artisans, but only crimson sleeves for the women whose husbands and fathers belonged to the humbler trades.[47]

In Italy, too, the laws were mocked as being unenforceable, as they were by Montaigne; but the point was not to eliminate luxury, but to control its utility in marking status:

> Luxury performed many useful functions within the city and it was precisely because of its symbolic importance that legislators were concerned to ensure the strict regulation of its use.[48]

Both the main studies of sumptuary legislation in Renaissance Italy agree that it was a way of talking about social order in a context of social fluidity generating by rising mercantilism.

On numerous occasions, however, governments used sumptuary laws as a conservative, or even repressive, force; as a means of providing order in society, both structural and behavioural, and of denying opportunities to the politically ambitious:[49]

> Italian sumptuary legislation was, among other things, an approach to easing tension caused by structural problems of a local social nature . . . But Europe did in a sense form a sumptuary whole, expressing its frustration over social problems it could not fully control through legislative control over their outward signs . . . In Italy, a society that dreamed of orders while facing the daily reality of class fluidity, they had to be controlled by legislation.[50]

In some ways, as we shall see, the Roman model is closer to that of Italian republics than of northern monarchies, with their emphasis on feudal nobilities. But the broad conclusions seem to be the same across Europe, from the city-states of Italy to the monarchies of France, England and Spain, or the cities of Germany and Switzerland. Luxury by definition was made possible by the increase of trade. But trade brought prosperity to merchants and craftsmen as well as the landed elite, and their participation in the language of luxury was perceived as a threat to social stability, to be controlled by a legislative assault on the use of that language. Sumptuary control was taken seriously by a very wide range of governments for at least 600 years. The abandonment of such legislative control led to a rethinking of the language

---

[47] Owen Hughes (1983) 98.   [48] Killerby (2002) 91.   [49] Killerby (2002) 61.
[50] Owen Hughes (1983) 99.

that defined society, a shift from a discourse of luxury, morality, rank and civility to the still-current modernist discourses of consumption, economy, class and culture. It is the fundamental nature of that change of language that makes it so hard to look back to past ways of structuring and talking about society and take them seriously in their own terms.

Roman luxury as a social discourse

In attempting to reassess the phenomenon of Roman luxury, the argument will not suggest that we should simply see here an earlier incarnation of the transformations of the modern world. Where there is an insight to be borrowed is that a society which regards luxury as a central concern is likely to be using it to articulate important concerns about social order. Rather than representing a failure to confront the more 'real' social and economic issues, it may prove to be antiquity's way of expressing them. We need therefore to listen to their discourse more attentively, not in the dismissive spirit of a Voltaire.

A convenient entry point to the discussion is Tacitus' account (*Annales* 3.52–5) of the senatorial debate of 22 CE, partly because this was the moment at which the Roman state stepped back from its attempt, sustained over the previous 200 years, to regulate consumption, and partly because it offers the perceptive commentary of a historian who, unlike his republican predecessors, did not identify luxury as a critical cause of crisis or decline. Insofar as it represents a moment of distance from the standard theme of luxury, it offers access to the limits of that discourse.

The complaint is raised in the senate by the aediles, as the magistrates responsible for the market, that the provisions of the sumptuary laws are being ignored and that 'utility' prices are rising beyond control.[51] Because our detailed knowledge of what Roman sumptuary laws provided is so fragmentary, it is not easy to say how they were being ignored. Our knowledge of the legislation largely depends on the two learned summaries written centuries after their abolition, by Aulus Gellius in the mid second century CE,[52] and by Macrobius in the fourth.[53] Sumptuary legislation was limited to the expenses of feasting (*luxus mensae* in Tacitus' terms). It regulated three aspects of feasting. The first was the number of guests who could be invited on any particular day. This, according to Macrobius, was the sole

---

[51] *Annales* 3.52.2: 'sperni sumptuariam legem vetitaque utilensium pretia augeri in dies.'
[52] *Noctes Atticae* 2.24.   [53] *Saturnalia* 3.17.

provision of the original law, the lex Orchia of 182 BCE,[54] and the equally learned Athenaeus of the late second century CE adds the detail that the limit was three guests outside the family except on market days, when five were permitted,[55] strikingly low limits that will have been raised by subsequent laws rather than abolished. The second limit was on the expense (*sumptus*) permissible for any single meal: the lex Fannia of 161 BCE placed a limit of 100 *asses* on festival days, and lower limits for lesser days; subsequent laws constantly refined these limits, raising them in the process.

The third limit was on precise foodstuffs and the prices payable for them. So we learn from Pliny that the lex Fannia limited consumption to one hen which should not be force-fed (*altilis*), a provision promptly evaded by finding a new way to make chickens plump by feeding them meal soaked in milk.[56] It was in the precise specification of foodstuffs that the legislation acquired its long-winded nature, and opened itself to constant satirical comment; it was in the specification of prices that it impacted directly on the market. Macrobius wonders at the long lists of types of fish and offal specified by Sulla's law,[57] while Pliny samples the names of some of the types of pig offal forbidden: *abdomina, glandia, testiculi, vulvae, sincipita verrina*.[58] Policing of the law is attested in the dictatorship of Caesar, who had guards posted round the market who seized any forbidden foodstuffs on sale.[59]

The Tiberian aediles were evidently concerned with the third of these aspects of the law, the control of market prices for luxury foodstuffs (*utensilia* seems to mean food in Tacitus' angular Latin).[60] They raised the matter encouraged by the knowledge that Tiberius, *princeps antiquae parsimoniae*, was himself a model of parsimony, seen as the virtue opposed to *luxuria*. That matches the claim of Suetonius' biography of the Emperor that he set such an enthusiastic model of parsimony as to serve reheated food at public feasts.[61] The biographer in the same passage reports Tiberius as complaining to the senate of exaggerated market prices, specifically of 3,000 sesterces for three mullet, and of asking the senate to set annual price-lists, and instructing the aediles to police public eating places, a reference which possibly coincides with the senatorial debate on luxury which Tacitus reports under the year 16 CE.[62] That is to say, at the moment the debate was raised in 22 CE, it was a familiar one, and one on which Tiberius could be supposed to have a firmly anti-luxury position.

---

[54] 3.17.2.   [55] *Deipnosophistae* 6.108.274c.   [56] *Natural History* 10.139.
[57] *Saturnalia* 3.17.11.   [58] *Natural History* 8.209.   [59] Suetonius, *Julius* 43.2.
[60] Woodman and Martin (1996) 381.   [61] *Tiberius* 34.1.   [62] *Annales* 2.33.1.

Yet the Emperor writes a letter (he is already in partial withdrawal in Campania, but prefers the excuse that he does not wish to embarrass the senators by looking the offenders in the eye),[63] which offers at least three cogent arguments against sumptuary control. The first is that the problem of luxury extends far beyond the remit of the law. He enumerates a list of phenomena which are indeed recurrent on Roman moralising discussions of luxury, which were never covered by legislation: the size of villas, the size of slave households, gold and silver plate, bronze statues and paintings, male and female clothing, and jewellery.[64] Though no sumptuary law touched any of these items, they were the field for a variety of expressions of public disapproval, especially by the censors. So, in the first such censorial act attested, the censors of 275 BCE, Fabricius Luscinus and Aemilius Papus, ejected Cornelius Rufinus from the senate for his possession of ten silver vases, a tale told in exemplary fashion in the reign of Tiberius by Valerius Maximus.[65] Tiberius' point, which we may find hard to dispute, was that the problem was so much larger than one of expensive eating that it was futile to focus on one aspect.

His second objection is that policing such a law may create yet greater problems, by being perceived as tyrannical. The senators will be the first to cry that the state is being turned upside down, that the most distinguished are being persecuted and that everyone is entrapped by the law.[66] This relates to a theme vital to Tacitus' own thinking, the potential of law for corrupting the state and creating tyranny. Earlier in the same book[67] he discussed the marriage laws, and put forward the thesis that in simple, primitive society, man is self-regulating through modesty and shame, and that the multiplication of laws is an index of corruption: *corruptissima re publica plurimae leges.*[68] In particular, the imperial order imposed by Augustus came at a price: *acriora ex eo vincula*, the chains thereafter were harsher, and specifically the marriage laws were a heavy and intrusive burden.[69] Tiberius now acknowledges the heavy burden of resentment generated by policing the sumptuary law, and prefers to limit his burden to the vital issues, not futile ones (*inanes et inritas*).[70] Chasing up table luxury, then, is a trivial matter, not worth the price in perception of tyrannical rule.

The third objection then puts table luxury in striking perspective. The real problem that concerns the ruler is the food supply from abroad: Italy and Rome are dependent on imported grain, and unless the emperor can guarantee the supply, the state risks being overthrown. This analysis of the

---

[63] *Annales* 53.1.   [64] 53.4.   [65] 4.4.3 and 2.9.4.   [66] 3.54.1.   [67] 3. 25–28.
[68] 3.27.3.   [69] 3.28.3.   [70] 3.54.6.

vital importance of the *cura annonae* was of course frequently vindicated.[71] The rhetorical power of the point lies in its relevant confrontation of related topics. One (insufficient) explanation for the inability of Rome to feed itself from its own hinterland was the prevalent villa culture, which focused precisely on the production of luxuries for the metropolis at the price of grain production: Varro's *de Re rustica* illustrates the fortunes made near Rome from *villatica pastio*, the breeding of poultry (a category of explicit concern to the sumptuary laws). But there is another obvious link: one of the prime sources of luxury goods was Alexandria, a main source of the grain supply. Such goods doubtless travelled in the same cargoes as the grain, and provided an incentive to the shippers to make the voyage. Emperors (notably Claudius) took care to maximise incentives for shippers. In a word: emperors were far more concerned about promoting the shipping trade to Rome than about limiting some of its excesses.

What makes this debate so interesting is that we seem to be witnessing a sort of paradigm shift comparable to Mandeville's *Fable.* For the eighteenth century, the issue was whether the boost to the economy of luxury consumption and trade was more important to the national interest than the perceived threat to social order. For the Roman emperors, the question is a political calculation: what will most strengthen their regime? The promotion of peaceful conditions of trade was a source of popularity for the regime: Augustus in his last days had taken pleasure on the Bay of Naples from the ecstatic greeting by the crew of a ship from Alexandria, who said they owed him their freedom and livelihood, and responded by giving his retinue money to spend on Alexandrian goods.[72] The grain supply was the best illustration of a fundamental interest of the imperial regime in promoting trade. On the other hand, was luxury legislation an effective instrument of social control? The imposition of the 'chains of law' on the elite had its downside in the creation of resentment. And Tacitus has a penetrating observation to add: though luxury continued to flourish for another half-century, it then tailed off, and one reason was the self-impoverishment of the richest and oldest families: *dites olim familiae . . . studio magnificentiae prolabebantur.*[73] One of the standard objections to luxury is that it squanders fortunes; a cynical but realistic interpretation is that emperors kept potential rivals under control by allowing elite families to self-destruct through competitive spending.[74]

On this argument, it is not enough for there to be widespread moral objection to luxury for the state to attempt to control it by legislation. Its control

---

[71] Rickman (1980), Sirks (1991).   [72] Suetonius, *Aug.* 98.2 (cited above, p. 38).   [73] 3.55.2.
[74] Hopkins (1983) 171ff., Edwards (1993) 162.

must map on to the desired social order. Despite the fact that Augustus reiterated republican sumptuary law, and despite the clear moral disapproval of Tiberius himself for luxury, policing the law ceased to be thought of as a critical issue for the maintenance of social order. What had changed? Tacitus' analysis makes it clear that luxury was still perceived as an effective instrument for enhancing social standing. He spells out the direct connection with clientelism: against the background of cultivation by the great houses of plebs, allies and kings, wealth, housing and 'parade' (*opibus domo paratu*) augmented fame and clientele (*per nomen et clienteles inlustrior*). In the stock-market of reputation, appearances are critical; the luxurious display of wealth added to the appearance of power and raised the stock of reputation, so increasing actual social power.[75] Luxury mapped effectively onto the traditional structures of social power (*clientela*). To this extent, the Roman hierarchy was, and remained, 'appearential' in Hunt's sense.

Remarkably, Tacitus goes on to link the demise of luxury to the rise of a new social group, the 'new men' from the *municipia* and *coloniae* and provinces who retained the old Roman tradition of *domestica parsimonia*. This is the same group which he identifies in his narrative of Nero's reign as disapproving of the Emperor's performative excesses, a group with which he and his contemporary the younger Pliny[76] evidently identified themselves.[77] But while Tacitus locates the discourse of luxury within that of social power and the emergence of new social groups, there are some obvious gaps in his argument. 'New men' from the towns and colonies of Italy had been penetrating the elite throughout the duration of the period characterised by the rise of luxury,[78] notably so in the figure of the elder Cato, a vociferous opponent of luxury: why should their presence only start to make a difference in the late first century CE? And where does this analysis find room for that other emergent group, so prominent in the rhetoric against luxury, of rich freedmen? A triangular relationship between an old elite, a new municipal elite, and the *parvenu* class of freedmen generates a rather different dynamic. On the basis of Tacitus' own narrative, the heyday of the power of the imperial freedman coincides with the heyday of luxury. The suppression of mention of freedmen in this context might be as instinctive for the 'municipal' Tacitus as his distasteful distancing from the standard word *luxuria* by the use of the rarer *luxus*, not 'luxury' but 'luxe'.[79]

If Roman sumptuary legislation ends with the debate of 22 CE, it begins with another, that over the lex Oppia, enacted in 215 BCE and repealed in 195.

---

[75] Cf. Saller (1982), Wallace-Hadrill (1989).   [76] *Letters* 1.14.4.
[77] Syme (1958b) 566ff., 593ff.   [78] Wiseman (1971).   [79] Woodman and Martin (1996) 379.

Some modern accounts of Roman sumptuary laws go back to one earlier moment, the lex Metilia of 217: this regulated the whitening of garments by fullers, and it is not at all clear that 'luxury' came into the argument.[80] Only in the case of the lex Oppia can we be confident that the argument was at least in part about luxury. It is not even certain that the original context of the law was more than a wartime austerity measure, though the case can be made that it was.[81] But the debate over its repeal fell in the consulship of Cato, and Livy uses it to introduce this founding figure of the anti-luxury crusade (Livy 34.1–8).

And yet this debate is a false dawn, in two senses. The first is that we can have little confidence that Livy is reporting a contemporary debate in its own terms, rather than projecting backwards onto the turning point of 195 BCE, just after the second Punic war, and on the verge of the great eastern conquests, a prescient anticipation of the issues that were to develop over the next two centuries. Scholarship is divided on the issue.[82] On the one hand, Cato's standing as one of Rome's great orators raises the possibility that his actual speech survived, though there are no citations from it in the numerous surviving fragments of his speeches.[83] On the other, his presentation of the fully fledged thesis of *avaritia* and *luxuria* as the two plagues that overthrow great empires, and his anticipation of the temptations to be presented by future Greek and Asiatic conquests, let alone the reference to Corinthian wares,[84] reflect the fully developed thinking of the second half of the second century, and must be anachronistic. To hope for contemporary authenticity in any speech reported by an ancient historian is to push one's luck.

But the lex Oppia debate is a false dawn in a second, more interesting sense. The consul Cato, self-styled model of *parsimonia*, loses the argument. Whether or not the law was initially intended as a wartime provision, the debate is cast in terms of *sumptus*, costly display of status. The law prevented women from displaying more than half an ounce of gold, any coloured (dyed? purple?) clothes, and from travelling in vehicles within the city.[85] Cato's objections are to any form of female display of wealth and status: the shame of poverty is concealed by a law that bans display.[86] The counter-arguments are about the inherent right to display status: just as purple is traditionally used to display the status of magistrates, and even minor neighbourhood magistrates, *vicomagistri* (a seeming anachronism by Livy, looking forward to the Augustan reform of these officials), so women are

---

[80] Sauerwein (1970) 39ff., Baltrusch (1989) 50ff., Bottiglieri (2002) 69ff.   [81] Culham (1982).
[82] Baltrusch (1989) 56, n. 119.   [83] Malcovati (1955) 12ff.   [84] Livy 34.4.1–2.   [85] 34.1.3.
[86] 34.4.13.

entitled to their status symbols; female ornament compensates for the lack of access to political and military decorations.[87] At least by Livy's time in the late first century BCE, it was self-evident that the debate was about the proprieties of wealth, status and social display.

These arguments were to be revived in fifteenth-century Italy by the formidable Nicolosa Sanuti, who cited them in her campaign against sumptuary provisions controlling women's dress.[88] In fact, the contrast between Renaissance and Roman sumptuary law is revealing. Women's dress was the single most important theme of Italian sumptuary control, both in legislation and enforcement,[89] and a strong misogynist cast to the legislation is often commented on.[90] After the repeal of the lex Oppia, Rome abandons any attempt to regulate female clothing, and the only context in which male clothing is regulated is that implicit in Livy's argument, of the use of purple on the toga to indicate office, rank (senatorial broad stripes versus equestrian narrow stripes), triumphal garb and so forth (see ch. 2 on the *toga*). Despite spasmodic attempts to restrict the use of silk (as in 16 CE, Tacitus, *Annals* 2.33), there is nothing to compare with the elaborate hierarchy of materials to mark status typical of European legislation.[91] Rome cannot match the highly innovative approaches to rule-evasion which drove fashion and, as Mandeville put it, 'turn'd the Wheel of Trade'. Perhaps, if Cato had succeeded in blocking the repeal, clothing might have achieved more of a role of a competitive status-marker; alternatively, we might argue, it was precisely because clothing had limited appeal for this purpose that the law was repealed, and subsequent legislation. Roman 'fashion' never became a hot topic.

Roman food, by contrast, was one of the prime obsessions. Not only was it the one obsessive concern of Roman sumptuary law; it appealed equally to social satirists[92] and to moralists like Seneca.[93] Lucilius, writing during the mid-second-century heyday of legislation, is constantly cited with reference to specific sumptuary laws; indeed, it was a significant reason why later antiquarians, especially Athenaeus and Macrobius, discussed the laws, because they were interested in consumption and the literature of consumption. It was one of the most effective ways of talking about society, its placements and distinctions. By a chiastic logic, just as Roman law ignores clothing to which European law devotes so much attention, European law shows only limited interest in food – the best parallels are in medieval

---

[87] 34.7.1–9.   [88] Owen Hughes (1983) 90ff.   [89] Killerby (2002) 36ff.
[90] Hunt (1996) 244ff.   [91] Friedlaender (1921–3) II, 312–27.
[92] Hudson (1989), Gowers (1993).   [93] Edwards (1993).

England, with attempts to restrict certain foodstuffs to the nobility, still reflected in the current restriction of swan-meat to royalty.[94]

Tiberius' question becomes more pressing. If the Romans really wanted to control the display of wealth for social standing, why not control villas, or buildings and interior furnishings, as did the Chinese and Japanese in enormous and loving detail?[95] Augustus could read to the senate with approval a speech of Rutilius Rufus, consul in 105 BCE, *de modo aedificiorum*, yet the only restrictions which Augustus legislated were on excessively tall apartment blocks in Rome, to limit dangers of fire and collapse. Censors could make a fuss about excessive luxury in housing, and in the early first century BCE, Licinius Crassus and Domitius Ahenobarbus put on a command performance of mutual reproof over the inflated value both of ten Hymettian marble columns in Crassus' portico and of the rare lotus or nettle-trees in Ahenobarbus' garden.[96] But despite endless complaints about domestic luxuries, whether the use of marble, or of expensive art works like bronze statues and paintings, which Tiberius also cites, no legislative attempt was made to restrict domestic architecture or furnishings. The quasi-public role of the elite house, and its acknowledged function in marking status and power, also promoted its potential for social differentiation,[97] though even here, had they wanted, Romans might in theory have drawn up restrictions about who might have what size of house (magistrates, senators and their family, *equites*, etc.), or what degree of lavishness of furnishing (e.g. by restricting imported coloured marbles by rank).

As Norbert Elias observed,[98] if the real preoccupation of European sumptuary law had been with providing restraints on the competitive struggle within the nobility, it should have been targeted at housing not clothes.[99] The same applies to Rome. It has frequently been urged that Roman sumptuary laws aimed to protect the cohesion and stability of the Roman ruling class by preventing excessive competition in luxury.[100] But Elias' objection applies with equal force here: had the ruling elite wished to avoid ruining themselves by luxury, to focus on the table and ignore the house was folly. The claim that the law was spurred by anti-hellenism is no more coherent:[101] whether or not table luxuries were identified as specifically hellenistic, so

[94] Hunt (1996) 299.   [95] Shiveley (1964–5).

[96] Valerius Maximus 9.1.4, Pliny, *Natural History* 17.1–6, cf. 36.7 and 114. The quarrel was much cited, see Broughton (1952) vol. 2, 17.

[97] Wallace-Hadrill (1994).   [98] Elias (1983), 53–65.   [99] Hunt (1996) 85.

[100] Daube (1969) 117ff., Beard and Crawford (1985) 79ff., Gabba (1988) 37ff., Baltrusch (1989) 43.

[101] Gruen (1992) 69ff.

much about domestic architecture and decoration was explicitly hellenistic that it will not explain the choice of focus.

Again, we may note the interesting failure of late republican sumptuary legislation to address funerary practice.[102] Weddings and funerals are prime occasions for public display by families, and consequently have been a frequent focus of legislation, for instance in medieval Italy.[103] They were the most important area which archaic Greek laws addressed; the Solonian laws at Athens mark the turning point between the great 'heroic' burial mounds of the late Iron Age, and the citizenly egalitarianism of classical Attic practice.[104] By no coincidence, funerary practice is the one area of sumptuary control addressed by the XII Tables, and Cicero's account in the *de Republica* describes the restriction on number of mourners, numbers of musicians and professional wailers, scale of monument and so on.[105] Great 'princely' burials with their incredibly lavish imported grave-goods of precious metals, like the Tomba Regolini-Galassi at Praeneste, give way in Latium to the more restrained and standardised burials of the sixth–fifth centuries.[106] But the late republic brings a notable boom in the monumentalisation of burials, with constant use of hellenistic models, and Polybius' description leaves us in no doubt of the centrality of funerary ritual in the reproduction of the elite (see above, pp. 218ff.). Why, then, does the revival of sumptuary law not bring a revival of the provisions of the XII Tables which, though no longer followed, were not forgotten?

The focus of European legislation on clothing, and of Roman legislation on the table, marks each out as a prime discursive field. And it is perhaps here that we have the best chance of understanding what made table luxury an appropriate target for legislation. Clothing was a good way of talking about, expressing and contesting the hierarchies of European societies in the middle ages and early-modern period. It was not the exclusive language of luxury; housing, too, had its vital role and consumed greater *per capita* investment. But its extensive diffusion in society, and its susceptibility to minute differentiation of grading, made it disproportionately eloquent, and susceptible to a type of control of which the whole essence was to enter into minutiae. Table luxury served a similar function in Rome: a well-diffused language with infinite gradations that allowed the law maker to draw numerous distinctions of occasion, cost, guest numbers and precise comestibles. The eloquence of this language of good eating has a great deal to do with

[102] Engels (1998).   [103] Killerby (2002) 36.
[104] Morris (1992) 128–55, Bernhardt (2003) 71–91.   [105] Engels (1998), Bernhardt (2003) 91–8.
[106] See Colonna (1977), Ampolo (1984), Bottiglieri (2002) 43.

the fact that the eastern Mediterranean, from which the Romans believed they had picked up their corrupting ways, had a highly evolved moralising discourse wrapped around luxury in general, and food in particular.

Tryphē and the fall of states

Romans learned luxury from Greeks, not just as a practice, but foremost as a concept. If Sallust blamed *luxuria* and *avaritia* for the loss of the virtues that had made Rome great, and for the corruption of contemporary politics, he was talking a language familiar to generations of Greek historians. His *Histories* were the chronological continuation of those of Posidonius, a major Stoic philosopher as well as historian, which in turn took up where Polybius left off with the sack of Carthage in 146 BCE. Both Polybius and Posidonius attributed a major role to luxury, or *tryphē*, in their explanatory frameworks. For Polybius, it was a significant element in the fall of Greece to its Roman conquerors; and his analysis of the Roman constitution and way of life ends with grave warnings of moral slippage. Posidonius, particularly if we can believe he was the source behind the detailed narrative of the Sicilian slave revolts of the 130 BCE, used the revolts to illustrate very vividly and precisely how the luxury and arrogance of wealthy slave-owners led to the alienation of their workforce and rebellion.

Polybius and Posidonius were writing, though in a Greek tradition, in close contact with Roman patrons, and specifically those like Scipio Aemilianus who took a strong position on luxury and moral decline; to this extent, they were reflecting the contemporary thought of the second and early first centuries BCE. But there is no doubt that they were also articulating those Roman preoccupations in a language long current among Greek historians. Since most hellenistic historiography before Polybius survives in a fragmentary state, it can be hard to grasp the context of what these historians were saying. But the emphasis they laid on the devastating consequences of *tryphē* is put on display by the collection of passages assembled by Athenaeus at the end of the second century CE – the entire 12th book of the *Deipnosophists* being dedicated to the theme. Theopompus, Timaeus and Phylarchus, Heraclides of Pontus and others repeatedly illustrated the theme of *tryphē* as the cause for the fall of cities, with Sybaris as the classic example,[107] but with Croton, Tarentum, Colophon, Siris, Miletus, Magnesia, Samos and others also wheeled on in evidence. On Phylarchus' account of the fall of

[107] 12.518c–522a.

Sybaris, far from legislating to restrain luxury, they promoted it, encouraging women to come to public festivals in rich dresses, allowing chefs who invented new dishes to enjoy a monopoly on their recipes for a year, and exempting eel-sellers and the importers of purple dye from tax. Such luxury led to arrogance (*hybris*), manifested in the murder of thirty legates from Croton, the anger of the gods, and the fall of the city.[108]

The schematic cycle of success leading to luxury to hybris to divine anger and revenge is one not invented by hellenistic historiography, but deeply embedded in Greek literature, from Homer to Attic tragedy (it is striking that in Phylarchus' account, mention of purple dye immediately precedes the act of *hybris* as Agamemnon's symbolic trampling of a purple carpet precedes his murder in Aeschylus). Yet interestingly, *tryphē* is not a word current in literature of the fifth century or earlier. Absent from Aeschylus, Sophocles and Herodotus, it first emerges in the plays of Euripides and Aristophanes around 415 BCE.[109] Bernhardt's thorough study of the critique and legislative control of luxury in the Greek world suggests a significant break between the period before this turning-point, when the vocabulary of indulgence and 'soft' ways is at worst ambivalent and legislation is limited to control of expenditure on funerals, and the marked rise in tempo and tone of criticism from the late fifth century onwards. Even then, legislative control of luxury is limited, and is scarcely met in the context of general moral control of the population, but is focused on control of conducts at funerals, religious festivals, and especially the control of female behaviour on specific occasions (through the *gynaeconomoi*), and control of the behaviour of the young in the *ephēbeia* (through *kosmētai* and *sōphronistai*).[110] But for philosophers, historians, and perhaps above all comic playwrights, *tryphē* becomes an obsessive theme.[111]

It is unlikely that Roman sumptuary legislation drew on any Greek precedents: indeed, the only attestation of a Greek restriction on eating is the ban on eggs and honey-cakes at weddings at Naukratis reported by Athenaeus, citing Hermias.[112] Nevertheless, the context in which the legislation is articulated is a discourse about society impregnated with current hellenistic thought. To answer the question of why the table, as opposed to clothing or housing, was the nodal point of such thinking, it is enough to refer to the abundant discussion of recent years over the key role of the *symposion* as a Greek social and political institution.[113] Whether in the religious banquets that gave community to the citizen body in the distribution of equal

---

[108] 12. 521c–e.   [109] Bernhardt (2003) 193.   [110] Bernhardt (2003) 248–87.
[111] Bernhardt (2003) 331ff.   [112] 4.150A; Bernhardt (2003) 248.   [113] Murray (1990).

shares, or in the commensality of aristocratic groups sharing the *symposion* in private homes but with more than private significance for the city,[114] the ritual sharing of food and wine played a critical role in Greek social practice and thought. Representations of the *symposion* saturate Greek iconography, whether the ceramic vessels used at these sharing rituals, or the grave monuments that projected the life of feasting into the hereafter.[115] From the archaic period onwards, the rituals of the banquet reach Latium and central Italy,[116] Etruria and Campania,[117] in close contact with the Greek 'frontier' cities of the south,[118] and of course archaic Rome itself.[119] The density of ideas, images and social practices that cluster around the consumption of food and wine in Greek and Italic societies made it incomparably rich as an area of discourse. 'Fishcakes', that consuming passion of classical Athens,[120] came to Rome with a cargo of ideas that fitted perfectly into Roman anxieties about what was happening to their society.

We can exemplify with some precision the transmission of ideas. One text about gastronomy which Athenaeus cites again and again is the mid-fourth-century poem on gastronomy, or *Hedypatheia*, of Archestratus of Gela, which now benefits from an excellent new edition and discussion.[121] Archestratus sailed around the Greek world (or at least represented himself as so doing), collecting information on the gastronomic delicacies of each city, especially the local fish, and the ways of serving them. In mock-heroic tones, he presents his work as the fruit of the circumnavigation of Europe and Asia, a *historiē*, or enquiry, to rival Herodotus.[122] The gourmet must understand which cities produce the best varieties:

Ainos has large mussels, Abydos oysters,
Parion bear-crabs, and Mitylene scallops . . .
You shall buy Peloriac clams in Messene, where the sea's strait is narrow,
And excellent smooth-shelled ones in Ephesos.[123]

At least in the fragments Athenaeus cites, fish predominate, as they generally did in Greek discussion of good eating, or *opsophagia*.[124] Not surprisingly for a Sicilian author, South Italy is an important source of delicacies, most of which were equally familiar to the Roman table: the eels of Rhegion,[125] the *elops* of Syracuse,[126] the gilthead (*sparus aurata*) of Selinus,[127] the *muraena* or moray eel of the straits of Messina,[128] the dentex of the same straits,[129]

---

[114] Schmitt Pantel (1992).   [115] Dentzer (1982).   [116] Rathje (1990).
[117] Pontrandolfo (1995).   [118] Lombardo (1995).   [119] Coarelli (1995).
[120] Davidson (1997).   [121] Dalby (1995), Olson and Sens (2000).   [122] Frs. 1–3.
[123] Fr. 7, trans. Olson and Sens (2000), 39.   [124] Davidson (1997) 11ff.   [125] Fr. 10.
[126] Fr. 12.   [127] Fr. 13.   [128] Fr. 17.   [129] Fr. 18.

the lobsters of Lipari,[130] the tuna of Sicily.[131] But fish was not the only food for high living, as his loving prescription for a feast shows:

Always cover your head at a feast with garlands
Of every variety with which the earth's rich plain blooms,
And treat your hair with fine perfumes dispensed in drops,
And all day long cast myrrh and frankincense,
The fragrant fruit of Syria, upon the fire's soft ash.
And to you as you are drinking your fill let someone bring a dainty such as
A sausage, and a stewed sow's womb that has embarked
In cumin and in pungent vinegar and silphium,
And the tender race of whatever roasted birds are in
Season. Pay no attention to these Syracusans,
Who act like frogs and merely drink without eating anything.[132]

Archestratus was known in Rome in the early second century, doubtless in some circles in the original Greek, but also directly in Latin thanks to the fact that the epic and dramatic poet Ennius, remarkably enough, produced his own mock-didactic *Hedyphagetica*, seemingly closely modelled on Archestratus:

Just as the sea-weasel at Clipea surpasses all others,
Mussels are most abundant at Ainos, rough-shelled oysters at Abydos.
The scallop is found in Mytilene and in Ambracian Charadrus.
The sargue is good in Brindisi; if it is big, buy it.
Be aware that the boar-fish is of the highest quality at Tarentum.
Be sure to buy the *elops* in Surrentum and the *glaukos* in Cumae.[133]

Such gastronomy is a system of knowledge, that extends beyond the mere training of slave-chefs to the higher reaches of research and literature. It is a system of knowledge in which Greece and Italy are bound together geographically, and in the direct transmission and exchange of codified knowledge. The gourmets and *piscinarii* of the Bay of Naples, who bred *muraena* and gilthead bream in their technologically advanced, concrete fish-tanks (the entrepeneur Sergius Orata owed his name to the *Sparus Aurata*, or gilthead), relied on the diffusion of such a body of knowledge for the effectiveness of their hospitality; and as they were well aware, they were geographically situated on the northern margin of the area already staked out by Greek gastronomic expertise (figures 7.4, 7.5).[134]

---

[130] Fr. 25. [131] Frs. 35 and 39. [132] Fr. 60, trans. Olson and Sens (2000).
[133] Olson and Sens (2000) 241. [134] D'Arms (1970).

Figure 7.4 South Italian fish plate from Paestum (photo courtesy Soprintendenza di Salerno, Museo di Paestum)

This body of knowledge feeds directly into sumptuary legislation and the discussion that surrounds it. A rare and precious example of a speech delivered in support of a sumptuary law, the lex Fannia of 161 BCE (though arguably not on the occasion of the original legislation, but of subsequent discussion), is a passage of C. Titius cited by Macrobius in his discussion of the sumptuary legislation.[135] Titius, an otherwise unheard-of figure, is praised by Cicero as an orator of wit and urbanity, 'almost of Attic style', though allegedly ignorant of Greek literature.[136] He depicts with indignation the modern youth, gambling, drenched with perfumes, surrounded by courtesans, and consequently neglecting their duties in the courts and in the assembly. They finally stagger drunkenly off to court, filling the amphorae in the alleyways with urine as they go, and struggle to stay awake during the court cases they are hearing. Rather than consider the case, they cry:

'What business do I have with these triflers, why don't we go instead and drink *mulsum* mixed with Greek wine, eat a good plump thrush (*turdus*) and a good fish, a pike caught between the two bridges?'

[135] *Saturnalia* 3.16.15–16, Malcovati (1955) no. 51, 201ff.   [136] Cicero, *Brutus* 167.

Figure 7.5 Mosaic from the House of the Faun, Pompeii illustrating varieties of fish
(Naples Museum inv. 9997, photo Alfredo Foglia)

Titius' young men seem to have stepped from the pages of Archestratus,[137]
dripping with perfume, craving for sausage and sow's womb. As Macrobius
knew, the pike caught between the two bridges was a gastronomical fashion
of the day, also mentioned by the satirist Lucilius:

Moreover, they had brought on whatever each wanted.
This one went for pig's tripe and a plate of fattened birds;
That one for a Tiber *catillo* caught between the two bridges.[138]

[137] Above, fr. 60.   [138] Lucilius, *Satires*, book XX, 601–3 (Loeb edn.), cited by Macrobius 3.16.18.

It is in the nature of this connoisseur's language that we now struggle to reconstruct the precise vocabulary – was Titius' *turdus* a thrush, or the fish of the same name, a wrasse, that occurs in Ennius' *Hedyphagetica*,[139] and was *catillo* the same as Titius' pike, *lupus germanus*, rather than the 'plate-licker' which Macrobius understands him to refer to? The point is that Titius and Lucilius are speaking the language of the *Hedyphagetica*, and Archestratus' gastronomy. Just where the fish was caught mattered to the epicure. Lucilius's plate of fattened birds, *altilium lanx*, belongs exactly to the vocabulary of the sumptuary laws: as we have seen, Pliny the Elder reports that the lex Fannia banned the force-fed fowl, *altilia*, that were a speciality of Delos, and since Delos' boom period as a Roman market starts in 167, the law of 161 was doubtless on to a very new fad. Pliny also reports the ban on various types of pig's offal, including *abdomina*, adding that Publilius the writer of mimes gave it the name of *sumen*. Lucilius' pig's tripe, *sumina*, is surely another item on the list of forbidden fruits. So, we may infer, was the pike, *lupus germanus* or *catillo*, at least as caught between the two bridges.

The sumptuary laws read like cookbooks. They entered in detail into a discourse of gastronomy and *tryphē*, the art of high living articulated by hellenistic texts, and shadowed in word as well as eating practice by the Roman elite.[140] We may recall that the lex Orchia, the first sumptuary law, limited the number of guests outside the household to three, except on market days when it rose to five. Given the traditional layout of the Roman *triclinium*, and the expectation of up to nine diners, that may seem excessive severity.[141] Yet Archestratus might actually have approved:

Everyone should dine at a single table set for an elegant meal.
Let the total company be three or four,
Or at any rate no more than five; for after that you would have
A mess-group of rapacious mercenary soldiers.[142]

Titius' speech may help us to understand where the discourse of gastronomic luxury was felt to have some purchase on elite behaviour. His focus is on the senatorial elite, and the gap between their luxurious private lives and their proper public role, of attendance at judicial and political gatherings in the Forum. Their private lives clash with their public *persona*. Their convivial style has many components: gambling, perfume, courtesans, drinking and eating. The sumptuary laws act like the grammatical figure of *synecdoche*, or *pars pro toto*: one thing stands for many. Placing limits on the pleasures of the

---

[139] Olson and Sens (2000) 244f.   [140] Wilkins, Harvey and Dobson (1995).
[141] Dunbabin (2003).   [142] Fr. 4, trans. Olson and Sens (2000).

table, on specific foodstuffs and their precise prices, is an attempt to strike at the heart of the whole undesirable lifestyle they represent. The pleasures of the table were the most susceptible to regulation because they were most discussed, written about, familiar from humorous mock-didactic, satire and mime. The relish of the telling detail caught the eye of the legislator, as it caught that of the elder Pliny, of Gellius, Athenaeus and Macrobius.

Consumerism and social anxieties

To attack table luxury was a way to address anxieties. The laws promised more than they could possibly deliver: how could they hold back the tide of transformation of material culture that swept through Italy? But they also offered a sort of alibi. Feasting was of course effective, not least in the context of political competition, and specific limitations placed upon candidates for office show the links to the *ambitus* laws that controlled electoral bribery.[143] But so, too, was housing, expressly so in Cicero's account of how a great house by the Forum catches votes (*suffragatur*) for its owner.[144] What the legislative focus on feasting paradoxically achieved was the legitimisation of other forms of conspicuous consumption, particularly in housing and funerary monuments, which become so embedded in the expression of social standing in the late republic that we scarcely question their use.

Whatever was not forbidden was implicitly sanctioned. What was the use, a Tiberius might ask, of limiting the budget for fancy foodstuffs if the guests were already stunned by the magnificence of the domestic setting, the regal peristyles, the *triclinia* richly decorated with vermiculate mosaics and richly coloured wall-painting imitating the colonnades of some hellenistic palace, the couches with the best bronze legs from Delos, *triclinia aerata*, an abundance of multi-coloured coverlets and hangings of Persian opulence, side-tables in exotic wooden inlays of citrus and terebinth, silver drinking vessels with rich decoration, lighting from elaborate bronze candelabra, an olfactory assault of oriental perfumes, rose-petals and garlands, and an army of slaves, waiters and entertainers, picked for their good looks? Far from preserving any sort of homogeneity among the elite or deterring them from conspicuous consumption, the narrow limits of the laws set them on a path of escalating competition. In this context, the sumptuary laws cannot rate as more than a minor nuisance, encouraging rather than blocking the advance of luxury.

---

[143] Bottiglieri (2002) 105–74.   [144] Cicero, *de Officiis* 1.138.

By a paradox familiar from early modern situations, legislation that addressed some manifestations of a widespread phenomenon only fuelled what we would now recognise as a consumer boom. Max Weber taught us to see the ancient city as a consumer city. He may have been thinking of consumption in a negative sense, as the non-productive absorption of the surpluses generated by agricultural production or conquest. But Mandeville's *Fable* has taught us that consumption, especially conspicuous consumption driven by the sociable evils of pride and vanity, of competitive assertion of social rank, is inescapably productive. The same luxury that 'Employ'd a Million of the poor' in the early eighteenth century was as hard at work in the late Roman republic. From the perspective of those who study the modern 'consumer revolution', the consumer city emerges as an engine of economic development.[145] Roman, like early-modern, morality favoured the saving and conservation of capital, and luxury laws often addressed the dangers of the young 'consuming' their patrimony in wasteful spending. But consumption, as Adam Smith argued, by releasing capital into the economy increased productivity and wealth. From this perspective, the waves of luxury that swept over Rome from the beginning of the second century BCE represent a major economic stimulus in a dynamic and mobile society.

So many starting-dates have been identified for the modern 'consumer revolution', from the seventeenth and eighteenth centuries,[146] to Joan Thirsk's earlier sixteenth-century projects,[147] to the boom of luxury goods in the cities of north Italy that dates back to the twelfth century,[148] that it has been suggested we should not think in terms of a single revolution but rather of 'a series of protracted and overlapping revolutions each of which has associated with it distinctive patterns of consumption'.[149] That vision of change is surprisingly close to that of the Elder Pliny. It may indeed seem mildly absurd to argue with the Roman historians over the exact date of the onset of the luxury that brought down the Roman republic, whether we point with Piso to Vulso's triumph of 186, or to the shameless developments of 154, or with Posidonius to the sack of Carthage, or with Sallust to the return of Sulla's army from Asia (see pp. 315–16). Historians overinvest in turning points to underpin their own narrative. But Pliny thought he was looking not at turning-points but at successive waves in a continuous process.

He twice discusses Asiatic triumphs as part of a repetitive phenomenon. If the conquest of Asia brought luxury to Italy, it is harder for him to say whether more damage was done by the triumph of Lucius Scipio in 189 BCE,

---

[145] Hunt (1996) 175, remarkably interpreting Weber's 'consumer city' as a positive analysis.
[146] Stearns (2001) 22.   [147] Thirsk (1978).   [148] Killerby (2002).   [149] Hunt (1996) 225.

with all its thousands of pounds of wrought silverware and golden vessels, or by Attalus' bequest of Pergamum in 133, which made men shameless about picking up at auction the contents of a royal palace. The conquest of Achaea by Mummius in 146 brought new fashions for statues and paintings to Rome; and in the same year the destruction of Carthage stimulated the appetite and gave the licence for luxury.[150]

Returning later to the same theme, Pliny focuses on new waves of fashion.[151] If the victories of Lucius Scipio and Manlius Vulso introduced Rome to chased silver, 'Attalic' cloth (maybe the equivalent, at least in prestige, of medieval 'cloth of gold') and bronze couches, that of Mummius in 146 brought in 'Corinthian' ware (a highly valued form of metal alloy inlay) and paintings, but that of Pompey in 61 brought pearls and gemstones, and along with them the novelty of 'myrrhine' ware. Myrrhine is defined by Pliny as a liquid solidified below ground, originating from Parthia; evidently a semi-precious stone, perhaps fluor-spar. He illustrates the process of a fashion wave:

The same victory first brought myrrhine ware to the city, and Pompey was the first to dedicate bowls and cups of myrrhine to Capitoline Jupiter. Immediately it spread to human use [i.e. in domestic not religious contexts]; sidetables (*abaci*) and eating vases in it became in demand. This luxury grows by the day.[152]

Pliny goes on to illustrate the absurd prices paid for myrrhine by various collectors, which culminate in the price of 1 million sesterces paid by Nero for a myrrhine wine-ladle.[153]

The idea that triumphs brought in novelties is clear. But just who was responsible for a fashion innovation could be disputed. Elsewhere, Pliny reveals that Pompey was not the only claimant to setting a fashion for pearls. The early imperial antiquarian Fenestella asserted that it was Augustus' triumph over Alexandria that brought pearls into 'promiscuous and frequent use', though an inferior smaller version had been in circulation since Sulla. Yet, as Pliny is happy to point out, an earlier writer, the antiquarian Aelius Stilo (of the early first century BCE), said the use of the Latin word *unio* (as opposed to the Greek *margarita*) went back to the Jugurthine wars of the late second century.[154]

They might dispute over details, but the common assumption was that fashion worked in waves, a restless competition ever in search of novelties, and ever frustrated by the rapid diffusion of the same novelties to 'promiscuous' usage. An emperor, to stay ahead, had to pay auction-room prices

---

[150] *Natural History* 33.148–150. See in general Carey (2003). [151] *Natural History* 37.12.
[152] *Natural History* 37.18. [153] *Natural History* 37.18–22. [154] *Natural History* 9.123.

that were the talk of the town. Putting your name to a novelty was a source of prestige, whether you were a general or a *bon viveur*. Who could lay claim to the invention of *foie gras* by fattening geese on milk and honey mixed with wine-lees (*mulsum*): the consular Metellus Scipio or the equestrian Marcus Seius?[155] The orator Hortensius, a well-known gourmet, scored his 'first' by serving peacock at his inaugural banquet to celebrate his priesthood: that evidently set a fashion, and one Aufidius Lurco in the mid first century made a handsome profit of 60,000 sesterces from his business in fattening peacocks.[156]

There is scarcely a corner of Pliny's encyclopaedic purview of the worlds of animals, plants and minerals which does not offer him material for complaint about the growth of luxury; his vision is of luxury as a pervasive phenomenon, of a Roman empire that sacks not only its own terrain, but the widest reaches, from the pearls of Sri Lanka and the Indian Ocean to the amber of the Baltic, to supply the taste for the exotic and 'unnatural'.[157] To arrive at an estimate of the sort of impact which such waves of luxury had on the Roman economy, there is no need to stay with the exotica relayed by Pliny: for that, the archaeological record can, and in chapter 8 will, prove a more trustworthy witness. Pliny's value is as a window on contemporary perceptions of how luxury worked, and to what effect.

The theme of this chapter has been the role of luxury and the debates surrounding it in defining and contesting the social order. Here, too, Pliny is an eloquent witness both of the perceived role of luxury in defining social standing, and of the abusive inversions of proper order which to him make it so objectionable. In the middle of a long section on pearls as luxury, in which his prize exhibits will be Lollia Paulina, daughter of an Augustan general and wife of Caligula, who appears at a betrothal feast wearing pearls to the value of 40 million sesterces (a not inconsiderable sum if right, the equivalent of the minimum census of 40 senators), and Cleopatra, who dissolves a pearl worth 10 million sesterces in vinegar,[158] he offers an aside on the popularity of pearl ear-rings, and specifically the variety of two or three dangling pearls called *crotalia* or castanets:

Now even poor women desire them, saying that a pearl is a woman's lictor in public.[159]

There is a reminiscence here (conscious or not) of the debate over the lex Oppia as reported by Livy: women, denied access to magistracies,

[155] *Natural History* 10.52.   [156] *Natural History* 10.45.   [157] Wallace-Hadrill (1990a).
[158] *Natural History* 9.117–21.   [159] *Natural History* 9.114.

priesthoods, and the insignia and decorations of war use cosmetics, dress and adornment as their *insignia*.[160] The image of the pearl as the women's lictor expresses equally forcefully the sense of substitution for a language of rank open only to men. But what is so striking about Pliny's observation is that he is talking about *pauperes*, poor women: luxury is a language of rank far from limited to the elite.

Despite Pliny's objection to the poor flaunting luxuries beyond their rank, he does not wish them to be deprived of their respect due as citizens. On the contrary, he protests explicitly against social differentiation by diet. That by *pauperes* he means the plebeian poor (not, for instance, the less wealthy members of the elite) is clear throughout his discussion of the market garden, the *hortus*.[161] The contrast he sets up is between the food of the poor man, in the old ideal with his allotment patch, and the (to him) inaccessible goods of the *macellum*, the luxury food market which the aediles policed, with its exotic birds from the river Phasis or Ethiopia. The art of the baker has produced so many refinements in the basic staple that

there is one bread for the elite (*proceres*) and one for the masses (*volgus*), with the grain supply going down in so many grades to the lowest of the plebs (*infima plebs*).[162]

Even simple herbs and vegetables like asparagus come in cultivated varieties that the plebs cannot afford.[163] Water itself is differentiated, and snow and ice are luxurious forms of water unavailable to the poor.[164] The ideal Pliny proffers is the familiar one of a simple peasant society of equal citizens, an ideal fixed in the Roman imagination by Cato. But though that is a historical fantasy, it does not affect the validity of his analysis of luxury as a system of social differentiation.

Perhaps the fullest of Pliny's disquisitions on luxury and social order is his attempt to provide what we might call 'the social history of the gold ring'.[165] These chapters are well known to the discussion of the definition of the equestrian order,[166] and their apparently rambling and incoherent attempt to bring together a number of themes (the use of gold rings, changes in judiciary law and practice, the political emergence of a self-conscious elite body of non-senators, etc.) have caused frustration. Here, however, we may focus on Pliny's attempt to implicate *luxuria* in the growth of social differentiation. He opens his essay (having warmed up previously with a diatribe against gold and gems, noxious products of mining)[167] by declaring that the

---

[160] Livy 34.7.8–9.   [161] *Natural History* 19.51ff.   [162] *Natural History* 19.53.
[163] *Natural History* 19.54.   [164] *Natural History* 19.55.   [165] *Natural History* 33.8–36.
[166] Nicolet (1966), Wiseman (1970), Brunt (1988) 144ff., etc.   [167] *Natural History* 33.1–7.

first man to put a ring on his finger committed the worst of crimes, though his identity lies hid.[168] The search for the first inventor, *protos heuretes*, is of course a standard feature of Greek philosophic discourse.

He now pursues the theme that rings were initially both rarities, and normally of iron not gold, in order to establish the case for the narrow social diffusion of gold rings in early Roman society. Thus the usage of the senate in granting gold rings to its envoys proves them to be exceptional,[169] and the fact that Marius took one only in his third consulship shows, at least for Pliny, that iron rings were still standard at the end of the second century BCE.[170] Then (after a passage on the rarity of gold in early Rome), he takes us back to the late fourth century with the election of the scribe Cn. Flavius to the aedileship (304 BCE) despite his lowly origins as son of a freedman, and the consequent indignation of the nobility who laid down their gold rings in protest. Pliny underlines that it was the nobility, not the senate, let alone, as some authors wrongly alleged, the equestrians, who made the protest, to underline the social restriction of the use of gold rings.[171] Whether or not his inference (or, indeed, his information) was valid, there is good evidence for the removal of gold rings as a sign of mourning, including historically on the death of Augustus.[172]

After establishing (at least to his own satisfaction) this original exclusivity of the gold ring, he begins to depict a catastrophic spread to promiscuous use from the second Punic war, when Hannibal could find rings only on the fingers of the *equites* (3.20), though he pulls back and illustrates again that not even all senators had gold rather than iron (3.21). An excursus on the deplorable ingenuity of luxury in making gold rings even more complicated with gemstones and engraving introduces the theme of the use of rings for signing (3.22–23). Indeed were it not for the key role of witnessing and signature in Roman society, and the capacity of the witness signature-lists from Pompeii and Herculaneum to illustrate the highly formalised hierarchies of early imperial society,[173] we might feel that Pliny was protesting too much about their social significance.

Pliny's social world is one threatened at every point by slaves and ex-slaves. We have already met the symbolic gesture of the nobility at the ascent of a freeman's son. Pliny now complains that slaves are using the goldsmith's skills to produce iron rings bound in gold – presumably a legal evasion.[174] After a breathless return to the regal period to establish which fingers rings

---

[168] *Natural History* 33.8.   [169] *Natural History* 3.11.   [170] *Natural History* 3.12.
[171] *Natural History* 3.17–18.   [172] Suetonius, *Augustus* 100; Zehnacker (1983) 134.
[173] Camodeca (1996), Camodeca (2002).   [174] *Natural History* 3.23.

were worn on,[175] he contrasts the innocence of our ancestors to the dangers of the present, when you need signet rings to seal everything in the house to protect it from the thieving hands of the army of slaves, and the danger of having your ring stolen to forge your signature as you sleep or even as you die.[176]

These chapters set the essential background for the more famous passage that follows on the equestrian order. He has established with some clarity (muddy though his exposition is) that the gold ring was no mere ornament, but a socially charged symbol, something to be awarded to ambassadors, to be put off in mourning, to indicate a legal signature, and to mark and secure possession. He has established a social world that spreads down from nobility to senate to lower ranks (including equestrians), and in which excessive growth of slavery and the upward mobility of freed slaves represent a threat. He now launches into his analysis of the insertion of a 'third order' between senate and plebs: the gold ring is guilty.[177] He is, let us remember, pleading a case; so that while we may find the judiciary reform from Gaius Gracchus on, and the rhetoric of Cicero about the equestrian order[178] more significant elements in the historical emergence of the order, Pliny's focus is on luxury, gold and its socially corrosive effect.

From this point of view, his key witness is the law of Tiberius of 23 CE (a *senatus consultum* confirmed next year by the lex Visellia), which regulated not the membership of the equestrian order but the wearing of the gold ring.[179] The date and context of the law are highly significant for the history of luxury: the year immediately following the debate reported by Tacitus that effectively abandoned the attempt to restrain table luxury (see pp. 329ff.). Pliny says that the law was passed as the result of the efforts of the young C. Sulpicius Galba (a relative of the future emperor), trying to win Tiberius' approval by strict policing of the *popinae*, and finding himself blocked by their managers (*institores*) brandishing the gold ring. Part of the outcome of the luxury debate of 22 CE was that Tiberius urged the aediles to police the *popinae* more strictly, and here is a magistrate busy repressing one face of luxury only to find himself confronted by another. The assumption is that an *institor* would have been slave-born; but the fact that a gold ring could be a protection against magisterial intervention shows that it was a privilege conveying social status, presumably equestrian rank. The new law explicitly limited the wearing of the ring to the free-born over three generations, in addition to a minimum property qualification and the right to privileged

---

[175] *Natural History* 3.24–5.   [176] *Natural History* 3.26–8.
[177] *Natural History* 3.29.   [178] *Natural History* 3.34.   [179] *Natural History* 3.29–30.

seating at the theatre. The insistence on three generations of freeborn status matches with the language of the *senatus consultum* preserved from Larinum, and belonging to the same year, 23 CE, which in excluding senators from participating in gladiatorial games, makes senatorial rank a three-generation obligation (sons and grandsons of senators are equally excluded), and makes the infamy of having been a gladiator last three generations. The senate in 23 CE was fretting greatly about social mobility.

Pliny, alas, leaves some critical missing pieces out of the puzzle. He never actually explains when, if ever, the gold ring came to indicate equestrian status, nor what role that privilege played in creating a third order between senate and plebs.[180] Since the *ius anuli* was granted by Verres to members of his entourage, including a scribe,[181] it must already by the 70s BCE have been a recognisable mark of privilege, though if Pliny is right it was not enshrined in law before Tiberius. Pliny also notably fails to discuss the vital role played by the symbolic privilege of sitting in the front fourteen rows of the theatre, from the lex Roscia of 67 BCE onwards, in visibly setting apart this 'middle rank', nor how that related to the wearing of gold rings.[182] No matter: what interests him is the inescapable social descent of luxurious social markers. No sooner is the law of 23 CE passed to set a barrier against the rising tide of successful traders of servile origin, than it is overwhelmed. By a process only too familiar to critics of luxury laws, the moment any marker has been identified as a limited privilege, it becomes more desirable. The 'ornaments of the gold ring' became a privilege to grant freedmen. Such promiscuity of the use of the gold ring ensued that, during the censorship of the emperor Claudius, one equestrian, Flavius Proculus, charged 400 individuals with breaking the law.[183] And so, in the very attempt, laments Pliny, to keep the order distinguished by free birth, it was shared with the servile (*ita dum separatur ordo ab ingenuis, communicatus est cum servitiis* – the expression is tangled but the sense clear).

Whatever Pliny's failings in terms of coherent exposition, the underlying sentiments are those familiar from the luxury debate. Luxuries are seen constantly to trickle-down, from noble to slave. Because the essence of the luxury is to mark social superiority, the process of trickle-down is seen as a dissolution of the vital distinctions of rank, leading to the danger of 'social promiscuity', a society where there is a sort of free-for-all, and the servile newcomer inverts the hierarchy. Pliny, it would appear, blames the innocent signifier (the ring) for the evolution of the rank it signified (the equestrian order).

---

[180] See Nicolet (1966) 139–43.   [181] Cicero, *Verrines* 3.185–7.   [182] Rawson (1991) 530ff.
[183] *Natural History* 3.33.

But Pliny, living in his pre-Mandeville world, is caught in a bind. If you do not want inferiors to 'ape' their superiors, it is best not to allow luxury goods to become status-markers, as Pliny repeatedly argues. The anxiety is about new wealth being able to afford the status-markers. So long as social, economic and demographic changes ensure that the social order is contested, policing the markers is a losing strategy. Pliny takes refuge in the ideal of a simple citizen society: better to have a two-tier senate-and-plebs model, and avoid any further social distinction. Hence his protest extends not merely to the differentiation of the equestrian order as a third body, but to differentiations within it (or more precisely, the judicial order): the 'superb usurpation' of titles means that jurors make much of their rank as *nongenti*, or *selecti*, or *tribuni*.[184]

Pliny's pose as enemy of social distinction is a paradox. Here is a leading member of the *equester ordo*, a senior officer in the imperial service, beneficiary of the changes emerging in Cicero's day, and consolidated by the imperial system, harking back to a simpler society in which his own rank would not exist. If there is incoherence in his position, it flows directly from the dissonance between two systems of describing social order which trouble him. On the one hand, there is the ascriptive system whereby the state assigns the ranks proper to a citizen society; on the other, the competitive system of a prosperous consumer society in which the display of wealth and its symbols established its own hierarchy. The attempt by the state to impose limits on the second system has the undesired effect of actually legitimising it: define who may or may not wear gold rings, and the display of rings becomes more potent as a social marker.

The imperial social order, one may suggest, depended more on reinforcing the first system than on regulating the second. Augustus' attempts to regulate luxury through legislation were a blind alley, and recognised as such by Tiberius. His attempts to reinforce the grades of social hierarchy and multiply grades of differentiation were fundamental for the new social order. Patrician, senatorial and equestrian rank, and citizen status itself, were basic building blocks of a ramifying system of imperial patronage. Regulating grades of honour for freedmen, introducing the *vicomagistri* of Rome and the Augustales of the *municipia* and colonies, generated a vast industry in status display, visible in the epigraphic record. Petronius' figure of Trimalchio suggests, and the archaeological record confirms, the energies and resources invested by the socially emergent in 'luxury' as an affirmation of status, success and belonging.

---

[184] *Natural History* 33.31.

Conclusion

Luxury, it is argued, comes into its own not in defining a stable and uncontested social hierarchy, but in the dynamic situation where there is expansion, new money and new social groups contesting a claim for prominence. The debate about luxury is rooted in the transformations and upheavals of society that characterise this period. To speak of a Roman 'middle class' is not helpful, not only because it is wrong to confuse the equestrian order with a merchant class,[185] but because the language of class was developed, as we have seen, in the context of the replacement of the discourse of rank and luxury by the post-industrial discourse of class and economy. It remains valid to characterise the Roman social order, as did Finley, as one of rank not class. That does not mean it was a society in which rank was fixed and uncontested, and the parallels of early-modern societies show the potential of luxury in contesting and modifying rank. We may end this chapter with two passages that suggest the hot breath of that competition as clearly as the fright caused among the ladies of Mandeville's court by the fashions of the merchants' wives.

In the lex Oppia debate, Livy has the tribune Valerius justify the desire of the Roman women for their *insignia* of status by reference to their rivals among the provincial elites:

> But by Hercules, they all feel pain and indignation when they see that the wives of our allies in Latin towns are allowed the ornaments which they are refused, when they see them distinguished by gold and purple, travelling in vehicles through the city, while they follow on foot, as if it was the allied cities, not theirs, which ruled an empire.[186]

Given the other anachronisms of the speech, we need not believe that this was an argument used at the time. But that the underlying tensions went back at least to the mid second century is confirmed by the report of Macrobius that the main reason for passing the lex Didia in 143 BCE, replacing the lex Fannia of 161 was so that all Italy (*universa Italia*), not just the city of Rome, should be subject to sumptuary control, since the Italian cities did not regard the lex Fannia as applicable to themselves.[187] The remarkable monumental development of the cities of central Italy in the second century BCE leaves no doubt of the extent to which the profits of empire, whether from war-booty or trade in the lucrative eastern markets, reached beyond the Roman elite.[188]

---

[185] Brunt (1988) 162ff.   [186] *Natural History* 34.7.5–6.   [187] Macrobius 3.17.6.
[188] See ch. 3.

Luxuries of table, clothing, housing and funerary practice were as accessible to the elites of the Italic allies as to Romans. Their contestation of the Roman hierarchy of *imperium* led eventually to rebellion and war; but, short of that, luxury was a powerful language in which to assert their claims to respect.

Once they had established those claims, there were plenty of others to assert their own claims. Nothing makes Pliny quite so uncomfortable as the luxury of freedmen; and we can find the same anxieties in the Rome emerging from social and civil wars at the end of Sulla's dictatorship, articulated by the young Cicero defending Sextus Roscius of Ameria. His defence hinges on a contrast of social personalities. On the one side, Sextus Roscius, descendent of a line of major land-owners in Umbrian Ameria, with a network of connections to the Roman nobility,[189] a paragon of the values of the local gentry, rooted in the land and its cultivation, who remained steeped in the frugal, ancestral qualities of the country and steered clear of the city and its temptations.[190] On the other, L. Cornelius Chrysogonus, the potent and corrupt freedman of Sulla, exemplar of the decadence of urban luxury, his house on the Palatine stuffed with luxury goods: Corinthian and Delian vessels, a prize piece called an *authepsa* or 'self-boiler' (probably, as we shall see, one of those elegant bronze vessels from Pompeii referred to now as 'samovars'), which had fetched a price at auction the value of an estate, embossed silver plate, fabric spreads, paintings, bronze and marble statues; not to speak of the swarm of slaves, cooks, bakers, litter-bearers, singers, musicians and entertainers who disturb the entire neighbourhood; and then his personal appearance with perfumed locks, flitting round the Forum with an escort of togas.[191]

What is at stake is a choice between two models of social dignity. Given the contrast, Cicero could count on his senatorial jury to understand who was the true villain:

It is in the city that luxury is created, from luxury is necessarily born avarice, from avarice bursts out audacity, and from it are born all crimes and wrongdoings; this country life which you call 'rustic' is the teacher of parsimony, diligence and justice.[192]

---

[189] *Pro Sex Roscio* 15.   [190] *Ibid*. 39.   [191] *Ibid*. 133–5.   [192] *Ibid*. 75.

8 | Waves of fashion

New luxuries reached Rome on the back of conquest: and never so dramatically, as the Elder Pliny saw, as in a triumphal procession. Triumphs transformed Rome. A triumph might be no more than a punctuation mark in the narrative of conquest, yet it required the centre to engage directly in the cultural consequences of expansion.[1] The economic impact of the arrival of prodigious quantities of bullion,[2] and the social impact of the importation of war captives as slaves in their tens and hundreds of thousands,[3] had as their cultural correlate a transformation of lifestyles. The physical transformation of the capital by major building projects is the direct, and frequently, as expressed by the words *ex manubiis*, explicit consequence of war-booty. Contemporaries knew that public building schemes had their 'trickle-down' effect in the private sphere: Velleius Paterculus was to comment on how swiftly the use of marble passed from the earliest public building, that of Jupiter Stator built by Metellus Macedonicus in 146 BCE, to the enhancement of private dwellings;[4] and a neat symbol of the ease with which goods passed from the public to the private sphere was the reuse by Licinius Crassus of the six 12-ft columns of Hymettan marble which originally decorated a stage building, *scaenae frons*, in his aedileship in the last decade of the second century BCE, to the embellishment of his own atrium.[5] In parallel with Rome, many cities of central Italy, as we have seen (ch. 3) transformed their urban fabric in the late second and early first centuries BCE, a phenomenon that scarcely makes sense except in the context of conquest and booty.

Granted the general point that conquest, culminating in the moment of triumph, transformed the economy, society and culture of Rome, it is worth paying attention to Pliny's observation that specific triumphs introduced specific waves of fashion.[6] If we can set aside our prejudices against

---

[1] See now Beard (2007).   [2] Frank (1933) 127–37.   [3] Hopkins (1978), Harris (1979).

[4] Velleius 1.11.5; on the temple, to be identified with that in the Porticus Metelli designed by Hermodorus, Viscogliosi, *Lexicon Topographicum Urbis Romae*, ed. E. M. Steinby. Rome 3 (1996) 157–9.

[5] Valerius Maximus 9.1.4; Pliny, *Natural History* 17.6, 36.7. On the influence of public on private architecture, Coarelli (1996c) 327–43.

[6] See ch. 7.

the idea that one moment marks the great collapse of Roman morality, we can welcome Pliny's understanding that Roman material culture had a myriad of components, each subject to its own chronological rhythms, with its own specific geographical sources, circumstantial stories, and consequent trajectories. When he argues that specific triumphs brought in specific fashions,[7] Pliny offers no more than examples: the chased silver, 'Attalic' cloth and bronze couches of the early second century (Lucius Scipio and Manlius Vulso), the Corinthian bronzes and paintings of Mummius in 146 BCE, the pearls, gemstones and myrrhine ware of Pompey's triumph of 61 BCE. He does not even mention the triumph of Lucullus over Mithridates of Pontus and Tigranes of Armenia in 63 BCE, though, according to Nicolaos of Damascus the Peripatetic, it was with this triumph that Lucullus was the first to introduce luxury to Rome.[8]

Archaeological evidence does not allow us to check all Pliny's examples: while we can trace the spread of bronze couches with some accuracy (see pp. 421ff.), the perishable (Attalic cloth) and the precious (gemstones and myrrhine ware) elude the record. The fashion wave which is easiest to trace is one which Pliny, strangely, omits: the impact of Octavian/Augustus' conquest of Egypt and the 'Egyptomania' that followed it.[9] The vast economic impact of the conquest of Egypt is famously illustrated by Cassius Dio's observation that the influx of wealth with the triumph of 29 BCE was such that interest rates dropped from 12 to 4%.[10] The antiquarian Fenestella alleged that this triumph introduced a new fashion for large pearls.[11] What we can measure better is the impact of the triumph on the decorative arts.

Alexandrian art had already made its impact felt in Italy over the preceding century, most spectacularly in the Nilotic mosaics of Palestrina and the House of the Faun in Pompeii (both dated to the late second century BCE). But the outbreak of Egyptianising motifs in wall decoration of the 'third style' represents a distinctive new wave of fashion, and one that seemingly starts with court circles.[12] It goes hand in hand with the new fashion for funerary monuments in the form of pyramids, of which that of Cestius, of 18–12 BCE, is the most conspicuous surviving example, with the appearance of obelisks in public monuments, starting with the Horologium of 10 BCE, and with the purely decorative use of Egyptian motifs in bronze-work and terracotta plaques.[13] The popularity of 'Pharaonic' motifs in court circles is

---

[7] *Natural History* 37.12.   [8] Athenaeus 6.274e–f; 12.543a.
[9] De Vos (1980), De Vos (1983), De Vos (1994), Bricault, Versluys and Meyboom (2006), De Caro (2006).
[10] Dio 51.21.5, cf. Suetonius, *Augustus* 41.1.   [11] Pliny, *Natural History* 9.123, cf. ch. 7.
[12] De Vos (1980) 75–95.   [13] De Vos (1980) 78–9.

the more striking against a background of repeated repression of the popular cult of Isis at Rome, in 28 BCE shortly after the Egyptian triumph, again in 21 BCE, and again under Tiberius.[14] The uncomprehending distortion by artists of details of liturgical significance has been read as a confirmation that the artistic mode was a purely aesthetic phenomenon without religious underpinning;[15] but the significant growth of a popular cult of Isis, and of Egyptian theophoric names in the port cities like Puteoli and Ostia,[16] makes it hard to keep artistic fashion and belief completely separate, though a distinction can be drawn between the use of 'Pharaonic' motifs, and Isiac cult images.[17] Nor can the artistic fashion be limited to court circles, even if it plausibly started there: the House of the Fruit Orchard, as several other of the Pompeian houses where this style is attested, is a middle-level town house, below that of the local municipal elite, and far below the level of the great villas like that of Livia at Prima Porta or of Agrippa Postumus at Boscoreale (figure 8.1).[18]

This much seems to confirm Pliny's observations on the social diffusion of such fashions. They may start with triumphant generals and the Roman elite; but they rapidly reach the levels at least of municipal bourgeoisie. At this point, however, the Plinian model of diffusion shows its shortcomings, and archaeology can begin to give more substance to the picture. It is not enough to observe that a particular material (a type of cloth, or metal, or precious stone) becomes popular at Rome and spreads through society. The example of Egyptomania suggests that style itself may change and spread; and that in turn raises a set of questions about artistic production. Are we talking about Egyptian art physically imported from (say) Alexandria; about artistic fashions made possible by the arrival of artists from Alexandria in Italy; or about home-made products that take over Egyptian styles or motifs, produced by 'local' craftsmen (who might by chance be former slaves from Egypt, or equally from Greece or Asia Minor, or home-born in Italy itself)?

The misinterpretation of Pharaonic motifs observed by De Vos is as much about the distance of the decorators from direct experience of Egypt as about their possession or otherwise of religious knowledge. Cultural goods become separated in transmission between societies from their surrounding context of knowledge.[19] The artist who misinterprets a motif which has a cultural and ideological significance in the context of the export culture reveals his separation from a body of knowledge; but he is also in the process of creating

---

[14] Malaise (1972) 378–95.   [15] De Vos (1980) 80.   [16] Malaise (1972) 31.
[17] See the nuanced account of Bragantini (2006).   [18] De Vos (1983), Bragantini (2006) 163–5.
[19] Kopytoff (1986).

Figure 8.1 Third-style decoration with Egyptianising motifs, the House of the Fruit Orchard, Pompeii (watercolour Nicholas Wood, courtesy British School at Rome)

a new body of knowledge whereby the motif is reincorporated into its new context. The Alexandrianising art of third-style Italian wall-decoration has separated from its origin and become part of Roman culture.

As it happens, a neat example of the process by which the imported Egyptian material good is transformed into a local product is attested in Puteoli in the late Republic: the fortune of Cicero's friend Vestorius depended partly on his production of an 'Egyptian blue', *caeruleum*, based on the imported Alexandrian pigment:[20] Vitruvius speaks with admiration of Vestorius' invention and gives the recipe,[21] and Pliny can cite the high price, 11 denarii a pound, for Vestorian blue.[22] Vestorius' production was developed in the port which was Italy's major destination for Alexandrian trade, Puteoli; his workshops thus had the right 'address' for convincing dissemination in Italy. The discovery of traces of blue and other pigments on a wreck south of Marseilles at Planier which carried amphorae stamped with the name of a likely associate of Vestorius, M. Tuccius Galeo, raises the possibility that Vestorius actively exported his Alexandrian-inspired pigments further afield across the empire.[23] He may thus be taken as the embodiment of the three stages of a wave pattern that characterizes Roman material culture at this period: initial importation from the eastern Mediterranean, secondary production in Italy, and tertiary exportation outwards from Italy across the Mediterranean.

This chapter proposes that this three-stage wave pattern is an underlying rhythm which knits together the apparently separate processes of 'hellenisation' and 'romanisation' in one continuous cultural transformation. The necessary first stage is the importation of the exotic, above all from the east. Conquest and booty constitute only the most dramatic and conspicuous mode of importation; booty creates an appetite and desire satisfied by trade and renewed local production in the east. The second stage consists in the appropriation of this production by Italian centres, working initially no doubt with imported craftsmen, but significantly transforming the product in the process. In the third stage, Italian products not only reach empire-wide markets, but stimulate a further diffusion of production, generating provincial products on Italian models, but with local characteristics. Every artefact has its own rhythms; yet there seems to be an overarching chronology whereby the importation phase is typical of the second and early first centuries BCE, the evolution of home-grown Italian production belongs to a

---

[20] D'Arms (1981) 49–55.   [21] Vitruvius 7.11.1.   [22] *Natural History* 33.162.
[23] Tchernia (1969).

transition of the very late republic and Augustan periods, and the outwards wave characterises the empire.

From this perspective, it makes no sense to speak of 'hellenisation' and 'romanisation' as if they were separate phenomena. They are no more separable than the diastole and systole phases of the cardiac cycle. Think of Rome as a great heart, at the centre of the arterial system of its empire. In the diastolic phase, the heart draws blood from the entire system, literally sucking blood, drawing to itself all the wealth, the goods, the ideas, crafts and technology of the Mediterranean. In the systolic phase it pumps the blood back out again, transformed by oxygenation into 'Roman' blood.[24] The process is continuous. Wealth, skills and people are drawn to the centre so long as Rome serves its cardiac function; but the flow is two-way, and far from draining the system of blood, the imperial capital increases the circulation around the Mediterranean to levels never seen before nor, since the separation of the Islamic world, thereafter. To speak of hellenisation is to focus on one moment of what is a deeply interconnected process, that in which the wealth, skills and people of the eastern Mediterranean are first drawn into Rome on a global scale, to be re-circulated not only westwards but also back eastwards. But the inwards flow of new ideas, fashions and wealth from the east continues so long as the system operates, as does the return flow of 'romanisation'.

The Mahdia wreck: luxury catalogued

The late republican inflow of luxury goods from Greece to Italy has its best archaeological testimony in the wreck found in 1907 off Mahdia, at Cap Africa in Tunisia (figure 8.2). A notable collaboration between the Bardo Museum and the Rheinisches Landesmuseum of Bonn to conserve, reassess, study and exhibit this material generated a magnificent two-volume catalogue, entitled *Das Wrack*, which offers far more than a catalogue of a particular wreck but what amounts to a virtual catalogue of Roman luxury in the early first century BCE.[25]

The Mahdia wreck is one of a group of late republican wrecks with freights composed partly or largely of luxury objects. As with the Antikythera and Spargi wrecks (figure 8.2), no precise dating is possible, and consequently the precise historical context is hard to pin down, though at least in the

---

[24] See above p. 27.   [25] Hellenkemper Sallies (1994a).

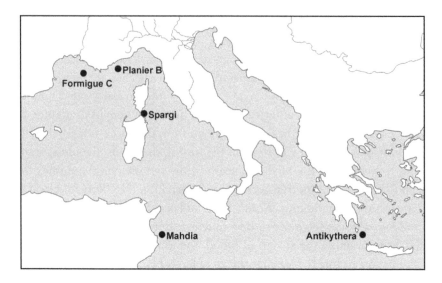

Figure 8.2 Map of shipwrecks mentioned in text (drawn by Amy Richardson)

case of Antikythera, an astrolabe seemingly set for the year 80 BCE gives a more precise peg than the very broad date-ranges normally permitted by cargos of amphorae.[26] The original interpretation was that Mahdia must be a ship laden with war-booty from Sulla's sack of Athens in 86 BCE. That assumption is the consequence of the attention which Roman sources, not least Pliny, devote to art works as war-booty in the late Republic, from Marcellus' sack of Syracuse in 211 BCE onwards.[27] But, as Coarelli showed, this interpretation is not compatible with the most significant component of the cargo, weighing over 200 tons, consisting of sixty–seventy marble columns. Since these are of Attic marble, and are only roughed out (i.e. without fluting and final polish), they are evidently not plunder from any Greek temple, but a fresh consignment from the Attic quarries, laded at the Piraeus.[28] Coarelli appropriately recalls the incident around 105 BCE when Licinius Crassus utilised his Attic marble columns first for a stage, then for his home (see p. 336), an example followed in 58 BCE by Aemilius Scaurus, from whose stage building came the four massive columns of his atrium.[29] We might indeed envisage the Mahdia cargo as bound for Rome, to grace first some public display, then some aristocratic home.

But the fluid boundary between public and private in Rome, and between booty and Rome-targeted export production in Greece, emerges from the

---

[26] Parker (1992) 56.   [27] Pape (1975), Hölscher (1994).

[28] Coarelli (1983) = Coarelli (1996c) 312–26; Galsterer (1994).

[29] Pliny, *Natural History* 36.6–8; Asconius, *in Scaurum* 26–7; Quintilian 5.13.40.

careful studies of the wreck catalogue.[30] The columns are not the only products that seem fresh-made for export to Rome. They are accompanied by a mixed bag of capitals of Pentelic marble, twenty Ionic, three Doric and five with elegant chimaera designs (figure 8.6, p. 368),[31] apparently equally new and of Attic craftsmanship, as is also the case with the four massive marble *craters*[32] and the five or more ponderous marble candelabra.[33] More striking evidence of vigorous production for the Italian market is provided by the bronze bed fittings for twenty-two couches, examples of the very *triclinia aerata* which Piso and Pliny saw as the symbols of luxury in the triumph of Manlius Vulso (p. 315). Sabine Faust interpreted the numerals which emerged from the conservation cleaning as pointing to a very substantial production, of perhaps as many as 2,000 per year, based probably on Delos.[34]

But alongside such examples of 'factory-fresh' specimens, there was also clear evidence of re-use. The exquisite bronze Herm is signed by the artist Boethus, possibly Boethus son of Athanaion from Calchedon, working in the early second century on Delos and Rhodes (figure 8.3). Scientific analysis showed the traces of the marble base on which it has originally stood. The famous bronze statue of a winged Eros, known as the 'Agon', still had the lead attachments on its feet of a previous installation. The fine bronze ship's figureheads of Dionysus and Ariadne, which did not form part of the fixings of this wrecked ship, had nail holes showing previous use; and the series of marble heads on circular *tondi* seem to have come from a public building.[35] In a word, it is mixed cargo, with some new and some old material, showing the simultaneous impact of Rome in both looting what was already in Greece, and stimulating the production of new material to satisfy the desires of a growing market. We may doubt whether the Roman purchasers wished or were able to distinguish.[36]

Equally telling are the results of reconsidering the copying processes that lie behind the production. As Carol Mattusch stresses, the old contrast between Greek 'originals' and Roman 'copies' mistakes the processes of production.[37] The 'lost wax' process allowed, or even required, a sculptor to start with a copy of a standard type and add his own details and finish to the specific wax version on which he was working, or indeed to produce

---

[30] Hellenkemper Sallies (1994b) 24f.   [31] Von Hesberg (1994).
[32] Grassinger (1994).   [33] Cain and Dräger (1994).
[34] Faust (1994).   [35] Hellenkemper Sallies (1994b) 20.
[36] For the credibility of a market for copies, see Hallett (2005a), questioning Gazda (2002) and Perry (2005) on the Roman pursuit of originality.
[37] Mattusch (1996) 168–97. On replication, see also MacMullen (2000) 124–31.

Figure 8.3 The Boethus Herm of Dionysus from the Mahdia wreck (photo Rheinisches Landesmusem Bonn, courtesy Musée Nationale du Bardo, Tunis)

Figure 8.4 The Boethus Herm of Dionysus from the Getty Museum (79.AB.138, courtesy the J. Paul Getty Museum)

a series of similar pieces with small individualising differences. Hence the magnificent Herm of Boethus from the Mahdia wreck is extremely close to the bronze Herm in the Getty Museum, yet is different enough in the modelling of the turban and grape clusters around the head to merit an artist's signature (figure 8.4). The Roman market was certainly big enough to stimulate mechanised reproduction; yet it is not quite Benjamin's 'Art in the age of mechanical reproduction'. Far from seeking individuality and originality in taking distance from the tools of copying, the Greek artist stamps his mark in the variation on a theme. The fact that the Boethus Herm had already been used before shipping overseas suggests that it was not simply the Roman market that stimulated the practice of multiple copying, but that this was a feature of the hellenistic artistic landscape they could exploit.

We thus move away from a picture of Romans ignorantly plundering and then debasing an innocent world of Greek pure aesthetics to a more complex picture of Romans participating in a hellenistic context in which art in multiples already serves a world of luxury, and in which the Greeks are keen that the Romans should join, for it can only do good for trade. In moving away from the distinction between booty (genuine 'Greek'

Figure 8.5 Marble Herm of Dionysus from
Pompeii, inv. 2914 (photo Alfredo Foglia, courtesy
Soprintendenza Archeologica di Napoli e Pompei)

originals reserved for conquering generals) and reproduction (a downmarket 'Roman' form of art, pandering to the nouveaux riches), we can
make better sense of the speed with which Italy can benefit from the example of the numerous centres of production in the east, Athens, Aegina,
Megara, Delos, Rhodes, Pergamum, Alexandria and elsewhere. Migrant
craftsmen could bring with them existing traditions of production and
reproduction.

What was the destination of this cargo of luxuries? It is tempting indeed to
imagine that it was a specific Roman client of the level of Licinius Crassus, of
whom we happen to know not only that he was fond of marble columns, but
also that he had a large collection of bronze couches, *triclinia aerata*.[38] Who
but such a major political figure could afford such a cargo, which Coarelli
conservatively valued at a million sesterces?[39] The parallel is strong with
Cicero's attempts, revealed in letters to Atticus in 67 BCE, to acquire from
Greece a collection of Herms (in Pentelic marble with bronze heads) and
other suitable ornaments for his villa; his references to the ship of Lentulus
in which he wishes the goods to be transported suggests the involvement
of the high aristocracy in such shipping.[40] But here, too, we are making

---

[38] Pliny, *Natural History* 34.14.   [39] Coarelli (1996c) 320f.   [40] Cicero, *ad Atticum* 1.8.2, 1.9.2.

assumptions. Cicero tells Atticus that if Lentulus' ship is not available, he may use any other. Numerous ships criss-crossed the Mediterranean, carrying the wine of Italian estates in Dressel I amphorae, remarkable stacks of black-glaze pottery (notably on the Spargi wreck), and luxury objects in marble and bronze (not to speak of precious metals). Just as the eighteenth-century British aristocracy could not build up their collections of antiquities to grace their stately homes without the services of a network of agents, we must imagine behind even an Atticus a network of agents, with many buyers to satisfy. They might export from Greece 'bespoke' items; but in so far as most buyers seemed to want the same, or indeed like Cicero showed clear signs of wanting to be told what to want ('something suitable for a gymnasium, *gymnasiodes*'), they could well take a risk on a shipment that would rapidly find its buyers, in Puteoli or Ostia, maybe speculating in their turn as objects changed hands repeatedly.

Without a detailed bill of lading, how could we do more than speculate where the Mahdia ship was bound, and whether for one client or several, or for the open market? Mattusch cites with approval Dorothy Kent Hill's words on the decorative features of Roman gardens:

I am not ready to assert that there was an ancient mail-order house, and that from a catalogue one could select a subject, in marble or bronze, large or small, perforated as a fountain or not. But for our purposes, as we try to recreate Roman gardens after many centuries and perhaps feel some of their calm and beauty, might it not be useful to make such a catalogue?[41]

She does well to stop short of the suggestion of a mail-order catalogue; after all, had there been one, Cicero might have been able to place his orders with less imprecision. But the point is that in the end everyone from Cicero downwards ends up with more or less the same sort of stuff in their gardens, larger or smaller, better or worse in quality. The Mahdia exhibition catalogue ends up as coming some considerable way to the sort of catalogue Dorothy Kent Hill had in mind.

Consider the sheer frequency with which parallels for the fine objects on the wreck are found in Pompeii. This is surely not because Pompeii was exceptional in anything but the mode of its preservation, but because it reflects accurately the culture diffused across the Bay of Naples, of which Puteoli was a major point of distribution, and Baiae and the other luxury resorts major points of consumption. Take the bronze Herm. The best

---

[41] Hill (1981) 94.

parallel in bronze is in the Getty Museum (alas, without provenance). The closest parallel in marble is from Pompeii, found as a garden ornament beside a *piscina* (house II.5.2); the workmanship is exquisite, the dimensions and face closely match the Mahdia example, but the turban is substituted with vine leaves, a variation on the theme (figure 8.5).[42] The marble is Italian, from Luna, so one can be reasonably confident of Italy as place of manufacture.[43] Other examples turn up, in terracotta, as a marble tondo, as a red jasper gem or an amethyst ring-stone; their findspots range from a well by the Porta Latina in Rome to Vaison-la-Romaine in Provence. Had we a dozen sites like Pompeii scattered across the Empire, we might be able to begin to grasp the scale of diffusion of such themes-with-variations.

Again, the five chimaera capitals (figure 8.6) belong to a class with forty specimens, most frequently in Athens and other Roman Greek sites (Patras, Corinth, Corfu), but also widespread in Rome. However, the parallel closest in workmanship and date is a pair of capitals from a grave in Pompeii (figure 8.7).[44] That bronze candelabra and couch ornaments such as are found in large numbers on the wreck are also common at Pompeii is obvious, and to these we will return; but when it comes to understanding an unattached candelabrum arm in the form of a luxuriant branch of acanthus, it is the more elaborate candelabra of Pompeii that provide the parallel.[45] The magnificent bronze calyx *crater* fragmentarily preserved from Mahdia has its best parallels in the Vesuvian cities, especially one example from Pompeii in the Naples Museum which Petrovsky says corresponds in all details, with virtually identical workmanship of the handles.[46] A rolling brazier from Mahdia, a rectangular bronze frame to contain hot coals, with little wheels set in the legs (figure 8.8), finds a number of parallels in Naples Museum, especially one with a similar arrangement of legs and wheels, though its lacks the elegant appliqué heads (figure 8.9).[47] Even so, the same appliqué heads can be found on another fine Pompeian bronze brazier, albeit one without wheels.[48] Finally, the five bronze lamps from the wreck are important enough for the classic type of lamp with long volutes framing the nozzle to be known as the 'Mahdia type'; but again Pompeii provides the closest parallels. The more elaborate the type, the more striking the parallel: an unusual three-nozzle lamp decorated with masks from new comedy found on the wreck has two of the masks missing, but the similarities to the

[42] Mattusch (1996) 186–7.   [43] *Rediscovering Pompeii* (1990) 264.
[44] Heinrich (1994), *Rediscovering Pompeii* (1990).
[45] Naumann-Steckner, Raeder and Willer (1994).   [46] Petrovsky (1994).
[47] Barr-Sharrar (1994b).   [48] *Rediscovering Pompeii* (1990) 173.

Figure 8.6 Marble capital from Mahdia wreck with Chimaera design (photo Rheinisches Landesmusem Bonn, courtesy Musée Nationale du Bardo, Tunis)

Figure 8.7 Marble capital from Pompeii with Chimaera design (author's photo)

Figure 8.8 Bronze rolling brazier from the Mahdia wreck (photo Rheinisches Landesmusem Bonn, courtesy Musée Nationale du Bardo, Tunis)

Figure 8.9 Bronze braziers from Pompeii (drawing from *Real Museo Borbonico* (Naples 1830), vol. VI, tav. XLV)

Pompeii example are so great that it is quite likely that the missing two masks can be supplied from the Pompeii example; nevertheless, the differences in size, details of garlands and craftsmanship show they do not come from the same production line.[49]

Enough has been said to make the point: suppose there had been a mail-order firm, and our Mahdia catalogue represented part of their wares, there were people in provincial Pompeii a century and a half later who were picking items from the same catalogue. But of course there was no mail-order firm, just an complex network of producers and suppliers, criss-crossing the waters of the Mediterranean, with production centres maybe at Athens or on Delos, maybe in Puteoli or Capua, turning out stuff that was inter-related because ancient art had the concept of theme and variation running through its veins. In a circulation system pumped by the heart of the conquest city of Rome, ideas and goods diffused over a wide distance. It is simply not true that everything becomes one homogeneous sameness, as in a world of brands and franchises, because the mechanical means of reproduction have not yet been industrialised. Each object is still, to some extent, individual. But the close parentage to a circulating language of ideas is unmistakable.

How this process works in detail can be suggested by examining some of the classes of luxury goods which have been sufficiently studied. But in pursuing a number of examples, the discussion will by no means be limited to luxury goods on the level of the Mahdia wreck. As was suggested in chapter 7, luxury cannot be understood by looking at the culture of the elite in isolation. Indeed, in the world of Mandeville, the restless pursuit of fashions by the elite is driven by the hot breath of competition from emergent groups below. Emulation is the counterpart to distinction, the urge to maintain a social distance expressed in the material superiority of luxury. Luxury must be understood, then, in the context of what we might term 'sub-luxury', that is the downmarket imitations of luxury which reach a wider diffusion than the true luxuries of the elite, but which nevertheless serve to maintain distinctions at lower levels. The most remarkable feature of Roman luxury is the degree to which it proliferates at the levels of sub-luxury, and the close liaison maintained between the two worlds. We might just get away with our image of the Roman world as elitist, populated by late republican nobles like Licinius Crassus and Aemilius Scaurus, and living in rich villas like the Villa of the Papyri, were it not for the survival in Pompeii and Herculaneum of

---

[49] Barr-Sharrar (1994a) 641–2.

clear documentation of the enthusiasm with which sub-elite levels embraced if not luxury, then at least sub-luxury.

Lighting in bronze: candelabra

The Mahdia wreck, as we have seen, contained a number of bronze objects that served for illumination. Practical and utilitarian though lighting may often be, it had a vital role in the context of dining. Consequently the apparatus of illumination had associations of high prestige. None of the lighting equipment on the wreck descends to the level of the quotidian. Of the five bronze lamps, one is an elaborate three-nozzle type decorated with swags and comic masks, while three others have two nozzles and elaborate vegetal handles and volutes.[50] The more nozzles a lamp had, the brighter it burned and the more oil it consumed. But in any case, it is likely that the lamps should be associated with the candelabra: whereas Etruscan candelabra were made with spikes for true candles, the hellenistic and Roman examples have flat tops for lamps.[51] A prestigious bronze lamp-stand should be capped by a bronze rather than terracotta lamp, and where the Pompeian evidence is good enough, they are indeed found in association (see p. 379). The five Mahdia candelabra, as Baratte warns, are not easy to count, because one can have little confidence in the way their constituent elements have been reassembled.[52] Since feet, shaft and top were manufactured separately, even in different centres, their recomposition is a little arbitrary. One may imagine equally that the bronze lamps were not specifically made for the ensemble, but that the purchaser would make their own match.

The standard lamp-holder has a base with three feet, a long, thin shaft, and a top in a variety of forms, in the examples from Mahdia of Corinthian capitals (figures 8.10 and 8.11). But there could be more elaborate supports. In addition to the acanthus stem, provisionally identified as part of a candelabrum,[53] there are also two statuettes, a third life-size, of running figures carrying torches, one a winged Eros, the other a Hermaphrodite (figures 8.12 and 8.13). The tops of their heads are ingeniously hinged so that their bodies can function as oil reservoirs, while the wicks for the flame are set in the torches in their hands.[54] The fluid boundary between representational art and the function of illumination, one common in the theme of the *lychnouchos*, or lamp-bearer, underlines the prestige attached to illumination (figures 8.13–8.15).

[50] Barr-Sharrar (1994a).   [51] Pernice (1925) 43.   [52] Baratte (1994).
[53] Naumann-Steckner, Raeder and Willer (1994).   [54] Hiller (1994).

Figure 8.10 Bronze candelabra from the
Mahdia wreck (drawing Rheinisches
Landesmusem Bonn, courtesy Musée
Nationale du Bardo, Tunis)

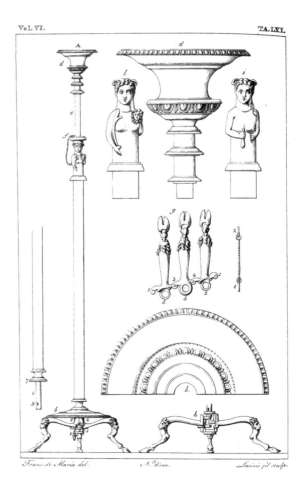

Figure 8.11 Bronze candelabra from Naples Museum
(drawing from *Real Museo Borbonico* (Naples 1830),
vol. VI, tav. LXI)

Finally, we should take note of the five massive marble candelabra in the
same cargo.[55] It may indeed be imprecise to call them candelabra; in form
they evoke the tradition of incense-burners or *thymiateria* that go back to the
fifth century and were particularly common in Etruria.[56] But the constant
confusion in the literature between lamp-stands and incense-burners suggests that they are closely related, and belong to the same world of luxury.
The production of these ostentatious marble objects is a distinctive feature
of the furnishings of Italian sites of the late republic and early Empire.[57]

---

[55] Cain and Dräger (1994).   [56] Testa (1989), Zaccagnino (1998).   [57] Cain (1985).

Figure 8.12 Bronze winged Eros as lamp-stand from the Mahdia wreck (photo Rheinisches Landesmusem Bonn, courtesy Musée Nationale du Bardo, Tunis)

Figure 8.13 Bronze *ephebe* as gilded *lychnouchos* from the House of Ephebe, Pompeii (photo Alfredo Foglia, courtesy Soprintendenza Archeologica di Napoli e Pompei)

The prestige attached to candelabra emerges equally from the elder Pliny's account of their place in bronze-working.[58] One of the marks of prestige in Roman collecting practice is the attachment of Greek place-names to objects of value. It seems from Pliny's slightly confused account that at least some candelabra were called 'Corinthian', though they were not made of 'Corinthian bronze', that prestigious alloy of bronze, silver and gold which aroused exceptional passions in Roman collectors (figure 8.14). Pliny thinks the name is due to the dispersion of bronzes caused by the sack of Corinth, but in any case explains that the prime centres of production were Aegina and Tarentum, in a striking collaborative arrangement by which Aegina made the tops and Tarentum the shafts. Candelabrum experts are disinclined to believe Pliny here; yet what the whole account perhaps reveals most clearly

---

[58] *Natural History* 34.10–12.

Figure 8.14 Example of 'Corinthian bronze': inlaid bronze statuette base from Herculaneum, inv. 77281 (photo Soprintendenza Archeologica di Napoli e Pompei)

is the confusion in the minds of the Roman buyers, who were aware of the importance of prestigious centres of production, and aware that Greece and Italy were interlocked in the whole business, but attached labels more as desirable brand-names than authentic marks of origin.

Indeed, 'Corinthian bronze' is itself one of the most curious of Roman brand-names. Pliny's own explanation, repeated by others, was that Mummius' destruction of Corinth caused the discovery of the alloy, through the casual fusing of bronze with silver and gold.[59] This is certainly wrong, and it has been argued that the discovery of the highly complex technique which involves not only alloying, but inlaying and careful chemical treatment of the surface to achieve a black patina, was developed in the eastern Mediterranean as early as the second millennium, and was transmitted to the far east where it survives in Japanese *shaduko*.[60] Yet the Roman snobbery involved emerges from Pliny's attempt to correct the ignorant. He accuses the collectors of ignorance:

> But the majority of them seem to me to pretend to scientific knowledge in order to set themselves apart from the others rather than to understand anything more subtle. (Pliny, *Natural History* 34.3.6)

Perhaps he wrote in conscious recall of Petronius' parody of conceited ignorance in Trimalchio, who first teases his guests by claiming to have the only

---

[59] *Natural History* 34.6.   [60] Craddock and Giumlia-Mair (1995).

true Corinthian ware because made by a bronze-smith called Corinthus, and then offers the 'true' origin in the sack of Troy by Hannibal.[61] Few episodes illustrate so well how luxury goods form a system of knowledge, and owe their value to their capacity for discourse. Both expense and discourse helped the rich collectors 'to set themselves apart from others', and the snobbery of Pliny and Petronius is visible in their conviction that their false story about the sack of Corinth is more authentic than the jumbled versions offered by the upstart Trimalchio.

One of the favourite commonplaces of Roman luxury discourse is the protest about exaggerated prices paid, one that stretches from Cato's lamentations of the decline of a republic in which men can pay the price of a farm for a jar of Pontic pickled fish (*tarichos*), to Tiberius' censure of a senator who paid the equally astronomical price of 30,000 sesterces for three fish.[62] Pliny compares the prices paid for bronze candelabra to the annual salary of a military tribune, and goes on to tell the illuminating story of the hunchback Clesippus, who was thrown in as part of a job-lot with a candelabrum (implying that the life of a human was worth a small percentage of the price of a lamp-stand). The unlovely Clesippus became the lover of his mistress Gegania, and inherited her fortune; he cultivated his lucky lamp-stand with religious fervour, and celebrated his story by representing it on his funerary monument. (By a freak of fortune, his monument survives, off the via Appia at Posta di Mesa.)[63] The story is again curiously reminiscent of Trimalchio's account of his own rise to fortune, from his purchase as a little slave-boy – 'I came from Asia the size of this candelabrum here'– to his success as his mistress's favourite.[64]

Whether the candelabra on the Mahdia wreck would have auctioned for astronomical prices seems a little dubious, but undoubtedly they were prestige items. Baratte is rather more cautious than other contributors to the catalogue in suggesting a place of production; but if the columns, capitals and marble *craters* and candelabra were fresh from Attic workshops, it seems reasonable to imagine that the bronze lamps came from the nearby centre of prestige production, Aegina. (The ship evidently had no chance to put in at Tarentum before it foundered.)

---

[61] *Satyricon* 50.2–6.

[62] Polybius 31.25.5, cited also by Athenaeus, *Deipnosophists* 6.274f, cf. Malcovati (1955) 40, Cato fr. XIX; Suetonius, *Tiberius* 34.1.

[63] Coarelli (1982) 282: the inscription reads: 'Clesipus Geganius, magister Capitolinus, magister Lupercorum, viator tribunicius', demonstrating his success in accumulating recognition (I thank Filippo Coarelli for this reference).

[64] *Satyricon* 75.10; see Whitehead (1993) for the links between the fictional Trimalchio and archaeological evidence.

The best confirmation that Pliny is right in saying that the Roman market attached enormous importance to candelabra is in wall-decoration. The characteristic decorative schemes of the first century BCE, in the 'second style', use as the prime vertical element of articulation columns, painted with three-dimensional realism. This is true both of those 'open' schemes with perspective depth which have attracted most study, and of the no less frequent 'closed' schemes where columns frame solid panels.[65] Candelabra or *thymiateria* occasionally form features in some of the more ambitious open schemes, as at Oplontis or Boscoreale. However, towards the end of the first century there starts the fashion, explicitly criticised by Vitruvius, for reducing the columns to thin, elongated elements, such as could certainly not be made of marble, but might be of metal. In this context, the candelabrum comes into its own.[66] Bronze candelabra play with two themes: the marble column with its Corinthian capital, and vegetation, such as a stalk of hemlock, or a palm. Already the Corinthian capital is based on vegetation, with fronds of acanthus. Metalwork enabled this game to be pushed to further extremes. The decorative representation of a candelabrum allowed a further step, and stems may grow out of absurdly small flower calyxes, or even be inverted and grow downwards. The dining room wall so decorated with candelabra allowed the same sort of play between painted representation and context that we see in Corinthian *oeci*, where a row of real columns stands in front of the painted ones, or garden paintings where wall and actual garden play off one another.[67] We may readily imagine the effect of dining by the flickering light cast from lamps on elegant bronze candelabra set in front of wall-decoration with a polished black background offset by the elegant details of attenuated candelabra with rampant vegetal flourishes and miniature flying figures.

Vitruvius' protests are those which characterise each step of the luxury game. Columns and architectural elements evoked a world of public magnificence. Candelabra evoked a world of private luxury. What outraged the moralist was effective in social discourse. The candelabra mimicked columns in form, yet drew them into the private sphere. The movement from the Mahdia wreck to these 'third-style' decorations reflects the underlying rhythm of the waves of luxury. At the beginning of the first century BCE, bronze candelabra are prestige import items from Greece, even if manufactured for a Roman market. By the end of the century, this luxury has been domesticated, absorbed into a standard decorative scheme that may be found in the villas of the rich, but also in more modest houses from Pompeii to Glanum.

[65] Heinrich (2002).   [66] Ehrhardt (1987).   [67] Yerkes (2005).

We would be able to follow both the chronological and the social diffusion of bronze candelabra in the Roman world had the numerous candelabra of Pompeii and Herculaneum been catalogued. These sites count as the biggest single source of Roman candelabra;[68] yet despite the passion with which the Romans regarded them, nobody has devoted a general study to Vesuvian candelabra since Pernice (figure 8.11).[69] Writing before the new excavations of Maiuri in Pompeii and Herculaneum, he counted well over a hundred examples, saying that it was the single most numerous class of bronze ware from the sites. That observation alone underlines the extent of their diffusion. They are by no means an everyday domestic object; bronze wares are never common in the way of terracotta. Yet it is evident that their use has passed from elite to sub-elite. To take the example of a single *insula*, I.9: its eight houses produce four examples of candelabra, and two of small lamp-stands. Two are fine bronze candelabra and occur in two of the houses with finest decoration, the House of the Beautiful *Impluvium* (I.9.1) and the House of the Fruit Orchard (I.9.5); two are disintegrated fragments of iron candelabra, found in a workshop full of a striking assemblage of diverse finds. The two bronze lamp-stands are found in the modest house attached to the bar of Amarantus (I.9.12) (figure 8.15).

It may be imagined that the candelabra of Pompeii were not up to the standards of luxury of those of the Mahdia wreck. Doubtless some examples will be downmarket, and the fragmentary iron examples from the workshop cited exemplify something which may otherwise be missed, thanks to the lower survival rates of iron as opposed to bronze. But the best of Pompeii can certainly compete with Mahdia. The wreck has two ingenious examples with extendable stems;[70] but Pernice knew six such examples in the Naples Museum[71] and, as his illustration shows, they were of great elegance.[72] Indeed, Pernice considers these specimens as hellenistic imports; the bronze candelabrum could enjoy a long life-cycle and the earliest specimens at Pompeii are Etruscan products of the fourth century or earlier. But Pernice assigns the major grouping of examples to the Augustan period, one in which we can register a boom in production of numerous luxury items, including marble candelabra.

For the highest levels of luxury, a columnar candelabrum was not enough. We have seen on the Mahdia wreck the figures of Eros and a Hermophrodite adapted as 'living torches'. Such *lychnophoroi* are well attested at Pompeii

[68] Pettinau (1990) 100.   [69] Pernice (1925) 43–63.
[70] Baratte (1994) 608–13.   [71] Pernice (1925) 55–6.
[72] Pernice (1925) Abb. 74; see the colour illustration in Pirzio Biroli Stefanelli (1990) 210, figures 187–8.

Figure 8.15 Bronze lamp-stand from the House of Amarantus (I.9.12), Pompeii, inv. 10026 (photo Hay/Sibthorpe, courtesy British School at Rome)

and elsewhere.[73] The most famous example is the Ephebe from the house of that name,[74] though others have been found in the house of Fabius Rufus,[75] and of Julius Polybius, in addition to a likely workshop outside the Porta Vesuvio (figure 8.13).[76]

Lucretius, in exposing the Epicurean ideal of living within the simple necessities of nature, exemplifies the superfluous luxuries desired by Romans, starting:

unless there are golden images of young men through the houses
holding in their right hands flame-bearing lamps
to supply light to nocturnal banquets.[77]

He may well have had in mind not only the Homeric description of Alcinoos' palace in Phaeacia,[78] but also the conduct of his contemporaries. The

[73] Mattusch (1996).   [74] I.7.10–12; *Rediscovering Pompeii* (1990) 257, no. 180.
[75] Ins. Occidentalis VII.16.19.   [76] Salskov Roberts (2002).
[77] *De Rerum Natura* 2.24–6.   [78] *Odyssey* 7.700.

ephebe from Pompeii, though not golden, was originally gilded, and it is in direct descent from the conduct of the late republican elite which Lucretius attacked. Yet the house, despite some touches of luxury, is by no means architecturally ambitious, and is attributed to a freedman, Cornelius Tages.

Lighting in bronze: lamps

Candelabra were an empire-wide phenomenon, attested from the first to the fourth centuries in centres from Gaul (Arras) to Germany (Kaiseraugst) to Romania (Callatis) to Morocco (Lixus, Volubilis and Banasa).[79] When the great catalogue of Roman imperial candelabra is written we will understand better the rhythms and mechanisms of diffusion. But for now, we are better off following the humbler, but infinitely better studied, lamp. In its bronze form at least, the lamp belongs closely with the candelabrum. On several occasions in Pompeii, lamp and stand were found together, and have been displayed and catalogued together.[80] In our sample *insula* at I.9, bronze lamps were found in the same three houses that had candelabra.[81] In the case of the Mahdia wreck, too, we have noted the association of lamps and stands. The bronze lamp may not rank quite so high in the sources as the candelabrum; but it, too, was the object of significant artistic effort and skill, and may be followed as part of the same world of luxury.

Lamps are among the characteristic boom products of the Roman imperial period. Bronze and pottery lamps, though distinct in their typologies and trajectories, nevertheless run in close parallel with each other, and the dissimilarities are as interesting as the similarities. The growth in popularity of bronze lamps in this period is starkly illustrated by the statistics of the collection in the British Museum. Despite Bailey's warnings of the dangers of assigning chronology or place of production to items that largely come from collectors, without provenance let alone stratigraphic context, internal similarities and comparisons to pottery allow him to make reasonable assignations: two bronze lamps belong to the late Cypriot bronze age; four are categorised as 'Greek'; twenty-one as 'Hellenistic and late Republican'; 110 as early imperial; and sixty-eight as 'Roman, high and late empire'. If this sample is remotely representative, we are looking at a fashion that has its origins in the hellenistic eastern Mediterranean, but with a significant peak under Roman imperial rule. For lack of an authoritative overall study of bronze lamps, it is hard to say whether the pattern applies to other

---

[79] Baratte (1994) 610 and n. 11.   [80] *Rediscovering Pompeii* (1990) 176–7.   [81] I.9.1, 5 and 8.

collections, though it certainly borne out by the smaller holdings of the Museo Nazionale Romano[82] and the Biblioteca Apostolica Vaticana,[83] which have no pre-hellenistic examples.

It is particularly difficult to distinguish bronze lamps produced by late hellenistic centres like Ephesos, Delos and Alexandria from local Italian production, which is taken to be centred on Capua, certainly a major centre of bronze production.[84] We have already seen how closely paralleled the bronze lamps from the Mahdia wreck are in the Pompeian material; this is both because the wares being imported from the east in the early first century BCE reached sites like Pompeii, and continued in use over a long period, and because they formed the basis of local production, which both copied hellenistic forms and derived from them a family of other forms.

It is the Vesuvian cities which have produced comfortably the largest surviving collections of bronze lamps. The Naples Museum has easily the largest collection: of 385 entries, one is an isolated Ionic–Cycladic piece, four are late Roman, and the rest Vesuvian.[85] To these should be added the 151 examples from twentieth-century excavations kept on site in Pompeii and Herculaneum, which have the enormous benefit of precise provenance.[86] Thus over 500 bronze lamps certainly derive from excavation in Pompeii and Herculaneum, and bearing in mind the dispersal of such finds in the late eighteenth and early nineteenth century around the museums of Europe, the true number is likely to be higher (a significant proportion of the British Museum holdings derives, via collectors like Sir William Hamilton and Richard Payne Knight, from these sites).[87] To put those numbers in proportion, the pottery lamps of the Naples Museum run to just short of 5,000, to which probably another thousand should be added from the uncatalogued collections on site, including 226 from Herculaneum.[88] Pottery outnumbers bronze by over 10:1.

The most interesting issue for the understanding of the 'waves of fashion' is how bronze and pottery lamps relate to one another. If we accept that luxury does not merely operate in isolation, as a closed circle of prestige goods accessible to only the richest social strata, but as one element in a system of goods charged with social meaning, that range from the most exclusive luxuries to the most reduced levels of 'sub-luxury', it is helpful to see bronze and pottery as working together in a single semantic system. The close relationship is always stressed by the typological studies that dominate

---

[82] 102 specimens; De' Spagnolis and De Carolis (1983).

[83] Fifty specimens; De' Spagnolis and De Carolis (1986).

[84] Willers (1907), Valenza Mele (1981) IX.   [85] Valenza Mele (1981).

[86] De' Spagnolis and De Carolis (1988).   [87] Bailey (1996) vii.   [88] Bissi Ingrassia (1977).

the field: particularly in the first centuries BCE and CE, the forms are closely linked, with a presumed dependence of pottery forms on bronzes ones; yet bronze typologies are seen as relatively conservative, remaining faithful to hellenistic models, while pottery shapes progressively develop away from these models and by the second century CE achieve their own independent development.[89]

At the risk of oversimplification, bronze lamps may be divided into four main families: those with nozzles rising from the body like the spout of a teapot, those with nozzles attached to the body by decorative volutes, those in which body and nozzle form an interconnected pear-shape, and 'plastic lamps' in the form of a wide variety of models, including heads, feet and animals. The earliest forms come from the eastern Mediterranean, and it is their links with pottery forms that allow us to say this. The earliest 'teapot' form (figure 8.16) is the 'Spargi' type, met in the form of a *trilychnos* with three spouts in examples from the Spargi and Mahdia wrecks (figure 8.17), paralleled by one from Pompeii and one from Herculaneum (figure 8.18);[90] it is very close to the pottery lamps found on Delos of the late second/early first centuries BCE, which include a *trilychnos* with comic masks like the examples in bronze from Mahdia and Pompeii[91] – such masks are fairly common on Delian lamps, but also on those of Cnidos.[92] This coincidence might, or might not, suggest that the model comes from Delos itself.

The 'volute' type (figure 8.19), of which there are four examples on the Madhia wreck, four from the Naples Museum, and one more on site in Pompeii, is supposedly related to the 'Ephesus' type of pottery, found commonly not only in Ephesus[93] but on Delos;[94] parallels in Antioch suggest that the form moved gradually westwards.[95] The pear-shaped form (figure 8.20) likewise has pottery parallels on Delos, but the suggested origin of the bronze form is Alexandria.[96] Finally, 'plastic' forms, usually of a humorous or grotesque taste, notably of heads of satyrs or Africans, have pottery analogues going back to the third century, including Egypt,[97] and may be an Alexandrian inspiration.

The general point, that the models move from east to west, seems clear. That fits in with the Roman perception that luxury was an eastern import. But what seems even more striking is the degree to which the forms are taken over and transformed in local Italian production. The 'pure' forms,

---

[89] De' Spagnolis and De Carolis (1988) 19–20.   [90] Valenza Mele (1981) 11–12, nos. 3–4.
[91] Bruneau (1965) 102, no. 4418.   [92] Bailey (1975) 129f., plates 69–71.
[93] Bailey (1975) 88ff.   [94] Bruneau (1965) 51ff.   [95] Valenza Mele (1981) 29–30.
[96] De' Spagnolis and De Carolis (1988) 137–9.   [97] Bailey (1975) 258, Q554.

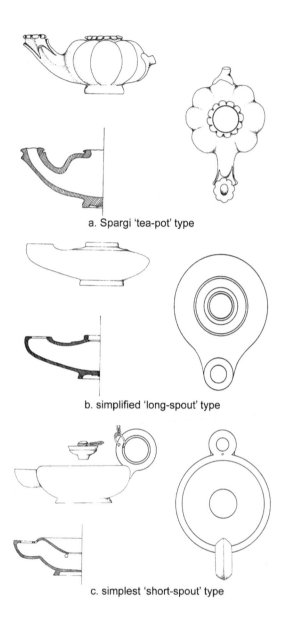

a. Spargi 'tea-pot' type

b. simplified 'long-spout' type

c. simplest 'short-spout' type

Figure 8.16 Forms of lamps of 'Spargi' or 'tea-pot' type
(drawing, after Valenza Mele 1981, figures 5, 9, 39)

like the Spargi teapot or the Mahdia volute, are great rarities in Pompeii. Each of these forms generates simplified or reduced types. The distinctive long spout of the Spargi type is reduced to a shorter nozzle, then to one actually attached to the body of the lamp. The long sweeping volutes of the Mahdia type become reduced volutes then semi-volutes. The 'pear-forms'

Figure 8.17 Bronze *trilychnos* lamp from the Mahdia wreck (photo Rheinisches Landesmusem Bonn, courtesy Musée Nationale du Bardo, Tunis)

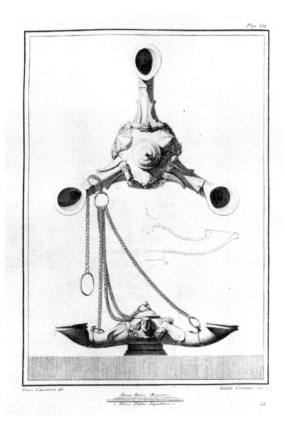

Figure 8.18 Bronze *trilychnos* lamp from Herculaneum, Naples Museum inv. 72180 (drawing from *Le Antichità di Ercolano Esposte* vol. VIII (Naples 1792), tav. L)

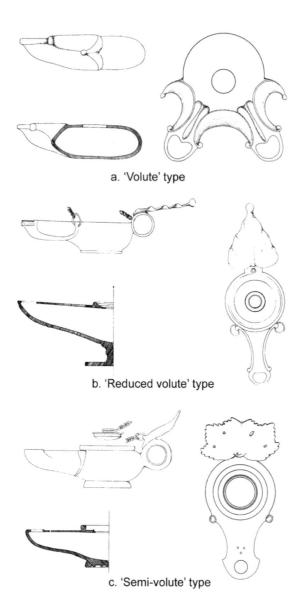

a. 'Volute' type

b. 'Reduced volute' type

c. 'Semi-volute' type

Figure 8.19 Forms of lamps of 'volute' type (drawing after Valenza Mele 1981, figures 44, 47, 119)

are reduced to the simplified shapes known as Loeschke XX and XXI, in which the flowing elongated lines are compacted. It may also be possible to see in the distinctively chunky shapes of the *Firmalampen* that became a standard shape of the empire an ultimate derivative of the pear-form. Production is transferred to Italy, domesticated, simplified, replicated and

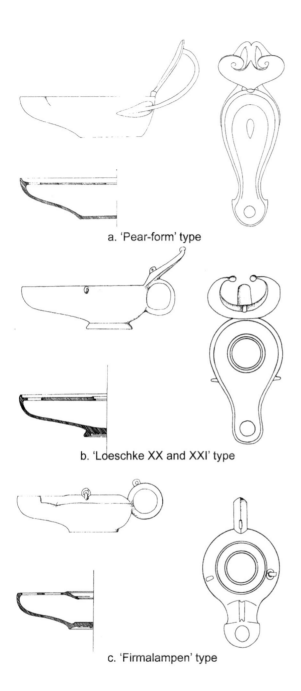

a. 'Pear-form' type

b. 'Loeschke XX and XXI' type

c. 'Firmalampen' type

Figure 8.20 Forms of lamps of 'pear-form' type (drawing after Valenza Mele 1981, figures 209, 300, 314)

so diffused through the empire. Pear-form bronze lamps have been found in Gaul, Spain, Germany, Pannonia, Dalmatia, Syria and Morocco.[98] But they also provide the point of reference for the development of pottery forms, which then develop their own simplifications and diffusions.

Lighting in clay

It is by no means necessary to posit a precise bronze model for each of the new pottery types, even though sometimes there are extremely close parallels, like *Firmalampen* in both media. The experts find themselves arguing over which was the original;[99] both are common in Pompeii, though supposed they came in only during the final decades of the site. It is enough to say that the standard pottery lamp forms, whether of first-century CE Italy represented in the Vesuvian cities, or of the empire at large, bear a generic relationship to the bronze forms, with the varieties of nozzles flanked by volutes (Bailey Types A–D) related to the Mahdia volute type, and those with short, rounded nozzles (Bailey Types O–Q) linked to the most reduced form of the Spargi 'teapot' type. If we concede that *Firmalampen* (Bailey Type N) are a reduction of the pear-form, we can say that all the main bronze forms have their standardised empire-wide offspring.

But does this mean that the users of mass-produced, cheap, pottery lamps thought of themselves as using something related to the elite luxuries of the Mahdia wreck, any more than British labourers in worsted socks were aware that their fashion started on the legs of courtiers wearing silk stockings,[100] or the inhabitants of cabins on the Delaware using Staffordshire crockery for their tea in the 1760s realised they were following a fashion set by the court of Queen Anne?[101] Or, since we have no chance of entering into the minds of the consumers, were pottery lamps produced and openly marketed as downmarket versions of bronze ones? The answer is complex and elusive, but some points can be made.

The first is that they were related in mode of production, being mould-made. Before the third century BCE, pottery lamps were wheel-thrown, like other forms of ceramics. Body and nozzle were separately thrown and then attached; hence the tendency to long spouts still reflected in the Spargi 'teapot' type, one which made less sense in mould-made production, and leads to the 'reduction' of forms observed.[102] The use of moulds starts in

---

[98] De' Spagnolis and De Carolis (1988) 138.   [99] Bailey (1980) 278.
[100] Thirsk (1978).   [101] Breen (2004) 170ff.   [102] Bailey (1972) 9.

Greece and the eastern Mediterranean in the early third century,[103] though wheel-made production continues in the east, as indeed in Sicily, well into the first century BCE.[104] The transition is gradual. Cosa, the Italian site with the best-studied sequence of lamps, has only wheel-made lamps down to the middle of the second century BCE;[105] the last century of the republic is characterised by mould-made lamps closely derived from hellenistic types, including the unattractively named *Warzenlampen* or wart lamps, 'probably based on a bronze prototype'.[106] The destruction layers of Cosa around 70 BCE, and its reoccupation in the Augustan period, allow particularly fine dating, and it is already before 70 BCE that a critical development emerges, in the form of a central discus, providing a potential field for decoration.[107]

However, it is with Augustus that the major break comes, and it is significant that in cataloguing the British Museum lamps, Bailey could include late republican Italy in the volume on the Greek and hellenistic world,[108] arranged geographically, whereas all the imperial lamps of Italy from early Augustus onwards form a single, typologically arranged volume.[109] A new and distinctive nozzle form, with volutes, emerges; the potential of the central discus for varied decoration is fully embraced; and the much finer and thinner clay is covered with a red glaze, contrasting with the black and brown glazes of earlier pottery. This 'picture lamp' is indeed in some ways a typological derivative of bronze lamps (notably in the use of volutes). But it is also a realisation of the independent potential of mould-based pottery production. The development of the central discus as a decorative field has no real precedent in bronze ware. In bronze, decorative elaboration focuses above all on the handle and heat-shield, and to some extent on the curved body and nozzle attachment. It also exploits to the full the potential of bronze for three-dimensional, 'plastic', elaboration. Augustan volute lamps create a new shape that has left behind the wheel and uses the potential of the large flat discus for low-relief moulded decoration. It also adopts a 'new look' in colour: the high-quality red glaze is related to that of contemporary Arretine ceramics, though in fact the shift from black ware to red ware is earlier in lamps than pottery (figures 8.21 and 8.22). We can say, if we like, that it is imitating metal, but if so, not bronze but gold: a fashion which has been linked to Lucullus' triumph of 63 BCE.[110]

As Michael Vickers has often stressed, ancient ceramics reveal their status as a downmarket version of more expensive metal wares by constant

---

[103] Howland (1958) 129.   [104] Bailey (1975) 15f.   [105] Fitch and Goldman (1994) 19.
[106] Fitch and Goldman (1994) 53.   [107] Fitch and Goldman (1994) 69f.
[108] Bailey (1975).   [109] Bailey (1980).   [110] Vickers (1994).

Figure 8.21 Examples of discus lamps from Pompeii Reg. I ins. 9 (photo Hay/Sibthorpe, courtesy British School at Rome)

Figure 8.22 Discus lamp from Pompeii I.9.8, inv. 9033, in its mould (photo Hay/Sibthorpe, courtesy British School at Rome)

imitation of form, decorative features and colour. The argument here is precisely that ceramic lamps acted as a downmarket extension of a luxury market in metals. Bronze is the metal in which lamps most frequently survive, but there will doubtless have been silver and even gold versions for the truly wealthy: a gold lamp was found in the temple of Venus at Pompeii. But having made the point that pottery lamps were a 'poor man's' version of this luxury, we must add the qualification that, far from acting as a mere reflection of tastes dictated by metal forms, pottery lamp production was independent, innovative, vigorous – and, indeed, in its Augustan apogee set new standards of artistic quality. 'The fineness of the clay, the crisp execution, and the sophistication of the design testify to its being the golden era of Roman lamp production.'[111]

It is this combination of independence, innovation and artistic aspiration that makes it impossible to view the Augustan picture lamps as a cheap substitute for something else. They set the pattern for most of the common types of Roman lamps for four centuries. The decoration of the central discus, and the adherence to red glaze, remain constant, though there are many variations in form. The range of images applied to the central disc is remarkable: ranging from religious and mythological scenes, through historical personages, daily life, particularly military life, gladiators, circus scenes, the theatre and scenes of sex, to animals, and plants and floral patterns.[112] The registers of mood are equally varied, from imperial propaganda of the type of Victory with the Augustan oak-wreath OB CIVES SERVATOS, or a shield celebrating an anniversary, to allusions to high poetry (Virgil's Tityrus shown beneath his spreading beech tree), to the mass appeal of gladiatorial scenes, bawdy humour and parody (Cleopatra on a crocodile with a large phallus), and the outright pornography of the scenes of sex, the largest single group within the British Museum collection (though that may also reflect the tastes of the collectors). The sheer variety defies the dismissal of these lamps as a downmarket, purely utilitarian, product.

Utilitarian these lamps may have been, but the association with the rituals of evening entertainment may give them some measure of symbolic potency. It is notable that the range of images, from the mythological to the erotic, is related to the range of imagery encountered in domestic wall-decoration. A striking control on the proposition that lamps did not merely spread at random is their distribution pattern in Switzerland. Of 3,000 lamps studied by Annalis Liebundgut, 96% were of the first century CE, a period of military occupation, only 3% from the second and third centuries, only 1% from the fourth. Their distribution proved to be heavily concentrated in sites of military occupation (Augst, Avenches, Baden and Basel), and extremely rare in rural sites including villas. The implication is that the Celtic population continued to use tallow lamps; Roman oil lamps constituted a cultural choice, what has frequently been called an index of romanisation.[113]

---

[111] Fitch and Goldman (1994) 86.   [112] Bailey (1980) 6–88.   [113] Liebundgut (1977).

In the Vesuvian cities, by contrast, lamps were an essential part of a way of life that penetrates in a capillary fashion to all levels. Pottery lamps, as we have seen, outnumbered bronze by at least 10:1. But even bronze lamps were well spread, albeit through the larger houses, of Pompeii and Herculaneum. The findspots of the twentieth-century excavations show a spread of between two and six bronze lamps per *insula* in each of the *insula* 6–14 of Region I. They tend to be found in the larger and better-decorated houses in each block, though none of these houses, not even the House of the Menander, has more than two specimens. Only the house of Fabius Rufus in the *Insula* Occidentalis has an exceptional six lamps, and this spreading complex is composed of the nuclei of several separate units. In Herculaneum, the twenty-eight bronze lamps with findspots are spread over thirteen houses; the cluster of six in the Colonnato Tuscanico seems to be the result of earlier treasure-hunting.[114] The crippling absence of a catalogue of the pottery lamps from these sites prevents reliable statistics on their spread, though the 6,000 or so specimens must come from virtually every corner of each Vesuvian site. Joanne Berry's analysis of the finds of insula I.9 shows lamps spread in low numbers in every unit in the *insula* except shop 6 (which probably lost its finds to earlier excavations).

The sheer success of the Italian lamp production of the first century CE can be measured from the geographic extension of the market it reached. The biggest single success story is that of the *Firmalampen* or factory lamps; their production, based in north Italy, especially around Modena, starts around the middle to third quarter of the first century CE.[115] They are characterised by a simple linear form without decorative discus; the only variation is in the names stamped on the underside, of which the commonest is FORTIS. Not only is the output enormous, but it is spread throughout the western provinces (North Africa, Spain, Gaul, Germany, the Alps and the Balkans). This, combined with the restricted number of makers' signatures, led William Harris to argue for a system of provincial branches, based on the legal structure of *institores* or agents.[116] However it was organised, the effect was a massive outwards spread of an Italy-based production, to an extent unparalleled in the essentially localised production of the hellenistic period.

Roman imperial lamp production in its outwards, spreading ripples, documented by the third volume of the British Museum catalogue, thus represents the outcome of a process that starts with the cultural dominance of the hellenistic east. One striking case-study is Athens, a centre which throughout

[114] Conticello De' Spagnolis (1988). For Pompeii insula 1.9, see Berry (1997).
[115] Buchi (1975).   [116] Harris (1980).

the second and early first centuries BCE set the artistic fashion for Rome. Throughout the first century BCE, long after the traumatic sack by Sulla in 86, Athenian potters remained loyal to their hellenistic traditions. Only in the early first century CE do imports of Roman lamps begin, becoming dominant towards the end of the century and generating new Athenian forms based on Roman shapes, with the characteristic volutes on the nozzle.[117], Athens develops its own distinctive 'alpha-globule' lamps based on Roman voluted nozzle shapes; in the third, under the influence of Corinth, which as a Roman colony is always keener to embrace Roman styles, it develops a line in decorated discs, including a scene of a horse making love to a woman, curiously reminiscent of the scenes set in Corinth in Apuleius' *Metamorphoses*.[118]

The transformation, as Rotroff stresses, is not the instant consequence of conquest, and the old idea that Athenian pottery was hellenistic down to 86 BCE, and Roman thereafter, is plainly wrong. But the rhythm of Roman cultural change lags behind that of conquest. The first result of conquest is the inwards pull to Rome. Only in a second stage does Italy become a major production centre in its own right, and only in a third do the styles and tastes formed in Italy spread outwards. Expressed in the image of the cardiac cycle, the Sullan sack of Athens is still part of the diastole phase, when goods, ideas and tastes are pumped towards Rome; the systole phase where ideas and tastes pump back out belongs to the first century CE, with the Augustan period as the critical transition when Italy establishes itself as a major producer of goods and tastes. This pattern is borne out by the parallel trajectory of vessels in bronze and clay, particularly drinking vessels.

Vessels of metal

The sheer range of variety, the quality of craftsmanship, and the astonishing quantity of the bronze vessels that served a Roman household of the late first century CE are scarcely imaginable to anyone who has not visited the storerooms of Pompeii and Naples, and seen them in their serried ranks. It is an aspect of the Roman household concealed from us both by the systematic (and necessary) removal of finds from their findspots to museums and storerooms, and by the heavy bias of art-historical study to the 'high genres' of mural decoration and statuary. Some insight can be gained from exhibition catalogues, particularly those of *Rediscovering Pompeii, Homo*

---

[117] Rotroff (1997).   [118] Bailey (1988) 406–11, Perlzweig (1961).

Faber and *Storie di un'eruzione*, in which the detailed catalogue entries are especially valuable.[119] A valuable overview with excellent illustrations of the most spectacular pieces is offered by *Il bronzo dei Romani*.[120] But the single most valuable contribution is the full catalogue of the bronze vessels of Pompeii by Suzanne Tassinari,[121] which not only analyses typologically the remarkable range of vessels, but where possible restores them to the houses in which they were found, so providing an unique insight into the social context of their usage.

Tassinari's catalogue covers the 1,678 bronze vessels preserved on site in Pompeii. Up till 1890, finds were automatically sent back to the Museum in Naples, and even thereafter the better pieces were often consigned. The collection in Naples is significantly larger. No count is available, but to judge from the proportions of bronze lamps (see p. 380), it is likely to be over twice the size. If we add in Herculaneum, the total probably approaches 4,000, and that of course excludes the numerous pieces that have passed to museums abroad, as gifts, sales, or thefts. We are looking at a formidable *corpus* of material. No less impressive is the range of shapes and sizes. Between the four prime functions of vessels for ablution, toilette, cooking and table, Tassinari distinguishes twenty-five principal vessel types, indicated by the letters A–Y, and each of these is subdivided into its variants, in some cases several dozen. Some shapes are very common, particularly the jugs (*brocche*) divided into six distinct types (A–F) with numerous variants, and saucepans (*casseruole*), with 190 examples, the largest single type. Others, like the varia lumped together as Y, are rarities indeed: five *craters*, two water-boilers, six stands (including lamp-stands), and a single *askos*, shaped like a leather flask. No two pieces are identical: production by the lost wax process means that every piece is individually moulded.

Where in all this dazzling array are we to identify the world of luxury? Again, the Mahdia wreck provides a convenient repertory of the sort of wares that might be shipped from east to west across the Mediterranean in the early first century BCE. Petrovsky examined thoroughly the forty-three pieces from sixteen or seventeen separate bronze vessels, noting the absence of previous study of these pieces, neglected in favour of statuary and marble.[122] The vessels comprise three *hydriae*, three buckets, a basin, a water heater, two *craters*, an incense burner, a beaker and a ladle, together with an assortment of attachments. As Petrovsky observes, they are mostly

---

[119] *Rediscovering Pompeii* (1990), Ciarallo and De Carolis (1999), D'Ambrosio, Guzzo and Mastroroberto (2003).
[120] Pirzio Biroli Stefanelli (1990).   [121] Tassinari (1993).   [122] Petrovsky (1994).

showpieces (*Prunkgefäße*): only the beaker is suspected of forming part of the crew's equipment rather than the freight. With the exception of the incense burner and the ladle, they are large objects; the incense burner and ladle or *simpulum* may well be religious. Their manufacture is evidently eastern, and they exemplify the hellenistic taste which Romans admired. But they are all, with the possible exception of the incense burner, models imitated in Roman production, and represent forms to be found in Pompeii and Herculaneum in more or less magnificent examples.

The *craters* from the wreck represent the two principle forms of bronze *crater*: the volute *crater*, with ovoid body and handles rising to meet the lip in elaborate volutes (figure 8.25), and the calyx *crater*, in the bell-shape familiar also from the marble varieties (figure 8.23). *Craters* are rarities in Pompeii and Herculaneum, true collectors' items. Petrovsky points to three examples close to the Mahdia calyx *crater*, from Pompei, Herculaneum and Boscotrecase.[123] Tassinari registers five *craters* (Y1100 and 1200), of which four are the calyx type. The houses in which they were found include a magnificent house built over the western wall of the town next door to Fabius Rufus (Insula Occidentalis 17), one which produced no less than 111 bronze vessels; likewise the House of the Ephebe (I.7.10–12), a far less grand house but one which we have met as the source of a lamp-bearing *ephebe*; but then descend to the more modest Ara Massima (IV.16.15), and finally the little house of Epidius Primus (I.8.14), one which despite its small size and out-of-the way location has a treasure trove of objects of bronze and silver.[124] But the best parallel comes from the house of Julius Polybius, published after Tassinari's catalogue. Here Fausto Zevi discovered an exceptional collection of bronzes: they include a magnificent calyx *crater* (plate 75) (figure 8.24), a lamp-bearing statue in the form of an archaising Apollo (plate 17), and a fifth-century BCE *hydria* from Argos.[125]

The houses where the *craters* were found in Pompeii are by no means the most important in town, nor even exceptional; what they have in common was that their owners show an exceptional interest in quantity as well as quality of bronze. The owner of the House of Julius Polybius (perhaps Julius Philippus) looks like a serious collector: how did he come to acquire a bronze *hydria* of exceptional quality which was made, as its inscription reveals, for the festival of Hera at Argos in the mid fifth century? Zevi recalls

[123] Petrovsky (1994) 673. For colour illustrations, see Pirzio Biroli Stefanelli (1990), plates 237–240.

[124] For illustrations of the silver, see *Rediscovering Pompeii* (1990) 195–7.

[125] These have yet to be published in full, but are illustrated in the exhibition catalogue, *Pompei: abitare sotto il Vesuvio*: Zevi (1996a); Lazzarini and Zevi (1988–9).

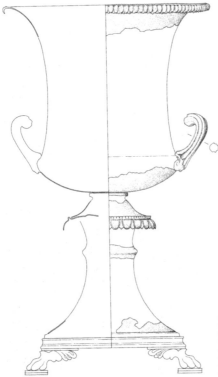

Figure 8.23 Calyx *crater* from the Mahdia wreck (drawing Rheinisches Landesmusem Bonn, courtesy Musée Nationale du Bardo, Tunis)

Figure 8.24 Calyx *crater* from the House of Julius Polybius, Pompeii (courtesy Soprintendenza Archeologica di Napoli e Pompei)

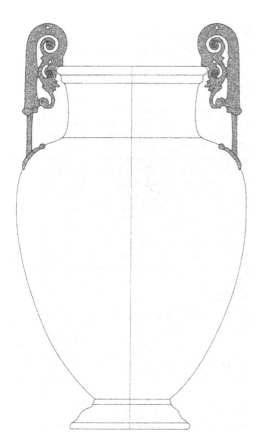

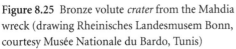

Figure 8.25 Bronze volute *crater* from the Mahdia wreck (drawing Rheinisches Landesmusem Bonn, courtesy Musée Nationale du Bardo, Tunis)

Figure 8.26 Bronze calyx and volute *craters* from Herculaneum (from Carlo Ceci, *Piccoli bronzi del Real Museo Borbonico* (Naples 1854), tav. IV)

Strabo's vivid account of how the Caesarian colonists of Corinth, whom he characterizes as 'mostly of the freedman class', ransacked old graves in pursuit of valuable loot, terracottas and bronzes (doubtless hoping for 'Corinthian' ones), which they sold in Rome as 'Necrocorinthia';[126] it is plausible enough that the piece reached Italy as such loot or plunder, for the passions of collectors doubtless generated the antiquities trade then as now. That the *hydria* was a prized object to acquire is also suggested by the three *hydriae* on the Mahdia wreck.

By coincidence, the volute *crater* from Mahdia (figure 8.25) takes us to another example of collectors' passion. Pompeii seems to produce no example of the type, but Petrovsky points to a close parallel from Herculaneum (figure 8.26).[127] But what is its date? The closest parallels to the Herculaneum

[126] Strabo 8.6.23.   [127] Petrovsky (1994) 671.

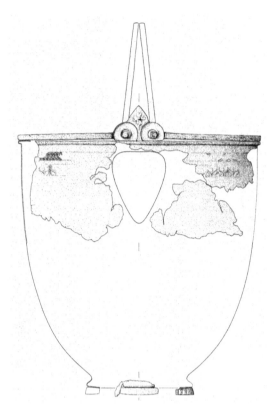

Figure 8.27 Bronze bucket from the Mahdia wreck
(drawing Rheinisches Landesmusem Bonn, courtesy
Musée Nationale du Bardo, Tunis)

example are from a fourth-century tomb at Derveni, a late fifth-
century tomb at Agrigento, and an unknown context in Apulia (Vasta).
Claude Rolley suggests that the Herculaneum piece is a fourth-century
collector's item from Apulia; but concedes that it is virtually impossible
to exclude the possibility of a later reproduction.[128] The point is that the
Roman passion for collection flowed directly into production and reproduction, in Greece and then locally, and it is extraordinarily hard for us to
draw the line. The Mahdia cargo merely confirms that these are the sort of
goods Romans wanted to import.

The overlap between bronzes found on the wreck, and those found in
the Vesuvian cities is nearly, but not quite, perfect. Pompeii produces no
incense burners (unless they are hidden away in the Naples collection); on

---

[128] Rolley (1995).

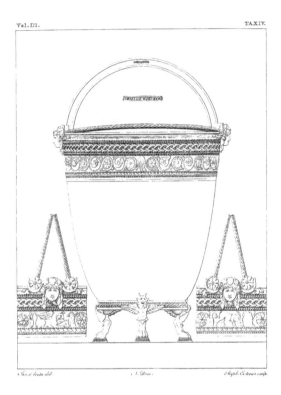

Figure 8.28 *Situla* of Cornelia Chelidon, Naples
Museum (drawing from *Real Museo Borbonico* (Naples
1827), tav. XIV, etc.)

the other hand, they are represented on the walls of Pompeii in 'second-style'
paintings.[129] Pompeii also seems to lack *hydriae*, apart from the spectacular
example in the House of Julius Polybius. On the other hand, it can match
the buckets (*situlae*) of Mahdia (figure 8.27). These are no common or
garden buckets, but richly decorated showpieces, especially the type with
ovoidal bodies (Tassinari's type X1200): of the two examples of these, one
comes from the magnificent House of the Menander (I.10.4), the other
from the bizarre back-street collection of Epidius Primus (I.8.14). But the
finest example is from the Naples Museum, known as the '*Situla* of Cornelia
Chelidon' from the name stamped in the rim (figure 8.28).[130] The inlaid
ornamentation in copper and silver against the dark tone of the bronze
suggests that this must be a specimen of what Romans called Corinthian
bronze, a collector's item indeed. Yet the Latin name stamped during the

[129] Riz (1990) 96, no.195.
[130] For fine colour illustrations, see Pirzio Biroli Stefanelli (1990) 112, plates 190–191.

lost wax manufacturing process confirms its Italian manufacture, perhaps in the mid first century BCE.

If the Mahdia wreck offers a decent sample of early first-century BCE luxury bronzes, it is certainly not a complete selection (and the battered and fragmentary state of the bronzes indicates that other pieces were lost). One well-documented example of a missing item much valued at this period is the *authepsa* or 'automatic boiler'. We met above Cicero's attack on Sulla's powerful freedman Chrysogonus, with his collection of Corinthian and Delian vessels, including an *authepsa*, which he bought at auction for the price of an estate (p. 355).[131] The passage is an important reminder both of who acquired luxuries, and how. The buyer is not a member of the senatorial elite, but one of those powerful freedman dependants who foreshadow the imperial freedman (such as C. Julius Polybius of Pompeii, evidently either an imperial freedman or a freedman of an imperial freedman); the status exclusion of such men is precisely the motor for the investment in luxury as an alternative expression of status. He buys neither by direct order from Greece (like Cicero), nor from an importer, but at an auction, presumably of the estate of one of the proscribed. Goods that enter the system with conquest rapidly pass into circulation within the internal market system.

The automatic boiler is a characteristic piece of hellenistic ingenuity, of the application of science to comfort, and especially to 'automata', devices that work without slave labour, that is typical of centres like Alexandria. The construction of one such is described in the *Pneumatics* (2.34) of the prolific author of engineering, Heron of Alexandria, probably of the mid first century CE (assuming that he refers to an eclipse of 62 CE).[132] The principle is to create an internal system of tubing within a bronze cylinder so that water circulates around the hot coals and even, in Heron's example, uses the steam to blow on the coals (figure 8.29). Heron refers to the device as a *miliarium*, which is the name also used by Seneca in his *Natural Questions*.[133] It is thus an appliance familiar both to scientists and the world of luxury by the first century CE. Technology serves social need, and as Katherine Dunbabin has demonstrated, the use of the appliance presupposes a significant change from the consumption rituals of the classical Greek symposium. Instead of mixing wine and water in the communal *crater* to the same strength for all guests, Roman diners took their water individually to taste, hot or cold.[134] We may recall the ingenious device by which Nero

---

[131] *pro Roscio Amerino* 133.   [132] Drachmann (1948).
[133] Seneca, *Natural Questions* 3.24.1 and 4.9; Hilgers (1969) 118, 221.   [134] Dunbabin (1993).

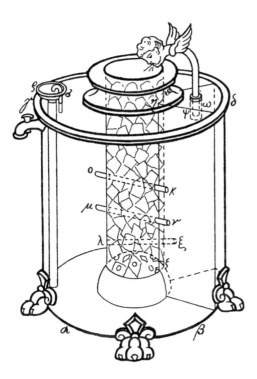

Figure 8.29 Illustration of 'automatic' boiler from
Heron of Alexandria (drawing from Dunbabin
1993, figure 15b, after Schmidt)

is said to have poisoned his half-brother Britannicus at an open feast, by
having the poison added in the water which he asked for after the poison-
taster had checked the wine.[135] Seneca waxes indignant against the luxurious use of snow to cool wine in summer;[136] the addition of hot water to
taste from an automatic boiler was the flip side of this luxury, and Dunbabin
finds the appliance featuring in representations of the *convivium* on mosaics
from Ephesus, Malaga, Carthage, Hippo Regius and Piazza Armerina, on
the Sevso silver plate, and on sarcophagi and catacomb paintings from Rome
(figure 8.30).

The latest study of surviving specimens identifies twenty-seven examples from across the Empire, stretching from the first to fifth centuries CE
(figure 8.31).[137] The largest number (eight) is from the Vesuvian area; otherwise only one is registered from Italy outside Campania, five from North
Africa (including three from Cyrene), four from Bulgaria, three each from
Switzerland and Turkey, one each from France, Hungary and Spain. The

[135] Tacitus, *Annals* 13.16.2.   [136] *Natural Questions* 4B, 13.   [137] Buck (2002).

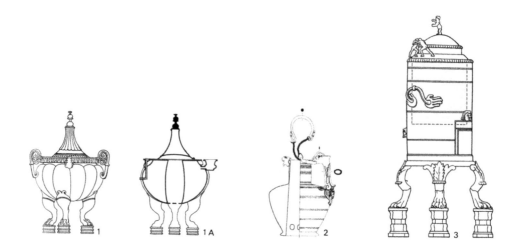

Figure 8.30 Types of *authepsa* from Roman world (drawing after Buck 2002, Abb. 2 by E. Weber)

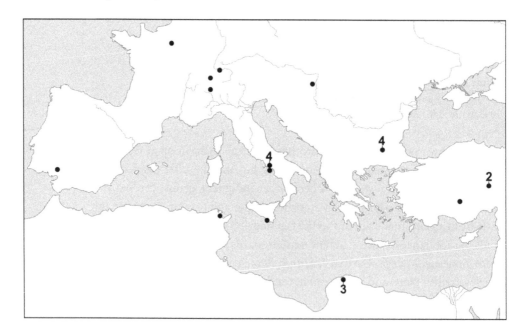

Figure 8.31 Distribution map of finds of *authepsae* in the Roman world (by Amy Richardson)

concentration in the Vesuvian area might indeed indicate that it was a centre of production for this, as for so much other, bronze ware. But above all it illustrates the chances of survival: bronze is too easily melted down to survive under normal, non-volcanic, circumstances. The Pompeian examples are splendid pieces, which lend themselves to illustration. The *Bronzo*

Figure 8.32 Bronze boiler from Pompeii (photo Alfredo Foglia, courtesy Soprintendenza Archeologica di Napoli e Pompei)

dei Romani catalogue offers three varied examples: one a samovar with a melon shaped body on lion's paws, one a complex rectangular brazier with a cylindrical boiler and rich decoration including Siren feet, and one an ovoidal body decorated with Medusa's heads (figure 8.32).[138] There were evidently many variations in design in this prestige item. Tassinari registers two examples from the site collection in Pompeii (Y2000), and at last we can comment on the context of these notable finds. They come, strikingly,

[138] Pirzio Biroli Stefanelli (1990), plates 207, 216–17 and 218–19, respectively.

from two medium-sized but well-decorated houses, the House of the Ceii (I.6.15), and the House of the Fruit Orchard (I.9.5).[139] A third, found in house V.4.1, was sent to Naples;[140] this was a bakery, of too little distinction to pick up a modern name. We are reminded yet again that the rarest and most sought-after objects are not found exclusively in the grandest houses.

Craters, *situlae* and *authepsae* are evidently *de luxe* objects. Is it reasonable to speak of other bronze vessels in similar terms, or are they rather standard household utensils? It is, according to the present argument, scarcely helpful to draw such a distinction. The wide range of bronze vessels catalogued by Tassinari seem to come from the same workshops, produced by the same lost wax techniques, and there is an enormous consistency in the language of decorative details (masks, bird's heads, animal feet etc.) which cross the typological boundaries. Moreover, they are found in close association with one another: we need only think of the way that the owners of the House of Julius Polybius had piled all their bronze wares together, including antique collector's items, in one corner of the house during building works. It never occurred to them to separate domestic utensils from collectables. Inherent in the language of any world of goods is that some items were more valued and prized than others; size, elaboration, richness of decoration will be among the criteria. This does not mean that the humblest items do not belong to the same semantic system.

We have already seen that when the findspots of the more conspicuous items are known in Pompeii, they do not adequately map onto their hierarchy of the houses themselves. This is closely linked to another striking phenomenon: the degree to which bronze vessels are distributed throughout the housing stock. If one takes a stretch of houses like insulae 6–12 of Regio I, for which the archival records are relatively well preserved,[141] there is scarcely a house that that does not have at least some bronze vessels. It is virtually impossible to establish a meaningful correlation between size of house and richness of room-decoration on the one hand, and frequency of bronze vessels on the other. There is a considerable gap between the numbers of vessels now possible to inventory, and the numbers originally found. So the 'bronze-smith' Verus in I.6.3 originally had thirty-three vessels among a total of 134 bronze objects, but only sixteen are inventoried.[142] These difficulties are part of the larger question of the turmoil of the finds of Pompeii, that cascade from poor excavation and recording, to robbing of

---

[139] Illustrated in *Rediscovering Pompeii* (1990) 189.   [140] Tassinari (1993) 233.
[141] Tassinari (1993) 123–52, Berry (1995).   [142] Tassinari (1993) 223.

Figure 8.33 Examples of domestic bronze ware from Pompeii (photo Hay/Sibthorpe, courtesy British School at Rome)

the site after the eruption, to the disruptive force of the eruption itself, to the confused state of the city before the eruption due to the effect of repeated earthquakes.[143] Suffice it to say that the Pompeian evidence indicates that bronze wares were as much a part of the everyday life of each and every inhabitant as was terracotta (figure 8.33).

That phenomenon is surely linked to the existence of local centres of production. The common assumption that the centre was Capua stems from the combination of Cato's statement to that effect with the observation of the frequency of bronzes in the Campanian sites.[144] Bettina Gralfs was able to identify twelve metal workshops in and around Pompeii.[145] Rather than seeing Capua as the sole place of production, we are surely looking at an activity widespread in Campania.[146] Though the scale may be 'industrial', the methods are were not mechanical, and are unlikely to have involved large numbers of workers in any workshop but rather, as suggested by Tassinari's ethnographic parallels, a concentration of numerous small workshops, each turning out more or less the same products to the same models. The ultimate models for many vessels, and most of the decorative details, have come from the eastern Mediterranean, and the occasional valuable 'import' survives among the collectors' items. But production has gone local by the first

---

[143] Allison (2004).   [144] Cato, *de Agricultura* 135.
[145] Gralfs (1988).   [146] Tassinari (1993) 222–4.

century CE, if not earlier, and reaches a massive scale capable of penetrating not only all Pompeian houses, but far-flung reaches of the empire.

The best illustration of this process, because the most intensively studied, is the production of the handled dishes misleadingly called *casseruole* and *paterae*. The reasons for the intensity of study of these forms are to do both with the frequency of their occurrence in Germany, and with the frequency of maker's stamps. German research focused on *Kleinaltertümer* long before Italian, with its predilection for the 'high' arts, and in the long absence of the necessary cataloguing work of the Italian material, the fundamental studies were based on the material in Germany[147] or Hungary,[148] at least until the renewed interest in material culture promoted by Andrea Carandini.[149] In particular, the production of the workshop or workshops of the Cipius family attracted attention, with two studies published in the same year, one by a German scholar,[150] one by two Italians.[151] A major study by Petrovsky is still awaited.

It is ironical and symptomatic of the state of the evidence that we cannot even agree as to the use of these vessels. What is traditionally called a *casseruola* or saucepan is a small but deep pan with steep sides and a flat, horizontal handle, ideally designed for stacking in multiples.[152] With 190 examples catalogued from Pompeii, it is the commonest type of bronze vessel after the varieties of jug. The Italian name suggests cooking, but there are no traces of burning on the Pompeian examples, and there is a strong argument that it belongs to the context of washing and *toilette*.[153] The *patera* is also a pan with a handle, but it is shallower and more sloped, and its handle is round in section, making stacking awkward. In artistic terms, it is a more elaborate object, both in the grooving of the underside, caused by the turning of the wax patrix on the lathe (the 'patrix' being the positive from which the negative 'matrix' is formed),[154] and in the elaboration of the handle, most frequently with a ram's head. There are sixty-two such *paterae* at Pompeii, the majority of which have ram's heads, each of which, thanks to the lost wax process, is individually executed (figure 8.34).[155] The Latin word is certainly a misnomer, since it is appropriate neither for pouring offerings in sacrifice nor for drinking wine.[156] It is particularly unlikely that such fine objects should be put anywhere near a fire. In the burial contexts of northern Europe it is frequently found associated with a pouring jug, and it is suggested that *patera* and jug form a pair in ritual washing, since

---

[147] Willers (1907), Eggers (1951).   [148] Radnóti (1938).   [149] Carandini (1977).
[150] Kunow (1985).   [151] Massari and Castoldi (1985).   [152] Tassinari (1993) 210–12.
[153] Nenova-Merdjanova (2002).   [154] Poulsen (1995).
[155] Tassinari (1993) 210, 227.   [156] Hilgers (1969) 242–4.

Figure 8.34 Bronze ram's-head *patera* from the House of C. Iulius Polybius, Pompeii, inv. 21798 (photo Soprintendenza Archeologica di Pompei)

a slave can hold the dish with his left hand as he pours with his right.[157] At least one test case confirms the association in Pompeii, too, and underlines the importance of studying the precise locations and associations of artefacts.[158]

Two points can be made relevant to the present argument. The first is that these pans, though exceptionally widely diffused among Pompeian households, are certainly not mere cooking ware; at least in the *patera* version, they are objects of some elegance, and their use belonged either to domestic religious ritual, or to social rituals of washing. The second is that while we are certainly looking at a local production, it enjoys extraordinary success in diffusion, not just to the provinces, but across the frontiers, where such objects are eagerly acquired by barbarians across the German and British frontiers, and into Denmark, the Baltic and the Black Sea, to form part of their grave-goods. At least for the barbarians, these objects were associated with prestige not utility; they represent the point at which, unwilling though the tribes might be to 'romanise' politically, they could exchange cultural goods and ideas.

---

[157] Nuber (1972).   [158] Sarnataro (2002).

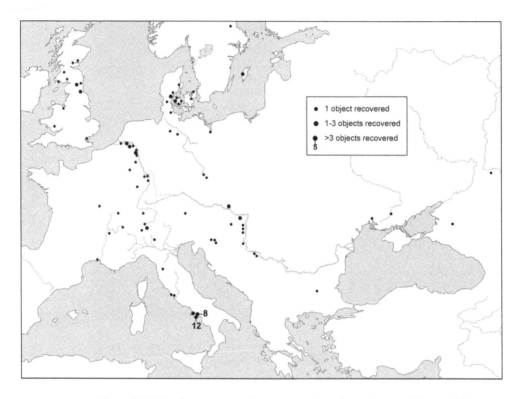

Figure 8.35 Distribution map of bronze ware from the workshop of the Cipii (by Amy Richardson after Kunow 1985)

The range of names stamped on these pans attests to the vigour and diversity of the Campanian bronze industry. The Cipii alone have twelve separate names, all of freedmen; each stamp is individual, and even the spellings of the names vary (so POLYBI/POLIBI/POLIBY/POLVYBI), suggesting they were not written by the person named (figure 8.35). Well over thirty different names are found on the stamps attested in the Vesuvian cities: it was a large and ramifying business. This is an astonishing boom in terms of production and, as Carandini suggests, it belongs to a tightly defined chronological period, starting under Augustus and already petering out by the Flavians. It runs parallel to the story of production in many other areas of consumer goods; and it runs parallel to the evident economic success of freedmen on the Bay of Naples in the first century CE.[159] Spurred by a fashion wave that starts with Roman desire for the hellenistic, it generates under Augustus a productive mechanism that can reach beyond the frontiers of empire, with profound consequences for the sub-elite.

[159] Carandini (1977) 167–8.

Pottery: from Samian to Arretine

Pottery lamps, as we have seen, functioned to some degree as a downmarket version of bronze lamps; yet though the ultimate parentage is of hellenistic bronze forms, the enormous imperial production establishes its own styles and its own aesthetic aspirations. Pottery vessels were similarly a downmarket version of metal, especially silver, ones: they allude in several ways to their metal parentage, and yet within their earthy limitations offered a luxury ware that reached far beyond the elite.

Roman sources leave us in no doubt that they considered pottery as a cheap alternative to metal; yet acknowledge that pottery merited its own respect. The labels typically attached to such pottery were 'Samian' and 'Arretine'. One vivid passage, an imaginary speech from an early-first-century rhetorical manual describing the behaviour of a pretentious rogue, sets out the contrast.[160] Mr Pretentious is a social climber, bluffing his way in company. He takes a group of friends into a house where a banquet is being prepared, and pretends it is his own. The silver is laid out, the *triclinium* is spread for dinner. He invites his friends back at dinner time, and disappears. They arrive to discover the fraud. But when they question him the next day, he pretends that they had got the wrong address, and invites them anew. He gets his smart slave-boy, Sannio, to find vessels (*vasa*), coverings (for the *triclinium* couches), and slaves to wait. When the guests arrive, the host explains to them he has lent his principal house for a wedding. Sannio then spins a story about the silver ware being requested for the wedding. The rogue waxes ironical: 'To hell with him! I have lent him my house and my staff, and now he wants my silver? Well, even though I have guests to dinner, I'll let him have it; we'll enjoy the Samian ware.' The scene, written in the style of contemporary comedy, with boastful masters and scheming slaves, nevertheless evokes with some precision the social context of the usage of luxury items. The sign of social success is to entertain your guests to dinner in a large house with a large slave staff, with silver laid and rich coverlets spread at the *triclinium*. 'Samian' pottery has to be excused.

A series of other passages make plain this contrast of prestigious silver with non-prestigious Samian was proverbial.[161] It goes back to the early second century in Plautus.[162] Cicero cites a speech of the orator Laelius

---

[160] *ad Herennium* 4.51.64.   [161] Gatti and Onorati (1992) 244–7.

[162] *Bacchides* 202, a *vas Samium* for something proverbially easy to break; *Menaechmi* 178, easily broken doors described as 'Samian'; *Captivi* 292, a miser uses *Samia vasa* for household sacrifice in case the household genius steals the plate; *Stichus* 694 contrasts a rich household with our 'Samiolum poterium'.

in the second century BCE asserting that the (presumably silver) sacrificial ware of the pontiffs was as welcome to the gods as Samian; while in his defence of Murena he notes as an example of unrealistic Stoic ideology the setting of a *triclinium* for a funerary feast with goat-skin and *vasa Samia*.[163] This Stoic gesture however suggests a counter-ideology, one favoured by the Augustan poets in the context of the theme that the luxuries of the rich are superfluous to the simple life of a decent person, that preferred a stance of ironical modesty. So Tibullus elaborates the contrast between himself, the poor poet living in the country, and the sort of rich man to whom girls are attracted, with vast acres and flocks of sheep, a private jetty on the sea and well-stocked fishponds: he, the poet, dines in happy companionship with Samian crockery, and the smooth pottery thrown on the wheels of Cumae.[164] Simultaneously, the poetic theme underlines the gulf between the lifestyle of the rich and the poor, and reclaims dignity for that of the poor. As Martial puts it, 'you would do well not to be too contemptuous of Arretine ware, for king Porsena dined elegantly from pottery':

Arretina nimis ne spernas vasa monemus:
lautus erat Tuscis Porsena fictilibus.[165]

Similarly, he stands up for the dignity of the chalices of Sorrento, one of Pliny's 'noble' productions, using the language of metal ware, *toreuma*: 'accept (the gift of) chalices made of no cheap dust, but the smooth turning of a Sorrentine wheel':

accipe non vili calices de pulvere natos
    sed Surrentinae leve toreuma rotae.[166]

It is to this moralising, anti-luxury context that Pliny's comments on the 'ennoblement' of centres of pottery production belong. After his invectives against the use of precious metals, he is more than happy to celebrate the generosity of the earth in providing the material for storage jars, water tubes, bath tiles, roof tiles and building bricks:

The majority of mankind use earthenware vessels. Samian vases are still, even now, praised as eating wares. This nobility is attained in Italy by Arretium, and for chalices only by Surrentum, Hasta and Pollentia; in Spain, by Saguntum; and in Asia, by Pergamum. In Asia too are the workshops of Tralles, and in Italy those of Mutina, since this too is a way by which peoples are ennobled, and these products too, from

---

[163] *Republic* 6.2.2; *pro Murena* 36.75.
[164] *Elegies* 2.3.47–8: 'at mihi laeta trahant Samiae convivia testae, fictaque Cumana lubrica terra rota', cf. Horace, *Satires* 1.6.117f, Statius, *Silvae* 4.9.43, etc.
[165] Martial, *Epigrams* 14.98f.   [166] 14.102.1–2, cf. 4.46.16 and 12.74.5.

famous workshops of the wheel, are transported hither and thither across land and sea.[167]

Pliny emphatically claims the high status of major pottery production (*nobilitatem, nobilitantur, insignibus*), and appreciates the role of cross-Mediterranean trade on a vast scale in stimulating the growth of centres like Arretium or Pergamum. He is thinking about an economic phenomenon, even if not in a modern economic way.[168]

The transformation of Italian pottery production that takes place in the second half of the first century BCE is one of the most remarkable aspects of the Roman consumer revolution. The body of study dedicated to this material is so enormous that the salient issues relevant here may be summed up with relative brevity. Italian pottery production between the fourth and first centuries BCE is dominated by the black-glaze ware labelled Campanian, though Etruria, to a lesser extent Sicily, and Rome itself were as important as centres of production as was Campania (figure 8.36). While these black-glaze wares are distinctive, and readily recognised by the non-expert, not least from their high-gloss black finish, it takes the eye of the expert to detect the progression of forms and decoration over the course of three hundred and more years; the massive achievement of Morel's catalogue is to provide a fairly tight dating-range for each of his morphologically distinguished types.[169] The relative consistency of appearance of this black-glaze ware over an extended period makes it virtually impossible to see in it the impact of the 'hellenisation' supposedly typical of the second century BCE. Though its styles may ultimately derive from classical Greek precedents, and the Etruscan-produced Campana B had strong affinities to the toreutic tradition of silver vases,[170] it shows no impact of the major waves of fashion that affect eastern production in the third and second centuries.[171] Alongside Campanian black-glaze are a variety of other styles; perhaps most notably as a more lavish decorated style, the 'Gnathian' pottery, from central and south Italian centres as well as Egnatia, which with its decorative details in white and orange slip is closely parallel to the 'West Slope' wares of Athens. 'Thin wall' wares, in unglazed red clay, come in towards the end of the second century, and overlap in use both with black-glaze ware and its successor.[172]

Easily the most significant change in the face of Italian pottery is the displacement of black-glaze in the second half of the first century BCE by the red-glaze wares variously called Samian, Arretine or terra sigillata Italica (figure 8.37). 'Samian' is certainly a misnomer. We have seen that as early as the second century, it was the name for standard pottery in contrast

[167] *Natural History* 35.160–1.   [168] Pucci (1985) 365–6.   [169] Morel (1981).
[170] Morel (1981) 522–31.   [171] Morel (1976).   [172] Ricci (1985).

Figure 8.36 Examples of Campanian black-glaze wares from Pompeii (photo Hay/Sibthorpe, courtesy British School at Rome)

Figure 8.37 Examples of Arretine wares from Pompeii (photo Hay/Sibthorpe, courtesy British School at Rome)

to silverware. The label must therefore have been applied to black-glazed Campanian, and since this had nothing to do with the island of Samos, an attractive suggestion is that it was associated with the Praenestine family of Samiarii which played a prominent role in production.[173] That the Samiarii were named as 'makers of Samian ware' is more convincing than the converse, and the passage of Pliny which names Samian ('still, even now') and Arretine alongside each other both implies a succession, and suggests that Pliny at least assumed that Samian came from Samos. That it did not creates no problem, given how frequent it was for false geographical origins to be used as labels ('Corinthian' bronzes are another case).

If 'Samian' was used by the Romans for black-glaze, 'Arretine' surely was indeed their term for the new red-glaze style, in contrast to 'terra sigillata' which despite its reassuring Latin formation, is a completely modern invention to create a bogus technical terminology, and in so far as it implies stamping with decorative punches, applies only to the decorated, and not the commoner plain wares.[174] That the new style was known after its largest single centre of production in Arezzo is confirmed not only by Pliny and other literary references like Martial, but most impressively by the potters' stamps themselves, which refer several times to *Arretin*(um, i.e. *poculum*), and even to the potter as an 'Arretine potter', such as 'A Titi figul(i) Arret(ini)'.[175] That evidence is the more impressive when found on a vessel evidently not from Arezzo itself: the fact that ARRETI and the like are especially common on pots produced in Pozzuoli and outside Arezzo shows that 'Arretine' had become a brand name, like Champagne, used beyond its proper home.[176] If the potter Scotius from Le Graufesenque in south Gaul could describe his pots as 'Arretine' – 'Scotius fec(it) Arretinu(m)' – it had truly become a household name.[177]

There seems to be a substantial contrast in the contemporary perceptions of Samian and Arretine. Samian was proverbially cheapskate: you had to be a Stoic or a lovesick poet to be proud of it. Arretine was indeed, as Martial suggested, not to be sniffed at, and as Pliny claimed, it made a name for Arezzo. The sheer quality of the new red-glaze was of a different order. It differed visibly from the old wares in at least four ways. First, its colour. The difference between a red and black glaze lies simply in the firing, in how the oxidisation takes place in the kiln. There is no great technological advance, and indeed it is actually simpler to produce red. It is a clear example

[173] Gatti and Onorati (1992) 226–31.   [174] Comfort (1966) 726.
[175] *Thesaurus Linguae Latinae* II, 636, 28ff.; Kenrick (2000) 440, no. 2169.
[176] Kenrick (2000) 11.   [177] Hoffmann (1995) 399.

of change of taste. The choice of black is probably driven by the desire to imitate silver; as Vickers has argued, the oxidised finish of ancient silver meant that it was black, and closely comparable to the high-gloss black achieved by Campanian wares.[178]

The argument that the switch to red is driven by the new popularity of gold[179] is weakened both by the fact that gold had always been more prestigious than silver, and by the need to explain a similar shift in the eastern Mediterranean at least a century earlier, though it may be right in broad principle. What is referred to as Eastern Sigillata A developed in a still unidentified centre in the eastern Mediterranean from the mid second century BCE, and achieved a wide circulation, spreading to Italy, too.[180] The model for red-glaze was in circulation in Italy for up to a century, and it is as interesting that this was not imitated earlier as that it was later. But if the recent suggestion is right that this ware is the same as what Cicero called *Rhosica vasa* and despatched from Cilicia to Atticus in 50 BCE, we catch a vivid glimpse of the process by which the new red-glaze wares became collectables for the rich and powerful of Rome, and of how even a provincial governor might play a role in the spread of fashions.[181]

The second major contrast is that the upper range at least of Arretine was mould-made. A similar shift took place in Athens in the third century BCE. What are called 'Megarian bowls' represented a new-look pottery, based on imitation of metalwork (silver or gold) which, given the fondness for certain vegetal motifs like the lotus flower, probably came from Alexandria.[182] Susan Rotroff has argued for a precise context of Athenian friendship with Ptolemy III Euergetes in the 220s BCE.[183] From the third century on, this style of black-glaze pottery, in complete contrast to the wheel-made wares of the classical Attic tradition, dominates the finds, and is widespread in the eastern Mediterranean. It is imitated in Italy, too, in a red but unglazed version, in the class of wares known either after one production centre, in Otricoli, or more commonly after one potter, Popilius; yet it only gains a restricted circulation in central Italy north of Rome, is scarcely found south of Rome and has no impact on Campanian black-glaze.[184] As with the choice of red glaze, the model for moulded wares had long been to hand, and it is testimony to the conservatism of the dominant Campanian wares that it was not adopted sooner.

---

[178] Vickers, Impey and Allan (1986).   [179] Vickers (1994).

[180] Hayes (1985) 9–13.   [181] Malfitana, Poblome and Lund (2005).

[182] Hayes (1997) 40 illustrates the debt to metal ware.   [183] Rotroff (1982) 9–13.

[184] Paribeni (1963), Del Chiaro (1961).

Figure 8.38 Arretine bowl from Perennius workshop (photo Ashmolean Museum, Oxford, AN 1966.250/EKTK11)

The third innovation of Arretine lay in the forms and decorative motifs it chose. Red-glaze plain wares were much closer to black-wares in manufacture and style; but even they adopted some distinctive forms that do not come out of the previous repertory, especially the flat dishes and sloping-wall bowls which are so typical.[185] But it is the moulded wares that mark out Arretine's exceptional quality. This technique, which we have met repeatedly as fundamental to the hellenistic style of bronze work and lamp-making, allowed decoration of high quality in relief. Though the same techniques are used by the Megarian bowls of Athens and elsewhere, the decoration on them is not nearly so ambitious, being in lower relief and more standardised, primarily revolving around vegetal patterns. The complex scenes of Arretine make heavy use of figures, including sympotic and erotic themes, executed in sharp detail (figure 8.38). There are precedents for these in pottery: for instance, the copulating couples are anticipated by the appliqués on Pergamene wares of the second and first centuries BCE, which surely provided an actual model.[186] But even more important must be the silver ware on which the Pergamene pottery was based. Silver vessels, as we gather from Verres' attempts to appropriate the prize specimens of his Sicilian hosts,

---

[185] Ettlinger, Hedinger and Hoffmann (1990) 52ff., forms 1–16.   [186] Garbsch (1982) 30.

were highly desirable collectables for the Roman elite, prized in particular for their high-relief decoration. Arretine in its new forms, especially the 'chalice', and its introduction of a decorative repertoire effectively new to pottery, modelled itself closely on silver.

The fourth innovation lies in the use of potter's stamps. Over 90% of Arretine pots, both moulded and plain, bear maker's stamps. These stamps are a major focus of study, not least for the light they cast on the production processes. Kenrick's new edition of the *Corpus Vasorum Arretinorum* lists 2,585 stamps, each with several variants. They reflect the work of hundreds of different workshops, concentrated particularly in and around Arezzo, but with important production centres also in Pisa, Pozzuoli, the Po Valley and Lyon. Many workshops name separate slave-potters, including P. Cornelius with sixty-nine dependants, Rasinius with sixty-three, L. Titius with sixty, and C. Annius with thirty-seven.[187] As a source of information about the production of any class of material, it is exceptional, though it runs parallel to the stamping of certain bronze wares, as by the workshop of the Cipii (see p. 406). The function of these stamps has been endlessly discussed, not least for the potential light cast on the productive process: the suggestion that they served to distinguish the work of different potters placed in the same kiln for firing is attractive.[188] Rather than seeing modern 'firms', we are probably looking at a hierarchy very like that of brick production, with the equipment of production, from land and furnaces to the punches for decorating moulds, belonging to high-status *domini*, individual *officinae* or workshops leased under *locatio-conductio* to *officinatores*, and the potters or *figuli* working under contract for them.[189] What is interesting is that whatever purpose they served, there was no corresponding systematic marking of Campanian black ware, or any other earlier Italian wares. It is hard to resist the conclusion that the stamps were also (whatever productive function they had) marks of pride, of Plinian 'nobility'. The Arretine potters were genuinely interested in brand recognition, in making their names, like the name of Arezzo, known.[190] Their pottery was innovative, whatever the models, and demanded recognition in its own right.

All this raises the more acutely the question of why, and why now? These questions would be easier to answer if there was agreement about the precise date of introduction of Arretine. The chronology has long depended on the excavation of Augustan military camps, especially on the Rhine frontier, such as those at Oberaden and Haltern; it is frustrating that there is still no Italian

---

[187] Fülle (1997) 147–55.   [188] Fülle (1997) 117.
[189] Mees (2002).   [190] Kenrick (2000) 11–12.

site to provide a firm sequence for the early phases. On the military evidence, the production starts under Augustus, and many place it in the 20s BCE. Oxé tied the start explicitly to a Plinian wave of fashion, suggesting that M. Perennius Tigranes brought a troupe of eastern slaves to Arezzo immediately following the fall of Alexandria in 30 BCE, though it is now no longer accepted that M. Perennius was the first.[191] Others have pushed for an earlier date, especially in the light of the dating to the 40s of the Planier B wreck (figure 8.2, p. 362), which contained Arretine, and in this context an alternative 'wave of fashion' is the passion for gold following the eastern triumphs of Lucullus and Pompey in the late 60s and 50s BCE.[192] Philip Kenrick cautiously places the first phase of production in the span 40–20/15.[193]

The lack of clear archaeological evidence is the more frustrating because the decades of the 40s and 30s represent ones of significant upheaval in Italy. What is so remarkable is the way the Arretine simply displaces the black ware production of many centuries. It does not happen overnight, and the earliest Arretine forms are produced in black glaze as well as red, with many of the new red forms derived directly from the old Campanian ware; it looks as if the new styles took over within the same production centres, and especially those of Arezzo.[194] Etruria remained a focus of civil disturbance as a result of the triumviral land-distributions in the late 40s BCE; one might argue that it was not until the resistance of Lucius Antonius was broken by the siege of Perusia in 41 that any degree of stability returned to the area. The speed with which the new style spreads from Arezzo to other centres, including the Bay of Naples, the speed of displacement of the old Campanian production, and the rapid spread of products to the frontiers of military activity all surely point to the new conditions of stability that hold in Italy only from the 30s.

While it is hard to imagine that Octavian/Augustus took any direct hand in organising the pottery industry, it surely does respond to the conditions he creates. It may be no coincidence that Maecenas, who enjoyed his period of influence in the 30s and 20s, came from Arretium. Economic benefits flowed down the channels of political influence, and if we accept that behind the work of the relatively humble *officinatores* and *figuli* lie the interests of land-owners, renting out their plant, it is easy to imagine a scenario by which Maecenas benefits his rich and powerful friends locally. The frequency of these wares in military camps may be no coincidence. The Roman army on the march was encumbered by vessels, so much that 'collect your vessels',

---

[191] Wells (1990) 24.   [192] Vickers (1994).
[193] Kenrick (2000) 36–7.   [194] Ettlinger, Hedinger and Hoffmann (1990) 3–4.

'*vasa conclamari*', was a signal to the army to pack up and march.[195] It would only take Maecenas' influence in the assignment of contracts for the supply of Octavian/Augustus' armies with *vasa* to create a new boom in Arezzo. And why else should Augustus teasingly refer to his friend as 'jewel among potters', *iaspis figulorum*?[196]

The role of Maecenas must remain conjectural.[197] The broader question is of the consumers of the new Arretine. Again, the military camps can help us. Officers may well have carried silver ware on the march, like Pompeius Paulinus of Arles who carried 12,000 lb of plate with him on campaign,[198] though we should not assume too rapidly that officers were all above Arretine. But the sheer quantities of this pottery found indicate that its use was spread throughout the troops. We will recall that the new picture lamps are found in Switzerland only where there was a Roman military presence, and that the bronze ware of the Cipii and their like followed the armies to the Rhine frontier and beyond. The citizen-soldier of the Augustan legions, and his correlate, the veteran colonist, beneficiary of the massive land-distributions that transformed so many Italian cities, represent the target market for the new consumption of lesser luxuries. A key to the new Augustan social order is the restoration of dignity not only to the elite but to the citizen. The aspiration to new 'quality' wares by the citizen is part of an assertion of social dignity in a world re-emerging from chaos.

One point illustrated again from the development of Roman table wares is that the process of hellenisation by no means occurred by an automatic osmosis, spreading constantly from east to west. Campanian black-gaze remained uninfluenced by the mould-made 'Megarian' fashion dominant in the eastern Mediterranean for two centuries (despite notorious hellenistic influence in other fields), just as Athenian production shows no influence from the red Eastern sigillata current from the mid second century. Influence, as Rotroff underlines, is neither the automatic result of the emergence of new models, nor of conquest.[199] When the great shift in taste comes in Italy, it is not the result of the availability of new models, nor of the growth of fashion of one model, but of the deliberate creation of a new style which has precedents in numerous models: Campanian black, eastern red-glaze, 'Megarian' moulded wares, possibly Pergamene appliqués and even the lead-glazed wares of western Asia Minor,[200] not to speak of embossed silver wares. This is not a passive influence, but an active appropriation.

---

[195] Cicero, *Verrines* 6.49; Caesar, *Civil War* 1.66.   [196] Macrobius, *Saturnalia* 2.4.12.
[197] Pucci (1985) 366 denies a connection.   [198] Pliny, *Natural History* 33.143.
[199] Rotroff (1997).   [200] Hochuli-Gysel (1977).

Other classes of luxury and sub-luxury goods already discussed have suggested a pattern of distinct chronological phases. The major phase of importation of hellenistic goods belongs to the late republic, the second century and the first half of the first century BCE. In the Augustan phase of transition, around the turn of the era, production shifts to Italy, and goods based on hellenistic models but showing their own aesthetic independence are produced both for a much wider Italian market and are exported to the provinces. In the third, early imperial phase, production moves outwards in the wake of imports. Arretine is a text-book example of this model. The speed of this provincial diffusion is illustrated by the distribution maps for Kenrick's four phases of Arretine production (figure 8.39): in period A (40–20/15 BCE) finds are concentrated in Italy and South Gaul, with a small scattering further afield; in period B (20 BCE–15 CE), the dots spread densely up the Rhine and Danube frontiers, and throughout Gaul, Spain, North Africa, with a lighter presence in the eastern Mediterranean (Athens, Asia Minor, Cyprus, Syria, Egypt, Cyrene); by period C (15–50 CE), the dots have almost disappeared from Gaul and Spain, growing only in Italy and North Africa; while period D (50+ CE) represents a further contraction to Italy and North Africa.[201]

The last two phases of contraction correspond to the rise of provincial centres of production (figure 8.40). Arretine workshops are already active at Lyon (La Muette) between 10 BCE and 10 CE. Their wares can only be distinguished from those of Italian workshops by chemical analysis, and as much as half of the Arretine from Haltern confidently assigned by Loescke to Arezzo in fact comes from Lyon, which is a major reason for renaming 'Italian terra sigillata' as 'Italian-style terra sigillata'.[202] The southern Gallic centres enter serious production in the early first century CE, at Le Graufesenque (peaking in the late first century CE with over 260 potters), and Montans, and soon take over the market; these centres in turn see a shift to numerous central Gallic (Lezoux, Clermont-Ferrand, etc., peaking in the mid second century) and north-eastern sites like Rheinzabern, starting in the mid second, and flourishing until the mid third century, with over 600 named potters.[203] By an inescapable law of the market, as the production centres spread and the productivity increases, the levels of artistic input drop, leading to simpler and less deeply punched decorative moulds, that never match the aspirations of the original Augustan Arretine.

---

[201] Kenrick (2000) 38–50.   [202] Ettlinger, Hedinger and Hoffmann (1990) 1 and 19–20.
[203] Garbsch (1982) 41–61, Hofmann (1986).

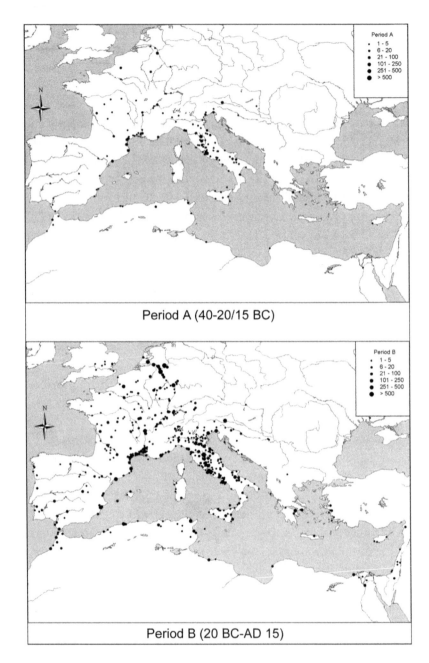

Figure 8.39 Spread of phases of Arretine production (drawing from Kenrick 2000, figures 5, 6, 7, 8)

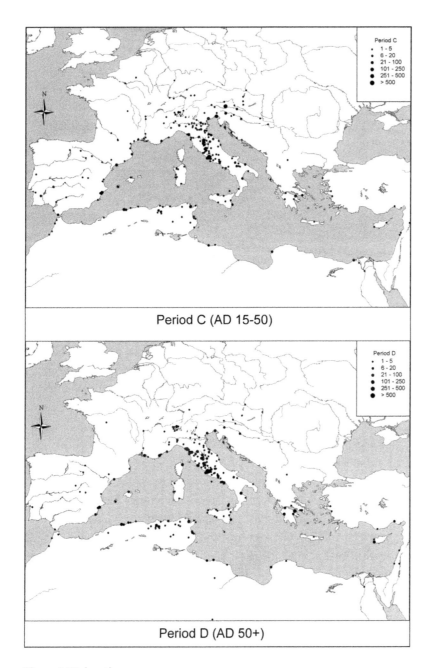

Period C (AD 15-50)

Period D (AD 50+)

Figure 8.39 (*cont.*)

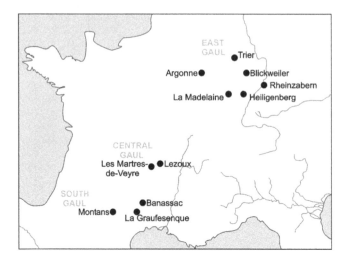

Figure 8.40 Map of Gallic and Rhenish centres of Arretine production (drawn by Amy Richardson)

Study of 'terra sigillata' focuses on the products of the western provinces, but it is important to note their impact in the eastern Mediterranean. Arretine reaches eastern centres from the first. The substantial presence in well-reported sites like Athens, Corinth and Olympia leads to the strong suspicion of underreporting elsewhere.[204] Rotroff, while playing down the presence and influence of Italian wares in Athens in the first century BCE, concedes that the picture is very different in the first century CE.[205] While there is no suggestion of Arretine 'branch offices' opening in the east, its style is deeply influential: the Eastern Sigillata A which may have initially provided a model for Italian red-glaze, shows the influence of Arretine from the first century CE, including the name stamps of the potters; the new and different production distinguished as Eastern Sigillata B, possibly from Tralles, mentioned by Pliny as an important centre, is a direct derivative of Arretine, and among the stamps, in Latin lettering, is the eloquent ARRETINA.[206] What Italy takes from the east, it transforms, and pumps back out.

It would be especially helpful for understanding who were the consumers of Arretine to be able to study its distribution house by house in Pompeii and Herculaneum; but again we are hampered by lack of a catalogue. Pucci's helpful overview examined 1,675 pieces from Pompeii, Herculaneum and Naples.[207] He counted thirty-four pieces with twenty-five different stamps from Arezzo workshops, thirty-nine with eighteen stamps from Pozzuoli, and seventy-seven with fifty-four stamps from uncertain Italian centres;

---

[204] Kenrick (2000) 38.   [205] Rotroff (1997).   [206] Hayes (1985).   [207] Pucci (1977).

together this material constituted only 19% of the total. 'Late Italic' pottery was enormously better represented: 767 examples from only fifteen work-shops, some in considerable quantities, like the 113 pieces of L. Rasinius Pisanus and the 133 of Xanthus. Evidently the pottery produced in the final three decades was the dominant presence. But alongside these is a signifi-cant number of foreign imports, 203 from South Gaul (including a famous batch of ninety pieces found together in house VIII.5.9, mainly from La Graufesenque), but also 210 examples of Eastern Sigillata A and 104 of East-ern Sigillata B. This is vivid testimony of the way pottery criss-crossed the Mediterranean, 'hither and thither across land and sea' as Pliny put it.[208] With pots just as with wines, we find imports and local products alongside each other at Pompeii.

As for the distribution of these wares between houses, there is little that can be said until we have more of the work pioneered by Pim Allison and Jo Berry to trace the full range of finds house by house. But even their samples show that red-glaze wares were common in virtually every house. In *Insula* I.9, this ranges from the relatively smart house of Ceres (13), with a large collection of Arretine stacked together in a single room, to the mish-mash of finds of the workshop/house I.9.8. Studies of individual houses, such as Sarnataro's of Volusius Faustus (I.2.10),[209] or Gallo's of Helvius Severus (I.13.2),[210] suggest that bronze, terracotta and glass, with the occasional piece of silver ware, worked together in close association to provide the needs of the ordinary household. It would be particularly helpful to understand better the social diffusion of the decorated moulded wares, as opposed to the much commoner plain ones. It is perhaps with these that we are best justified in describing terra sigillata as a *Luxusgeschirr* or 'luxury ware'.[211] It is luxury in the special sense of a consumer good that ultimately evokes a world of luxury, but gains its power from its wide penetration of the population.

Couches: recline to decline

Lamps and vessels offer a more or less consistent picture of fashions that come in with imported eastern luxuries, but develop an independent char-acter once produced in Italy, above all in the great Augustan boom, and then rapidly spread outwards to the provinces. It has only been possible to make the case for the spread of fashion from the elite to a broad sub-elite by looking at terracotta production. But this is not to suggest that all luxuries automatically developed their 'downmarket' versions, nor that all fashions

---

[208] *Natural History* 35.161.　　[209] Sarnataro (2002).
[210] Gallo (1994).　　[211] Garbsch (1982).

necessarily spread widely. Some of the limits to this picture emerge when we consider couches.

Bronze beds enjoy a special place in the annals of luxury. We have seen that Pliny cites the histories of Piso as authority for the claim that *triclinia aerata*, bronze-decorated dining couches, along with the tables called *abaci* and *monopodia*, were first brought to Rome in the triumph of Manlius Vulso in 187 BCE, a moment symbolic of the invasion of Asian luxury.[212] The taste grew. He reports another historian, Valerius Antias, as stating that the heirs of the orator Licinius Crassus (who died in the civil war in 87 BCE), sold many *triclinia aerata*. Pliny has several other titbits to offer on the history of bronze couches. In his discussion of the hierarchy of bronzes (Corinthian the best, followed by Delian and Aeginetan), he claims that Delos has the oldest reputation for bronze work, thanks to its position as an international market, and that their first claim to distinction (*prima aeris nobilitas*) was for making the feet and supports (*fulcra*) of dining couches.[213] He adds that their expertise then passed to images of gods, men and animals, surely a slightly garbled reference to the use of these themes on couches. The word *antiquissima* apparently implies that Delos had been producing couches for centuries, but the reference to the market makes clear that he is talking about the period from 168 BCE. Bronze couches could be trumped by silver ones. He states that the Roman *eques* Carvilius Pollio was the first to apply silver, and even gold, to couches, then rather confusingly adds that these were not of the Delian but the Punic type, and that Delian beds came to be silvered not long after.[214] A time frame is suggested by the elliptical remark that these things were 'expiated' by the Sullan civil war. Shortly after, he adds another citation suggesting that Sulla was in some way a turning-point: Cornelius Nepos reported that before Sulla's victory, there were only two silver couches in Rome.[215]

Pliny is not attempting to write a history of the Roman couch, and the titbits he feeds us give only a general impression: of bronze couches representing the first wave of hellenisation from the early second century, growing to a major luxury item, and becoming common enough by the 80s BCE for it to be worth raising the stakes by introducing silver. But here the archaeological record is relatively generous, and bears Pliny out in some surprising ways. A consignment of bronze couches formed part of the freight of the Mahdia wreck consisting, if Faust's calculations are right, of not less than twenty-two items (figure 8.41). Certainly, the high serial numbers on the bronze parts,

---

[212] *Natural History* 34.8.14.   [213] *Natural History* 34.9.
[214] *Natural History* 33.144.   [215] *Natural History* 33.146.

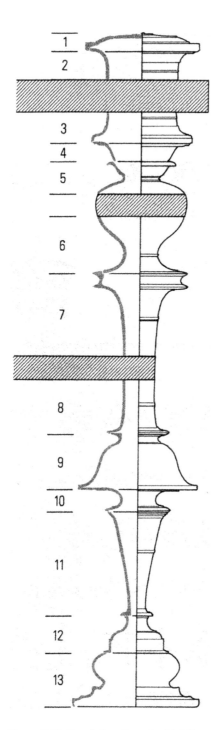

Figure 8.41 Couch legs from the Mahdia
wreck (drawing Rheinisches
Landesmusem Bonn, courtesy Musée
Nationale du Bardo, Tunis)

rising as high as 7,760, even if we do not accept the unspoken assumption that workshops started numbering at 1 each year, point to a manufacture of considerable volume, targeted at the Roman export market.[216] Bronze beds' parts are found on two other wrecks of approximately the same date, Antikythera and Formigue C (figure 8.2, p. 362), and the impression is of a much-shipped commodity. Interestingly enough, the presumed dates of these wrecks, in the 80s or 70s, coincide with the cluster of references in Pliny to the same period, the sale of Crassus' estate, Carvilius Pollio's experiments before the Sullan war and Nepos' count of two silver beds in this period.

There is some measure of archaeological confirmation, too, for Delos as the centre of production. Bronze is generally not well preserved on Delos, but excavations in the 1960s in the *îlot du quartier de Skardhana* produced several bronze pieces, including decorative appliqués for *fulcra*, particularly a Silenus head that has an almost exact parallel in marble on the same island. More important, three complete plaster moulds for bed-legs, together with a number of fragments, confirm one essential bronze-casting activity for couch manufacture.[217] There is no reason to doubt that Pliny was right in identifying Delos as the major centre for bronze beds in the second century BCE; the heavy Roman and Italic presence on the island makes it likely enough that *negotiatores* played a key role in organising a major production destined for export to Italy.

Is not Pliny, and behind him a row of moralising authors like Piso, Antias, Nepos and Fenestella, simply making too much fuss about a standard domestic item? The answer is no. Two considerations underline just how exotic and luxurious these bronze couches were. The first is the sheer quality of the craftsmanship repeatedly encountered in the numerous surviving examples, and the second the interesting misfit between the shape and size of such a dining couch and the customary practice of Roman dining. It is hard to get into the mind of the collector in another world; what we have to understand is that these were no ordinary domestic objects, but prized possessions to be displayed to guests at the critical social moment of the day, the *convivium*. One of the finest surviving examples, on display in the Palazzo dei Conservatori in Rome, is the couch found in a chamber tomb of the early first century BCE at Amiternum in Abruzzo: its richness and delicacy of detail is such that it occupies twenty illustrations in the *Bronzo dei Romani* catalogue, easily the largest number for any one item.[218]

Highly finished with coatings and inlays in silver, copper and glass-paste enamel, the Amiternum couch gives us an idea of what a Carvilius Pollio

---

[216] Faust (1994).   [217] Siebert (1973) 581ff.
[218] Pirzio Biroli Stefanelli (1990) 162–71, plates 118–37.

may have been up to in the addition of silver to his couches and, if this is as it must surely be, an example of what was called 'Corinthian' bronze, both alloyed and inlaid with precious metals (see pp. 374f.), it offers an insight into what drove collectors to pay small fortunes for it (figures 8.42–8.44). The legs, cast in the sort of mould met on Delos, in the complex lines of turned wood, are of a more coppery alloy of a warm gold colour; the feet are decorated with palmettes and tendrils in inlaid silver. Round the wooden bed-frame runs a decorative element in a dark bronze richly inlaid with floral motifs in silver, copper and red glass-paste. The crowning elements are, as always, the *fulcra* on which the diners rested their arms (softened, of course, by pillows); here, as often, there are rests at either end of the couch, in the pattern referred to an *amphithalamos* (double-bed). The *fulcra* are composed of three main elements: an S-shaped frame, following the lines of the arm-rest; a round medallion affixed to the bottom part where the rest meets the frame; and the decorative finial or *protome* at the top of the rest. The themes are drawn, as normally, from the Dionysiac repertoire: Maenads' heads for the medallion, the head of the braying donkey of Silenus for the *protome*, and a lush scene of vintage inlaid in the flat plate of the S-frame. The donkey's head is half-turned in alarm: its mouth open in a bray, its ears turned back in fear, its eyes wide open, shining out brightly in silver against the dark bronze background. Round its head runs a Bacchic garland of vines, the leaves and berries picked out in golden copper.

Not all examples were so lavishly decorated, though it is enough to look at the dozens of donkeys' and horses' heads (with the occasional lion or wolf, and even one elephant) and Maenad, satyr or Silenus medallions catalogued by Faust to see the high standards of bronze casting that prevailed – each element, we must remember, individually cast by the lost wax method so that no two examples are ever quite the same, familiar though the motifs may be.[219] We may be struck too by how common silver inlays are on surviving examples: eighty-six of 321 bronze couch elements catalogued have silver inlay, and three are of solid silver.[220]

The second observation which should make us hesitate before dismissing these couches as standard household furniture is the misfit between such a Greek *klinē* and the standard Roman *convivium* setting. The Latin '*triclinium*' is indeed a Greek loan-word, indicating a three-couch setting; but, as is familiar, the Roman convention was to place up to three diners on each couch. In the numerous examples of solid masonry couches that survive,

---

[219] Faust (1989) plates 34–53 for donkey heads, 54–60 for variants, 61–77 for Maenad/satyr/ Silenus medallions.
[220] Nos. 41, 386, 457.

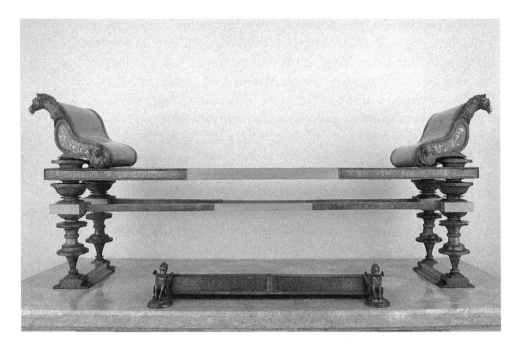

Figure 8.42 Amiternum couch, Capitoline Museum (photo Araldo De Luca, courtesy Musei Capitolini)

Figure 8.43 Amiternum couch, Capitoline Museum, detail of leg (photo Araldo De Luca, courtesy Musei Capitolini)

like the spectacular marble-lined examples from Murecine near Pompeii, the couch shape is longer and considerably wider than that of a Greek *klinē*, sloping downwards towards the back, and is without arm-rests. This arrangement comfortably accommodates three to a couch, in a way impossible on a narrow wooden *klinē*. The *fulcra* at the ends of the Greek couches

Figure 8.44 Amiternum couch, Capitoline Museum, detail of *fulcrum* (photo Zeno Colantoni, courtesy Musei Capitolini)

imply a symposiast reclining the entire length of a couch; any partner on the couch must lie in the intimacy presupposed by the standard Greek sympotic images of men with female or male sexual partners. The double *fulcrum* of the *amphithalamos* would be particularly awkward at a Roman table, where all guests lean on their left arms, leaving the right free for eating; whereas it would suit well a *hetaira* sitting at the end of the couch. These practical considerations seem so obvious that it is the more remarkable that none of the experts in the abundant literature that surrounds these couches raises the problem, or its implications for social practice.[221]

One answer might be that Roman dining practice was affected by the waves of luxury and hellenisation of the second century BCE, and that richer households abandoned the awkward Roman tradition of putting three diners

---

[221] The contrasts of Greek and Roman practice are discussed by Dunbabin (2003) 36–50, n. 9 for the problem of *fulcra*.

together on a couch. Yet this is abundantly contradicted by the archaeological evidence, which shows the three-by-three setting at its normative peak in the late republic and early empire, whether in masonry *triclinia*, or in the T + U patterns in floor-decoration which so neatly define the expected position of the couches.[222] Indeed, some argue that the *triclinium* setting itself is no older than the second century, and is the product of hellenistic influence.[223] Yet it is hard to see where in Greek practice an insistence on a three-couch setting might come from; it is surely much older, and the sheer awkwardness of a three-couch setting based on the *klinē* tells strongly against the hypothesis.

The tenacity of the Roman insistence on three couches emerges obliquely from Varro's recurrent use of the 'setting' of a dining room to explain the principles of similarity and dissimilarity that govern linguistic usage. He puts the counter-factual case that if you followed the strict principles of similarity or *analogia*, you would not have beds that were not all of the same size or shape: they would all be of the same form, either with or without *fulcrum*, either triclinium-type or *cubiculum*-type; nor could you have decorative distinctions like the use on some of ivory.[224] But to this *reductio ad absurdum* of the analogist position, there is a good answer: you can have different types of bed within the household, but not in the same setting. Anybody who set a *triclinium* and had one of the three couches unequal would be corrected.[225] He returns to the problem again: you may ask, if you follow the principles of similitude, why do we prefer to have some beds of ivory, some of tortoiseshell, and some of other types? But who would dream of setting the *triclinium* except with beds of the same material and height and shape? Who wouldn't ensure the *triclinium* spreads matched? Or the cushions?[226]

Varro's insistence on the importance of matched settings should have made Mau hesitate before suggesting that the *fulcra* were placed by Romans at the bottom end of the first couch of a three-couch setting and the top end of the last.[227] The hateful asymmetry would have had Varro's friends wagging their fingers. But Varro also points to a better answer. Not all the couches in the house had to be the same, nor used in the same place. There was room in the Roman household for all types of beds, in all shapes or forms, with or without *fulcra*. The standard Roman *triclinium* was evidently no place for a set of Delian *klinai*, though of course one could make a setting consisting of three *klinai*.

[222] Dunbabin (2003) 41.   [223] Dunbabin (2003) 46.   [224] *De Lingua Latina* 8.32.
[225] *De Lingua Latina* 9.9.   [226] *De Lingua Latina* 9.47–8.   [227] Mau (1896).

Faust catalogues the remains of decorative elements from forty-five couches in Pompeii, thirty-one of bronze, five of ivory and nine of bone. Among these, there are only two from groups of three found in the same room: one from the house of C. Vibius (VII.2.8), one from that of Julius Polybius (IX.13.1–3).[228] In addition, three finely inlaid couches were found in a *triclinium* in the villa at Boscoreale.[229] It is true that it is not always easy for the excavator to distinguish the number of couches from the jumble of bronze appliqués found. Maiuri described finding the mixed remains of two couches in the *tablinum* of the House of the Menander and, worried by their presence there and their absence from the *triclinium*, suggested the placing was temporary.[230] Faust distinguishes parts of four couches rather than two. It is hard indeed to say whether the finds of 79 CE are in their proper places or not,[231] but we should not leap to the conclusion that *klinai* belonged to a *triclinium*. Otherwise we must start worrying about the numerous grand houses, like that of Fabius Rufus, where remains of a single couch only have been found.[232] What are we to make of the House of the Ephebe (I.7.11), from which we have met a fine hellenistic bronze ephebe serving as a lampstand, where again a single mule *protomē* was found in the *triclinium*?[233] While the numbers suggest that couch decorations were reasonably well spread in domestic use, Herculaneum with its organic remains usefully reminds us of the many items of furniture made of wood and leather that do not show up in the Pompeian record.[234]

One context in which decorated couches are especially common is not convivial, but funerary. The Amiternum couch described in figures 8.42–8.44 is one of two coming from a chamber tomb, and to that it owes its excellent condition. But particularly favoured for burials were couches of ivory, or its cheaper version, bone. Ivory and bone couches certainly also served a domestic function; Varro mentions ivory as a typical variant, and a number are attested at Pompeii, though not nearly so common as bronze. The number of ivory and bone couch decorations known has increased dramatically since conservators started to recognise them from among the burned remains of incineration burials. The Fitzwilliam Museum in Cambridge acquired the parts of a bone couch in 1973, initially not recognised as such, and when Nicholls published them in 1979, he catalogued nineteen other examples from around the Roman world (figure 8.45).[235] Five years later, Cesare Letta published the remains of two bone couches from the

---

[228] Faust (1989) nos. 223–224A, 312–314.   [229] Faust (1989) nos. 36–38, now in Berlin.
[230] Maiuri (1933) 423ff.   [231] Allison (2004).   [232] Faust (1989) no. 310.
[233] Faust (1989) no. 305   [234] Faust (1989) nos. 122–127, Mols (1999).
[235] Nicholls (1979).

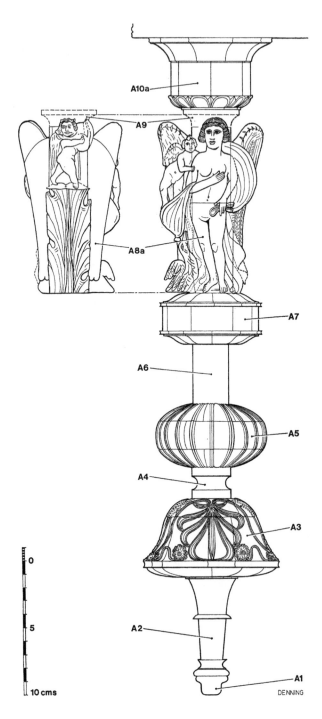

Figure 8.45 Ivory couch leg, Fitzwilliam Museum (illustration by Denning, Fitzwilliam Museum, Cambridge)

Figure 8.46 Distribution of ivory and bone couches in the Roman world (drawing by Amy Richardson)

Valle d'Amplero in Abruzzo; his catalogue, subsequently definitive, runs to 186 examples, divided into three classes, ivory beds (thirty-three examples), bone beds imitating ivory (forty-one), and bone beds imitating bronze (fifty-one). Knowledge of ivory beds was significantly increased by the conservation and reconstitution of a magnificent example, preserved in 1,100 fragments in the Palazzo dei Conservatori, from a burial on the Esquiline (Piazza Vittorio Emanuele).[236] Jean-Claude Béal, in publishing the fragments of a bone bed from the mausoleum of Cucuron (Vaucluse), was able to supplement Letta's list with eleven further examples from France, one from Spain, three from Italy, and one from Greece, and provide a new distribution map of the seventy-two different locations – from Palencia in Spain in the west, to Birten in Germany to the north, to Sabratha in the south, to Ai Khanoum in Afghanistan in the east.[237] Chiara Bianchi's publication of bone

---

[236] Talamo (1987–8), Talamo (1993).   [237] Béal (1991) 314–17

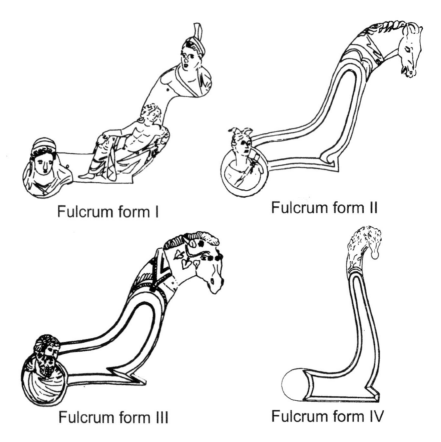

Fulcrum form I

Fulcrum form II

Fulcrum form III

Fulcrum form IV

Figure 8.47 Four forms of *fulcra* according to Faust (drawing by Amy Richardson, after Faust 1989)

beds from the necropolis of S. Lorenzo in Cremona offers a valuable update, including five new sites in northern Italy, and others at Haltern, Flavia Solva in Noricum, and Fréjus.[238] Another example can be reported from the excavations of the British School at Rome at Forum Novum (Vescovio) in Sabina (figure 8.46 for the distribution).

What emerges is a strong fashion, starting in the early second century BCE, peaking in the late first century BCE and gradually fading in the first century CE, for displaying the body of the dead on an ivory or bone bed, and then cremating them together, or in the areas of central Italy, particularly Abruzzo, where inhumation persisted, of burying them together. Letta places the earliest occurrences in the early second century in central and eastern Italy, near Rome at Praeneste and Ostia, eastwards at Ancona, and Norcia. In the late second and early first BCE, they spread to Umbria, and in the course

[238] Bianchi (2000) esp. 125ff.

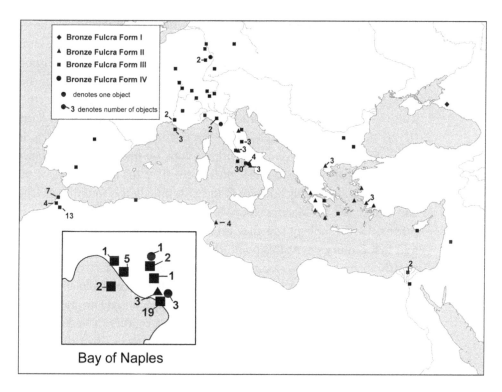

Figure 8.48 Distribution map of forms of *fulcra* (drawing by Amy Richardson, after Faust 1989)

of the first BCE extend to central Abruzzo. The peak is at the turn of the era, with numerous examples from Abruzzo, Umbria, Etruria, Latium and Campania (Pompeii). It is at the end of the first century BCE that the spread into northern Italy starts, with Cremona and Modena, and in the early first century CE that provincial finds become common, in Narbonensis, Tarraconensis and the islands (Sardinia and Sicily). As the finds die out in Italy in the mid first century CE, they extend northwards to the Rhine frontier. The pattern seems not to extend beyond the first century CE.

The by now familiar wave pattern of growth in Italy peaking under Augustus, leading immediately to a provincial spread, especially towards the north, maps well onto the evidence of bronze beds, to which should be added the interesting category of terracotta, which clusters in north Italy around Lomello. Faust was able to establish a clear chronological typology for bronze *fulcra*. They occur in four distinct forms (figure 8.47). The first form (I) is a plaque in an attenuated S-shape cast in a single piece. This is the original hellenistic form, emerging only in the late third century and lasting till the end of the second. The findspots are eastern (figure 8.48). A second form (II) introduces a *fulcrum* in multiple pieces, with the wider framed centre piece, and attached medallion and *protome*. This starts in the early second century BCE, and lasts into the early first century CE. Its findspots are concentrated the eastern Mediterranean, in Greece, Asia Minor, the Black Sea and Egypt; this reaches central Italy in limited numbers, together with the familiar wrecks. A third form (III) is distinguished from Form (II) by the detail of the angle where the *fulcrum* rests on the bed-leg: in place of a blunt angle decorated with a volute, we find the sharply-angled reversed Z-shape of the 'double-spur'. Form III is the best attested of the forms, common in Italy but rare in the east, though it is found at Athens, and indeed on the Mahdia wreck, a cargo that seems to have started in Athens. Its chronology stretches from the early first century BCE to the mid first century CE. At this point, there seems to be a significant change in fashion, and the low, sloping arm-rest is replaced by a vertically rising, box-like enclosure. This type of boxed bed is attested at Herculaneum in a wood and leather version in the House of the Carbonised Furniture, and is represented on the Haterii tomb of the late first century CE and on a Flavian mirror-back. The *fulcrum* first adapts itself to the new bed-shape, then disappears.

What we have here is the familiar pattern of the introduction, domestication and spread of a new luxury form, but without the full mid-imperial follow-through. Application of bronze decoration to the dining couch is indeed a fashion without classical precedent created in the hellenistic east Mediterranean. But its boom, even in the east, takes place in the period of Roman domination, and given the strong association of Delos with the fashion, it is hard to imagine there is not already an input of Roman taste in the development of Form II. The classical Form III of the first century BCE and early first century CE also seems to have developed on Delos, and presumably in response to the Italian market. What is impossible to make out is just when production shifts to Italy, but it is hard to imagine that Campania would have missed out on the opportunities in the late first century BCE. Form IV is presumably produced in Italy in direct response to changing taste in Italy.

What fails to take place is the development of a downmarket form, an 'everyman's' *fulcrum*. Bone is certainly available as a downmarket version of ivory. Ivory was the material of the beds on which Julius Caesar and Augustus were cremated: these are luxury goods indeed. But despite its broad diffusion, bone was also an expensive material to work, if not to buy, requiring enormous labour, and it is to be assumed that only the rich could indulge in this form of potlatch. Terracotta is the obvious downmarket version, capable of being run off moulds in large quantities; and the north Italian examples demonstrate that the experiment was made. Yet it did not 'take'. The reason surely lies in the misfit observed between the couch form and the normal eating practices of the *triclinium*. In developing the *klinē* into a boxed bed with high surrounds, its irrelevance to the *triclinium* setting was made explicit. As in the House of the Carbonised Furniture in Herculaneum, it was a sort of day-bed for an individual, rather than one of a group of beds for socialising. Italy flirts for a couple of centuries with an item of prestige furniture which it regards as the cutting edge of luxury; adapts it successfully to funerary rituals; and tries to make sense of it in a domestic setting. But it neither enjoys the social diffusion, nor ultimately the provincial expansion, of the luxuries that proved more practical.

Conclusions

Luxury revels in diversity. There are countless other aspects of Roman material culture that tell the same story of eastern derivation in the late republic, leading to a boom in Italian production under Augustus, and a progressive provincial spread in the early Empire. We could look at marble furniture, like the massive candelabra (which should properly be called *thymateria*) met on the Mahdia wreck,[239] or the Herms and other items that decorated gardens far more humble than Cicero's peristyle, or the *oscilla* roundels with carved reliefs that swung between columns;[240] marble tables, like the sphinx-footed *trapezophoroi*, which are found in virtually identical versions in Pompeii and on Delos[241] and of which no fewer than 850 have been found in Italy;[242] or the single-footed *monopodia*, like the example from Pompeii in the Metropolitan Museum in New York which combines the metal-worker's skill in its frame of Corinthian bronze, and the stonemason's skill in its veined and coloured marble. We could extend the analysis to glass wares which, coming from eastern workshops in Syria and Alexandria, become a major industry under Augustus in Puteoli, then in Aquileia, the Murano of antiquity,[243] then in Lyon, Belgium and Cologne,[244] along with the working of amber from the Baltic;[245] even rock-cut crystal 'myrrhine' ware, originally from Persia, and sweeping Rome in the first century CE.[246] These and many other consumer goods, that seem to interest only the specialists in material

---

[239] Cain (1985).   [240] Corswandt (1982).   [241] Coarelli (1983), Moss (1988).
[242] Moss (1988).   [243] Calvi (1968).
[244] Isings (1957), Newby and Painter (1991), Fleming (1999).   [245] Strong (1966).
[246] Vickers (1996), Loewenthal and Harden (1949), Harden (1954), Grose (1989).

culture on whose knowledge the interpretation of excavations rests, could illuminate our understanding of Roman culture, society and economy. This chapter does not aspire to write the history of Roman luxury, only to tease out the underlying rhythms and their implications.

The argument parted from recent studies of consumption in the early-modern period. Behind the 'industrial revolution' lies not only a transformation of the means of production, but a revolution in consumer appetites. Those appetites cannot be understood except in the context of the social use of goods. The model of 'emulation' embraced by Mandeville and other eighteenth-century commentators has its limitations, though it is a good deal more powerful than the version of the 'trickle-down' effect made familiar by Veblen. The drive is not merely to 'ape' social superiors, but to create distance from inferiors. It is the product of a dynamic society with ample resources in circulation, and new money creating the pressure of competition in the social game.

Pliny's waves of fashion sweep in successively from the eastern Mediterranean to break on the shores of Roman consumer appetite. Like the moralists with whom Mandeville took issue, Pliny saw luxury as purely destructive, not transformational or productive. While he commented repeatedly on the phenomenon of the social diffusion of luxuries far beyond the elite, he had no appreciation of the social function of consumer goods, or their role in constructing social identities in a rapidly changing world. Because his model of social order was essentially static, he disapproved of the use of commodities in a competitive and fluid society, and could not grasp the wider sense of belonging which shared possession of objects disseminated across a community of users might bring.

The waves of fashion here proposed have a different pattern: they do not merely flow in to a shore, break and dissipate, but have a longer rhythm as the inward ripples are transformed to outward ripples. It may indeed be the case that different commodities and fashions reached Rome progressively in the course of two centuries of conquest. Nevertheless, there is a fundamental contrast to register between those periods politically defined as 'Republic' and 'Empire'. The late republic is indeed a period when foreign exports invade Italy – or, rather, are sucked into Italy by the desire of the conquerors. But even if luxury products are mostly manufactured in the east, it is with the active involvement of Roman *negotiatores*. The growth of Delos as a production centre for luxury bronze couches falls exactly in the period of Roman domination of the island. The slave trade brought many spin-offs, and the massive presence of *Italici* is intimately linked to the sort of cargo we find on the Mahdia wreck. Marble table-stands and bronze couches might be manufactured on Delos; Neo-Attic marble products in Athens; bronze candelabra on Aegina: the Romans and their Italian allies could keep their fingers on the pulse of production, acting as effective middle-men between Greek productive skills and Italian taste. It is in this period, too, that new fashions in house-decorating spread through Italy; it is no coincidence that the best eastern parallels are on Delos.

But the new tastes spread in Italy to a point where importation could no longer satisfy a growing market. The shift seems to start in the mid first century BCE: Cicero's friend Vestorius, manufacturing Egyptian blue in Puteoli, points the way. But the real transformation takes place under Augustus: in an Italy traumatised by civil war, disrupted by large-scale redistributions of land, and its citizen body massively enlarged first by the enfranchisement of Italian cities then by the rapid expansion that allowed Augustus to register a rise from 4 million citizens to 5 million. The market for consumer goods in Italy creates its own production. Banal household commodities aspire to new levels of quasi-luxury. Ambitious new production lines, like the red-glaze pottery of Arezzo, or picture lamps, or the bronze *paterae* of the Cipii, or the new passion for blown-glass, prove massively successful in this market. The Vesuvian towns show us how these little luxuries could penetrate quite ordinary households. The legionary camps and even the barbarian burials of northern Europe show how swiftly they spread outwards geographically.

By the end of Augustus' reign, the new rhythms that characterise the Empire are set. Appetites that have grown in Italy become the hallmark of Roman living, however far from home: already under Augustus, the elite of south Gaul eat off Arretine (produced nearby at Lyon), light their dinners with picture lamps, decorate their houses with the 'third-style' fashion of the day, and are laid out for burial on decorated couches carved from bone. The 'romanisation' process of the provinces is not, except in its initial stages, about importation of Italian manufactures, but about learning to generate their own consumer goods only originally derived from a Roman model. The barbotine slip decorations on the terra sigillata of Lezoux have no precedent or parallel in Italian manufacture. Imitation does not exclude invention or independence. 'Becoming Roman' does not imply ceasing to be Gallic.[247]

There are, of course, implications in this for the Roman economy, but they are not the focus of the argument. The growth of consumer goods is now seen as a vital part of the transformation of the early-modern economy. In arguing for a boom in the appetite for, and production of, consumer goods in Augustan Italy, there is no suggestion at all that the Roman economy

---

[247] Woolf (1998).

was on the verge of industrialisation. None of the evidence for production centres considered, most explicitly attested in the stamping of red-glaze ware with the names of the free and slave-potters, suggests mechanisation of production, nor creation of concentrated production units on the scale of factories. Had the potters of Arezzo established one or two large factories, they might conceivably have been able to dominate the market; instead, there are numerous small-to-medium-sized sites around Arretium, which proliferate further sites in Pisa and then Lyon. The scale is impressive, but the organisation is not of the large-scale type we call 'industrial'.

Why did an engineer of the talent of Heron of Alexandria focus his ingenuity on automatic drink-warmers rather than the steam engine? The classic answer is to blame slavery for the low price of labour and the lack of urge to save costs by mechanisation. Maybe: but then there were plenty of slaves at the rich man's table, so why bother to develop the *authepsa*? Luxury, not cost-cutting, is the mother of this invention. And while it may be ideologically satisfying to blame slavery for the lack of an industrial revolution in the Roman world, it is forgotten that the British industrial revolution was itself rooted in slavery. How to explain the cotton mills of Manchester without the forced labour of tens of thousands of African slaves in the cotton fields of the Mississippi delta, the product of a systematic brutality which matches the Roman Empire at its worst? How to account for the new fashion drinks of tea, coffee and chocolate without the colonial domination of India and the sugar plantations of the Caribbean? If modern economic progress has been built on colonialism and exploitation, it is irrelevant to identify the same causes as retardants to the Roman economy. Why not simply say that the Roman world, impressive though its Mediterranean extent, was very much smaller than a colonial world which stretched from the Americas to India? Rome fell well short of an industrial revolution, but the impact of the new consumer boom on the economy was enormous.

Without statistics, we are hard put to measure this impact. But the concern of this chapter is with the social impact of a consumer revolution. The proposition is that luxuries and their downmarket derivatives or 'sub-luxuries' played a central role in redefining the social order of the Empire. In the late republic, there is still a case for seeing hellenistic fashions as restricted to a fairly narrow elite. It is of crucial importance that this elite is not limited to the Roman political class. It also includes the political elites of Italian cities; at a time when they stood outside Roman citizenship, luxury spending was a way of asserting equality of standing, just as ambitious municipal building programmes asserted the dignity of the cities themselves. The luxurious House of the Faun in late second-century BCE Pompeii is the correlate of the architectural transformation of the city. Centres like Delos served an important function in forging a community of taste between the Roman and Italian elites. It is arguably the desire of these Italian elites to assert their belonging to the Roman project of conquest that provides the most important motor behind competitive luxury. Simultaneously, we should remember the figure of Cornelius Chrysogonus: the ex-slaves on whom the Roman elite depended found luxury an ideal language for asserting their own identity. The *authepsa* is not a device for saving slave labour: it is the symbol by which the ex-slave can demonstrate his power, his taste and his equality with the elite.

Chrysogonus points the way to the world of early imperial Italy. The image is familiar of the Bay of Naples as one full of Trimalchios, flaunting the lifestyle of the free, rich and successful.[248] But it is perhaps in the veterans of the triumviral and Augustan settlements, in Italy and overseas, that we should look for the initial markets for the new Augustan consumer goods. Deracinated from their own local origins and support networks, anxious to settle down and build up a new peace and prosperity, and anxious to have their cut, too, of the Mediterranean conquest in which they had participated, they could find in the new sub-luxury consumer goods a measure of their own dignity. That would explain, too, the speed with which this language spreads to the provinces, like Narbonensis, where they settle, and the community of language with the material cultural of the legionary camps on the Rhine and Danube frontier. We have seen an element so banal as pottery lamps follow closely the pattern of military presence in Switzerland. The soldier serving abroad, like the colonist settling abroad, has a need to display the reassurance of a home culture. The new material culture served a purpose, and its success allowed it to spread in an Empire defined by colonisation and extension of citizenship.

There is, however, a potential convergence of motives between the veteran colonist trying to build a new life and the freed slave trying to build the life of a citizen. Behind the Arretine vessel lies an army of slaves, digging the clay, washing and purifying it by levigation, turning the potters' wheels, lugging the batches to the kilns, stoking the furnaces, let alone the privileged slave who gets to stamp his name on the pot. Most of the dossiers that survive from early imperial Italy, like the Murecine dossier of the Sulpicii, or the Pompeii dossier of Caecilius Iucundus, show a world of business that depends on slavery for its functioning. Manumission is an instrument for making business work effectively, by promoting the successful. The tombstones of

[248] See now Petersen (2006).

Rome or Pompeii, and the citizen lists of Herculaneum, tell the same story of a substantial preponderance of freedmen in the citizen population of the mid first century CE. Consumer goods and a lifestyle aspiring to luxury offered a language to the ex-slave asserting his freedom and success.

What drives the elder Pliny's objections to luxury, as is apparent in his account of the wearing of gold rings, is the effectiveness of luxury goods in achieving this aim of assimilating the ex-slave to the freeborn population. Luxury bridged the gap opened by the dissonance between ascribed legal status and wealth. It flourished on the tension and competition between different social groups, the freeborn and the freed, the veteran farmer and the successful trader. It not only consumed wealth but generated it, raising the standards of material culture by a considerable margin, recycling surplus into the production of more goods, and spreading the pattern of enrichment to the provinces.

Epilogue: a cultural revolution?

The 'Roman Revolution' made familiar by Syme's title is notoriously problematic: so paradoxical indeed as to be provocatively ironical.[1] No class struggle; no transference of the means of production to the working class; indeed, no challenge to the dominance of landed wealth. It is almost perverse to grace this *rivoluzione mancata* with the name of 'revolution'.[2] Syme was evidently well aware of an alternative, Marxist, view of revolution, and went out of his way to underline that this did not apply to the Roman case:

the rich were in power – conspicuous in their serried ranks were hard-headed and hard-faced men like Lollius, Quirinus and Tarius Rufus. With such champions, property might rest secure.[3]

Revolution has many faces: the 'Glorious Revolution' of 1688 that replaced the Catholic monarchy with a Protestant monarchy might be cited as an English precedent.[4] More significantly, the American Revolution might be seen as a reverse precedent: rooted in Roman political ideology, the Roman republic provided explicit models for the overthrow of monarchy, and the Augustan revolution could be seen as a reversal of this process.[5] In terms of Greek political theory of *metabolē*, explicitly applied to Rome by Polybius, the replacement of *dēmokratia* by *monarchia* was the revolution most apparent in the victory of Augustus.[6] Yet again, Syme went out of his way to deny a mere political revolution:

In all ages, whatever the form and name of government, be it monarchy, republic, or democracy, an oligarchy lurks beneath the façade.[7]

The epigrammatic formulation dismisses with equal impatience Polybius and Marx, searching behind the rhetoric for the realities of power, seen as inescapably controlled by the rich and few.

---

[1] See previous discussions in Wallace-Hadrill (1997a) 3–7, Wallace-Hadrill (2000b) 287–91.
[2] See Heuss (1982) for the debate.   [3] Syme (1939) 452.
[4] Brunt (1988) 9–10; discussed by North (1989), who prefers to avoid the term.
[5] E.g. Bailyn (1967).   [6] Note the implications of the title of Millar (2002).
[7] Syme (1939) 7.

Consistent with his rejection of political theory and constitutional analysis, Syme located his revolution firmly in the replacement of the traditional ruling families by a new elite drawn from the cities of Italy:

In the Revolution the power of the old governing class was broken, its composition transformed. Italy and the non-political orders in society triumphed over Rome and the Roman aristocracy.[8]

Occasionally, the ascendant elite is described as a 'bourgeoisie', conveying a tacit implication of a class-based struggle:

The Principate itself may, in a certain sense, be regarded as a triumph of Italy over Rome . . . The Italian bourgeoisie had their sweet revenge when the new State was erected at the expense of the *nobiles*, as a result of their feuds and follies.[9]

Here Syme took his cue from the thesis explicitly proposed in the first chapter of Rostovtzeff's *Social and Economic History of the Roman Empire* (1926). That thesis was of a growth of wealth and urbanisation in second-century Italy, producing a new class simultaneously dependent on landed wealth and engaged in business:

The developments which we have described, which took place in Italy in the second century B.C., had far-reaching consequences for the political, social, and economic life of the country. Rome ceased to be a peasant-state ruled by an aristocracy of landowners, who were mostly richer peasants. There arose now all over Italy not only an influential class of business men, but a really well-to-do city *bourgeoisie*. In fact it was in the second century that Italy became for the first time urbanized . . . This was due to the growing importance of the already mentioned class of municipal shopowners and landed proprietors, who during their stay in the Hellenistic East had become habituated to the comfort of city life and had assimilated the ideals of the *bourgeois* class, and returned to promote city life and *bourgeois* ideal in Italy.[10]

Syme attempts no analysis of the social and economic composition of his Italian *bourgeoisie*, though in his characterisation of the municipal man as 'priggish and parsimonious, successful in business life'[11] he implicitly accepts Rostovtzeff's thesis of a confluence of landed wealth and trade. He cites Rostovtzeff only to disagree with him, dismissing the suggestion that Celtic army recruits could pass for 'members of the Italian bourgeoisie'.[12]

---

[8] Syme (1939) 8.   [9] Syme (1939) 453.   [10] Rostovtzeff (1957) 21.   [11] Syme (1939) 453.
[12] Syme (1939) 457; but Rostovtzeff (1957) 41–2 actually falls short of stating as much.

Rostovtzeff's emphasis on a *bourgeoisie* would find few supporters now, and tells us more about his own background in revolutionary Russia,[13] but that is not damaging to Syme, whose focus was not on the socio-economic base, but the geographical origin, of these *domi nobiles*. In charting the rise of the 'new men' of the Italian elite, he opened up a rich seam, to be developed in detail by Wiseman,[14] and by a generation of research, whether couched in the language of *bourgeoisie* or of *élite*.[15] The same theme was to be developed for the provincial elites across the empire in his later works, especially his study of Tacitus; and as his *Colonial Elites* made explicit, he was drawing on his experience as a New Zealander in Oxford to confront the Roman with the British Empires.[16] In this sense, *The Roman Revolution*, far from continuing Rostovtzeffian class-analysis, was a precocious essay in post-colonialist history.

The success of Syme lay not only in his use of the dictatorships of the 1930s to cast the Augustan regime in a new, and brutally realistic, light, but in his relation of Roman history to one of the fundamental themes of imperialism: the impact on imperial power of the gradual penetration of the periphery to the centre.[17] Much of the cultural change described in the present book can be mapped onto Syme's revolution: the transformation of the fabric of the towns of Italy, the collapse of the basis of authority of the Roman nobility through privileged knowledge of the Roman way, the rise in luxury of a new face of power for a new elite. But though this is a compelling story, it is not the full story: it is a fragment of a larger story which Syme refused to tell. His insistent focus on the elite, to whom he felt he could give faces, was at the expense of a conscious refusal to confront the sub-elite.

The transformation of the elite is an integral part of a larger picture of the transformation of the citizenship. There is a persistent tendency to regard Roman culture as an elite culture, achieved by focusing on the 'high culture' of Latin literature.[18] But if culture is about the construction of identities, we cannot stop with the construction of elite identity. Roman identity must start with citizenship, and the transformation of the citizenship over this same period is as dramatic and profound. Just how dramatic is affected only partly by a critical uncertainty about demography. Peter Brunt's *Italian Manpower*, in addressing this problem, and supplying the dimension missing from Syme, moves from an inherent contradiction in the sources. What was the impact on the citizen body of the enfranchisement of the cities of Italy

---

[13] Finley (1975) 78, Shaw (1992) esp. 219–20.   [14] Wiseman (1971).
[15] Cébeillac-Gervasoni (1983), Cébeillac-Gervasoni (1996).   [16] Syme (1958a).
[17] Woolf (1990).   [18] Questioned by Dench (2005) 13.

under the lex Iulia of 90 BCE? The statistics for the second century BCE are reasonably consistent, and tell a story of a stable citizen body. Between 168 and 130 BCE, the censors returned a number fluctuating between 313,000 and 337,000 adult male citizens; allowing for soldiers serving abroad and under-registration, Brunt raises the numbers to between 373,000 and 414,000.[19] The most reliable figure for the aftermath of the Social War is 910,00, raised on the same principles to 980,000. The numbers certainly double, probably treble. The repeated failure of the censors of the first century BCE to complete their census and return a figure not only increases our uncertainty about precise growth, but reflects, despite Brunt's scepticism on this point, the controversial impact of the extension of the citizenship.[20] Statistical firm ground returns with Augustus, whose *Res Gestae* provide the figures for his three censuses, 4,063,000 in 28 BCE, 4,233,000 in 8 BCE and 4,937,000 in 14 CE.

The leap from 1 to 4 to 5 million in less than a century remains as problematic today as it was for Beloch. Brunt, following Beloch, regarded the quadrupling of the citizen body, even after the enfranchisement of Transpadana and Sicily, as a demographic impossibility. He consequently accepted the argument that Augustus had changed the rules of the census count by including women and children, and thereby reduced the Augustan numbers to 35 per cent: the figure for 28 BCE so becomes 1,422,000, corrected to allow for under-recording to 1,706,000–1,777,000.[21] Elio Lo Cascio, by contrast, on the basis of demographic statistics, has argued that this gives an impossibly low figure, and maintains that Beloch systematically underestimated the populations of the ancient world as a result of a false assumption.[22] Without new evidence, there is no way to resolve this crux. But the debate, while remaining fundamental for demography, does nothing to diminish the importance of the phenomenon in terms of transformation of identity. Second-century Italy had something around a third of a million Roman citizens, with a substantial majority living within a radius of 100 miles from Rome. The outcome of the Social War was to treble the citizen body, and treble the radius within which they lived, starting a process of further growth that was to see a further doubling or quadrupling of numbers by the start of Augustus' reign, and a further 25 per cent increase by its end. Even on Brunt's cautious figures, there were five to six more times Roman citizens in 14 CE than there had been in the late second century BCE. Citizenship had

[19] Brunt (1971) 70.

[20] Wiseman (1969) seems to me convincing on this point, though dismissed by Brunt (1971) 83 n. 2.

[21] Brunt (1971) 117.   [22] Lo Cascio (1994).

not merely expanded: it had changed its nature.[23] No account of Roman identity and culture that ignores this can be adequate.

One self-image which Rome presents is of the permeability of its citizenship. Romulus offers the founding myth by establishing from the outset a city of immigrants and vagrants, not of autochthonous natives. Romulus' asylum, as Emma Dench's subtle study has shown, is a potent but ambivalent myth.[24] In Plutarch's version, the asylum welcomed all fugitives, 'surrendering neither slave to masters, nor debt-bondsman to creditors nor murderer to magistrates' (*Romulus* 9.3). Other versions make less of the low, even criminal status of the asylum-seekers, but even Cicero's contemptuous label for the Roman populace as *faex Romuli*, the 'dregs of Romulus' has the idea of scraping the barrel to make Rome.[25] Dench sums up the ambiguity:

> Thus, while Romulus' asylum *could* be made to stand for 'traditional' Roman 'openness' to noble refugees, it was hard ever to write out entirely overtones of ignobility, the implication that Rome and the citizen body were descended from slaves, sinners, a deeply uncomfortable mixture of races and classes that upset a socially and cosmically pleasing emphasis on distinction.[26]

The most eloquent presentation of a noble Roman tradition of openness to outside talent is the speech of the Emperor Claudius, partially preserved in bronze at Lyon, and paraphrased by Tacitus. Extension of the right of access to the senate to the elite of Gallia Comata is justified in terms of welcoming strangers to the citizen body, with the kings themselves as examples – Numa the Sabine, Tarquin the son of a Greek from Corinth and an Etruscan mother, Servius Tullius the son of a slave. In this rhetoric, the welcome extended to new members of the elite, *primores*, kings and senators, is closely tied to the welcoming of new citizens: as Tacitus puts it, 'our founder Romulus had such strength of wisdom as to hold several peoples on the same day enemies, and then citizens. Immigrants reigned over us; promotion of the sons of freedmen to magistracies is not recent, as many falsely suppose, but an old practice' (11.24). The permeability of the elite and that of the citizen body were inseparable.

But that is a perspective possible only after Augustus. Senatorial opinion was split even in the mid first century CE: Claudius makes his speech only

---

[23] A phenomenon about which A. N. Sherwin-White's *The Roman Citizenship*, first published in 1939, the same year as *The Roman Revolution*, is disappointingly reticent: Sherwin-White (1973).

[24] Dench (2005).

[25] Dench (2005) 3, 15–16 translates '*faex*' vigorously as 'crap'; but the sense of excrement is not present in Ciceronian Latin.

[26] Dench (2005) 3.

because so many complain at this invasion of the alien, of privileges given to the descendents of those who besieged Caesar at Alesia, of the hard lot of the poor senators from Latium. Xenophobia and resistance is the opposite side of the coin to openness. There was doubtless a similar debate in the second century BCE, but the balance between the 'asylum' tradition of welcoming newcomers on the one side and of xenophobic resistance on the other was the other way round. Even Cicero, that champion of the Italian 'bourgeoisie', recalled with approval the speech made in 122 BCE by C. Fannius against the proposal of C. Gracchus to extend citizenship to the Latins.[27] The surviving fragment appeals to basic instincts of preserving vested privilege:

were you to grant citizenship to the Latins, I think, do you imagine that you would still, as is now the case, find place in an assembly or take part in the games and festivals? Don't you imagine they would occupy all the places?[28]

Scholars have repeatedly asked why the allies were so keen to obtain Roman citizenship. A better question might be: why were the Romans so unwilling to let them have it? The great tradition that those who served the Roman state virtuously merited citizenship, which could be invoked by Cicero in the following century, had no purchase in the second. The Romans remained astonishingly consistent in expecting their Italian allies to fight for their cause, and put up with a variety of subaltern statuses – citizenship without the vote, Latin rights, allies (with 'equal' or 'unequal' treaties). If the Romulean myth of embracing their former enemies had ever had currency before this point, they had forgotten it, and the steady census figures for numbers of citizens confirm the lack of expansion of the citizen body at a peak period of imperial expansion.

It is true that one of the most powerful external testimonies to Roman generosity with citizenship dates to the late third century. As we know from an inscription, Philip V of Macedon wrote in 214 BCE to the magistrates and people of Larisa urging them to follow the example of others who ensure that their states are strong by extending the citizenship:

Among these are the Romans, who when they manumit their slaves admit them to the citizen body and grant them a share in the magistracies, and in this way have not only enlarged their country but have sent out colonies to nearly 70 places.[29]

The enfranchisement of formally manumitted slaves is indeed a key aspect of the Roman citizenship with long roots that distinguishes it from Greek

[27] Cicero, *Brutus* 99 = Malcovati (1955) no. 32, 1.   [28] Malcovati (1955) no. 32, 3.
[29] *Sylloge* ed.3, 543; trans. Austin (1981) no. 60; discussed Dench (2005) 93.

practice. But in the present context, we may be equally struck by what Philip does *not* say. No suggestion here that the Romans made their polity stronger by recruiting their allies to their ranks, let alone immigrants or former enemies. It is the distance between what Philip V and Claudius could say that marks the revolution in the Roman citizenship. Implicit in that revolution is one of identities. The audience to which C. Fannius appealed in 122 BCE sensed their identity under attack: they were unwilling to share the political rights and religious festivals that marked them as Romans. The Social War was a battle over identities for the citizen as well as the member of the elite; and the Augustan census figures, however we interpret them, indicate the outcome of the battle.

A traditional model of cultural change has been questioned throughout this book. Summed up in the binomial pair, hellenisation–romanisation, it sees a process by which first Roman culture is transformed in contact with the eastern Mediterranean, and then in turn can transform the provinces, especially of the west. It is seen in the context of imperialism: it is the conqueror's contact with the 'superior' civilisation of the conquered that leads to their transformation, and thus their ability to transform others. This model, with its roots in an image of world history that goes back to Droysen, proves unsatisfactory in accounting for the identities constructed by culture, and the consequent implications of cultural change. So long as hellenisation is read not as a part of the process of imperialism but as a sort of side-effect, cultural change remains excluded from mainstream historical discourse.

More recently, especially since the 1974 conference on *Hellenismus in Mittelitalien*,[30] the place of hellenisation has been reassessed. It has been granted a more dynamic role, as an integral part of the process of romanisation. So in Italy, hellenism is seen as the cultural arm of Roman conquest: to make Italy Roman, the Romans made it hellenistic. But this model, in turn, has two flaws: it presupposes a Roman desire to give Italy a cultural identity that was Roman, and it assumes that Rome was the trend-setter, and that the hellenistic model always reached the Italian cities via Rome. On the contrary, I have argued, Romans before the Social War were more concerned to keep their identity exclusive than to impose it on others, and in many cases it can be shown that Rome, far from setting hellenistic trends, lagged significantly behind. The eagerness of the cities and communities of central Italy to transform their urban fabric in the period up to the Social War is

---

[30] Zanker (1976).

better explained, I have argued, in terms of desire to assert local pride in a context of multiple identities than as an aspiration to Roman identity.

Indeed, rather than seeing Rome as keen to assimilate Italy to its own identity, it is the exclusiveness of the Romans, in denying allies participation in an identity defined by citizenship, that provides the motor for cultural change. Unable to assert their share in Roman conquest and success in the accepted language of Roman identity, the Italian allies adopted an alternative language of power. Its diffusion in the Greek east established architecture and material culture as a potent language of expression of power and success; Italian familiarity with the eastern Mediterranean through military service and trade, best attested on Delos, made it a common tongue, a *koinē*, in which they could compete. They were not so much copying the Romans as engaging in a polemical counter-assertion of their own significance. It was only after the Social War that this language could form the basis of an expression of unity between the Italian and the Roman, and we see in Vitruvius the conscious attempt to represent the Italians and Romans, through their architecture, as an 'us' with common ancestors in opposition to the Greeks. It requires a major change in Roman attitudes, seen at its sharpest in the controversies over solid theatres, before such building can be accepted as a valid expression of Roman identity.

There are persistent signs of a deep Roman unhappiness with the new cultural definitions. The evidence was set out with eloquence and clarity by Erich Gruen in two major studies; it is not so clear why we should resist the conclusion that the Romans felt their identity to be under threat.[31] Criticisms of Romans abandoning the *toga* for the *pallium*, of nakedness in the gymnasium, of the use of Greek in public discourse, of its employment in writing Roman history, expulsions of philosophers, rhetors and professors, or simply of 'foreigners', notably including Latins, expulsions and suppressions of 'foreign' cults, burning of Pythagorean books and dangerous oracles, rejection or control of perceived luxuries: of course none of these, as Gruen subtly shows, tells the whole story about Roman attitudes, which are shot through with contradictions. And of course it is true that the Roman elite adopted new ways, and specifically Greek ways, with competitive if not indiscriminate alacrity. Nevertheless, the recurrent phrasing of objections to such phenomena as incompatible with ancestral tradition suggests the Romans were by no means free of the sort of existential anxieties and xenophobia typical of peoples confronted with population change. The second century BCE was indeed a period of vigorous cultural innovation, one that

[31] Gruen (1990), Gruen (1992).

saw the emergence of a self-consciously Roman literature, in epic, drama and history. But at the same time it was marked by acute caution in the articulation of a new identity, running parallel with the unwillingness to extend the circle of citizenship.

The Social War changed the situation radically, but not overnight. The period between 90 BCE and Augustus is one of transition, in which the full consequences of redefining the citizen body as Italy-wide only gradually percolate. It is striking, for instance, how long it took the 'new men' from the municipalities of Italy to penetrate to power. We constantly encounter the rhetoric of challenge to the power of the *nobiles* in favour of the *novi*, pervasively in Cicero, and presented as a historical leitmotif in Sallust. Yet the degree to which the old families continued to dominate is significant. Gelzer defined the *nobiles* as descendants of consuls, and explained their power by networks of friendship, obligation and dependence.[32] There is surely still some truth in that, even if patronage by itself is not a sufficient explanation, nor sufficiently attested in practice.[33] Hopkins analysed more precisely the extent to which consuls had consular ancestry in the immediately preceding generations, and consular descendants. His analysis showed that there were failures as well as successes – not all sons of consuls could count on political success. It also showed that there was indeed a steady penetration of the charmed circle by outsiders, though his statistics do not take account of Italian origins. But the figures show little sign of the weakening of the pattern of dominance in the post-Social War period. In Cicero's generation (79–50 BCE), 74 per cent of consuls had consular ancestors within three generations, a figure that rises steadily across the thirty-year generations from the 47 per cent of 249–220 BCE.[34] This is a far from permeable elite, that appears to be strengthening its stranglehold. Yet this is exactly the time when the credibility of the traditional authority of the nobility came under attack. Its ability to know and define what it meant to be Roman, follow the ancestral ways, religion, time, law, suffered catastrophic collapse. A rising generation of new Romans did not question their obligation to follow the ancestral ways, *mores maiorum*; they merely challenged the ability of the old elite to preserve the traditional standards and set the right *exempla* for the future.

For Rostovtzeff, the Italian bourgeoisie 'took no active part in the political life of the state'.[35] The vigour with which the *domi nobiles* participated in political and public life once Augustus made it possible suggests the degree of frustration pent up beforehand. *Honores* in the form of office at Rome

[32] Gelzer (1969).   [33] Brunt (1988) 382ff., Wallace-Hadrill (1989) 63ff., Millar (2002) 145ff.
[34] Hopkins (1983) 58.   [35] Rostovtzeff (1957) 22.

were one mechanism for conveying distinction, making the elite stand out. But the craving for recognition was not limited to the Roman nobility. It is in the context of frustrated ambitions that the enormous growth of 'luxury' can be seen in a different light. Just as the failure of Rome to extend citizenship in the second century may be seen as a factor behind the boom of building in Italian cities, so the frustrations of an Italy-wide elite, trapped in the bottleneck of the Roman political system and unable to express its distinction in the language of magistracies and public honours at Rome, found in luxury an alternative language for the expression of status. Its role as an alternative system is made explicit in Pliny's objections, contrasting luxury to the simplicity of traditional honours like the crown of grass, *corona graminea.*

When we encounter the material evidence of the high living of the late republic, spreading villas with their painted walls evoking fantastical architecture, mosaic pavements in the tiny tesserae of *opus vermiculatum,* marble statues and table legs, magnificent bronze mixing vessels and self-heating boilers, or beds with decoration in inlaid bronze of Dionysiac figures, nymphs and donkeys' heads, it is only too easy to attribute them instinctively to the 'Roman nobility'. The archaeological evidence firmly contradicts that assumption. They are found spread across Italy, and not just in the villas of Roman holiday-makers, but in the burials of the local elites. Luxury became not merely a possible way of indicating status, but perhaps the most important and indispensable. The focus of legislation at Rome on table luxury provided a focus for debate about the disquiet provoked by the effectiveness of this language, but left its principal manifestations to spread unimpeded. It might be argued that luxury would have spread, encouraged by the massive influx of wealth to Italy, even had the Roman elite been more willing, at an earlier stage, to share power and respect with a wider circle. Maybe so: but the consequence of using a system of honour and respect designed for a single city to satisfy the ambitions of an entire country is that there are inescapably more people seeking recognition and respect than the system can provide for. The growth of luxury is not about wealth alone, but about the relationships between wealth and systems of status-recognition.

The victory of Augustus did not initiate a process of cultural change. That had started long before, when the Romans embarked on the conquest of the Mediterranean and found themselves gradually forced to concede to those on whose manpower they depended for that conquest a full share in their state. Nor is the reign of Augustus a period of cultural innovation: the preceding two centuries are far more daring in that sense. Rather, it is a period when crisis is resolved by a new order, a new set of compromises is negotiated, and agreement is reached on a new Roman order and identity that is sustainable into the future. In this new deal, a redefinition of what constitutes the elite is indeed, as Syme saw, a vital part: but that is underpinned by a new understanding of what constitutes the citizen body. It is not so much the triumph of Italy as the triumph of a model that permits progressive expansion.

That Augustus marks a decisive break in the meaning of the Roman citizenship was firmly grasped by Sherwin-White:

> The spread of the Roman citizenship begins to follow new channels under the Principate. First the connection of citizenship with Italian birth or origin, and later its connection with Latin culture, is gradually loosened. At the same time, the value and meaning of the franchise change; it becomes a *passive* citizenship, in Mommsen's phrase, and is sought no longer for its political significance but as an honour, or out of sentiment; the old privileges and dues of a *civis Romanus* are effaced, and the extension of citizenship becomes the sign of the unification of the Empire within one abiding system of law.[36]

It is frustrating that he did not elaborate on what he meant by 'passive' citizenship, or what privileges and dues were effaced, but it is evident to what he was referring. The traditional model of citizenship involved the privilege of the vote and political participation in exchange for the obligations to bear arms and make financial contributions. That basic deal, characteristic of the city-states of the first millennium BCE, was 'effaced' in the sense that, in the course of the reign, the vote became meaningless, and the obligation to bear arms was limited to a 'professional' army. The steps of both processes are complicated by the lack of clean breaks: Augustus 'restored' free elections at first, and probably made a genuine attempt to give them new reality by looking for mechanisms to give more of a voice to local communities across Italy. Suetonius claims that he played with the idea of a postal vote, with voting for office at Rome conducted locally in colonies by local magistrates (*Augustus* 46.1). But without successfully installing some such system of local voting, the vote for the vast majority of citizens not living within easy reach of Rome was meaningless. In any case, reliance on imperial patronage rapidly overwhelmed reliance on popular favour, and with a large growth in the number of public offices directly appointed by the emperor, the networks of patronage were necessarily transformed.[37]

If what the Italian allies wanted was the vote, it may seem paradoxical that their moment of 'triumph' under Augustus should lead to its abandonment.

---

[36] Sherwin-White (1973) 222.   [37] Saller (1982); Wallace-Hadrill (1989).

But if what they wanted was the dignity and protection that came with the vote, this is what Augustus ensured that they had. When Suetonius, a century later, gave his account of Augustus' treatment of the citizenship, he said nothing of the massive increase of citizen numbers, from 4 to 5 million, nor of the transformational impact of his programme of planting colonies overseas in the provinces. These things could be taken for granted, since they were characteristic of the growth pattern of the empire. Instead, he pointed to Augustus' emphasis on the dignity of the citizenship: his avoidance of 'pollution' of the stock by an uncontrolled influx of foreign and servile blood; his refusal of requests from Tiberius for citizenship for a Greek, and of Livia for a Gaul, lest he debase the honour of citizenship (*civitatis Romanae vulgari honorem*); the legal difficulties placed on excessive manumission, and the ban on manumission for those with criminal records; and finally the insistence on the wearing of the *toga* in the Forum, complete with citation of Virgil (Suetonius, *Augustus* 40.3–5). Suetonius' attitudes fit in well with those of early second-century Rome, as encapsulated in Juvenal's protests at the flood of Greeks and easterners (*Satire* 3). The anxiety of the citizen is no longer whether his vote counts (long since, as Juvenal puts it, sacrificed for bread and circuses), but whether he is having to share his privilege with others.

The transformation of citizenship from a reciprocal bundle of rights and obligations to a form of social dignity is basic for Roman cultural identity. Citizenship is no longer expressed through actions (voting, fighting) but through symbols: it becomes more urgent to define culturally what 'being Roman' is about when it is reduced to a socio-legal status. Consequently, the entire 'alternative' language evolved to express status distinction outside the Roman citizenship and its magistracies can be recruited as an expression of shared cultural values. Tacitus' list of what might make the Britons Roman shows this mixed origin: Latin language, liberal education, the *toga*, porticoes, baths and elegant parties (*Agricola* 21). Latin language and the *toga* are 'traditional' characteristics of the Roman citizen, though it remained the case so long as Latins were excluded from the full franchise that at least as many spoke Latin and wore the *toga* who were not citizens as who were. Liberal education (through Latin rhetors), baths (with their nudity) and elegant parties (risking contravention of the luxury laws) were all aspects of the cultural innovation of the late republic which were questioned and resisted.

Why did Augustus and his successors set such store by the citizenship when its political and military functions were superfluous? One type of answer is by reference to tradition: Augustus' 'restoration of the republic' was the compromise necessary for public opinion in the context of the civil wars, and was a convenient 'sham' with which to mask the realities of autocracy. That sort of approach appealed to Syme's analysis of *Machtpolitik*. But it also chooses to ignore the utility to the emperors of the structures of the citizen state, just as it ignores the citizen body beyond the elite. Augustus, the *civilis princeps*, chose to present himself as a fellow citizen for good political reasons.[38] By reinforcing the value and dignity of citizenship, and presenting himself as its champion and defender, he reaffirmed a social order based on attributable legal status which he himself could control, and use as the material for his patronage network. Not only could he control the elite by an effective distribution of the numerous ranks of senatorial and equestrian status, but he was the main font of patronage of the citizenship itself, whether distributed to individuals or communities. The anecdotes reported by Suetonius are telling: members of Augustus' family, his wife and adopted son, might ask him to grant citizenship to their protégés: he exercised control in refusal as well as granting favours.

Hence the paradox that Augustus both massively increased the citizenship, and yet put effort into maintaining its symbolic integrity. If citizenship was to be worth having, it should not be seen as too easy to come by. On the same principle, Claudius, widely criticised for being indiscriminate with his grants of citizenship, made a show of protecting its value and integrity. He had false claimants to citizen status beheaded on the Esquiline, displayed his fairness in a trial of such a claimant by allowing him to wear the *toga* only when pleading his defence. He also as censor struck a leading citizen from the province of Greece from the citizen list because of his ignorance of Latin.[39] The symbolic and cultural manifestations of citizen identity grew in importance as the functional link with the operations of the city-state was lost.

It is perhaps in this limited sense that we may allow ourselves to speak of a 'cultural revolution' under Augustus. The new order was at once profoundly conservative and revolutionary. In preserving the structures of the city-state of the republic, it gave them new meaning. Augustus' traditionalism, in reaffirming the *mores maiorum*, in morality, religion, social structures and social practices, was not a veil for an alternative reality; it was rather the language in which the alternative reality was formulated. Roman cultural identity is vigorously contested in the republican period, so long as the identity of the citizen body, and the distribution of power within it, was also contested. Augustus, in achieving a sort of consensus, one which allowed

---

[38] Wallace-Hadrill (1982).   [39] Suetonius, *Claudius* 25.3, 15.2, 16.2, respectively.

continuing expansion of the citizen body, and continuing penetration of the elite from the margins, was able to establish a sort of consensus about what Romans were like, how they behaved, what their cities were like, what customs and rituals they followed. To the extent that there was a consensus, and a recognisable package of Roman culture could be endorsed, to that extent 'romanisation' could spread to the provinces. Precisely because that spread involved more recruitment to the citizen body, and negotiation with new groups with their own cultural background, there was room for fluidity and change, and for a vast range of local difference within what even so could be recognised as 'Roman', from Hadrian's wall to Palmyra.

It is not helpful or accurate, so I would wish to underline, to characterise such a Roman culture as an 'elite' culture. It involved unashamed celebration of wealth, property and privilege. It depended on a steep hierarchy of statuses, which it reinforced and promoted. Provincial elites grow, with overt encouragement, to take over the roles and ambitions of the Italian *domi nobiles*. On the other hand, it did not promote exclusive and impenetrable elites, not even to the extent true of the late republic. Members of the Roman elite have a way of looking the same over the centuries, but they are the product of an ongoing percolation to power at the centre. At the same time, the culture is as concerned to distinguish the Roman from the non-Roman – the slave, the foreigner, the barbarian – as the elite from the masses. The boundaries are policed neurotically: under what precise conditions can a slave become a Roman? The culture of spectacle and bathing is designed for the masses. The language of luxury spreads to a broad segment of the urban population, flagging not so much elite status, as the respectability of the *plebs media*.[40] The freedmen *vicomagistri* of Rome, often, we must imagine, the sort of *tabernarius* or *opifex* whom Cicero saw as the core of the urban plebs, are a useful symbol of the participation of the freedman in Roman cultural identity. Such figures multiply through small or medium-sized towns like Pompeii and Herculaneum, where we see a society that is hierarchical, by all means, but also remarkably inclusive.

[40] Veyne (2002).

Bibliography

Abrahams, R. (1983) *The Man-of-words in the West Indies. Performance and the Emergence of Creole Culture.* Baltimore, MD

Abramenko, A. (1993) *Die munizipale Mittelschicht im kaiserzeitlichen Italien. Zu einem neuen Verständnis von Sevirat und Augustalität.* Frankfurt

Adamesteanu, D. and M. Torelli (1969) 'Il nuovo frammento della Tabula Bantina', *Archaeologia Classica* 21: 1–17

Adams, J. N. (2003) *Bilingualism and the Latin Language.* Cambridge

Adams, J. N., M. Janse and S. Swain (eds.) (2002) *Bilingualism in Ancient Society. Language Contact and the Written Text.* Oxford

Agnoli, N. (2002) *Museo Archeologico Nazionale di Palestrina. Le Sculture.* Rome

Alcock, S. E. (1993) *Graecia Capta. The Landscapes of Roman Greece.* Cambridge
(ed.) (1997) *The Early Roman Empire in the East.* Oxford

Alföldy, G. (2005) 'Romanisation-Grundbegriff oder Fehlbegriff? Überlegungen zum gegenwärtigen Stand der Erforschung von Integrazionsprozessen im römischen Weltreich', in *Limes XIX. Proceedings of the XIXth International Congress of Roman Frontier Studies,* ed. Z. Visy. Pécs: 25–56

Allison, P. M. (2004) *Pompeian Households. An Analysis of Material Culture.* Los Angeles

Ampolo, C. (1984) 'Il lusso funerario e la città arcaica', *AION (Annali Istituto Orientale Napoli, sez. Archeologia e Storia Antica)* 6: 71–102

Anselm, S. (2004) *Struktur und Transparenz: eine literaturwissenschaftliche Analyse der Feldherrnviten des Cornelius Nepos.* Stuttgart

Antonaccio, C. (2003) 'Hybridity and the Cultures within Greek Culture', in *The Cultures within Ancient Greek Culture. Contact, Conflict, Collaboration,* eds. C. Dougherty and L. Kurke. Cambridge

Appadurai, A. (ed.) (1986) *The Social Life of Things. Commodities in Cultural Perspective.* Cambridge

Arce, J. (1999) 'El inventario de Roma. Curiosum y Notitia', in *The Transformations of Urbs Roma in Late Antiquity,* ed. W. V. Harris. Providence, RI: 15–22

Austin, M. M. (1981) *The Hellenistic World from Alexander to the Roman Conquest. A Selection of Ancient Sources in Translation.* Cambridge

Ax, W. (2000) 'Dikaiarchs *Bios Hellados* and Varros *De Vita Populi Romani*', *Rheinisches Museum* 143: 337–69

Baglione, M. P. (1992) 'Osservazioni sui contesti delle necropoli medio-repubblicane di Praeneste', in *La Necropoli di Praeneste. 'Periodi orientalizzante e medio repubblicano*'. *Atti del 2° Convegno di Studi Archeologici, Palestrina 21/22 Aprile 1990*, ed. Palestrina: 163–88

Bailey, D. M. (1972) *Greek and Roman Pottery Lamps.* London

(1975) *A Catalogue of Lamps in the British Museum. I, Greek, Hellenistic, and Early Roman Pottery Lamps.* London

(1980) *A Catalogue of Lamps in the British Museum. II, Roman Lamps Made in Italy.* London

(1988) *A Catalogue of the Lamps in the British Museumc III Roman Provincial Lamps.* London

(1996) *A Catalogue of Lamps in the British Museum. IV, Lamps of Metal and Stone, and Lampstands.* London

Bailyn, B. (1967) *The Ideological Origins of the American Revolution.* Cambridge, MIT

Baldwin, B. (1990) 'The Date, Identity, and Career of Vitruvius', *Latomus* 49: 425–34

Baltrusch, E. (1989) *Regimen Morum. Die Reglementierung des Privatlebens der Senatoren und Ritter in der römischen Republik und frühen Kaiserzeit.* Munich

Baratte, F. (1994) 'Les candélabres', in *Das Wrack. Der antike Schiffsfund von Mahdia*, ed. G. Hellenkemper Sallies. Cologne, 1: 607–28

Barchiesi, A. (1992) *The Poet and the Prince. Ovid and Augustan Discourse.* Berkeley

Barr-Sharrar, B. (1994a) 'The Bronze Lamps', in *Das Wrack. Der antike Schiffsfund von Mahdia*, ed. G. Hellenkemper Sallies. Cologne, 1: 639–56

(1994b) 'Rolling Brazier', in *Das Wrack. Der antike Schiffsfund von Mahdia*, ed. G. Hellenkemper Sallies. Cologne, 1: 657–62

Barrett, J. C. (1997) 'Romanization: A Critical Comment', in *Dialogues in Roman Imperialism. Power, Discourse and Discrepant Experience in the Roman Empire*, ed. D. J. Mattingly. Ann Arbor

Barton, T. (1994) *Power and Knowledge. Astrology, Physiognomics and Medicine under the Roman Empire.* Ann Arbor

(1995) 'Augustus and Capricorn. Astrological Polyvalency and Imperial Rhetoric', *Journal of Roman Studies* 85: 33–51

Battaglia, G. B. and A. Emiliozzi (1979) 'Le Ciste Prenestine I Corpus 1'. Rome

(1990) 'Le Ciste Prenestine I Corpus 2'. Rome

(1992) 'Nuova apporti di conoscenza per la ciste prenestine', in *La necropoli di Praeneste. 'Periodi orientalizzante e medio-repubblicano'. Atti del 2° convegno di Studi archeologici, Palestrina 21/22 Aprile 1990*, ed. Palestrina: 147–61

Béal, J.-C. (1991) 'Le mausolée de Cucuron (Vaucluse), 2e partie. Le lit funéraire à décor d'os de la tombe no 1', *Gallia* 48: 285–317

Beard, M. (1986) 'Cicero and divination: The Formation of a Latin discourse', *Journal of Roman Studies* 33: 33–46

(1987) 'A Complex of Times: No More Sheep on Romulus' Birthday', *Proceedings of the Cambridge Philological Society* 33: 1–15

(2007) *The Roman Triumph.* Cambridge, MA and London

Beard, M. and M. H. Crawford (1985) *Rome in the Late Republic. Problems and Interpretations.* London

Beard, M. and J. A. North (eds.) (1990) *Pagan Priests. Religion and Power in the Ancient World.* London

Beard, M., J. A. North and S. Price (1998) *Religions of Rome. Volume I: A History.* Cambridge

Bénabou, M. (1976) *La Résistance africaine à la romanisation.* Paris

Bender, H. (1994) 'De habitu vestis: Clothing in the *Aeneid*', in *The World of Roman Costume*, eds. J. L. Sebesta and L. Bonfante Warren. Madison, WI: 146–52

Benelli, E. (1994) *Le inscrizioni bilingui etrusco-latine.* Firenze

    (2001) 'The Romanization of Italy through the Epigraphic Record', in *Italy and the West. Comparative Issues in Romanization*, eds. S. Keay and N. Terrenato. Oxford: 7–16

Berger, P. L. and T. Luckmann (1966) *The Social Construction of Reality. A Treatise in the Sociology of Knowledge.* New York

Bermingham, A. and J. Brewer (eds.) (1995) *The Consumption of Culture 1600–1800. Image, Object, Text.* London and New York

Bernhardt, R. (2003) *Luxuskritik und Aufwandsbeschränkungen in der griechischen Welt* (*Historia Einzelnschriften* 168)

Berry, C. J. (1994) *The Idea of Luxury. A Conceptual and Historical Investigation.* Cambridge

Berry, J. (1997) 'The Conditions of Domestic Life in Pompeii in AD 79: A Case-Study of Houses 11 and 12, Insula 9, Region I', *Papers of the British School at Rome* 65: 103–25

Bettini, M. (1986) *Antropologia e cultura romana. Parentela, tempo, immagini dell'anima.* Rome

Bhabha, H. K. (ed.) (1990) *Nation and Narration.* London and New York

    (1994) *The Location of Culture.* London and New York

Bianchi, C. (2000) *Cremona in età Romana. I letti funerari in osso dalla necropoli di S. Lorenzo.* Milan

Bichler, R. (1983) '*Hellenismus*'. *Geschichte und Problematik eines Epochenbegriffs.* Darmstadt

Bieber, M. (1959) 'Roman Men in Greek Himation (Romani palliati). A Contribution to the History of Copying', *Proceedings of the American Philosophical Society* 103: 374–417

    (1973) 'Charakter und Unterschiede der griechische und römische Kleidung', *Archäologischer Anzeiger* 88: 425–47

Bissi Ingrassia, A. M. (1977) 'Le lucerne fittili nei nuovi scavi di Ercolano', in *L'instrumentum domesticum di Ercolano e Pompei nella prima età imperiale*, ed. A. Carandini. Rome: 73–104

Boethius, A. and J. B. Ward-Perkins (1970) *Etruscan and Roman Architecture.* Harmondsworth

Bollinger, T. (1969) *Theatralis Licentia.* Winterthur

Bonfante Warren, L. (1973) 'Roman Costumes. A Glossary, and Some Etruscan Derivations', *Aufstieg und Niedergang der römischen Welt I*, 4: 242–9

(1975) *Etruscan Dress*. Baltimore, MD and London

(1989) 'Nudity as a Costume in Classical Art', *American Journal of Archaeology* 93: 543–79

Bonner, R. J. (1969) *Lawyers and Litigants in Ancient Athens*. New York

Borg, B. (ed.) (2004) *Paideia. The World of the Second Sophistic*. Berlin

Bottigliere, A (2002) *La legislazione sul lusso nella Roma repubblicana*. Naples and Rome

Bourdieu, P. (1977) *Outline of a Theory of Practice*. Cambridge

Bowie, E. (1970) 'The Greeks and their Past in the Second Sophistic', *Past & Present* 46

(1974) 'The Greeks and their Past in the Second Sophistic', in *Studies in Ancient Society*, ed. M. I. Finley. London: 166–209

Boyd, B. W. (2000) '*Celabitur auctor*. The Crisis of Authority and Narrative Patterning in Ovid *Fasti* 5', *Phoenix* 54: 64–98

Bradley, G. (2000) *Ancient Umbria. State, Culture and Identity in Central Italy from the Iron Age to the Augustan Era*. Oxford

(2008) 'Romanisation: The End of the Peoples of Italy', in *Ancient Italy: Regions Without Boundaries*, eds. G. Bradley, E. Isayev and C. Riva. Exeter: 295–322

Bragantini, I. (2006) 'Il culto di Iside e l'Egittomania antica in Campania', in *Egittomania. Iside e il mistero*, ed. S. de Caro. Naples: 159–67

Brandizzi Vittucci, P. (1968) *Cora. Forma Italiae I.5*. Rome

Breen, T. H. (2004) *The Marketplace of Revolution. How Consumer Politics Shaped American Independence*. Oxford and New York

Brendel, O. J. (1953 (n.p.1973)) 'Prolegomena to a Book on Roman Art', *Memoirs of the American Academy in Rome* 21: 7–73

Brentano, R. (1974) *Rome before Avignon. A Social History of Thirteenth-century Rome*. London

Brewer, J. and R. Porter (eds.) (1993) *Consumption and the World of Goods*. London and New York

Bricault, L. B., M. J. Versluys and F. Meyboom (eds.) (2006) *Nile into Tiber. Egypt in the Roman World: Proceedings of the IIIrd International Conference of Isis Studies, Leiden, May 11–14, 2005*. Leiden and Boston

Brödner, E. (1983) *Die römischen Thermen und das antike Badewesen. Eine kulturhistorische Betrachtung*. Darmstadt

Broughton, T. R. S. (1952) *The Magistrates of the Roman Republic*. New York

Bruneau, P. (1965) *Délos – XXVI. Les Lampes*. Paris

Brunt, P. A. (1971) *Italian Manpower 225 B.C.–A.D. 14*. Oxford

(1988) *The Fall of the Roman Republic and Related Essays*. Oxford

Bruun, C. (1991) *The Water Supply of Ancient Rome. A Study of Roman Imperial Administration*. Helsinki

Buchi, E. (1975) *Lucerne del Museo di Aquileia. Vol 1*. Aquileia

Buchner, E. (1982) *Die Sonnenuhr des Augustus*. Mainz von Rheim

Buck, T. T. (2002) 'Römische *Authepsae*, auch ein Instrument der ärzlichen Versorgung?', in *From the Parts to the Whole. Volume 2 Acta of the International Bronze Congress, held at Cambridge, Massachusetts, May 28–June 1, 1996*, eds. C. C. Mattusch, A. Brauer and S. E. Knudsen. Cambridge, MA: 213–32

Bürge, M. (2001) 'Das Laconicum – eine Neuebetrachtung nach dem Fund von Monte Iato', in *Zona archeologica. Festschrift für Hans Peter Isler zum 60. Geburtstag*, eds. S. Buzzi *et al.* Bonn, 3, 42: 57–66

Burkert, W. (1992) *The Orientalizing Revolution: Near Eastern Influence on Greek Culture in the Early Archaic Age*, trans. M. E. Pinder and W. Burkert. Cambridge, MA and London

Burnett, A. (1998) 'The Coinage of the Social War', in *Coins of Macedonia and Rome. Essays in Honour of Charles Hersch*, eds. A. Burnett, H. Wartenburg and R. Witschonke. London: 165–72

Burroughs, C. (1994) 'Absolutism and the Rhetoric of Topography', in *Streets. Critical Perspectives on Public Space*, eds. Z. Çelik, D. Favro and R. Ingersoll. Berkeley: 189–202

Bursche, A. (1996) 'Archaeological Sources as Ethnical Evidence. The Case of the Eastern Vistula Mouth', in *Cultural Identity and Archaeology. The Construction of European Communities*, eds. P. Graves-Brown, S. Jones and C. Gamble. London and New York: 228–37

Caiazza, D. (2004) 'Il problema della civiltà sannita', in *Safinim. Studi in onore di Adriano La Regina per il premio I Sanniti*, ed. D. Caiazza. Piedimonte Matese: 39–51

Cain, H.-U. (1985) *Römische Marmokandelaber*. Mainz am Rhein

Cain, H.-U. and O. Dräger (1994) 'Die Marmorkandelaber', in *Das Wrack. Der antike Schiffsfund von Mahdia*, ed. G. Hellenkemper Sallies. Cologne, 1: 239–57

Calvi, M. C. (1988) *Vetri del museo di Aquileia*. Aquileia

Calza, G. (1941) 'La Popolazione di Roma antica', *Bullettino Comunale* 69: 142–65

Cameron, A. (1986) 'Redrawing the Map: Early Christian Territory after Foucault', *Journal of Roman Studies* 76: 266–71

Camodeca, G. (1996) 'La ricostruzione dell'élite municipale Ercolanese degli anni 50–70. Problemi di metodo e risultati preliminari', *Cahiers Centre Glotz* 7: 167–78

(2001) 'Albi degli Augustales di Liternum della seconda metà del II secolo', *Annali Istituto Orientalii Napoli* n.s. 8: 163–82

(2002) 'Per una riedizione dell'archivio ercolanese di L. Venidius Ennychus', *Cronache Ercolanesi* 32: 257–80

Campanile, E. (1976) 'La latinazzazione del "osco"', in *Scritti in onore di Giuliano Bonfante*, ed. Brescia, 1: 109–20

Canciani, F. and F.-W. von Hase (1979) *La Tomba Bernardini di Palestrina*. Rome

Canfora, L. (1987) *Ellenismo*. Rome and Bari

Cappelli, R. (ed.) (2000) *Studi sull'Italia dei Sanniti*. Rome

Carandini, A. (1977) 'Alcune forme bronzee conservate a Pompei e nel Museo Nazionale di Napoli', in *L'instrumentum domesticum di Ercolano e Pompei nella prima età imperiale.*, eds. A. Carandini *et al.* Rome: 163–82

(ed.) (1985) *Settefinestre. Una Villa schiavistica nell'Etruria Romana.* Modena

(1997) *La nascita di Roma. Dèi, Lari, eroi e uomini all'alba di una civiltà.* Torino

Carandini, A. and P. Carafa (1995) *Palatium e Sacra Via I.* Rome

Cardauns, B. (1976) *M. Terentius Varro. Antiquitates Rerum Divinarum.* Mainz

(2001) *Marcus Terentius Varro. Einführung in sein Werk.* Heidelberg

Carettoni, G., A. Colini, L. Cozza and S. Gatti (eds.) (1960) *La pianta marmorea di Roma antica. Forma urbis Romae.* Rome

Carey, S. (2003) *Pliny's Catalogue of Culture: Art and Empire in the Encyclopaedia.* Oxford

Carl, P., B. Kemp and R. Laureuce (2000) 'Were Cities Built as Images?' *Cambridge Archaeological Journal* 10:2: 327–65

Cartledge, P. and A. Spawforth (1989) *Hellenistic and Roman Sparta: A Tale of Two Cities.* London and New York

Cébeillac-Gervasoni, M. (ed.) (1983) *Les "bourgeoisies" municipales italiennes aux IIe et Ie siècles av. J.-C.* Institut Français de Naples, 7–10 décembre 1981. Paris and Naples

(ed.) (1996) *Les élites municipales de l'Italie péninsulaire des Gracques à Néron.* Actes de la table ronde de Clermont-Ferrand, 28–30 novembre 1991. Naples and Rome

Cecconi, G. A. (2006) 'Romanizzazione, diversità culturale, politicamente corretto', *Mélanges de l'École Française de Rome. Antiquités* 118–1: 81–94

Chartier, R. (1988) *Cultural History. Between Practices and Representations.* Oxford

(1991) *The Cultural Origins of the French Revolution.* Durham, NC and London

Childe, V. G. (1929) *The Danube in Prehistory.* Oxford

Chioffi, L. (1995) 'Fornix Fabianus', in *Lexicon Topographicum Urbis Romae*, ed. E. M. Steinby. Rome, 2: 264–6

Ciarallo, A. and E. De Carolis (eds.) (1999) *Homo Faber. Natura, scienza e tecnica nell'antica Pompei.* Napoli, Museo Archeologico Nazionale 27 marzo–18 luglio 1999. Milan

Cifarelli, F. M. (1995) 'Un ninfeo repubblicano a Segni con la firma di Q. Mutius architetto', in *Tra Lazio e Campania* Quaderni del Dipartmento di Scienze dell' Antichita, Universita di Salerno, 16

(2003) *Il tempio di Giunone Moneta sull'acropoli di Segni. Storia, topografia e decorazione architettonica.* Rome

Clanchy, M. T. (1979) *From Memory to Written Record. England 1066–1307.* London

Clauss, M. (1977) 'Die Epigraphik und das Fortuna Primigenia Heiligtum von Praeneste. Der Versuch einer Zusammenfassung.' *Arheoloski Vestnik Acta archaeologica* 28: 131–5

Clemente, G. (1981) 'Le leggi sul lusso e la società romana tra III e II secolo a.C.' in *Società Romana e Produzione Schiavistica. 3. Modelli etici, diritto e trasformazione sociale*, eds. A. Giardina and A. Schiavone. Rome and Bari: 1–14

Coarelli, F. (1972) 'Il sepolcro degli Scipioni', *Dialoghi di Archeologia* 6: 36–106

(1977a) 'Il Campo Marzio occidentale. Storia e topografia', *Mélanges de l'École Française de Rome. Antiquités* 89: 807–46

(1977b) 'Public Buildings in Rome between the Second Punic War and Sulla', *Papers of the British School at Rome* 45: 1–23

(1978) *Studi su Praeneste*. Perugia

(1982) *Lazio (Guide archeologiche Laterza)*. Rome and Bari

(1983) 'Il commercio delle opera d'arte in età tardo-repubblicana', *Dialoghi di Archeologia* ser. 3, 1: 45–53

(1985) *Il Foro Romano 2 Periodo Repubblicano e Augusteo*. Rome

(1987) *I santuari del Lazio in età repubblicana*. Rome

(1988) 'Colonizzazione romana e viabilità', *Dialoghi di Archeologia* 3, 6: 35–48

(1991) 'Le plan de Via Anicia: Un nouveau fragment de la Forma Marmorea de Rome', in *L'Urbs, l'espace urbain et ses répresentations*, ed. Paris: 65–81

(1992) 'Praeneste in età repubblicana. Società e politica', in *La Necropoli di Praeneste. 'Periodo orientalizzante e medio repubblicano' (Atti 2° convegno di studi archeologici, Palestrina 21/22 Aprile 1990)*, ed. Palestrina: 253–68

(1993) 'Argei, sacraria', in *Lexicon Topographicum Urbis Romae*, ed. E. M. Steinby. Rome, 1: 120–5

(1995) 'Vino e ideologia nella Roma arcaica', in *In Vino Veritas*, eds. O. Murray and M.-M. Tecusan. London: 196–213

(1996a) 'Da Assisi a Roma. Architettura pubblica e promozione sociale in una città dell'Umbria', in *Assisi e gli Umbri nell'Antichità (Atti del Convegno Internazionale Assisi 18–21 dicembre 1991)*, eds. G. Bonamente and F. Coarelli. Assisi: 245–63

(1996b) 'Il sepolcro degli Scipioni', in *Revixit Ars. Arte e ideologia, dai modelli ellenistici all tradizione repubblicana*, ed. Rome: 179–238

(1996c) *Revixit Ars. Arte e ideologia a Roma, dai modelli ellenistici alla tradizione repubblicana*. Rome

(1997a) *Il Campo Marzio, dalle origini alla fine della repubblica*. Rome

(1997b) 'La consistenza della città nel periodo imperiale. *Pomerium, vici, insulae*', in *La Rome impériale: démographie et logistique*, Collection de l'École Française de Rome 230. Rome

(1999) 'Praefectura Urbana', *Lexicon Topographicum Urbis Romae*, ed. E.M. Steinby. Rome, 4: 159–60

(2000) 'Gli spazi della vita sociale', in *Roma imperiale. Un metropoli antica*, ed. E. Lo Cascio. Rome: 221–47

(2002) 'I ritratti di "Mario" e "Silla" a Monaco e il sepolcro degli Scipioni', *Eutopia* n.s. 2.1: 47–75

Coarelli, F. and A. La Regina (1984) *Abruzzo, Molise (Guide archeologiche Laterza).* Rome and Bari

Coarelli, F., D. Musti and H. Solin (eds.) (1982) *Delo e l'Italia.* Opuscula Instituti Romani Finlandiae II. Rome

Coarelli, F. and F. Pesando (eds.) (2005) *Rileggere Pompei I. L'insula 10 della Regio VI.* Studi della Soprintendenza archeologica di Pompei 12. Rome

Cole, T. (2004) 'Ovid, Varro and Castor of Rhodes: The Chronological Architecture of the *Metamorphoses*', Harvard Studies in Classical Philology: 355–422

Colledge, M. (1987) 'Greek and Non-Greek Interaction in the Art and Architecture of the Hellenistic East', in *Hellenism in the East*, eds. A. Kuhrt and S. Sherwin-White. Berkley and London: 134–62

Colonna, G. (1977) 'Un aspetto oscuro del Lazio antico. Le tombe del VI–V secolo', *Parola del Passato* 32: 131–65

(1992) 'Praeneste arcaica e il monde Etrusco-italico', in *La necropoli di Praeneste. 'Periodi orientalizzante e medio-repubblicano'. Atti del 2° convegno di Studi archeologici, Palestrina 21/22 Aprile 1990*, ed. Palestrina: 13–45

Comfort, H. (1966) 'Terra sigillata', in *Enciclopedia dell'Arte Antica Classica e Orientale*, ed. Rome, VII: 726–59

Conticello De' Spagnolis, M. and E. de Carolis (1988) *Le lucerne di bronzo di Ercolano e Pompei.* Roma

Coppola, F. (2000) *Le Ciste Prenestine I Corpus 3 Manici isolati* Rome

Corbeill, A. (2001) 'Education in the Roman Republic. Creating Traditions', in *Education in Greek and Roman Antiquity*, ed. Y. L. Too. Leiden: 261–87

(2004) *Nature Embodied: Gesture in Ancient Rome.* Princeton and Oxford

Cornell, T. J. (1995) *The Beginnings of Rome. Italy and Rome from the Bronze Age to the Punic Wars (c. 1000–264 BC).* London

Corswandt, I. (1982) *Oscilla. Untersuchungen zu einer römischen Reliefsgattung.* Berlin

Craddock, P. T. and A. Giumlia-Mair (1995) 'The Identity of Corinthian Bronze: Rome's *shakudo* Alloy', in *Acta of the 12th International Congress on Ancient Bronzes*, eds. S. T. A. M. Mols *et al.* Nijmegen 1992: 137–57

Crawford, M. (1974) *Roman Republican Coinage.* Cambridge

(1996a) 'Italy and Rome from Sulla to Augustus', in *Cambridge Ancient History. The Augustan Empire, 43 B.C.–A.D. 69*, eds. A. Bowman, E. Champlin and A. Lintott. Cambridge, X: 414–33, 979–89

(ed.) (1996b) *Roman Statutes.* London

Cresci Marrone, G. and M. Tirelli (eds.) (1999) *Vigilia di romanizzazione. Altino e il Veneto orientale tra II e I sec. a.C.* Studi e ricerche sulla Gallia Cisalpina 11. Rome

Cristofani, M. (ed.) (1990) *La Grande Roma dei Tarquini.* Catalogo della mostra, Roma, Palazzo delle Esposizioni 12 giugno–30 settembre 1990. Rome

Crowther, N. B. (1980–1) 'Nudity and Morality. Athletics in Italy', *Classical Journal* 76: 119–23

Crystal, D. (2000) *Language Death*. Cambridge

Culham, P. (1982) 'The lex Oppia', *Latomas* 41: 786–93

Curti, E., E. Dench and J. R. Patterson (1996) 'The Archaeology of Central and Southern Roman Italy. Recent Trends and Approaches', *Journal of Roman Studies* 86: 170–89

d'Agostino, B. (1977) 'Tombe "principesche" dell'orientalizzante antico da Pontecagnano', *Memorie dell'Accademia dei Lincei* 49

D'Ambra, E. (1996) 'The Calculus of Venus. Nude Portraits of Roman Matrons', in *Sexuality in Ancient Art*, ed. N. Kampen. Cambridge: 219–32

D'Ambrosio, A., P. G. Guzzo and M. Mastroroberto (eds.) (2003) *Storie di un'eruzione. Pompei Ercolano Oplontis*. Napoli, Museo Archeologico Nazionale 20 Marzo – 31 agosto 2003. Milan

D'Arms, J. H. (1970) *The Romans on the Bay of Naples. A Social and Cultural Study of the Villas and their Owners from 150 B.C. to A.D. 400*. Cambridge, MA

  (1981) *Commerce and Social Standing in Ancient Rome*. Cambridge, MA and London

Dahlmann, H. (1935) 'M. Terentius Varro', in *Paulys Real-Encyclopädie der Classischen Alterthumswissenschaft*, eds. G. Wissowa and W. Kroll. Stuttgart, Suppl. VI: 1171–1277

Dalby, A. (1995) 'Archestratos: Where and When?', in *Food in Antiquity*, eds. J. Wilkins, D. Harvey and M. Dobson. Exeter: 400–12

Daremberg, C. and E. Saglio (1877–1912) 's.v. Pallium', in *Dictionnaire des antiquités grecques et romaines*, 4.285–93. Paris

Daube, D. (1969) *Roman Law. Linguistic, Social and Philosophical Aspects*. Edinburgh and Chicago

David, J.-M. (1994) *La Romanisation de l'Italie*. Paris

Davidson, J. N. (1997) *Courtesans & Fishcakes. The Consuming Passions of Classical Athens*. London

Davies, G. (2005) 'What Made the Roman Toga *virilis?*' in *The Clothed Body in the Ancient World*, eds. L. Cleland, M. Harlow and L. Llewellyn-Jones. Oxford: 121–30

De' Spagnolis, M. and E. De Carolis (1983) *Museo Nazionale Romano. I Bronzi IV, 1 Le Lucerne*. Rome

  (1986) *Musei della Biblioteca Apostolica Vaticana, Inventari e studi, 1. Le Lucerne di Bronzo*. Vatican City

  (1988) *Le lucerne di bronzo di Ercolano e Pompei*. Rome

De Caro, S. (ed.) (2006) *Egittomania. Iside e il mistero*. Exhibition catalogue. Napoli, Museo Archeologico Nazionale 12 ottobre 2006–26 febbraio 2007. Milan

De Rossi, G. M. (ed.) (1992) *Segni*. Quaderni del dipartimento di Scienze dell'antichità. Salerno

De Vos, M. (1980) *L'egittomania in pitture e mosaici romano-campani della prima età imperiale*. Leiden

  (1983) '"Egittomania" nelle case di Pompei ed Ercolano', in *Civiltà dell'antico Egitto (Catalogo della mostra, Napoli, giugno-settembre 1983)*, Naples: 59–71

  (1994) 'Aegyptiaca Romana', in *Alla ricerca di Iside. Atti della giornata di studio, Napoli, 5 giugno 1993*, eds. S. Adamo Muscettola and S. De Caro. Naples: 130–59

De Waele, J. A. K. E. (2001) *Il tempio Dorico del Foro triangolare di Pompei*. Rome

Degrassi, A. (1947) *Inscriptiones Italiae, vol. XIII Fasti e elogia. Fasciculus 1 Fasti Consulares et triumphales*. Rome

  (1963) *Inscriptiones Italiae, vol. XIII Fasti et Elogia. Fasciculus II Fasti Anni Numiani et Iuliani*. Rome

  (1969) 'Epigraphica IV', in *Atti della Accademia nazionale dei Lincei. Memorie. Classe di Scienze morali, Storiche e filologiche* ser. viii, *vol. XIV, 2*, ed.: 111–41

Del Chiaro, M. A. (1961) 'Megaresi vasi', in *Enciclopedia dell'Arte Antica Classica e Orientale*, Rome, IV: 970–4

DeLaine, J. (1988) 'Recent Research on Roman Baths', *Journal of Roman Archaeology* 1: 14–17

  (1989) 'Some Observations on the Transition from Greek to Roman Baths in Hellenistic Italy', *Mediterranean Archaeology* 2, 111-25

  (1997) *The Baths of Caracalla. A Study in the Design, Construction, and Economics of Large-scale Building Projects in Imperial Rome*. Portsmouth, RI

DeLaine, J. and D. E. Johnston (1999) 'Roman Baths and Bathing. Part 1. Bathing and Society'. *Proceedings of the First International Conference on Roman Baths held at Bath, England, 30 March–4 April 1992*

Delbrück, R. (1907) *Hellenistische Bauten in Latium*. Strassburg

Delorme, J. (1960) *Gymnasion: étude sur les monuments consacrés a l'education in Grèce (des origines à l'Empire romain)*. Paris

  (1986) 'Gymnasium', in *Reallexicon für Antike und Christenum*, 13: 155ff

Delplace, C. (1993) *La romanisation du Picenum. L'exemple d'Urbs Salvia*. Rome

Dench, E. (1995) *From Barbarians to New Men. Greek, Roman, and Modern Perceptions of Peoples in the Central Apennines*. Oxford

  (2005) *Romulus' Asylum. Roman Identities from the Age of Alexander to the Age of Hadrian*. Oxford

Dentzer, J.-M. (1982) *Le motif du banquet couché dans le Proche-Orient et le monde grec du VIIe au IVe siècle avant J.-C.* Rome

Derks, T. (1998) *Gods, Temples and Ritual Practices. The Transformation of Religious Ideas and Values in Roman Gaul*. Amsterdam

Di Iorio, A. (1995) *Immagini quasi inedite da Bovianum Vetus*. Rome

Díaz-Andreu, M. (1996) 'Constructing Identities through Culture: The Past in the Forging of Europe', in *Cultural Identity and Archaeology: The Construction of European Communities*, eds. P. Graves-Brown, S. Jones and C. Gamble. London and New York: 48–61

Dickmann, J.-A. (1997) 'The peristyle and the Transformation of Domestic Space in Hellenistic Pompeii', in *Domestic Space in the Roman World. Pompeii and Beyond*, eds. R. Laurence and A. Wallace-Hadrill. Portsmouth, RI: 121–36

(1999) *Domus frequentata. Anspruchvolles Wohnen im pompejanischen Stadthaus.* Munich

Dobbins, J. J. and L. F. Ball (2005) 'The Pompeii Forum Project', in *Nuove recherche archeologiche a Pompei e Ercolano*, eds. P. G. Guzzo and M. P. Guidobaldi. Naples: 60–72

Dodwell, E. (1834) *Views and Descriptions of Cyclopian, or Pelasgic Remains in Greece and Italy.* London

Dohrn, T. (1968) *Der Arringatore. Bronzestatue im Museo archeologico von Florenz.* Berlin

Dondero, I. and P. Pensabene (eds.) (1982) *Roma repubblicana fra il 509 e il 270 a.C.* Rome

Dondrin-Payre, M. (1987) 'Topographie at propaganda gentilice. Le compitum Acilium et l'origine des Acilii Glabriones', in *L'Urbs. Espace urbain et histoire (Ier siècle av. J.-C.- IIIe siècle ap. J.-C.)*, Rome, 98: 87–109

Dougherty, C. and L. Kurke (eds.) (2003) *The Cultures within Ancient Greek Culture. Contact, Conflict, Collaboration.* Cambridge

Douglas, M. and B. Isherwood (1979) *The World of Goods. Towards an Anthropology of Consumption.* London, New York and Harmondsworth

Dover, K. (1978) *Greek Homosexuality.* London

Drachmann, A. G. (1948) *Ktesibios, Philon and Heron. A Study in Ancient Pneumatics.* Copenhagen

Dreyfus, H. L. and P. Rabinow (1982) *Michel Foucault. Beyond Structuralism and Hermeneutics.* Brighton

Dunbabin, K. (1993) 'Wine and Water at the Roman *convivium*', *Journal of Roman Archaeology* 6: 116–41

(2003) *The Roman Banquet. Images of Conviviality.* Cambridge

Duthoy, R. (1978) 'Les "Augustales"', in *Aufstieg und Niedergang der römischen Welt*, II 16.2 ed. W. Haase. Berlin and New York: 1254–309

Eagleton, T. (2000) *The Idea of Culture.* Oxford

Earl, D. C. (1961) *The Political Thought of Sallust.* Cambridge

(1967) *The Moral and Political Tradition of Rome.* London and Ithaca

Edwards, C. (1993) *The Politics of Immorality in Ancient Rome.* Cambridge

Edwards, J. (1985) *Language, Society and Identity.* Oxford

Eggers, H. J. (1951) *Der römische Import im freien Germanien.* Hamburg

Ehrhardt, W. (1987) *Stilgeschichtliche Untersuchungen an römischen Wandmalereien zweiten Stils.* Mainz

Elias, N. (1978) *The History of Manners.* Oxford

(1983) *The Court Society.* Oxford

Engels, J. (1998) *Funerum sepulcrorumque magnificentia. Begräbnis- und Grabluxu- sgesetze in der griechisch-römischen Welt mit einigen Ausblicken auf*

Einschränkungen des funeralen und sepulkralen Luxus im Mittelalter und in der Neuzeit. Stuttgart

Erickson, B. and T. Lloyd-Jones (1997) 'Experiments with Settlement Aggregation Models', *Environment and Planning B: Planning and Design* 24: 903–28

Eschebach, H. (1979) *Die stabianer Thermen in Pompeji.* Berlin

Esposito, D. (2007) 'Pompei, Silla e la villa dei Misteri', in *Villas, maisons, sanctuaires et tombeaux tardo-républicains: découvertes et relectures récentes, Actes du colloque international de Saint-Romain-en-Gal en l'honneur d'Anna Gallina Zevi,* ed. B. Perrier. Rome: 441-65

Etienne, R. (1966) 'La naissance de l'amphithéâtre, le mot et la chose', *Revue des Etudes Latines*: 213–20

Ettlinger, E. D. Hedinger and D. Hoffmann (1990) *Conspectus formarum terrae sigillatae Italico modo confectae.* Bonn

Fagan, G. G. (1999) *Bathing in Public in the Roman World.* Ann Arbor

Fairchilds, C. (1993) 'The Production and Marketing of Populuxe Goods in Eighteenth-century Paris', in *Consumption and the World of Goods,* eds. J. Brewer and R. Porter. London and New York: 228–48

Farrington, A. (1999) 'The Introduction and Spread of Roman Bathing in Greece', in *Roman Baths and Bathing. Part 1: Bathing and Society,* eds. J. DeLaine and D. E. Johnston. Portsmouth, RI: 57–65

Fasolo, F. and G. Gullini (1953) *Il santuario della Fortuna Primigenia a Palestrina.* Rome

Faust, S. (1989) *Fulcra. Figürlicher und ornamentaler Schmuck an antiken Betten.* Mainz

(1994) 'Die Klinen', in *Das Wrack. Der antike Schiffsfund von Mahdia,* ed. G. Hellenkemper Sallies. Cologne, 1: 573–606

Favro, D. (1996) *The Urban Image of Augustan Rome.* Cambridge

Feeney, D. C. (1998) *Literature and Religion at Rome. Cultures, Contexts and Beliefs.* Cambridge

(2007) *Caesar's Calendar. Ancient Time and the Beginnings of History.* Berkeley and Los Angeles

Fentress, E. (1998) 'The House of the Sicilian Greeks', in *The Roman Villa. Villa Urbana,* ed. A. Frazer. Philadelphia: 29–41

(ed.) (2000) *Romanization and the City: Creation, Transformations and Failures. Journal of Roman Archaeology Supplementary Series* 38

(2003) *Cosa V. An Intermittent Town, Excavations 1991–1997.* Ann Arbor

Ferrary, J. L. (1988) 'Philhellénisme et impérialisme. Aspects idéologiques de la conquête romaine du monde hellénistique, de la guerre de Macédoine à la guerre contre Mithridate', *Mélanges de l'École Française de Rome. Antiquités* 271

Fine, B. and L. Ellen (1993) *The World of Consumption.* London and New York

Finley, M. I. (1971) *The Ancestral Constitution.* Cambridge

(1975) *The Ancient Economy.* London

Fitch, C. R. and N. W. Goldman (1994) *Cosa. The Lamps*. Ann Arbor

Flambard, J.-M. (1977) 'Clodius, les collèges, la plèbe et les esclaves. Recherches sur la politique populaire au milieu du 1er siècle', *Mélanges de l'École Française de Rome. Antiquités* 89: 115–53

Fleming, S. J. (1999) *Roman Glass. Reflections on Cultural Change*. Philadelphia

Fleury, P. (1990) *Vitruve de l'Architecture livre 1. Texte établi, traduit et commenté*. Paris

Flower, H. I. (1996) *Ancestor Masks and Aristocratic Power in Roman Culture*. Oxford

Foucault, M. (1970) *The Order of Things. An Archaeology of the Human Sciences*. London

   (1977) *Discipline and Punish. The Birth of the Prison*. London

   (1979) *The History of Sexuality (The Care of the Self)*, trans. R. Hurley. London

   (1980) *Power/Knowledge. Selected Interviews and other Writings 1972–1977*. New York and Brighton

   (1986) *The Care of the Self*, trans. Robert Hurley. London

Fox, M. (1993) 'History and Rhetoric in Dionysius of Halicarnassus', *Journal of Roman Studies* 83: 31–47

   (1996) 'History and Rhetoric in Dionysius of Halicarnassus', in *Roman Historical Myths. The Regal Period in Augustan Literature*, ed. M. Fox. Oxford: 49–95

Fraenkel, E. (1964) 'Greek and Roman Culture', *Kleine Beiträge zur klassischen Philologie* 2: 583–98

Franciosi, G. (ed.) (2002) *La romanizzazione della Campania antica*. Naples

Frank, T. (1933) *An Economic Survey of Ancient Rome. Rome and Italy of the Republic*. Baltimore. MD

Fraschetti, A. (1990) *Roma e il principe*. Rome

   (1996) 'Montes', in *Lexicon Topographicum Urbis Romae*, ed. E. M. Steinby. Rome, 3: 282–7

Frazer, A. (ed.) (1998) *The Roman Villa. Villa Urbana*. Philadelphia

Freeman, P. W. M. (1997) 'Mommsen to Haverfield. The Origins of Studies of Romanization in late 19th-c. Britain', in *Dialogues in Roman Imperialism. Power, Discourse and Discrepant Experience in the Roman Empire*, ed. D. J. Mattingly. Ann Arbor

Frézouls, E. (1982) 'Aspects de l'histoire architecturale du théâtre romain', in *Aufstieg und Niedergang der römischen Welt* II 12.1, ed. H. Temporini. Berlin and New York, 343–41

Friedlaender, L. (1921–3) *Darstellungen aus der Sittengeschichte Roms in der Zeit von August bis zum Ausgang der Antonine*. Leipzig

Frier, W. B. (1985) *The Rise of the Roman Jurists. Studies in Cicero's pro Caecina*. Princeton

Fröhlich, T. (1991) *Lararien- und Fassadenbilder in den Vesuvstädten. Untersuchungen zur 'volkstümlichen' pompejanischen Malerei*. Mainz

Frow, J. (1995) *Cultural Studies and Cultural Value*. Oxford

Frutaz, A. P. (1962) *Le piante di Roma*. Rome

Fulford, M. G. and A. Wallace-Hadrill (1999) 'Towards a History of pre-Roman Pompeii. Excavations beneath the House of Amarantus (I.9.11–12), 1995–8', *Papers of the British School at Rome* 67: 37–144

Fülle, G. (1997) 'The Internal Organization of the Arretine *Terra Sigillata* Industry. Problems of Evidence and Interpretation', *Journal of Roman Studies* 87: 111–55

Gabba, E. (1988) 'Ricchezza e classe dirigente romana fra III e I sec. a.C.', in *Del Buon Uso della Ricchezza. Saggi di storia economica e sociale del mondo antico*, ed. E. Gabba. Milan: 27–44

  (1994) *Italia Romana*. Como

Galinsky, K. (1996) *Augustan Culture. An Interpretive Introduction*. Princeton

Gallini, C. (1973) 'Che cosa intendere per ellenizzazione. Problemi di metodo', *Dialoghi de Archeologia* 7: 175–91

Gallo, A. (1994) *La Casa di Lucio Elvio Severo a Pompei*. Naples

Galsterer, H. (1994) 'Kunstraub und Kunsthandel im republikanischen Rom', in *Das Wrack. Der antike Schiffsfund von Mahdia*, ed. G. Hellenkemper Sallies. Cologne, 2: 857–66

Gambaro, L. (1999) *La Liguria costiera tra III e I secolo a.C. Una lettura archeologica della romanizzazione*, Documenti di archeologia 18

Garbsch, J. (1982) *Terra Sigillata. Ein Weltreich im Spiegel seines Luxusgeschirrs. Einführung und Katalog*. Munich

Gatti, S. and M.-T. Onorati (1992) 'Praeneste medio-repubblicana. Gentes ed attività produttive', in *La necropoli di Praeneste. 'Periodi orientalizzante e medio-repubblicano'. Atti del 2° convegno di Studi archeologici, Palestrina 21/22 Aprile 1990*, ed. Palestrina: 189–252

Gazda, E. K. (ed.) (2002) *The Ancient Art of Emulation. Studies in Artistic Originality and Tradition from the Present to Classical Antiquity*. Memoirs of the American Academy in Rome, Suppl. vol.1. Ann Arbor

Geertz, C. (1973) *The Interpretation of Cultures*. New York

Geiger, J. (1985) *Cornelius Nepos and Ancient Political Biography*. Wiesbaden

Gelsomino, R. (1975) *Varrone e i sette colli di Roma. Per il bimillenario varroniano*. Rome

Gelzer, M. (1969) *The Roman Nobility*. Oxford

Gilbert, F. (1931) *Johann Gustav Droysen und die preussisch-deutsche Frage*. Munich and Berlin

Gildenhard, I. (2007) *Paideia Romana. Cicero's Tusculan Disputations*. Cambridge

Ginouvès, R. (1962) *Balaneutikè. Recherches sur le bain dans l'antiquité grecque*. Paris
  (1998) *Dictionnaire Méthodique de l'Architecture Grecque et Romain, Tome III. Espaces Architecturaux, Bâtiments et Ensembles*. Rome

Gleason, M. W. (1995) *Making Men. Sophists and Self-presentation in Ancient Rome*. Princeton

Gleason, P. (1983) 'Identifying Identity. A Semantic History', *Journal of American History* 69: 910–31

Goette, H. R. (1990) *Studien zu römischen Togadarstellungen.* Mainz

Golden, M. and P. Toohey (eds.) (1997) *Inventing Ancient Culture. Historicism, Periodization, and the Ancient World.* London and New York

Goldhill, S. (ed.) (2001) *Being Greek under Rome. Cultural Identity, the Second Sophistic and the Development of Empire.* Cambridge

Goldhill, S. and R. Osborne (eds.) (2006) *Rethinking Revolutions through Ancient Greece.* Cambridge

Gosden, C. (2004) *Archaeology and Colonisation. Cultural Contact from 5000 BC to the Present.* Cambridge

Gowers, E. (1993) *The Loaded Table: Representations of Food in Roman literature.* Oxford

Gralfs, B. (1988) *Metalverarbeitende Produktionstätten in Pompeji.* Oxford

Granger, F. (ed.) (1970) *Vitruvius On Architecture.* Loeb Classical Library. London and Cambridge, MA

Grassi, M. T. (1991) *I Celti in Italia.* Milan

(1995) *La romanizzazione degli Insubri. Celti e romani in Transpdana attraverso la documentazione storica ed archeologica.* Milan

Grassinger, D. (1994) 'Die Marmorkratere', in *Das Wrack. Der antike Schiffsfund von Mahdia,* ed. G. Hellenkemper Sallies. Cologne, 1: 259–83

Graves-Brown, P., S. Jones and C. Gamble (eds.) (1996) *Cultural Identity and Archaeology. The Construction of European Communities.* London and New York

Gregori, G. L. and M. Mattei (eds.) (1999) *Supplementa Italica. Imagines. Supplementi fotografici italiani del CIL. Roma (CIL, VI) 1. Musei Capitolini.* Rome

Gros, P. (1976) *Aurea Templa. Recherches sur l'architecture religieuse de Rome à l'époque d'Auguste.* Rome

(1989) '*L'auctoritas* chez Vitruve. Contribution à l'étude de la sémantique des ordres dans le *De Architectura*', in *Munus non ingratum. Proceedings of the International Symposium on Vitruvius' De Architectura and the Hellenistic and Roman Architecture, Leiden 20–23 January,* eds. H. Geertman and J. J. De Jong. Leiden: 126–33

(1994) 'Munus non ingratum. Le traité Vitruvien et la notion de service', in *Le projet de Vitruve. Objet, destinataires et réception du De Architectura. Actes du Colloque international organisé par l'École française de Rome, l'Institut de recherche sur l'architecture antique du CNRS et la Scuola normale superiore de Pise (Rome, 26–27 mars 1993),* ed. Rome: 75–90

(1999) 'Theatrum Pompeü', in *Lexicon Topographicum Urbis Romae,* ed. M. Steinby, vol. 5: 35–8

(2001) *L'Architecture romaine du début du IIIe siècle av. J.-C. à la fin du Haut-Empire. 2, Maisons, palais, villas et tombeaux.* Paris

(2006) *Vitruve et la tradition des traités d'architecture. Fabricatio et ratocinatio, receuil d'études.* Rome

Gros, P., A. Corso and E. Romano (eds.) (1997) *Vitruvio. De Architectura.* Turin

Gros, P. and M. Torelli (1988) *Storia dell'urbanistica. Il mondo romano.* Rome

Grose, D. (1989) *Early Ancient Glass.* New York

Grossi Bianchi, L. and E. Poleggi (1980) *Una città portuale del medioevo. Genova nei secoli X–XVI.* Genoa

Gruen, E. S. (1990) *Studies in Greek Culture and Roman Policy.* Leiden and New York

(1992) *Culture and National Identity in Republican Rome.* Ithaca

(1996) 'The Roman Oligarchy. Image and Perception', in J. Linderski (ed.), *Imperium sine fine. T. Robert S. Broughton and the Roman Republic* (Historia Einzelschriften 105). Stuttgart: 215–34.

(1998) *Heritage and Hellenism. The Reinvention of Jewish Tradition.* Berkeley, Los Angeles and London

(2002) *Diaspora. Jews amidst Greeks and Romans.* Cambridge, MA

Guaitoli, M. (ed.) (2003) *Lo Sguardo di Icaro. Le collezioni dell'Aerofototeca Nazionale per la conoscenza del territorio.* Rome

Guidobaldi, F. (1995) 'Domus: L. Fabius Cilo', *Lexicon Topographicum Urbis Romae,* ed. E. M. Steinby. 95–6

Guidobaldi, M. P. (1995) *La romanizzazione dell'ager Praetutianus (secoli III–I a.C.).* Naples

Guilhembet, J.-P. (1995) 'Habitavi in oculis (Cicéron, *Planc.* 66). Recherches sur la résidence urbaine des classes dirigeantes romaines des Gracques à Auguste'. *Préhistoire, archéologie, histoire et civilization de l'Antiquité et du Moyen-Age.* Doctorat, Université de Provence

(1996) 'La densité des domus et des insulae dans les XIV régions de Rome selon les Régionnaires représentations cartographiques', *Mélanges de l'École Française de Rome. Antiquités* 108: 7–26

Guzzo, P. G. (2000) 'Alla ricerca della Pompei sannitica', in *Studi sull'Italia dei Sanniti,* ed. R. Cappelli. Rome: 107–17

Guzzo, P.G. and M.P. Guidobaldi (eds.) (2008) *Nuove ricerche archeologiche nell'area vesuviana (scavi 2003–2006), Atti del Convegno Internazionale Roma 2007.* Rome

Habinek, T. and A. Schiesaro (eds.) (1997) *The Roman Cultural Revolution.* Cambridge

Hagemajer Allen, K. (2003) 'Becoming the "Other". Attitudes and Practices at Attic Cemeteries?' in *The Cultures within Ancient Greek Culture: Contact, Conflict, Collaboration,* eds. C. Dougherty and L. Kurke. Cambridge: 207–36

Hales, S. (2003) *The Roman House and Social Identity.* Cambridge

Hall, E. (1989) *Inventing the Barbarian. Greek Self-definition through Tragedy.* Oxford

Hall, J. M. (1997) *Ethnic Identity in Greek Antiquity.* Cambridge

(2002) *Hellenicity. Between Ethnicity and Culture.* Chicago

Hallett, C. (2005a) 'Emulation *versus* Replication. Redefining Roman Copying', *Journal of Roman Archaeology* 18: 419–35

(2005b) *The Roman Nude. Heroic Portrait Statuary 200 BC–AD 300.* Oxford

Hallier, G. (1989) 'Entre les règles de Vitruve et la réalité archéologique. l'*atrium toscan*', in *Munus non ingratum. Proceedings of the International Symposium on*

Vitruvius' De Architectura and the Hellenistic and Roman Architecture, Leiden 20–23 January, eds. H. Geertman and J. J. de Jong. Leiden: 194–211

Hannah, R. (2005) *Greek and Roman Calendars. Constructions of Time in the Classical World*. London

Hano, M. (1986) 'A l'origine du culte impériale. Les autels des Lares Augusti. Recherces sur les thèmes iconographiques et leur signification'. *Aufstieg und Niedergang der römischen Welt* II 16.3, ed. W. Haase. Berlin and New York: 2333–81

Hanson, J. A. (1959) *Roman Theatre Temples*. Princeton

Harden, D. B. (1954) '*Vasa murrina* Again', *Journal of Roman Studies* 44: 53

Hardie, P. (ed.) (2002) *The Cambridge Companion to Ovid*. Cambridge

Harlow, M. (2005) 'Dress in the *Historia Augusta*. The Role of Dress in Historical Narrative', in *The Clothed Body in the Ancient World*, eds. L. Cleland, M. Harlow and L. Llewellyn-Jones. Oxford: 143–53

Harris, H. A. (1976) *Greek Athletics and the Jews*. Cardiff

Harris, W. V. (1971) *Rome in Etruria and Umbria*. Oxford

(1979) *War and Imperialism in Republican Rome 327–70 B.C.* Oxford and New York

(1980) 'Roman Terracotta Lamps. The Organization of an Industry', *Journal of Roman Studies* 70: 126–45

Harrison, E. B. (1989) 'Hellenic Identity and Athenian Identity in the Fifth Century B.C.' in *Cultural Differentiation and Cultural Identity in the Visual Arts*, eds. S. J. Barnes and W. S. Melion. Washington, DC, 27: 41–61

Hartog, F. (1988) *The Mirror of Herodotus. The Representation of the Other in the Writing of History*. Berkeley

Harvey, P. (1975) 'Cicero leg. agr. 2,78 and the Sullan Colony at Praeneste', *Athenaeum n.s.* 53: 33–56

Haselberger, L. and D. G. Romano (2002) *Mapping Augustan Rome*. Portsmouth, RI

Hatzfeld, J. D. (1919) *Les trafiquants italiens dans l'Orient hellénique*. Paris

Hayes, J. W. (1985) 'Sigillate Orientali', in *Atlante dell Forme Ceramiche II. Ceramica fine romana nel bacino del Mediterraneo (tardo ellenismo e primo impero)*, ed. Rome: 1–96

(1997) *Handbook of Mediterranean Roman Pottery*. London

Heers, J. (1977) *Family Clans in the Middle Ages. A Study of Political and Social Structures in Urban Areas*. Amsterdam and Oxford

Heinrich, H. (1994) 'Die Chimärenkapitelle', in *Das Wrack. Der antike Schiffsfund von Mahdia*, ed. G. Hellenkemper Sallies. Cologne, 1: 209–38.

(2002) *Der zweite Stil in pompejanischen Wohnhäusern*. Munich.

Heinze, R. (1930) *Von den Ursachen der Grösse Roms*. Leipzig and Berlin

(1938) *Vom Geist der Römertums*. Leipzig and Berlin

Hellenkemper Sallies, G. (ed.) (1994a) *Das Wrack. Der antike Schiffsfund von Mahdia*. Cologne

(1994b) 'Der antike Schiffsfund von Mahdia Entdeckung und Erforschung', in *Das Wrack. Der antike Schiffsfund von Mahdia*, ed. G. Hellenkemper Sallies. Cologne, 1: 5–29

Heller, M. (ed.) (1988) *Codeswitching. Anthropological and Sociolinguistic Perspectives*. Berlin

(1995) 'Code-switching and the Politics of Language', in *One Speaker, Two Languages. Cross-disciplinary Perspectives on Code-switching*, eds. L. Milroy and P. Muysken. Cambridge: 158–74

Hengel, M. (1980) *Jews, Greeks and Barbarians. Aspects of the Hellenization of Judaism in the pre-Christian Period*. London and Philadelphia

Herbert, C. (1991) *Culture and Anomie. Ethnographic Imagination in the Nineteenth Century*. Chicago

Herbert-Brown, G. (1994) *Ovid and the Fasti. An Historical Study*. Oxford

Hermansen, G. (1978) 'The Population of Imperial Rome. The Regionaries', *Historia* 27: 129–68

(1982) *Ostia. Aspects of Roman City Life*. Edmonton

Heskel, J. (1994) 'Cicero as Evidence for Attitudes to Dress in the Late Republic', in *The World of Roman Costume*, eds. J. L. Sebesta and L. Bonfante Warren. Madison, WI: 133–45

Heuss, A. (ed.) (1982) *La rivoluzione romana. Inchiesta tra gli antichisti*. Naples

Hilgers, W. (1969) *Lateinischen Gefässnamen. Bezeichnungen, Funktion und Form römischer Gefäße nach den antiken Schriftquellen*. Düsseldorf

Hill, D. K. (1981) 'Some Sculpture from Ancient Roman Gardens', in *Ancient Roman Gardens*, eds. E. B. MacDougall and W. F. Jashemski. Washington, DC: 83–94

Hiller, H. (1994) 'Zwei bronzene Figurenlampen', in *Das Wrack. Der antike Schiffsfund von Mahdia*, eds. G. Hellenkemper Sallies. Cologne, 1: 515–30

Himmelmann, N. (1990) *Ideale Nacktheit in der griechischen Kunst*. Berlin and New York

Hobsbawm, E. and T. Ranger (1983) *The Invention of Tradition*. Cambridge

Hochuli-Gysel, A. (1977) *Kleinasiatische glasierte Reliefkeramik (50 v.Chr. bis 50 n.Chr.) und ihre oberitalienischen Nachahmungen*. Bern

Hoffman, A. (1990), 'Elemente bürgerlicher Repräsentation. Eine Späthellenistische Haufassade in Pompeii', *Akten des XIII Internationalen Kongresses für Klassische Archäologie, Berlin 1988*. Berlin, Beilage 4: 490–5

Hoffmann, B. (1995) 'À propos des relations entre les sigillées de La Graufesenque et les sigillées de l'Italie', *Annali della scuola normale superiore di Pisa* 25: 389–402

Hoffmann, M. (1999) *Griechische Bäder*. Munich

Hofmann, B. (1986) *La Céramique Sigillée*. Paris

Hofter, M. (ed.) (1988) *Kaiser Augustus und die verlorene Republik*. Eine Ausstellung im Martin-Gropius-Bau, Berlin 7.Juni-14.August 1988. Mainz

Hölkeskamp, K.-J. (1987) *Die Entstehung der Nobilität. Studien zur sozialen und politischen Geschichte der römischen Republik im 4. Jhdt. v. Chr.* Stuttgart

Hollnsteiner-Racelis, M. (1988) 'Becoming an Urbanite. The Neighbourhood as a Learning Environment', in *The Urbanization of the Third World*, eds. J. Gugler *et al.* Oxford: 230–41

Hölscher, T. (1987) *Römische Bildsprache als semantisches System*. Heidelberg

(1988) 'Historische Reliefs', in *Kaiser Augustus und die verlorene Republik.*, ed. M. Hofter. Mainz: 351–400

(1990) 'Römische nobiles und hellenistische Herrscher', in *Akten des XIII Internationalen Kongresses für klassische Archäologie Berlin 1988*, ed. Mainz: 73–84

(1994) 'Hellenistische Kunst und römische Aristokratie', in *Das Wrack. Der antike Schiffsfund von Mahdia*, ed. G. Hellenkemper Sallies. Cologne, 2: 875–87

(2000) 'Discussion', in *La Révolution Romaine après Ronald Syme. Bilans et Perspectives. Sept exposés suivis de discussions*, eds. A. Giovannini and B. Grange. Geneva: 317–21

(2008) 'The Concept of Roles and the Malaise of "Identity". Ancient Rome and the Modern World', in *Role Models in the Roman World*, eds. S. Bell and I. L. Hansen. Ann Arbor: 41–56

Homeyer, H. (1957) 'Some Observations on Bilingualism and Language Shift in Italy from the Sixth to the Third Century B.C.', *Word* 13: 415–40

Hopkins, K. (1978) *Conquerors and Slaves*. Cambridge

(1983) *Death and Renewal. Sociological Studies in Roman History*, 2. Cambridge

Horden, P. and N. Purcell (2000) *The Corrupting Sea. A Study of Mediterranean History*. Oxford

Horsfall, N. (1989) *Cornelius Nepos. A Selection, Including the Lives of Cato and Atticus, Translated with Introductions and Commentary*. Oxford

(1993) 'Roma', in *Lo spazio letterario della Grecia antica, 1, 2 L'ellenismo*. Rome: 791–816

Howland, R. H. (1958) *The Athenian Agora IV. Greek Lamps and their Survivals*. Princeton

Hudson, N. (1989) 'Food in Roman Satire', in *Satire and Society in Ancient Rome*, ed. S. H. Braund Exeter: 67–89

Hundert, E. G. (1994) *The Enlightenment's Fable. Bernard Mandeville and the Discovery of Society*. Cambridge

Hunt, A. (1996) *Governance of the Consuming Passions. A History of Sumptuary Law*. Basingstoke

Hunt, L. (ed.) (1989) *The New Cultural History. Essays*. Berkeley and Los Angeles

Ingersoll, R. (1994) 'Piazza di Ponte and the Military Origins of Panopticism', in *Streets. Critical Perspectives on Public Space*, eds. Z. Çelik, D. Favro and R. Ingersoll. Berkeley: 177–88

Inglebert, H. (2005) 'Le processus de romanisation', in *Histoire de la civilisation romaine*, ed. H. Inglebert. Paris: 421–49

Insalaco, A. (2003) 'Rilettura di un gruppo di frammenti della Forma Urbis', in *Caelius 1. Santa Maria in Domnica, San Tommaso in Formis e il Clivus Scauri*, ed. A. Englen. Rome: 106–12

Isings, C. (1957) *Roman Glass from Dated Finds*. Groningen

Isler, H.-P. (1989) 'Vitruvius Regeln und die erhaltenen Theaterbauten', in *Munus non ingratum. Proceedings of the International Symposium on Vitruvius' De Architectura and the Hellenistic and Roman Architecture*, eds. H Geertman, and J. J. de Jong. Leiden: 141–53

Jackson, R. (1999) 'Spas, Waters, and Hydrotherapy in the Roman World', in *Roman Baths and Bathing. Part 1. Bathing and Society (Proceedings of the First International Conference on Roman Baths held at Bath, England, 30 March–4 April 1992)*, eds. J. DeLaine and D. E. Johnston. Portsmouth, RI: 107–16

Jaeger, W. W. (1946–7) *Paideia. The ideal of Greek culture*. Oxford

Johannowsky, W. (2000) 'Appunti sui teatri di Pompei, Nuceria Alfaterna, Ercolano', *Rivista di Studi Pompeiani* 11: 17–32

Jones, A. H. M. (1940) *The Greek City. From Alexander to Justinian*. Oxford

Jones, S. (1997) *The Archaeology of Ethnicity. Constructing Identities in the Past and Present*. London and New York

Jost, K. (1936) *Das Beispiel und Vorbild der Vorfahren bei den attischen Redern und Geschichtsschreibern bis Demosthenes*. Paderborn

Jurgeit, F. (1986) *Le Ciste Praenestine II. Studi e contributi 1. 'Cistenfüsse' etruskische und praenestiner Bronzewerkstätten*. Rome

Kaimio, J. (1975) 'The Ousting of Etruscan by Latin in Etruria', in *Studies in the Romanization of Etruria. Acta Instituti Romani Finlandiae*, eds. P. Bruun *et al.* Rome

(1979) *The Romans and the Greek Language*. Helsinki

Kaster, R. A. C. (1988) *Guardians of Language*. Berkeley

(ed.) (1995) *Suetonius Tranquillus. De grammaticis et rhetoribus*. Oxford

Kaye, F. B. (1924) *Bernard Mandeville, The Fable of the Bees or Private Vices, Publick Benefits, With a Commentary Critical, Historical and Explanatory*. Oxford

Keay, S. and N. Terrenato (eds.) (2001) *Italy and the West. Comparative Issues in Romanization*. Oxford

Kenrick, P. (2000) *Corpus Vasorum Arretinorum. A Catalogue of the Signatures, Shapes and Chronology of Italian Sigillata by August Oxé and Howard Comfort. Second edition completed revised and enlarged*. Bonn

Killerby, C. (2002) *Sumptuary Law in Italy, 1200–1500*. Oxford

Kleiner, D. E. E. (1977) *Roman Group Portraiture. The Funerary Reliefs of the Late Republic and Early Empire*. New York

Kolb, F. (1973) 'Römische Mäntel: *paenula, lacerna, mandué*', *Römische Mitteilungen* 80: 69–167

Koller, D., J. Trimble, T. Najbjerg, N. Gerfand and M. Lexoy (2006) 'Fragments of the City. Stanford's Digital Forma Urbis Romae Project', in *Imaging Ancient Rome. Documentation – Visualization – Imagination. Proceedings of the Third Williams Symposium on Classical Architecture*: 237–52

Kopytoff, I. (1986) 'The Cultural Biography of Things. Commoditization as Process', in *The Social Life of Things*, ed. A. Appadurai. Cambridge: 64–91

Kostof, S. (1991) *The City Shaped. Urban Patterns and Meanings through History.* London

(1992) *The City Assembled. The Elements of Urban Form through History.* London

Kraus, C. S. and A. J. Woodman (1997) *Latin Historians.* Oxford

Kreeb, M. (1985) 'Das delische Wohnhaus. Einzelprobleme', *Archäologischer Anzeiger*: 95–111

Kroeber, A. L. and C. Kluckholm (1952) *Culture. A Critical Review of Concepts and Definitions.* Cambridge, MA

Kunow, J. (1985) 'Die capuanischen Bronzegefässhersteller L Ansius Epaphroditus und P Cipius Polybius', *Bonner Jahrbücher* 185: 215–42

Kuper, A. (1998) 'Les origines de l'idee moderne de culture en anthropologie', in *La Culture est-elle naturelle? Hitoire, épistémologie et application récents du concept de culture*, eds. A. Ducros, J. Ducros and J. F. Joulian. Paris: 55–69

La Regina, A. (1966) 'Le iscrizioni osche di Pietrabbondante e la questione di Bovianum Vetus', *Rheinisches Museum* 109: 223ff

(1976) 'Il Sannio', in *Hellenismus in Mittelitalien. Kolloquium in Göttingen vom 5. bis 9. Juni 1974*, ed. P. Zanker. Göttingen: 219–54

(1989) 'I sanniti', in *Italia Omnium Terrarum Parens. La Civiltà degli Enotri, Choni, Ausoni, Sanniti, Lucani, Brettii, Sicani, Siculi, Elimi*, ed. G. Pugliese Carratelli. Milan: 301–432

Laffi, V. (1967) 'Le inscrizioni relative all'introduzione nel 9 a.c. del nuovo calendario della provincia d'Asia', *Studi Classici e Orientali* 16: 5–98

Lampe, G. W. H. (1961) *A Patristic Greek Lexicon.* Oxford and New York

Lanciani, R. (1893–1901, 1988) *Forma Urbis Romae.* Rome

Laqueur, R. (1928) 'Hellenismus'. *Die Religion in Geschichte und Gegenwart.* Tübingen. 2: 1781–7

Laurence, R. (1991) 'The Urban Vicus. The Spatial Organisation of Power in the Roman City', in *Papers of the Fourth Conference of Italian Archaeology. The Archaeology of Power*, eds. E. Herring, R. Whitehouse and J. Wilkins. London, 1: 145–52

(1999) *The Roads of Roman Italy. Mobility and Cultural Change.* London

Lauter, H. (1975) 'Zur Siedlungstruktur Pompejis in samnitischer Zeit', in *Neue Forschungen in Pompeji und den anderen vom Vesuvausbruch 79 n. Chr. verschütteten Städten*, eds. B. Andreae and H. Kyrieleis. Recklinghausen: 147–52

(1976) 'Die hellenistiche Theater der Samniten und Latiner in ihrer Beziehung zur Theaterarchitektur der Griechen', in *Hellenismus in Mittelitalien*, ed. P. Zanker. Göttingen, 2: 413–30

(1998) 'Hellenistische Vorläufer der römischen Villa., in *The Roman Villa. Villa Urbana*, ed. A. Frazer. Philadelphia: 21–7

Lazzarini, M. L. and F. Zevi (1988–9) 'Necrocorinthia a Pompei. Una idria bronxea per le gare di Argo', *Prospettiva* 53–6: 33–48

Le Roux, P. (2004) 'La romanisation en question', *Annales, histoire, sciences sociales* 59: 287–311

Lejeune, M. (1990) *Méfitis d'après les dédicaces lucaniennes de Rossano di Vaglio.* Louvain-le-Neuve

Lepik, W. (1949) 'Mathematical Planning of Ancient Theaters as Revealed in the Work of Vitruvius and Detected in Ancient Monuments', *Travaux de la Société des Lettres de Wroclaw. Seria A*

Liebeschuetz, J. H. W. G. (1979) *Continuity and Change in Roman Religion.* Oxford

Liebundgut, A. (1977) *Die römischen Lampen in der Schweiz. Eine kultur- und handelsgeschichtliche Studie.* Bern

Lintott, A. W. (1982) 'Imperial Expansion and Moral Decline in the Late Republic', *Historia* 21: 626–38

　(1990) 'Electoral Bribery in the Roman Republic', *Journal of Roman Studies* 80: 1–16

Lo Cascio, E. (1994) 'The Size of the Roman Population. Beloch and the Meaning of Augustan Census Figures', *Journal of Roman Studies* 84: 23–40

　(1997) 'Le procedure di "recensus" dalla tarda repubblica al tardo antico e il calcolo della popolazione di Roma', in *La Rome impériale. Démographie et logistique,* (Collection de l'École Française de Rome 230): 365–85

　(2007) 'I valori romani tradizionali e le culture delle periferie dell'impero', *Athenaeum* 95.1: 75–96

Loewenthal, A. and D. B. Harden (1949) '*Vasa murrina*', *Journal of Roman Studies* 39: 31–7

Lomas, K. (1993) *Rome and the Western Greeks, 350 BC–AD 200. Conquest and Acculturation in Southern Italy.* London and New York

Lombardo, M. (1995) 'Food and "Frontier" in the Greek Colonies of South Italy', in *Food in Antiquity,* eds. J. Wilkins, D. Harvey and M. Dobson. Exeter: 256–72

Lorenzini, C. (2002) 'La necropoli di Palestrina. Una sintesi', *Eutopia n.s.* 2.1: 33–46

Lott, J. B. (2004) *The Neighbourhoods of Augustan Rome.* Cambridge and New York

Lowenthal, D. (1965) *Montesquieu, Considerations on the Causes of the Greatness of the Romans and their Decline, Translated with Introduction and Notes.* Indianapolis and Cambridge

Lugli, G. (1941–2) 'Il valore topografico e giuridico dell'insula in Roma antica', *Rendiconti Pontifica Accademia Romana* 18: 191–208

Macdonald, W. M. (1986) *The Architecture of the Roman Empire. Vol. II: An Urban Appraisal.* New Haven

MacMullen, R. (1991) 'Hellenizing the Romans (2nd century B.C.)', *Historia* 40: 419–38

　(2000) *Romanization in the Time of Augustus.* New Haven and London

Mairie-Vigueur, J.-C. (ed.) (1989) *D'une ville a l'autre. Structures materielles et organisation de l'espace dans les villes européennes (XIII–XVI siècles). Collection École Francaise de Rome. Antiquités* 122. Rome

Maiuri, A. (1931) *La Villa dei Misteri.* Rome

　(1933) *La Casa del Menandro e il suo tesoro di argenteria.* Rome

Malaise, M. (1972) *Les conditions de pénétration et de diffusion des cultes Egyptiens en Italie*. Leiden

Malcovati, H. (1955) *Oratorum Romanorum Fragmenta Liberae Rei Publicae*. Turin

Malfitana, D., J. Poblome and J. Lund (2005) 'Eastern Sigillata A in Italy. A Socio-economic Evaluation', *Bulletin antieke Beschaving* 80: 199–212

Manacorda, D. (1996) 'Nymphae, Aedes', in *Lexicon Topographicum Urbis Romae*, ed. E. M. Steinby. Rome, 3: 350–1

Mancini, G. (1935) 'Fasti consolari e censorii ed elenco di vicomagistri rinvenuti in via Marmorata', *Bullettino della Comisscone archeologica comunale di Roma*. 53: 35–79

Manderscheid, H. (2004) *Ancient Baths and Bathing. A Bibliography for the Years 1988–2001*. Portsmouth, RI

Mar-Molinero, C. (2000) 'Conflicting and Competing Identities. Language and Nationalism in the Spanish-speaking World', in *Identity and Discursive Practices. Spain and Latin America*, ed. F. Dominguez. Berlin: 123–34

Marotta, V. (2006) 'Cittadinanza imperiale romana e britannica a confronto: le riflessioni di James Bryce', *Mélanges de l' École Française de Rome. Antiquités* 118(1)–1: 95–106

Marrou, H. (1956) *A History of Education in Antiquity*. New York

Martelli, A. (2002) 'Per una nuova lettura dell'inscrizione Vetter 61 nel contesto del santuario di Apollo a Pompei', *Eutopia. Rivista di studi sull'Europa antica* II, 2: 71–81

Massari, G. and M. Castoldi (1985) *Vasellame in bronzo romano. L'officina dei Cipii*. Como

Mattingly, D. (2002) 'Vulgar and Weak "Romanization", Or Time for a Paradigm Shift?', *Journal of Roman Archaeology* 15: 536–40

(2004) 'Being Roman. Expressing Identity in a Provincial Setting', *Journal of Roman Archaeology* 17: 5–25

(2006) *An Imperial Possession. Britain in the Roman Empire*. London

Mattusch, C. (1996) *Classical Bronzes. The Art and Craft of Greek and Roman Statuary*. Ithaca and London

Mau, A. (1896) 'Fulcra lectorum. Testudines alveorum', *Nachrichten von den Königlichen Gesellshaft der Wissenschaften zu Göttingen. Philogisch-historische Klasse*: 72–86

McEwen, I. K. (2003) *Vitruvius. Writing the Body of Architecture*. Cambridge, MA and London

McGinn, T. A. J. (1998) *Prostitution, Sexuality, and the Law in Ancient Rome*. New York and Oxford

McKendrick, N., J. Brewer and J. Plumb (1982) *The Birth of a Consumer Society. The Commercialization of Eighteenth-century England*. London

McKitterick, R. (1989) *The Carolingians and the Written Word*. Cambridge

Mees, A. W. (2002) *Organisationsformen römischer Töpfer-manufakturen am Beispeil von Arezzo und Rheinzabern. Unter Berücksichtingung von Papyri, Inschriften und Rechtsquellen.* Mainz

Meinzer, M. (1992) *Die französische Revolutionskalender (1792–1805). Planung, Durchführung und Scheitern einer politischen Zeitrechnung.* Munich

Meneghini, R. and R. Santangeli Valenzani (2006) *Formae urbis Romae. Nuovi frammenti di piante marmoree dallo scavo dei Fori Imperiali.* Rome

Metzler, J., M. Millett, N. Roymans and J. Slofstra (eds.) (1995) *Integration in the Early Roman West. The Role of Culture and Ideology.* Luxembourg

Meyboom, F. (1995) *The Nile Mosaic of Palestrina. Early Evidence of Egyptian Religion in Italy.* Leiden, New York and Cologne

Michels, A. K. (1967) *The Calendar of the Roman Republic.* Princeton

Mielsch, H. (1989) *Die römische Villa. Architektur und Lebensform.* Munich

Millar, F. (1968) 'Local Cultures in the Roman Empire. Libyan, Punic and Latin in Roman Africa', *Journal of Roman Studies* 58: 126–34

   (1987) 'The Problem of Hellenistic Syria', in *Hellenism in the East*, eds. A. Kuhrt and S. Sherwin-White. London and Berkeley: 110–33

   (1993) *The Roman Near East, 31 BC–AD 337.* Cambridge, MA

   (1998) *The Crowd in Rome in the Late Republic.* Ann Arbor

   (2002) *The Roman Republic and the Augustan Revolution.* Chapel Hill and London

Miller, M. C. (1997) *Athens and Persia in the Fifth Century B.C.. A Study in Cultural Receptivity.* Cambridge

Millett, M. (1990) *The Romanization of Britain. An Essay in Archaeological Interpretation.* Cambridge

Milnor, K. (2005) *Gender, Domesticity, and the Age of Augustus.* Oxford

Moatti, C. (1991) 'La crise de la tradition à la fin de la république romaine à travers la littérature juridique et la science des antiquaires', in M. Pani (ed.), *Continuità e trasformazione fra repubblica e principato. Istituzioni, politica, società.* Bari

   (1997) *La Raison de Rome. Naissance de l'esprit critique à la fin de la République (IIe–Ier siècle avant Jésus-Christ).* Paris

Mols, S. T. A. M. (1999) *Wooden Furniture in Herculaneum. Form, Technique and Function.* Amsterdam

Momigliano, A. (1955) 'Per il centenario dell' "Alessandro Magno" di J. G. Droysen', in *Contributo alla storia degli studi classici.* Rome: 263–73

   (1966) 'Ancient History and the Antiquarian', in *Studies in Historiography*, London: 1–39

   (1975) *Alien Wisdom. The limits of Hellenization.* Cambridge

   (1977) 'J.G. Droysen between Greeks and Jews', in *Essays in Ancient and Modern Historiography*, ed. A. Momigliano. Oxford: 307–23

Morel, J.-P. (1976) 'Céramiques d'Italie et céramiques hellénistiques (150–30 av. J.-C.)', in *Hellenismus in Mittelitalien*, ed. P. Zanker. Göttingen: 471–501

   (1981) *Céramique campanienne. Les formes.* Rome

(1989) 'The Transformation of Italy, 300–133 B.C.' *Cambridge Ancient History* VII (2nd edn.): 477–516

(1991a) 'Artisanat, importations et romanisation dans le Samnium aux IIe et Ier siècles av. J.-C.', in *La Romanisation du Samnium aux IIe et Ier siècles av. J.-C.. Actes du colloque organisé par le Centre Jean Bérard en collaboration avec la Soprintendenza archeologica e per i BAAS del Molise et al Soprintendenza archeologica per la province di Salerno, Avellino e Benevento: Naples Centre Jean Bérard, 4–5 Novembre 1988*, ed. Naples: 187–203

(1991) 'La Romanisation de Samnium et de la Lucanie aux IVe et IIIe siècles av. J.-C. D'après l'artisanat et le commerce', in *Communità indigene e problemi della romanizzazione nell'Italia centro-meridionale (IV–III sec. av. C.). Actes du colloque international organisé à l'occasion du 50e anniversaire de l'Academia Belgica et du 40e anniversaire des fouilles belges en Italie (1er–3 février 1990)*, eds. J. Mertens and R. Lambrechts. Rome

Morel, W. (ed.) (1927) *Fragmenta Poetarum Latinorum Epicorum et Lyricorum praeter Ennium et Lucilium*. Stuttgart

Morgan, M. G. (1990) 'The Perils of Schematism. Polybius, Antiochus Epiphanes and the "Day of Eleusis"', *Historia* 39: 37–76

Morgan, T. (1998) *Literate Education in the Hellenistic and Roman Worlds*. Cambridge

Morris, I. (1992) *Death-ritual and Social Structure in Classical Antiquity*. Cambridge

(1998) 'Remaining Invisible: The Archaeology of the Excluded in Classical Athens', in *Women and Slaves in Greco-Roman Culture. Differential Equations*, eds. S. Joshel and S. Murnaghan. London: 193–220

Moss, C. F. (1988) *Roman Marble Tables*. Princeton

Mouritsen, H. (1998) *Italian Unification. A Study in Ancient and Modern Historiography*. London

Müller, C. and C. Hasenohr (eds.) (2002) *Les Italiens dans le monde grec, IIe siècle av. J.-C.-Ier siècle ap. J.-C. Circulation, activités, intégration: actes de la table ronde, Ecole normale supérieur, Paris 14–16 mai 1998*. Athens and Paris

Murray, O. (ed.) (1990) *Sympotica. A Symposium on the Symposion*. Oxford

Musti, D. (1988) 'I Greci e l'Italia', *Storia di Italia* 1: 39ff

Myers-Scotton, C. (1990) 'Codeswitching and Borrowing. Interpersonal and Macrolevel Meaning', in *Codeswitching as a Worldwide Phenomenon*, ed. R. Jacobson. New York: 85–110

(1993) *Social Motivations for Codeswitching. Evidence from Africa*. Oxford and New York

Myres, S. (1999) 'The Metamorphosis of a Poet. Recent Work on Ovid', *Journal of Roman Studies* 89: 190–204

Nappo, S. C. (1997) 'Urban Transformation at Pompeii in the Late Third and Early Second Centuries BC', in *Domestic Space in the Roman World. Pompeii and Beyond*, eds. R. Laurence and A. Wallace-Hadrill. Portsmouth, RI: 91–120

Naumann-Steckner, F., T. Raeder and F. Willer (1994) 'Ein Kandelaber mit Akanthusranken?', in *Das Wrack. Der antike Schiffsfund von Mahdia*, ed. G. Hellenkemper Sallies. Cologne, 1: 629–38

Nenova-Merdjanova, R. (2002) 'Bronze Vessels and the Toilette in Roman Times', in *From the Parts to the Whole. Volume 2, Acta of the 13th International Bronze Congress*, eds. C. C. Mattusch, A. Brauer and S. E. Knudsen. Cambridge, MA: 201–4

Neudecker, R. (1988) *Die Skulpturenausstattung römischer Villen in Italien*. Mainz
    (1994) *Die Pracht der Latrine. Zum Wandel öffentlicher Bedürfnisanstalten in der kaiserzeitlichen Zeit*. Munich
    (1998) 'The Roman Villa as a Locus of Art Collections', in *The Roman Villa. Villa Urbana*, ed. A. Frazer. Philadelphia: 77–91

Nevett, L. C. (1999) *House and Society in the Ancient Greek World*. Cambridge

Newby, M. and K. S. Painter (eds.) (1991) *Roman Glass. Two Centuries of Art and Innovation*. Society of Antiquaries Occasional Papers 13. London

Newlands, C. (2002) '*Mandati memores*. Political and Poetic Authority in the *Fasti*', in *The Cambridge Companion to Ovid*, ed. A. Schiesaro. Cambridge: 200–16

Nicholls, R. V. (1979) 'A Roman Couch from Cambridge', *Archaeologia* 106: 1–32

Nicolet, C. (1966) *L'ordre équestre. L'époque républicaine (312–43 av. J.-C.): Tome 1 Définitions juridiques et structures sociales*. Paris
    (1976) 'Le temple des Nymphes et les distributions frumentaires à Rome à l'époque républicaine d'après des découvertes récentes', *Comptes rendues de l'Académie des Inscriptions et belles lettres*: 29–51
    (1980) *The World of the Citizen in Republican Rome*. London
    (1987) 'La table d'Héraclée et les origines du cadastre romain', in *L'Urbs. Espace urbain et histoire*, ed. Rome: 1–25
    (1991) *Space, Geography, and Politics in the Early Roman Empire*. Ann Arbor

Nielsen, I. (1985) 'Considerazione sulle prime fasi dell'evoluzione dell'edificio termale romano', *Analecta Romana Instituti Danici* 14: 81–112
    (1990) *Thermae et Balnea. An Architectural and Cultural History of Roman Public Baths*. Aarhus

Niethammer, L. (2000) *Kollektive Identität. Heimliche Quellen einer unheimlichen Konjunktur*. Reinbeck bei Hamburg

Nippel, W. (1984) 'Policing Rome', *Journal of Roman Studies* 74: 20–9
    (1995) *Public Order in Ancient Rome*. Cambridge

Nissen, H. (1877) *Pompeianische Studien zur Städtekunde des Altertums*. Leipzig

Nordh, A. (1949) *Libellus de regionibus urbis Romae*. Lund

North, J. A. (1976) 'Conservatism and Change in Roman Religion', *Papers of the British School at Rome* 44: 1–12
    (1989) 'The Roman Counter-revolution', *Journal of Roman Studies* 79: 151–6
    (1990) 'Family Strategy and Priesthood in the Late Republic', in *Parenté et stratégies familiales dans l'antiquité*, eds. J. Andreau and H. Bruhns. Rome: 527–43

Noy, D. (1999) "'Peace upon Israel". Hebrew Formulae and Names in Jewish Inscriptions from the Western Roman Empire', in *Hebrew Study from Ezra to Ben-Yehuda*, ed. W. Horbury. Edinburgh: 135–46

Nuber, H. U. (1972) 'Kanne und Griffschale', *Bericht der römisch-germanischen Kommission*: 1–232

Ober, J. (2003) 'Postscript. Culture, Thin Coherence and the Persistence of Politics', in *The Cultures within Ancient Greek Culture. Contact, Conflict, Collaboration*, eds. C. Dougherty and L. Kurke. Cambridge: 237–55

Olson, S. D. and A. Sens (2000) *Archestratos of Gela. Greek Culture and Cuisine in the Fourth Century BCE. Text, Translation and Commentary*. Oxford

Ong, W. J. (1982) *Orality and Literacy. The Technologizing of the Word*. London and New York

Oppermann, H. (ed.) (1967) *Römische Wertbegriffe*. Darmstadt

Osborne, R. (1997) 'Men Without Clothes. Heroic Nakedness and Greek Art', *Gender and History* 9(3): 504–28

Ostrow, S. E. (1985) 'Augustales along the Bay of Naples. A Case for their Early Growth', *Historia* 34: 64–101

Owen Hughes, D. (1983) 'Sumptuary Laws and Social Relations in Renaissance Italy', in *Disputes and Settlements. Law and Human Relations in the West*, ed. J. Bossy. Cambridge: 69–99

Pairault Massa, F.-H. (1992) 'Aspetti e problemi della società prenestina tra IV e III sec. a.C.', in *La necropoli di Praeneste. 'Periodi orientalizzante e medio-repubblicano'. Atti del 2° convegno di Studi archeologici, Palestrina 21/22 Aprile 1990*, ed. Palestrina: 109–45

Palmer, L. R. (1954) *The Latin Language*. London

Pape, M. (1975) *Griechische Kunstwerke aus Kriegesbeute und ihre öffentliche Aufstellung in Rom von der Eroberung von Syrakus bis in augusteische Zeit*. Hamburg

Paribeni, E. (1963) 'Otricolensi vasi', in *Enciclopedia dell'Arte Antica Classica e Orientale*, ed. Rome, V: 804–5

Parker, A. J. (1992) *Ancient Shipwrecks of the Mediterranean and the Roman Provinces*. Oxford

Percival, J. (1976) *The Roman Villa. An Historical Introduction*. London

Perlzweig, J. (1961) *The Athenian Agora VII. Lamps of the Roman Period*. Princeton

Pernice, E. (1925) *Die hellenistische Kunst in Pompeji IV. Gefässe und Geräte aus Bronze*. Berlin and Leipzig

Perry, E. (2005) *The Aesthetics of Emulation in the Visual Arts of Ancient Rome*. Cambridge

Pesando, F. (1987) *Oikos e Ktesis. La casa greca in età classica*. Perugia

(1996) 'Autocelebrazione aristocratica e propaganda politica in ambiente privato. La casa del Fauno a Pompei', *Cahiers du Centre Gustav-Glotz* 7: 189–228

(1997) *Domus. Edilizia privata e società pompeiana fra III e I secolo a.C.* Rome

(2003) 'Appunti sulla cosidetta Basilica di Ercolano', *Cronache Ercolanesi* 33: 331–7

Petersen, L. H. (2006) *The Freedman in Roman Art and Art History*. Cambridge

Petrovsky, R. (1994) 'Die Bronzegefäße', in *Das Wrack. Der antike Schiffsfund von Mahdia*, ed. G. Hellenkemper Sallies. Cologne, 1: 663–700

Pettinau, B. (1990) 'L'illuminazione della domus. Lucerne e candelabri', in *Il Bronzo dei Romani. Arredo e Suppellittile*, ed. L. Pirzio Biroli Stefanelli. Rome: 81–101

Pfeiffer, R. (1968) *History of Classical Scholarship from the Beginnings to the End of the Hellenistic Age*. Oxford

Pirzio Biroli Stefanelli, L. (ed.) (1990) *Il Bronzo dei Romani. Arredo e suppellettile*. Rome

Pisani Sartorio, G. (1988) 'Compita Larum. Edicole sacre nei crocicchi di Roma antica', *Bollettino della Unione Storia ed Arte* 1–4: 23–34

  (1993a) 'Compitum Acilium', in *Lexicon Topographicum Urbis Romae*, ed. E. M. Steinby. Rome, 1: 314–15

  (1993b) 'Compitum vici Aesc(u)leti', in *Lexicon Topographicum Urbis Romae*, ed. E. M. Steinby. Rome, 1: 316

Plumpe, J. C. (1932) *Wesen und Wirkung der Auctoritas Maiorum bei Cicero*. Münster

Poccetti, P. (1979) *Nuovi documenti italici a complemento del Manuale di E. Vetter*. Pisa

Pontrandolfo, A. (1995) 'Simposio e élites sociali nel mondo Etrusco e Italico', in *In Vino Veritas*, eds. O. Murray and M.-M. Tecusan. London: 176–95

Pöschl, V. (1940) *Grundwerte römischer Staatsgesinnung in den Geschichtswerken des Sallust*. Berlin

Poulsen, E. (1995) 'Remarks on Roman Bronze Skillets with Deep Grooves under the Base', in *Acta of the 12th International Congress on Ancient Bronzes*, ed. S. T. A. M. Mols *et al.* Nijmegen: 59–67

Pucci, G. (1977) 'Le terre sigillate italiche, galliche e orientali', in *L'Instrumentum domesticum di Ercolano e Pompei*, ed. A. Carandini. Rome: 9–21

  (1985) 'Terra Sigillata Italica', in *Atlante dell Forme Ceramiche II. Ceramica fine romana nel bacino del Mediterraneo (tardo ellenismo e primo impero)*. Rome: 359–406

Purcell, N. (1986) 'Livia and the Womanhood of Rome', *Proceedings of the Cambridge Philological Society* 32: 83f

  (1994) 'The City of Rome and the *plebs urbana* in the Late Republic', in *Cambridge Ancient History*. Cambridge, IX: 644–88

Quilici, L. (1983) 'Il Campo Marzio occidentale', in *Città e Architettura nella Roma Imperiale*, ed. K. de Fine Licht. Rome: 59–85

  (1992) 'Studio topografico delle necropoli', in *La necropoli di Praeneste. 'Periodi orientalizzante e medio-repubblicano'. Atti del 2° convegno di Studi archeologici, Palestrina 21/22 Aprile 1990*, ed. 53–75

Radnóti, A. (1938) *Die römischen Bronzegefässe von Pannonien*. Budapest

Raeder, J. (1988) 'Vitruv, de architectura VI 7 (*aedificia Graecorum*) und die hellenistische Wohnhaus- und Palastarchitektur', *Gymnasium* 95: 316–68

Rainbird, J. S. (1986) 'The Fire Stations of Imperial Rome', *Papers of the British School at Rome* 54: 147–69

Rainer, J. M. (1987) *Bau- und nachbarrechtliche Bestimmungen im klassischen römischen Recht.* Graz

Ramieri, A. M. (1990) *I vigili del fuoco nella Roma antica.* Rome

Rathje, A. (1990) 'The Adoption of the Homeric Banquet in Central Italy in the Orientalizing Period', in *Sympotica. A Symposium on the Symposion*, ed. O. Murray. Oxford: 279–88

Rauh, N. K. (1993) *The Sacred Bonds of Commerce. Religion, Economy and Trade Society at Hellenistic Roman Delos, 166–87 B.C.* Amsterdam

Rawson, E. D. (1985) *Intellectual Life in the Late Roman Republic.* London and Baltimore, MD

(1987) 'Discrimina Ordinum. The Lex Julia Theatralis', *Papers of the British School at Rome* 55: 83–114

(1989) 'Roman Tradition and the Greek World', in *Cambridge Ancient History*, 2nd edn., VIII eds. A. E. Astin, F. W. Walbank, M. W. Frederiksen and R. M. Ogilvie. Cambridge: 422–76

(1991a) *Roman Culture and Society. Collected Papers.* Oxford

(1991b) 'Discrimina Ordinum. The Lex Julia Theatralis', in *Roman Culture and Society. Collected Papers*, ed. E. Rawson. Oxford and New York: 508–45

Reber, K. (1988) 'Aedificia Graecorum. Zu Vitruvs Beschreibung des griechischen Haus', *Archäologischer Anzeiger*: 653–66

Rech, H. (1936) *Mos Maiorum. Wesen und Wirkung der Tradition in Rom.* Marburg

Rediscovering Pompeii (1990) *Rediscovering Pompeii. Exhibition by IBM-ITALIA New York City, IBM Gallery of Science and Art 12 July–15 September 1990.* Rome

Renfrew, C. (1987) *Archaeology and Language. The Puzzle of Indo-European Origins.* London

(1996) 'Prehistory and the Identity of Europe', in *Cultural Identity and Archaeology. The Construction of European Communities*, eds. P. Graves-Brown, S. Jones and C. Gamble. London and New York: 125–37

Reynolds, D. W. (1996) 'Forma Urbis Romae. The Severan Marble Plan and the Urban Form of Ancient Rome'. PhD, Ann Arbor

Reynolds, J. M. and J. B. Ward Perkins (eds.) (1952) *The Inscriptions of Roman Tripolitania.* London

Ricci, A. (1985) 'Ceramica a pareti sottili', in *Atlante dell Forme Ceramiche II. Ceramica fine romana nel bacino del Mediterraneo (tardo ellenismo e primo impero).* Rome

Rickman, G. (1980) *The Corn Supply of Ancient Rome.* Oxford

Rix, H. (2002) *Sabellische Texte. Die Texte des Oskischen, Umbrischen und Südpikenischen.* Heidelberg

Riz, A. E. (1990) *Bronzegefässe in der römisch-pompejanischen Wandmalerei.* Mainz

Robert, L. (1968) 'De Delphes à Oxus. Inscriptions grècques nouvelles de la Bactriane', *Comptes rendues de l' Académie des Inscriptions et belles letters*: 416–57

Robinson, O. F. (1992) *Ancient Rome. City Planning and Administration.* London

Roche, D. (2000) *A History of Everyday Things. The Birth of Consumption in France, 1600–1800.* Cambridge

Rodríguez-Almeida, E. (1981) *Forma Urbis Marmorea. Aggiornamento Generale 1980.* Rome

(1983) 'Un nuovo frammento della Forma Urbis Marmorea', in *Città e architettura nella Roma Imperiale. Atti del seminario del 27. ottobre 1981 nel 25o anniversario dell'Accademia di Danimarca.* Odense: 87–92

(1988) 'Un frammento di una nuova pianta marmorea di Roma', *Journal of Roman Archaeology* 1: 120–31

(2002) *Formae Urbis Antiquae. Le mappe marmoree di Roma tra la Repubblica e Settimio Severo.* Rome

Rolley, C. (1995) 'Datations impossibles. À propos de quelques cratères de bronze', in *Acta of the 12th International Congress on Ancient Bronzes*, eds. S. T. A. M. Mols and R. M. van Heeringen. Nijmegen: 69–75

Roloff, H. (1937) *Maiores bei Cicero.* Leipzig

Rostovtzeff, M. (1957) *The Social and Economic History of the Roman Empire.* Oxford

Rotroff, S. I. (1982) *The Athenian Agora XXII. Hellenistic Pottery, Athenian and Imported Moldmade Bowls.* Princeton

(1997) 'From Greek to Roman in Athenian Ceramics', in *The Romanization of Athens. Proceedings of an International Conference held at Lincoln, Nebraska (April 1996)*, eds. M. C. Hoff and S. I. Rotroff. Oxford: 97–116

Rowland, I. and T. N. Howe (1999) *Vitruvius. Ten Books on Architecture.* Cambridge

Roymans, N. (ed.) (1996) *From the Sword to the Plough. Three Studies on the Earliest Romanisation of Northern Gaul.* Amsterdam

Rumpf, A. (1950) 'Die Entstehung des römischen Theaters', *Römische Mitteilungen* 3: 40–50

Rüpke, J. (1995) *Kalender und Öffentlichkeit. Die Geschichte der Repräsentation und religiösen Qualifikation von Zeit in Rom.* Berlin and New York

(1998) 'Les archives des petits collèges. Le cas des Vicomagistri', in *La Mémoire perdue. Recherches sur l'administration romaine* (Collection École Française de Rome) 243: 27–44

Russo Tagliente, A. (1992) *Edilizia domestica in Apulia e Lucania. Ellenizzazione e società nella tipologia abitativa indigena tra VIII e III secolo a.C.* Galatina

Sahlins, M. D. (1981) *Historical Metaphors and Mythical Realities. Structure in the Early History of the Sandwich Islands Kingdom.* Ann Arbor

Said, E. W. (1978) *Orientalism.* New York

Saliou, C. (1994) *Les lois des bâtiments. Voisinage et habitat urbain dans l'Empire romain.* Beirut

Saller, R. P. (1982) *Personal Patronage under the Early Empire.* Cambridge

Salmon, E. T. (1982) *The Making of Roman Italy.* London

Salskov Roberts, H. (2002) 'A Bronze Statuette with Hook-like Hands Found in Denmark', in *I bronzi antichi. Produzione e tecnologia: atti del XV Congresso internazionale sui bronzi antichi organizzato dall'Università di Udine, sede di Gorizia, Grado-Aquilieia, 22–26 maggio 2001*, ed. A. Giumlia-Mair, Montagnac: 456–61

Salway, B. (1994) 'What's in a Name? A Survey of Roman Onomastic Practice from c.700 B.C. to A.D. 700', *Journal of Roman Studies* 84: 124–45

Salzman, M. R. (1990) *On Roman Time. The Codex-Calendar of 354 and the Rhythms of Urban Life in Late Antiquity*. Berkeley

Samuel, A. E. (1972) *Greek and Roman Chronology. Calendars and Years in Classical Antiquity*. Munich

Sarnataro, T. (2002) 'Le patere con manico dell'area vesuviana e la loro funzione domestica. Case-study: la Casa di *L. Volusius Faustus* (I 2,10)', in *I bronzi antichi. Produzione e tecnologia: atti del XV Congresso internazionale sui bronzi antichi organizzato dall'Università di Udine, sede di Gorizia, Grado-Aquilieia, 22–26 maggio 2001*, ed. A. Giumlia-Mair, Montagnac: 393–405

Sauerwein, I. (1970) *Die leges sumptuariae als römische Maßnahme gegen den Sittenverfall.* Hamburg

Sauron, G. (1987) 'Le complexe pompéien du champ de Mars', in *L'Urbs. Espace urbain et histoire.* Rome: 457–73

Schadewaldt, W. (1973) 'Humanitas Romana', in *Aufstieg und Niedergang der römischen Welt* I 4, ed. H. Temporini. Berlin and New York: 43–62

Scheid, J. (1992) 'Myth, Cult and Reality in Ovid's *Fasti*', *Proceedings of the Cambridge Philological Society* 38: 118–31

Schiesaro, A. (2002) 'Ovid and the Professional Discourses of Scholarship, Religion, Rhetoric', in *The Cambridge Companion to Ovid*, ed. P. Hardie. Cambridge: 62–75

Schmitt Pantel, P. (1992) *La cité au banquet. Histoire des repas publics dans les cités grecques.* Rome

Schutz, M. (1990) 'Zur Sonnenuhr des Augustus auf dem Marsfeld', *Gymnasium* 97: 432–57

Scott, K. (1931) 'Greek and Roman Honorific Months', *Yale Classical Studies* 2: 241–63

Sear, F. (1990) 'Vitruvius and Roman Theatre Design', *American Journal of Archaeology* 94: 249–58

(2006) *Roman Theatres. An Architectural Study.* Oxford

Sekora, J. (1977) *Luxury. The Concept in Western Thought, Eden to Smollett.* Baltimore, MD

Shaw, B. D. (1992) 'Under Russian Eyes', *Journal of Russian Studies* 82: 216–28

Shennan, S. J. (1989a) *Archaeological Approaches to Cultural Identity.* London and New York

(1989b) 'Introduction. Archaeological Approaches to Cultural Identity', in *Archaeological Approaches to Cultural Identity*, ed. S. J. Shennan. London: 1–32

Sherwin-White, A. N. (1973) *The Roman Citizenship.* Oxford

Shiveley, D. (1964–5) 'Sumptuary Legislation and Status in Early Tokugawa Japan', *Harvard Journal of Asiatic Studies* 25: 123–64

Siebert, G. (1973) 'Mobilier délien en bronze', *Études déliennes*. Bulletin de Correspondance héllenique Supp. 1: 555–87

Sirks, A. J. B. (1991) *Food for Rome. The Legal Structure of the Transportation and Processing of Supplies for the Imperial Distributions in Rome and Constantinople.* Amsterdam

Sisani, S. (2001a) 'Aquilonia. Una nuova ipotesi di identificazione', *Eutopia n.s.* I.2: 131–47

(2001b) *Tuta Ikuvina. Sviluppo e ideologia della forma urbana a Gubbio.* Rome

(2007) *Fenomenologia della conquista. La romanizzazione dell'Umbria tra il IV sec. a.C. e la guerra sociale.* Rome

Skutsch, O. (1985) *The Annals of Quintus Ennius.* Oxford

Small, D. B. (1983) 'Studies in Roman Theatre Design', *American Journal of Archaeology* 87: 55–68

Smith, C. J. (1996) *Early Rome and Latium. Economy and Society c. 1000 to 500 BC.* Oxford

Smith, R. R. R. (1998) 'Cultural Choice and Political Identity in Honorific Portrait Statues in the Greek East in the Second Century A.D.', *Journal of Roman Studies* 88: 56–93

Solin, H. (1982) 'Appunti sull'onomastica romana a Delo', in *Delo e l'Italia*, eds. F. Coarelli, D. Musti and H. Solin. Rome: 101–17

Sombart, W. (1967) *Luxury and Capitalism.* Ann Arbor

Spagnolo Garzoli, G. (ed.) (1999) *Conubia gentium. La necropoli di Oleggio e la romanizzazione dei Vertamocori, 23 gennaio-30 aprile.* Oleggio

Spinazzola, V. (1953) *Pompei alla luce degli scavi nuovi di via dell' Abbondanza (anni 1910–1923),* 2 vols. Rome

Spivak, G. C. (1987) *In Other Worlds. Essays in Cultural Politics.* New York

Stearns, P. N. (2001) *Consumerism in World History. The Global Transformation of a Desire.* London and New York

Steinby, E. M. (ed.) (1993–2000) *Lexicon Topographicum Urbis Romae.* Rome

Sternini, M. (2004) *La romanizzazione della Sabina tiberina.* Bari

Stevenson, T. (1998) 'The "Problem" with Nude Honorific Statuary and Portraits in Late Republican and Augustan Rome', *Greece and Rome ser.* 2(45): 45–69

Stone, S. (1994) 'The Toga. From National to Ceremonial Costume', in *The World of Roman Costume*, eds. J. L. Sebesta and L. Bonfante Warren. Madison, WI

Stray, C. (1998) *Classics Transformed. Schools, Universities, and Society in England, 1830–1960.* Oxford

Strong, D. E. (1966) *Catalogue of the Carved Amber in the Department of Greek and Roman Antiquities.* London

Swain, S. (1996) *Hellenism and Empire. Language, Classicism and Power in the Greek World, AD 50–250.* Oxford

Swan, P. M. (2004) *The Augustan Succession. An Historical Commentary on Cassius Dio's* Roman History *Books 55–56 (9 B.C.–A.D.14).* Oxford

Syme, R. (1939) *The Roman Revolution.* Oxford

  (1958a) *Colonial Élites. Rome, Spain and the Americas.* Oxford

  (1958b) *Tacitus.* Oxford

  (1988) 'Rome and the Nations', in *Roman Papers IV*, ed. A. R. Birley. Oxford: 62–73

  (2002) *Sallust*, with a New Foreword by Ronald Mellor. Berkeley, Los Angeles and London

Tagliamonte, G. (1996) *I Sanniti. Caudini, Irpini, Pentri, Carricini, Frentani.* Milan

Talamo, E. (1987–8) 'Un letto funerario da una tomba dell'Esquilino', *Bullettino Comunale.* 92(1): 17–102

  (1993) 'Ricostruzione di un letto funerario da una tomba dell'Esquilino', *Bullettino Comunale* 95: 285–7

Tamm, B. (1970) *Nero's Gymnasium in Rome.* Stockholm

Tarpin, M. (2002) *Vici et pagi dans l'occident romain.* Rome

Tassinari, S. (1993) *Il vasellame bronzeo di Pompei.* Rome

Tchernia, A. (1969) 'Les fouilles sous-marines de Planier (Bouches-du-Rhone)', *Comptes rendues de l'Académie des Inscriptions et belles lettres*: 292–309

Terrenato, N. (1998) '*Tam Firmum Municipium.* The Romanization of Volaterrae and its Cultural Implications', *Journal of Roman Studies* 88: 94–114

  (2001) 'A Tale of Three Cities. The Romanization of Northern Coastal Etruria', in *Italy and the West. Comparative Issues in Romanization*, eds. S. Keay and N. Terrenato. Oxford: 54–67

Testa, A. (1989) *Candelabri e thymiateria.* Rome

Thébert, Y. (2003) *Thermes romains d'Afrique du nord et leur contexte méditerranéen. Études d'histoire et d'archéologie.* Rome

Thirsk, J. (1978) *Economic Policy and Projects. The Development of a Consumer Society in early Modern England.* Oxford

Thomas, R. (1992) *Literacy and Orality in Ancient Greece.* Cambridge and New York

  (2000) *Herodotus in Context. Ethnography, Science and the Art of Persuasion.* Cambridge

Tomlinson, R. (1989) 'Vitruvius and Hermogenes', in *Munus non ingratum. Proceedings of the International Symposium on Vitruvius' De Architectura and the Hellenistic and Roman Architecture, Leiden 20–23 January*, eds. H. Geertman and J. J. De Jong. Leiden: 71–5

Torelli, M. (1992) 'Conclusioni', in *La necropoli di Praeneste. 'Periodi orientalizzante e medio-repubblicano'. Atti del 2° convegno di Studi archeologici, Palestrina 21/22 Aprile 1990*, ed. 269–80

  (1995) *Studies in the Romanization of Italy.* Edmonton

  (1999) *Tota Italia. Essays in the Cultural Formation of Roman Italy.* Oxford

Traina, G. (2006) 'Romanizzazione, "métissages", ibridità', *Mélanges de l'École Française de Rome. Antiquités* 118(1): 151–8

Trevor-Roper, H. (1983) 'The Invention of Tradition. The Highland Tradition of Scotland', in *The Invention of Tradition*, eds. E. Hobsbawm and T. Ranger. Cambridge: 15–41

Trimble, J. (2008) 'Process and Transformation on the Severan Marble Plan of Rome', in *Cartography in Antiquity and the Middle Ages: Fresh Perspectives, New Methods*, eds. R. J. A. Talbert and R.W. Unger (Leiden)

Tucci, P. L. (1994) 'Il tempio dei Castori in circo Flaminio', in *Castores, l'immagine dei Dioscuri a Roma*, ed. L. Nista. Rome: 123–8

(2006) 'Navalia', *Archeologia Classica* 57 n.s. 7: 175–202

Valenza Mele, N. (1981) *Museo Nazionale Archeologico di Napoli. Catalogo delle Lucerne in Bronzo*. Rome

Vallat, J.-P. (1995) *L'Italie et Rome, 218–31 av. J.-C.* Paris

van Andringa, W. (2000) 'Autels de carrefour, organisation vicinale et rapports de voisinage à Pompéi', *Rivista di Studi Pompeiani* 11: 47–86

Various authors (1973) *Roma medio-repubblicana. Aspetti culturali di Roma e del Lazio nei secoli IV e III a.C.* Rome

(1991) *La Romanisation du Samnium aux IIe et Ier sièclesav. J.-C.. Actes du colloque organisé par le Centre Jean Bérard en collaboration avec la Soprintendenza archeologica e per i BAAS del Molise et al Soprintendenza archeologica per la province di Salerno, Avellino e Benevento: Naples Centre Jean Bérard, 4–5 Novembre 1988.* Naples

(1994) *Le Fortune dell'età arcaica nel Lazio e loro posterità*. Palestrina

Veeser, H. A. (ed.) (1989) *The New Historicism*. New York

Veit, U. (1989) '"Ethnic Concepts in German Prehistory". A Case Study on the Relationship between Cultural Identity and Archaeological Objectivity', in *Archaeological Approaches to Cultural Identity*, ed. S. J. Shennan. London: 35–56

Versluys, M. J. (2002) *Aegyptiaca Romana. Nilotic Scenes and the Roman Views of Egypt*. Leiden, Boston and Cologne

Vetter, E. (1953) *Handbuch der italienischen Dialekte*. Heidelberg

Veuve, S. (1987) *Fouilles d'Aï Khanoum, 6. Le gymnase: Architecture, céramique, sculpture*. Paris

Veyne, P. (1979) 'The Hellenization of Rome and the Question of Acculturations', *Diogenes* 106: 1–27

(1980) 'L'Empire romain', in *Le Concept d'Empire*, ed. M. Duverger. Paris

(2002) 'La "plèbe moyenne" sous le Haut-Empire romain', *Annales, histoire, sciences sociales* 55.6: 1169–99

Vickers, M. (1994) 'Nabataea, India, Gaul and Carthage. Reflections on Hellenistic and Roman Gold Vessels and Red-Gloss Pottery', *American Journal of Archaeology* 48: 231–48

(1996) 'Rock Crystal. The Key to Cut Glass and *diatreta* in Persia and Rome', *Journal of Roman Archaeology* 9: 48–65

Vickers, M., O. Impey and J. Allan (1986) *From Silver to Ceramic. The Potter's Debt to Metalwork in the Graeco-Roman, Oriental and Islamic Worlds*. Oxford

Virlouvet, C. (1995) *Tessera frumentaria. Les procédures de la distribution du blé public à Rome à la fin de la République et au début de l'Empire*. Rome

Vitali, D. (ed.) (1987) *Celti ed Etruschi nell'Italia centro-settentrionale dal V a.C. alla romanizzazione. Atti del Colloquio internazionale Bologna 12–14 aprile 1985.* Bologna

Volpe, G. (1990) *La Daunia nell'età della romanizzazione. Paesaggio agrario, produzione, scambi.* Bari

von Hesberg, H. (1984) 'Vitruv und die italische Tradition', in *Vitruv-Kolloquium 17./18. Juni 1982 Technische Hoschule Darmstadt,* eds. H. Knell and B. Wesenberg. Darmstadt: 123–40

(1986) 'Archäologische Denkmäler zum römischen Kaiserkult', in *Aufstieg und Niedergang der römischen Welt* II 16.2 ed. W. Haase. Berlin and New York. 911–95

(1994) 'Die Architekturteile', in *Das Wrack. Der antike Schiffsfund von Mahdia,* ed. G. Hellenkemper Sallies. Cologne, 1: 175–94

Vout, C. (1996) 'The Myth of the Toga. Understanding the History of Roman Dress', *Greece and Rome ser.* 2 43 (2): 204–20

(2006) 'What's in a Beard? Rethinking Hadrian's Hellenism', in *Rethinking Revolutions through Ancient Greece,* eds. S. Goldhill and R. Osborne. Cambridge: 96–123

Wachter, R. (1987) *Altlateinische Inschriften. Sprachliche und epigraphische Untersuchungen zu den Dokumenten bis etwa 150 v.Chr.* Bern

Walbank, F. (1981) *The Hellenistic World.* Brighton

Wallace-Hadrill, A. (1982) 'Civilis princeps. Between Citizen and King', *Journal of Roman Studies* 72: 32–48

(1983) *Suetonius. The Scholar and his Caesars.* London

(1986) 'Image and Authority in the Coinage of Augustus', *Journal of Roman Studies* 76: 66–87

(1987) 'Time for Augustus. Ovid, Augustus and the Fasti', in *Homo Viator. Classical Essays for John Bramble,* eds. M. Whitby *et al.* Bristol: 221–30

(1989) 'Patronage in Roman Society', in *Patronage in Ancient Society,* ed. A. Wallace-Hadrill. London: 63–87

(1990a) 'Pliny the Elder and Man's Unnatural History', *Greece and Rome* 37: 80–96

(1990b) 'Roman Arches and Greek Honours. The Language of Power at Rome', *Proceedings of the Cambridge Philological Society* 37: 143–81

(1994) *Houses and Society in Pompeii and Herculaneum.* Princeton

(1995) 'Public Honour and Private Shame. The Urban Texture of Pompeii', in *Urban Society in Roman Italy,* eds. T. Cornell and K. Lomas. London: 39–62

(1997a) '*Mutatio morum.* The Idea of a Cultural Revolution', in *The Roman Cultural Revolution,* eds. T. Habinek and A. Schiesaro. Cambridge: 3–22

(1997b) 'Rethinking the Roman Atrium House', in *Domestic Space in the Roman World. Pompeii and Beyond,* eds. R. Laurence and A. Wallace-Hadrill. Portsmouth, RI, Supp. 22: 219–40

(1998) 'The Villa as a Cultural Symbol', in *The Roman Villa. Villa Urbana,* ed. A. Frazer. Philadelphia: 43–53

(2000a) 'Case e abitanti a Roma', in *Roma imperiale. Una metropoli antica*, ed. E. Lo Cascio. Rome: 173–220

(2000b) 'The Roman Revolution and Material Culture', in *La Révolution Romaine après Ronald Syme. Bilans et Perspectives: sept exposés suivis de discussions*, eds. A. Giovannini and B. Grange. Geneva: 283–321

(2001a) 'Emperors and Houses in Rome', in *Childhood, Class and Kin in the Roman World*, ed. S. Dixon. London and New York: 128–43

(2001b) 'Rome Finds its Pevsner (Review of *Lexicon Topographicum Urbis Romae*)', *Times Literary Supplement* (11 May): 3–4

(2003) 'Domus and Insulae in Rome. Families and Housefuls', in *Early Christian Families in Context. An Interdisciplinary Dialogue*, eds. D. L. Balch and C. Osiek. Grand Rapids, MI

(2004) 'Imaginary Feasts. Pompeii and the Image of Success', in *Ostia, Cicero, Gamala, Feasts, & the Economy. Papers in memory of John H. D'Arms*, eds. A. Gallina Zevi and J. H. Humphrey. Portsmouth, RI: 109–26

Walton, J. K. (1983) *The English Seaside Resort. A Social History 1750–1914*. Leicester

Warrior, V. M. (1992) 'Intercalation and the Action of M'. Acilius Glabrio (cos 191 BC)', in *Studies in Latin Literature and Roman History VI*, ed. C. Deroux. Brussels: 119–44

Weatherill, L. (1988) *Consumer Behaviour and Material Culture in Britain 1660–1760*. London and New York

Webster, J. (2001) 'Creolizing the Roman Provinces', *American Journal of Archaeology* 105 n. 2: 209–25

(2003) 'Art as Resistance and Negotiation', in *Roman Imperialism and Provincial Art*, eds. S. Scott and J. Webster. Cambridge: 24–51

Welch, K. (1994) 'The Roman Arena in Late-Republican Italy. A New Interpretation', *Journal of Roman Archaeology* 7: 59–80

(1999) 'Subura', in *Lexicon Topographicum Urbis Romae*, ed. E. M. Steinby. Rome, 4: 379–83

(2007) *The Roman Amphitheatre. From its Origins to the Colosseum*. New York

Wells, C. M. (1990) '"Imitations" and the Spread of sigillata Manufacture', in *Conspectus formarum terrae sigillatae Italico modo confectae*, ed. E. Ettlinger *et al.* Bonn: 24–5

West, M. (1997) *The East Face of Helicon. West Asiatic Elements in Greek Poetry and Myth*. Oxford

Whitehead, J. (1993) 'The "Cena Trimalchionis" and Biographical Narration in Roman Middle-class Art', in *Narrative and Event in Ancient Art*, ed. P. J. Holliday. Cambridge: 299–325

Whitmarsh, T. (2001a) '"Greece is the World". Exile and Identity in the Second Sophistic', in *Being Greek under Rome. Cultural Identity, the Second Sophistic and the Development of Empire*, ed. S. Goldhill. Cambridge: 269–305

(2001b) *Greek Literature and the Roman Empire. The Politics of Imitation.* Oxford

Wiessner, P. (1983) 'Style and Social Information in Kalahari San Projectile Points', *American Antiquity* 48: 253–76

Wilkins, J., D. Harvey and M. Dobson (eds.) (1995) *Food in Antiquity.* Exeter

Willers, H. (1907) *Neue Untersuchungen über die römische Bronzeindustrie von Capua und von Niedergermanien.* Hanover and Leipzig

Williams, R. (1961) *Culture and Society 1780–1950.* Harmondsworth

(1983) *Keywords. A Vocabulary of Culture and Society.* New York

Wilson, A. J. N. (1966) *Emigration from Italy in the Republican Age of Rome.* Manchester

Wilson Jones, M. (1989) 'Designing the Roman Corinthian Order', *Journal of Roman Archaeology* 2: 35–69

(2000) *Principles of Roman Architecture.* New Haven and London

Wiseman, T. P. (1969) 'The Census in the First Century B.C.' *Journal of Roman Studies* 59: 59–75

(1970) 'The Definition of "eques Romanus" in The Late Republic and Early Empire', *Historia* 19: 67–83

(1971) *New Men in the Roman Senate 139 BC–AD 14.* Oxford

(1974) *Cinna the Poet and other Roman Essays.* Leicester

(1994) *Historiography and Imagination. Eight Essays on Roman Culture.* Exeter

(2004) *The Myths of Rome.* Exeter

Woodman, A. J. and R. H. Martin (1996) *The Annals of Tacitus Book 3, Edited with a Commentary.* Cambridge

Woolf, G. (1990) 'World Systems Analysis and the Roman Empire', *Journal of Roman Archaeology* 3: 44–58

(1996) 'Becoming Roman, Staying Greek. Culture, Identity and the Civilizing Process in the Roman East', *Proceedings of the Cambridge Philological Society* 40: 116–43

(1997) 'The Roman Urbanization of the East', in *The Early Roman Empire in the East*, ed. S. Alcock. Oxford: 1–14

(1998) *Becoming Roman. The Origins of Provincial Civilization in Gaul.* Cambridge

Yarrow, L. (2006) 'Lucius Mummius and the Spoils of Corinth', *Scripta Classica Israelica* 25: 57–70

Yegül, F. (1992) *Baths and Bathing in Classical Antiquity.* Cambridge, MA and London

Yerkes, S. R. (2005) '"Living Architecture". Living Column and Vegetal Urn: Shared Motifs in Roman Wall Painting and "neo-Attic" Furnishings', in *Terra Marique*, ed. J. Pollini. Oxford: 149–68

Young, R. C. (1995) *Colonial Desire. Hybridity in Theory, Culture and Race.* London and New York

Zaccagnino, C. (1998) *Il Thymiaterion nel mondo greco. Analisi delle fonti, tipologia, impieghi.* Rome

Zanker, P. (1970/1) 'Über die Werkstätten augusteischer Larenaltäre und damit zusammenhangende Probleme der Interpretation', *Bullettino Comunale.* 82: 147–55

(1975) 'Grabreliefs römischer Freigelassener', *Jahrbuch des deutschen archäologischen Instituts* 90: 267–315

(ed.) (1976) *Hellenismus in Mittelitalien. Kolloquium in Göttingen vom 5. bis 9. Juni 1974.* Göttingen

(1979) 'Die Villa als Vorbild des späten pompejanischen Wohngeschmacks', *Jahrbuch des deutschen archäologischen Instituts* 94: 460–523

(1981) 'Zur Bildnisräpresentation führender Männer in mittelitalischen und campanischen Städten zur Zeit des späten Republik und der Julisch-Claudischen Kaiser', in *Les 'bourgeoisies' municipales italiennes aux IIe et Ier siècles av.J.C.*, Paris and Naples: 251–66

(1988) *The Power of Images in the Age of Augustus.* Ann Arbor

(1995) *Die Maske des Sokrates. Das Bild des Intellectuellen in der antiken Kunst.* Munich

(1998) *Pompeii. Public and Private Life.* Cambridge, MA

Zehnacker, H. (1983) *Pline l'Ancien Histoire Naturelle livre XXXIII. Texte établi, traduit et commenté.* Paris

Zevi, F. (1976) 'Alatri', in *Hellenismus in Mittelitalien. Kolloquium in Göttingen vom 5. bis 9. Juni 1974*, ed. P. Zanker. Göttingen: 84–96

(1994) 'Considerazioni vecchie e nuove sul santuario della Fortuna Primigenia. L'organizzazione del santuario, i Mucii Scaevolae e l'architettura "mariana". *Le Fortune dell'età arcaica nel Lazio ed in Italia e loro posterità.* Atti 3° convegno di studi archaeologici, Palestrina: 137–83

(1996a) 'La casa di Giulio Polibio', in *Pompei. Abitare sotto il Vesuvio*, eds. M. Borriello, A. d'Ambrosio, S. De Caro and P. G. Guzzo Ferrara: 73–80

(1996b) 'Les elites municipali, Mario e l'architettura del tempo', *Cahiers du Centre Gustav-Glotz* 7: 229–52

(1998) 'Die Casa del Fauno in Pompeji und das Alexandermosaik', *Römische Mitteilungen* 105: 21–65

Index

Lightning Source UK Ltd.
Milton Keynes UK
UKHW050808230619

344860UK00006B/97/P